ts 13-16:

itle Route

gement

rse Book

In this September 2004 first edition

- full and comprehensive coverage of the revised Edexcel
  Guidelines, effective from September 2004

- activities, examples and quizzes

- practical illustrations

- practice assignments

- glossary and index

BPP
PROFESSIONAL EDUCATION™

EDEXCEL HNC & HND BUSINESS

First edition September 2004

ISBN 07517 1252 3

British Library Cataloguing-in Publication Data

A catalogue record for this book is available from the British Library

Printed in Great Britain by WM Print
45-47 Frederick Street
Walsall, West Midlands
WS2 9NE

Published by

BPP Professional Education

Aldine House, Aldine Place

London W12 8AW

www.bpp.com

We are grateful to Edexcel for permission to reproduce the Guidelines.

CONTENTS

(iv)

INTRODUCTION

Edexcel has revised the structure of the HND/HNC qualifications in Business, and its Guidelines covering the content of each Unit. These changes are effective from September 2004. This book has been **written specifically to cover the revised Guidelines** and provides concise yet comprehensive coverage.

The HNC and HND qualifications in Business have always been very demanding. The suggested content, set out by Edexcel in Guidelines for each unit, includes topics which are normally covered at degree level. Students therefore need books which get straight to the core of these topics, and which build upon the student's existing knowledge and experience. BPP's series of Course Books have been designed to meet that need.

This book has been written specifically for specialist Units 13 to 16. These units form the endorsed title route in Management. The book covers the Edexcel guidelines and suggested content in full, and includes the following features.

- The Edexcel guidelines

- A study guide explaining the key features of the book and how to get the most from your studies

- A full index

Each chapter contains:

- An introduction and study objectives

- Summary diagrams and signposts, to guide you through the chapter

- Numerous activities, topics for discussion, definitions and examples, all designed to bring the subject to life and enable students to apply their learning to practical situations

- A chapter roundup, a quick quiz with answers and answers to activities

Unit 13 Professional Development

Unit 13, Professional Development, has been put at the end of this book as it is a Unit that learners are likely to do on an ongoing basis throughout the course of their HND/HNC studies. Although it forms part of the Management endorsed title route, it will not necessarily be covered at the same time as the other Units, and therefore has been placed separately.

BPP Professional Education are the leading providers of targeted texts for professional qualifications. Our customers need to study effectively. They cannot afford to waste time. They expect clear, concise and highly-focused study material. This series of Course Books for HNC and HND Business has been designed and produced to fulfil those needs.

BPP Professional Education
2004

Other titles in this series:

Mandatory units

Unit 1	Marketing
Unit 2	Managing Financial Resources and Decisions
Unit 3	Organisations and Behaviour
Unit 4	Business Environment
Unit 5	Common Law 1
Unit 6	Business Decision Making
Unit 7	Business Strategy
Unit 8	Research Project

Endorsed title routes

Units 9-12	Finance
Units 13-16	Management
Units 17-20	Marketing
Units 21-24	Human Resource Management
Units 25-28	Law

For more information, or to place an order, please call 020 8740 2211, or fill in the order form at the back of this book.

If you would like to send in your comments on this book, please turn to the review form on the last page.

EDEXCEL GUIDELINES FOR UNIT 13 PROFESSIONAL DEVELOPMENT

Description of the Unit

This unit is designed to enable learners to assess and develop a range of professional and personal skills in order to promote future personal and career development. The unit also aims to develop learners' abilities to organise, manage and practise a range of approaches to improve their performance as self-organised learners, in preparation for work or further career development.

The unit emphasis is on the needs of the individual but within the context of how the development of self-management corresponds with effective team management in meeting objectives.

Summary of learning outcomes

To achieve this unit a learner must:

1   Undertake responsibility for own **personal and career development**

2   **Evaluate progress** and achievement of personal development and learning targets

3   Develop a range of **interpersonal and transferable skills**

4   Demonstrate **self-managed learning in a professional context**

Content

Outcomes and assessment criteria

The learning outcomes and the criteria used to assess them are shown in the table below.

Outcomes	Assessment criteria for pass To achieve each outcome a learner must demonstrate the ability to:
1 Undertake responsibility for own **personal and career development**	• Identify, review and assess own performance of current management skills • conduct a self-assessment inventory • devise and maintain a current CV and/or portfolio of work • devise a personal development plan to achieve personal targets and short and long-term learning objectives
2 **Evaluate progress** and achievement of personal development and learning targets	• evaluate learning and development with original aims and objectives set in the development plan • reset objectives in the light of evaluation and feedback
3 Develop a range of **interpersonal and transferable skills**	• create or identify solutions to a range of work-based problems • communicate in a variety of styles and appropriate manner at various levels • identify a range of effective time management strategies
4 Demonstrate **self-managed learning** in a professional context	• apply an awareness of how people learn to identify suitable methods for development • suggest ways in which lifelong learning could be encouraged • use a range of research methods and sources • give a presentation evaluating progress in achieving learning objectives outlined in the personal development plan

Guidance

Delivery

This unit would benefit from a series of skills-based workshops or a residential period to facilitate personal development.

Guest speakers from businesses would be helpful in describing their job roles and identifying the skills needed to run and work in a business environment.

Assessment

For the personal profile the learner should self-evaluate their current skills and experiences using a skills audit and then construct a personal portfolio.

Assessment for the career development could be via a personal journal or skills log compiled throughout the programme. It should be based on the learner's own personal and career aims and needs.

Evidence for interpersonal and transferable skills should involve role play and use examples of 'real-life' situations. Learners should also analyse qualities of existing business entrepreneurs.

Links

The unit has links with *Unit 14: Working with and Leading People, Unit 15: Managing Activities to Achieve Results* and *Unit 16: Managing Communications, Knowledge and Information*. It should be developed throughout the programme in order to influence the selection of an appropriate project and career route.

Support materials

Textbooks

Sufficient library resources should be available to enable learners to achieve this unit. Particularly relevant texts are:

Adair J – *Effective Leadership* (Pan Books, 1988) ISBN: 0330302302

Adair J – *Effective Time Management* (Pan Books, 1989) ISBN: 0330302299

Hartley P – *Interpersonal Communication* (Routledge, 1993)

Dubrin A – *10 Minute Guide to Leadership* (John Wiley & Sons, 1997) ISBN: 0028614062

Glass N – *Management Masterclass: A Practical guide to the New Realities of Business* (Nicholas Brealey Publishing, 1996) ISBN: 1857881079

Godefroy and Clark – *The Complete Time Management System* (Piatkus, 1990) ISBN: 0749910445

Jay – *How to Write Proposals and Reports That Get Results* (FT Prentice Hall 2000) ISBN: 0273622021

Mullens – *Management and Organisational Behaviour* (Pitman Publishing, 1996) ISBN 0415013852

Perkins – *Killer CVs and Hidden Approaches* (FT Prentice Hall 2001) ISBN: 027365246X

EDEXCEL GUIDELINES FOR UNIT 14 WORKING WITH AND LEADING PEOPLE

Description of the Unit

This unit develops the knowledge and skills needed to work with and lead people. The unit recognises that leadership operates within the internal framework of organisational values, culture, policies and practices. It also recognises that, externally, leadership should meet the requirements of current legislation and ensure ethical and environmentally friendly behaviour.

The unit also considers the requirements for recruitment, selection and retention. It examines team working and leadership roles and identifies the work and development needs of individuals in the workplace.

Summary of learning outcomes

To achieve this unit a learner must:

1   Explore **recruitment, selection and retention procedures**

2   Understand how to **build winning teams**

3   Evaluate the styles and impact of **leadership**

4   Analyse the **work and development needs of individuals considering performance monitoring and assessment**

Content

Outcomes and assessment criteria

The learning outcomes and the criteria used to assess them are shown in the table below.

Outcomes	Assessment criteria for pass To achieve each outcome a learner must demonstrate the ability to:
1 Explore **recruitment, selection and retention procedures**	• identify characteristics of the person(s) required and inform potential applicants • suggest suitable methods for selection • contribute to the selection process • apply legal, regulatory and ethical considerations to the selection process
2 Understand how to **build winning teams**	• identify the mix of knowledge, skills and experience necessary for a team to fulfil its functions • analyse dynamics within teams and stimulate and promote a team spirit which helps motivate and provides support to its members • clarify expectations of relationships • encourage team members to develop roles during team assignments • empower teams to develop their own ways of working independently and to rely on their own capabilities within pre-set boundaries
3 Evaluate the styles and impact of **leadership**	• evaluate theories and styles of leadership • effectively communicate visions, goals and values to colleagues and promote understanding of how delegated objectives support these • enthuse and motivate colleagues to achieve objectives • promote confidence among colleagues to engage with change • empower colleagues to present their own ideas, develop their own ways of working within agreed boundaries and to provide a lead in their own areas of expertise

Outcomes	Assessment criteria
	To achieve each outcome a learner must demonstrate the ability to:
4 Analyse the **work and development needs of individuals considering performance monitoring and assessment**	• plan to analyse work activities using appropriate objective-setting techniques and processes • negotiate assignments with colleagues using suitable delegation techniques to motivate and enable colleagues • review development needs and activities and evaluate the effectiveness of activities • use suitable methods, with clearly defined and relevant criteria and objectives, to assess the performance of colleagues • identify factors affecting the quality of performance and use these to provide clear and constructive feedback on performance to colleagues • incorporate results of assessments into personal development plans and other organisational procedures for dealing with performance issues

Guidance

Delivery

Delivery will normally be through a mixture of lectures and seminars. Learners will be required to work on case studies and to participate in role play to allow them to practise skills.

Tutors should be aware that this unit is intended to cover the requirements of general managers working with and leading people, rather than being concerned with the needs of human resource management as a specialist function.

Assessment

Evidence could be generated through assignments, examinations and/or case studies and may encompass performance in role-play situations. Learners who are in work or who are able to participate in relevant work experiences may be able to generate evidence from real workplace situations. Where the working situation of a learner renders this impractical, learners should be encouraged to use a 'host' organisation or a job situation with which they are familiar to simulate the role of a manager. Good use could be made of managerial situations even if these are unpaid and/or part-time in nature.

Links

This unit has links with *Unit 13: Professional Development, Unit 15: Managing Activities to Achieve Results* and *Unit 16: Managing Communications, Knowledge and Information*. There may also be links with units in the Human Resources Management pathway and with *Unit 56: Project Management*.

The unit links with the following units from the Management Standards Centre National Occupational Standards:

- Unit B5:   Provide leadership for your team

- Unit D3:   Recruit, select and keep colleagues

- Unit D5:   Allocate and check work in your team

- Unit D6:   Allocate and monitor the progress and quality of work in your area of responsibility

- Unit D7:   Provide learning opportunities for colleagues

Support materials

Textbooks

Biddle D and Evenden R – *Human Aspects of Management 2nd Edition*(Chartered Institute of Personnel and Development, 1989) ISBN: 0852923953

Huczynski A and Buchanan D – *Organisational Behaviour An Introductory Text* (Pearson Higher Education, 2003) ISBN: 0582843219

Maund L – *An Introduction to Human Resource Management: Theory and Practice* (Palgrave Macmillan, 2001) ISBN: 033391242X

Mullins L – *Management and Organisational Behaviour 6th Edition* (FT Prentice Hall, 2004) ISBN: 0273651471

Price A – *Human Resource Management in a Business Context 2nd Edition*(Thomson Learning, 2004) ISBN: 186152966X

Journals and newspapers

A daily broadsheet eg *The Times, The Guardian*

Management Today

People Management

Websites

Websites can provide reports on research and current theories as well as case study materials. The following are examples of useful websites.

www.belbin.co.uk	Website of R M Belbin, expert on team building
www.cipd.co.uk	Chartered Institute of Personnel and Development
www.eoc.org.uk	Equal Opportunities Commission
www.greatplacetowork.gov.uk	Advice on involving and developing personnel to achieve results
www.human-resources.org	Human resources learning centre
www.humanresources.about.com	Advice on human resources issues
www.managing-people-performance.com	Advice on performance management and appraisal
www.peoplemanagement.co.uk	Online magazine of Chartered Institute of Personnel and Development

EDEXCEL GUIDELINES FOR UNIT 15 MANAGING ACTIVITIES TO ACHIEVE RESULTS

Description of the Unit

This unit focuses on the effective and efficient planning and management of work activities. It provides learners with the knowledge and skills to design, implement and change operational systems to improve their effectiveness and efficiency and to achieve the desired results.

Learners are encouraged to consider the importance and interrelationship of business processes and the implementation of operational plans, together with quality systems and health and safety in achieving satisfactory results.

Summary of learning outcomes

To achieve this unit a learner must:

1 Evaluate the importance of **business processes in delivering outcomes based upon business goals and objectives**

2 Develop **plans for their areas of responsibility and implement operational plans**

3 Design and monitor **appropriate systems to ensure quality of product and services**

4 Manage **health and safety in the workplace**

5 Improve **organisational performance**

Content

Outcomes and assessment criteria

The learning outcomes and the criteria used to assess them are shown in the table below.

Outcomes	Assessment criteria for pass To achieve each outcome a learner must demonstrate the ability to:
1 Evaluate the importance of **business processes in delivering outcomes based upon business goals and objectives**	• describe the structure and culture of an organisation and evaluate the inter-relationships between the different processes and functions of an organisation • identify the mission, aims and objectives of an organisation and analyse the effect of these on the structure and culture of the organisation • define the methodology to be used to map processes to the organisation's objectives and functions and evaluate the output of the process and analyse quality gateways
2 Develop **plans for their areas of responsibility and implement operational plans**	• develop plans which promote goals and objectives for area of responsibility and ensure plans are consistent with legal, regulatory and ethical requirements • use objectives which are specific, measurable, achievable, realistic and time-based to align people and other resources in an effective and efficient way • prepare and agree implementation plans which translate strategic targets into practical efficient and effective actions • manage work activities to prevent ineffective and inefficient deviations from the operational plan through effective monitoring and control • implement appropriate systems to achieve objectives and goals of the plan in the most effective and efficient way, on time and to budget and to meet organisational standards of quality

Outcomes	Assessment criteria To achieve each outcome a learner must demonstrate the ability to:
3 Design and monitor **appropriate systems to ensure quality of product and services**	• define the resources, tools and systems required to support the business process • define and implement quality audit systems/practice to manage and monitor quality to standards specified by the organisation and process operated • embed a quality culture to ensure continuous monitoring and development of the process
4 Manage **health and safety in the workplace**	• carry out risk assessments as required by legislation, regulation and organisational requirements and ensure appropriate action is taken • identify health and safety regulations and legislation applicable in specific work situations and ensure these are correctly and effectively applied • systematically review organisational health and safety policies and procedures in order to ensure they are effective and that they comply with the appropriate legislation and regulations • ensure practical application of health and safety policies and procedures in the workplace
5 Improve **organisational performance**	• monitor systems and work activities and identify problems and opportunities for improvement • recommend improvements which align with the organisation's objectives and goals and which result in a reduction in the variation between what customers and other stakeholders want and what products, processes and services deliver • identify the wider implications of proposed changes within the organisation • plan, implement and evaluate changes within an organisation

Guidance

Delivery

Delivery will normally be through a mixture of lectures and seminars. Learners will be required to work on case studies and to participate in role play to allow them to practise skills.

Tutors should be aware that this unit is intended to cover the requirements of managers who are responsible for managing activities, rather than being concerned with the needs of specialist managerial functions, such as, for example, professional quality managers.

Assessment

Evidence may be generated through assignments, examinations and/or case studies and may encompass performance in role-play situations. Learners who are in work or who are able to participate in relevant work experience may be able to generate evidence from real workplace situations. Where the working situation of a learner renders this impractical, learners should be encouraged to use a 'host' organisation or a job situation with which they are familiar to simulate the role of a manager. Good use could be made of managerial situations even if these are unpaid and/or part-time in nature.

Links

This unit has links with *Unit 13: Professional Development, Unit 14: Working with and Leading People* and *Unit 16: Managing Communications, Knowledge and Information*. There may also be links with *Unit 39: Quality Management, Unit 53: Contemporary Issues in Marketing Management, Unit 56: Project Management* and *Unit 60: Environmental Management*.

The unit links with the following units from the draft Management Standards Centre National Occupational Standards.

- Unit B1: Develop and implement operational plans for your area of responsibility
- Unit B8: Ensure compliance with legal, regulatory, ethical and social requirements
- Unit B10: Manage risk
- Unit C2: Encourage innovation in your area of responsibility
- Unit C3: Encourage innovation in your organisation
- Unit C4: Lead change
- Unit C5: Plan change
- Unit C6: Implement change
- Unit E5: Ensure your own actions reduce risks to health and safety
- Unit E6: Ensure health and safety requirements are met in your area of responsibility
- Unit E7: Ensure an effective organisational approach to health and safety
- Unit F12: Improve organisational performance

Support materials

Textbooks

Harrison A et al – *Cases in Operations Management 3rd Edition*(FT Prentice Hall, 2003) (ISBN 0273655310)

Naylor J – *Introduction to Operations Management 2nd Edition* (FT Prentice Hall, 2002) ISBN: 0273655787

Oakland J S and Porter L J – *TQM: Text with Cases 3rd Edition* (Butterworth-Heinemann, 2003) ISBN: 0750657405

Slack N et al – *Operations Management* (FT Prentice Hall, 2003) ISBN: 0273679066

Journals and newspapers

A daily broadsheet, eg *The Times, The Guardian, The Financial Times.*

Many professional and academic institutions publish journals relevant to this unit. Examples are:

Production, Planning and Control

International Journal of Productivity & Performance Management

The TQM Magazine

Websites

Websites can provide reports on research and current theories as well as case study materials. Examples are:

www.businesscases.org/newInterface	Provides business case studies
www.dti.gov.uk/mbp	Department of Trade and Industry
www.efqm.org	Management advice for European businesses
www.hbsworkingknowledge.hbs.edu	Harvard Business School
www.hse.gov.uk	Health and Safety Executive
www.hsl.gov.uk	Health and Safety Laboratory
www.managerwise.com	Provides information on management practice
www.praxiom.com	Praxiom Research Group – provides information on ISO 9001:2000 quality standards
www.quality.co.uk	Provides advice on quality management

EDEXCEL GUIDELINES FOR UNIT 16 MANAGING COMMUNICATIONS, KNOWLEDGE AND INFORMATION

Description of the Unit

This unit recognises that communications do not automatically take place effectively in organisations and thus both information and work-based knowledge is often deficient when decisions are made. This suggests that managers need to look to improve the planning of their communications processes as well as improving their communication skills. It also promotes the need for managers to adopt a more inclusive approach to stakeholders affected by the decisions they make and thus maintains the need for managers to network on a more structured basis. It also suggests that managers need to make the information and knowledge they gain accessible to other parts of the organisation.

This unit is designed to develop an understanding of the interaction between communications, knowledge and information. The unit also looks at how IT systems can be used as a management tool for collecting, storing, disseminating and providing access to knowledge and information.

Summary of learning outcomes

To achieve this unit a learner must:

1 Assess **information and knowledge needs** internally and externally to improve decision making and taking

2 Create strategies to increase **personal networking** to widen involvement in the decision-making process

3 Develop **communication processes** to improve the gathering and dissemination of information and organisational knowledge

4 Design and improve **appropriate systems** for the collection, storage and dissemination of and access to the information and knowledge gathered

Content

Chapter coverage

1 **Information and knowledge needs**

Sources: internal and external, primary and secondary, formal and informal, team workers, customers and other stakeholders

13

Types: qualitative and quantitative, tacit and explicit, official and unofficial, policy and opinion

2 **Personal networking**

Sources: stakeholders and useful contacts, internal and external

Methods: formal, informal

14

Strategies: formal and informal, direct or via media, relating and interacting trust and confidentiality, forming business relationships, decision making and decision taking

3 **Communication processes**

Types: meetings and conferences, workshops and training events, internet and email, written, telephone, video conferencing, one-to-one meetings

Approaches: structured and coordinated, planned, formal and informal

15

Strategy: advantages, disadvantages; informal, face-to-face, formal in writing, emotional, intelligence

4 **Appropriate systems**

Type: hard and soft, websites and mailings, access and dissemination

15

Style: trends and patterns, diagrams and text, consistent and reliable, current and valid; legal and confidential

Outcomes and assessment criteria

The learning outcomes and the criteria used to assess them are shown in the table below.

Outcomes	Assessment criteria for pass To achieve each outcome a learner must demonstrate the ability to:
1 Assess **information and knowledge needs** internally and externally to improve decision making and taking	• identify the range of decisions to be taken • review information and knowledge needed to ensure effective decision taking • assess internal and external sources of information and understanding • make recommendations for improvement
2 Create strategies to increase **personal networking** to widen involvement in the decision-making process	• identify personnel including customers, other stakeholders and other experts • make contact with those identified and develop business relationships • involve those identified in decision making as appropriate • suggest strategies for improvement
3 Develop **communication processes** to improve the gathering and dissemination of information and organisational knowledge	• evaluate existing processes of communication in an organisation and look to ensure and improve appropriateness • implement and justify improvements to ensure greater integration of systems of communication in that organisation • on a personal level, identify weaknesses and develop a personal plan to improve communication skills
4 Design and improve **appropriate systems** for the collection, storage and dissemination of and access to the information and knowledge gathered	• evaluate existing approaches to the collection, formatting, storage, disseminating information and knowledge • implement and justify appropriate changes to improve the collection, formatting, storage, disseminating information and knowledge • implement a strategy to improve access to systems of information and knowledge to others as appropriate

Guidance

Delivery

Variety in delivery beyond seminars and tutorials will be of value in developing this unit to ensure that learners have opportunities to gain experience through a range of avenues of discovery and learning. The unit requires an investigative approach through research, background reading, case studies and, where possible, workplace experience with an emphasis on exchanges of learning and understanding between learner groups and teams.

Assessment

Evidence of outcomes may be in the form of at least two of the following:

- a reflective investigation into the communication, information and knowledge flows of an organisation familiar to the learner

- a critical appraisal of current management thinking

- an assignment into the issues of managing communications, information and knowledge in any organisation

- development of new approaches to existing models of communication, information and knowledge flow

- implementation of an innovative approach to improve the flow of communication, information and knowledge

Links

This unit has links with *Unit 13: Professional Development, Unit 14: Working with and Leading People* and *Unit 15: Managing Activities to Achieve Results.*

The unit links with many of the Management NVQ units particularly:

- Unit A3:   Develop your personal networks

- Unit D1:   Develop productive relationships with colleagues and stakeholders

- Unit F3:   Manage business processes

- Unit F12:   Improve organisational performance

Resources

Learners should have access to the internet to provide them with case studies and other information.

Whilst there is a technical element to this unit, the stress on the effective development of systems to support management decision making needs to remain the focus. There is a developing literature in this area of debate, indicated below although appropriate articles need to be sought in either the more technical or more general management journals.

Support materials

Textbooks

Avgerou C – *Information Systems and Global Diversity* (Oxford University Press, 2003) ISBN: 0199240779

Boddy D, Boonstra A and Kennedy G – *Managing Information Systems: An Organisational Perspective* (FT Prentice Hall, 2002) ISBN: 0273655957

Kovacic B – *New Approaches to Organizational Communication*(State University of New York Press, 1994) ISBN: 0791419185

Little S, Quintas P and Ray T – *Managing Knowledge: An Essential Reader* (Sage Publications, 2002) ISBN: 0761972137

McKenzie J and van Winkelen C – *Understanding the Knowledgeable Organisation* (Thomson Learning, 2004) ISBN: 1861528957

Preston P – *Reshaping Communications* (Sage Publications, 2001) ISBN: 0803985630

Quirke B – *Communicating Corporate Change* (McGraw-Hill, 1996) ISBN: 0077093119

Stewart T A – *Intellectual Capital: The New Wealth of Organisations* (Nicholas Brealey Publishing Ltd, 1998) ISBN: 1857881834

Video

The BBC and the Centre for Tomorrow's Company – *Communications* from the 'Building Tomorrow's Company' series.

BPP
PROFESSIONAL EDUCATION

STUDY GUIDE

This Course Book gives full coverage of the Edexcel guidelines. It also includes features designed specifically to make learning effective and efficient.

(a)   Each chapter begins with a summary diagram which maps out the areas covered by the chapter. You can use the diagrams during revision as a basis for your notes.

(b)   After the summary diagram there is an introduction, which sets the chapter in context. This is followed by learning objectives, which show you what you will learn as you work through the chapter.

(c)   Throughout the Course book, there are special aids to learning. These are indicated by the following symbols.

 **Signposts** guide you through the text, showing how each section connects with the next.

 Definitions give the meanings of key terms.

 Activities help you to test how much you have learnt. An indication of the time you should take on each is given. Answers are given at the end of each chapter.

 Topics for discussion are for use in seminars. They give you a chance to share your views with your fellow students. They allow you to highlight holes in your knowledge and to see how others understand concepts. If you have time, try 'teaching' someone the concepts you have learnt in a session. This helps you to remember key points and answering their questions will consolidate your knowledge.

 **Examples** relate what you have learnt to the outside world. Try to think up your own examples as you work through the Course book.

 Chapter roundups present the key information from the chapter in a concise format. Useful for revision.

NOTES

(d)   The wide **margin** on each page is for your notes. You will get the best out of this book if you interact with it. Write down your thoughts and ideas. Record examples, question theories, add references to other pages in the Course book and rephrase key points in your own words.

(e)   At the end of each chapter, there is a **chapter roundup**, and a **quick quiz** with answers. Use these to revise and consolidate your knowledge. The chapter roundup summarises the chapter. The quick quiz tests what you have learnt (the answers refer you back to the chapter so you can look over subjects again).

(f)   At the end of the book you will find a number of assignments on key topics. Practice these under timed conditions

(g)   At the end of the text, there is a bibliography and an index.

WORKING WITH AND LEADING PEOPLE

Chapter 1 :
RECRUITMENT, SELECTION AND RETENTION PROCEDURES

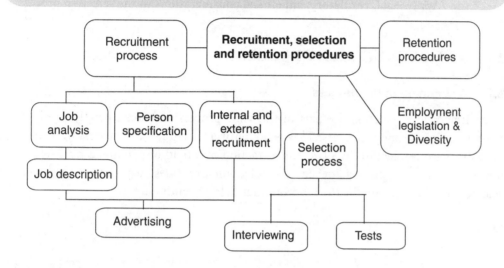

Introduction

The outcome of this chapter is for you to be able to implement recruitment, selection and retention procedures. The overall aim of the recruitment and selection process in an organisation is to obtain the quantity and quality of employees to fulfil the objectives of the organisation.

The process can be broken down into three main stages.

- Defining requirements, including the preparation of job descriptions, job specifications and personnel specifications

- Attracting potential employees, including the evaluation and use of various methods of reaching sources of applicants

- Selecting the appropriate person for the job

Once a person is recruited, it is management's responsibility to ensure that the individual is retained. A retention strategy will ensure the employee's needs are satisfied and means are found to keep him or her motivated towards achieving the organisation's goals.

The recruitment and selection process is covered by legislation that relates to equal opportunities and discrimination. However, most organisations will go beyond the requirements of equal opportunity and discrimination regulations and will encourage diversity in terms of sex, race, culture, age, religion, disability, sexual orientation and ethnicity.

Your objectives

After completing this chapter you should be able to:

(a) Identify characteristics of the person(s) required and inform potential applicants

(b) Suggest suitable methods for selection

(c) Contribute to the selection process

(d) Apply legal, regulatory and ethical considerations to the selection process

1 THE RECRUITMENT PROCESS

1.1 A summary of the process

Recruitment and selection are part of the same process and some people often refer to both as the recruitment process. This is not entirely accurate; the process of recruitment as distinct from selection involves the attraction of a field of suitable candidates for the job. Once this has been achieved, the selection processes begin; these are aimed at selecting the best person for the job from that field of candidates.

Definitions

Recruitment is the process of selecting a supply of possible candidates for positions within an enterprise.

Selection is the choosing from a number of candidates the one most suitable for a specified position.

The recruitment process involves:

(a) Detailed human resource planning defines what resources the organisation needs to meet its objectives.

(b) The sources of labour should be forecast. Internal and external sources, and media for reaching both, will be considered.

(c) Job analysis produces two outputs.

(i) A job description: a statement of the component tasks, duties, objectives and standards

(ii) A person specification: a reworking of the job specification in terms of the kind of person needed to perform the job.

(d) Recruitment as such begins with the identification of vacancies, from the requirements of the manpower plan or by a job requisition from a department, branch or office that has a vacancy.

(e) Preparation and publication of advertising information will have three aims.

(i) Attract the attention and interest of potentially suitable candidates

NOTES

(ii)   Give a favourable (but accurate) impression of the job and the organisation

(iii) Equip those interested to make an attractive and relevant application (how and to whom to apply, desired skills, qualifications and so on)

(f)   Recruitment merges into selection at the stage of processing applications and short-listing applicants for interview

(g)   Interviewing and selecting the best person for the job

(h)   Notifying applicants of the results of the selection process is the final stage of the combined recruitment and selection process.

1.2   Recruitment policy

Detailed procedures for recruitment should only be devised and implemented within the context of a coherent **policy**, or code of conduct. A typical recruitment policy might deal with:

- Internal advertisement of vacancies
- Efficient and courteous processing of applications
- Fair and accurate provision of information to potential recruits
- Selection of candidates on the basis of suitability, without discrimination

1.3   The Recruitment Code

The Institute of Personnel and Development has issued a Recruitment Code.

The IPD Recruitment Code

1   Job advertisements should state clearly the form of reply desired, in particular whether this should be a formal application form or by curriculum vitae. Preferences should also be stated if handwritten replies are required.

2   An acknowledgement of reply should be made promptly to each applicant by the employing organisation or its agent. If it is likely to take some time before acknowledgements are made, this should be made clear in the advertisement.

3   Applicants should be informed of the progress of the selection procedures, what there will be (eg group selection, aptitude tests, etc), the steps and time involved and the policy regarding expenses.

4   Detailed personal information (eg religion, medical history, place of birth, family background, etc) should not be called for unless it is relevant to the selection process.

5   Before applying for references, potential employers must secure permission of the applicant.

6   Applications must be treated as confidential.

7   The code also recommends certain courtesies and obligations on the part of the applicants.

Detailed **procedures** should be devised in order to make recruitment activity systematic and consistent throughout the organisation (especially where it is decentralised in the hands of line managers). Apart from the manpower resourcing requirements which need to be effectively and efficiently met, there is a **marketing** aspect to recruitment, as one 'interface' between the organisation and the outside world: applicants who feel they have been unfairly treated, or recruits who leave because they feel they have been misled, do not enhance the organisation's reputation in the labour market or the world at large.

1.4 Creating equal opportunities in recruitment

In order to encourage diversity and social inclusion it is essential to develop robust processes that allow those from all backgrounds to succeed. It may be necessary to hold open days and 'drop in' recruitment events and re-design application forms, or even discard forms altogether. A key opportunity is to go into target areas or communities rather than expecting potential applicants to seek the organisation out. In this way the organisation can genuinely encourage a broader staff base.

Activity 1 (30 minutes)

Find out, if you do not already know, what are the recruitment and selection procedures in your organisation, and who is responsible for each stage. The procedures manual should set this out, or you may need to ask someone in the personnel department.

Get hold of and examine some of the documentation your organisation uses. We show specimens in this chapter, but practice and terminology varies, so your own 'house style' will be invaluable. Compare your organisation's documentation with our example.

---

2 JOB ANALYSIS

The management of the organisation needs to analyse the sort of work needed to be done.

Definition

Job analysis is:

'the process of collecting, analysing and setting out information about the content of jobs in order to provide the basis for a job description and data for recruitment, training, job evaluation and performance management. Job analysis concentrates on what job holders are expected to do.' (Armstrong)

The definition shows why job analysis is important – the firm has to know what people are doing in order to recruit effectively.

2.1 Information that might be obtained from a job analysis.

Information	Comments
Purpose of the job	This might seem obvious. Someone being recruited to the accounts department will be expected to process or provide financial data. But this has to be set in the context of the organisation as a whole.

Information	Comments
Content of the job	The tasks you are expected to do. If the purpose of the job is to ensure, for example, that people get paid on time, the tasks involved include many activities related to payroll.
Accountabilities	These are the results for which you are responsible. In practice they might be phrased in the same way as a description of a task.
Performance criteria	These are the criteria which measure how good you are at the job. For a payroll technician, performance criteria includes task-related matters such as the timeliness and accuracy of your work – which are easily assessed.
Responsibility	This denotes the importance of the job. For example, a person running a department and taking decisions involving large amounts of money is more responsible that someone who only does what he or she is told. Similarly, someone might have a lot of discretion in determining what he or she will do or how he or she spends the day, whereas other people's tasks might be programmed in some detail according to a predictable routine.
Organisational factors	Who does the jobholder report to directly (line manager) or on grounds of functional authority?
Developmental factors	Relating to the job, such as likely promotion paths, if any, career prospects and so forth. Some jobs are 'dead-end' if they lead nowhere.
Environmental factors	Working conditions, security and safety issues, equipment etc.

2.2 Carrying out a job analysis

A job analysis has to be done systematically – that is why it is called an **analysis** – as the purpose is to obtain facts about the job. Therefore the job analysis involves the use of a number of different techniques to gather the data. The stages should be:

Step 1. Obtain documentary information, for main tasks and so on.

Step 2. Ask managers about more general aspects such as the job's purpose, the main activities, the responsibilities involved and the relationships with others.

Step 3. Ask the job holders similar questions about their jobs – perceptions might differ.

Step 4. Watch people at work – but they may not like it, and they may think you are engaged on a time and motion study.

2.3 Techniques of job analysis

Interviews establish basic facts about the job, from the job holder's point of view. You'll need to get hold of two sorts of information.

(a) **Basic facts** about the job, such as the job title, the jobholder's manager or team leader, people reporting to the jobholder, the main tasks or duties, official targets or performance standards.

(b) More **subjective issues**, which are harder to test which are still important, such as:

- The amount of supervision a person receives
- How much freedom a person has to take decisions
- How hard the job is
- The skills/qualifications you need to carry out the job
- How the job fits in elsewhere with the company
- How work is allocated
- Decision-making authority

This information should always be checked for accuracy.

2.4 Advantages and disadvantages of interviewing

Advantages	Disadvantages
Flexibility	Time consuming
Interactive	Hard to analyse
Easy to organise and carry out	Interviewee might feel on the defensive and might not be entirely frank
New or follow-on questions can be asked in the light of information received	
Reveals other organisational problems	

Interviewing procedures will be covered in greater detail later in this chapter.

Other techniques include:

(a) **Questionnaires**

Questionnaires are sometimes used in job analysis. Their success depends on the willingness of people to complete them accurately.

- They gather purely factual information
- They can cover large numbers of staff
- They provide a structure to the process of information gathering

(b) **Checklists and inventories**

A checklist would contain a list of activities and the job holder would have to note down how important these are in the job.

Activity description	Time spent on activity	Importance of activity
Processes sales invoices	Less than 10%	Unimportant
	10% to 20%	Not very important
	20-30%	Important
	...and so on	Very important

(c) **Observation**

People are watched doing the job. This is easy enough for jobs which can be easily observed or which are physical, but is harder for knowledge based work. But observation is quite common in assessing performance – trainee school teachers are observed in the classroom.

(d) **Self description**

Jobholders are asked to prepare their own job descriptions and to analyse their own jobs. This is quite difficult to do, because people often find it hard to stand back from what they are doing.

(e) **Diaries and logs**

People keep records of what they do over a period of time, and these can be used by the analyst to develop job descriptions. You may come across something like this in your working life, if, say, you have to keep a timesheet covering work for a particular client, or if it is part of your training record.

Which method should you use?

It depends. Any job analysis exercise might involve a variety of methods: Questionnaires or checklists save time. Interviews give a better idea of the detail. Self-description to shows how people perceive their jobs, which may be very different from how managers perceive their jobs. Diaries and logs are useful for management jobs, in which a lot is going on.

It is not always easy to carry out a job analysis, especially for managers and supervisors. The case example below shows how job analysis techniques can be adapted

CASE EXAMPLE

People Management, 6 March 1997, described **workset**, a job analysis system developed by Belbin. Workset uses colour coding to classify work and working time into seven types.

1	Blue: tasks the job holder carries out in a prescribed manner to an approved standard
2	Yellow: individual responsibility to meet an objective (results, not means)
3	Green: tasks that vary according to the reactions and needs of others
4	Orange: shared rather than individual responsibility for meeting an objective
5	Grey: work incidental to the job, not relevant to the four core categories
6	White: new or creative undertaking outside normal duties
7	Pink: demands the presence of the job holder but leads to no useful results

The manager gives an outline of the proportion of time which the manager expects the jobholder to spend on each 'colour' of work. The job holder then briefs the manager on what has actually been done. This highlights differences: between managers' and jobholders' perceptions of jobs; between the perceptions of different jobholders in the same nominal position, who had widely different ideas as to what they were supposed to do.

Important issues arise when there is a gap in perception. Underperformance in different kinds of work can be identified, and people can be steered to the sort of work which suits them best.

NOTES

Activity 2 (10 minutes)

Analyse your own working time according to the Workset classification above. Do the results surprise you?

2.5 Competences

A more recent approach to job design is the development and outlining of competences.

Definition

A person's **competence** is 'a capacity that leads to behaviour that meets the job demands within the parameters of the organisational environment and that, in turn, brings about desired results', (Boyzatis). Some take this further and suggest that a competence embodies the ability to transfer skills and knowledge to new situations within the occupational area.

2.6 Different sorts of competences.

(a) **Behavioural/personal** competences: underlying personal characteristics people bring to work (eg interpersonal skills); personal characteristics and behaviour for successful performance, for example, 'ability to relate well to others'. Most jobs require people to be good communicators.

(b) **Work-based/occupational competences** refer to 'expectations of workplace performance and the outputs and standards people in specific roles are expected to obtain'. They cover what people have to do to achieve the results of the job. For example, a competence of a Certified Accountant includes 'produce financial and other statements and report to management'.

(c) **Generic competences** can apply to all people in an occupation.

Many lists of competences confuse the following.

- Areas of **work** at which people are competent
- Underlying aspects of behaviour

2.7 Examples of competences for managers.

Competence area	Competence
Intellectual	• Strategic perspective • Analytical judgement • Planning and organising
Interpersonal	• Managing staff • Persuasiveness • Assertiveness and decisiveness • Interpersonal sensitivity • Oral communication

Competence area	Competence
Adaptability	
Results	• Initiative
	• Motivation to achievement
	• Business sense

These competences can be elaborated by identifying **positive** and **negative** indicators.

3 JOB DESCRIPTION

The job analysis is used to develop the job description.

Definition

> **Job description**. A job description sets out the purpose of a job, where it fits in the organisation structure, the context within which the job holder functions and the principal accountability of job holders and the main tasks they have to carry out.

3.1 Purpose of job description

Purpose	Comment
Organisational	The job description defines the job's place in the organisational structure
Recruitment	The job description provides information for identifying the sort of person needed (person specification)
Legal	The job description provides the basis for a contract of employment
Performance	Performance objectives can be set around the job description

3.2 Contents of a job description

(a) **Job title** (eg Assistant Financial Controller). This indicates the function/department in which the job is performed, and the level of job within that function.

(b) **Reporting to** (eg the Assistant Financial controller reports to the Financial Controller), in other words the person's immediate boss. (No other relationships are suggested here.)

(c) **Subordinates** directly reporting to the job holders.

(d) **Overall purpose** of the job, distinguishing it from other jobs.

(e) **Principal accountabilities or main tasks**

　(i) Group the main activities into a number of broad areas.

　(ii) Define each activity as a statement of accountability: what the job holder is expected to achieve (eg **tests** new system to ensure they meet agreed systems specifications).

(f) The current fashion for multi-skilled teams means that **flexibility** is sometimes expected.

Here are two examples of job descriptions.

JOB DESCRIPTION

1 *Job title:* Baking Furnace Labourer.

2 *Department:* 'B' Baking.

3 *Date:* 20 November 20X0.

4 *Prepared by:* H Crust, baking furnace manager.

5 *Responsible to:* baking furnace chargehand.

6 *Age range:* 20-40.

7 *Supervises work of:* N/A.

8 *Has regular co-operative contract with:* Slinger/Crane driver.

9 *Main duties/responsibilities:* Stacking formed electrodes in furnace, packing for stability. Subsequently unloads baked electrodes and prepares furnace for next load.

10 *Working conditions:* stacking is heavy work and requires some manipulation of 100lb (45kg) electrodes. Unloading is hot ($35° – 40°C$) and very dusty.

11 *Employment conditions:*

Wages £5.20 ph + group bonus (average earnings £257.46 pw).

Hours: Continuous rotating three-shift working days, 6 days on, 2 days off. NB must remain on shift until relieved.

Trade Union: National Union of Bread Bakers, optional.

MIDWEST BANK PLC

1 *Job title:*   Clerk (Grade 2).

2 *Branch:*   All branches and administrative offices.

3 *Job summary:*   To provide clerical support to activities within the bank.

4 *Job content:*   Typical duties will include:

(a) Cashier's duties
(b) Processing of branch clearing
(c) Processing of standing orders
(d) Support to branch management.

5 *Reporting structure*

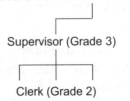

Administrative officer/assistant manager

Supervisor (Grade 3)

Clerk (Grade 2)

6 *Experience/education:* experience not required, minimum 3 GCSEs or equivalent.

7 *Training to be provided:* initial on-the-job training plus regular formal courses and training.

8 *Hours:* 38 hours per week.

9 *Objectives and appraisal:* Annual appraisal in line with objectives above.

10 *Salary:* refer to separate standard salary structure.

Job description prepared by: Head office personnel department.

Activity 3 (20 minutes)

Studying has placed you in a role in which you have to perform a fairly consistent set of duties, in fairly consistent conditions, within a structure that requires you to interact with other people, both superiors and peers (and possibly subordinates). Draw up a job description for yourself.

3.3 Alternatives to job descriptions

Detailed job descriptions are perhaps only suited for jobs where the work is largely repetitive and therefore performed by low-grade employees: once the element of **judgement** comes into a job description it becomes a straitjacket. Many difficulties arise where people adhere strictly to the contents of the job description, rather than responding flexibly to task or organisational requirements.

Perhaps job descriptions should be written in terms of the **outputs and performance levels** expected. Some firms are moving towards **accountability profiles** in which outputs and performance are identified explicitly.

Armstrong suggests a crucial difference between:

(a) A job – a group of tasks.

(b) A role. A part played by people in meeting their objectives by working competently and flexibly within the context of the organisation's objectives, structures and processes.

A **role definition** is wider than a job description. It is less concerned with the details of the job content, but how they interpret the job, and how they perceive them.

Activity 4 (30 minutes)

Without looking at the real thing, to start with, draw up a job description for your own job and for the job of a personnel/HR officer in your organisation. Now look at the official job descriptions. Are they true, detailed and up-to-date compared with the actual jobs as you saw them?

If not, what does this tell you about (a) job descriptions and (b) perceptions of the personnel/HR function?

---

4 PERSON SPECIFICATION

Definition

'A **person specification**, also known as a job or personnel specification, sets out the education, qualifications, training, experience personal attributes and competences a job holder requires to perform her or his job satisfactorily.' (Armstrong)

The job description outlines the job: the person specification describes the person needed to do the job. For example, a position of secretary or personal assistant normally requires the holder to have word processing skills.

4.1 Traditional approaches to the person specification

The **Seven Point Plan** put forward by Professor Rodger in 1951 draws the selector's attention to seven points about the candidate.

- **Physical attributes** (such as neat appearance, ability to speak clearly)
- **Attainment** (including educational qualifications)
- **General intelligence**
- **Special aptitudes** (such as neat work, speed and accuracy)
- **Interests** (practical and social)
- **Disposition** (or manner: friendly, helpful and so on)
- Background **circumstances**

4.2 Problems with the Seven Point Plan.

(a) Physical attributes or disposition might include a person's demeanour. **Eye contact** is considered a sign of honesty and frankness in some cultures, but a sign of disrespect in others.

(b) **General intelligence** is not something that can be measured easily. A criticism of IQ tests is that test scores tell you that you are good at doing IQ tests – and not much else.

(c) **Attainment**: educational qualifications – no attention is paid to the circumstances in which these were obtained.

The plan does not identify a person's **potential**, or suggest how it can be aligned precisely to the organisation's requirements.

4.3 Five-Point Pattern

Munro-Fraser's Five Point Pattern is one alternative.

- **Impact on others**: physical attributes, speech, manner
- **Acquired knowledge** and qualifications
- **Innate abilities**: ability to learn, mental agility
- **Motivation**: What sort of goals does the individual set, how much effort goes into achieving them, how successful.
- **Adjustment**: emotional stability, tolerance of slips.

4.4 New approaches: competences

The two methods described above have been in use for many years. More recruiters are using **competences** (see paragraph 2.5) in designing the person specification.

4.5 Preparing the specification

Each feature in the person specification should be classified as:

(a) **Essential.** For instance, honesty in a cashier is essential whilst a special aptitude for conceptual thought is not.

(b) **Desirable.** For instance, a reasonably pleasant manner should ensure satisfactory standards in a person dealing with the public.

(c) **Contra-indicated.** Some features are actively disadvantageous, such as an inability to work in a team when acting as project leader.

PERSON SPECIFICATION: Customer Accounts Manager			
	ESSENTIAL	DESIRABLE	CONTRA-INDICATED
Physical attributes	Clear speech Well-groomed Good health	Age 25-40	Age under 25 Chronic ill-health and absence
Attainments	2 'A' levels GCSE Maths and English Thorough knowledge of retail environment	Degree (any discipline) Marketing training 2 years' experience in supervisory post	No experience of supervision or retail environment
Intelligence	High verbal intelligence		
Aptitudes	Facility with numbers Attention to detail and accuracy Social skills for customer relations	Analytical abilities (problem solving) Understanding of systems and IT	No mathematical ability Low tolerance of technology
Interests	Social: team activity		Time-consuming hobbies 'Solo' interests only
Disposition	Team player Persuasive Tolerance of pressure and change	Initiative	Anti-social Low tolerance of responsibility
Circumstances	Able to work late, take work home	Located in area of office	

Activity 5   **(30 minutes)**

Turn your job description for A student into a corresponding Personnel Specification, using the 'essential; desirable; contra-indicated' framework, and either the Seven Point Plan or Five Point Pattern. If you did not do Activity 3, do it now! (You might like to consider into which section of your personnel specification 'laziness' would fall....)

NOTES

5 INTERNAL AND EXTERNAL RECRUITMENT PROCESSES

5.1 Recruit or promote?

Apart from the preliminary decision as to whether the job needs filling and the determination of the job description and personnel specification, a recruitment policy will outline the factors to be considered when deciding whether to recruit someone from outside to fill a vacancy *or* to promote or transfer someone from within the existing workforce.

Some of the factors to be considered in this decision are as follows.

(a) **Availability in the current staff** of the skills and attributes required to fill the vacancy. If the lead time to develop current staff to 'fit' the vacancy is too long, there may be no immediate alternative to external recruitment.

(b) **Availability in the external labour pool** of the skills and attributes required. Where there are skill shortages, it may be necessary to develop them within the organisation.

5.2 Internal recruitment

Internal recruitment occurs when a vacant position is filled by one of the existing employees. It generally applies to those jobs where there is some kind of career structure, as in the case of management or administrative staff. If a policy of internal recruitment is to be pursued the following advantages and disadvantages should be noted:

Advantages	Disadvantages
• Quick and inexpensive and no induction necessary	• Limited number of applicants
• Career progression – internal promotion is evidence of the organisation's willingness to develop people's careers	• External candidates might be better
• Reduces the risk of employing the wrong person – selection can be made on the basis of known data	• Creates another vacancy
• Will be familiar with the culture, structures, systems and procedures, objectives and other people in the organisation. This gives a head start for performance in the new position	• Could be difficulties if promoting someone to a job of supervising ex-workmates.
• No need to replace an internal post	• No suitable candidate
• Can act as a source of motivation and may be good for the general morale of the workforce (and avoid resentments)	• May create ill feeling among those not selected

5.3 External recruitment

External recruitment occurs when an organisation seeks to bring in someone from outside the organisation to fill a vacancy. In general its advantages and disadvantages are opposite to those of internal recruitment, but the following specific points should be noted.

Advantages	Disadvantages
• Wider pool of labour – may be necessary to restore manning levels, depleted by employee wastage and internal promotion policies	• Can be a long and expensive process and induction is still necessary
• May be more suitable especially if an organisation is seeking specific skills and expertise not available internally	• Increased risk of employing the wrong person
• Can inject new blood into an enterprise. External recruits bring new ideas and different approaches to the job, gleaned from their experience working in other organisations	• May block promotion for internal candidates
• No need to replace an internal post	• May create dissatisfaction among existing employees

5.4 Finding and attracting suitable candidates

There are a number of ways for organisations to find and attract suitable candidates but whatever method is chosen, it should deter people who do not meet the requirements without discouraging those who have much to offer but do not quite match the job specification. The objectives are to attract candidates of the right quality in the right number.

(a) As we have already noted, **internal promotion** is the cheapest way to recruit, and can help to motivate and keep existing employees. Using training and development programmes can also prepare employees for promotion. If internal recruitment is proposed, methods of finding and attracting candidates include a form of direct invitation where assessments are made of employees, and on the basis of these, management decide who will be offered a promotion opportunity. Some firms, however, allow employees to compete for vacancies by advertising internally, either on their website, through newsletters or by using notice boards; normal selection procedures then follow. Even where external recruitment is the main policy it does not prevent an existing employee from applying.

(b) **Nomination of existing employees** – some companies rely on recommendations from their existing staff and occasionally offer incentive schemes for successful introductions.

(c) **Casual applications** can be kept on file – sometimes applicants will write to the company on-spec, saving the time and money involved in a full-scale recruitment campaign.

(d) **Adverts** to attract candidates can be placed in appropriate publications eg, national newspapers, specialist trade magazines or local newspapers.

(e) The cheapest way to advertise is on a **website**. But this may be inefficient if a site does not attract enough visitors.

(f) **Recruitment consultants** – assist clients in selecting the best staff to fill particular vacancies. They tend to specialise in separate market sectors such as clerical and secretarial, accounting or computing.

(g) **Hiring temporary staff** can be a good way to get to know employees before offering them permanent positions.

(h) The **government employment services** – the unemployed register presents firms with a reservoir of potential employees categorised according to skill and pre-selected according to suitability.

(i) Building **relationships with local schools**, **colleges** and **universities** can attract promising candidates for trainee positions.

6   ADVERTISING THE POSITION

The object of recruitment advertising is to attract suitable candidates and deter unsuitable candidates.

6.1   Content of the advertisement

An advert should be:

(a) **Concise,** but comprehensive enough to be an accurate description of the job, its rewards and requirements.

(b) **Attractive** to the maximum number of the right people.

(c) **Positive and honest** about the organisation. Disappointed expectations will be a prime source of dissatisfaction when an applicant actually comes into contact with the organisation.

(d) **Relevant and appropriate to the job and the applicant**. Skills, qualifications and special aptitudes required should be prominently set out, along with special features of the job that might attract – on indeed deter – applicants, such as shiftwork or extensive travel.

The advertisement, based on information set out in the job description, job and person specifications and recruitment procedures, should contain information about:

(a) The **organisation**: its main business and location, at least.

(b) The **job**: title, main duties and responsibilities and special features.

(c) **Conditions**: special factors affecting the job.

(d) **Qualifications and experience** (required, and preferred); other attributes, aptitudes and/or knowledge required.

(e) **Rewards**: salary, benefits, opportunities for training, career development, and so on.

(f) **Application process**: how to apply, to whom, and by what date.

It should encourage a degree of **self-selection**, so that the target population begins to narrow itself down. The information contained in the advertisement should deter unsuitable applicants as well as encourage potentially suitable ones.

6.2 Factors influencing the choice of advertising medium

(a) **The type of organisation**. A factory is likely to advertise a vacancy for an unskilled worker in a different way to a company advertising for a member of the Institute of Personnel and Development for an HRM position.

(b) **The type of job**. Managerial jobs may merit national advertisement, whereas semi-skilled jobs may only warrant local coverage, depending on the supply of suitable candidates in the local area. Specific skills may be most appropriately reached through trade, technical or professional journals, such as those for accountants or computer programmers.

(c) **The cost of advertising**. It is more expensive to advertise in a national newspaper than on local radio, and more expensive to advertise on local radio than in a local newspaper etc.

(d) The **readership and circulation** (type and number of readers/listeners) of the medium, and its suitability for the number and type of people the organisation wants to reach.

(e) The **frequency** with which the organisation wants to advertise the job vacancy, and the duration of the recruitment process.

NOTES

Activity 6 (20 minutes)

Dealing with individuals demands a certain... ...um...

You've heard the old line...
'You don't have to be mad to work here, but it helps'. It's like that at AOK, but in the nicest possible way. We believe that our Personnel Department should operate for the benefit of our staff, and not that staff should conform to statistical profiles. It doesn't make for an easy life, but dealing with people as individuals, rather than numbers, certainly makes it a rewarding one.

We're committed to an enlightened personnel philosophy. We firmly believe that our staff are our most important asset, and we go a long way both to attract the highest quality of people, and to retain them.

AOK is a company with a difference. We're a highly progressive, international organisation, one of the world's leading manufacturers in the medical electronics field.

...Character

As an expanding company, we now need another experienced Personnel Generalist to join us at our UK headquarters in Reigate, Surrey.

Essentially we're looking for an individual, a chameleon character who will assume an influential role in recruitment, employee relations, salary administration, compensation and benefits, or whatever the situation demands. The flexibility to interchange with various functions is vital. Within your designated area, you'll experience a large degree of independence. You'll be strong in personality, probably already experienced in personnel management in a small company. Whatever your background you'll certainly be someone who likes to help people help themselves and who is happy to get involved with people at all levels within the organisation.

Obviously, in a fast growing company with a positive emphasis on effective personnel work, your prospects for promotion are excellent. Salaries are highly attractive and benefits are, of course, comprehensive.

So if you're the kind of personnel individual who enjoys personal contact, problem solving, and will thrive on the high pace of a progressive, international organisation, such as AOK, get in touch with us by writing or telephoning, quoting ref: 451/BPD, to AOK House, Reigate, Surrey.

What do you think of this advertisement? How can you improve it?

6.3 Media for recruitment advertising

(a) **In-house magazine, notice-boards,** e-mail or its 'intranet'. An organisation might invite applications from employees who would like a transfer or a promotion to the particular vacancy advertised.

(b) **Professional and specialist newspapers or magazines,** such as *Accountancy Age, Marketing Week* or *Computing.*

(c) **National newspapers** are used for senior management jobs or vacancies for skilled workers, where potential applicants will not necessarily be found through local advertising.

(d) **Local newspapers** would be suitable for jobs where applicants are sought from the local area.

(e) **Local radio, television and cinema.** These are becoming increasingly popular, especially for large-scale campaigns for large numbers of vacancies.

(f) **Job centres.** Vacancies for unskilled work (rather than skilled work or management jobs) are advertised through local job centres, although in theory any type of job can be advertised here.

(g) **School and university careers offices.** Ideally, the manager responsible for recruitment in an area should try to maintain a close liaison with careers officers. Some large organisations organise special meetings or **careers fairs** in universities and colleges (the so-called 'milk round'), as a kind of showcase for the organisation and the careers it offers.

(h) The **Internet**. Any personal computer user may access the network, independently or via an Internet service provider such as CompuServe.

7 THE SELECTION PROCESS

7.1 Procedure

Selection is the process that leads to a decision being made as to whether an individual is offered and takes up employment with an organisation. It is really a two–way process, not only is the firm selecting the individual but invariably the individual is making decisions as to the suitability of the job offered, the terms of employment and the organisation.

The stages include the following.

Step 1. Deal with responses to job advertisements. This might involve sending **application forms** to candidates. Not all firms bother with these, however, preferring to review CVs.

Step 2. Assess each application or CV against **key criteria** in the job advertisement and specification. Critical factors may include age, qualifications, experience or whatever.

Step 3. **Sort applications** into 'possible', 'unsuitable' and 'marginal'.

'Possibles' will then be more closely scrutinised, and a shortlist for interview drawn up. Ideally, this should be done by both the personnel specialist and the prospective manager of the successful candidate.

Step 4. **Invite candidates for interviews.**

Step 5. Reinforce interviews with **selection testing,** if suitable.

Step 6. Review un-interviewed 'possibles', and 'marginals', and put potential future candidates on hold, or in reserve.

Step 7. Send standard letters to unsuccessful applicants, and inform them simply that they have not been successful. Reserves will be sent a holding letter: 'We will keep your details on file, and should any suitable vacancy arise in future...'.

Step 8. Make a provisional offer to the recruit.

7.2 Selection methods

Attracting a wide choice of applicants will be of little use unless there is a way of measuring how people differ eg, in intelligence, attitudes, social skills, physical characteristics, experience etc and extending this to a prediction of performance in the workplace.

Successful selection means matching the organisation's and the applicant's requirements through the exchange of information.

The organisation provides applicants with an objective description of the company and the job, while the applicants provide information about their capabilities.

A number of techniques can reveal this information. Selecting is choosing from among the applicants the one that meets the position requirements. Methods of selection include the following:

- Application forms
- CVs and covering letters
- Shortlists
- Interviews
- Tests
- References
- Medical examinations
- Group selection methods
- Situational tests
- Assessment centres.

The selection process starts with the sifting and sorting of paper details – the application forms and submitted CVs. Once the shortlist is drawn up, the next stage is to determine the best methods of further assessment. The selection interview is probably the most popular of these methods, although other techniques – assessment centres, psychometric testing and ability testing – will all be considered.

We will discuss interviews and tests after briefly examining the other methods identified.

7.3 Application forms

The **application form** usually seeks information about the applicant on several fronts, namely:

(a) Personal details of address, age, family background, nationality
(b) Education and experience history
(c) Present employment terms and experience
(d) Social and leisure interests.

The application form should be regarded by the applicant as an opportunity to qualify for the interview. It usually includes a general section enabling the applicant to express career ambitions, personal preferences, etc, in his or her own words. This can be an important section in gauging an applicant's ability to express himself/herself in writing and perhaps even aspects of motivation, ambition and character.

As well as obtaining all the essential information about the applicant, the purposes of the application form are:

- To eliminate totally unsuitable candidates

- To act as a useful preliminary to selection interviews. Basic information can be gained which would otherwise take up valuable interview time. Some interviewers use the form as the framework for the interview itself; it can be a particularly useful guide for inexperienced interviewers. It forms the nucleus of the personal record of individual employees.

> **Activity 7**   **(10 minutes)**
>
> Suggest four possible design faults in job application forms. You may be able to draw on your own personal experience.

7.4 CVs and covering letters

A CV or 'Curriculum Vitae' will provide prospective employers with a summary of the applicant's relevant life experiences and skills to date. It is essentially a record of his or her personal, educational and work details, which emphasises the experience, knowledge and skills relevant to the type of job vacancy. The purpose of the CV is to generate enough interest for the employer to want to take the application further.

Many job adverts ask for a CV and a covering letter. A good covering letter introduces the author to the reader and stimulates interest in the attached CV and is essential when applying speculatively to an advertised position. Also, if there are further points that need to be mentioned in addition to an application form, it may be appropriate to attach a brief covering letter.

7.5 References

References are used by most employers as a key part of their selection process, but mainly to verify facts about the candidate rather than as an aid to decision making. The reference check is usually the last stage in the selection process and referees should be contacted only after the applicant has given permission. Good referees are almost certain to know more about the applicant than the selector and it would be foolish not to seek their advice or treat the reference check as a mere formality.

A reference should contain two types of information.

(a) Straightforward **factual information.** This confirms the nature of the applicant's previous job(s), period of employment, pay, and circumstances of leaving.

(b) **Opinions** about the applicant's personality and other attributes. These should obviously be treated with some caution. Allowances should be made for prejudice (favourable or unfavourable), charity (withholding detrimental remarks), and possibly fear of being actionable for libel (although references are privileged, as long as they are factually correct and devoid of malice).

As well as the applicant's suitability for employment, the reference may provide information on strengths and weaknesses, training needs and potential for future development.

Written references save time, especially if a standardised letter or form has been pre-prepared. A simple letter inviting the previous employer to reply with the basic information and judgements required may suffice. A standard form to be completed by the referee may be more acceptable, and might pose a set of simple questions about:

- Job title
- Main duties and responsibilities
- Period of employment
- Pay/salary
- Attendance record

If a judgement of character and suitability is desired, it might be most tellingly formulated as the question: 'Would you re-employ this individual? (If not, why not?).'

Telephone references may be timesaving if standard reference letters or forms are not available. They may also elicit a more honest opinion than a carefully prepared written statement. For this reason, a telephone call may also be made to check or confirm a poor or grudging reference, which the recruiter suspects may be prejudiced.

7.6   Shortlists

Shortlisting applicants is undertaken by comparing information provided about the applicants against the essential and desirable characteristics listed in the person specification. This information comes from application forms, CVs, references and testimonials; university, college or school reports; service discharge documents; and possibly a medical report. They can be sorted into 'probable', 'possible' and 'rejected' or some similar set of headings. The aim is to find about six candidates who meet most of the essential requirements and some of the desirable ones.

Six is considered 'ideal' as they can all be interviewed during a single working day and compared with one another while impressions are still fresh in the interviewers' minds. More than six 'probables' allows more stringent standards to be implemented to reduce the numbers. Less than six means sorting through the 'possibles' to select enough to make up the numbers.

After short-listing, selected applicants are referred to as 'candidates'. They are placed on a shortlist and generally invited to interviews.

7.7   Group selection methods

Group selection methods might be used by an organisation as the final stage of a selection process as a more 'natural' and in-depth appraisal of candidates. Group assessments tend to be used for posts requiring leadership, communication or team-working skills: advertising agencies often use the method for selecting account executives, for example.

They consist of a series of tests, interviews and group situations over a period of two days, involving a small number of candidates for a job. After an introductory session to make the candidates feel at home, they will be given one or two tests, one or two individual interviews, and several group situations in which the candidates are invited to discuss problems together and arrive at solutions as a management team.

A variety of tools and techniques are used in group selection, including:

(a) **Group role-play exercises,** in which they can explore (and hopefully display) interpersonal skills and/or work through simulated managerial tasks

(b) **Case studies,** where candidates' analytical and problem-solving abilities are tested in working through described situations/problems, as well as their interpersonal skills, in taking part in (or leading) group discussion of the case study

These group sessions might be thought useful because of the following reasons.

(a) They give the organisation's selectors a longer opportunity to study the candidates.

(b) They reveal more than application forms, interviews and tests alone about the ability of candidates to persuade others, negotiate with others, and explain ideas to others and also to investigate problems efficiently. These are typically management skills.

(c) They reveal more about how the candidate's personality and attributes will affect the work team and his own performance.

7.8 Work sampling

Work sampling is a technique used for two purposes.

(a) It is used to discover the proportions of total time devoted to the various components of a job. It is also known as job sampling. Data obtained from work sampling can be used to establish allowances applicable to a job, to determine machine utilisation, and to provide the criteria for production standards. Although the same information can be obtained by time-study procedures, work sampling usually provides the information faster and at less cost.

(b) It is also used to describe a performance test designed to be a miniature replica of behaviour required on-the-job, which attempts to measure how well an employee will perform in the particular occupation. Such tests are considered a more precise device for measuring particular occupational abilities than simple motor skills or verbal ability tests.

7.9 Assessment centres

The assessment centre is really a combination of many forms of selection, but at present its use is confined more to the selection of employees for promotion. Groups of around six to ten candidates are brought together for one to three days of intensive assessment. They are presented, individually and as a group, with a variety of exercises, tests of ability, personality assessments, interviews, work samples, team problem solving and written tasks. As well as being multi-method, other characteristics of assessment centres are that they use several assessors and they assess several dimensions of performance required in the higher-level positions.

Traditionally, the main purpose of assessment centres has been to contribute to management decisions about people, usually the assessment of management skills and potential as a basis for promotion decisions. Assessment centres are better at predicting future performance than are judgements made by unskilled managers, and it is the

BPP
PROFESSIONAL EDUCATION

combination of techniques which contributes to their apparent superiority over other approaches.

8 INTERVIEWS

Most firms use the selection interview as their main source for decision-making.

8.1 Purpose of the interview

(a) Finding the best person for the job, by giving making the organisation a chance to assess applicants (and particularly their interpersonal communication skills) directly.

(b) Making sure that applicants understand the job, what the career prospects are and have suitable information about the company.

(c) Giving the best possible impression of the organisation – after all, the candidate may have other offers elsewhere.

(d) Making all applicants feel that they have been given **fair treatment** in the interview, whether they get the job or not.

8.2 Conducting selection interviews: matters to be kept in mind

(a) The **impression** of the organisation given by the interview arrangements.

(b) The **psychological effects** of the location of the interview and seating arrangements.

(c) The **manner and tone** of the interviewers.

(d) Getting the candidates to talk freely (by asking open questions) and honestly (by asking probing questions), in accordance with the organisation's need for **information.**

(e) The **opportunity for the candidate to learn** about the job and organisation.

(f) The control of **bias** or hasty judgement by the interviewer.

8.3 Preparation for the interview

Welcoming the candidate. Candidates should be given:

(a) Clear instructions about the date, time and location – perhaps with a map.
(b) The name of a person to contact.
(c) A place to wait (with cloakroom facilities), perhaps with tea or coffee.

The interview room

(a) The interview is where the organisation 'sells' itself and the candidate aims to give a good impression. The layout of the room should be carefully designed. Being 'interrogated' by two people from the other side of a desk may be completely unsuitable.

(b) Some interviews are deliberately tough, to see how a candidate performs under pressure.

The agenda. The agenda and questions will be based on:

(a) The job description and what abilities are required of the jobholder.

(b) The personnel specification. The interviewer must be able to judge whether the applicant matches up to the personal qualities required from the jobholder.

(c) The application form or the applicant's CV: the qualities the applicant claims to possess.

8.4 Conduct of the interview

Questions should be paced and put carefully. The interviewer should not be trying to confuse the candidate, plunging immediately into demanding questions or picking on isolated points; neither, however, should s(he) allow the interviewee to digress or gloss over important points. The interviewer must retain control over the information-gathering process.

Type of question	Comment
Open questions	('Who...? What...? Where...? When...? Why....?') These force candidates to put together their own responses in complete sentences. This encourages them to talk, keeps the interview flowing, and is most revealing ('Why do you want to be a marketing assistant?')
Probing questions	Similar to open questions, these aim to discover the deeper significance of the candidate's answers, especially if they are initially dubious, uninformative, too short, or too vague. ('But what was it about marketing that **particularly** appealed to you?')
Closed questions	Invite only 'yes' or 'no' answers: ('Did you...?, 'Have you...?').
	These elicit an answer **only** to the question asked. This may be useful where there are small points to be established ('Did you pass your exam?'), but they do not encourage the same degree of revelation as an open question, and may only give part of the picture. (Did candidate pass their exam first time, or with top grades, for example.)
	Candidates cannot express their personality, or interact with the interviewer on a deeper level.
	They make it easier for candidates to conceal things ('You never asked me...').
	They make the interviewer work very hard.
Multiple questions	Two or more questions are asked at once. ('Tell me about your last job? How did your knowledge of accountancy help you there, and do you think you are up-to-date or will you need to spend time studying?'). This encourages the candidate to talk at some length, without straying too far from the point. It might also test the candidate's ability to listen, and to handle large amount of information.

NOTES

Type of question	Comment
Problem solving questions	Present the candidate with a situation and ask him/her to explain how he/she would deal with it. ('How would you motivate your staff to do a task that they did not want to do?'). Such questions are used to establish whether the candidate will be able to deal with the sort of problems that are likely to arise in the job.
Leading questions	Encourage the candidate to give a certain reply. ('We are looking for somebody who likes detailed figure work. How much do you enjoy dealing with numbers?' or 'Don't you agree that...?' 'Surely...?'). The danger with this type of question is that the candidate will give the answer that he thinks the interviewer wants to hear.

Activity 8   **(10 minutes)**

Identify the type of question used in the following examples, and discuss the opportunities and constraints they offer the interviewee who must answer them.

(a) 'So, you're interested in a Business Studies degree, are you, Jo?'

(b) 'Surely you're interested in Business Studies, Jo?'

(c) 'How about a really useful qualification like a Business Studies degree, Jo? Would you consider that?'

(d) 'Why are you interested in a Business Studies degree, Jo?

(e) 'Why particularly Business Studies, Jo?'

8.5 Evaluating the response

(a) The interviewer must **listen carefully** to the responses and evaluate them so as to judge what the **candidate** is:

- Wanting to say
- Trying **not** to say
- Saying, but does not mean, or is lying about
- Having difficulty saying

(b) In addition, the interviewer will have to be aware when he/she is hearing:

- Something he/she needs to know

- Something he/she **doesn't** need to know

- Only what he/she **expects** to hear

- Inadequately – when his or her own attitudes, perhaps prejudices, are getting in the way of an objective response to the candidate

Candidates should be given the opportunity to ask questions. The choice of questions might well have some influence on how the interviewers assess a candidate's interest in and understanding of the job. Moreover, there is information that the candidate will need to know about the organisation, the job, and indeed the interview process.

8.6 Types of interview

Individual or **one-to-one interviews**. These are the **most common** selection method.

(a) **Advantages**

    (i) **Direct** face-to-face communication.

    (ii) **Rapport** between the candidate and the interviewer: each has to give attention solely to the other, and there is potentially a relaxed atmosphere, if the interviewer is willing to establish an informal style.

(b) The **disadvantage** of a one-to-one interview is the scope it allows for a biased or superficial decision.

    (i) The **candidate** may be able to **disguise** lack of knowledge in a specialist area of which the interviewer knows little.

    (ii) The **interviewer's** perception may be selective or **distorted**, and this lack of objectivity may go unnoticed and unchecked.

    (iii) The greater opportunity for personal rapport with the candidate may cause a **weakening of the interviewer's objective judgement**.

Panel interviews are designed to overcome such disadvantages. A panel may consist of two or three people who together interview a single candidate: most commonly, an HR specialist and the departmental manager who will have responsibility for the successful candidate. This saves the firm time and enables better assessment.

Large formal panels, or **selection boards**, may also be convened where there are a number of individuals or groups with an interest in the selection.

(a) **Advantage**. A number of people see candidates, and share information about them at a single meeting: similarly, they can compare their assessments on the spot, without a subsequent effort at liaison and communication.

(b) **Drawbacks**

    (i) Questions tend to be more varied, and more random, since there is **no single guiding force** behind the interview strategy. The candidate may have trouble switching from one topic to another so quickly, especially if questions are not led up to, and not clearly put – as may happen if they are unplanned. Candidate are also seldom allowed to expand their answers and so may not be able to do justice to themselves.

    (ii) If there is a **dominating member** of the board, the interview may have greater continuity – but that individual may also influence the judgements of other members.

    (iii) Some candidates may not perform well in a formal, artificial situation such as the board interview, and may find such a situation extremely stressful.

    (iv) Research shows that **board members rarely agree** with each other in their judgements about candidates.

8.7 The limitations of interviews

Interviews are criticised because **they fail to provide accurate predictions** of how a person will perform in the job, partly because of the nature of interviews, partly because of the errors of judgement by interviewers.

Problem	Comment
Scope	• An interview is **too brief** to 'get to know' candidates in the kind of depth required to make an accurate prediction of work performance. • An interview is an **artificial situation**: candidates may be on their best behaviour or, conversely, so nervous that they do not do themselves justice. Neither situation reflects what the person is really like.
The halo effect	A tendency for people to make an initial **general judgement** about a person based on a **single obvious attribute**, such as being neatly dressed or well-spoken. This single attribute will colour later perceptions, and might make an interviewer mark the person up or down on every other factor in their assessments.
Contagious bias	The interviewer changes the behaviour of the applicant by suggestion. The applicant might be led by the wording of questions or non-verbal cues from the interviewer, and change what (s)he is doing or saying in response.
Stereotyping	Stereotyping groups people together who are assumed to share certain characteristics (women, say, or vegetarians), then attributes certain traits to the group as a whole (emotional, socialist etc). It then (illogically) assumes that each individual member of the supposed group will possess that trait.
Incorrect assessment	Qualitative factors such as motivation, honesty or integrity are very difficult assess in an interview.
Logical error	An interviewer might decide that a young candidate who has held two or three jobs in the past for only a short time will be unlikely to last long in any job. (Not necessarily so.)
Inexperienced interviewers	• Inability to evaluate information about a candidate properly • Failure to compare a candidate against the requirements for a job or a personnel specification • Bad planning of the interview • Failure to take control of the direction and length of the interview • A tendency either to act as an inquisitor and make candidates feel uneasy or to let candidates run away with the interview • A reluctance to probe into fact and challenge statements where necessary

While some interviewers may be experts for the human resources function, it is usually thought desirable to include **line managers** in the interview team. They cannot be full-time interviewers, obviously: they have their other work to do. No matter how much training they are given in the interview techniques, they will lack continuous experience, and probably not give interviewing as much thought or interest as they should.

9 TESTS

In some job selection procedures, an interview is supplemented by some form of **selection test**. Tests must be:

(a) **Sensitive** enough to discriminate between different candidates.

(b) **Standardised** on a representative sample of the population, so that a person's results can be interpreted meaningfully.

(c) **Reliable**: in that the test should measure the same thing whenever and to whomever it is applied.

(d) **Valid**: it measures what it is supposed to measure.

9.1 Types of tests

The science of measuring mental capacities and processes is called 'psychometrics'; hence the term **psychometric testing**. Types of test commonly used in practice are:

- Intelligence tests
- Aptitude tests
- Personality tests
- Proficiency tests

Intelligence tests

Tests of **general intellectual ability** typically test memory, ability to think quickly and logically, and problem solving skills.

(a) Most people have experience of IQ tests and the like, and few would dispute their validity as good measure of **general** intellectual capacity.

(b) However, there is no agreed definition of intelligence.

Aptitude tests

Aptitude tests are designed to **measure** and predict an individual's potential for performing a job or learning new skills.

- **Reasoning**: verbal, numerical and abstract
- **Spatio-visual ability**: practical intelligence, non-verbal ability and creative ability
- **Perceptual speed and accuracy**: clerical ability
- **'Manual' ability**: mechanical, manual, musical and athletic

Personality tests

Personality tests may measure a variety of characteristics, such as an applicant's skill in dealing with other people, his ambition and motivation or his emotional stability.

CASE EXAMPLE

Probably the best known example is the 16PF, originally developed by Cattell in 1950.

The 16PF comprises 16 scales, each of which measure a factor that influences the way a person behaves.

The factors are functionally different underlying personality characteristics, and each is associated with not just one single piece of behaviour but rather is the source of a relatively broad range of behaviours. For this reason the factors themselves are referred to as source traits and the behaviours associated with them are called surface traits.

The advantage of measuring source traits, as the 16PF does, is that you end up with a much richer understanding of the person because you are not just describing what can be seen but also the characteristics underlying what can be seen.

The 16PF analyses how a person is likely to behave generally including, for example, contribution likely to be made to particular work contexts, aspects of the work environment to which the person is likely to more or less suited, and how best to manage the person.

The validity of such tests has been much debated, but is seems that some have been shown by research to be valid predictors of job performance, so long as they are used **properly.**

Proficiency tests

Proficiency tests are perhaps the most closely related to an assessor's objectives, because they **measure ability to do the work involved**. An applicant for an audio typist's job, for example, might be given a dictation tape and asked to type it.

9.2 Trends in the use of tests

(a) Continuing enthusiasm for personality tests.

(b) The continuing influence of cognitive ability intelligence tests.

(c) A focus on certain popular themes – sales ability or aptitude, customer orientation, motivation, teamworking and organisational culture are mentioned.

(d) The growing diversity of test producers and sources (meaning more choice, but also more poor quality measures).

(e) Expanded packages of tests, including tapes, computer disks, workbooks and so on.

(f) A growing focus on fairness: the most recent edition of the 16PF test, for example, has been scrutinised by expert psychologists to exclude certain types of content that might lead to bias.

9.3 Limitations of testing

(a) There is not always a direct relationship between ability in the test and ability in the job: the job situation is very different from artificial test conditions.

(b) The **interpretation of test results is a skilled task,** for which training and experience is essential. It is also highly subjective (particularly in the case of personality tests), which belies the apparent scientific nature of the approach.

(c) Additional difficulties are experienced with particular kinds of test. For example:

   (i) An aptitude test measuring arithmetical ability would need to be constantly revised or its content might become known to later applicants.

   (ii) Personality tests can often give misleading results because applicants seem able to guess which answers will be looked at most favourably.

   (iii) It is difficult to design intelligence tests which give a fair chance to people from different cultures and social groups and which test the **kind** of intelligence that the organisation wants from its employees: the ability to **score highly in IQ** tests does not necessarily correlate with desirable traits such as mature **judgement** or **creativity**, merely mental ability.

   (iv) Most tests are subject to coaching and practice effects.

(d) **It is difficult to exclude bias from tests.** Many tests (including personality tests) are tackled less successfully by women than by men, or by some candidates born overseas than by indigenous applicants because of the particular aspect chosen for testing.

10 EMPLOYMENT LEGISLATION AND DIVERSITY

10.1 Employment

After the selection process, the formal offer of employment is made and (hopefully) acknowledged.

The Employment Protection (Consolidation) Act 1978 defines the terms of a contract of employment. The express terms are specifically stated in the contract, which must provide the names of the parties concerned, the date of the commencement of the job, its title, terms of payment, working hours, holiday, sick pay and pension entitlements, notice of termination of employment, discipline and grievance procedures.

A medical examination may be required. This ensures the person is physically suited to the job and safeguards the organisation from the engagement of anyone who suffers from infectious diseases and strictly forms part of the selection process.

10.2 Equal opportunities and discrimination legislation

'Equal opportunities' is a generic term describing the belief that there should be an equal chance for all workers to apply and be selected for jobs, to be trained and promoted in employment and to have that employment terminated fairly. Employers should only discriminate according to ability, experience and potential. All employment decisions should be based solely on a person's ability to do the job in question; no consideration should be taken of a person's sex, age, racial origin, disability or marital status.

Discrimination against various groups in an organisation has been made unlawful and legislation, which relates to equal opportunities and discrimination includes the following.

(a) The *Equal Pay Act 1970* – this Act is intended to prevent discrimination between men and women with regards to the terms and conditions of employment. It aims to ensure that where men and women are employed in like work or work of an equivalent nature, they will receive the same terms and conditions of employment.

(b) The *Sex Discrimination Act 1975* – renders it unlawful to make any form of discrimination in employment affairs because of marital status or sex. The Act applies to offers of employment, dismissal and opportunities for promotion, transfer, training and other benefits. It applies especially to the selection process as it offers protection to both sexes against unfair treatment on appointment. Note that there are two kinds of discrimination, direct and indirect.

Direct discrimination – occurs when someone is treated less favourably than someone of the opposite sex – perhaps by being banned from applying for a job because of being a woman. This type is not difficult to discover.

Indirect discrimination – in this case, an employer may relate a condition to an applicant for a job that does not actually seem relevant to it, but which suggests that only one sex would be acceptable. An example of this may be advertising so that only men are encouraged to apply.

(c) The *Disability Discrimination Act 1995* – Provides for disabled people not to be discriminated against in a variety of circumstances including employment.

(d) The *Race Relations Act 1976* – discrimination is expressed in terms of 'racial grounds' and 'racial groups' and relate to colour, race, nationality or other ethnic or national origins. The term ethnic has been held to be much wider than race. The Race Relations Act uses a broadly similar approach to that of the Sex Discrimination Act and uses the same categorisations of direct and indirect discrimination and victimisation.

(e) The *Rehabilitation of Offenders Act 1974* – provides that a conviction, other than one involving imprisonment for more than 30 months, may become erased if the offender commits no further serious offences during the rehabilitation period, which varies according to the age of the person convicted and the length of the sentence imposed.

10.3 Formulating an effective equal opportunities policy

A number of employers label themselves as equal opportunity employers, establishing their own particular kind of equal opportunity policy. While some protection is afforded by employment legislation, the majority of everyday cases must rely on good practice to prevail.

The main areas where good practice can be demonstrated are:

- **Job analysis** – person specifications must not be more favourable to men or women.

- **Advertisements and documentation** – must not discriminate on sex or marital status grounds. This means that job titles must be sexless eg 'salesman' becomes 'sales person'.

- **Employee interviewing and selection** – questions must not be asked at interviews which discriminate by implication eg asking a woman whether or not she intends to have children.

Some employers have begun to address the underlying problems of equal opportunities, with further measures such as the following.

(a) Putting equal opportunities high on the agenda by appointing Equal Opportunities Managers who report directly to the Personnel/HR Director.

(b) Flexible hours or part-time work, term-time or annual hours contracts (to allow for school holidays) to help women to combine careers with family responsibilities. Terms and conditions, however, must not be less favourable.

(c) Career-break or return-to-work schemes for women.

(d) Fast-tracking school-leavers, as well as graduates, and posting managerial vacancies internally, giving more opportunities for movement up the ladder for groups (typically women and minorities) currently at lower levels of the organisation.

(e) Training for women-returners or women in management to help women to manage their career potential. Assertiveness training may also be offered as part of such an initiative.

(f) Awareness training for managers, to encourage them to think about equal opportunity policy.

(g) The provision of workplace nurseries for working mothers.

(h) Positive action to encourage job and training applications from minority groups.

(i) Alteration of premises to accommodate wheelchair users, blind or partially sighted workers and so on.

10.4 Diversity and equal opportunities

Definition

Diversity: 'all the ways in which we are different and similar along an infinite number of lines.'

Diversity refers to a broad range of characteristics including: gender, age, race, disability, cultural background, sexual orientation, education, religious belief, class and family responsibilities. Four distinct dimensions characterise the many facets of differences and similarities of diverse employees. These four dimensions are as follows.

(a) **Personality dimensions:** The unique characteristics of each individual that directly impact communication with others, which may include, patient or impatient, doer or thinker, assertive or non-assertive, listener or talker, flexible or inflexible, rational or emotional.

(b) **Internal dimensions:** Diversity characteristics that for the most part are not within a person's control, but shape expectations, assumptions and opportunities such as, age, gender, ethnicity, race, physical ability and sexual orientation.

(c) **External dimensions:** Social factors and life experiences that are more under a person's control and also exert a significant impact on behaviour and attitude. Examples of these include religion, marital status, parental status, educational background, income, appearance, geographic location, and work experience.

(d) **Organisational dimensions:** Characteristics of a person's experience within an organisation that impact assumptions, expectations, and opportunities. This may include functional level or classification, management status, department/division/unit and work group, union affiliation, work location, seniority, work content or field.

From the employer's point of view, an organisation's workforce is **representative** when it reflects or exceeds the demographic composition of the external work force. A representative work force reflects or exceeds the current proportions of women, visible minorities and persons with disabilities in each occupation as are known to be available in the external work force and from which the employer may reasonably be expected to draw.

A representative work force is a good indication that an employer is not limiting access to the skills and talents of workers by discriminating on the basis of sex, race, colour or disability. A non-representative work force signals the need for evaluation and action, so that whatever is blocking or discouraging certain groups from employment and advancement may be corrected.

Some organisations set themselves goals on the representation of certain groups eg, there is an under-representation of certain ethnic groups within the police force. To address this type of problem, a **diversity assessment** will show how an organisation's systems may provide support or may act as a barrier to diversity.

Diversity assessment

A diversity assessment is a structured process to gather information about the experience of current employees and, if desired, former employees using employee focus groups, personal interviews with senior managers, and telephone interviews with employees who have left the organisation.

The three general approaches for implementing diversity in an organisation are:

(a) **Affirmative action** – an approach with a goal to gain representation and upward mobility for ethnic minorities and women. It is focused on special efforts for targeted groups who are under-utilised.

(b) **Valuing diversity** – an approach with a goal to improve the quality of relationships between people. It is focused on understanding the cultural similarities and differences within an organisation. There is strong research evidence (Meredith Belbin's 1981 studies on team effectiveness) to support the view that groups that have a diverse mix of experiences, skills, knowledge and working approaches are generally more creative and productive than groups with a more uniform profile. Diversity is therefore a valuable organisational asset, and needs to be perceived as such.

(c) **Managing diversity** – an approach with a goal to improve the full use of all human resources in the organisation. The process is focused on creating a diversity friendly management system. It opens up the whole system to change and questions the policies and practices of the organisation in light of the current diverse environment.

Managing diversity

Managing diversity is a strategic decision and commitment is more than adherence to legal responsibilities – it means creating an environment which values and uses the contributions of people with different backgrounds, experiences and perspectives. It is a value that needs to be taken on by all levels of staff and translated into a working culture.

The equal opportunities approach is often seen as trying to 'right a wrong' for certain groups and create a level playing field. Those working within a diversity framework, on the other hand, embrace different employees or customers as individuals and not members of a disadvantaged social group, and see difference as potentially a resource. It introduces equity.

Equality and equity

Definition

> **Equality** = sameness. When we treat people equally we ignore differences.
>
> **Equity** = fairness. When we treat people equitably we recognise differences.

Equity relates to the fairness of outcomes and of the procedures used to determine the outcomes.

Barriers to managing diversity

The two things that might get in the way of this are:

1 **Intentional discrimination** (attitudes) eg, sexism, racism, ageism, nationalism, nepotism, favouritism and protectionism

2 **Systemic discrimination** (behaviours) eg, seniority systems, referral systems, old boys/new girls networks, unnecessary language barriers, non-*bona fide* job requirements, limited advertising, unfair communications systems and non recognition of qualifications

A 'managing diversity' orientation implies the need to be proactive in managing the needs of a diverse workforce in areas (beyond the requirements of equal opportunity and discrimination regulations) such as:

- Tolerance of individual differences

- Communicating effectively with (and motivating) ethnically diverse work forces

- Managing workers with increasingly diverse family structures and responsibilities

- Managing the adjustments to be made by an increasingly aged work force

- Managing increasingly diverse career aspirations/patterns and ways of organising working life (including flexible working)

- Confronting issues of literacy, numeracy and differences in qualifications in an international work force

- Managing co-operative working in ethnically diverse teams.

As the workforce becomes more diverse, organisations need to create cultures in which all employees can develop their potential and flourish. Recognising 'individuality' is not only the right thing to do, but it can have a measurable impact on productivity and its profitability.

The 'business case' approach is shown in the figure below.

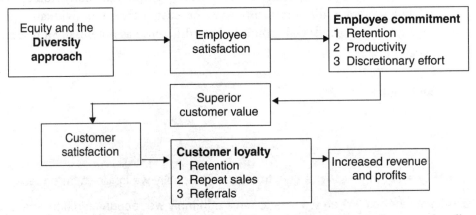

Figure 1.1 Business case for managing diversity

Benefits to the business of managing diversity

Management believe that the benefits will be:

(a) A more positive working environment. By respecting difference, individuals are made to feel more valued and consequently employee loyalty and productivity is increased, and staff turnover decreased.

(b) A contribution to raising the profile of the organisation in the community. A more diverse workforce better reflects the diversity of the customer base.

Encouraging the employment of diverse individuals can help to provide a working environment that can negate the destructive effects of direct and indirect discrimination, victimisation and harassment. A positive culture can be created where individual differences are welcomed and supported and a deeper level of understanding of the nature of diversity permeates the entire organisation.

10.5 Behaving ethically

By adopting a diversity approach the organisation's stakeholders perceive it as behaving 'ethically'. Within the organisation ethics might also be called morality, since it reflects the general expectations of any person in any society, acting in any capacity. It covers the principles we try to instil in our children, and expect of one another without needing to articulate the expectation or formalise it in any way. It includes:

- Concern for the well being of others
- Respect for the autonomy of others
- Trustworthiness and honesty
- Willing compliance with the law (with the exception of civil disobedience)
- Basic justice; being fair
- Refusing to take unfair advantage
- Benevolence: doing good
- Preventing harm

Managing ethics in the workplace involves identifying and prioritising values to guide behaviour in the organisation, and establishing associated policies and procedures to ensure they are carried out. One might call this 'values management'.

11 RETENTION PROCEDURES

11.1 Monitoring the HRM plan

Monitoring is a crucial component of the HRM plan. It is here that an employer can determine whether goals are being attained and problems resolved. Evaluation of the HRM plan can indicate levels of success, and indicate where further planning is needed to achieve the overall goals of the organisation.

Mission statements often talk about the success of the business, but as a part of the recruitment and retention strategy, companies should also include a well-conceived succession plan for employees. Retention issues are vital to the success of any organisation. Companies devote tremendous resources to recruiting good people, but they must be just as diligent about retaining them. To do this, effective retention strategies must be created that are based on a combination of all workplace conditions, such as issues of health and safety, employee treatment, motivating employees through recognition and rewards and enhancing employee loyalty. An organisation earns loyalty by creating a positive working environment that is stimulating and emphasises an employee's personal growth. Succession planning aims to establish the identity of individuals who will step in and take over key positions as and when the need arises.

Other areas included in a retention strategy are:

(a) **Analysis of wastage statistics**. This will establish where wastage is taking place, as it is unlikely to be the same throughout the firm and more likely to be concentrated in certain jobs, locations or departments.

(b) **Exit Interviewing**. The reasons why staff are leaving may be established by conducting exit interviews so that any organisational problems or failings can be dealt with.

(c) **Remuneration package**. The package needs to be regularly reviewed to ensure it is flexible (adjusted to employee needs) and competitive.

(d) **Career and development policies**. Employees need career prospects and career development to sustain their motivation.

(e) **Job redesign programmes**. These are motivating as they make work more varied and therefore interesting.

(f) **Grievance handling**. Effective and efficient procedures (informal and formal) for dealing with grievances are required.

(g) **Equal opportunity policies**. Special policies may need to be developed and monitored for particular groups of staff such as women and those from ethnic minorities.

11.2 Health, safety and welfare

Because of concern by successive governments to avoid exploitation and discrimination, human resource management is perhaps more subject to legislation than any other aspect of corporate management.

In 1972, a Royal Commission on Safety and Health at Work reported that unnecessarily large numbers of days were being lost each year through industrial accidents, injuries and diseases, because of the 'attitudes, capabilities and performance of people and the efficiency of the organisational systems within which they work'. Since then, major legislation has been brought into effect in the UK, most notably:

(a) Health and Safety at Work Act 1974;

(b) The regulations introduced in January 1993 implementing EU directives on Health and Safety.

Some of the most important regulations are as follows.

- Reporting of Injuries, Diseases and Dangerous Occurrences Regulations (RIDDOR) 1995

- The Health and Safety (First Aid) Regulations 1981

- The Noise at Work Regulations 1989

- The Control of Substances Hazardous to Health Regulations 1994

- The Manual Handling Operations Regulations 1992

- The Workplace (Health, Safety and Welfare) Regulations 1992

- The Provision and Use of Work Equipment Regulations 1992

- The Health and Safety (Display Screen Equipment) Regulations 1992

- The Management of Health and Safety at Work Regulations 1992

- The Personal Protective Equipment at Work Regulations 1992

We will not be covering their provisions in detail here. Just be aware that the framework for personnel policy in the area of health and safety is extensive and detailed!

In the UK, the Health and Safety at Work Act 1974 provides for the introduction of a system of approved codes of practice, prepared in consultation with industry. Thus an employee, whatever his/her employment, should find that his/her work is covered by an appropriate code of practice.

Employers also have specific duties under the 1974 Act.

(a) All systems (work practices) must be safe.

(b) The work environment must be safe and healthy (well-lit, warm, ventilated and hygienic).

(c) All plant and equipment must be kept up to the necessary standard (with guards on machines and so on).

In addition, information, instruction, training and supervision should be directed towards safe working practices. Employers must consult with safety representatives appointed by a recognised trade union, and appoint a safety committee to monitor safety policy, if asked to do so. Safety policy and measures should be clearly communicated in writing to all staff.

The employee also has a duty:

1   To take reasonable care of himself/herself and others,

2   To allow the employer to carry out his or her duties (including enforcing safety rules), and

3   Not to interfere intentionally or recklessly with any machinery or equipment.

Under the Workplace (Health, Safety and Welfare) Regulations 1992 employers have additional general duties including:

- A written risk assessment of al work hazards
- Controls to reduce risks – with new or revised safety policies as required
- Informing employees (including temps) about health and safety
- Training in safety matters

These Regulations deal with matters such as machinery, temperature and ventilation, lighting, washroom facilities, doors and gates, fire and first aid that have been statutory requirements for many years in the UK under legislation such as the Offices, Shops and Railway Premises Act 1963. These are now expected and accepted by employees and employers and the modern role of welfare in organisations is less easy to define.

In its widest context, welfare, as the concern for people as individuals, can be seen in most personnel management policies, in selection interviewing, counselling, appraisal schemes and so on. In a narrow context, welfare can be viewed as a set of provisions that have a great deal of overlap with fringe benefits. These provisions have been identified by Thomason as canteen and recreational facilities, information services such as legal aid, the provision of houses, nurseries, transport and the like, further education provision and medical services. For example, because of the increased attention to equal opportunities and also the need to recruit more women returnees to the workforce, many organisations are improving their childcare arrangements. Thomason feels that such provisions may enable people to work better within the normal functioning of the enterprise and may have an effect on such factors as recruitment, loyalty and length of service.

BPP
PROFESSIONAL EDUCATION

11.3 Health and Safety Policy

An organisation's health and safety policy will include some or all of the following courses of action.

(a) **Job descriptions,** which stress health and safety aspect of the job.

(b) The **design of work systems** to reduce health and safety hazards; using engineering design to build in safety controls.

(c) **Creating patterns of work** to reduce accidents directly, eg the introduction of rest pauses, or indirectly, eg by reducing stress by introducing flexitime, job enrichment and so on.

(d) The **training of employees** – identifying what employees must know concerning health and safety and then devising the most appropriate method of instruction.

(e) **Formal procedures** are set up by most organisations. They range from employing a safety officer and a medical officer, to establishing disciplinary procedures to deal with rule breaking.

(f) **Accident prevention** by carrying out an analysis of accidents.

(g) **Participative management** in an attempt to involve the workforce in the question of health and safety. Involvement has been institutionalised in the Health and Safety at Work Act by the introduction of safety representatives. In some industries, such as mining, there is an obvious commitment on the part of employees toward a shared objective of safe working. In other firms, involving the workforce in safety matters is a problem that no amount of committees or publicity has yet solved. The problem may lie in an attitude generated by management who may see safety work as having a low status.

(h) **Employee counselling** has met with some success, particularly in reducing stress, an area of a great deal of current concern and research.

11.4 Motivating employees through recognition and rewards

Understanding what motivates people is necessary at all levels of management. On a basic level (according to Maslow) people need to be fed and to walk around without holes in their shoes. However, feeding people's minds, helping them to realise their potential, making them feel that their jobs are worth doing and they are contributing to the good of the whole organisation are just as important.

Motivation is frequently based on reward. Many writers describe rewards as having basically two dimensions – intrinsic and extrinsic.

Extrinsic rewards are those forms of reward that are outside the control of the individual and at the disposal of others; sometimes the individual's superior but more often the organisation itself. Extrinsic rewards can be 'seen' and are akin to Herzberg's hygiene (or maintenance) factors. Because extrinsic rewards are obvious and can be 'seen,' not only by the individual concerned but also by others, lack of attention can lead to job dissatisfaction and motivation problems. These rewards include salaries and conditions, incentive arrangements, share schemes, pension provision, sickness and holiday pay, family leave, parking, open access to learning and development opportunities, insurance and wider facilities such as crèches.

Intrinsic rewards are to a great extent within the control of the individual. They include feelings of personal satisfaction, a sense of achievement, status, recognition, the opportunities for advancement, responsibility and pride in the work. This form of reward forms part of Maslow's higher order thinking on motivation and is also often seen as akin to Herzberg's motivators (or 'satisfiers'); ie, those factors directly concerned with the satisfaction gained from the job itself.

While it is true that higher salaries offered by other organisations may be a threat to employee retention efforts, research shows that traditional pay programmes are ineffective for motivating high-performing, committed employees. Compensation has become a right – an expected reward for simply coming to work. Companies will lose their most valued employees if they fail to offer them the intangible intrinsic rewards that money cannot buy. Studies have found that recognition for a job well done is the top motivator of individual performance.

In fact, study after study has shown that what tends to stimulate and encourage top performance, growth and loyalty is praise and recognition. Employees want to:

- Feel they are making a contribution
- Have a manager who tells them when they do a good job
- Have the respect of peers and colleagues
- Be involved and informed about what's going on in the organisation
- Have interesting, challenging work.

Another key part of any retention strategy should include adopting flexible work arrangements. This addresses many work/life and childcare issues. Progressive companies are realising that restructuring full-time work to include alternative work options, such as flexitime, a compressed work week, and telecommuting, can be beneficial to both the employee and the employer.

Retaining employees today is harder than ever. Skilled workers are, and will continue to be, the most important asset of any organisation. Managers must realise this and must create a culture that fosters a sense of trust, loyalty, and commitment. Employees must know that if they work hard and are loyal they will be appreciated and valued.

11.5 Succession planning

Management and employee succession planning are both important issues. In an environment of rapid social and technical change, where knowledge, expertise and skill requirements are constantly changing, succession planning should be a fundamental part of the overall corporate plan. Unless dealing with a retirement or other planned departure, it is difficult, if not impossible, for a company to know exactly when it will encounter an employee loss. The departure can occur at any location or time, but will ultimately produce the same result: a void that the company must fill in order to successfully continue operations. Although it is not feasible to plan for every possible scenario, and particularly for the loss of several key leaders at the same time, it is entirely realistic to map out a chain of command and understand who will assume control if and when a key employee is lost.

Succession plans establish the identity of the individual who will step in and assume the role of a departed CEO, executive, project manager, or other key employee, allowing companies to make the transition and continue performing.

The planning process starts with:

(a) An **assessment of current staff resources**, analysed by departments, identifying the types of jobs at each level (job description) and the number and quality of staff in those jobs (staff appraisal).

(b) A **forecast of the staffing requirements**, by grades and skills, should then be agreed within the corporate plan (both the short and long-term needs) to highlight any surplus staff as well as shortages.

(c) In the case of a **mismatch** between job specification and existing employees, every opportunity should be made to provide retraining or to undertake staff development. Again, the personnel appraisal records should indicate staff who have been willing or who are keen to widen or change their skills.

(d) Where there are **shortages**, recruitment programmes should be agreed. Vacancies should be identified and using the job description and job specification, recruitment and selection of appropriate staff should be carried out. The plan may require that training should then be provided for new recruits, as they will be unlikely to have the specific job knowledge required. In such cases, recruitment would be geared to the selection of people with the necessary ability and aptitude.

Management succession planning will probably entail compiling for each post, a list of perhaps three potential successors; and for each person (at least from a certain level upwards) a list of possible development moves. These lists then form the basis for long-term plans and development moves.

Succession planning is a difficult task. Whilst the process must seek to achieve the organisation's goals and objectives, it must also take into account the aspirations of individuals and try to achieve a realistic fit between the person and the job.

Glaxo Wellcome's succession planning process is based on retaining 'star' employees as well as ensuring that key positions are filled. In addition to identifying critical positions and any gaps in the corporate structure, Glaxo seeks to develop – and thereby retain – employees with extraordinary skills and/or performance. The company also emphasises female and minority employees as part of its commitment to diversity.

Chapter roundup

- Effective recruitment practices ensure that a firm has enough people with the right skills.

- Most recruitment practices aim to fit the person to the job by identifying the needs of the job and finding a person who satisfies them.

- The recruitment process involves personnel specialists and 'line' managers, sometimes with the help of recruitment consultants.

- First the overall needs of the organisation have been identified in the recruitment process.

- To account for each individual position a job analysis is prepared, which identifies through various investigative techniques, the content of the job.

Chapter rounded (continued)

- A job description is developed from the job analysis. The job description outlines the tasks of the job and its place within the organisation.

- A person specification identifies the characteristics of a person who will be recruited to do the job identified in the job description.

- The person specification can be used to develop the job advertisement. The Seven Point Plan and Five Point Pattern are examples.

- In recent years, recruiters have been using 'competences' as a means to select candidates. A competence is a person's capacity to behave in a particular way, for example to fulfil the requirements of a job, or to motivate people. Work-based competences directly relate to the job (eg the ability to prepare a trial balance); behavioural competences relate to underlying issues of personality.

- The process of selection begins when the recruiter receives details of candidates interested in the job, in response, for example, to a job advert, or possibly enquiries made to a recruitment consultant.

- Many firms require candidates to fill out an application form. This is standardised and the firm can ask for specific information about work experience and qualifications, as well as other personal data. Some firms do not bother with an application form, being happy to accept CVs with a covering letter.

- Most firms use interviews, on a one-to-one basis, using a variety of open and closed questions. The interviewer should avoid bias in assessing the candidate.

- Selection tests can be used before or after interviews. Intelligence tests measures the candidate's general intellectual ability, and personality tests identify the type of person. Other tests are more specific to the job (eg proficiency tests).

- Interviews are unreliable as predictors of actual job performance for many posts, but they are traditional and convenient. A combination of interviews with other methods may be used.

- Current legislation that applies to recruitment and selection includes laws on equal pay, sex discrimination, the employment of disabled people, race relations and the rehabilitation of offenders.

- Motivation theories suggest that individuals have needs that must be satisfied. There are a number of different theories. Satisfaction theories are based on the assumption that a 'satisfied' worker will work harder. Extrinsic theories believe that individuals will work harder to obtain a desired reward, eg more money and intrinsic theories argue that effective performance is its own reward.

- As the workforce becomes more diverse in terms of gender, race, culture, age, religion, disability, sexual orientation and ethnicity, organisations need to create cultures in which all employees can develop their potential and flourish. Not only is this the 'right' thing to do, but also how an

Chapter rounded (continued)

organisation manages diversity will have a measurable impact on productivity, retention and its profitability.

- Having gone to the trouble of employing suitable people, organisations must strive to retain them within the workforce. Retention strategies must be created that are based on a combination of all workplace conditions, such as issues of health and safety, employee treatment, motivating employees through recognition and rewards and enhancing employee loyalty.

- Succession planning aims to establish the identity of individuals who will step in and take over key positions as and when the need arises.

Quick quiz

1 What, in brief, are the stages of the recruitment and selection process?

2 Briefly summarise job analysis.

3 What is a currently fashionable approach to drawing up jobs analysis, job descriptions etc?

4 List the components of the Five Point Pattern.

5 What are the characteristics of a good job advertisement?

6 What should application forms achieve?

7 What factors should be taken into account in an organisation's interview strategy?

8 Why are open questions useful?

9 Why do interviews fail to predict performance accurately?

10 List the desirable features of selection tests

11 What are the provisions of the Sex Discrimination Act 1975?

Answers to quick quiz

1 Identifying/defining requirements; attracting potential employees; selecting candidates. (See para 1.1)

2 **Job analysis**. The process of examining a 'job' to identify the component parts and the circumstances in which it is performed. (2)

3 The use of competences – work based and behavioural. (2.5)

4 Impact on others; acquired knowledge and qualifications; innate abilities; motivation; adjustment. (4.3)

5 Concise; reaches the right people; gives a good impression; relevant to the job, identifying skills required etc. (6.1)

6 They should give enough information to identify suitable candidates and weed out no-hopers, by asking specific questions and by getting the candidate to volunteer information. (8.1)

7   In brief, giving the right impression of the organisation and obtaining a rounded, relevant assessment of the candidate. (8.1)

8   They allow the candidate to volunteer more, and open avenues for further questions. (8.4)

9   Brevity and artificiality of interview situation combined with the bias and inexperience of interviewers. (8.7)

10 Sensitive; standardised; reliable; valid. (9)

11 Sex Discrimination Act 1975 renders it unlawful to make any form of discrimination in employment affairs because of marital status or sex. (10.2)

Answers to activities

1   Large organisations tend to have standard procedures. In order to ensure a standard process, you might have seen a specialist from the personnel/HR department only. Smaller organisations cannot afford such specialists so you might have been interviewed by your immediate boss – but perhaps someone else might also have interviewed you (your boss's boss) to check you out.

2-5 Your own research. Keep this documentation; it might be helpful in your Professional Development studies for Unit 13.

6   (a) Goods points about the advertisement and points for improvement

    (i)   It is attractively designed in terms of page layout.

    (ii) The tone of the headline and much of the body copy is informal, colloquial and even friendly. It starts with a joke, implying that the company has a sense of humour.

    (iii) The written style is fluent and attractive.

    (iv) It appears to offer quite a lot of information about the culture of the company – how it feels about personnel issues, where it's going etc – as well as about the job vacancy.

Improvements that could be made

Job advertisements carry certain 'responsibilities': they are a form of pre-selection, and as such should be not be just attractive and persuasive, but accurate and complete enough to give a realistic and relevant picture of the post and the organisation.

    (i)   There is too much copy. Readers may not have the patience to read through so much (rather wordy) prose, particularly since the same phrases are repeated ('progressive international organisation', for example), or look rather familiar in any case ('in the nicest possible ways', 'our staff are our most important asset', 'a company with a difference' etc) and there is very little 'hard' information contained in the ad.

    (ii) There are many words and expressions which sound good, and seem to imply good things, but are in fact empty of substance, and commit the organisation to nothing. They are usually the 'stock' expressions like 'committed to an enlightened personnel philosophy': what does that actually mean?

NOTES

(iii) There are confusing contradictions, eg between the requirements for flexibility, 'interchange with various functions', do 'whatever the situation demands' etc and the more cautious 'within your designated area ...'.

(iv) The copywriters are in places too 'clever' for their own good. The first three lines, for example, could backfire quite badly if a reader failed to catch the next line, or simply didn't appreciate the self-deprecating tone.

(v) The advertisement does not give enough 'hard' information to make effective response likely – and then fails to do its job of facilitating response at all! Despite the invitation to telephone, no number is given. No named corespondent is cited, merely a reference number – despite the claimed emphasis on people as people, not numbers.

(b) **What is learnt about AOK**

The advertisement claims to say quite a lot about AOK, its culture, its people-centredness, its expansion and progressive outlook, flexibility, sense of humour etc. Such claims should always be taken with a pinch of salt. We may, however, infer some things about the company.

(i) It has a strong cultural 'flavour', and believes in 'selling' that culture quite hard. It likes, for example, telling people what it is 'committed to', what it 'firmly believes' etc.

(ii) It tends to stress its good points and opportunities: it certainly sees itself (even allowing for advertising hyperbole) as go-ahead, successful and expanding, flexible, people-oriented.

(iii) It is possibly not as deeply people oriented as it tries to project. The areas of involvement for the Personnel Department enumerated, for example, seem rather limited and administrative: there is no suggestion of a wider strategic role for personnel, such as would indicate that 'people issues' really do affect management outlook.

7 (a) Boxes too small to contain the information asked for.

(b) Forms which are (or look) so lengthy or complicated that a prospective applicant either completes them perfunctorily or gives up (and applies to another employer instead).

(c) Illegal (eg discriminatory) or offensive questions.

(d) Lack of clarity as to what (and how much) information is required.

8 (a) Closed. (The only answer is 'yes' or 'no', unless Jo is prepared to expand on it, at his or her own initiative.)

(b) Leading. (Even if Jo was interested, (s)he should get the message that 'yes' would not be what the interviewer wanted, or expected, to hear.)

(c) Leading closed multiple! ('Really useful' leads Jo to think that the 'correct' answer will be 'yes': There is not much opportunity for any other answer, without expanding on it unasked.)

(d) Open. (Jo has to explain, in his or her own words.)

(e) Probing. (If Jo's answer has been unconvincing, short or vague, this question forces a more specific answer.)

Chapter 2 :
BUILD WINNING TEAMS

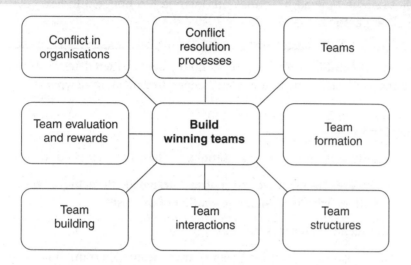

Introduction

The outcome of this chapter is for you to be able to develop an understanding of how to build winning teams. We begin by looking at the existence of conflict in organisations from different viewpoints and discuss the causes and outcomes of it. Management responses to the handling of conflict range from denial to encouraging co-operation. The win-win model identifies three ways to approach conflict resolution.

Teams have been described as collections of people who must rely on group collaboration if each member is to experience the optimum of success. We identify the mix of knowledge, skills and experience necessary for a team to fulfil its functions. The process known as team building or team maintenance has become an important element in helping work groups to function more effectively and we will be looking at some of the skills and methods used in the process.

Your objectives

After completing this chapter you should be able to:

    (a)   Identify the main cause of conflict within an organisation

    (b)   Outline procedures for managing conflict

    (c)   Define the purpose of a team

    (d)   Identify mix of knowledge, skills and experience necessary for a team to fulfil its functions

    (e)   Explain the stages in team development

    (f)   Analyse dynamics within teams and promote a team spirit

    (g)   Encourage team members to develop roles during team assignments

    (h)   Identify appropriate methods to evaluate team performance

    (i)   Describe the main ways of rewarding a team

1   CONFLICT IN ORGANISATIONS

1.1   Differing perspectives

Definition

> **Conflict** can be defined as 'behaviour intended to obstruct the achievement of some other person's goals.'

The existence of conflict in organisations might be considered inevitable (the conflict view) or unnatural (the happy family view), depending on your viewpoint.

The happy family view

The happy family view presents organisations as essentially harmonious

- They are co-operative structures, designed to achieve agreed common objectives, with no systematic conflict of interest

- Management power is legitimate

- Conflicts are exceptional and arise from aberrant incidents, such as misunderstandings, clashes of personality and external influences

This kind of view is reasonably common in managerial literature, which attempts to come up with training and motivational techniques for dealing with conflicts that arise in what are seen as potentially 'conflict-free' organisations. Conflict is thus blamed on bad management, lack of leadership, poor communication, or 'bloody-mindedness' on the part of individuals or interest groups that impinge on the organisation. The theory is that a strong culture, good two-way communication, co-operation and motivational leadership will eliminate conflict. Co-operation is assumed to be desirable and achievable.

The conflict view

The conflict view in contrast, sees organisations as arenas for conflict on individual and group levels. Members battle for limited resources, status, rewards and professional values. Organisational politics involve constant struggles for control, and choices of structure, technology and organisational goals are part of this process. Individual and organisational interests will not always coincide.

Organisations may be seen as political coalitions of individuals and groups that have their own interests. Management has to create a workable structure for collaboration, taking into account the objectives of all the stakeholders in the organisation. A mutual survival strategy, involving the control of conflict through compromise, can be made acceptable in varying degrees to all concerned.

Activity 1 **(15 mins)**

How accurate is the 'happy family' perspective when applied to your own organisation, or to any organisation with which you are sufficiently familiar?

To what extent would you subscribe to the claim that the 'happy family' view is publicised by managers within their own organisations, not so much as an accurate description of reality, but rather because adoption of the 'happy family' perspective itself helps to reduce the level of articulated conflict?

The 'evolutionary' view

This view regards conflict as a means of **maintaining the status quo**, as a useful basis for **evolutionary change**.

- **Conflict** keeps the organisation **sensitive to the need to change**, while reinforcing its essential framework of control.

- The **legitimate pursuit of competing interests** can balance and preserve social and organisational arrangements.

The constructive conflict view

This '**constructive conflict**' view may perhaps be the most useful for managers and administrators of organisations, as it neither:

(a) Attempts to dodge the issues of conflict, which is an observable fact of life in most organisations; nor

(b) Seeks to pull down existing organisational structures altogether.

Conflict can be highly desirable. Conflict is constructive, when its effect is to:

- Introduce different **solutions** to problems
- **Define power relationships** more clearly
- Encourage **creativity**, the testing of ideas
- **Focus attention** on individual contributions
- **Bring emotions** out into the open
- **Release hostile feelings** that have been, or may be, repressed otherwise

Conflict can also be destructive. It may:

- **Distract attention** from the task
- **Polarise** views and 'dislocate' the group
- Subvert **objectives** in favour of secondary goals
- Encourage **defensive** or 'spoiling' behaviour
- Force the group to **disintegrate**
- Stimulate emotional, **win-lose conflicts**, ie hostility

1.2 Conflict between groups

Conflicts of interest may exist throughout the organisation – or even for a single individual. There may be conflicts of interest between local management of a branch or subsidiary and the organisation as a whole.

- Sales and production departments in a manufacturing firm (over scheduling, product variation)

- Trade unions and management.

Interest groups such as trade unions tend to wield greater power in conflict situations than their members as individuals. Trade Unions are organisations whose purpose it is to promote their members' interests. (Strike action has to be preceded by a ballot.)

Activity 2   **(10 mins)**

What other examples of 'conflicts of interest' can you identify within an organisation? Having selected some instances, can you detect any common patterns in such conflicts?

CASE EXAMPLE

Conflict can also operate **within** groups.

In an experiment reported by Deutsch (1949), psychology students were given puzzles and human relation problems to work at in discussion groups. Some groups ('co-operative' ones) were told that the grade each individual got at the end of the course would depend on the performance of his group. Other groups ('competitive' ones) were told that each student would receive a grade according to his own contributions.

No significant differences were found between the two kinds of group in the amount of interest and involvement in the tasks, or in the amount of learning. But the co-operative groups, compared with the competitive ones, had greater productivity per unit time, better quality of product and discussion, greater co-ordination of effort and sub-division of activity, more diversity in amount of contribution per member, more attentiveness to fellow members and more friendliness during discussion.

1.3   Conflict and competition

Sherif and Sherif conducted a number of experiments into groups and competing groups.

(a)   People tend to identify with a group.

(b)   New members of a group quickly learn the norms and attitudes of the others, no matter whether these are 'positive' or 'negative', friendly or hostile.

(c)   When a group competes, this is what happens to it **within the group**.

   (i)   Members close ranks, and submerge their differences; loyalty and conformity are demanded.

   (ii)   The 'climate' changes from informal and sociable to work and task-oriented; individual needs are subordinated to achievement.

(iii) Leadership moves from democratic to autocratic, with the group's acceptance.

(iv) The group tends to become more structured and organised.

(v) The opposing group begins to be perceived as 'the enemy'.

(vi) Perception is distorted, presenting an idealised picture of 'us' and a negative stereotype of 'them'.

(vii) Communication between groups decreases.

In a 'win-lose' situation, where competition is not perceived to result in benefits for both sides.

(a) The **winning** group will:

- Retain its cohesion
- Relax into a complacent, playful state
- Return to group maintenance and concern for members' needs
- Be confirmed in its group 'self-concept' with little re-evaluation

(b) The **losing** group might behave as follows.

(i) Deny defeat if possible, or place the blame on the arbitrator, or the system

(ii) Lose its cohesion and splinter into conflict, as 'blame' is apportioned.

(iii) Be keyed-up, fighting mad.

(iv) Turn towards work-orientation to regroup, rather than members' needs or group maintenance.

(v) Tend to learn by re-evaluating its perceptions of itself and the other group. It is more likely to become a cohesive and effective unit once the 'defeat' has been accepted.

Members of a group will act in unison if the group's existence or patterns of behaviour are threatened from outside. Cohesion is naturally assumed to be the result of positive factors such as communication, agreement and mutual trust – but in the face of a 'common enemy' (competition, crisis or emergency) cohesion and productivity benefit.

Activity 3 (10 mins)

How applicable are Sherifs' 1965 research findings to the cause, symptoms and treatment of conflict in a modern organisation? In what ways, if at all, could Sherifs' findings be used as a means of improving employee performance within an organisation?

1.4 Causes of conflict

(a) **Differences in the objectives** of different groups or individuals.

(b) **Scarcity of resources**.

(c) **Interdependence of two departments** on a task. They have to work together but may do so ineffectively.

(d) **Disputes about the boundaries of authority**.

    (i)   The technostructure may attempt to encroach on the roles or 'territory' of line managers and usurp some of their authority.

    (ii)   One department might start **'empire building'** and try to take over the work previously done by another department.

(e) **Personal differences**, as regards goals, attitudes and feelings, are also bound to crop up. This is especially true in **differentiated organisations**, where people employed in the different sub-units are very different.

1.5 Symptoms of conflict

- Poor communications, in all 'directions'

- Interpersonal friction

- Inter-group rivalry and jealousy

- Low morale and frustration

- Widespread use of arbitration, appeals to higher authority, and inflexible attitudes

1.6 The tactics of conflict

(a) **Withholding information** from one another

(b) **Distorting information**. This will enable the group or manager presenting the information to get their own way more easily.

(c) **Empire building**. A group (especially a specialist group such as research) which considers its influence to be neglected might seek to impose rules, procedures, restrictions or official requirements on other groups, in order to bolster up their own importance.

(d) **Informal organisation**. A manager might seek to by-pass formal channels of communication and decision-making by establishing informal contacts and friendships with people in a position of importance.

(e) **Fault-finding** in the work of other departments: department X might duplicate the work of department Y – hoping to prove department Y 'wrong' – and then report the fact to senior management.

2 CONFLICT RESOLUTION PROCESSES

2.1 Management responses to the handling of conflict

Not all of these are effective.

Response	Comment
Denial/withdrawal	'Sweeping it under the carpet'. If the conflict is very trivial, it may indeed blow over without an issue being made of it, but if the causes are not identified, the conflict may grow to unmanageable proportions.

Response	Comment
Suppression	'Smoothing over', to preserve working relationships despite minor conflicts. As Hunt remarks, however: 'Some cracks cannot be papered over'.
Dominance	The application of power or influence to settle the conflict. The disadvantage of this is that it creates all the lingering resentment and hostility of 'win-lose' situations.
Compromise	Bargaining, negotiating, conciliating. To some extent, this will be inevitable in any organisation made up of different individuals. However, individuals tend to exaggerate their positions to allow for compromise, and compromise itself is seen to weaken the value of the decision, perhaps reducing commitment. **Negotiation** is: 'a process of interaction by which two or more parties who consider they need to be jointly involved in an outcome, but who initially have different objectives seek by the use of argument and persuasion to resolve their differences in order to achieve a mutually acceptable solution'.
Integration/ collaboration	Emphasis must be put on the task, individuals must accept the need to modify their views for its sake, and group effort must be seen to be superior to individual effort.
Encourage co-operative behaviour	Joint problem-solving team, goals set for all teams/departments to follow.

Activity 4   **(25 mins)**

In the light of the above consider how conflict could arise, what form it would take and how it might be resolved in the following situations.

(a) Two managers who share a secretary have documents to be typed.

(b) One worker finds out that another worker who does the same job as he does is paid a higher wage.

(c) A company's electricians find out that a group of engineers have been receiving training in electrical work.

(d) Department A stops for lunch at 12.30 while Department B stops at 1 o'clock. Occasionally the canteen runs out of puddings for Department B workers.

(e) The Northern Region and Southern Region sales teams are continually trying to better each others results, and the capacity of production to cope with the increase in sales is becoming overstretched.

2.2 The win-win model

One useful model of conflict resolution is the **win-win model**. This states that there are three basic ways in which a conflict or disagreement can be worked out.

Method	Frequency	Explanation
Win-lose	This is quite common.	**One party gets what (s)he wants at the expense of the other party**: for example, Department A gets the new photocopier, while Department B keeps the old one (since there were insufficient resources to buy two new ones). However well-justified such a solution is (Department A needed the facilities on the new photocopier more than Department B), there is often lingering resentment on the part of the 'losing' party, which may begin to damage work relations.
Lose-lose	This sounds like a senseless outcome, but actually **compromise** comes into this category. It is thus very common.	**Neither party gets what (s)he really wanted**: for example, since Department A and B cannot both have a new photocopier, it is decided that neither department should have one. However 'logical' such a solution is, there is often resentment and dissatisfaction on *both* sides. (Personal arguments where neither party gives ground and both end up storming off or not talking are also lose-lose: the parties may not have lost the argument, but they lose the relationship ...) Even positive compromises only result in half-satisfied needs.
Win-win	This may not be common, but working towards it often brings out the best solution.	**Both parties get as close as possible to what they really want**. How can this be achieved?

It is critical to the **win-win approach** to discover **what both parties really want** – as opposed to:

- What they think they want (because they have not considered any other options)

- What they think they can get away with

- What they think they need in order to avoid an outcome they fear

For example, Department B may want the new photocopier because they have never found out how to use all the features (which do the same things) on the old photocopier; because they just want to have the same equipment as Department A; or because they fear that if they do not have the new photocopier, their work will be slower and less professionally presented, and they may be reprimanded (or worse) by management.

The important questions in working towards win-win are:

- What do you want this for?
- What do you think will happen if you don't get it?

These questions get to the heart of what people really need and want.

In our photocopier example, Department A says it needs the new photocopier to make colour copies (which the old copier does not do), while Department B says it needs the new copier to make clearer copies (because the copies on the old machine are a bit blurred). Now there are **options to explore**. It may be that the old copier just needs fixing, in order for Department B to get what it really wants. Department A will still end up getting the new copier – but Department B has in the process been consulted and had its needs met.

EXAMPLE: THE WIN-WIN APPROACH

Two men are fighting over an orange. There is only one orange, and both men want it.

(a) If one man gets the orange and the other does not, this is a **win-lose** solution.

(b) If they cut the orange in half and share it (or agree that neither will have the orange), this is a **lose-lose** solution – despite the compromise.

(c) If they talk about what they each need the orange for, and one says 'I want to make orange juice' and the other says 'I want the skin of the orange to make candied peel', there are further options to explore (like peeling the orange) and the potential for both men to get exactly what they wanted. This is a **win-win** approach.

Win-win is not always possible: It is **working towards it** that counts. The result can be mutual respect and co-operation, enhanced communication, more creative problem-solving and – at best – **satisfied needs all round**.

Activity 5 (30 mins)

Suggest a (i) win-lose, (ii) compromise and (iii) win-win solution in the following scenarios.

(a) Two of your team members are arguing over who gets the desk by the window: they both want it.

(b) You and a colleague both need access to the same file at the same time. You both need it to compile reports for your managers, for the following morning. It is now 3.00pm, and each of you will need it for two hours to do the work.

(c) Manager A is insisting on buying new computers for her department before the budgetary period ends. Manager B cannot understand why – since the old computers are quite adequate – and will moreover be severely inconvenienced by such a move, since her own systems will have to be upgraded as well, in order to remain compatible with department A. (The two departments constantly share data files.) Manager B protests, and conflict erupts.

3 TEAMS

3.1 Teams and teamwork

Definition

> A **team** is a 'small number of people with *complementary skills* who are committed to a *common* purpose, performance goals and approach, for which they hold themselves *mutually accountable'.* (Katzenbach & Smith)

The dictionary defines **teamwork** as the joint action of a group of people in which the individual interests of group members become secondary to achieving the goals of the group.

The essential difference between a team and a group lies in the fact that a group works together without a common purpose – a team working together is a unified whole, a selection of individuals working towards the same goal. It cannot be said that a number of people brought together by work are a team, and even a group of people who share a common interest will not necessarily achieve anything by discussing it together. Teamwork starts when a group of individuals have a **common goal** and work together to achieve it, regardless of personal preference or personality. It means taking an objective view for the greater good of the team.

The basic work units of organisations have traditionally been specialised hierarchical departments. Team working can break down 'departmental barriers', provide developmental challenges, free-up management, or improve customer service. Teams allow work to be shared among a number of individuals, so that it gets done faster and with a greater range of skills and information than by individuals working alone.

A team may be called together temporarily, to achieve specific task objectives (project team), or may be more or less permanent, with responsibilities for a particular product, product group or stage of the production process (a product or process team).

There are two basic approaches to the organisation of teamwork:

(a) **Multi-disciplinary teams -** bring together individuals with different skills and specialisms so that their skills, experience and knowledge can be pooled or exchanged. They:

- increase workers' awareness of their overall objectives and targets

- aid co-ordination and communication across functional boundaries

- help to generate new ideas and solutions to problems, since the team has access to more perspectives and 'pieces of the jigsaw'.

(b) **Multi-skilled teams –** bring together a number of individuals who can perform any of the group's tasks. These tasks can then be shared out in a more flexible way between group members, according to who is available and best placed to do a given job at the time it is required.

Multi-skilling is the cornerstone of team empowerment, since it cuts across the barriers of job descriptions and demarcations to enable teams to respond flexibly to changing demands.

3.2 Self-managed teams

Self-managed teams are the most highly developed form of team working. They are permanent structures in which team members collaboratively decide all the major issues affecting their work: work processes and schedules, task allocation, the selection and development of team members, the distribution of rewards and the management of group processes (problem-solving, conflict management, internal discipline and so on). The team leader is a member of the team, acting in the role of coach and facilitator: leadership roles may be shared or rotated as appropriate.

Self-managed teamworking is said to have advantages in:

- Saving managerial costs

- Gains in quality and productivity, by harnessing the commitment of those who perform the work

- Encouraging individual initiative and responsibility, enhancing organisational responsiveness (particularly in front-line customer-facing units)

- Gains in efficiency, through multi-skilling, the involvement of fewer functions in decision-making and co-ordinating work, and (often) the streamlining of working methods by groups.

3.3 Applications of team working

The collaborative nature of teams makes them particularly effective for **increasing communication,** generating new ideas and evaluating ideas from different viewpoints. Common applications of teamworking therefore include the following.

- **Problem-solving or brainstorming groups:** generating creative ideas for problem solving and innovation. Small groups of people are invited to contribute ideas, without any initial evaluation or censorship: this freedom encourages people to 'bounce' ideas off each other and build on each other's ideas, creating more innovative ideas than would otherwise be possible.

- **Quality and service circles:** drawing people together from different disciplines to share ideas about quality and service issues. This has been a popular technique in involving employees at different levels of the organisation in quality assurance, as part of a Total Quality Management (TQM) orientation. Such discussions are said to result not only in specific suggestions for quality improvements, but to a greater awareness and discussion of performance issues in the organisation, and to higher morale in employees. Similar options include **health and safety circles** and other groups that meet regular to discuss matters of concern.

- **Project teams:** set up to handle particular tasks or projects. This enables a range of cross-functional expertise to collaborate on a project, creating a 'horizontal' organisation. In the case of account teams, dedicated to particular customers or clients (eg advertising agency accounts), this offers the customer a more satisfying 'horizontal' experience of the organisation than having to be constantly transferred between departments.

- **Representative groups:** set up to discuss and put forward the views of interest groups in the organisation. An employee representative team (a works council, the local branch of a trade union or staff association, say) might consult and negotiate with management, for example, representing the views and interests of employees. This is often an important channel of upward communication, so that management can benefit from 'grass roots' knowledge of issues at the front line of the organisation.

- **Briefing groups:** allowing information and instructions to be presented to a number of people together.

Activity 6   **(10 mins)**

What functions do teams perform in your own organisation? List a number of different teams of which you are aware (or perhaps a member). What is their function – and why is this function most effectively performed by a team (as opposed to individuals working on their own)?

---

4   TEAM FORMATION

4.1   Establishing objectives

Every team must have something to work on that supports the goals of the organisation, its stakeholders, customers, suppliers and employees. Unfortunately, most teams are established without clear and actionable objectives. Therefore it should come as no surprise that research shows that nearly nine out of every ten teams fail to achieve the desired results.

So before the first team is formed, someone must provide very specific answers to the following questions:

- What is the team empowered to do? Is it going to accomplish a specific task, make a recommendation or actually manage itself? Has the organisation defined the team's authority to make recommendations and to implement its plan? Is there a defined review process so both the team and the organization are consistently aligned in direction and purpose?

- Will it solve a problem, complete a project, meet an objective, make a consensus decision, redesign a process or manage a particular aspect of the business? At the same time, do team members clearly understand their boundaries?

- How far may members go in pursuit of solutions? Are limitations (i.e. monetary and time resources) defined at the beginning of the project before the team experiences barriers and rework?

- What indices and indicators will the team track to measure and verify its results?

- What resources, support, coordination, training, coaching and tools will the team need to gain its objectives and achieve the desired results?

- How will the team and the organisation know when the team has completed its mission?

- How will they know if and when the team should be disbanded, reformulated or continue on with new challenges?

4.2 Team formation – Tuckman

Developing the characteristics outlined above is the first stage of building an effective and enjoyable team. There are many theories on how teams form and, while each theory has unique characteristics, most agree on two things. First, that there are predictable stages every team goes through on its way to becoming a highly productive, efficient team. And second, that leaders and group members who are aware of these stages can improve the quality of their team's interactions during each stage. Tuckman, identified four stages of team development: Forming, Storming, Norming, and Performing. It describes the interaction between team members in two-dimensions: task and relations.

The Forming stage – involves the introduction of team members, either at the initiation of the team, or as members are introduced subsequently. Members are likely to be influenced by the expectations and desires they bring with them, and will be keen to understand how the group will operate. They will be wary about introducing new ideas. The objectives being pursued may as yet be unclear and a leader may not yet have emerged. This is a stage of transition from a group of individuals to a team. As team members grow more confident, the team are likely to enter the next stage.

The **Storming** phase – frequently involves more or less open conflict between team members who will have different opinions as to how the team should operate. There may be changes agreed in the original objectives, procedures and norms established for the group. If the team is developing successfully this may be a fruitful phase as more realistic targets are set and trust between the group members increases. The best teams will understand the conflict, actively listen to each other, and navigate an agreed way forwards. Other teams may disintegrate as they bolster their own opinions to weather the storms of the group. As the team emerges with an agreed method of operating, it enters the next stage.

The **Norming** phase – a period of settling down: there will be agreements about work sharing, individual requirements and expectations of output. Norms and procedures may evolve which enable methodical working to be introduced and maintained. During this phase, team members are able to reconcile their own opinions with the greater needs of the team. Co-operation and collaboration replace the conflict and mistrust of the previous phase.

Finally the team reaches the final phase,

The **Performing** phase -emphasis is now on reaching the team goals, rather than working on team process. The team sets to work to execute its task. The difficulties of growth and development no longer hinder the group's objectives. Relationships are settled, and team members are likely to build loyalty towards each other. The team is able to manage more complex tasks, and cope with greater change.

Teams have a finite life. They form for a specific purpose and must disband once their mission is complete. Consequently there is a fifth and final stage, sometimes called **Adjourning**. Achieving closure, acknowledging the end of a project and moving on is a vital part of the lifecycle of every team.

4.3 Moving through the phases

The action steps for moving through team development:

Forming to storming

- Build a shared purpose/mission and continuously clarify team outcomes.

- Create a sense of urgency and rationale for the purpose/mission.

- Select members based on resource and skill needs.

- Invest time getting to know each member's skills, experience and personal goals.

- Bring individuals together to work on common tasks.

- Define recognition and rewards, both individual and team-based.

- Work on personal commitment by linking personal goals to team roles.

Storming to norming

- Build a common understanding by periodically communicating the team's purpose/mission.

- Acknowledge times when the team is struggling and take time to discuss ways to move toward 'Norming'.

- Set out to achieve a few performance goals and tasks.

- Encourage members to express their differing opinions, ideas, and feelings by asking open-ended questions.

- Make connections between divergent perspectives; acknowledge where there are differences.

- Build a set of operating agreements (rules for team behaviour).

- Raise issues, confront deviations from commitments, and allow conflict to occur.

Norming to performing

- Develop shared leadership based on expertise and development needs.

- Translate common purpose and team expectations into performance goals that are specified and measurable.

- Build consensus on overarching goals and approaches.

- Formally give and receive feedback within the team.

- Maintain focus on external relationships: commitments, requirements, feedback, and competitive realities.

- Celebrate successes, share rewards, recognise team and individual achievements.

- Continue to evaluate team against performance goals.

NOTES

Activity 7 (10 mins)

Read the following descriptions of team behaviour and decide to **which** category they **belong** (forming, storming, norming, performing, dorming).

(a) Two of the group arguing as to whose idea is best

(b) Progress becomes static

(c) Desired outputs being achieved

(d) Shy member of group not participating

(e) Activities being allocated

4.4 Woodcock

An alternative model was developed by Woodcock, who classified teams into four categories showing different stages of development.

Category	Comment
Undeveloped	The team-leader takes most decisions. People are not quite sure what the objectives should be. Personal interaction is based on hiding feelings.
Experimenting	The group turns in on itself, with people raising and facing key issues.
Consolidating	The task and its objectives become clear, people begin to get along with each other on a personal level, and people begin to agree on procedures
Mature	Working methods are methodical, people are open with their feelings leadership style is contributory and the group recognises its responsibilities to the rest of the organisation

4.5 Effective and successful teams

Effective and successful teams are characterised by:

Size and composition – ideally a team should have seven to nine people and no delegates. You do not want people who have to take the team's ideas back to someone else to get authorisation. In the best teams, no one hesitates to act out of a fear that what they are about to do is not in their area of responsibility. Good team players take action.

Diversity – members must have adequate levels of complementary skills. A team should be made up of people who have different opinions about things, people who approach their work in different ways, intuitive thinkers as well as logical thinkers. Diversity (of skills and opinions) is one of the keys to a successful team.

Shared culture - to have a successful team, you must have a shared organisational culture. People from different parts of a company will, in all likelihood, have disparate styles, expectations, and reward systems. A shared organisational culture will mitigate the differences.

Well-defined goals - **the team must have a specific goal or goals** and have a well-defined purpose or vision of what the team will accomplish. The team's mission and mode of operation must be clearly defined and every team member has to understand it. That includes an understanding of the project's purpose, the strategy for getting the work accomplished, the ultimate goal, the benefits people will receive if the goal is met, the measurement system that's going to be used, and how differences of opinion (conflicts) are going to be handled.

Positive attitude and cooperative spirit – in successful teams all team members are positive thinkers. A team cannot function with excuse-driven, 'no-can-do' members on board. Team members need to be fiercely independent, and at the same time, intensely collaborative. They constantly ask questions and challenge ideas to achieve results as part of an open and positive feedback process.

Mutual respect and accountability – successful teams have three things in common:

(a) mutual respect among team members – team members know each other's individual strengths and preferences as well as working styles;

(b) a **sense of mutual accountability;** and

(c) a common vision about where the team is going.

Each member of the team must know that he or she can influence the team's agenda. When there exists a feeling of trust among team members and open and honest communication is encouraged the team has an even better chance of success. Team members are confident in each other ability – there is mutual trust and support. Unfortunately, there is going to be contention in any team, but team members have to respect one another and appreciate each other's contribution.

5 TEAM STRUCTURES

5.1 Flexible structures

The structures that most organisations adopt are line organisations, project organisations or matrix organisations.

- A line organisation is based on a hierarchy of managers responsible for ongoing operations supported by staff organisations, which exist to serve the goals of the line. Companies that produce products typically have a line organisation structure

- Staff functions are those, which need to serve all the lines, such as human resources and accounting. In a for-profit company, line managers will be responsible for the bottom line profitability of their line of business.

- In service-based businesses such as architecture or design, the project organisation is more common. In such a business, a senior manager will be responsible for one or more projects and the staff on those projects will report directly to the project manager. Each project manager then has responsibility for personnel development as well as for project delivery.

- Due to the rapidly changing environment and the need for effective co-ordination in very complex situations, most large corporate projects today operate in a matrix environment. In this setting the leader needs to be sensitive to a larger array of political arenas than in a project or line structure. In a matrix structure, the project manager may have little written authority, but needs to rely primarily on personal relationships and 'personal power.' The diagram below gives an indication of how the matrix structure works.

Central policy. Eg Board of directors

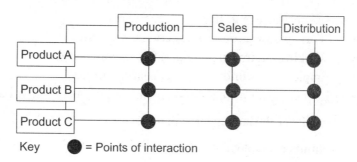

Figure 2.1 Matrix structure

It shows that the team working on Product C would be responsible not only to the head of that product, but also to the heads of the production, sales and distribution departments.

Within a team you will find a mixture of different people with different assignments – but that does not necessarily require a specific structure. For each issue or process someone needs to be the recognised leader; someone has to believe it is his or her responsibility to drive an issue otherwise it may become forgotten. There will also be a sub-set of people most appropriate to make contributions. It could mean that a leader for one issue might be a contributor for another.

The team structure that develops (either formally or informally) will be flexible such that the right people work together for any given topic.

5.2 Linking pin

Rensis Likert proposed that the structure of an organisation should be formed around effective work groups rather than around individuals. He devised an overlapping structure that involved a linking pin process in which the leader/superior member of one team/group was a subordinate member of the team/group above – see diagram below of a project organisation:

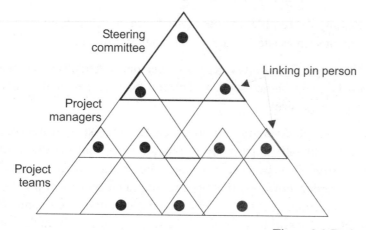

Figure 2.2 Project organisation

Likert argued that this type of structure improved communications, increased co-operation, more team commitment and faster decision-making.

5.3 Working culture

The working culture of an organisation is determined by the following elements:

- Labour force (e.g. size, characteristics).
- Work organisation (e.g. functions, structures).
- Working environment (e.g. safety, health issues).
- Employment conditions (e.g. salary, training).
- Labour relations (e.g. union membership, sector organisation).

The key elements of the labour force include:

- Numbers employed
- Social characteristics (diversity)
- Contractual status (type of contracts)
- Recruitment sources

From its mix of personnel, policies and environment, every organisation represents a unique working culture, which will affect the way it performs.

The working culture of most British organisations – whether service sector, public sector or manufacturing – has yet to move beyond the traditional highly controlled, 'head down', 'assembly line' model, characterised by measurable targets and a rigid chain of command.

Teamwork has become an important part of the working culture and many businesses now look at teamwork skills when evaluating a person for employment. Most companies realise that teamwork is important because either the product is sufficiently complex that it requires a team with multiple skills to produce, and/or a better product will result when a team approach is taken.

5.4 Diversity issues within teams

Diversity can be defined as the presence of differences among members of a social unit. It is an increasingly important factor in organisational life as organisations worldwide become more diverse. Jackson *et al* (1995) differentiate between two sources of diversity – readily detectable attributes and underlying attributes.

- **Readily detectable attributes** are those, which can be easily recognised in a person such as age, gender, or national/ethnic origin.

- **Underlying attributes** represent personal characteristics, which are not so easily identifiable, such as cultural beliefs, personality characteristics, or knowledge level.

Frequently, critics of diversity initiatives charge that such initiatives operate as an outgrowth of a 'politically correct' environment. They contend that organisations have diversity initiatives just because they are the 'right thing to do'. It has become increasingly apparent, however, that appropriate management of a diverse workforce is critical for organisations that seek to improve and maintain their competitive advantage. Focusing on diversity and looking for more ways to be a truly inclusive organisation –

one that makes full use of the contributions of all employees – is not just a nice idea; it is good business sense that yields greater productivity and competitive advantage.

Teams with members from varied backgrounds can bring different perspectives, ideas and solutions, as well as devise new products and services, challenge accepted views and generate a dynamic synergy.

Winning team players are aware of and appreciate diversity in their team member's individual styles, perspective, and opinions. A team that does not appreciate and value diversity among its team members defeats the purpose of a team. At their best, winning teams bring together players with diverse talents, experience, and perspective to accomplish results that no one team member could accomplish on their own. Teams that lack diversity in breadth of skills, experience, and point of view are poorly prepared to solve complex problems or succeed at challenging tasks that, by their nature, require diversity

5.5 Anti-discriminatory practice

Everyone is unique. Working practices and behaviours that discriminate, stereotype or label people are limiting and impact negatively on group levels of motivation. A team that can acknowledge and appreciate difference is strong. There is no simple short cut to integrating the values of equality and diversity into an organisation's culture. There can be commitment across the top team and a superb set of policies but, in the end, many elements of the working culture are actually determined at team level. That means everyone has a part to play in developing an inclusive (rather than exclusive) culture.

Team leaders should:

- Promote a flexible approach to work.

- Use team meetings to discuss equalities issues including the development, progress and monitoring of the operational team equality action plan.

- Support their team, and the individuals in it, to feel comfortable in raising equalities issues in meetings and performance reviews.

- Include a discussion and review of equalities targets and equalities issues, including any training and development needs, in the team meetings.

- Act promptly, confidentially, sympathetically and appropriately to informal or formal complaints by individuals in the team concerning discrimination, victimisation or harassment.

- Promote opportunities for their team and themselves to receive training, support and development opportunities on equalities issues.

6 TEAM INTERACTIONS

6.1 Team roles

Belbin researched business game teams and drew up a widely used framework for understanding roles within work groups. He identifies nine team roles.

Role and description	Team-role contribution	Allowable weaknesses
1 **Plant** – creative, imaginative, unorthodox	Solves difficult problems	Ignores details, too preoccupied to communicate effectively
2 **Resource investigator** – extrovert, enthusiastic, communicative	Explores opportunities, develops contacts	Over-optimistic, loses interest once initial enthusiasm has passed
3 **Co-ordinator** – mature, confident, a good chairperson	Clarifies goals, promotes decision-making, delegates well	Can be seen as manipulative, delegates personal work
4 **Shaper** – challenging, dynamic, thrives on pressure	Has the drive and courage to overcome obstacles	Can provoke others, hurts people's feelings
5 **Monitor evaluator** – sober, strategic and discerning	Sees all options, judges accurately	Lacks drive and ability to inspire others, overly critical
6 **Team worker** – mild, co-operative, perceptive and diplomatic	Listens, builds, averts friction, calms the waters	Indecisive in crunch situations, can be easily influenced
7 **Implementer** – reliable, disciplined, conservative and efficient	Turns ideas into practical actions	Somewhat inflexible, slow to respond to new possibilities
8 **Completer** – anxious, painstaking, conscientious	Searches out errors and omissions, delivers on time	Inclined to worry unduly, reluctant to delegate, can be a nitpicker
9 **Specialist** – single-minded, self-starting, dedicated	Provides knowledge and skills in rare supply	Contributes only on a narrow front, dwells on technicalities, overlooks the 'big picture'

These team roles are not fixed within any given individual. Team members can occupy more than one role, or switch to 'backup' roles if required: hence, there is no requirement for every team to have nine members. However, since role preferences are based on personality, it should be recognised that:

- Individuals will be naturally inclined towards some roles more than other
- Individuals will tend to adopt one or two team roles more or less consistently
- Individuals are likely to be more successful in some roles than in others

The nine roles are complementary, and Belbin suggested that an ideal team should represent a mix or balance of all of them. If managers know employees' team role preferences, they can strategically select, 'cast' and develop team members to fulfil the required roles.

Belbin insists that a sharp distinction needs to be made between:

(a) **Team role** ('a tendency to behave, contribute and interrelate with others at work in certain distinctive ways'), and

(b) **Functional role** ('the job demands that a person has been engaged to meet by supplying the requisite technical skills and operational knowledge')

Activity 8 (10 mins)

The following phrases and slogans project certain team roles: identify which. (Examples drawn from Belbin, 1993)

(a) The small print is always worth reading.

(b) Let's get down to the task in hand.

(c) In this job you never stop learning.

(d) Without continuous innovation, there is no survival.

(e) Surely we can exploit that?

(f) When the going gets tough, the tough get going.

(g) I was very interested in your point of view

(h) Has anyone else got anything to add to this?

(i) Decisions should not be based purely on enthusiasm.

6.2 Dynamics within teams

In order to evaluate and manage team dynamics, it may be helpful for the team leader to:

(a) Assess who (if anybody) is performing each of Belbin's team roles. Who is the team's plant, co-ordinator, monitor-evaluator and so on? There should be a mix of people performing task and team maintenance roles.

(b) Analyse the frequency and type of individual members' contributions to group discussions and interactions.

    (i) Identify which members of the team habitually make the most contributions, and which the least (eg by taking a count of contributions from each member, during a sample 10-15 minutes of group discussion).

    (ii) If the same people tend to dominate discussion whatever) is discussed (ie regardless of relevant expertise), the team has a problem in its communication process.

Additional factors influencing team dynamics include team members' attitudes – excitement and enthusiasm are valuable commodities and can be encouraged through praise and appreciation. Praise where it is due costs very little. Being overly critical and cynical towards other's work can lead to a dulling of the critical faculty by blocking one's openness to alternative ideas, reducing the will to experiment. The team should be always looking for ideas that are fresh, fun and effective. Having found such ideas, studying and copying the methods of their realisation can lead to the development of new ones.

NOTES

Good communications between team members and with employees inside and outside the organisation are also important for success. Acknowledging and talking through problems can be helpful in lifting mind-blocks, even with team members who do not specialise in the same area. Sometimes a suggestion from a completely different direction can be just what is needed in reengaging one's creative thought processes.

Neil Rackham and Terry Morgan have developed a helpful categorisation of the types of contribution people can make to team discussion and decision-making

Category	Behaviour	Example
Proposing	Putting forward suggestions, new concepts or courses of action	'Why don't we look at a flexi-time system?'
Building	Extending or developing someone else's proposal.	'Yes. We could have a daily or weekly hours allowance, apart from a core period in the middle of the day'.
Supporting	Supporting another person or his/her proposal.	'Yes, I agree, flexi-time would be worth looking at'
Seeking information	Asking for more facts, opinions or clarification.	'What exactly do you mean by flexi-time?'
Giving information	Offering facts, opinions or clarification.	'There's a helpful outline of flexi-time in this article.'
Disagreeing	Offering criticism or alternative factors or opinions, which contradict a person's proposals or opinions.	'I don't think we can take the risk of not having any staff here at certain periods of the day'.
Attacking	Attempting to undermine another person or their position: more emotive than disagreeing.	'In fact, I don't think you've thought this through at all.'
Defending	Arguing for one's own point of view.	'Actually, I've given this a lot of thought, and I think it makes sense.'
Blocking/ difficulty stating	Putting obstacles in the way of a proposal, without offering any alternatives.	'What if the other teams get jealous? It would only cause conflict.'
Open behaviour	Risking ridicule and loss of status by being honest about feelings and opinions.	'I thing some of us are afraid that flexi-time will show up how little work they really do in a day.'
Shutting-out behaviour	Interrupting or overriding others; taking over.	'Nonsense. Let's move onto something else – we've had enough of this discussion.'
Bringing-in behaviour	Involving another member; encouraging contribution	'Actually, I'd like to hear what Fred has to say. Go on, Fred.'

Category	Behaviour	Example
Testing understanding	Checking whether points have been understood.	'So flexi-time could work over a day or a week; have I got that right?'
Summarising	Drawing together or summing up previous discussion.	'We've now heard two sides to the flexi-time issue: on the one hand, flexibility; on the other side possible risk. Now ...'

Each type of behaviour may be appropriate in the right situation at the right time. A team may be low on some types of contribution – and it may be up to the team leader to encourage, or deliberately adopt, desirable behaviours (such as bringing-in, supporting or seeking information) in order to provide balance.

6.3 Politics of working relationships

An important aspect of management studies is politics in the work place. By this we mean political behaviour rather than preference for one party rather than another. Political behaviour is broadly concerned with competition, conflict, rivalry, influence and power relationships in organisations. Organisations are political systems in the sense that they are composed of individuals and groups who have their own interests, priorities and goals: there is competition for finite resources, power and influence; there are cliques, alliances, pressure groups and blocking groups, centred around values, opinions and objectives which may be opposed by others. Managers are constantly involved in compromise, reconciling or controlling differences, and settling for 'reality' rather than 'ideal'.

Political behaviour is based around the notion of coalitions and the assumption that individuals and groups can succeed together where they might fail alone. Various coalitions will seek to protect their interests and positions of authority.

Office politics, when viewed as a negative influence, can reduce organisational productivity, create a lack of trust, undermine staff morale, exclude key people from the decision-making processes and increase internal conflict that leads to a drain of its talent pool.

The workplace politicians are characterised with animal stereotypes based on the model devised by management development experts Simon Baddeley and Dr Kim James.

The donkey	Unprincipled and unethical, they are useless at interpersonal skills but like to stay close to authority figures within the firm. They make judgments based on feelings rather than knowledge of the organisation's procedures or bureaucracy.
The fox	Unsurprisingly in the cunning and clever category, they are quick to exploit weaknesses in their allies and opponents alike. In human terms fox-like behaviour is demonstrated through being interested in power and in fraternising with powerful people. These individuals may seem unprincipled, self-driven, typically seen as unethical and they have trouble showing their feelings.

| The sheep | They are the innocents. Loyal yet politically clueless, they do not put themselves about to build networks in the organisation. Sheep act with integrity, sticking to ethical, corporate and professional rules. |
| The owl | Politically astute, wise owls can cope with being disliked, are non-defensive, use coalitions but are aware of other people's concerns. |

If office politics are a fact of life, individuals who want to reach the upper echelons must master the scheming. The recommended strategies for surviving and thriving in a political landscape are as follows.

Agenda setting	Politically, agendas combine a vision for change with a strategy for achieving that vision. Effective leaders develop this agenda from a sense of what they want and what they are prepared to trade off against something more desirable in the longer term. In setting an agenda, effective politicians recognise the concerns of major stakeholders.
Mapping the political terrain	Office politics work within the informal system and there are no route maps to what is a changing and hazardous territory. So before entering, determine the channels of communication to find the best ways to hear and be heard. Then identify the main players with political influence, not always the most senior people but those who have their ear and thus maximise the chances of your ideas being adopted.
Coalition building	A memo to your superior can be effective, but is often a sign of impotence and betrays a lack of political sophistication. The rules of engagement dictate that no strategy will work without a power base and line managers face a power gap. Moving up the food chain brings more authority but it also brings more dependence because success hinges on the efforts of a diverse group of people.
Bargaining and negotiation	Horse-trading among different interest groups presents the toughest challenge to many managers. The principled search for an agreement beneficial to all parties rests on separating the people from the problem. The trick is to focus on interests not positions.
Building a power base	Managers should build up elements of their power base by being sensitive to what others consider legitimate behaviour in acquiring and using power. Politically astute managers will develop an intuitive understanding of various types of power and methods of influence which bolster their authority.
Selling your ideas	As a manager you need friends and allies to get things done. To promote change or innovation get preliminary agreement from those most affected. Make them your cheer-leaders and build your resource base on the way to securing the necessary approvals from higher management.

A good team will experience heightened creativity in each other's company, compared to that which is achievable individually. But sometimes there is conflict between team members, resulting in work taking a back seat to relationships and office politics. This, in turn, leads to the marginalisation of certain members of the team and the accompanying elevation of others to positions of power. This can only cause unrest as raised expectations followed by disappointment and demotivation will result from the breakdown of communications within the team.

7 TEAM BUILDING

7.1 Issues involved in team building

Woodcock suggests that to achieve a successful team, the following nine aspects of its functioning and performance must have taken place.

- (a) Clear objectives and agreed goals
- (b) Openness and confrontation
- (c) Support and trust
- (d) Co-operation and conflict
- (e) Sound procedures
- (f) Appropriate leadership
- (g) Regular reviews
- (h) Individual development
- (i) Sound inter-group relations

Definition

Team-building may be described as a systematic attempt to develop the processes of collaborative functioning within a team (such as communication, problem-solving, decision-making and conflict resolution) in such a way as to help the team to overcome any barriers to effective pursuit of its shared goals.

In its simplest terms, the stages involved in team building are:

- To clarify the team goals

- To identify those issues which inhibit the team from reaching their goals

- To address those issues, remove the inhibitors and enable the goals to be achieved

There are three main issues involved in team building.

1   **Team identity:** get people to see themselves as part of the group. A manager might seek to reinforce the **sense of identity** of the group.

- **Name** – staff at McDonald's restaurants are known as the Crew

- **Badge or uniform** – this often applies to service industries, but it is unlikely that it would be applied within an organisation

- Expressing the team's **self-image:** teams often develop their own jargon, especially for new projects

- Building a team **mythology** – in other words, stories from the past ('classic mistakes' as well as successes)

- **A separate space:** it might help if team members work together in the same or adjacent offices, but this is not always possible

2 **Team solidarity:** implies cohesion and loyalty inside the team. A team leader might be interested in:

- Expressing solidarity

- Encouraging interpersonal relationships – although the purpose of these is to ensure that work does get done

- Dealing with conflict by getting it out into the open; disagreements should be expressed and then resolved

- Controlling competition – the team leader needs to treat each member of the team fairly and to be seen to do so; favouritism undermines solidarity

- Encouraging some competition with other groups if appropriate. For example, sales teams might be offered a prize for the highest monthly orders; London Underground runs best-kept station competitions

Getting commitment to the team's shared objectives may involve a range of leader activity.

3 **Shared objectives:** encourage the team to commit itself to shared work objectives and to co-operate willingly and effectively in achieving them.

7.2   Belbin – putting the team together

Meredith Belbin, one of the most influential modern writers on teams, identifies a number of basic steps in the early stages of team building.

(a) Articulating the purpose and terms of reference of the team: setting clear and meaningful goals

(b) Selecting team membership and 'casting' team members in appropriate roles

(c) Deciding the 'style' in which the team will operate: whether through meetings, independent working, working in pairs – or whatever suits the members

Team members may be pre-selected as representatives of specific functions/departments or interest groups. Members may be selected on the basis of:

(a) The skills, knowledge and expertise required by the task

(b) Power or influence in the wider organisation, required to champion the team's interests or to mobilise resources

(c) The skills required for task processes: skills in stimulating discussion, skills in checking and attending to detail, skills in implementation and follow-through

(d) The skills required for teamworking: skills in discussion, conflict resolution and so on

Belbin suggested that process roles – the ways people contribute to discussion, decision-making and teamworking – are at least as important as functional roles: whether a person is an accounting, marketing or technical expert.

7.3 Team spirit

The most important and fundamental aspect of teambuilding is developing and fostering a **team spirit.** It increases the chances of successful performance and winning but what is team spirit?

- It is a combination of **respect**, **trust**, **interconnectedness** and **enjoyment** amongst a group of individuals who work towards agreed common goals. These qualities are essential to success, for every individual must feel needed, valued, respected and wanted if he or she is to contribute fully to the group.

- It is a feeling of **loyalty** that the members of a group have toward others in the group.

- It is a group of people who **pull together**. Team members begin to envision what they can create together, begin to sense the possibilities for developing breakthrough solutions or delivering unparalleled service. Here they realise they can accomplish far more collectively than separately.

- It is the **desire** to work as a team. It helps the team as a whole develop a sense of solidarity and single-minded purpose, while empowering individual team members to assume responsibility for the goals, roles, competencies and resources needed to realise their shared vision.

- **Selflessness** (acting with less concern for yourself than for the success of the joint activity). Remember it's working together with commitment, allegiance, loyalty, dedication, (intellectually or emotionally) to a course of action.

7.4 Building blocks

Woodcock adopts a practical approach to team building. He argues that to build an effective team you must first identify the blockages to team building then decide on the building blocks to be used. He then discusses the general issues to be taken into account and outlines an action plan for implementation.

Identifying the best building blocks to use to overcome the blockages is a very important stage in team building. Inappropriate and misjudged team building activities can lead to a misuse of time, a waste of money and other resources, a lowering in morale because of the wasted effort and an increase in cynicism from the members.

The factors that lead to blockages in effectiveness and the building blocks used to overcome them are as follows.

Blockages	Building block
Inappropriate leadership	The leader can adopt a suitable leadership style
Insufficient mix of member skills and personalities	Ensure team members are suitably qualified. If necessary, get members to adopt another role than they would normally

NOTES

Blockages	Building block
Unconstructive climate	Strive to achieve an atmosphere of co-operation
An absence of clear and agreed goals and objectives	The team has been brought together for a purpose so this can be clarified and developed into sub-objectives which are agreed
Poor achievement	Performance is improved in a climate of trust and learning
Ineffective work methods	Develop sensible procedures for performing the team's tasks
Lack of communication – people afraid to challenge key issues	Develop a climate so that people can speak their minds constructively
Individual development needs not addressed	Individuals are given opportunities to grow or develop within the team
Low creativity	Techniques such as brainstorming can improve creativity. Much depends on how new ideas are treated
Poor and unconstructive interpersonal relationships	Some people will never get on or have much in common but they can still work together effectively. Induction exercises might be required to break the ice
Non existent or inadequate review and control of performance	The performance of the team can be reviewed at regular intervals

7.5 Team building tools

Once the difficulties or blockages have been identified, team building can be greatly accelerated by the use of special team-building events, activities, and exercises to help group members change individual behaviour to improve team performance. A range of techniques can be employed, including participation, empowerment, leadership development, outward-bound courses, team building games, team building exercises, team building activities and team building adventures and the use of formal processes, which evaluate the performance of teams and team members as a basis for feedback and for improvement.

(a) **Participation** is the first step in the process of involving team members in the company's decision-making processes. Instead of planning everything from the top level of the organisation, a participative leader would invite the team members to contribute their ideas to the process so that everyone will feel as though they have contributed and that their voice has been heard.

(b) **Empowerment** goes much further. It allows team members to have the discretion to make decisions that are relevant to their own sphere of operations, without the need to refer to a higher level of management.

(c) **Adventure courses** – with all the participants being involved in quite physical tasks with a need for the group members to help each other. There are less physical versions, like building bridges in competitive groups.

PROFESSIONAL EDUCATION

Whatever the format, a debriefing stage is an essential part of the exercise. 'How did we perform as a team?' or 'Where did we go wrong?' are the key kinds of question to consider.

(d) **Team volunteering** – is also an effective team-building tool. Teams connect with their community, develop new working skills and make a difference to people's lives. Examples include decorating classrooms, planting trees, taking disabled people for outings or visiting old people to have a chat.

Activity 9 (20 mins)

Why might the following be effective as team-building exercises?

(a) Sending a project team (involved in the design of electronic systems for racing cars) on a recreational day out karting.

(b) Sending two sales teams on a day out playing 'War Games, each being an opposing combat team trying to capture the other's flag, armed with paint guns

(c) Sending a project team on a conference at a venue away from work, with a brief to review the past year and come up with a vision for the next year

These are actually commonly used techniques. If you are interested, you might locate an activity centre or company near you that offers outdoor pursuits, war games or corporate entertainment and ask them about team-building exercises and the effect they have on people.

---

8 TEAM EVALUATION AND REWARDS

8.1 Supporting teams

Organisations succeed because of teams – people working together to accomplish common objectives. In most organisations, however, the process of establishing teams and managing their accomplishment of projects and tasks is haphazard at best. One of the main reasons teams fail to function at their best is that there are no systems to support best team practices. Many of the problems teams have, such as poor communication, personality conflicts, weak accountability, missed deadlines, cost overruns and so on can be diminished or eliminated by implementing improved team practices.

A supportive environment, which is genuinely interested in the results the team is going to produce, can energise a team to perform beyond anyone's expectations. A hostile environment can doom a team to failure no matter how good the people are in it. However, a supportive environment is more than just interest in the team – it is a whole culture that values teams and is characterised by informal teams forming and disbanding in response to the needs of the organisation.

8.2 Supervising teams

Proper supervision, neither too loose nor too tight, also contributes to team success. Team leaders need to be involved enough to know what the teams needs and to provide it. But they must never meddle in the team's functioning. Leaders have four primary roles in a team environment:

- to resolve conflicts that cannot be resolved by the team
- to give direction and functional expertise to the team and to members needing help
- to find the needed resources
- to judge the performance of the team and its individual members

8.3 Establish a way to monitor progress

For all teamwork, it is important to create a method for tracking how well the team is moving towards its objectives. A measurement system can be used on a regular basis to review progress, identify opportunities for improvement and learn from mistakes.

Metrics and measurements may be viewed as a time consuming activity with no real benefit, however this is just what is required in order to create and sustain high performance teamwork. Teams must know if what they are doing is effective and if they are on track to meet their goals. If they are not on track they need to know this and more importantly, they need to know why they are not on track so that they can modify their performance, get back on track and achieve their goals.

8.4 Evaluating teams

The task of the team leader is to build a 'successful' or an 'effective' team. The criteria for team effectiveness include:

- **Task performance**: fulfilment of task and organisational goals. Effectiveness is the degree to which goals are accomplished and efficiency is the use of resources in attaining goals
- **Team functioning**: constructive maintenance of team working, managing the demands of team dynamics, roles and processes
- **Team member satisfaction**: fulfilment of individual development and relationship needs

In most cases effectiveness and efficiency are related. The team could be effective in accomplishing its goals but it may not be efficient in its use of machinery or human resources. In circumstances where there is some physical or countable task, the measurement is relatively straightforward and there are certain elements that can be used to evaluate the team's performance, these include:

- The quantity of work performed
- The quality of work performed and
- The association of work performed with time allowed

Given the type of work done by teams, there may be no obvious objective measures, such as sales figures, number of complaints or components made per hour, available for assessing their performance. Therefore, some form of subjective measure is required. There are various ways of judging the performance of teams in the absence of objective measures. One way is to observe and rate the team's behaviour on some set of agreed criteria. Another is to interview all who may have a view about the team and its performance. A third is to administer a pre-prepared questionnaire to team members and their managers. Some researchers have used senior management as judges of a team's performance as well as, and sometimes instead of, team members' own judgements.

Concerns about working as a member of a team often revolve around issues of assessment – people fear they will receive a lower evaluation as a member of a team than they would if they worked alone. Or, there is the fear that other team members will not carry their share of the work, yet receive the same amount of credit as the harder-working members of the team.

Credit for work in a team project may be based on:

(a) A **single evaluation** provided to the group – all individuals would receive the same amount of credit for the work in a team regardless of their actual contributions.

(b) **Evaluations of individual team members** – each individual team member would receive an individual score, which may be the same or different than the credit given to their team mates

(c) A **combined assessment** using both group and individual assessment scores to determine the final credit given each team member – this matches the needs for individual accountability as well as evaluation of teams for reaching a group goal(s).

8.5 Rewarding effective teams

Organisations may try to encourage effective team performance by designing reward systems that recognise team, rather than individual success. Indeed, individual performance rewards may act against team co-operation performance because:

(a) They emphasise individual rather than team performance

(b) They encourage team leaders to think of team members only as individuals rather than relating to them as a team

For **team rewards** to be effective, the team must have certain characteristics.

- Distinct roles, targets and performance measures
- Significant autonomy and thus influence over performance
- Maturity and stability
- Co-operation
- Interdependence of team members

Reward schemes that focus on team (or organisation) performance include:

(a) **Profit sharing** schemes, based on a pool of cash related to profit

(b) **Gainsharing** schemes, using a formula related to a suitable performance indicator, such as added value. Improvements in the performance indicator must be perceived to be within the employees' control, otherwise there will be no incentive to perform

(c) **Employee share option** schemes, giving staff the right to acquire shares in the employing company at an attractive price

Chapter roundup

- Conflict can be viewed as inevitable owing to the class system; a continuation of organisation politics by other means; something to be welcomed as it avoids complacency; something resulting from poor management, or something that should be avoided at all costs.

- Conflict can be constructive, if it introduces new information into a problem, if it defines a problem, or if it encourages creativity. It can be destructive if it distracts attention from the task or inhibits communication.

- Causes of conflict include operative goal incompatibility, differentiation, interdependence, resource scarcity, power, uncertainty and rewards.

- Conflict can be managed by separating the conflicting parties, restricting communication or imposing a solution, a number of techniques are available actively to promote co-operative behaviour.

- Teams have a 'sense of identity' that a random crowd of individuals does not possess.

- A team is more than a group. It has joint objectives and accountability and may be set up by the organisation under the supervision or coaching of a team leader, although self-managed teams are growing in popularity.

- Teamworking may be used for: organising work; controlling activities; generating ideas; decision-making; pooling knowledge.

- Multidisciplinary teams contain people from different departments, pooling the skills of specialists.

- Multi-skilled teams contain people who themselves have more than one skill.

- Ideally team members should perform a balanced mix of roles. Belbin suggests: co-ordinator, shaper, plant, monitor-evaluator, resource-investigator, implementer, team-worker, finisher and specialist.

- Team members make different types of contribution (eg proposing, defending, blocking)

- A team develops in stages: forming, storming, norming, performing (Tuckman) and adjourning.

- Team development can be facilitated by active team building measures to support team identity, solidarity and commitment to shared objectives.

Quick quiz

1 What are the features of the 'happy family' view of the organisation?

2 Give an alternative to the happy family view

3 When can conflict be constructive?

4 What happens when two groups are put in competition with each other?

5 What are the possible outcomes of conflict, according to the 'win-win' model?

6   What causes conflict?

7   What is a team?

8   List Belbin's nine roles for a well-rounded team?

9   Who described the stages of group development?

(i)   Woodcock
(ii)   Belbin
(iii) Tuckman
(iv) Rackham and Morgan

10   List the teambuilding issues identified by Woodcock.

11   List six of Rackham and Morgan's categories of contribution to group discussion.

Answers to quick quiz

1   Organisations are co-operative and harmonious. Conflict arises when something goes wrong. (See para 1.1)

2   Conflict is inevitable, being in the very nature of the organisation. Conflict can be constructive. (1.1)

3   It can introduce solutions, define power relations, bring emotions, hostile or otherwise, out into the open. (1.2)

4   They become more cohesive internally and more achievement-orientated. (1.4)

5   Win-lose, lose-lose, win-win. (2.2)

6   Different objectives, scarcity of responses, personal differences, interdependence of departments. (2.5)

7   A small number of people with complementary skills who are committed to a common purpose, performance goals and approach for which they hold themselves basically accountable. (3.1)

8   Co-ordinator, shaper, plant, monitor-evaluator, resource-investigator, implementer, teams worker, finisher, specialist. (6.1)

9   (iii): Tuckman. You should be able to identify the team-relevant theories of Woodcock and Belbin as well. (4.2)

10   Leaders, Members. Climate. Objectives. Achievement. Work methods. Communications. Individuals, Creativity. Interpersonal communications. Review and control. (7.4)

11   Proposing, building, supporting, seeking information, giving information, disagreeing. (6.2)

Answers to activities

1   The 'happy family' perspective rarely fits most organisations, even those pursuing a common ideological goal, like a political party. Such organisations regularly face conflict (eg the Conservatives' divisions over Europe), if only about how to attain their goals. Cynics argue that managers promote the 'happy family' view to suppress conflict. Asda at one time referred to all its staff as 'colleagues'.

NOTES

2   Conflicts occur anywhere in an organisation. Individuals, groups, departments or subsidiaries compete for scarce (financial/human/physical) resources.

3   Sherifs' work applies to conflict in organisations. To improve employee performance, win-lose conflict can be turned towards competitors, who become 'the enemy'.

4   (a)   Both might need work done at the same time. Compromise and co-ordinated planning can help them manage their secretary's time.

     (b)   Differential pay might result in conflict with management – even an accusation of discrimination. There may be good reasons for the difference (eg length of service). To prevent conflict such information should be kept confidential. Where it is public, it should be seen to be not arbitrary.

     (c)   The electricians are worried about their jobs, and may take industrial action. Yet if the engineers' training is unrelated to the electricians' work, management can allay fears by giving information. The electricians cannot be given a veto over management decisions: a 'win-lose' situation is inevitable, but both sides can negotiate.

     (d)   The kitchen should plan its meals better – or people from both departments can be asked in advance whether they want puddings.

     (e)   Competition between sales regions is healthy as it increases sales. The conflict lies between sales regions and the production department. In the long-term, an increase in production capacity is the only solution. Where this is to be possible, proper co-ordination methods should be instituted.

5   (a)   (i)   Win-lose: one team member gets the window desk, and the other does not. (Result: broken relationships within the team.)

            (ii)   Compromise: the team members get the window desk on alternate days or weeks. (Result: half satisfied needs.)

            (iii) Win-win: what do they want the window desk for? One may want the view, the other better lighting conditions. This offers options to be explored: how else could the lighting be improved, so that both team members get what they really want? (Result: at least, the positive intention to respect everyone's wishes equally, with benefits for team communications and creative problem-solving.)

     (b)   (i)   Win-lose: one of you gets the file and the other doesn't.

            (ii)   Compromise: one of you gets the file now, and the other gets it later (although this has an element of win-lose, since the other has to work late or take it home).

            (ii)   Win-win: you photocopy the file and both take it, or one of you consults his or her boss and gets an extension of the deadline (since getting the job done in time is the real aim – not just getting the file). These kinds of solutions are more likely to emerge if the parties believe they can both get what they want.

     (c)   (i)   Win-lose: Manager A gets the computers, and Manager B has to upgrade her systems.

            (ii)   Compromise: Manager A will get some new computers, but keep the same old ones for continued data-sharing with Department B.

Department B will also need to get some new computers, as a back-up measure.

(ii) Win-win: what does Manager A want the computers for, or to avoid? Quite possibly, she needs to use up her budget allocation for buying equipment before the end of the budgetary period: if not, she fears she will lose that budget allocation. Now, that may not be the case, or there may be other equipment that could be more usefully purchased – in which case, there is no losing party.

6   Your own observation: remember, these will be useful examples to use, if asked in an assessment.

7   Categorising the behaviour of group members in the situations described results in the following: (a) storming, (b) dorming, (c) performing, (d) forming, (e) norming.

8   Completer/finisher
      Implementer
      Specialist
      Plant
      Resource investigator
      Shaper
      Teamworker
      Co-ordinator
      Monitor evaluator

9   • Recreation helps the team to build informal relationships: in this case, the chosen activity also reminds them of their tasks, and may make them feel special, as part of the motor racing industry, by giving them a taste of what the end user of their product does.

      • A team challenge purses the group to consider its strengths and weaknesses, to find it's natural leader. This exercise creates and 'us' and 'them' challenge: perceiving the rival team as the enemy heightens the solidarity of the group.

      • This exercise encourages the group the raise problems and conflicts freely, away from the normal environment of work and also encourages brainstorming and the expression of team members' dreams for what the team can achieve in the future.

Chapter 3 :
LEADERSHIP

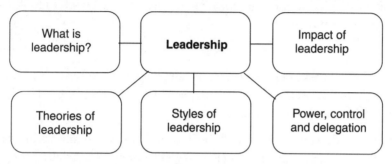

Introduction

The outcome of this chapter is for you to be able to evaluate the styles and impact of leadership. There are many ways of looking at leadership, and many interpretations of its meaning. Essentially it is a relationship through which one person influences the behaviour or actions of other people. Leadership is related to motivation, communication and delegation, as well as the activities of groups.

This chapter describes and comments on a number of the theoretical and practical aspects of leadership. A review of the main leadership theories is followed by a discussion on the alternative leadership styles available to a person in a management or supervisory position.

Your objectives

After completing this chapter you should be able to:

(a) Evaluate theories and styles of leadership

(b) Effectively communicate visions, goals and values to colleagues and promote understanding of how delegated objectives support these

(c) Enthuse and motivate colleagues to achieve objectives

(d) Promote confidence amongst colleagues to engage with change

(e) Empower colleagues to present their own ideas, develop their own ways of working within agreed boundaries and to provide a lead in their own areas of expertise.

NOTES

1 WHAT IS LEADERSHIP?

1.1 Defining leadership

There are many different definitions.

Definition

> **Leadership** is the process of influencing others to work willingly towards goals, to the best of their capabilities, perhaps in a manner different to that which they would otherwise have chosen.

Buchanan and Huczynski define a leader as 'someone who exercises influence over other people'. Leadership is seen as 'a social process in which one individual influences the behaviour of others without the use or threat of violence'.

The essence of leadership is followership. In other words it is the willingness of people to follow that makes a person a leader (Koontz, O'Donnell, Weihrich).

Most definitions of leadership reflect the assumptions that it is a relationship through which one person influences the behaviour or actions of other people in an organisational context. It is a dynamic two-way process of leading and following that can affect both individual and organisational performance. For example, a leader can influence the interpretation of events, the choice of objectives and strategies, the organisation of work activities, the motivation of people to achieve the objectives, the maintenance of co-operative relationships, the development of skills and confidence by members and the enlistment of support and co-operation from people outside the group or organisation.

1.2 Differences between leadership and management

The terms 'management' and 'leadership' are often used interchangeably. In some cases, management skills and theories have simply been relabelled to reflect the more fashionable term. However, there have been many attempts to distinguish meaningfully between them.

(a) **Yukl** suggests that while management is defined by a prescribed role and position in the structure of the organisation, leaders are given their roles by the perception of others, through election, choice or influence. Leadership is an interpersonal process. In other words, managers have subordinates, but leaders have followers.

(b) **Zaieznik** suggests that managers are mainly concerned with order and maintaining the status quo, exercising their skills in diplomacy and focusing on decision-making processes within the organisation. Leaders, in contrast, direct their energies towards introducing new approaches **and ideas.** They create excitement and vision in order to arouse motivation, and focus with empathy on the meanings of events and actions for people. Leaders search out opportunities for change.

(c) **Katz and Kahn** point out that while management aims to secure compliance with stated organisational objectives, leadership aims to secure willingness, enthusiasm and commitment. Leadership is the **influential increment** over and above mechanical compliance with the routine directives of the organisation.

(d) John Kotter (*The Leadership Factor*, 1988) has made one of the most detailed and helpful distinctions between leadership and management, and in so doing has further described both. According to Kotter, management involves the following activities.

(i) **Planning and budgeting** – target-setting, establishing procedures for reaching the targets, and allocating the resources necessary to meet the plans.

(ii) **Organising and staffing** – designing the organisation structure, hiring the right people and establishing incentives.

(iii) **Controlling and problem-solving** – monitoring results against the plan, identifying problems, producing solutions and implementing them.

Everything here is concerned with logic, structure, analysis and control. If done well, it produces predictable results on time. Leadership requires a different set of actions and, indeed, a completely different mindset.

(i) Creating a sense of direction – usually borne out of dissatisfaction with the *status quo*. Out of this challenge a vision for something different is created.

(ii) Communicating the vision – which must meet the realised or unconscious needs of other people and the leader must work to give it credibility.

(iii) Energising, inspiring and motivating – in order to stimulate others to translate the vision into achievement.

All of these activities involve dealing with people rather than things. But remember that leadership is a conscious activity. If you yawn and others around you do the same, it is more properly called 'behavioural contagion' than leadership.

Activity 1   **(10 minutes)**

Suppose you were in a cinema and smelt smoke. How would you categorise the following possible actions on your part? Your options are behavioural contagion, management and leadership.

(a) You rush to the door screaming 'Fire' and everyone follows you.

(b) You rush to the door, switch on the lights, hit the fire alarm, and, grabbing a fire extinguisher, start looking for the source of the fire. People start moving towards the exits when they hear the fire alarm.

(c) You rush to the door, switch on the lights, shout for people not to panic but to move towards the exits (which they do) and ask for help to locate the fire and get the fire extinguishers (which you get).

(d) You do any or all of the above, but nobody takes any notice.

1.3 Why should managers be leaders?

Whether or not we make the distinction between management and leadership, attempts to define what makes leadership 'special' have suggested some key points about the benefits effective leadership can bring and why it is valuable.

(a) Leaders energise and support **change,** which is essential for survival in highly competitive and fast-changing business environments. By setting visionary goals, encouraging contribution from teams, leaders create environments that:

- Seek out new information and ideas
- Allow challenges to existing procedures and ways of thinking
- Invite innovation and creativity in finding better ways to achieve goals
- Support and empower people to cope with the turbulence.

(b) Leaders secure **commitment,** mobilising the ideas, experience and motivation of employees – which contributes to innovation and improved quality and customer service. This is all the more essential in a competitive, customer-focused, knowledge- based business environment

(c) Leaders set **direction,** helping teams and organisations to understand their purpose, goals and value to the organisation. This facilitates team-working and empowerment (allowing discretion and creativity about how to achieve the desired outcomes) without loss of co-ordination or direction

(d) Leaders support, challenge and develop **people,** maximising their contribution to the organisation. Leaders use an influence-based facilitate-empower style rather than a command-control style, and this is better suited to the expectations of empowered teams and the need for information sharing in modern business environments.

Activity 2 (10 minutes)

Reflect on your own experience of working under the direction of others. Identify the 'best' leader you have ever 'followed'. (You may need to think about non-work leaders such as a sports coach or school teacher.) Think about how this person behaved and interacted with you and others.

What qualities make you identify this person as a 'great leader', from your point of view as a follower?

---

2 THEORIES OF LEADERSHIP

2.1 Different approaches

Theories of leadership can be classified as follows:

- **Trait** – based on analysing the *personality characteristics* or preferences of successful leaders.

- **Activity based,** based on analysing what designated leaders actually do, and how they do it.

- **Contingency – based** on the belief that there is no 'one best way' of leading, but that effective leaders adapt their behaviour to the specific and changing variables in the leadership context: the nature of the task, the personalities of team members, the organisation culture and so on.

- **Style – based** on the view that leadership is an interpersonal process whereby different leader behaviours influence people in different ways. More or less effective patterns of behaviour (or 'styles') can therefore be adopted.

Yukl (1989) identified four approaches for studying leadership. The 'power influence approach' attempts to understand leadership effectiveness in terms of the amount and type of power possessed by the leader. This approach would examine how power is acquired, lost, and maintained. The 'behaviour approach' looks at the actual tasks performed by leaders. This involves evaluating daily activities and behavioural characteristics of leaders. The 'trait approach' looks at the personal attributes of leaders, such as energy, intuition, creativity, persuasiveness, and foresight. The 'situational approach' examines leadership in terms of its relationships with environmental factors, such as superiors, subordinates, and peers. This approach is often referred to as contingency theory because the role of the leader is contingent on the situation.

2.2 Trait theories of leadership

Early theories suggested that there are certain qualities, personality characteristics or 'traits' that make a good leader. These might be aggressiveness, self-assurance, intelligence, initiative, a drive for achievement or power, appearance, interpersonal skills, administrative ability, imagination, a certain upbringing and education, the 'helicopter factor' (ie the ability to rise above a situation and analyse it objectively) etc.

This approach has much in common with the 'great man' theory of history, which states that great men set the great events of history in motion. Thus, those who display leadership in one situation would probably be the leader in any other situation. They are leaders because of some unique and inherent set of traits that set them apart from normal people. Lists of leadership qualities were compiled that included:

- Physical traits, such as drive, energy, appearance and height
- Personality traits, such as adaptability, enthusiasm and self-confidence and
- Social traits, such as co-operation, tact, courtesy and administrative ability

Trait theory, although superficially attractive, is now largely discredited, in favour of other theories.

2.3 Adair's action-centred leadership

Professor Adair's action-centred or situational model sees the leadership process in a context made up of three interrelated variables – task needs, the individual needs of group members and the needs of the group as a whole.

(a) The total situation dictates the relative priority that must be given to each of the three sets of needs

(b) Effective leadership is identifying and acting on that priority.

The diagram below shows the overlap of the task, group and individual needs, and indicates some measure of interrelation between these factors.

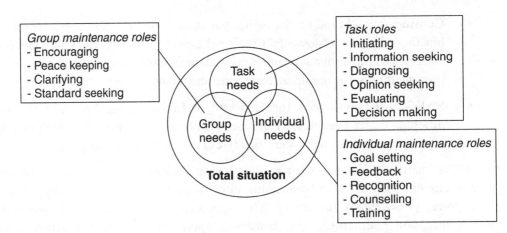

Figure 3.1 Adair's situational model of leadership

Adair's model of leadership is more a question of appropriate behaviour than of personality or of being in the right place at the right time. His model stresses that effective leadership lies in what the leader does to meet the needs of task, group and individuals. This takes the model nearer the contingency approaches of modern theorists, whose concern is with a variety of factors – task, people and situation – all having a bearing on leadership and leadership styles.

2.4 A contingency approach to leadership

A contingency approach to leadership is one that argues that the ability of a manager to lead and to influence his work group will vary according to:

(a) The leader's personality, character and preferred style of operating.

(b) The subordinates: their individual and collective personalities, and their preference for a particular style of leadership.

(c) The task: If the tasks of a work group are simple, few in number and repetitive, the best style of leadership will be different from a situation in which tasks are varied and difficult.

(d) The context

    (i) The position of power held by the leader in the organisation and the group. A person with power is better able to choose a personal style and leadership, select subordinates and re-define the task of the work group

    (ii) Organisational norms and the structure and technology of the organisation. No manager can act in a manner which is contrary to the customs and standards of the organisation.

For each of the three factors, a spectrum can be drawn ranging from 'tight' to 'flexible'. Handy argues that the most effective style of leadership in any particular situation is one which brings the first three factors – a leader, subordinates and task – into a 'best fit'.

The spectrum		
	Tight	**Flexible**
The leader	Preference for autocratic style, high estimation of his own capabilities and a low estimation of his subordinates. Dislikes uncertainty	Preference for democratic style with confidence in his subordinates, dislikes stress, accepts reasonable risk and uncertainty
The subordinates	Low opinion of own abilities; do not like uncertainty in their work and like to be ordered. They regard their work as trivial; past experience in work leads to acceptance of orders, cultural factors lean them towards autocratic/dictatorial leaders	High opinion of own abilities; likes challenging important work; prepared to accept uncertainty and longer time scales for results; cultural factors favour independence.
The task	Job requires no initiative – it is routine, repetitive or has a certain outcome. It has a short time scale for completion. Trivial tasks	Important tasks with a longer time scale. It can involve problem-solving or decision-making and complex work

A best fit occurs when all factors are on the same level in the spectrum. In practice, there is likely to be a misfit. Confronted with a lack of fit, the leader must decide which factor(s) should be changed to bring all three into line. In the short-term, the easiest is to change the leadership style. There are often long-term benefits to be achieved from re-defining the task (eg job enlargement) or from developing the work group.

Activity 3   **(20 minutes)**

List four ways in which an organisation, by dealing with 'environmental constraints' can help its managers to adopt an appropriate management style.

3   STYLES OF LEADERSHIP

Leaders accept responsibility for the outcomes of the groups they lead. While leaders have to exercise authority, the way in which this is done (the *style* of leadership) might vary. It is generally accepted that a leader's style of leading can affect the motivation, efficiency and effectiveness of the leader's followers.

There are various classifications of leadership style. Although the labels and definitions of styles vary, style models are often talking about the same thing: a continuum of behaviours from:

- Wholly task-focused, directive leadership behaviours (representing high leader control) at one extreme, and

- Wholly people-focused, supportive/relational leadership behaviours (representing high subordinate discretion) at the other

3.1 Styles of leadership

Huneryager and Heckman identified four different styles of leadership:

(a) **Dictatorial style** – where the leader forces subordinates to work by threatening punishment and penalties.

(b) **Autocratic style** – where decision-making is centralised in the hands of the leader, who does not encourage participation by subordinates. Many of the most successful businesses have been led to success by autocrats who are paternalistic leaders, offering consideration and respect to the workforce, but retaining full rights in decision-making. This is typified by the Quaker companies in the early years of this century (eg, Cadbury, Rowntree, Reckitt and Colman). Such a style is frequently found today in professional firms. Often they find it hard to delegate, to bring on successors, to stand down at the right moment, to switch off and go home, and to appreciate the views of others.

(c) **Democratic style** – where decision-making is decentralised, and shared by subordinates in participative group action. It is important not to allow a preference for democratic social systems to blind managers into favouring democratic management styles in all situations. Businesses can stand (and often need) firmer, more single-minded management than nation states would generally find healthy. Those who lead using the democratic approach suffer from being unable to move as quickly as competitor businesses led by autocrats and from people in the ranks not being clear as to exactly which direction they should be pulling in.

(d) **Laisser-faire style** – where subordinates are given little or no direction at all, and are allowed to establish their own objectives and make all their own decisions.

As we shall see from various studies a considerate style of leadership is frequently found to be the most effective and leads to greater job satisfaction, though task centred styles are often associated with high employee performance and, on occasions, with employee satisfaction as well.

3.2 A continuum of leadership styles

Tannenbaum and Schmidt proposed a continuum of behaviours (and associated styles), which reflected the balance of control exercised in a situation by the leader and the team.

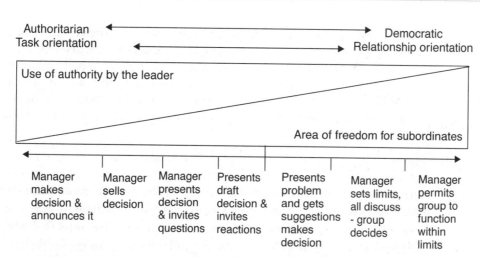

Figure 3.2 Tannenbaum and Schmidt's continuum of leadership styles

The continuum suggests a range of styles between authorisation and democratic without any suggestion that any one style is right or wrong. Tannenbaum and Schmidt's continuum recognises that the appropriate style depends upon:

- The leader (personality, values, natural style etc)

- The subordinates (their knowledge, experience, attitude etc)

- The situation (such forces as the organisation's culture, time pressures, levels of authority and responsibility etc)

3.3 Ashridge Management College

A further development of the continuum was published by the Ashridge Management College in 1966. Basically, they suggest four distinct management styles.

(a) **Tells** – the autocratic dictator. The manager makes all the decisions, and issues instructions, which must be obeyed without question. Communication is downward with no feedback until after the event. The strengths are that quick decisions can be made when speed is required and it is the most efficient type of leadership for highly programmed routine work. The weaknesses are that it does not encourage the subordinates to give their opinions when these might be useful and communications between the manager and subordinate will be one-way and the manager will not know until afterwards whether the orders have been properly understood

(b) **Sells** – the persuader. The manager still makes all the decisions, but believes that subordinates have to be motivated to accept them in order to carry them out properly. The strengths are that employees are made aware of the reasons for decisions. Selling decisions to staff might make them more committed. Staff will have a better idea of what to do when unforeseen events arise in their work because the manager will have explained his intentions. The weaknesses are that communications are still largely one-way. Subordinates might not accept the decisions and it does not encourage initiative and commitment from subordinates.

(c) **Consults** – partial involvement. The manager confers with subordinates and takes their views into account, but has the final say. Ashridge points out that this must be an honest approach not an attempt to hoodwink staff where the manager has no intention of changing a predetermined decision. The benefits are that employees are involved in decisions before they are made. This encourages motivation through greater interest and involvement. An agreed consensus of opinion can be reached and for some decisions consensus can be an advantage rather than a weak compromise. The weaknesses are that it might take much longer to reach decisions and subordinates might be too inexperienced to formulate mature opinions and give practical advice. Consultation can too easily turn into a façade concealing, basically, a sells style.

(d)   **Joins** – the democrat. Leader and followers make the decision on the basis of consensus. It is clearly most effective where all members within the group have knowledge and experience to contribute so that an evenly balanced informed discussion can lead to the best decision. It can provide high motivation and commitment from employees. It shares the other advantages of the consultative style (especially where subordinates have expert power). The problems are that the authority of the manager might be undermined. Decision-making might become a very long process, and clear decisions might be difficult to reach and subordinates might lack enough experience.

The Ashridge studies came to the following conclusions.

(a)   In an ideal world, subordinates preferred the 'consults' style of leadership.

(b)   People led by a 'consults' manager had the most favourable attitude to their work.

(c)   Most subordinates feel they are being led by a 'tells' or 'sells' manager.

(d)   In practice, **consistency** was far more important to subordinates than any particular style. The least favourable attitudes were found amongst subordinates who were unable to perceive any consistent style of leadership in their superiors.

Activity 4   **(20 minutes)**

Suggest an appropriate style of management for each of the following situations. Think about your reasons for choosing each style in terms of the results you are trying to achieve, the need to secure commitment from others, and potential difficulties with both.

(a)   Due to outside factors, the personnel budget has been reduced for your department and one-quarter of your staff must be made redundant. Records of each employee's performance are available.

(b)   There is a recurring administrative problem which is minor, but irritating to every one in your department. Several solutions have been tried in the past, but without success. You think you have a remedy, which will work, but unknown problems may arise, depending on the decisions made.

(c)   A decision needs to be made about working hours. The organisation wishes to stagger arrival and departure times in order to relieve traffic congestion. Each department can make its own decisions. It doesn't really matter what the times are, so long as department members conform to them.

> (d) Even though they are experienced, members in your department don't seem to want to take on responsibility. Their attitude seems to be: 'You are paid to manage, we are paid to work: you make the decisions.' Now a decision has come up which will personally affect every person in your department.

3.4 Rensis Likert

Likert (*New patterns of Management*) also described a range of four management styles or 'systems'.

System 1: Exploitative authoritative. The leader has no confidence or trust in his subordinates, imposes decisions, never delegates, motivates by threat, has little communication with subordinates and does not encourage teamwork.

System 2: Benevolent authoritative. The leader has only superficial trust in subordinates, imposes decisions, never delegates, motivates by reward and, though sometimes involving others in problem solving, is basically paternalistic.

System 3: Participative. The leader has some confidence in subordinates, listens to them but controls decision making, motivates by reward and a level of involvement, and will use the ideas and suggestions of subordinates constructively.

System 4: Democratic. The leader has complete confidence in subordinates who are allowed to make decisions for themselves. Motivation is by reward for achieving goals set by participation, and there is a substantial amount of sharing of ideas, opinions and co-operation.

Likert recognised that each style is relevant in some situations; for example, in a crisis, a System 1 approach is usually required. Alternatively when introducing a new system of work, System 4 would be most effective. His research shows that effective managers are those who adopt either a System 3 or a System 4 leadership style. Both are seen as being based on trust and paying attention to the needs of both the organisation and employees.

3.5 Blake and Mouton's Managerial Grid

Robert Blake and Jane Mouton carried out research (The Ohio State Leadership Studies) into managerial behaviour and observed two basic dimensions of leadership: concern for **production** (or task performance) and **concern for people.**

Along each of these two dimensions, managers could be located at any point on a **continuum** from very low to very high concern. Blake and Mouton observed that the two concerns did not seem to correlate, positively or negatively: a high concern in one dimension, for example, did not seem to imply a high or low concern in the other dimension. Individual managers could therefore reflect various permutations of task/people concern.

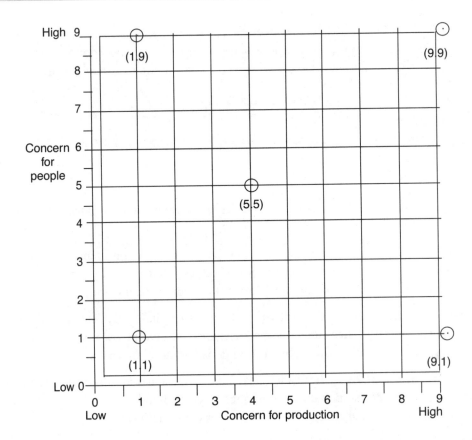

Figure 3.3 Blake and Mouton's managerial grid

The extreme cases shown on the grid are:

(a) 1.1 **impoverished:** the manager is lazy, showing little interest in either staff or work.

(b) 1.9 **country club:** the manager is attentive to staff needs and has developed satisfying relationships. However, there is little attention paid to achieving results.

(c) 9.1 **task management:** almost total concentration on achieving results. People's needs are virtually ignored.

(d) 5.5 **middle of the road** or the **dampened pendulum:** adequate performance through balancing the necessity to get out work while maintaining morale of people at a satisfactory level.

(e) 9.9 **team:** high performance manager who achieves high work accomplishment through 'leading' committed people who identify themselves with the organisational aims.

The managerial Grid was intended as an appraisal and management development tool. It recognises that a balance is required between concern for task and concern for people, and that a high degree of both is possible (and highly effective) at the same time.

The Grid thus offers a number of useful insights for the identification of management training and development needs. It shows in an easily assimilated form where the behaviour and assumptions of a manager may exhibit a lack of balance between the dimensions and/or a low degree of concern in either dimension or both. It may also be used in team member selection, so that a 1.9 team leader is balance by a 9.1 co-leader, for example.

However, the grid is a simplified model, and as such has practical limitations.

(a) It assumes that 9.9 is the desirable model for effective leadership. In some managerial contexts, this may not be so. Concern for people, for example, would not be necessary in a context of comprehensive automation: compliance is all that would be required.

(b) It is open to oversimplification. Scores can appear polarised, with judgements attached about individual managers' suitability or performance. The Grid is intended as a simplified snapshot of a manager's preferred style, not a comprehensive description of his or her performance.

(c) Organisational context and culture, technology and other 'givens' influence the manager's style of leadership, not just the two dimensions described by the grid.

(d) Any managerial theory is only useful in so far as it is useable in practice by managers: if the grid is used only to inform managers that they 'must acquire greater concern for people', it may result in stress, uncertainty and inconsistent behaviour.

Activity 5 (10 minutes)

Here are some statements about a manager's approach to meetings. Which position on Blake's Grid do you think each might represent?

(a) I attend because it is expected. I either go along with the majority position or avoid expressing my views

(b) I try to come up with good ideas and push for a decision as soon as I can get a majority behind me. I don't mind stepping on people if it helps a sound decision

(c) I like to be able to support what my boss wants and to recognise the merits of individual effort. When conflict arises I do a good job of restoring harmony.

---

4 POWER, CONTROL AND DELEGATION

4.1 Power

Organisations feature a large number of different activities to be co-ordinated, and large numbers of people whose **co-operation and support** is necessary for the manager to get anything done. As you have probably noticed if you have worked for any length of time, organisations rarely run as clockwork, and all depend on the directed energy of those within them.

Definition

Power is the **ability** to get things done.

BPP
PROFESSIONAL EDUCATION

NOTES

A manager without power, of whatever kind, cannot do his/her job properly, and this applies to leaders too. Power is not something a person has in isolation: it is exercised over other individuals or groups. Neither is it the exclusive preserve of managers. The following types of power from different sources have been identified.

Type of power	Description
Physical, coercive power	This is the power of physical force or punishment. Physical power is absent from most organisations, but organisations can sometimes use hidden forms of coercion to get what they want
Resource power	Access to or control over valued resources is a source of power. For example, managers have a resource of information or other contacts. The amount of resource power a person has depends on the scarcity of the resource, how much the resource is valued by others, and how far the resource is under the manager's control
Legitimate or position power	This is power associated with a particular job or position in the hierarchy. For example, your boss has the power to authorise certain expenses, or organise work. This is equivalent to **authority**
Expert power	A person may have power if his/her experience, qualifications or expertise are recognised. Typically, accountants have a type of expert power because of their knowledge of the tax system
Personal power	A person may be powerful simply by force of personality, which can influence other people, inspire them etc.
Negative power	This is the power to disrupt operations, such as strike, or refusal to communicate information

4.2 Influence

Influence denotes any 'changes in behaviour of a person or group due to anticipation of the response of others'.

The term influence is often used in conjunction with other terms such as power and/or authority. In some cases, they are considered as mutually exclusive concepts, with influence covering those ways of influencing behaviour that cannot be termed power or authority. A range of ways to influence behaviour is outlined below.

(a) **Emulation** – although it requires no direct contact between individuals, it is a powerful influence on behaviour. People often pick out certain behaviour patterns and strive to equal or surpass them. In organisations, participants are aware of the behavioural patterns of co-workers and various executives. Certain individuals become 'models' with their behaviour patterns being adopted by others, hoping to attain similar success.

(b) **Suggestion** – is an explicit attempt to influence behaviour by presenting an idea or advocating a particular course of action. Typically this mode is used when several alternative behaviour patterns for individuals or groups are acceptable and the person influencing is merely suggesting a preferred pattern. If this tolerance for different behaviour were not present, the influencer would use some other mode such as persuasion or even coercion.

(c) **Persuasion** – implies urging and the use of some inducement in order to evoke the desired response. It involves more pressure than a mere suggestion but falls short of the type of force implied by the term coercion.

(d) **Coercion** – involves forcible constraint, which may include physical pressure (arm-twisting). In organisations, salaries and / or promotions can be used to constrain or influence behaviour. In many cases the threat of dismissal is also a powerful influencer.

More recently, the interest in corporate culture also recognises the importance of people identifying with their employer. One of the reasons this is important is that it makes conflict less likely, and therefore power in the traditional sense becomes less important. It is less necessary to exercise tight control over employees, and there is more scope for delegation.

Some, however, have argued that this is really power use in a more subtle form. Managers, by manipulating an organisation's culture are effectively influencing people's attitudes and beliefs, in the same way that politicians might use 'propaganda' to influence people. Managers are clearly much more able to achieve this than anyone else in the organisation. In so doing they may be able to get people to do the same things they could by using more overt power – the 'carrot and stick approach,' – but without any overt conflict. So, the ability to influence people in this way could be seen as a very effective form of power, even though it does not fit easily into the standard definition.

4.3 Authority

If an organisation is to function as a co-operative system of individuals, some people must have authority or power over others. Authority and power flow downwards through the formal organisation.

It is also important to know Weber's contribution to our understanding of authority. Weber identified three forms of authority.

(a) Traditional
(b) Charismatic
(c) Rational/legal

Traditional and charismatic authority are vested in particular individuals. Rational/legal authority is vested in an office (or the person occupying it for the time being). Traditional authority is vested in someone by virtue of tradition and custom. The most obvious examples are royalty. They are considered to be able to give orders (and have them obeyed) purely by virtue of their 'station in life', and not as a result of any abilities they might have. Charismatic authority is vested in someone by virtue of his or her personality. A religious leader, for example, might generate strong feelings of loyalty and commitment among his or her followers.

Where someone has authority, however, it is clearly a particularly useful form of power since you can expect your orders to be carried out without the implicit bargaining that is involved in the dependency model. Nevertheless, there are limits even to authority. If people make demands that are seen as unreasonable, this will eventually undermine their authority. If people give subordinates reason to believe they are not in fact well qualified for the job, their authority will be undermined. Authority is rarely, if ever, granted unconditionally.

4.4 Control

Control is the general ability to direct and organise the efforts of the workforce. Different types of control have been identified.

(a) **Simple control** - refers to control by straightforward direct supervision.

(b) **Technical control** - refers to control that is imposed by the technology used in a factory. For example, the pace at which people must work on a production line is determined in part by the speed at which the line runs. The use of power here is more subtle, but is nevertheless clearly in the hands of the managers that control the technology.

(c) **Bureaucratic control** - refers to control by means of formal rules and regulations. Bureaucratic organisations typically have large books of rules that specify things like hours of work, entitlement to time off under various circumstances (eg annual leave, compassionate leave, maternity leave, etc.), grievance procedures, and so on). There are also rules or 'standard operating procedures' that people must follow in the course of their work. This form of control involves a still more subtle form of power. One might almost think of the rules as having a sort of authority, legitimated by people's understanding about the way in which the rules were derived – typically assumed to be some sort of 'rational' process. Further legitimacy might be obtained by the involvement of employee representatives in writing the rules.

The exercise of control is also an expression of leadership style and systems of management. The style of managerial leadership is a function of the manager's attitudes towards people and assumptions about human nature and behaviour eg, McGregor's Theory X and Theory Y.

McGregor's Theory X and Theory Y

The central principle of Theory X is that people have an inherent hatred of work, and as such must be cajoled, coerced (Etzioni), directed, threatened and even punished if corporate objectives are to be achieved. In many instances people prefer to be directed, wish to avoid responsibility, and prefer security rather than satisfying ambition.

The basis of Theory Y is that people do not hate work and find it a natural function. They are motivated on their own initiative and will strive for Maslow's self-actualisation. There is some support for Theory Y. If the right conditions can be developed for employees to work and satisfy their personal ambitions within their work, then high levels of motivation and productivity can be achieved. Theory Y is about creating a climate whereby people will motivate themselves.

4.5 Delegation

Leadership is the art of getting someone else to do something you want done because he/she wants to do it. This is delegation of authority and it refers to the successful transfer of authority to someone else.

We begin our discussion of delegation with an investigation into the nature of authority.

Definition

> **Authority** is the *right* of a person to ask someone else to do something and expect it to be done. Authority is thus another word for 'position power'.

Managerial authority consists of:

(a) **Making decisions within the scope of authority** given to the position. For example, a supervisor's authority is limited to his/her team and with certain limits. For items of expenditure more than a certain amount, the supervisor may have to go to someone else higher up the hierarchy.

(b) **Assigning tasks** to subordinates, and expecting satisfactory performance of these tasks.

> **Activity 6** (15 minutes)
>
> What types of authority and power are being exercised in the following case?
>
> Marcus is an accountant supervising a team of eight technicians. He has to submit bank reconciliation statements every week to the chief accountant. However, the company runs four different bank accounts and Marcus gets a team member, Dave, to do it for him.
>
> Marcus asks Isabella to deal with the purchase ledger – the company obtains supplies from all over the world, and Isabella, having worked once for an international bank, is familiar with letters of credit and other documentation involved with overseas trade. Isabella has recently told Marcus that Maphia Ltd, a supplier, should not be paid because of problems with the import documentation, even though Marcus has promised Maphia to pay them.
>
> Marcus is getting increasingly annoyed with Sandra, the departmental PA, who seems to be leaving Marcus's typing until last, although she says she has piles of other work to do. 'Like reading the newspaper,' thinks Marcus, who is considering pulling rank by giving her an oral warning.

Definition

> **Line authority** is the authority a manager has over a subordinate, arising from their respective positions in the organisation hierarchy. In other words, if you have line authority you an exercise position power over someone immediately below you.

There are other forms of authority which individuals (or departments) may exercise in the organisation.

PROFESSIONAL EDUCATION

NOTES

Definition

> **Staff authority** is the influence wielded when an expert gives specialist **advice** to another manager or department, even if there is no direct line authority. (An example might be the influence of legal advice from the legal department, or advice on budgetary constraints from the accounts department.)
>
> **Functional authority** is staff authority which has been built into the structure and policies of the organisation, for example where a specialist department lays down *procedures* and *rules* for other departments to follow within the area of its expertise. (The Personnel/HR department, for example, may impose certain recruitment and selection procedures on other departments.)

Definition

> **Delegation** of authority is when a superior gives to a subordinate part of his or her own authority to make decisions.

Note that delegation can only occur if the superior initially possesses the authority to delegate; a subordinate cannot be given organisational authority to make decisions unless it would otherwise be the superior's right to make those decisions personally.

Managers and leaders must delegate some authority because:

(a) There are **physical and mental limitations** to the work load of any individual or group in authority.

(b) Managers and leaders are free to **concentrate on the aspects of the work** (such as planning), which only they are competent (and paid) to do.

(c) The **increasing size and complexity** of some organisations calls for specialisation, both managerial and technical.

However, by delegating authority to assistants, the supervisor takes on the extra tasks of:

- **Monitoring their performance**
- **Co-ordinating** the efforts of different assistants.

The process of delegation is as follows.

Step 1. **Specify the expected performance** levels of the assistant, keeping in mind the assistant's level of expertise.

Step 2. **Formally assign tasks** to the assistant, who should formally agree to do them.

Step 3. **Allocate resources and authority** to the assistant to enable him or her to carry out the delegated tasks at the expected level of performance.

Step 4. **Maintain contact** with the assistant to review the progress made and to make constructive criticism. **Feedback** is essential for control, and also as part of the learning process.

Remember that ultimate **accountability** for the task remains with the leader: if it is not well done it is at least partly the fault of poor delegation, and it is still the leader's responsibility to get it re-done.

Disadvantages of delegation

Of course there are problems with delegation.

Many managers and leaders are **reluctant to delegate** and attempt to do many routine matters themselves in addition to their more important duties.

(a) **Low confidence and trust** in the abilities of their staff: the suspicion that 'if you want it done well, you have to do it yourself'.

(b) The burden of **accountability for the mistakes of subordinates**, aggravated by (a) above.

(c) A **desire to 'stay in touch'** with the department or team – both in terms of workload and staff – particularly if the manager does not feel 'at home' in a management role.

(d) **Feeling threatened.** An unwillingness to admit that assistants have developed to the extent that they could perform some of the leader's duties. The leader may feel threatened by this sense of 'redundancy'.

(e) **Poor control and communication systems** in the organisation, so that the manager feels he has to do everything himself, if he is to retain real control and responsibility for a task, and if he wants to know what is going on.

(f) An **organisational culture** that has failed to reward or recognise effective delegation, so that the manager may not realise that delegation is positively regarded (rather than as shirking responsibility).

(g) **Lack of understanding** of what delegation involves – not giving assistants total control, or making the manager himself redundant.

To overcome the reluctance of manager to delegate:

(a) **Train the subordinates** so that they are capable of handling delegated authority in a responsible way. If assistants are of the right 'quality', supervisors will be prepared to trust them more.

(b) Have a system of **open communications,** in which the leader and assistants freely interchange ideas and information. If the assistant is given all the information needed to do the job, and if the supervisor is aware of what the assistant is doing:

   (i) The assistant will make better-informed decisions.

   (ii) The supervisor will not panic because he does not know what is going on.

(c) **Ensure that a system of control is established**. If responsibility and accountability are monitored at all levels of the management hierarchy, the dangers of relinquishing authority and control to assistants are significantly lessened.

NOTES

> **Activity 7** (15 minutes)
>
> You are the manager of an accounts section of your organisation and have stopped to talk to one of the clerks in the office to see what progress he is making. He complains bitterly that he is not learning anything. He gets only routine work to do and it is the same routine. He has not even been given the chance to swap jobs with someone else. You have picked up the same message from others in the office. You discuss the situation with Jean Howe the recently appointed supervisor. She appears to be very busy and harassed. When confronted with your observations she says that she is fed up with the job. She is worked off her feet, comes early, goes late, takes work home and gets criticised behind her back by incompetent clerks.
>
> What has gone wrong?

5 IMPACT OF LEADERSHIP

5.1 Style and effectiveness

Much has been written on the subject of what constitutes good leadership but it is probably most true to say that the effectiveness of leaders is best measured by looking at the impact they have on the performance of those they lead. Excellent leadership can deliver results from an organisation well above what could reasonably be predicted, while at the same time morale among employees is high; conversely, poor leadership often results in under performing businesses, unhappy employees and highly defensive organisational behaviours.

Rensis Likert's research showed that **effective managers** display each of the four characteristics below, in relation to leadership skills. Such managers:

(a) **Expect high levels of performance** from subordinates, other departments and themselves.

(b) **Are employee-centred.** They spend time getting to know their workers and develop a situation of trust whereby their employees feel able to bring their problems to them. Such managers face unpleasant facts in a constructive manner and help their staff to do the same.

(c) **Do not practise close supervision.** The truly effective manager knows performance levels that can be expected from each individual and has helped them to define their own targets. The manager judges results and does not closely supervise the actions of subordinates.

(d) **Operate the participative style of management as a natural style.** If a job problem arises they do not impose a favoured solution. Instead, they pose the problem and ask the staff member involved to find the best solution. Having then agreed their solution the participative manager would assist his staff in implementing it.

5.2 Organisational climate and culture

Organisational climate is directly related to the leadership and management style of the leader, based on the values, attributes, skills, and actions, as well as the priorities of the leader. The ethical climate then is the 'feel of the organisation' about the activities that have ethical content or those aspects of the work environment that constitute ethical behaviour. The ethical climate is the feel about whether we do things right; or the feel of whether we behave the way we ought to behave. The behaviour (character) of the leader is the most important factor that impacts the climate.

On the other hand, culture is a long-term, complex phenomenon. Culture represents the shared expectations and self-image of the organisation. The mature values that create 'tradition' or the 'way we do things here.' Things are done differently in every organisation. The collective vision and common folklore that define the institution are a reflection of culture. Individual leaders cannot easily create or change culture because culture is a part of the organisation. Culture influences the characteristics of the climate by its effect on the actions and thought processes of the leader. But, everything a leader does will affect the climate of the organisation. It also influences the decision-making processes, the styles of management and what everyone determines as success.

Research published in the March-April 2000 *Harvard Business Review* (Goleman, 'Leadership that gets results') investigated how each of six distinctive leadership styles correlated with specific components of an organisation's culture.

These cultural components are:

- **Flexibility** – employees' ability to innovate without excessive rules and regulations

- **Responsibility** – how responsible employees feel towards the organisation

- **Standards** – the level of standards expected in the organisation

- **Rewards** – the accuracy of performance feedback and rewards

- **Clarity** – how clear employees are about the mission, vision and core values

- **Commitment** – employees' commitment to a common purpose

Daniel Goleman suggests that effective leaders choose from six distinctive leadership styles.

(i) **Coercive** (Do what I tell you) – this describes a leader that demands immediate compliance. This style can destroy an organisational culture and should only be used with extreme caution. It is useful in an emergency, and may work in a crisis or as a last resort with a problem employee. This leadership style has the most negative impact on the overall organisational culture.

(ii) **Pacesetting** (Do as I do, now) – describes a leader who sets extremely high standards for performance. This style can also destroy a good culture and only works with a highly motivated and competent team who are able to 'read' the leader's mind. Others will feel overwhelmed and give up because they cannot see themselves reaching unrealistic standards. This style also has a negative impact on the overall organisational culture, especially on rewards and commitment.

(iii) **Coaching** (Try this) – describes a leader who is focused on developing people for the future. These leaders are good at delegating, and are willing to put up with short-term failures, provided they lead to long-term development. This style works best when wanting to help employees improve their performance or develop their long-term strengths and has a positive impact on the overall organisational culture.

(iv) **Democratic** (What do you think?) – describes a leader who achieves consensus thorough participation. This style builds trust, respect and commitment, and works best when wanting to receive input or get employees to 'buy-in' or achieve consensus. If handled correctly, this style has a positive impact on the overall organisational culture.

(v) **Affiliative** (People come first) – this describes a leader who is interested in creating harmony and building emotional bonds with employees. This style works best when motivating employees, building team harmony, improving communication, increasing morale or repairing broken trust and has a positive impact on the overall organisational culture. Because this style has virtually no downside, it is often described as the best overall approach.

(vi) **Authoritative** (Come with me) – describes a visionary leader who gives people lots of scope to innovate and take calculated risks, provided that they move in the direction of the stated vision. This style works best when change requires a new vision or when employees are looking for a new direction but fails when employees are more knowledgeable or experienced than the leader, or if the authoritative style becomes overbearing. Provided that it is used subtly, this style has the most positive impact on the overall organisational culture.

Activity 8 (15 minutes)

In your career so far, you might have worked for a number of managers. Jot down the following features of each situation on a scale of 1-5 for comparative purposes.

(a) The degree to which you had autonomy over your own work.

(b) The degree to which you were consulted on decisions that affected you.

(c) The degree to which your advice was sought about decisions affecting your section.

If you worked for managers who had different approaches to these issues, do you think these approaches influenced your effectiveness? What score to questions (a), (b) and (c) would you give your ideal boss? and your current boss?

5.3 Leadership and vision

Leadership is a dynamic process in a group (or team), where one individual influences the others to contribute voluntarily to the achievement of group tasks in a given situation. The role of the leader is to direct the group towards their goals.

Leadership starts with having a vision of the future, then developing a plan to achieve it.

In the literature concerning leadership, vision has a variety of definitions, all of which include a mental image or picture, a future orientation, and aspects of direction or goal. Vision provides guidance to an organisation by articulating what it wishes to attain. By providing a picture, vision not only describes an organisation's direction or goal, but also the means of accomplishing it. It has a compelling aspect that serves to inspire, motivate, and engage people. It answers the questions: Who is involved? What do they plan to accomplish? Why are they doing this? Vision therefore does more than provide a picture of a desired future; it encourages people to work, to strive for its attainment.

Given a clear vision and a strategy the leader can empower people to achieve the goals. Empowerment means giving employees control of the decision-making process and allowing them to be independent of the leader.

5.4 Empowerment

Empowerment and delegation are related.

Definition

> **Empowerment** is the current term for making workers (and particularly work teams) responsible for achieving, and even setting, work targets, with the freedom to make decisions about how they are to be achieved.

Empowerment goes in hand in hand with:

(a) **Delayering** or a cut in the number of levels (and managers) in the chain of command, since responsibility previously held by middle managers is, in effect, being given to operational workers.

(b) **Flexibility**, since giving responsibility to the people closest to the products and customers encourages responsiveness – and cutting out layers of communication, decision-making and reporting speeds up the process.

(c) **New technology**, since there are more 'knowledge workers'. Such people need less supervision, being better able to identify and control the means to clearly understood ends. Better information systems also remove the mystique and power of managers as possessors of knowledge and information in the organisation.

According to Max Hand, the main reason for empowerment is the people lower down the organisation possess the knowledge of what is going wrong with a process but lack the authority to make changes. Those further up the structure have the authority to make changes, but lack the profound knowledge required to identify the right solutions. The only solution is to change the culture of the organisation so that everyone can become involved in the process of improvement and work together to make the changes.'

The change in organisation structure and culture as a result of empowerment can be shown below.

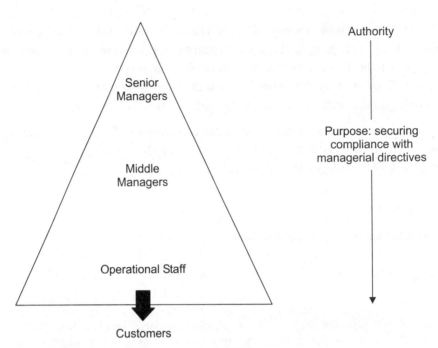

Traditional hierarchical structure: fulfilling management requirements

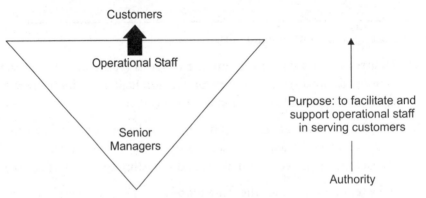

Empowerment structure: supporting workers in serving the customer

Figure 3.4 The hierarchical and empowerment structure compared

The argument, in a nutshell, is that by empowering workers (or 'decentralising' control of business units, or devolving/delegating responsibility, or removing levels in hierarchies that restrict freedom), not only will the job be done more effectively but the people who do the job will get more out of it.

CASE EXAMPLE

The validity of this view and its relevance to modern trends appears to be borne out by the approach to empowerment adopted by *Harvester Restaurants*, as described in *Personnel Management*. The management structure comprises a branch manager and a 'coach', while everyone else is a team member. Everyone within a team has one or more 'accountabilities' (these include recruitment, drawing up rotas, keeping track of sales targets and so on) which are shared out by the team members at their weekly team meetings. All the team members at different times act as 'co-ordinator' to the person responsible for taking the snap decisions that are frequently necessary in a busy restaurant. Apparently all of the staff involved agree that empowerment has made their jobs more interesting and has hugely increased their motivation and sense of involvement.

5.5 Motivating and empowering employees

The goal of leadership should be to move away from the old forms of bureaucracy that rely on position, reward and coercion power towards an organisational culture that relies on information, expertise, personality and moral power. In order for this to happen, the leader has to be less controlling.

Four forms of power can be used to motivate employees by empowering them – **information, expertise, personality** and **moral power**. When these forms of power are used, the employees decide the course of action. If they decide to follow their leader, the form of motivation is intrinsic because they see that course of action as a good thing to do. Further, they are allowed the independence of choice and they are empowered in the process. As employees become more mature, the leadership style can become more collaborative and less directive.

(a) **Information** can be used by a leader to involve the employee in the decision-making process and empower them. For example, if the leader wants the employee to change the way they were doing something, the leader could explain the benefits of the change. Handouts, videos, or other information extolling the advantages of the change could also be made available. The employee on analysing the information would have to make a decision. If the employee decided to change, the employee would be empowered, the motivation for the change would be intrinsic, and the decision would be made independent of the leader.

(b) A leader who has **expertise** can demonstrate how to perform a task. The employee who watches the demonstration decides whether they are able to perform that task. Competence or expertise is the root of power and leaders without competence cannot maintain power. However, a leader cannot be expert in all things. Consequently, he or she must use the expertise of others to motivate employees to change. For example, if a new technique will benefit an organisation, the leader needs to send key employees to another place where that technique is being successfully used. The employees observe the new process and decide whether it is beneficial and if it will work in their organisation. Employees who are exposed to this form of power frequently choose to imitate what they have observed. It is their choice, the motivation is intrinsic, they are independent of the person with the expertise, and they have been empowered.

(c) A leader who has **personality** or referent power is described as a person who is generally liked and admired by others because of it. When a leader uses this form of power it usually comes in the form of a request (verbal) or a signal (non-verbal). The subordinate hears the request or sees the signal and changes their behaviour to comply with the leader's wishes. The change in behaviour is done willingly, is intrinsically motivated, and the employee remains independent of the leader. The employee has made a conscious decision to grant the leader's wishes.

(d) A leader who has **moral power** has communicated a shared set of values and obligations which lay out the right thing to do for the good of employees, the organisation, the stakeholders and possibly the community as a whole. These values may be set out as a mission statement or vision, possibly arrived at through discussion with followers and explained through procedures, rules and regulations. This type of power requires the least maintenance as following the standards laid down becomes a matter for the individual's conscience and will be enforced through personal values, peer pressure and organisational culture.

5.6 Leadership and change

Change can be classified into two categories – planned and unplanned.

- **Planned change** – is a deliberate and conscious effort designed to meet forthcoming input changes that can be seen or predicted. For example, changes in the buying patterns or customer requirements.

- **Unplanned change** – is thrust upon the organisation by environmental events beyond its control. For example, changes in the bank rate, sudden changes in the value of a currency, unexpected scarcity of a raw material or a serious fire.

The role of the leader is to anticipate the need for change, create an atmosphere of acceptance of change and manage the stages of introduction and implementation. He or she can expect resistance to change since all major changes threaten somebody's security or somebody's status.

One of the most important factors in the successful implementation of organisational change is the style of managerial behaviour. In certain situations, and with certain members of staff, it may be necessary for leaders to make use of hierarchical authority and attempt to impose change through a coercive, autocratic style of behaviour. In most cases, however, the introduction of change is more likely to be effective with a participative style of behaviour. If staff are kept informed of proposals, are encouraged to adopt a positive attitude and have personal involvement in the implementation of the change, there is a greater likelihood of their acceptance of the change.

Chapter roundup

- Leadership is the process of influencing others to work willingly towards the achievement of organisational goals.

- There are many different definitions of leadership. Key themes (which are also used to distinguish leadership from management) include interpersonal influence, securing willing commitment to shared goals, creating direction and energy and an orientation to change.

- There are three basic schools of leadership theory: trait theories, style theories and contingency theories.

- Leadership styles are clusters of leadership behaviour that are used in different ways in different situations. While there are many different classifications of style, they mainly relate to the extent to which the leader is focused primarily on task/performance (directive behaviour) or relationships/people (supportive behaviour).

- Leaders need to adapt their style to the needs of the team and the situation. this is the basis of contingency approaches such as Handy's best 'fit' model.

- Power is the ability to get things done. There are many types of power in organisations: position or legitimate power, expert power, personal power, resource power and negative power.

- Authority is the right to take certain decisions within boundaries.

- Empowerment means giving employees control of the decision-making process and allowing them to be independent of the leader.

Quick quiz

1. How do people become leaders in a group or situation?

2. What type of task makes tight control a suitable style?

3. What is the difference between a 'sells' and 'consults' style of management?

4. What factors in the environment influence the choice of a tight or loose style?

5. What might be the disadvantages of a 'tells' style of management?

6. Why is consistency of management style important – and why might this be a problem?

7. Do teams need to have a leader? Would they be as effective without one?

8. What is the most effective style suggested by Blake and Mouton's managerial grid and why is it so effective in theory? Why might it not be effective in practice?

9. What is the difference between power and authority?

10. What is expert power?

Answers to quick quiz

1   Through different forms of influence such a vision, inspiration and motivation. (See para 1.2)

2   Those which lack initiative, are routine, trivial or have a short time scale. (2.4)

3   'Sells' – the manager still makes all decisions but explains them to subordinates to get them to carry them out willingly. 'Consults' – the manager confers with subordinates, takes their views and feelings into account, but retains the right to make the final decision. (3.3)

4   The position of power held by the leader, organisational norms, structure and technology, the variety of tasks and subordinates. (2.4)

5   'Telling' is one-way, there is no feedback. It does not encourage contributions or initiative. (3.3)

6   Inconsistency results in subordinates feeling unsure and distrusting the manager. (3.3)

7   Someone has to ensure the objective is achieved, make decisions and share out resources. If everyone on the team is equally able and willing to do these things (unlikely in practice) a good information system is probably all that is needed, not a leader. (3.4)

8   9.9. It is effective if there is sufficient time and resources to attend fully to people needs, if the manager is good at dealing with people and if the people respond. It is ineffective when a task has to be completed in a certain way or by a certain deadline even if people don't like it. (3.5)

9   Authority is the right to do something; power is the ability to do it. (4)

10 Power based on the acknowledgement of expertise. (4.1)

Answers to activities

1   Categorisation of different behaviour on smelling smoke in a cinema is as follows.

   (a) Behavioural contagion: people are simply copying you, without any conscious intention to lead on your part.

   (b) Management. You are dealing with logistics: planning and organising. You are not, however, concerned with influencing the people: they simply respond to the situation.

   (c) Leadership. You intend to mobilise others in pursuit of your aims, and you succeed in doing so.

   (d) Whatever it is, it isn't leadership – because you have gained no followers.

2   This will depend on your own observations and opinions.

3   The environment can be improved for leaders if senior management ensure that:

   (a) Managers are given a clear role and the power (over resources and information) to back it up

(b) Organisational norms can be broken without fear of punishment – ie, the organisation culture is adaptive and managers can change things if required

(c) The organisational structure is not rigid and inflexible: managers can redesign task and team arrangements

(d) Team members are selected or developed so that they are, as far as possible, of the same 'type' in terms of their attitudes to work and supervision

(e) Labour turnover is reduced as far as possible (by having acceptable work conditions and terms, for example) so that the team does not constantly have to adjust to new members or leaders.

4   Styles of management suggested in the situations described, using the tells-sells-consults-joins model.

(a) You may have to 'tell' here: nobody is going to like the idea and, since each person will have his or her own interests at heart, you are unlikely to reach consensus. You could attempt to 'sell', if you can see a positive side to the change in particular cases: opportunities for retraining, say.

(b) You could 'consult' here: explain your remedy to staff and see whether they can suggest potential problems. They may be in a position to offer solutions – and since the problem affects them too, they should be committed to solving it.

(c) We prefer a 'joins' style here, since the team's acceptance of the decision is more important than the details of the decision itself.

(d) We would go for 'consult' despite the staff's apparent reluctance to participate. They may prefer you to 'tell' – but may resist decisions they disagree with anyway. Perhaps their reluctance is to do with lack of confidence – or lack of trust that you will take their input seriously, in which case, persistent use of a 'consults' style may encourage them. You could use a 'sells' approach initially, to get them used to a less authoritarian style than they seem to expect.

5   Blake's Grid positioning of the given managerial approaches are:

(a) 1.1: low task, low people
(b) 9.1: High task, low people
(c) 1.9: high people, low task

6   Marcus exercises position power because he has the right, given to him by the chief accountant, to get his staff, such as Dave, to do bank reconciliations. Dave does not do bank recs because of Marcus's personality or expertise, but because of the simple fact that Marcus is his boss. Marcus also exercises position power by getting Isabella to do the purchase ledger. However, Isabella exercises expert power because she knows more about import/export documentation than Marcus. She does not have the authority to stop the payment to Maphia, and Marcus can ignore what she says, but that would be a bad decision. Sandra is exercising negative power as far as Marcus is concerned, although she is claiming, perhaps, to exercise resource power – her time is a scarce resource. No-one appears to be exercising physical power as such, although Marcus's use of the disciplinary procedures would be a type of coercive power.

7   The problem appears to be that the new supervisor is taking too much of the department's work on to herself. While she is overworked, her subordinates are apparently not being stretched and as a result motivation and morale amongst them are poor. The supervisor herself is unhappy with the position and there is a danger that declining job satisfaction will lead to inefficiencies and eventually staff resignations.

There could be a number of causes contributing to the problem.

(a) Jean Howe may have been badly selected, ie she may not have the ability required for a supervisory job.

(b) Alternatively she may just be unaware of what is involved in a supervisor's role. She may not have realised that much of the task consists of managing subordinates; she is not required to shoulder all the detailed technical work herself.

(c) There may be personality problems involved. Jean Howe regards her clerks as incompetent and this attitude may arise simply from an inability to get on with them socially. (Another possibility is that her staff actually are incompetent.)

(d) The supervisor does much of the department's work herself. This may be because she does not understand the kind of tasks which can be delegated and the way in which delegation of authority can improve the motivation and job satisfaction of subordinates.

As manager you have already gone some way towards identifying the actual causes of the problem You have spoken to some of the subordinates concerned and also to the supervisor. You could supplement this by a review of personnel records relating to Jean Howe to discover how her career has progressed so far and what training she had received (if any) in the duties of a supervisor. You may then be in a position to determine which of the possible causes of the problems are operating in this case.

8   This will depend on your own experience.

Chapter 4 :

DEVELOPMENT NEEDS, LEARNING STYLES AND PROCESSES

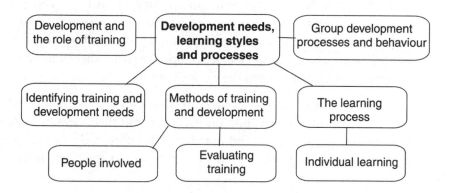

Introduction

Human resource development is the process by which the knowledge, skills and attitudes of employees are enhanced to the benefit of the organisation, the individual and the group. Development is the growth or realisation of a person's ability through conscious or unconscious learning. Training is a planned process to modify attitude, knowledge, skill or behaviour through learning experiences to achieve effective performance in an activity or range of activities.

The different types of learning theory we will be looking at in this chapter include the behaviourist and the cognitive approaches. Learning theory highlights the importance of feedback in sustaining and improving performance.

Lifelong learning should be the concern of all employees in the organisation and, despite its title, it is arguable that the concept of continuing professional development (CPD) should not be seen as applying only to professionals or managers. Clearly, however, CPD does have particular significance for management development.

Your objectives

After completing this chapter you should be able to:

(a) Identify training and development needs

(b) Discuss the methods of development and training

(c) Identify the people involved in training and development

(d) Evaluate training

(e) Outline the learning process

(f) Review development needs and activities and evaluate the effectiveness of activities

(g) Understand how groups develop

1 DEVELOPMENT AND THE ROLE OF TRAINING

1.1 Training requirements

Training can be considered as the creation of learning opportunities. The required needs can be said to consist of:

- **Knowledge** – basic knowledge for the job; this usually comes from education in the early stages of work, or before employment.

- **Skills and experience** - related closely to the job content.

- **Attitude** – the development and conditioning of attitudes and patterns of behaviour depend more upon *learning experiences*. A person will, for example, benefit more by experiencing co-operation than reading about it, and a person's ability to adapt to change, co-operate with others and be more self-confident, comes partly from the work situation.

People learn better when they see the *relevance* of what they are learning in relation to their own jobs. They should be given opportunities to try out their ideas in a situation as near as possible to real life conditions and practices. Therefore, training that is relevant and provides persons or groups with an opportunity to use the ideas learnt will be preferred.

Effective learning can take place according to Bass and Vaughan (1966) when the following four requirements exist.

- **Drive** – the motivation of the individual who must accept and be committed to the need for training.

- **Stimulus** – the signal received and interpreted by a trainee.

- **Response** – the behaviour resulting from a stimulus. This can be developed through training.

- **Reinforcement** – information that the learner receives giving an indication of progress – ideally as soon as possible to enable more effective learning to occur.

It is important to distinguish between the terminology used when discussing training and development.

Education. Instruction in knowledge and skills to enable people to be prepared for various roles in society. Its focus is broadly-based for the needs of the individual and to a lesser extent the needs of society.

Training. The acquisition of knowledge and skills for the purposes of an occupation or task. Its focus is much more narrowly-based than education or development, and is job or task-orientated.

Development. Concerned more with changes in attitude, behaviour and employee potential than with immediate skill. It relates more to *career* development than *job* development. It is a learning activity concentrating on the future needs of an organisation.

1.2 Factors affecting job performance

There are many factors affecting a person's performance at work, as shown in the diagram below. Training and development are the ways by which organisations seek to improve the performance of their staff and, it is hoped, of the organisation.

Figure 4.1 Factors affecting job performance

1.3 What is development?

Definition

Development is 'the growth or realisation of a person's ability and potential through the provision of learning and educational experiences'.

Training is 'the planned and systematic modification of behaviour through learning events, programmes and instruction which enable individuals to achieve the level of knowledge, skills and competence to carry out their work effectively'.

(Armstrong, *Handbook of Personnel Management Practice*)

1.4 Overall purpose of employee and management development

- **Ensure** the firm meets current and future performance objectives by...

- **Continuous improvement** of the performance of individuals and teams, and...

- **Maximising people's** potential for growth (and promotion).

1.5 Development activities

- Training, both on and off the job
- Career planning
- Job rotation
- Appraisal
- Other learning opportunities

Activity 1	(10 minutes)

Note down key experiences which have developed your capacity and confidence at work, and the skills you are able to bring to your employer (or indeed a new employer!).

Organisations often have a **training and development strategy,** based on the overall strategy for the business. We can list the following steps.

Step 1. Identify the skills and competences are needed by the **business plan**

Step 2. Draw up the **development strategy** to show how training and development activities will assist in meeting the targets of the corporate plan.

Step 3. **Implement** the training and development strategy.

The advantage of such an approach is that the training is:

- Relevant
- Problem-based (ie corrects a real lack of skills)
- Action-oriented
- Performance-related

1.6 Training and the organisation

Benefits for the organisation of training and development programmes

Benefit	Comment
Minimise the learning costs of obtaining the skills the organisation needs	Training supports the business strategy
Lower costs and **increased productivity,** thereby improving performance	Some people suggest that higher levels of training explain the higher productivity of German as opposed to many British manufacturers
Fewer accidents, and better health and safety	EU health and safety directives require a certain level of training. Employees can take employers to court if accidents occur or if unhealthy work practices persist
Less need for detailed supervision	If people are trained they can get on with the job, and managers can concentrate on other things. Training is an aspect of **empowerment**

Benefit	Comment
Flexibility	Training ensures that people have the **variety** of skills needed – multi-skilling is only possible if people are properly trained
Recruitment and succession planning	Training and development attracts new recruits and ensures that the organisation has a supply of suitable managerial and technical staff to take over when people retire
Change management	Training helps organisations manage change by letting people know why the change is happening and giving them the skills to cope with it
Corporate culture	(1) Training programmes can be used to build the corporate culture or to direct it in certain ways, by indicating that certain **values** are espoused. (2) Training programmes can **build relationships** between staff and managers in different areas of the business
Motivation	Training programmes can increase commitment to the organisation's goals

Training cannot do everything. Look at the wheel below Paragraph 1.2 again. Training only really covers:

Aspect of performance	Areas covered
Individual	Education; Experience; possibly Personal Circumstances (if successful completion of training is accompanied by a higher salary)
Physical and job	Methods of work
Organisational and social	Type of training and supervision

In other words, **training cannot improve performance problems** arising out of:

- Bad management

- Poor job design

- Poor equipment, factory layout and work organisation

- Other characteristics of the employee (eg intelligence)

- Motivation – training gives a person the ability but not necessarily the willingness to improve

- Poor recruitment

Activity 2 (10 minutes)

Despite all the benefits to the organisation, many are still reluctant to train. What reasons can you give for this?

NOTES

1.7 Training and the individual

For the individual employee, the benefits of training and development are more clear-cut, and few refuse it if it is offered.

Benefit	Comment
Enhances portfolio of **skills**	Even if not specifically related to the current job, training can be useful in other contexts, and the employee becomes more attractive to employers and more promotable
Psychological benefits	The trainee might feel reassured that he/she is of continuing value to the organisation
Social benefit	People's social needs can be met by training courses – they can also develop networks of contacts
The job	Training can help people do their job better, thereby increasing job satisfaction

2 IDENTIFYING TRAINING AND DEVELOPMENT NEEDS

2.1 The training process in outline

In order to ensure that training meets the real needs of the organisation, large firms adopt a planned approach to training. This has the following steps.

Step 1. Identify and define the **organisation's training needs**. It may be the case that recruitment might be a better solution to a problem than training.

Step 2. **Define the learning required** – in other words, specify the knowledge, skills or competences that have to be acquired. For technical training, this is not difficult: for example all finance department staff will have to become conversant with a new accounting system.

Step 3. **Define training objectives** – what must be learnt and what trainees must be able to do after the training exercise.

Step 4. **Plan training programmes** – training and development can be planned in a number of ways, employing a number of techniques, as we shall learn about in Section 3. (Also, people have different approaches to learning, which have to be considered.) This covers:

- Who provides the training

- Where the training takes place

- Divisions of responsibilities between trainers, managers and the individual.

Step 5. Implement the training.

Step 6. Evaluate the training: has it been successful in achieving the learning objectives?

Step 7. Go back to Step 2 if more training is needed.

> **Activity 3** **(15 minutes)**
>
> Draw up a training plan for introducing a new employee into your department. Repeat this exercise after you have completed this chapter to see if your chosen approach has changed.

2.2 Training needs analysis

Training needs analysis covers three issues.

Current state	Desired state
Organisation's current results	Desired results, standards
Existing knowledge and skill	Knowledge and skill needed
Individual performance	Required standards

The difference between the two columns is the **training gap**. Training programmes are designed to improve individual performance, thereby improving the performance of the organisation.

CASE EXAMPLE

Training for quality

The British Standards for Quality Systems (BS EN ISO 9000: formerly BS 5750) which many UK organisations are working towards (often at the request of customers, who perceive it to be a 'guarantee' that high standards of quality control are being achieved) includes training requirements. As the following extract shows, the Standard identifies training needs for those organisations registering for assessment, and also shows the importance of a systematic approach to ensure adequate control.

The training, both specific to perform assigned tasks and general to heighten quality awareness and to mould attitudes of all people in an organisation, is central to the achievement of quality.

The comprehensiveness of such training varies with the complexity of the organisation. The following steps should be taken:

1. Identifying the way tasks and operations influence quality in total

2. Identifying individuals' training needs against those required for satisfactory performance of the task

3. Planning and carrying out appropriate specific training

4. Planning and organising general quality awareness programmes

5. Recording training and achievement in an easily retrievable form so that records can be updated and gaps in training can be readily identified

BSI, 1990

Training surveys

Training surveys combine information from a variety of sources to discern what the training needs of the organisation actually are. These sources are:

(a) The **business strategy** at corporate level.

(b) **Appraisal and performance reviews** – the purpose of a performance management system is to improve performance, and training maybe recommended as a remedy.

(c) **Attitude surveys** from employees, asking them what training they think they need or would like.

(d) **Evaluation of existing training** programmes.

(e) **Job analysis** can be used. To identify training needs from the job analysis, the job analysis can pay attention to:

   (i) Reported difficulties people have in meeting the skills requirement of the job

   (ii) Existing performance weaknesses, of whatever kind, which could be remedied by training

   (iii) Future changes in the job.

   The job analysis can be used to generate a training specification covering the knowledge needed for the job, the skills required to achieve the result and attitudinal changes required.

2.3 Setting training objectives

The training manager will have to make an initial investigation into the problem of the gap between job or competence **requirements** and current performance of **competence**.

If training would improve work performance, training **objectives** can then be defined. They should be clear, specific and related to observable, measurable targets, ideally detailing:

- **Behaviour** – what the trainee should be able to do

- **Standard** – to what level of performance?

- **Environment** – under what conditions (so that the performance level is realistic)?

EXAMPLE: TRAINING OBJECTIVE

'At the end of the course the trainee should be able to describe ... or identify ... or distinguish x from y ... or calculate ... or assemble ...' and so on. It is insufficient to define the objectives of training as 'to give trainees a grounding in ...' or 'to encourage trainees in a better appreciation of ...': this offers no target achievement which can be measured.

Training objectives link the identification of training needs with the content, methods and technology of training. Some examples of translating training needs into learning objectives are given in *Personnel Management, A New Approach* by D Torrington and L Hall.

Training needs	Learning objectives
To know more about the Data Protection Act	The employee will be able to answer four out of every five queries about the Data Protection Act without having to search for details.
To establish a better rapport with customers	The employee will immediately attend to a customer unless already engaged with another customer.
	The employee will greet each customer using the customer's name where known.
	The employee will apologise to every customer who has had to wait to be attended to.
To assemble clocks more quickly	The employee will be able to assemble each clock correctly within thirty minutes.

Having identified training needs and objectives, the manager will have to decide on the best way to approach training: there are a number of types and techniques of training, which we will discuss below.

3 METHODS OF TRAINING AND DEVELOPMENT

3.1 Formal training

Formal training

(a) **Courses** may be run by the organisation's training department or may be provided by external suppliers.

(b) **Types of course**

    (i) **Day release**: the employee works in the organisation and on one day per week attends a local college or training centre for theoretical learning.

    (ii) **Distance learning, evening classes and correspondence courses,** which make demands on the individual's time outside work.

    (iii) **Revision courses** for examinations of professional bodies.

    (iv) **Block release** courses which may involve four weeks at a college or training centre followed by a period back at work.

    (v) **Sandwich courses,** usually involve six months at college then six months at work, in rotation, for two or three years.

    (vi) A **sponsored full-time course** at a university for one or two years.

(c) **Computer-based training** involves interactive training via PC. The typing program, Mavis Beacon, is a good example.

(d) **Techniques** used on the course might include lecturers, seminars, role play and simulation.

3.2 Disadvantages of formal training

(a) An individual will not benefit from formal training unless he or she **is motivated to learn**.

(b) If the **subject matter** of the training course does not **relate to an individual's job**, the learning will quickly be forgotten.

3.3 On the job training

Successful on the job training

(a) The assignments should have a **specific purpose** from which the trainee can learn and gain experience.

(b) The organisation must **tolerate any mistakes** which the trainee makes. Mistakes are an inevitable part of on the job learning.

(c) The work should **not be too complex**.

Methods of on the job training

(a) **Demonstration/instruction:** show the trainee how to do the job and let them get on with it. It should combine **telling** a person what to do and **showing** them how, using appropriate media. The trainee imitates the instructor, and asks questions.

(b) **Coaching:** the trainee is put under the guidance of an experienced employee who shows the trainee how to do the job.

   (i) **Establish learning targets**. The areas to be learnt should be identified, and specific, realistic goals (eg completion dates, performance standards) stated by agreement with the trainee.

   (ii) **Plan a systematic learning and development programme.** This will ensure regular progress, appropriate stages for consolidation and practice.

   (iii) **Identify opportunities for broadening the trainee's knowledge and experience:** eg by involvement in new projects, placement on inter-departmental committees, suggesting new contacts, or simply extending the job, adding more tasks, greater responsibility etc.

   (iv) **Take into account the strengths and limitations of the trainee** in learning, and take advantage of learning opportunities that suit the trainee's ability, preferred style and goals.

   (v) **Exchange feedback**. The coach will want to know how the trainee sees his or her progress and future. He or she will also need performance information in order to monitor the trainee's progress, adjust the learning programme if necessary, identify further needs which may emerge and plan future development for the trainee.

(c) **Job rotation:** the trainee is given several jobs in succession, to gain experience of a wide range of activities. (Even experienced managers may rotate their jobs, to gain wider experience; this philosophy of job education is commonly applied in the Civil Service, where an employee may expect to move on to another job after a few years.)

(d) **Temporary promotion:** an individual is promoted into his/her superior's position whilst the superior is absent due to illness. This gives the individual a chance to experience the demands of a more senior position.

(e) **'Assistant to' positions:** a junior manager with good potential may be appointed as assistant to the managing director or another executive director. In this way, the individual gains experience of how the organisation is managed 'at the top'.

(f) **Action learning:** a group of managers are brought together to solve a real problem with the help of an 'advisor' who exposes the management process that actually happens.

(g) **Committees:** trainees might be included in the membership of committees, in order to obtain an understanding of inter-departmental relationships.

(h) **Project work:** work on a project with other people can expose the trainee to other parts of the organisation.

Activity 4 **(15 minutes)**

Suggest a suitable training method for each of the following situations.

(a) A worker is transferred onto a new machine and needs to learn its operation.

(b) An accounts clerk wishes to work towards becoming qualified with the relevant professional body.

(c) An organisation decides that its supervisors would benefit from ideas on participative management and democratic leadership.

(d) A new member of staff is about to join the organisation.

3.4 Induction training

On the first day, a manager or personnel/HR officer should welcome the new recruit. He/she should then introduce the new recruit to the person who will be their **immediate supervisor.**

The immediate supervisor should commence the **on-going process of induction.**

Step 1. Pinpoint the areas that the recruit will have to learn about in order to **start the job.** Some things (such as detailed technical knowledge) may be identified as areas for later study or training.

Step 2. Explain first of all the nature of the job, and the goals of each task, both of the recruit's job and of the department as a whole.

Step 3. Explain about hours of work, and stress the importance of time-keeping. If flexitime is operated, the supervisor should explain how it works.

Step 4. Explain the structure of the department: to whom the recruit will report, to whom he/she can go with complaints or queries and so on.

Step 5. Introduce the recruit to the people in the office. One particular colleague may be assigned to the recruit as a **mentor**, to keep an eye on them, answer routine queries, 'show them the ropes'.

Step 6. Plan and implement an appropriate **training programmes** for whatever technical or practical knowledge is required. Again, the programme should have a clear schedule and set of goals so that the recruit has a sense of purpose, and so that the programme can be efficiently organised to fit in with the activities of the department.

Step 7. Coach and/or train the recruit; and check regularly on their progress, as demonstrated by performance, as reported by the recruit's mentor, and as perceived by the recruit him or herself.

Note that induction is an **on-going process**, embracing mentoring, coaching, training, monitoring and so on. It is not just a first day affair! After three months, six months or one year the performance of a new recruit should be formally appraised and discussed with them. Indeed, when the process of induction has been finished, a recruit should continue to receive periodic appraisals, just like every other employee in the organisation.

Appraisal is covered in detail in Chapter 6.

Activity 5 (30 minutes)

'Joining an organisation with around 8,500 staff, based on two sites over a mile apart and in the throes of major restructuring, can be confusing for any recruit. This is the situation facing the 20 to 30 new employees recruited each month by the Guy's and St Thomas' Hospital Trust, which was formed by the merger of the two hospitals in April.

In a climate of change, new employees joining the NHS can be influenced by the negative attitudes of other staff who may oppose the current changes. So it has become increasingly important for the trust's management executive to get across their view of the future and to understand the feelings of confusion new staff may be experiencing.'

Personnel Management Plus, August 1993

See if you can design a **one day** induction programme for these new recruits, in the light of the above. The programme is to be available to **all** new recruits, from doctors and radiographers to accountants, catering and cleaning staff and secretaries.

---

4 PEOPLE INVOLVED IN TRAINING AND DEVELOPMENT

4.1 The trainee

Many people now believe that the ultimate responsibility for training and development lies, not with the employer, but with the **individual**. People should seek to develop their own skills, to improve their own careers rather than wait for the organisation to impose training upon them. Why? The current conventional wisdom is that:

(a) **Delayering** means there are fewer automatic promotion pathways; promotion was once a source of development but there might not be further promotions available.

(b) **Technological change** means that new skills are always needed, and people who can find new work will be learning new skills.

Activity 6   **(2 minutes)**

You are currently studying for the HNC/HND Business qualification. Was this your own decision, or were you encouraged to do so by your employer? Do you think that this will have any impact on your training and development?

4.2 The human resources department or training department

The human resources department is ideally concerned with developing people. Some organisations have extensive development and career planning programmes. These shape the progression of individuals through the organisation, in accordance with the performance and potential of the individual and the needs of the organisation. Of course, only large organisations can afford to use this sort of approach.

The HR department also performs an **administrative** role by recording what training and development opportunities an individual might be given – in some firms, going on a training programme is an entitlement that the personnel department might have to enforce.

4.3 The supervisor and manager

Line managers and supervisors bear some of the responsibility for training and development within the organisation by identifying:

- The training needs of the department or section
- The current competences of the individuals within the department
- Opportunities for learning and development on the job
- When feedback is necessary

The **supervisor** may be required to organise training programmes for staff.

NOTES

4.4 Mentoring

Definition

> **Mentoring** is the use of specially trained individuals to provide guidance and advice which will help develop the careers of those allocate to them. A person's line manager should not be his or her mentor.

Mentors can assist in:

- Drawing up personal development plans
- Advice with administrative problems people face in their new jobs
- Help in tackling projects, by pointing people in the right direction

Mentoring is covered in more depth in Chapter 6.

4.5 The training manager

The training manager is a member of staff appointed to arrange and sometimes run training. The training manager generally reports to the **human resources** or **personnel director,** but also needs a good relationship with line managers in the production and other departments where the training takes place.

4.6 Responsibilities of the training manager

Responsibility	Comment
Liaison	With HRM department and operating departments
Scheduling	Arranging training programmes at convenient times
Skills identifying	Discerning existing and future skills shortages
Programme design	Develop tailored training programmes
Feedback	The trainee, the department and the HR department

5 EVALUATING TRAINING

Definition

> **Validation of training** means observing the results of the course and measuring whether the training objectives have been achieved.
>
> **Evaluation of training** means comparing the actual costs of the scheme against the assessed benefits which are being obtained. If the costs exceed the benefits, the scheme will need to be redesigned or withdrawn.

Ways of validating and evaluating a training scheme

(a) **Trainees' reactions to the experience.** This form of monitoring is rather inexact, and it does not allow the training department to measure the results for comparison against the training objective.

(b) **Trainee learning:** measuring what the trainees have learned on the course by means of a test at the end of it.

(c) **Changes in job behaviour following training.** This is possible where the purpose of the course was to learn a particular skill.

(d) **Organisational change as a result of training:** finding out whether the training has affected the work or behaviour of **other** employees not on the course – seeing whether there has been a general change in attitudes arising from a new course in, say, computer terminal work. This form of monitoring would probably be reserved for senior managers in the training department.

(e) **Impact of training on organisational goals:** seeing whether the training scheme has contributed to the overall objectives of the organisation. This too is a form of monitoring reserved for senior management, and would perhaps be discussed at board level in the organisation. It is likely to be the main component of a cost-benefit analysis.

Activity 7   **(10 minutes)**

Outline why it is important to evaluate and validate a training programme and describe possible methods for achieving this.

---

6   THE LEARNING PROCESS

6.1   Learning theories

There are different schools of learning theory, which explain and describe how people learn.

(a) **Behaviourist psychology** concentrated on the relationship between **stimuli** (input through the senses) and **responses** to those stimuli. 'Learning' is the formation of **new** connections between stimulus and response, on the basis of **conditioning.** We modify our responses in future according to whether the results of our behaviour in the past have been good or bad. We are continually looking for ways to achieve more positive reinforcement, in terms of rewards, and avoid negative reinforcement, ie punishment.

The principles for learning underlying this approach include:

• The learner must be able to respond **actively**
• **Frequency of repetition** of responses is important in acquiring skills
• **Immediate feedback** of results is strongly motivating
• Learning is helped when **objectives are clear**

(b) The **cognitive approach** argues that the human mind takes sensory information and imposes organisation and meaning on it: we interpret and rationalise. We use feedback information on the results of past behaviour to make **rational decisions** about whether to maintain successful behaviours or modify unsuccessful behaviours in future, according to our goals and our plans for reaching them. The principles for learning associated with cognitive theories are:

- Instruction should be **well organised** and be clearly structured – making it easier to learn and to remember.

- The way a **problem is displayed** is important if learners are to understand it.

- **Prior knowledge** is important – things must fit with what is already known

6.2 Effective training programmes

Whichever approach it is based on, learning theory offers certain useful propositions for the design of **effective training programmes**.

Proposition	Comment
The individual should be **motivated** to learn	The advantages of training should be made clear, according to the individual's motives – money, opportunity, valued skills or whatever.
There should be clear **objectives and standards** set, so that each task has some meaning	Each stage of learning should present a challenge, without overloading the trainee or making them lose confidence. Specific objectives and performance standards for each will help the trainee in the planning and control process that leads to learning, and providing targets against which performance will constantly be measured.
There should be timely, relevant **feedback** on performance and progress	This will usually be provided by the trainer, and should be concurrent – or certainly not long delayed. If progress reports or performance appraisals are given only at the year end, for example, there will be no opportunity for behaviour adjustment or learning in the meantime.
Positive and negative **reinforcement** should be judiciously used	Recognition and encouragement enhance an individual's confidence in their competence and progress: punishment for poor performance – especially without explanation and correction – discourages the learner and creates feelings of guilt, failure and hostility
Active **participation** is more telling than passive reception (because of its effect on the motivation to learn, concentration and recollection)	If a high degree of participation is impossible, practice and repetition can be used to reinforce receptivity. However, participation has the effect of encouraging 'ownership' of the process of learning and changing – committing the individual to it as their **own** goal, not just an imposed process.

6.3 Learning styles

The way in which people learn best will differ according to the type of person. That is, there are **learning styles** which suit different individuals. Peter Honey and Alan Mumford have drawn up a popular classification of four learning styles.

(a) **Theorists**

- Seek to understand basic principles and to take an intellectual, 'hands-off' approach based on logical argument. They prefer training to be:

    o Programmed and structured

    o Designed to allow time for analysis

    o Provided by teachers who share his/her preference for concepts and analysis

(b) **Reflectors**

- Observe phenomena, think about them and then choose how to act

- Need to work at their own pace

- Find learning difficult if forced into a hurried programme

- Produce carefully thought-out conclusions after research and reflection

- Tend to be fairly slow, non-participative (unless to ask questions) and cautious

(c) **Activists**

- Deal with practical, active problems and do not have patience with theory

- Require training based on hands-on experience

- Excited by participation and pressure, such as new projects

- Flexible and optimistic, but tend to rush at something without due preparation

(d) **Pragmatists**

- Only like to study if they can see its direct link to practical problems
- Good at learning new techniques in on-the-job training
- Aim is to implement action plans and/or do the task better
- May discard good ideas which only require some development

Training programmes should ideally be designed to accommodate the preferences of all four styles. This can often be overlooked especially as the majority of training staff are activitists.

6.4 The learning cycle

Another useful model is the **experiential learning cycle** devised by David Kolb. Experiential learning involves **doing**, however, and puts the learners in an active problem-solving role: a form of **self-learning** which encourages the learners to formulate and commit themselves to their own learning objectives.

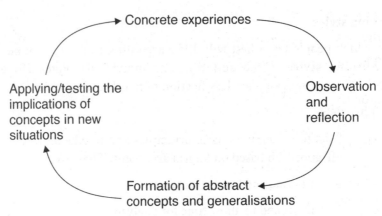

Figure 4.2 Kolb's experiential learning cycle

EXAMPLE

An employee interviews a customer for the first time (concrete experience). He observes his own performance and the dynamics of the situation (observation) and afterwards, having failed to convince the customer to buy his product, the employee analyses what he did right and wrong (reflection). He comes to the conclusion that he failed to listen to what the customer really wanted and feared, underneath his general reluctance: he realises that the key to communication is listening (abstraction/ generalisation). In his next interview he applies his strategy to the new set of circumstances (application/testing). This provides him with a new experience with which to start the cycle over again.

Simplified, this 'learning by doing' approach involves:

Act → Analyse action → Understand principles → Apply principles

Activity 8 **(15 minutes)**

With reference to Kolb's learning cycle, think of a situation on your present course where you have been involved in a practical exercise or 'experiential learning'. Illustrate the stages of the learning cycle using your chosen example.

6.5 Barriers to learning

According to Peter Senge, there are seven sources of **learning disability** in organisations which prevent them from attaining their potential – which trap them into 'mediocrity', for example, when they could be achieving 'excellence'.

(a) **'I am my position'**. When asked what they do for a living, most people describe the tasks they perform, not the **purposes** they fulfil; thus they tend to see their responsibilities as limited to the boundaries of their position.

(b) **'The enemy is out there'**. If things go wrong it is all too easy to imagine that somebody else 'out there' was at fault.

(c) **The illusion of taking charge.** The individual decides to be more active in fighting the enemy out there, trying to destroy rather than to build.

(d) **The fixation on events.** Conversations in organisations are dominated by concern about events (last month's sales, who's just been promoted, the new product from our competitor), and this focus inevitably distracts us from seeing the longer-term patterns of change.

(e) **The parable of the boiled frog.** Failure to adapt to gradually building threats is pervasive. (If you place a frog in a pot of boiling water, it will immediately try to scramble out; but if you place the frog in room temperature water, he will stay put. If you heat the water gradually, the frog will do nothing until he boils: this is because 'the frog's internal apparatus for sensing threats to survival is geared to sudden changes in his environment, not to slow, gradual changes'.)

(f) **The delusion of learning from experience.** We learn best from experience, but we never experience the results of our most important and significant decisions. Indeed, we never know what the outcomes would have been had we done something else.

(g) **The myth of the management team.** All too often, the management 'team' is not a team at all, but is a collection of individuals competing for power and resources.

Activity 9   **(20 minutes)**

How far do Senge's seven learning disabilities apply to your own organisation, or to some other significant organisation with which you may be familiar?

For individuals, the barriers may be:

- 'A waste of time': people see no personal benefit from training

- Training programmes employ the wrong techniques for people's learning styles

- Unwillingness to change

6.6 Encouraging learning: what managers can do

Managers can try to **develop the learning organisation** learning organisation:

- Encourages continuous learning and knowledge generation at all levels
- Has the processes to move knowledge around the organisation
- Can transform knowledge into actual behaviour

Definition

Learning organisation is 'An organisation that facilitates the learning of all its members and continuously transforms itself'.

6.7 The building of the learning organisation

Characteristics	Comments
Systematic problem solving	Problems should be tackled in a scientific way
Experimentation	Experimentation can generate new insights
Learn from experience	Knowledge from past failures can help avoid them in future
Learn from others	Customers and other firms can be a good source of ideas. Learning opportunities should be sought out
Knowledge transfer	Knowledge should be transferred throughout the organisation

7 INDIVIDUAL LEARNING

7.1 Lifelong learning

Increasingly, and especially in the professional sectors, it is becoming the responsibility of the individual to ensure that they take responsibility for their own development.

Definition

> **Lifelong learning** 'Learning activity undertaken throughout life, with the aim of improving knowledge, skills and competence within a personal and/or employer-related perspective.'

The idea that learning goes on throughout our lives and that learning opportunities are presented to us continuously has been formally reflected in the government's commitment to Lifelong Learning and its aim to develop that same commitment in organisations and individuals everywhere.

Pedler, Burgoyne and Boydell acknowledge the same concept in *The Learning Company*, McGraw-Hill (1991).

> 'Each of us is in a process of development as a person and as a worker. We can become aware of the process and, to some extent, direct ourselves towards desired ends – towards becoming the person and professional we want to be.'

From a professional point of view, your objective should be to ensure 'growth' during your career. This objective can obviously benefit your organisation as well as you. The growth should be triggered by a job that provides challenging, stretching goals. The clearer and more challenging the goals, the more effort you will exert, and the more likely it is that good performance will result. If you do a good job and receive positive feedback, you will feel successful (psychological success). These feelings will increase your feelings of confidence and self-esteem. This should lead to you becoming more involved in your work, which in turn leads to the setting of future stretching goals.

7.2   Support for personal learning

A Continuing Professional Development (CPD) process, a Personal Development Planner (PDP) and Learning Logs are all tools that are designed to enable and support an individual to take charge of his or her own development. They do this by simply providing a mechanism that helps the individual to assess development needs, record action plans, goals and progress towards those goals.

The goals can be professional or personal and are often both. For example, it is difficult to consider how to improve your skills in managing a team of people without reflecting on how you yourself communicate. A Personal Development Planner can be as simple or as sophisticated as the individual wishes. It can be:

- **Structured or informal** – planners range from the commercially prepared ring binder with printed sections and templates to complete, to a personal diary where you keep private notes.

- **Solo or supported activity** – some people work privately on their development whilst others seek support from a colleague, mentor or group.

All of the processes that support personal development are based on the principles of the learning cycle, which shows that to learn from an experience a person needs to reflect upon that experience and as a result of it to identify the learning that can be taken into the next experience.

The core of any process for planning and recording learning should include:

- A procedure for planning the learning in relation to a person's current abilities, future work and the requirements of the organisation

- A procedure for describing the learning that has taken place

- A procedure for showing how that learning will be applied to the individual's work.

The discipline of planning one's own development effectively will require time and energy; resources that managers frequently complain are in short supply, so, what are the arguments for investing this time and energy?

(a) **Accurate investment of resources** – investing time in a personally-driven and determined development process means that any energy, time and money that is spent can be directed into achieving goals that really matter to the individual, be they personal or professional. Learning can be deeper, more significant and more permanent when it is self–managed.

(b) **Discipline** – adopting a discipline, such as the format of a PDP, can help bring clarity and direction to a person's activities. Some people find the process of writing something down to be very helpful in formulating ideas and making sense of things.

(c) **Life enhancing** – individuals find the process of planning their own development, requires them to explore what it is they personally want to achieve and what it is about themselves that will enable or hinder the achievement of those goals. All of this requires that they reflect on and learn about themselves in the process.

(d) Improving your **employability** – as the labour market changes, there is a greater onus on each person to take more responsibility for their ongoing development and learning, so that they remain equipped for whatever roles they may need to undertake in the future.

(e) **Liberating and exciting** – many people find that taking control of their own development is more satisfying than simply responding to the organisation's direction. Setting goals, seeking opportunities for learning and measuring success can be both exciting and liberating.

(f) **Good professional practice** – many of the professional institutes now require evidence of the recording of continuous professional development (CPD) by each of their members as a condition of continued membership. Some institutes have produced paper and disk-based templates for such recording. An Institute of Continuous Professional Development has also been formed to promote good practice in this area.

7.3 Planning personal development

When planning your own personal development, clarity is the key to achieving your goals and objectives. So, before you set yourself specific development objectives, you need to clarify:

(a) Your **development needs** in terms of current challenges, what your organisation will be asking of you in the next three years and career (and personal) plans and aspirations. It is important that your plan reflects a balanced mix of activities. It is also important that these are carefully recorded. These may relate to your current job and will include training to meet specific needs and self-driven updating. But at different stages of your career the emphasis may change. Those on a career break may find formal training impractical and may benefit more from networking or self-directed reading and learning. Those who are self-employed or who are not working for supportive organisations may find that much of their development comes from new, work-related projects or assignments.

(b) The **sort of person you are** and the ways in which you learn best – having a clear profile of yourself will enable you to choose learning opportunities that provide the best chance for you to realise your potential.

(c) Your **strengths and weaknesses** – sources to explore include your appraisal feedback, asking others informally and feedback from a mentor.

(d) Your **preferred learning style** – how you choose to pursue your development goals, what activities, and how much support you need will depend on what resources are available to you, but also on your preferred learning style.

Activity 10   **(10 minutes)**

With reference to the four learning styles drawn up by Honey and Mumford, which of these styles do you think most closely resembles your own? What implications has this got for the way you learn?

Once you have pinpointed your preferred learning style(s) then you will be better able to choose learning experiences and activities that suit your style. Choose from:

- Training courses
- Networking
- Problem solving activity with colleagues
- Working with a coach or mentor
- Work shadowing
- Learning on the job from others who are experienced
- Distance learning
- Personal reflection
- Feedback from others
- Joining a network

Consider the type of support that is available to you. Research shows that the support of another individual, either a peer coach or mentor, or even support within a group is very advantageous. A colleague who you can ask for feedback on your performance and who can occasionally offer a different perspective on things can be very useful. Having access to someone with coaching skills and a commitment to working regularly with you can bring much energy and discipline to your development process. A mentor is someone who can act as a guide, advisor and counsellor at various stages in your career or perhaps during a particular period of your development, such as studying for a professional qualification. Your mentor may be a colleague or someone more senior in your organisation. Often people choose a mentor from outside their organisation, who can bring an objectivity and greater breadth to their professional development.

7.4 The continuing professional development process

Continuing professional development (CPD) is an approach or process, which should be a normal part of how you plan and manage your whole working life, put simply, a life-long learning approach to planning, managing and getting the most from your own development. Learning and development becomes planned, rather than accidental.

- CPD is **continuing** because learning never ceases, regardless of age or seniority

- It is **professional** because it is focused on personal competence in a professional role

- It is concerned with **development** because its goal is to improve personal performance and enhance career progression and is much wider than just formal training courses.

Planning, recording and reflecting are the real key to successful CPD so before starting you will need to decide the means of recording your plan and achievements that will suit you best. Remember, as important as record keeping is, it is only a means to an end. It is the process of planning, reviewing, learning and reflecting that matters, not the particular method or format you adopt. However, the very process of writing will help to distil experiences, recognise patterns and discern trends. It enables you to remember what has gone before and capture lessons for the future. It also becomes a valuable and objective measure of your professional competence and, as such, it can be useful when preparing for staff appraisals or tailoring your CV for a specific promotion or career move.

It is important to keep records in two key areas.

(a) A **personal development plan** – this looks ahead and sets out your objectives and the action and activities you plan to take to achieve them.

(b) A **record of achievements** – this is a full record of the action and activities you have undertaken, together with their respective outcomes.

Your records demonstrate you have thoroughly reflected on your accomplishments to date, carefully assessed your present situation and coherently planned your future professional development.

The learning plan

Effective CPD is the production of a structured learning plan, which leads to increased and improved performance. The plan is a four stage cycle: appraisal, planning, development and reflection. This takes you through all the necessary steps to assess your current situation, identify your learning needs, set your learning objectives, find and participate in suitable activities and reflect on your progress.

Step 1 – Appraisal

Where am I now? In order to identify future learning and development needs it is important to review your personal and professional experience to date. It is often said that there is no point in deciding where you are going until you have established where you are now. As with other areas in business, identifying what you have already achieved (in this case in terms of skills and knowledge) can provide a sound basis for planning for the future.

An effective method of self-appraisal is to identify your strengths and weaknesses and to examine both the opportunities and the threats you may face.

(a) Identify your **strengths,** and your **positive assets:** physical, mental, behavioural and emotional. What are your core skills? What do you do well? You may dress well, have a good memory, be good with the telephone, be honest, calm under pressure, a good listener and so on.

(b) Identify your **weaknesses,** or **liabilities.** Where are your skills/knowledge lacking? What would you like to improve – from your own point of view and from the point of view of other people? You may have no head for numbers, have a tendency to fidget, be subject to stress, or impatient with other people.

(c) Identify the opportunities facing you. What are the interesting new trends? Are there changes in markets and professional practice, emerging new specialisms, promotion opportunities or developments in technology?

(d) What threats and obstacles do you face? Is your professional role changing? Can you foresee competition from other businesses, legislative changes, limited opportunities for progression or threat of redundancy?

There are a number of dimensions to this analysis for individuals.

(a) Do you have the skills necessary to do the job **today?** (You should have – but if not, training is essential.)

(b) Do you have the skills to do the job **tomorrow?** (This may be because of a change in the environment or an expansion of the department – if not, proactive training should be planned to ensure you are prepared.)

(c) Do you have the skills to do **tomorrow's job?** (Will you be promoted? If so, what new skills and knowledge will be needed? This is development and would be a pro-active approach to succession planning, or a personal strategy to increase the chances of promotion.)

(d) Do you have the skills for a **different job tomorrow?** (What will be the alternative employment options in the future and what skills and qualifications will be needed? This is personal career development planning and investment in which many managers are today taking personal responsibility.)

This kind of SWOT analysis should enable you to determine areas of interest and ambitions, which can be used to shape plans for further development. Although there are clear benefits in planning CPD to develop knowledge and skills in new or weaker areas, you should not overlook the potential for further development in your stronger areas. Building on existing strengths is as relevant an aim for CPD as improving in areas of weakness.

Step 2 – Planning

Where am I going? The first stage is to form an action plan before engaging in any development activities. The formulation of this plan will assist in monitoring and reflecting upon the activity being undertaken. On completion of the activity, you can then review, reflect upon and evaluate your actions. This whole process should generate evidence that would be documented and fed back into the appraisal/assessment stage allowing for the cycle of activities to be continuously repeated.

Having established areas for action, the next step is to detail your priorities for development. Following the completion of Step 1, you should be able to identify gaps in your skills and knowledge where you can set specific development objectives. These objectives should contain an element of challenge so that they carry you on to new ground, but they must also be realistic. At this stage it is useful to set targets in terms of required levels of competence.

Competences are the critical skills, knowledge and attitudes that a person must have to perform effectively at work. They are expressed in visible, behavioural terms and reflect the skills, knowledge and attitude (the main components of any job), which must be demonstrated to an agreed standard and must contribute to the overall aims of the organisation. The term is open to various interpretations because there are a number of competence-based systems and concepts of competence. As a general definition, a competent individual can perform a work role in a wide range of settings over an extended period of time.

When establishing your objectives, you should also work within practical constraints, which may influence methods of development. Factors you may wish to take into account include:

- What opportunities and support for learning are available?

- How much will it cost in terms of money, time, and conflict with other commitments?

- What added value will result – qualification, promotion, and new business?

Finally, objectives should be set within a realistic time frame. In some cases they will not be easily achievable within a 12-month cycle. However, it should be possible to determine some progress towards achieving an objective in this time period and to re-evaluate long-term objectives in the continuing cycle of development.

If this is the first time you have attempted to prepare such a plan, you may like to try a proven and easy to use method known by the acronym SMART. The letters will remind you of the five objective-setting rules as follows:

- Specific – use as few words as possible
- Measurable – plan small steps with objectively discernable outcomes
- Attainable – stay within your physical and intellectual reach
- Realistic – recognise the constraints of available time and resources
- Timed – set target dates for every step in your plan

Activity 11   **(20 minutes)**

Draw up a personal development plan for yourself over the next month, the next year and the next five years. You should include your HND/HNC activities.

Step 3 – Development

How will I get there? The achievement of development objectives requires involvement in a wide range of learning activities on a continuous basis. CPD may take the form of any appropriate learning activity and need not necessarily be biased towards course attendance. The decision as to what constitutes relevant learning and development must lie primarily with you as an individual. When arranging your CPD activities you will need to consider your preferred learning style. Different individuals perceive and process experience in different ways and these differences comprise a unique learning style.

When undertaking the activity, you need to maintain a progress file to record your achievements and review the actions you are taking. The record of achievement can be a vehicle for reviewing, making sense and perhaps for drawing implications for future practice and future learning.

Step 4 – Reflection

How will I know when I have got there? To gain the full benefit from any CPD activities undertaken, it is finally necessary to evaluate the outcomes and to establish whether you have achieved your objectives.

When reflecting on your activities you should consider whether you have experienced personal or business benefits from your efforts through the practical application of what you have learnt. Evidence of such achievement ie, skills acquisition and improved competence, can be demonstrated in various ways as illustrated below.

Recognised qualifications:	Organisation:
• short course completion certificates • credits for accumulated qualification • NVQ /HND/HNC	• adoption of recommendations as policy • improved business performance • cost efficiency savings • safer working environment
Self:	**Colleagues (peers/superiors):**
• measured against own criteria • discussion with manager/colleagues • favourable annual appraisal • recommendation for promotion • change in professional role/duties	• request to coach/advise colleagues • suggestion to join/lead project team

The evaluation stage deserves special attention as it produces a summary of achievements, which demonstrates how you have met your original objectives. For any areas of under-achievement, you should reconsider whether the target originally set remains valid or whether you require more time to achieve it. By reviewing the outcomes of your CPD activity in this way you will continue the learning and development cycle into the next year.

Although we have described CPD in terms of steps, the reality is that it is a circular process.

Personal growth is both interactive and incremental. Consequently, all lifelong learning plans should be 'living' documents. They should relate to life in the real world, where people and conditions constantly change.

Once you have written your development plan you should revisit each part of the process from time to time. Just follow these simple guidelines:

- Reflect on the overall process, not just when you first embark on CPD but at regular intervals throughout your working life

- Review your progress regularly and take stock

- Revise your plan when developments or circumstances so dictate

Together, these steps will ensure that you do not lose sight of your overall goals and that your development stays on track.

8 GROUP DEVELOPMENT PROCESSES AND BEHAVIOUR

We all belong to groups. They can be social, casual, formal or informal. Social groups include families, friends, clubs, voluntary organisations, religious societies and some work-related groupings of people, such as a regular lunch-time card school. Some groups are work groups, which may be formally established as part of the organisation or informally created by those working together or sharing an interest. Formal groups include committees.

NOTES

Definition

> **Group:** a collection of individuals with a common interest and who share a common identity. A group has a leader, a set of social norms and a reason for its existence. It may be informal or formally established and its existence may be permanent or temporary.

Groups may come together spontaneously or be formally established. However, they do not become teams until they have gone through the process of team formation.

8.1 Group formation

Organisations create formal groups (also referred to as official groups) automatically as departments and specialisms develop. Groups are also created to perform such tasks as exchanging ideas, sharing information, co-ordinating work and performing tasks that require the collective use of skills. The Board of Directors is a formal group; so are the Health and Safety Committee and the night shift operatives in machine shop four.

Informal (or unofficial) groups form at work because of:

(a) People's needs to socialise

(b) A need for self-help (for example, a baby sitting circle)

(c) A need for protection and collective action (for example, a union)

The aims of an informal group and the organisation may be different. It is important that organisations recognise the existence of informal groups and try to use them constructively, rather than making what are likely to be futile attempts to suppress them.

A group of people can be appointed to be a team, but a group has to go through the process of becoming a team before it can function as one. The composition of the group will affect its ability to become effective. Simply setting up a team does not make a group of people into a team, nor does it make it effective. Teams have to be formed with care.

8.2 Stages of group development

There are two dimensions – personal relations and task functions – that are central to the process of group development. This is illustrated in the figure below.

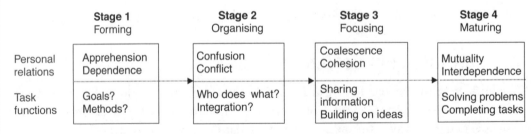

Figure 4.3 Stages of group development

As people progress through the stages towards becoming a group, personal relations evolve from apprehensive, tentative interactions and dependence on leaders or formal instructions through confusion and conflict (either overt or covert) to cohesiveness and ultimate interdependence. Obviously, some groups never reach the mature stage, which is the optimal use of human resources, even when tasks are accomplished reasonably well. Progress on task functions often parallels the development of personal relations, although one-to-one correlation is not necessary. The first stage involves understanding the task, group goals, and alternative means of achieving them. The organising stage means resolving issues/conflict such as leadership, authority-responsibility relationships, and methods of doing and co-ordinating the work. In stage three the group begins to share information and feelings and build on each other's ideas to get the job done. The mark of a mature group is its capacity to solve specific problems or to complete tasks, while at the same time improving its ability to do so. This calls for simultaneous attention to task accomplishment and group development.

8.3 Internal training and development methods for groups

Group training encourages participants to learn from each other through discussing issues, pooling experiences and critically examining opposite viewpoints. Instructors guide discussions rather than impart knowledge directly. They monitor trainee's understanding of what is going on, ask questions to clarify points and sometimes, but not always, prevent certain members from dominating the group. Some of the most popular methods follow.

(a) **The lecture method** – this is regarded as an economical way of giving a large amount of information to many people. Some people prefer listening to reading and good lecturers can help learning and assist understanding. Lectures are of little value if the aim of training is to change attitudes, or develop job or interpersonal skills.

(b) **Discussion methods** – discussion and participation are known ways of securing interest and commitment. Discussion methods in this respect are useful ways of shaping attitudes, encouraging motivation and securing understanding. Discussion methods can also underline the nature, and the difficulties of group problem solving.

(c) **Case study method** – in this approach to training, learning occurs through participation in the definition, analysis and solution of the problem or problems. It demonstrates the nature of group problem solving activity and usually underlines the view that there is no one best solution to a complex business problem. Casework creates interest and enthusiasm among members but, when they lack knowledge and experience, the exercise can fail.

(d) **Role playing** – this method requires trainees to project themselves into a simulated situation that is intended to represent some relevant reality, say, a confrontation between management and a trade union. The merit of role-playing is that it influences attitudes, develops interpersonal skills and heightens sensitivity to the views and feelings of others. However, it requires careful organising and giving tactful feedback is not easy unless the exercise is filmed in such a way that instant playback is possible.

(e) **Business games** – games simulate realistic situations, mergers, take-overs, etc in which groups compete with one another and where the effects of the decision taken by one group may affect others. The benefits are said to include development of an appreciation of the complex character of decision taking, understanding of risk and the nature of teamwork. Although business games and case studies can be devised to correspond to real life situations, the classroom environment means that participants might not take them seriously.

(f) **T-group exercises** (the T stands for training) leave the group to their own devices. The trainer simply tells them to look after themselves and remains as an observer. The group itself has to decide what to do and, understandably, the members feel helpless at first and then they pool their experiences and help each other. They eventually form a cohesive group, appoint a leader and resolve any conflicts within the group. The advantages claimed for T-group exercises are that members recognise the need to learn from experience and from each other. They also observe how others react to offers of help. Since the group begins in a leaderless state and ends by appointing a leader, it de-mystifies the process of leader selection. They exercise interpersonal communication skills and learn to understand group dynamics.

Next we look at group behaviour.

8.4 Group behaviour

Groups establish norms or acceptable standards of behaviour. The things which the group has in common and which characterise it are group norms. All members of the group are expected to conform to these. Groups put pressure on members to conform, and those who wish to belong will do so. Failure to conform can lead to conflict with the rest of the group. In extreme cases an individual can be excluded from all desirable groups and forced to seek another job.

Rituals

Groups develop their own rituals, such as meeting in a certain place for coffee breaks, going to the same pub for lunch or meeting after work on Fridays. Individuals may tend to seek acceptance and pretend to conform to such norms as working late, while regularly making excuses to go on time. Similarly, a member may conceal non-adherence to norms by avoiding some aspects of the social activities of the group – having to catch a particular train or getting a lift can be used to avoid after-work drinking sessions.

Where bonus payments are related to group performance there is much stronger pressure on members to conform. Unauthorised breaks and failure to meet targets that affect the performance of the group as a whole are likely to attract strong pressure to conform.

EXAMPLE: GROUP RITUALS IN THE WORKPLACE

An ice cream factory had several lines for filling different flavours of ice cream into tubs, cartons, choc ices and ice lollies. Each filling line had a team, with a leader who allocated jobs – usually in strict rotation so as to avoid boredom. The elite team worked on choc ices. The lowest level in the pecking order was the team responsible for stacking incoming supplies of cartons and loading delivery trucks.

Each team had its special table in the canteen. The ice lolly team brought in cakes they made and shared them. The stackers and loaders took their breaks elsewhere. The choc ice team took their break at a different time from everyone else. Entry to that group was by invitation and seniority. Managers had learned that it was not a good idea to try to allocate new members to choc ices: there would be an astonishing rise in the number of choc ices incorrectly wrapped or partly coated. Teams organised their own informal breaks on a rota basis. Anyone overstaying would lose the next break as the team leader would not relieve them.

The factory paid bonuses to teams that exceeded monthly targets for filling cartons and tubs. There were strict quality controls which included a variation of not more than $^1/_2\%$ either side of the declared weight. Quality checks showing unacceptable variations in fill weight led to the conveyor being slowed down and consequent loss of bonuses. Individuals who persistently underfilled in an attempt to earn bonuses were banished to the menial jobs of fetching boxes of empty cartons and removing filled tubs to the cold store. These people would also miss out on rounds of drinks in the Friday pub session.

8.5 Group cohesiveness

Group cohesiveness develops over time as the group moves through the stages to maturity. It refers to the ability of a group to stick together. A strongly cohesive group can become exclusive, with entry being virtually impossible. Individuals find it much easier to join less cohesive groups and groups in the earlier stages of formation.

Factors which affect the development of group cohesiveness are:

(a)   Similarity of work
(b)   Physical proximity in the work place
(c)   The work flow system and whether or not it gives continuing contact
(d)   The structure of tasks – whether individualised or group
(e)   Group size – smaller groups are more cohesive
(f)   Threats from outside – where a group sees other groups as the enemy
(g)   Prospects of rewards
(h)   Leadership style of the manager
(i)   Common social factors, such as race, social status and cultural origins

Next we look at the factors that affect the effectiveness of groups, and the features of effective and ineffective groups.

8.6 Group effectiveness

The personalities of group members and the traits they bring to the group play an important part in deciding its effectiveness. Personal goals also affect effectiveness. It is easy for groups, especially informal ones, to decide that a low level of productivity is the norm. Groups can be motivated to improve their performance. This requires:

(a)   A clearly defined task
(b)   Effective leadership
(c)   Small group size
(d)   Skills and abilities matched to the task
(e)   Proximity at work, for example an open-plan office
(f)   Rewards that are regarded as fair by the group

Factors for identifying effective work groups

A number of factors are involved in identifying effective and ineffective work groups. Some are quantifiable and others are qualitative.

Effective work group	Ineffective work group
Quantifiable factors	
(a) Low rate of labour turnover	(a) High rate of labour turnover
(b) Low accident rate	(b) High accident rate
(c) Low absenteeism	(c) High absenteeism
(d) High output and productivity	(d) Low output and productivity
(e) Good quality of output	(e) Poor quality of output
(f) Individual targets are achieved	(f) Individual targets are not achieved
(g) There are few stoppages and interruptions to work	(g) Time is lost owing to disagreements between supervisor and subordinates
Qualitative factors	
(a) There is a high commitment to the achievement of targets and organisational goals	(a) There is no understanding of organisational goals or the role of the group
(b) There is a clear understanding of the group's work	(b) There is a low commitment to targets
(c) There is a clear understanding of the role of each person within the group	(c) There is confusion and uncertainty about the role of each person within the group
(d) There is a free and open communication between members of the group and trust between members	(d) There is mistrust between group members and suspicion of the group's leader
(e) There is idea sharing	(e) There is little idea sharing
(f) The group is good at generating new ideas	(f) The group does not generate any good new ideas
(g) Group members try to help each other out by offering constructive criticisms and suggestions	(g) Group members make negative and hostile criticisms of each other's work
(h) There is group problem solving which gets to the root causes of the work problem	(h) Work problems are dealt with superficially, with attention paid to the symptoms but not the cause
(i) There is an active interest in work decisions	(i) Decisions about work are accepted passively
(j) Group members seek a united consensus of opinion	(j) Group members hold strongly opposed views
(k) The members of the group want to develop their abilities in their work	(k) Group members find work boring and do it reluctantly
(l) The group is sufficiently motivated to be able to carry on working in the absence of its leader	(l) The group needs its leader there to get work done

FOR DISCUSSION

Select a group you are involved in, for example a seminar or tutorial group, and analyse its effectiveness in terms of the features it shows from the above list. How valid are these factors in deciding whether or not a group is effective?

8.7   Relationships with other groups

A group's effectiveness is also affected by its relationships with other groups. Contact with other groups can bring power struggles, personal conflict between leaders, territorial disputes and distrust of motives. Relations in the work place often seem to parallel gang warfare in Los Angeles, where each group will go to any lengths to protect its turf.

Effectiveness can be improved and constructive competition encouraged by:

(a) Rewarding groups on the basis of their contribution to the organisation as a whole and their efforts to collaborate, rather than rewarding only individual group performance

(b) Encouraging staff to move across group boundaries so that understanding and co-operation are improved

(c) Avoiding putting groups into situations where one must emerge a winner and another a loser

(d) Encouraging communication between groups through committees, discussion groups, joint planning meetings and so on

Chapter roundup

- In order to achieve its goals, an organisation requires a skilled workforce. This is partly achieved by training.

- The main purpose of training and development is to raise competence and therefore performance standards. It is also concerned with personal development, helping and motivating employees to fulfil their potential.

- A thorough analysis of training needs should be carried out as part of a systematic approach to training, to ensure that training programmes meet organisational and individual requirements. Once training needs have been identified, they should be translated into training objectives.

- Individuals can incorporate training and development objectives into a personal development plan.

- There are a variety of training methods. These include:
  - Formal education and training
  - On-the-job training
  - Awareness-oriented training

- There are different schools of thought as to how people learn. Different people have different learning styles.

- Managers can design and manage the organisation to encourage learning.

- A SWOT analysis helps to identify your personal strengths and weaknesses and the opportunities and threats that affect your career opportunities and future prospects.

- Competences are the critical skills, knowledge and attitudes that you must have to perform effectively. They are expressed in visible, behavioural terms and reflect the skills, knowledge and attitude (the main components of any job), which must be demonstrated to an agreed standard and must contribute to the overall aims of the organisation.

- In your development plan you must establish targets that you are aiming for and remember that all good plans must be monitored and evaluated.

- Individuals find it much easier to join less cohesive groups and groups in the earlier stages of formation.

- Groups can be motivated to improve their performance using techniques such as clearly defined tasks, effective leadership, small groups sizes, proximity at work and fair rewards.

Quick quiz

1   List examples of development opportunities within organisations.

2   List how training can contribute to:
   (a) Organisational effectiveness
   (b) Individual effectiveness and motivation

3   According to ISO 9000, what are the main steps to be adopted in a systematic approach to training?

4   Define the term 'training need'.

5   How should training objectives be expressed?

6   What does learning theory tell us about the design of training programmes?

7   List the four learning styles put forward by Honey and Mumford.

8   List the four stages in Kolb's experiential learning cycle.

9   What is the supervisor's role in training?

10 What are the levels of training validation/evaluation?

Answers to quick quiz

1   Career planning, job rotation, deputising, on-the-job training, counselling, guidance, education and training. (See para 1.5)

2   (a) Increased efficiency and productivity; reduced costs, supervisory problems and accidents; improved quality, motivation and morale.

   (b) Demonstrates individual value, enhances security, enhances skills portfolio, motivates, helps develop networks and contacts. (1.6)

3   Identify how operations influence quality; identify individual training needs against performance requirements; plan and conduct training; plan and organise quality awareness programmes; record training and achievement. (2.2)

4   The required level of competence minus the present level of competence. (2.2)

5   Actively – 'after completing this chapter you should understand how to design and evaluate training programmes'. (2.3)

6   The trainee should be motivated to learn, there should be clear objectives and timely feedback. Positive and negative reinforcement should be used carefully, to encourage active participation where possible. (4.1)

7   Theorist, reflector, activist and pragmatist. (4.2)

8   Concrete experience, observation/reflection, abstraction/generalisation, application/testing. (4.3)

9   Identifying training needs of the department or section. Identifying the skills of the individual employee, and deficiencies in performance. Providing or supervising on-the-job training (eg coaching). Providing feedback on an individual's performance. (4.3)

10 Reactions, learning, job behaviour, organisational change, ultimate impact. (5)

Answers to activities

1   Few employers throw you in at the deep end – it is far too risky for them! Instead, you might have been given induction training to get acclimatised to the organisation, and you might have been introduced slowly to the job. Ideally, your employer would have planned a programme of tasks of steadily greater complexity and responsibility to allow you to grow into your role(s).

2   Cost: training can be costly. Ideally, it should be seen as an investment in the future or as something the firm has to do to maintain its position. In practice, many firms are reluctant to train because of poaching by other employers – their newly trained staff have skills which can be sold for more elsewhere. This got so bad that staff at one computer services firm were required to pay the firm £4,000 if they left (to go to another employer) within two years of a major training programme.

3   The answer to this activity will depend on your own personal situation and that of your employer. There is no 'right or wrong' answer which we can include here.

4   Training methods for the various workers indicated are as follows.

(a)   Worker on a new machine: on-the-job training, coaching.

(b)   Accounts clerk working for professional qualification: external course – evening class or day-release.

(c)   Supervisors wishing to benefit from participative management and democratic leadership: internal or external course. However, it is important that monitoring and evaluation takes place to ensure that the results of the course are subsequently applied in practice.

(d)   New staff: induction training.

5   Here is the actual programme for new recruits (of all types) at Guy's and St Thomas' Hospital Trust, as published in *Personnel Management Plus*.

9.00	Welcome	
9.05	Introduction	*Ground rules and objectives for the day*
9.25	Presentation	*The history of Guy's and St Thomas' hospitals*
10.25	Presentation	*Talk on structure of the management team, trust board and executive*
10.45	Group exercise	*With chief executive Tim Matthews on patient care, funding, hospital processes and measuring the care provided*
12.20	Lunch	
1.15	Tour of Guy's	
2.30	Presentation	*Looking at trust with new eyes – suggestions for change*
2.50	Presentation	*Information on staff organisations*
3.10	Presentation	*Security issues, fire drills, health and safety (including handouts)*
3.30	Presentation	*Session on occupational health*
3.40	Presentation	*Local areas and staff benefits*
3.45	Tour of St Thomas'	
4.30	Presentation	*Facilities management and patient care*
4.45	Closing session	*Evaluation and finish*

Particularly important is the focus on patient care and the group exercises. 'Feedback from the participants shows that they enjoy the discussions and learn a lot more about their colleagues and the trust by participating rather than being talked at.'

6   This will depend on your own situation.

7   Validation of a new course is important to ensure that objectives have been achieved. Evaluation of it is more difficult, but at least as important because it identifies the value of the training programme to the organisation.

8   Which part of Kolb's cycle you have experienced will be individual to you. For example, you may have been involved in a group project where you contributed less than other group members. Here the cycle is as follows.

- Concrete experience (make a poor contribution to group project)

- Observation/reflection (note that you felt unsure about the subject matter of the group project from the outset)

- Abstraction/generalisation (conclude that your style is to keep quiet when unsure in order to avoid showing your ignorance)

- Application/testing (at the next available opportunity speak out if you don't understand something – you will probably not be alone!)

9   The answers to this activity will depend on your own personal situation and that of your employer. There is no 'right or wrong' answer which we can include here.

10   You could have chosen any one of the following.

The Activist – you are open-minded, not sceptical and have an enthusiasm for anything new. You tend to act first and consider the consequences later. You are happiest faced with a new challenge and your preference is for learning by experience. So any opportunity for learning 'on the job' will appeal, such as getting involved in a project. Practical, activity-based training programmes are also good for you.

The Reflector – you are thoughtful and cautious and like to thoroughly consider something before concluding. You like to ponder things and prefer to take a back seat in meetings and discussions. You will value the learning you can gain from working closely with someone who already has the skills or knowledge you need to develop. You will learn through observation and can discuss your reflections and plans with a mentor. You are also happy learning from books, articles and case studies.

The Theorist – you are very logical in your thinking and enjoy analysing. You like working with principles, theories, models and systems. You prize rationality and logic. You learn well from theory-based courses with well-qualified and experienced trainers, well written books and articles.

The Pragmatist – you enjoy testing out theories and principles to see if they work in practice. Essentially, you like making practical decisions and solving problems. You see challenges as opportunities. You will respond well to flexible and practical learning experiences. You are particularly attracted to learning from real life projects and you value the help of someone who can offer good quality feedback and coaching to help you improve your performance.

11   The answer will depend on your own situation.

Chapter 5 :
PLANNING, WORK ORIENTATION AND JOB DESIGN

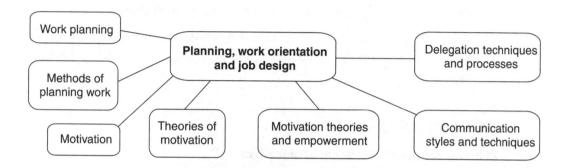

Introduction

Planning helps the organisation to define its purposes and activities. It enables performance standards to be set so that results can be compared with the standard to help managers to see how the organisation is progressing towards its goals.

Because organisations have goals they want to satisfy, they need to direct their activities by:

- Deciding what they want to achieve

- Deciding how and when to do it and who is to do it

- Checking that they do achieve what they want, by monitoring what has been achieved and comparing it with the plan

- Taking action to correct any deviation

Much research has been undertaken in an attempt to understand what motivates individual employees at work and how managers can improve it.

The motivational strategy that is decided on will depend on the beliefs held and the culture that prevails in the organisation. Maslow's theory holds that human needs form a hierarchy ranging from the lowest-order needs (physiological needs) to the highest order need – self-actualisation. According to Herzberg's two-factor theory, there are two sets of motivating factors. Vroom's expectancy theory suggests that people are motivated to reach a goal if they think the goal is worthwhile and can see that the activities will help them achieve the goal.

Delegation is one of the main functions of effective management. In essence, delegation is the process whereby a manager assigns part of his authority to a subordinate to fulfil those duties.

Your objectives

After completing this chapter you should be able to:

(a) Plan or analyse work activities using appropriate objective setting techniques and processes

(b) Negotiate assignments with colleagues using suitable delegation techniques to motivate and enable colleagues

(c) Enthuse and motivate colleagues to achieve objectives

(d) Promote confidence amongst colleagues to engage with change

(e) Empower colleagues to present their own ideas, develop their own ways of working within agreed boundaries and to provide a lead in their own areas of expertise.

1 WORK PLANNING

1.1 Planning for the achievement of objectives

Objectives represent the goals that direct the course of action taken by the organisation. Hence, they are a vital element within the planning process – representing as they do specific 'benchmarks' or points that indicate the direction the organisation is following – plus what it is to achieve and the time period involved. The objectives of the supervisor are the 4 Ms – to make the best use of:

- Machine capacity – this includes servicing and maintenance
- Manpower (Human resources) – this includes training
- Materials – including best type of ordering/delivery schedules
- Money – including cost reduction planning.

The setting of objectives is essential to the process of planning, since this activity:

- commits managers and their staff to the future plans and makes sure that they direct their efforts to those activities which will maximise results

- provides direction to the planning process at all organisational levels

- directs the organisational activities as a whole and provides co-ordination in pursuing established plans

- provides standards of performance allowing assessment of the organisational efficiency and effectiveness (the former relating to optimisation of resource-usage and the latter relating to attainment).

Individual objectives must be directed towards, or 'dovetailed' with organisational goals. Each managerial job must be focused on the success of the business as a whole, not just one part of it, so that the results can be measured in terms of his or her contribution. People must know what their targets of performance are.

Work objectives – at team level, they relate to the purpose of the team and the contribution it is expected to make to the goals of the department and the organisation. At individual level, they are related specifically to the job. They clarify what the individual is expected to do and they enable the performance of the individual to be measured.

Standing aims and objectives include qualitative aims – issues such as promptness and courtesy when dealing with customer requests – and quantified targets eg, for a sales team would be to ensure that all phone calls are picked up within three rings.

Output or improvement targets – have most of the features of SMART objectives. A sales person may be given a target of increasing the number of sales made in a particular district in a certain time. Many organisations have targets that involve the number of defects in goods produced, or seek to find ways of working more efficiently.

Development goals – deal with how an individual can improve his or her own performance and skills. These goals are set at the appraisal interview and are part of the performance management system.

1.2 Principles of planning work

The planning of work involves the allocation of time to the requirements of work to be done. This must be applied to the organisation as a whole, to individual departments and sections and to single employees. An important feature of the principles is the role of time. Planning must be geared to terms of time and the degree of flexibility built into planning will vary according to the length of time being planned for. The principles of planning will revolve around:

(a) the determination of the length of time the plans will be concerned with;

(b) planning by departments and groups of individuals;

(c) planning by individuals;

(d) the implementation of planning principles;

(e) the updating of and alterations to plans.

There are three time ranges that are normally involved in planning work – the long-term, the medium-term and the short-term. Different organisations will include different lengths of time under the same heading. For example, a length of five years might be considered long-term for an organisation producing footwear but short-term in, say, the aviation industry. It may well be that three years is short-term to an organisation but to a department within that organisation it may be medium-term. Indeed, to an individual employee it may be long-term.

Planning in the long term involves forecasting and as such may be somewhat inaccurate and is, therefore, normally expressed only in general terms. Medium-term plans are likely to be less inaccurate and less forecasting is required. In the short term forecasting will be fairly accurate and the plans made will probably be adhered to without alteration.

Within organisations departmental plans are devised to meet specific objectives, the origins of those objectives stemming directly from the goals, aims and objectives of the organisation as a whole. There are two aspects that should be considered here:

(i) the internal departmental/group planning via the determination of schedules etc;

(ii) the co-ordination of the work of all the departments/groups within the organisation to ensure that the overall objectives of the organisation are attained.

1.3 Work planning

Work planning is the establishment of work methods and practices to ensure that predetermined objectives are efficiently met at all levels. It is necessary to ensure that work is carried out in accordance with the organisation's requirements and needs, whether those requirements are clearly defined or are merely implied. It necessitates planning and organising on the part of the organisation and the employee.

(a) Task sequencing or prioritisation – ie considering tasks in order of importance for the objective concerned

(b) Scheduling to timetabling tasks and allocating them to different individuals within appropriate time scales

(c) Establishing checks and controls to ensure that:

    (i) Priority deadlines are being met and work is not 'falling behind'
    (ii) Routine tasks are achieving their objectives

(d) Contingency plans: arrangements for what should be done if a major upset were to occur eg if the company's main computer were to break down

(e) Co-ordinating the efforts of individuals

(f) Reviewing and controlling performance

The overall aim encompassing each of the individual objectives outlined above is to instil method into work – by working methodically existing systems can be improved and new systems will be effective from the date of implementation.

Some jobs (eg assembly line worker), are entirely routine, and can be performed one step at a time, but for most people, some kind of planning and judgement will be required.

1.4 Assessing where resources are most usefully allocated

A manager or supervisor is responsible for allocating resources between **competing areas,** where total resources are limited and in **different ways** to achieve the same objective (eg to increase total profits, sell more, or cut costs etc).

ABC analysis (Pareto analysis) suggests that only a small proportion of items will be significant. For example a business might have 99 customers who each spend £10 per month and 1 customer who spends £100,000 per month. Pareto's Law assumes that, for sales, approximately 80% of sales volume is accounted for by 20% of the customers. This means that the manager will:

(a) Concentrate scarce resources on the crucial 20%.
(b) Devise policies and procedures for the remaining 80%, or delegate.

A piece of work will be **high priority** in the following cases.

- If it has to be completed by a certain time (ie a deadline)
- If other tasks depend on it
- If other people depend on it

Routine priorities or regular peak times (eg tax returns etc) can be **planned ahead of time,** and other tasks planned around them.

Non-routine priorities occur when **unexpected demands** are made. Thus planning of work should cover routine scheduled peaks and contingency plans for unscheduled peaks and emergencies.

1.5 Methodical working

The majority of organisations approach work planning methodically. Employees, however, often do not realise that if they do not plan their own individual and personal approach to work then the results desired by the organisation will not be achieved despite the efforts of the organisation.

There are distinct advantages to be gained from ensuring that tasks are tackled in some semblance of order, be it chronological or priority. Once a task has been commenced it should be completed as far as is practically possible. Efficiency is impaired by moving from one task to another.

Efficiency requires working systematically or methodically

(a) Ensure that **resources** are available, in sufficient supply and good condition

(b) Organise work in **batches** to save time spent in turning from one job to another

(c) Work to **plans,** schedules, checklists etc

(d) Taking advantage of work **patterns**

(e) Follow up tasks:

- Check on the progress of an operation
- Checking the task is completed when the deadline is reached
- Check payments are made when they fall due
- Retrieve files relevant to future discussions, meetings, correspondence

It is important that routine in all aspects of the employee's work should be established:

- Important and difficult tasks should always be attempted when the employee is fresh, normally during the morning.

- Tasks, requests and instructions should be written down; memory often proves defective.

- The adage 'never put off until tomorrow what can be done today' should be put into action.

- Often there are tasks which need to be done daily. These tasks should indeed be carried out each day, preferably at the same time.

- The regular routine, once established, should be written down. This will enable the employee to use it as both a reminder and a checklist. Additionally, if the employee is absent or leaves the organisation the written routine will enable a substitute or replacement to function more effectively.

Although emphasis has been placed above on the employee working methodically, the method employed by the organisation in devising, implementing and operating administrative systems and procedures is of equal importance.

1.6 Work allocation

Managers and supervisors divide duties and allocate them to available staff and machinery. Here are all the considerations.

(a) **General tasks**. Some tasks (eg filing, photo-copying) may not have the attention of a dedicated employee. Who will do the work, and will it interfere with their other duties?

(b) **Peak periods in some tasks may necessitate re-distribution of staff to cope** with the work load.

(c) **Status and staff attitudes** must be considered. Flexibility in reassigning people from one job to another or varying the work they do may be hampered by an employee's perception of his or her own status.

(d) Individual **temperaments** and abilities may differ.

(e) Planning should allow for **flexibility** in the event of an employee proving unfit for a task, or more able than his present tasks indicate.

(f) Efforts will have to be **co-ordinated** so that all those involved in a process (eg sales orders) work together as a team or a number of groups.

2 METHODS OF PLANNING WORK

2.1 Methods and systems

We should recognise and understand that different organisations and different individuals have individual characteristics, tastes, styles, preferences and objectives. These particular objectives may well be attained via different methods and systems. It is thus difficult to state categorically that all methods apply to all organisations. All that can be given are guidelines to the methods available. The following are probably the most common:

- checklists;
- scheduling
- work programmes;
- action sheets;
- planning charts and boards,

2.2 Checklists

A checklist is often used at individual level and is perhaps the simplest system, being essentially a list of items or activities. The preparation of a typical checklist would involve:

(a) the formulation of a list of activities and tasks to be performed within a given period;

(b) the identification of urgent or priority tasks;

(c) the maintenance of a continuous checklist with the addition of extra activities and tasks as and when required.

This system is obviously limited in its application because of its simplicity. It is suited to fairly mundane or routine tasks but it is these tasks that are often the very essence of the attainment of objectives. Typical uses of checklists would include:

- purchasing requirements;
- points to cover at an interview;
- points to cover at a meeting eg, an agenda;
- organising a conference or meeting.

2.3 Scheduling

Scheduling is where priorities and deadlines are planned and controlled. A schedule establishes a timetable for a logical sequence of tasks, leading up to completion date.

(a) All involved in a task must be given adequate **notice** of work schedules.

(b) The schedules themselves should allow a **realistic time allocation** for each task.

(c) Allowance will have to be made for **unexpected events**.

(d) A **deadline** is the *end* of the longest span of time which may be allotted to a task, ie the last acceptable date for completion. Failure to meet them has a 'knock-on' effect on other parts of the organisation, and on other tasks within an individual's duties. Diary entries may be made on appropriate days (eg: – 'Production completed?' 'Payment received?' 'Bring forward file x' 'One week left for revision').

A number of activities may have to be undertaken in sequence, with some depending on, or taking priority over others.

(a) **Activity scheduling** provides a list of necessary activities in the order in which they must be completed. You might use this to plan each day's work.

(b) **Time scheduling** adds to this the time scale for each activity, and is useful for setting deadlines for tasks. The time for each step is estimated; the total time for the task can then be calculated, allowing for some steps which may be undertaken simultaneously by different people or departments.

2.4 Work programmes and other aids to planning

From activity and time schedules, detailed **work programmes** can be designed for jobs which are carried out over a period of time. Some tasks will have to be started well before the deadline, others may be commenced immediately before, others will be done on the day itself. **Organising a meeting**, for example, may include:

Step 1. Booking accommodation two months before
Step 2. Retrieving relevant files one week before
Step 3. Preparing and circulating an agenda 2-3 days before
Step 4. Checking conference room layout the day before
Step 5. Taking minutes on the day

The same applies to stock ordering in advance of production (based on a schedule of known delivery times), preparing correspondence in advance of posting etc.

Once time scales are known and final deadlines set, it is possible to produce **job cards**, **route cards** and **action sheets**.

	Activity	Days before	Date	Begun	Completed
1	Request file	6	3.9		
2	Draft report	5	4.9		
3	Type report	3	6.9		
4	Approve report	1	8.9		
5	Signature	1	8.9		
6	Internal messenger	same day	9.9		

Longer-term schedules may be shown conveniently on charts, pegboards or year planners, holiday planners etc. These can be used to show lengths of time and the relationships between various tasks or timetabled events.

Activity 1   **(30 mins)**

Choose a task or event that needs planning.

(a) Make a checklist

(b) Re-arrange items in order of priority and time sequence

(c) Estimate the time for each activity and schedule it, working back from a deadline

(d) Prepare an action sheet

(e) Draw a chart with columns for time units, and rows for activities

(f) Decide what items may have to be 'brought forward' later and how

---

3   MOTIVATION

3.1   Meaning of motivation

Definitions

Motivation is 'a decision-making process through which the individual chooses the desired outcomes and sets in motion the behaviour appropriate to acquiring them'. (Buchanan and Huczynski).

Motives: 'learned influences on human behaviour that lead us to pursue particular goals because they are socially valued'. (Buchanan and Huczynski).

In practice the words motives and motivation are commonly used in different contexts to mean the following.

(a) Goals or outcomes that have become desirable for a particular individual. We say that money, power or friendship are motives for doing something.

(b) The mental process of choosing desired outcomes, deciding how to go about them (and whether the likelihood of success warrants the amount of effort that will be necessary) and setting in motion the required behaviours.

(c) The social process by which other people motivate us to behave in the ways they wish. Motivation in this sense usually applies to the attempts of organisations to get workers to put in more effort.

From a manager's point of view motivation is the controlling of the work environment, rewards and sanctions in such a way as to encourage desired behaviours and performance from employees.

3.2 Organisational goals and motivation

An organisation has goals, which can only be achieved by the efforts of the people who work in the organisation. Individuals also have their own 'goals' in life and these are likely to be different from those of the organisation. Once recruited, the new employee might be subjected to a variety of techniques to enhance his or her performance at work and help the organisation achieve its goals. This means that the employee must be motivated.

You may be wondering why motivation is important. It could be argued that if a person is employed to do a job, he or she will do that job and no question of motivation arises. If the person does not want to do the work, he or she can resign. The point at issue, however, is the efficiency and effectiveness with which the job is done.

The claim is that if individuals can be 'motivated', they will perform better and more willingly – **above mere compliance** with rules and procedures. If their personal needs and goals are integrated with those of the team and organisation, individuals will work more efficiently (so that productivity will rise) or produce a better quality of work, or might contribute more of their creativity and initiative to the job.

There is on-going debate about exactly what motivation strategies can aim to achieve in the way of productivity, quality and other business benefits, but it has become widely accepted that **committed** employees add value to the organisation. This is particularly true in environments where initiative and flexibility are required of employees in order to satisfy customer demands and keep pace with environmental changes.

Job satisfaction is an even more ambiguous concept, although (as we will see) it is associated with motivation.

(a) It is difficult to prove that 'happy bees make more honey'.

(b) Job satisfaction is difficult to define: it means different things to different people, and over time – according to the individual's changing needs, goals and expectations.

On the other hand, low morale, dissatisfaction or de-motivation can cause direct and indirect performance problems, through effects such as:

(a) Higher than usual (or higher than acceptable) labour turnover

(b) Higher levels of absenteeism, and deterioration in time-keeping and discipline

(c) Reduction in upward communication, employee involvement (such as participation in suggestion schemes or quality circles)

(d) Higher incidence of employee disputes and grievances

(e) Restricted output quantity and/or quality (through lack of commitment or deliberate sabotage)

> **Activity 2**   **(10 mins)**
>
> What factors in yourself or your job or organisation motivate you to:
>
> - Turn up to work at all?
>
> - Do an average day's work?
>
> - 'Bust a gut' to do your best on a task, or for a boss or customer?

3.3 Rewards and incentives

Definitions

> A **reward** is a token (monetary or otherwise) given to an individual or team in recognition of some contribution or success.
>
> An **incentive** is the offer or promise of a reward for contribution or success, designed to motivate the individual or team to behave in such a way as to earn it

Not all the incentives that an organisation can offer its employees are directly related to **monetary** rewards. The satisfaction of **any** of the employee's wants or needs may be seen as a reward for past or incentive for future performance.

Different individuals have different goals, and get different things out of their working life: in other words they have different orientations to work. There are many reasons why a person works, or is motivated to work well.

(a) The **human relations** school of management theorists regarded **work relationships** as the main source of satisfaction and reward offered to the worker.

(b) Later writers suggested a range of 'higher-order' motivations, notably:

- **Job satisfaction,** interest and challenge in the job itself – rewarding work

- **Participation** in decision-making – responsibility and involvement

(c) **Pay** has always occupied a rather ambiguous position, but since people need money to live, it will certainly be part of the reward package.

Rewards offered to the individual at work may be of two basic types.

(a) **Extrinsic rewards** are separate from (or external to) the job itself, and dependent on the decisions of others (that is, also external to the control of the workers themselves). Pay, benefits, cash and non-cash incentives and working conditions are examples of extrinsic rewards.

(b) **Intrinsic rewards** are those which arise from the performance of the work itself. They are therefore psychological rather than material and relate to the concept of job satisfaction. Intrinsic rewards include the satisfaction that comes from completing a piece of work, the status that certain jobs convey, and the feeling of achievement that comes from doing a difficult job well.

4 THEORIES OF MOTIVATION

4.1 Content and process theories

Many theories try to explain motivation and why and how people can be motivated. One classification is between content and process theories.

(a) **Content theories** ask the question: '**What** are the things that motivate people?' They assume that human beings have a set of needs or desired outcomes. Maslow's hierarchy theory and Herzberg's two-factor theory, both discussed below, are two of the most important approaches of this type.

(b) **Process theories** ask the question: '**How** can people be motivated?' They explore the process through which outcomes **become** desirable and are pursued by individuals. This approach assumes that people are able to select their goals and choose the paths towards them, by a conscious or unconscious process of calculation. Expectancy theory and Handy's 'motivation calculus' are theories of this type.

4.2 Maslow's hierarchy of needs

Maslow outlined five needs, as in the diagram below, and put forward certain propositions about the motivating power of each need.

Figure 5.1 Maslow's hierarchy of needs

(a) Any individual's needs can be arranged in a '**hierarchy** of relative pre-potency'.

(b) Each level of need is **dominant until satisfied**; only then does the next level of need become a motivating factor.

(c)   A need which has been satisfied no longer motivates an individual's behaviour. The need for self-actualisation can rarely be satisfied.

Activity 3   **(10 mins)**

Decide which of Maslow's categories the following fit into.

(a) Receiving praise from your manager   (e) A pay increase

(b) A family party   (f) Joining a local drama group

(c) An artist forgetting to eat   (g) Being awarded the OBE

(d) A man washed up on a desert island   (h) Buying a house

4.3   Herzberg's two-factor theory

Herzberg's two-factor theory identified **hygiene factors** and **motivator factors**.

(a)   **Hygiene factors** are based on a **need to avoid unpleasantness.**

If inadequate, they cause **dissatisfaction** with work. Unpleasantness demotivates: pleasantness is a steady state. Hygiene factors (the conditions of work) include:

- Company policy and administration
- Salary
- The quality of supervision
- Interpersonal relations
- Working conditions
- Job security

(b)   **Motivator factors** are based on a **need for personal growth.**

They actively create job satisfaction and are effective in motivating an individual to superior performance and effort. These factors are:

- Status (this may be a hygiene factor too)
- Advancement
- Gaining recognition
- Responsibility
- Challenging work
- Achievement
- Growth in the job

Herzberg suggested that when people are dissatisfied with their work it is usually because of discontent with environmental factors. Satisfaction can only arise from the job. He recommended various approaches to job design, which would build motivator factor into the work.

4.4   Vroom's expectancy theory

Expectancy theory basically states that the strength of an individual's motivation to do something will depend on the extent to which he expects the results of his efforts to contribute to his personal needs or goals.

Victor Vroom stated a formula by which human motivation could be assessed and measured. He suggested that the strength of an individual's motivation is the product of two factors.

(i)   The strength of his preference for a certain outcome, Vroom called this **valence**: it can be represented as a positive or negative number, or zero – since outcomes may be desired, avoided or regarded with indifference.

(ii) His expectation that the outcome will in fact result from a certain behaviour. Vroom called this 'subjective probability' or **expectancy**. As a probability, it may be represented by any number between 0 (no chance) and 1 (certainty).

In its simplest form, the expectancy equation may be stated as: $F = V \times E$

Where

F = the force or strength of the individual's motivation to behave in a particular way

V = valence: the strength of the individual preference for a given outcome or reward and E = expectancy: the individual's perception that the behaviour will result in the outcome/ reward.

In this equation, the lower the values of either valence or expectancy, the less the motivation. An employee may have a high expectation that increased productivity will result in promotion (because of managerial promises, say), but if he is indifferent or negative towards the idea of promotion (because he dislikes responsibility), he will not be motivated to increase his productivity. Likewise, if promotion was very important to him -but he did not believe higher productivity would get him promoted (because he has been passed over before, perhaps), his motivation would also be low.

Activity 4   **(10 mins)**

How might a manager use this theory to improve the motivation of team members?

4.5 Handy's motivation calculus

Charles Handy suggests that for any individual decision, there is a conscious or unconscious **motivation calculus** which is an assessment of three factors.

(a) The individual's own set of needs.

(b) The desired results – what the individual is expected to do in his job.

(c) 'E' factors (effort, energy, excitement in achieving desired results, enthusiasm, emotion, and expenditure).

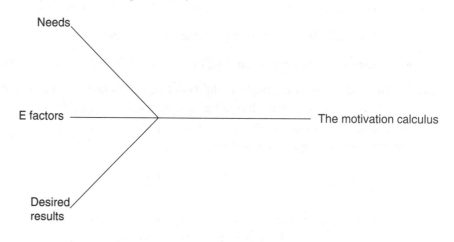

The **motivation decision** will depend on:

- The **strength of the individual's needs**
- The **expectancy** that expending 'E' will lead to a desired result
- How far the result will be **instrumental** in satisfying the individual's needs

Consequences for management

(a) **Intended results should be made clear,** so that the individual can complete the calculation by knowing **what is expected**, the **reward**, and **how much 'E'** it will take.

(b) Individuals are more committed to **specific goals** which they **have helped to set themselves**.

(c) **Feedback.** Without knowledge of **actual results**, there is no check that the 'E' expenditure was justified (and will be justified in future).

(d) If an individual is **rewarded** according to performance tied to standards (management by objectives), however, he or she may well set lower standards: the instrumentality part of the calculus (likelihood of success and reward) is greater if the standard is lower, so less expense of 'E' is indicated.

There are various ways of looking at motivation. Handy groups early motivation theories under three headings.

(i) **Satisfaction theories** are based on the assumption that a 'satisfied' worker will work harder (although there is little evidence to support the assumption). Satisfaction may reduce labour turnover and absenteeism, but will not necessarily increase individual productivity. Some theories hold that people work best within a compatible work group, or under a well-liked leader.

(ii) **Incentive theories** are based on the assumption that individuals will work harder to obtain a desired reward, ie positive reinforcement, although most studies are concentrated on money as a motivator. Handy notes that incentive theories can work if:

- the individual perceives the increased reward to be worth the extra effort

- the performance can be measured and clearly attributed to the individual

- the individual wants that particular kind of reward

- the increased performance will not become the new minimum standard

(iii) **Intrinsic theories** are based on the belief that higher-order needs are more prevalent in modern man than we give him credit for. People will work hard in response to factors in the work itself – participation, responsibility etc – effective performance is its own reward

4.6 Managerial implications of process theories

Expectancy theory suggests that:

(a) **Intended results should be made clear,** so that the individual can complete the calculation by knowing what is expected, the reward, and how much effort it will take.

(b) Individuals are likely to be more committed to **specific goals,** which they **have** helped **to set themselves,** taking their needs and expectations into account

(c) Immediate and on-going **feedback** should be given. Without knowledge of actual results, there is no check that 'E' expenditure was justified (or will be justified in the future).

(d) If an individual is **rewarded** according to performance tied to standards, he or she may well set lower standards: the expectancy part of the calculation (likelihood of success and reward) is-greater if the standard is lower, so less expense of 'E' is indicated.

5 MOTIVATION THEORIES AND EMPOWERMENT

5.1 The job as a motivator

The job itself can be used as a motivator or it can be a cause if dissatisfaction. Many attempts to improve the motivation and job satisfaction of employees have concentrated on job design.

Definition

Job design is the incorporation of the tasks the organisation needs to be done into a job for one person.

There are five core job dimensions that are thought to contribute to job satisfaction:

(a) skill variety- or the extent to which a job involves the use of several different skills and talents;

(b) task identity, or the extent to which a job involves completing an entire piece of work from beginning to end;

(c) task significance – the task is perceived to have a role, purpose, meaning and value, or the degree of impact the job is believed to have on other people;

(d) autonomy – the opportunity to exercise discretion or self-management (in areas such as target setting and work methods) – or the extent to which the worker feels freedom and discretion to act in different ways in relation to the job

(e) feedback – the extent to which workers are provided with information on the results of their work.

Frederick Herzberg suggest three ways of improving job design to make jobs more interesting to the employee, and hopefully to improve performance: job enrichment, job enlargement and job rotation.

Job enrichment – is planned, deliberate action to build greater responsibility, breadth and challenge of work into a job. Job enrichment is similar to **empowerment.** Job enrichment represents a 'vertical' extension of the job into greater levels of responsibility, challenge and autonomy. A job may be enriched by:

- Giving the job holder **decision-making tasks** of a higher order
- Giving the employee greater **freedom** to decide how the job should be done
- Encouraging employees **to participate** in the planning decisions of their superiors
- Giving the employee regular **feedback**

Job enlargement is the attempt to widen jobs by increasing the number of operations in which a jobholder is involved. It is a 'horizontal' extension of the job by increasing task variety and reducing task repetition.

(a) Tasks that span a larger part of the total production work should reduce boredom and add to task meaning, significance and variety.

(b) Enlarged jobs might be regarded as having higher status within the department, perhaps as stepping-stones towards promotion.

Job enlargement is, however, limited in its intrinsic rewards, as asking a worker to complete three separate tedious, unchallenging tasks is unlikely to be more motivating than asking him to perform just one tedious, unchallenging task.

Job rotation – is the planned transfer of staff from one job to another to increase task variety. It is a 'sequential' extension of the job. It is also sometimes seen as a form of training, where individuals gain wider experience by rotating as trainees in different positions.

It is generally admitted that the developmental value of job rotation is limited – but it can reduce the monotony of repetitive work.

5.2 Maccoby's social character types

Many theorists over the years have attempted to define what motivates people at work – ie, what drives them to be productive and deliver what the organisation wants of them.

Theorists such as Maslow believe that motivation is intrinsic. It comes from underlying needs that we all have. Such needs may be, for example, for power, achievement, or a sense of belonging. In their view it is management's task to diagnose and satisfy those needs if a worker is to perform adequately. Other theorists such as Vroom take the view that motivation is essentially extrinsic – we make a deliberate decision about how hard to work depending on our analysis of costs and rewards.

Herzberg's ideas were responsible for an emphasis in HRM on job enrichment and redesign during the 1960s and 1970s. The objective was to give employees responsibilities normally assumed by supervisors (vertical loading). Although these ideas lost popularity in the 1980s, they re-surfaced as 'Worker Empowerment' in the 1990s, partly due to the influence of Michael Maccoby's work. These ideas have helped to make the use of 'empowered' or 'semi-autonomous' teams popular in the workplace.

Maccoby compares the motivation of job enrichment with empowered teams – with its emphasis on skills development, problem solving, continuous improvement, quality products, improved customer service, flexible response to change:

Job enrichment, 1970s	Empowered teams, 1990's
• aimed to reduce costs of high turnover and increase productivity	• aims to improve organisational flexibility and quality for competitive advantage
• aimed to increase autonomy improves work experience and job satisfaction	• increased autonomy improves skill, decision-making, adaptability and use of new technology
• had little impact on management	• involves redefinition of management function
• quick fix, applied to problem groups only	• can take time to change culture
• Personnel administration technique	• human resource management strategy

Maccoby argues that people coming into employment today have different needs from employees of the past. These are due to changes in, for example, the way people are educated (learning is more self-directed) and social relationships (people are less prepared to do as they are told). Therefore, according to Maccoby, work has to match workers' dominant values for them to be motivated.

Maccoby identifies five 'social character types':

Type	Dominant Values
Expert	Mastery, control, autonomy
Helper	Caring for people, relatedness, sociability
Defender	Dignity, power, self esteem, protection
Innovator	Competition, glory, creating, experimenting
Self-developer	Balancing mastery and play, knowledge and fun

This 'new generation's work needs are:

- Clear management commitments on responsibilities and rewards
- Opportunities for expression, challenge and development
- Increased business
- Understanding and development
- Teamwork combined with individual growth
- Fair and meaningful rewards
- Reasons, information, to be included, to know why

Empowerment techniques

Empowerment is a feature of the new management model, based on managing resources and capabilities as opposed to the traditional method, based on managing assets.

Traditional model	New model
Built around assets	Built around capabilities
Directed at managing numbers with rationality and analysis	Focus on creating value with intuition and analysis

Traditional model	New model
Most tasks simplified. One best way to work defined by management	Enriched work; employees engaged in multiple tasks and expanding their knowledge. All employees learning continually and contributing to enterprise learning
Hierarchical with independent parts. Managers give orders; workers obey	The boundary-less organisation. Networked with interdependent parts. Participative management, self managing work teams
Reactive	Responsive
Command and control	Empowered employees
Risk-averse blame culture	Encouraging radical ideas and risk-taking

Definition

'Empowerment' is the term given to organisational arrangements that allow employees more autonomy, discretion and unsupervised decision-making responsibility.

Empowerment is motivational – it enables other people to act: it leaves them feeling strong, capable, and committed.

There are different degrees of empowerment and leadership within organisations:

Employee empowerment

Three levels

Degree of empowerment and leadership

ENABLING employees to make more and bigger decisions without having to refer to someone more senior

INVOLVING employees in taking responsibility for improving the way things are done

- Getting closer to the customer
- Improving service delivery
- Innovating continuously
- Increasing productivity
- Gaining the competitive edge

ENCOURAGING employees to play a more active role in their work

Organisational benefits

Figure 5.2 Degrees of empowerment and leadership within organisations

Bowen and Lawler (1992) describe three levels:

(i) **Suggestion involvement** – at a basic level staff may simply be able to contribute ideas and make suggestions but play no fundamental part in decision making and planning.

(ii) **Job involvement** – at a higher-level, employees' jobs may be redesigned to enable autonomous or semi-autonomous team working. Teams may be responsible for decision-making and planning in their own area of work with management offering support rather than control.

(iii) **High involvement** – at the highest level there may be a deliberate effort to enable 'vertical' teams which cut across hierarchical levels in the organisation, and there may be special provision for staff at all levels to be involved in strategic decision making. There are different degrees of empowerment. Bowen and Lawler (1992) describe three levels:

Employee empowerment can be meaningful only if three basic ingredients exist:

(i) **Trust** – as well as believing in a person's capabilities, you must trust them to perform or get on with the job.

(ii) **Competence** – there ought to be the mindset that individual employees can be expected to deliver to the best of their competence with the minimum of supervision.

(iii) **Teamwork** – not all company problems can be solved by one person. The sheer rate of change and turbulence implies that as fresh problems and challenges appear, individuals are likely to group together in flexible teams without barriers of hierarchy or status, to solve the problems within the framework of the company's values and objectives. The company is bound together by these beliefs and values – by people that are committed to one another and to their common goals. Remember, TEAM stands for 'Together Everyone Achieves More'.

There are four ways to breed empowerment:

(i) The **enlisting of support from employees** in tackling immediate organisational issues – empowerment is achieved by involving people in the development of their own solutions to specific issues. This is done by expecting teams to not just propose ways forward or to hope that someone else will do something; but to actually solve the problem in their part of the organisation, according to the constraints within which they work and the resources they have.

(ii) **Gaining the 'hearts and minds' of people** – empowerment is about winning both the hearts and minds of people so that they can take the opportunities made available to them for expanded responsibility. For example, at the management level, this could be achieved by sharing the vision and corporate values throughout the company.

(iii) **Structural means** (organisational and work grouping) – an organisation that is empowered has a flat structure with the minimum number of management layers. Work should be organised around basic operations to form 'whole tasks'. The basic organisational unit should be the primary workgroup – with a designated leader. Each workgroup and its leader should, as far a possible, plan and organise its own work, and be fully able to evaluate its performance against agreed standards of excellence. Jobs are to be structured so that workgroup members can personally plan, execute and evaluate at least one operation in the process. All workgroup members should have the opportunity to participate in the group's processes of planning, problem solving and evaluation

(iv) The **style or behaviour of individual managers** – leaders, managers and supervisors empower their team members not by abdicating or giving up control, but by changing the way control is exercised. They learn to delegate more, and allow individuals and teams more scope to act, monitor and plan their own performance; and to account for their acts and judgment calls. But at the end of it all, they (the managers) still have the responsibility of providing guidance and support to their staff. These leaders also need to help the staff to develop the competencies and skills required to function effectively in an empowered environment.

Leaders, managers or supervisors can empower others by:

- articulating a clear vision and goals
- helping them to master challenges
- modelling the correct behaviour
- providing support
- arousing positive emotions
- providing good information
- providing necessary resources
- connecting to outcomes
- being fair, reliable, open, caring, and competent

Activity 5 (10 mins)

Look back to Chapter 3 describing power and leadership and then outline the main differences between power and empowerment.

6 DELEGATION TECHNIQUES AND PROCESSES

6.1 Allocating work

Whatever its structure, the various operations of the organisation have to be distributed among its members. It is necessary to plan, organise, direct and control their activities. Delegation relates to the location of decision-making and, as we have already noted in an earlier chapter, one person cannot exercise all authority in making decisions as a firm grows. There is a limit to the number of persons that a manager can personally supervise. After this limit a manager must delegate authority to subordinates to make decisions.

The tasks delegated should be a mixture of different sorts of work – routine and non–routine, blended to suit the current circumstances and the subordinates' abilities and aspirations as well as those of their boss.

6.2 Delegation and empowerment

Delegation is the process of assigning tasks and granting sufficient authority for their accomplishment. The one to whom authority is delegated becomes accountable to the superior for doing the job, but the superior still remains responsible for getting the job done.

The idea of delegation is to make sure that responsibility and authority are equal for every job. When delegation is implemented correctly, people have the authority that they need to execute their responsibilities. However, assigning authority does not mean that someone has the ability, motivation and understanding necessary to perform.

In the new-generation adaptive organisation, delegation is replaced by empowerment, and responsibility by ownership. Authority and responsibilities are formal aspects of organising. They are based upon organisational properties and not individual capabilities. Empowerment and ownership are social aspects of organising. They are based on efficacy and initiative, and not just on roles and requirements. They belong to people.

6.3 The process of delegation

Delegation is a process where a manager or supervisor:

- determines the results expected

- allocates duties to subordinates

- grants them authority to enable those duties to be carried out

- holds them responsible for the completion of the work and achievement of results.

Remember that ultimate accountability for the task remains with the supervisor. If it is not well done it is the fault of poor delegation and is still the supervisor's responsibility to get it re-done.

There are immense differences between the processes of delegation employed in different organisations; you can find one firm where delegation flows freely and informally and another where it is only reluctantly employed. However, there is one feature that is common to almost all variants and that is its direction. It is almost always downward.

There is no 'correct procedure' for delegation, and even if there were you would not become a good delegator by learning it. 'It is not what you do, it is the way that you do it.' Let us take as examples different ways of delegation.

- *By abdication* – at one extreme, it is not uncommon to leave everything to a junior, which is a very crude and usually ineffective method.

- *According to custom and practice* – in some organisations it is customary to have work done by the age-old system whereby precedent rules. This method scarcely sounds progressive but it is common enough in the bureaucracies both of the Civil Service and major companies.

- *By explanation* – this more progressive way involves the manager in 'briefing' his subordinate along the lines of how the task should be done, without explaining too much because that could verge on actually doing the job. This is one of those cases when explanation is wanted – not too little and not too much – a fine balance that requires the art of management.

- *By consultation* – prior consultation was once quite novel in manager/union relations and also between managers and subordinates, but nowadays prior consultation is considered to be important and very effective. Another thing that has been realised by some, though not admitted by all, is that the middle grades of worker are immensely powerful; by contributing or withholding their cooperation they make the success of their seniors by no means automatic.

At least managers should have the humility to admit that sometimes good ideas come from below: indeed, the point of view of the person nearest the scene of action is more likely to be relevant. Delegation can benefit greatly from this sort of person.

What is more effective, more profitable and more humane, is for jobs to be apportioned to willing rather than merely to consenting subordinates, whose advice is sought before the method of doing the work is finally laid down. Again, there must be balances because managers cannot afford to spend most of their lives in consultation and only a residual portion in action.

In planning delegation therefore, a manager/ supervisor must ensure that:

- He/she does not delegate so much as to totally overload a subordinate.
- The subordinate has reasonable skill and experience in the area concerned.
- Appropriate authority is delegated.
- He/she remembers to monitor and control.
- He/she is not simply 'passing the buck' or 'opting out'.
- All concerned know that the task has been delegated.
- He/she puts time aside for coaching and guiding.
- If delegation goes well then the person will expect a reward, eg upgrade job/more pay.
- Delegation can be temporary and may be varied to give a rounded experience.

6.4 The techniques of delegation

Delegation is not just handing off work you don't want to do. Other things to consider when delegating include:

- qualifications of subordinate
- necessity of employee commitment
- expansion of employee capabilities
- evidence of shared values and perspectives
- sufficient time for delegation

Effective delegation is like starting a new exercise programme. You know it will be the right thing to do and you will love the results, but it is tough to make a commitment and get started. A delegation model outlining the techniques of delegation is shown below.

- Assess your current workload by reviewing and/or writing a job description and creating a time budget for your typical week (ie, x % spent on meetings, e-mail, sales, billing, etc.)

- Decide which tasks on your time budget consume too much time and don't effectively support your job description. These are the tasks that should be delegated!

- Decide what tasks need to be done and determine which employee would benefit most from the learning experience. Although most employees don't have extra time to do more work, many would welcome an assignment that stretches them.

- Clearly describe the assignment and where it fits in the "big picture" to the employee who will take responsibility for it. Giving the employee an understanding of why the task is so important and how it contributes to the company's goals will increase the employee's commitment and accountability.

- Jointly define the time, money, staff, training, and resources needed to accomplish the task. Doing this step together will clarify what is needed and show that you are working in partnership with your employee to help him or her succeed.

- Work together to outline initial ideas about how to proceed.

- Give the employee the appropriate level of authority to carry out the assignment.

- Both parties should come to an agreement about how success will be measured and how often. If the job is completed successfully, what would the result look like? Determining what constitutes success and how you will measure it before you start any job allows everyone to understand the expectations.

- Provide feedback and support during the process and at its completion. Staying on top of the work, while not actually doing it is critical. Feedback allows course corrections. It's disheartening to get to the end of a failed project and know that better communication with your employee could have influenced its success.

6.5 Problems of delegation

Many managers and supervisors are reluctant to delegate and attempt to do many routine tasks themselves in addition to their more important duties. This may happen for the following reasons:

(a) **Low confidence and trust** in the abilities of their staff: the suspicion that 'if you want it done well, you have to do it yourself.'

(b) The burden of **accountability for the mistakes of subordinates**.

(c) A **desire to 'stay in touch'** with the department or team – both in terms of workload and staff- particularly if the manager does not feel 'at home' in a management role.

(d) **Feeling threatened.** An unwillingness to admit that assistants have developed to the extent that they could perform some of the supervisor's duties.

(e) **Poor control and communication systems** in the organisation, so that the manager feels he has to do everything himself, if he is to retain real control and responsibility for a task.

(f) An **organisational culture** that has failed to reward or recognise effective delegation, so that the manager may not feel that delegation is positively regarded.

(g) **Lack of understanding** of what delegation involves – not giving assistants total control, or making the manager himself redundant.

(h) **Lack of training** and development of managers in delegation skills and related areas.

6.6 Overcoming the reluctance of managers to delegate

(a) **Train the subordinates** so that they are capable of handling delegated authority in a responsible way. If assistants are of the right 'quality', supervisors will be prepared to trust them more.

(b) Have a system of **open communications,** in which the supervisor and assistants freely interchange ideas and information. If the assistant is given all the information needed to do the job, and if the supervisor is aware of what the assistant is doing:

- The assistant will make better-informed decisions.

- The supervisor will not panic because he does not know what is going on.

(c) **Ensure that a** system **of control is established.** If responsibility and accountability are monitored at all levels of the management hierarchy, the dangers of relinquishing authority and control to assistants are significantly lessened.

6.7 Supervision styles

Effective delegation is best promoted by knowing how to delegate and how to overcome barriers to delegation.

How should a supervisor delegate?

The first thing to do is to prepare for delegation. It is essential to know what you want to delegate and to plan for it. Usually it is better to be precise about delegation and to decide that particular tasks will be delegated rather than responsibility for broad areas of work. Once you have made decisions on what is to be delegated then you can look around and select the individual who you think could, with your support and perhaps training, do the work that you intend to pass down. Of course, the failure to train and develop people for delegation is the most frequent cause of failure, so it really is important to consider what new skill, knowledge or experience the subordinate will need to do the delegated work.

The preparatory work done, the supervisor in delegating must brief the subordinate as to:

(a) precisely what is to be done;

(b) what results are required;

(c) the scale and scope of the authority that will accompany the delegation.

The supervisor must also communicate to all those who need to know what authority the person to whom work has been delegated now has.

There should be close control of delegated work, and the subordinate must know that the supervisor is prepared to help and give advice if this is required. Feedback is vital: a person in receipt of delegated work needs to know not only that he or she is doing the job properly, but also whether the job is being done well.

The people that are directly involved in doing the work are those that have the greatest knowledge of the process's inefficiencies and benefits. The supervisor will support these people by:

- soliciting their expertise and allowing them to take some operational decisions

- backing them up and helping them to become more efficient

- providing counselling and advice

- bringing the organisation's resources to bear on problems identified by the workforce

The climate of the organisation is a prime determinant of the effectiveness of delegation. If fear, distrust and uncertainty surround the process of delegation, people will become at best sceptical of the purpose and value of delegation and at worst cynical about and hostile to it.

The decision about when to delegate is also important:

(a) Is the acceptance of staff affected required for morale, relationships or ease of implementation of the decision?

(b) Is the **quality** of the decision most important? Many technical financial decisions may be of this type, and should be retained by the supervisor if he or she alone has the knowledge and experience to make them.

(c) Is the **expertise or experience** of assistants relevant or **necessary** to the task, and will it enhance the quality of the decision?

(d) Can **trust** be placed in the competence and reliability of the assistants?

(e) Does the **decision** require tact and confidentiality, or, on the other hand, maximum exposure and assimilation by employees?

Activity 6 (20 mins)

You are the manager of an accounts section of your organisation and have stopped to talk to one of the clerks in the office to see what progress he is making. He complains bitterly that he is not learning anything. He gets only routine work to do and it is the same routine. He has not even been given the chance to swap jobs with someone else. You have picked up the same message from others in the office. You discuss the situation with Jean Howe the recently appointed supervisor. She appears to be very busy and harassed. When confronted with your observations she says that she is fed up with the job. She is worked off her feet, comes early, goes late, takes work home and gets criticised behind her back by incompetent clerks.

What has gone wrong?

---

7 COMMUNICATION STYLES AND TECHNIQUES

7.1 The communication process

The efficient running of organisations requires that all the members of the organisation work together towards the achievement of the organisation's objectives. This working together requires the adequate understanding of what others are doing. It requires a high level of co-ordination and control, and fundamentally it requires communications, which are efficient and effective.

Communication is the transmission or exchange of information and, in any organisation, it is necessary for:

(i) Management decision-making

(ii) Interdepartmental co-ordination. All the interdependent systems for purchasing, production, marketing and administration can be synchronised to perform the right actions at the right times to co-operate in accomplishing the organisation's aims.

(iii) Individual motivation and effectiveness, so people know what they have to do and why.

Communication may take the following forms.

- Giving instructions
- Giving or receiving information
- Exchanging ideas
- Announcing plans or strategies
- Comparing actual results against a plan
- Rules or procedures
- Communication about the organisation structure and job descriptions

The communication process can be shown as follows.

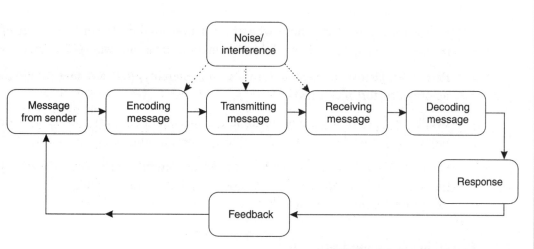

Figure 5.3 Communication process

Process	Comment
Coding of a message	The code or 'language' of a message may be verbal (spoken or written) or it may be non-verbal, in pictures, diagrams, numbers or body language.
Medium for the message	There are a number of channels for communication, such as a conversation, a letter, a notice board or via computer. The choice of medium used in communication depends on a number of factors such as urgency, permanency, complexity, sensitivity and cost.
Feedback	The sender of a message needs feedback on the receiver's reaction. This is partly to test the receiver's understanding of it and partly to gauge the receiver's reaction. Feedback can range from a smile or nod to a blank look or shrug, or from the desired action being taken to no action or the wrong action being taken. It is *feedback* that makes communication a two-way process rather than a series of send-receive events
Distortion	The meaning of a message can be lost in coding and decoding stages. Usually the problem is one of language and the medium used; it is easier to 'get the wrong end of the stick' in a telephone call than from a letter.
Noise	Distractions and interference in the environment in which communication is taking place may be physical noise (passing traffic), technical noise (a bad telephone line), social noise (differences in the personalities of the parties) or psychological noise (anger, frustration, tiredness).

Factors that can interfere with effective communication include:

- Semantics (occurs when the meaning of a message to the sender differs from its meaning to the recipient)

- Distraction (occurs when a recipient does not understand the sender's message because he/she is thinking about something else.

- Misrepresentation (includes things such as deliberate lies, focusing on positive results only)

- Information retention (those who control information are in a position of power in being able to channel the information in various ways)

- Perceptual factors (perceptual errors such as stereotyping can cause people to ignore or distort messages)

- Feedback repetitions, use of multiple channels, and simplified language can reduce problems due to semantics, selective perception, and distraction.

- Communication overload can be reduced by careful review of the material needed by the recipient and by use of the exception principle (ie, only exceptions should be reported).

7.2 Direction of communication flows

Communication flows can be:

- **Vertical** ie up and down the scalar chain (from superior to subordinate and back). This is mainly used for reporting and feedback, and sometimes also suggestions and problem solving input. Three forms of downward communication are manuals, handbooks, and newsletters. Three forms of upward communication are suggestion systems, grievances, and attitude surveys.

- **Horizontal or lateral:** between people of the same rank, in the same section or department, or in different sections or departments. Horizontal communication between 'peer groups' is usually easier and more direct then vertical communication, being less inhibited by considerations of rank.

  (a) **Formally:** to co-ordinate the work of several people, and perhaps departments, who have to co-operate to carry out a certain operation.

  (b) **Informally:** to furnish emotional and social support to an individual.

- **Diagonal.** This is interdepartmental communication by people of different ranks. Departments in the technostructure that serve the organisation in general, such as Human Resources or Information Systems, have no clear 'line authority' linking them to managers in other departments who need their involvement. Diagonal communication aids co-ordination, and also innovation and problem solving, since it puts together the ideas and information of people in different functions and levels. It also helps to by-pass longer, less direct channels, avoiding blockages and speeding up decision-making.

But communications can flow in all directions and across all boundaries via the grapevine. This is an informal network that can use any or all media available (eg, face-to-face, computer messaging). The grapevine can be the source of rumours, but most grapevine communications have been found to be accurate.

7.3 Patterns of communication

Communication networks structure the flow of information among network members. They influence decision quality, member satisfaction, message quality, and other variables. The patterns of communication that develop depend, in part, on the structure of the group. If there is little structure in a group, members communicate with anyone they want to. If the group is highly structured, group members might only communicate with certain other members.

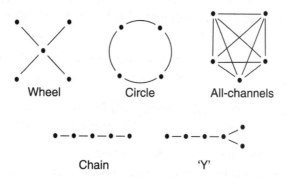

Wheel   Circle   All-channels

Chain   'Y'

Figure 5.4 Channel networks

We are most familiar with the **all-channel** network of a small group, where everyone can communicate to everyone else in the group. Another common network is the **inverted Y**, the normal hierarchy where each member communicates to the person above and the person(s) below, but levels are not skipped when communicating up or down the organisation.

Three other networks that have been studied are the wheel, the chain, and the circle. In the **wheel network** a central person can communicate with every other person, but they cannot talk to each other except through the centre. A taxi dispatcher, for instance, occupies the centre of a wheel and has a high degree of central control over information. Drivers who equip themselves with cellular telephones and take calls directly from their regular customers can bypass the dispatcher and create their own communication network.

In a **chain network,** individuals can communicate only to the two people next to them in the chain (or only one other person for the person at the end of the chain). For example, people on an assembly line may be restricted in whom they can talk to by their physical location on the line. A **circle network** is a closed chain. Though all members do not communicate with every other member, no one person controls the communication.

Network research began with individuals working on artificial tasks in behavioural laboratories, where the centralisation of networks was examined for its effects on leadership emergence and member satisfaction. Now that computer communication networks are becoming more important both within and across organisations, a person's link into the network is a real and important consideration. The person at the hub of a wheel network, the network manager, can expect to be very satisfied with communications and to assume a position of leadership within the network, even though average member satisfaction with communication may be low. While it is theoretically possible for all members of a computer network to send messages to all others (the all-channel network), such a system is inefficient when there are a large number people on the network.

Which type of network is better depends upon the type of task the group is working on. If the task is simple and there is only one right way to perform it, then a more structured group works best, because a central leader is necessary. If there are several ways to accomplish the task, a less structured group works better, because this allows members to generate ideas freely. Group members usually get the most satisfaction from the all channels network, because it gives them greater freedom and a feeling of control.

7.4 Styles and techniques

Communication styles include informing, influencing, being assertive, negotiating, consulting and counselling. The techniques associated with these styles are outlined below.

Informing techniques

(a) Consider the **information needs and priorities** of others: what do they need and want to know (which may not be the same thing)?

(b) Consider how much others **know already**: what background or explanation will (or will not) be required. Some people will be familiar with your subject matter, and some will not.

(c) **Avoid 'jargon'**: technical terminology, which you use in your specialisation, but may not mean anything to others.

(d) Communicate as **clearly, simply** and **directly** as possible – even (or especially) if the topic is complex.

(e) Use **visual aids** if this will help to make points more appealing, accessible or understandable.

(f) Provide an appropriate **volume** of information. This means:

    (i) Not **overloading** people with information they will not be able to get through or take in, in the time available.

    (ii) Not giving people more information than is **relevant** to them (or you).

    (iii) Not giving people **less** information than they need, or you want them to have

(g) Consider the degree of **accuracy** required. All information should be accurate in the sense of **correct** – without falsehood – but need not be minutely detailed: a summary or average figure may be all that is needed.

(h) Present factual information **objectively**: without emotional colour, exaggeration or bias.

Influencing techniques

There are two types of influencing techniques – push and pull:

Push	Pull
Identify the problem/opportunity and propose your solution.	State your view of the problem/ opportunity.
Invite reactions.	Clarify how the other person sees the situation.
Check that you understand each other's arguments.	Work towards agreement on the nature of the problem/opportunity

Push	Pull
Deal with objections: (a) by persuasion (if you want commitment) (b) by authority (if you only need compliance)	Look for solutions, using as many of the other person's ideas as possible.
Agree on the outcome and action plan.	Come to joint agreement on outcome and action plan.

Being assertive

Assertive behaviour involves standing up for your own rights and needs but also respecting the rights and needs of others. Assertive people stand up for their own rights in such a way that they do not violate another person's rights. They express their needs, wants, opinions, feelings and beliefs in direct, honest and appropriate ways.

Assertive behaviour must be carefully distinguished from aggressive behaviour – this is standing up for yourself at the expense of other people and involves:

- standing up for your own rights but doing so in such a way that you violate the rights of other people;

- ignoring or dismissing the needs, wants, opinions, feelings or beliefs of others;

- expressing your own needs, wants and opinions in inappropriate ways.

Aggression is some form of attack and may be verbal or physical. A frustrated employee may attack his or her supervisor or kick a machine that has broken down. Verbal aggression can take such forms as shouting, name-calling, sarcasm, swearing or making snide remarks.

Assertive behaviour must also be distinguished from passive or non-assertive behaviour – a 'flight' reaction that takes the form of giving in to others demands:

- Failing to stand up for your rights, or allowing others to disregard them
- Expressing your needs, wants, opinions and feelings apologetically or vaguely
- Failing to express honestly your needs, feelings and opinions

---

Activity 7   **(10 mins)**

A colleague telephones you when you are working on some invoices that you particularly want to finish. He says he wants to talk about next week's safety meeting. You prefer to discuss it later. Give (a) an assertive response and (b) an aggressive response

Negotiating techniques

Negotiating is a process of:

(a) Purposeful persuasion: each party attempts to persuade the other to accept its case, by marshalling persuasive arguments.

(b) Constructive compromise: each party accepts the need to move closer towards each other's position, so that they can explore common ground and areas where concessions and compromises can be made while still meeting the key needs of both parties.

Negotiation is a problem-solving technique. Its objective is that both parties reach agreement, so that they both go away with a decision they can live with – without damaging the relationship between them.

You can use negotiating as a style of communication to reach agreement and solve problems in all kinds of areas: asking your boss for permission to decorate your work space; asking your tutor for more time to complete an assignment; sorting out the demands of different people asking you to do things at the same time.

Consultation techniques

Definition

Consultation is where one party seeks the views of another party before either party takes a decision.

Consultation is the process where, on a regular basis, management genuinely seeks the views, ideas and feelings of employees before a decision is taken.

Consultation is not the same as negotiation. Negotiation implies acceptance by both parties that agreement between them is required before a decision is taken. Consultation implies a willingness to listen to the views of another while reserving the right to take the final decision, with or without agreement on both sides.

For the effective manager, using his or her interpersonal skills, a way of consulting subordinates is to discuss proposals with them. The 'I have decided to give you X approach is nowhere near as effective as the 'I've been thinking – do you feel that you can tackle X approach?'

Consulting implies decisions are only made after consultation. However, the final decision may not include any or all of the ideas put forward. Subordinates may feel cheated and not truly involved.

Counselling techniques

Counselling is client-centred and involves the client in solving the problem. A shorter definition is 'helping a person to help themselves'. Counselling is a specialist term and must be distinguished from telling, advising and manipulating.

- *Telling* is where the person giving help by telling the client what to do is problem centred and excludes the client from the problem solving process.

- *Advising* is also a problem centred person giving help and excluding the client in problem solving. The process usually involves the adviser identifying options and getting the client to select the one which the adviser favours.

- *Manipulating* is when the client is excluded from the problem solving process and the person doing the manipulating is satisfying his or her own needs.

Effective counselling shows an organisation's commitment to and concern for its staff and is likely to improve employee loyalty and enthusiasm. The techniques include:

- helping others to identify problems, issues and possible solutions for themselves;

- using a non-directive approach rather than advising or making specific suggestions;

- encouraging reflection and talking around issues;

- allowing others to lead and determine the direction;

- using open questions to help others explore ideas, feelings and thoughts;

- having more of a passive role, listening very actively and carefully;

- speaking only to clarify and probe.

7.5 Supervisor's role in communications and working culture

A supervisor plays a vital role in communication. He or she works not only as a receiver or sender but also as a facilitator. To make a communication system effective the supervisor needs to work as a developer as well as a maintenance person.

As a sender, the individual should be seen as:

- sharing, not telling

- trying to relate to other people, not to control them

- seeking truth rather than convincing others

- judging his or her own contribution by the feedback obtained from others rather than personal judgement ...

- looking for agreement and any disagreement and seeking the meaning the other person intends in the areas of difference

- seeking to be empathetic

- trying to eliminate from his behaviour actions that threaten

As a receiver the individual should:

- Try to help the sender clarify his or her meaning

- seek understanding ...

- identify what is not being said as much as he or she tries to understand what is being said

The supervisor's role in improving communications include the following measures:

- Encourage, facilitate and reward communication. Status and functional barriers can be minimised by improving opportunities for formal and informal networking and feedback.

- Give training and guidance in communication skills, including consideration of recipients, listening and giving feedback.

- Minimise the potential for misunderstanding. Make people aware of the difficulties arising from differences in culture and perception, and teach them to consider others' viewpoints. Solving the problems created by diversity involves:

    (a)   treating people first and foremost as individuals

    (b)   acknowledging the special circumstances or particular context that may lead to exclusion for some groups of people

    (c)   working to change that situation

    (d)   developing a workforce within which people are valued for the contribution they make

    While the main responsibility for eliminating discrimination and providing equal opportunity is that of the employer, individual employees at all levels have responsibilities too. They must not discriminate or knowingly aid their employer to do so.

- Adapt technology, systems and procedures to facilitate communication: making it more effective (clear mobile phone reception), faster (laptops for e-mailing instructions), more consistent (regularly reporting routines) and more efficient (reporting by exception).

- Manage conflict and politics in the organisation, so that no basic unwillingness exists between units.

- Establish rules, regulations and codes of practice and disciplinary procedures for non-conformance. Any successful organised activity requires that everyone concerned understands what behaviour is expected and is able and willing to behave in the required way. It is management's job to show that rules are necessary and to convince its employees that the observation of rules is not only a condition of employment but also a process that benefits everyone. If the employee understands the requirements of his or her own job, has the requisite skill and knowledge to perform, is convinced of its usefulness to related jobs and to the overall purposes of the organisation, he or she should be suitably disposed to organisational discipline. Provided penalties for poor performance are coupled with competent and fair supervision then employees' tolerance for discipline is unlikely to diminish.

- Establish communication channels and mechanisms in all directions: regular staff or briefing meetings, house journal or intranet and quality circles. Upward communication should particularly be encouraged using mechanisms such as inter -unit meetings, suggestion schemes, 'open door' access to managers and regular performance management feedback sessions.

The communication style of the manager/supervisor can also affect the working culture of the organisation. The term working culture can include employment characteristics such as working conditions, cooperation schemes, work-control, workload, degree of specialisation, ethical issues, etc. In many successful companies, leaders/supervisors serve as role models, set the standards for performance, communicate the regulations and codes of practice expected, motivate and discipline employees, make the company special and are a symbol to the external environment. The working culture created by leaders can result in many functions being carried out in quite different ways.

Chapter roundup

- Work objectives clarify what the individual is expected to do and they enable the performance of the individual to be measured.

- Work planning is the establishment of work methods and practices to ensure that predetermined objectives are efficiently met at all levels. It is necessary to ensure that work is carried out in accordance with the organisation's requirements and needs

- Supervisors often have to plan the use of resources in their section and schedule activities to ensure that work is done on time, to standard and to budget.

- Scheduling is where priorities and deadlines are planned and controlled. A schedule establishes a timetable for a logical sequence of tasks, leading up to a completion date.

- Motivation is the controlling of the work environment, rewards and sanctions in such a way as to encourage desired behaviours and performance from employees.

- Rewards offered to the individual at work may be of two basic types.

  - Extrinsic rewards are separate from (or external to) the job itself, and dependent on the decisions of others

  - Intrinsic rewards are those which arise from the performance of the work itself.

- Content theories of motivation suggest that each person has a package of needs: the best way to motivate an employee is to find out what his/her needs are and offer him/her rewards that will satisfy those needs.

  - Abraham Maslow identified a hierarchy of needs which an individual will be motivated to satisfy, progressing towards higher order satisfactions, such as self-actualisation.

  - Frederick Herzberg identified two basic need systems: the need to avoid unpleasantness and the need for personal growth. He suggested factors which could be offered by organisations to satisfy both types of need: 'hygiene' and 'motivator' factors respectively.

- Process theories of motivation do not tell managers what to offer employees in order to motivate them but help managers to understand the dynamics of employees' decisions about what rewards are worth going for.

NOTES

Chapter roundup (continued)

- Various means have been suggested or improving job satisfaction but there is little evidence that a satisfied worker actually works harder.

- Pay is the most important of the hygiene factors, but it is ambiguous in its effect on motivation.

- Ways in which managers can improve employees' motivation range from encouraging employees to accept responsibility to careful design of jobs (including job enrichment, job enlargement and job rotation) to increasingly sophisticated and performance-related pay and incentive schemes.

- Empowerment' is the term given to organisational arrangements that allow employees more autonomy, discretion and unsupervised decision-making responsibility.

- Delegation is the process of assigning tasks and granting sufficient authority for their accomplishment.

- Communication is the transmission or exchange of information. It is a two-way process: feedback is the signal returned form the recipient of a message indicating whether (and how accurately) the message has been received

- Communication styles include informing, influencing, being assertive, negotiating, consulting and counselling.

Quick quiz

1   List some planning and scheduling aids.

2   List the five categories in Maslow's Hierarchy of Needs.

3   List three ways in which an organisation can offer motivational satisfaction.

4   What is the difference between a reward and an incentive?

5   According to Herzberg, leadership style is a motivator factor. True or false?

6   'People will work harder and harder to earn more and more pay.' Do you agree? Why (or why not)?

7   A 'horizontal' extension of the job to increase task variety is called:

    A   Job evaluation
    B   Job enrichment
    C   Job enlargement
    D   Job rotation

8   List the stages in the process of delegation.

9   List some problems in delegation.

10   Is consultation the same as negotiation? If not, explain the difference.

Answers to quick quiz

1   The following are probably the most common:

- checklists;
- scheduling
- work programmes;
- action sheets;
- planning charts and boards. (See para 2.1)

2   Physiological, safety, love/social, esteem, self-actualisation. (4.2)

3   Relationships, belonging, challenge, achievement, progress, security, money. (3.3)

4   A reward is given for some contribution or success. An incentive is an offer or reward. (3.3)

5   False: it is a hygiene factor. (4.3)

6   See Paragraph 3.3.

7   C. Make sure you can define all the other terms as well. (5.1)

8   Specify performance levels; formally assign task; allocate resources and authority; back off; give feedback. (6.3)

9   Low trust, low competence, fear, worry about accountability. (6.4)

10 Consultation is not the same as negotiation. Negotiation implies acceptance by both parties that agreement between them is required before a decision is taken. Consultation implies a willingness to listen to the views of another while reserving the right to take the final decision, with or without agreement on both sides. (7.4)

Answers to activities

1   The answer will depend on the activity you have chosen.

2   This will depend on your own situation.

3   Maslow's categories for the listed circumstances are as follows:

(a) Esteem needs
(b) Social needs
(c) Self-actualisation needs
(d) He will have physiological needs
(e) Safety needs initially; esteem needs above a certain income level
(f) Social needs or self-actualisation needs
(g) Esteem needs
(h) Safety needs or esteem needs

4   Expectancy theory has various practical applications.

(a) Motivation can be measured and responses to incentives (to an extent) predicted, using attitude surveys or interviews in which team members are invited to state valence and expectancy.

(b) Managers need to fulfil their promises of rewards – otherwise expectancy will be lowered next time.

(c) Managers need to give some thought to the value of incentives and rewards to individual employees -otherwise valence will be low. (Some organisations offer a 'cafeteria' system of rewards and benefits, allowing employees to select those that they value.)

(d) Managers need to give employees clear information on expected results, offered rewards and progress -via on-going feedback – in order for them to make motivational calculations.

5

Power	Empowerment
• External source	• Internal source
• Ultimately, few people have it	• Ultimately, everyone can have it
• The capacity to have others do what you want	• The capacity to have others do what they want
• To get more implies taking it away from someone else	• To get more does not affect what others have
• Leads to competition	• Leads to cooperation

6 The problem appears to be that the new supervisor is taking too much of the department's work on to herself. While she is overworked, her subordinates are apparently not being stretched and as a result motivation and morale amongst them are poor. The supervisor herself is unhappy with the position and there is a danger that declining job satisfaction will lead to inefficiencies and eventually staff resignations.

There could be a number of causes contributing to the problem.

(a) Jean Howe may have been badly selected, ie she may not have the ability required for a supervisory job.

(b) Alternatively she may just be unaware of what is involved in a supervisor's role. She may not have realised that much of the task consists of managing subordinates; she is not required to shoulder all the detailed technical work herself.

(c) There may be personality problems involved. Jean Howe regards her clerks as incompetent and this attitude may arise simply form an inability to get on with them socially. (Another possibility is that her staff actually are incompetent.)

(d) The supervisor does much of the department's work herself. This may be because she does not understand the kind of tasks which can be delegated and the way in which delegation of authority can improve the motivation and job satisfaction of subordinates.

As manager you have already gone some way towards identifying the actual causes of the problem. You have spoken to some of the subordinates concerned and also to the supervisor. You could supplement this by a review of personnel records relating to Jean Howe to discover how her career has progressed so far and what training she had received (if any) in the duties of a supervisor. You may then be in a position to determine which of the possible causes of the problems are operating in this case.

7   (a)   an assertive response might be ' Fine. I'm happy to talk about the safety meeting, but right now I'd like to finish these invoices. How about me ringing you back later this afternoon?

    (b)   an aggressive response might be ' You can't expect me to think about a safety meeting. I'm in the middle of doing some invoices. You'll have to ring me back later.

Chapter 6 :

PERFORMANCE MONITORING AND EVALUATION

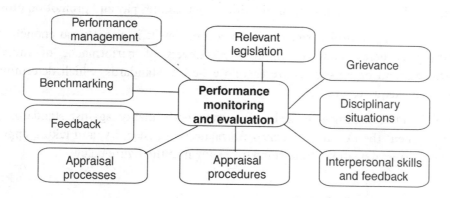

Introduction

The performance management process provides an opportunity for the employee and performance manager to discuss development goals and jointly create a plan for achieving those goals. Development plans should contribute to organisational goals and the professional growth of the employee. Achieving the overall goal requires several ongoing activities, including identification and prioritisation of desired results, establishing means to measure progress toward those results, setting standards for assessing how well results were achieved, tracking and measuring progress toward results, exchanging ongoing feedback among those participants working to achieve results, periodically reviewing progress, reinforcing activities that achieve results and intervening to improve progress where needed. Note that results themselves are also measures. Feedback is given and assistance with corrective actions is required where the performance does not match the standard set. The appraisal interview is the vehicle for giving feedback to the employee through which they can find out about their strengths and weaknesses and discuss what steps to take to improve future performance. As such it is a crucial part of the appraisal process.

Your objectives

After completing this chapter you should be able to:

(a)   Plan or analyse work activities using appropriate objective setting techniques and processes

(b)   Review development needs and activities and evaluate the effectiveness of activities

(c)   Use suitable methods, with clearly defined and relevant criteria and objectives, to assess the performance of colleagues

(d)   Identify factors affecting the quality of performance and use these to provide clear and constructive feedback on performance to colleagues

(e) Incorporate results of assessments into personal development plans and other organisational procedures for dealing with performance issues

1 PERFORMANCE MANAGEMENT

1.1 Controlled performance

Organisations are concerned with performance in the pursuit of their goals. The performance of an organisation as a whole determines its survival. The performance of a department determines its survival within the organisation and the amounts of resources allocated to it. The performance of individuals determines pay and promotion prospects.

It is necessary to control performance, to ensure that it is either good enough, or that something is being done to improve it. Levels of performance of individuals, departments and organisations are therefore tied to standards, which determine what counts as inadequate, satisfactory or good.

Control involves setting standards, measuring performance against standards, taking decisions about the extent to which performance is satisfactory, and taking appropriate action to correct deviations from standards, shown in the figure below.

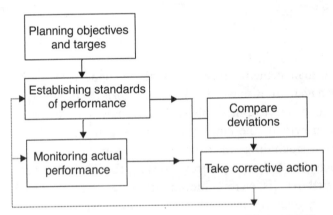

Figure 6.1 Controlling performance

The need for controlled performance leads to a deliberate and ordered allocation of functions, or division of labour, between organisation members. The activities and interactions of members are also intentionally programmed and structured. Admission to membership of organisations is controlled and the price of failure to perform to standard is usually loss of membership.

1.2 Features of performance management

Definition

> **Performance management** is: a means of getting better results by managing performance within an agreed framework of goals, standards and competence requirements. It is a process to establish a shared understanding about what is to be achieved, and an approach to managing and developing people.

This definition highlights key features of performance management.

Aspect	Comment
Agreed framework of goals, standards and competence requirements	The manager and the employee agree about a standard of performance, goals and the skills needed.
Performance management is a process	Managing people's performance is an on-going activity, involving continual monitoring, discussion and adjustment.
Shared understanding	The goals of the individual, unit and organisation as a whole need to be integrated: everyone needs to be 'on the same page' of the business plan.
Approach to managing and developing people	Managing performance is not just about plans, systems or resources: it is an **interpersonal** process of influencing, empowering, giving feedback and problem solving.
Achievement	The aim is to enable people to realise their potential and maximise their contribution to the organisation's success.

Other features of performance management described by Armstrong include:

(a) **Line management** – a performance management system is primarily the concern, not of experts in the personnel/HRM department, but of the managers responsible for driving the business.

(b) **Specific** – as each organisation has unique issues to face, performance management systems cannot really be bought off the shelf.

(c) **Future-based** – performance management is forward looking, based on the organisation's future needs and what the individual must do to satisfy them.

1.3 The process of performance management

A systematic approach to performance management might include the following steps.

Step 1. From the business plan, identify the requirements and competences required to carry it out.

Step 2. Draw up a performance agreement, defining the expectations of the individual or team, covering standards of performance, performance indicators and the skills and competences people need.

Step 3. Draw up a performance and development plan with the individual. These record the actions needed to improve performance, normally covering development in the current job. They are discussed with job holders and will cover, typically:

- The areas of performance the individual feels are in need of development

- What the individual and manager agree is needed to enhance performance

- Development and training initiatives

Step 4. Manage performance continually throughout the year, not just at appraisal interviews done to satisfy the personnel department. Managers can review actual performance, with more informal interim reviews at various times of the year.

High performance is reinforced by praise, recognition, increasing responsibility. Low performance results in coaching or counselling.

Work plans are updated as necessary.

Deal with performance problems by identifying what they are; establish the reasons for the shortfall; take control action (with adequate resources); and provide feedback.

Step 5. Performance review – at a defined period each year, success against the plan is reviewed, but the whole point is to assess what is going to happen in future.

Activity 1	**(10 mins)**

What are the advantages to employees of introducing such a system?

1.4 Goal setting

People are 'purposive' – that is, they act in pursuit of particular goals or purposes. The goals or objectives of an individual influence:

(a) What (s)he **perceives,** since we filter out messages not relevant to our goals and objectives and select those which are relevant

(b) What (s)he **learns,** since learning is a process of selecting and analysing experience in order to take it into account in acting in future, so that our goals and objectives may be more effectively met

(c) What (s)he **does,** since people behave in such a way as to satisfy their goals. This is the basis of motivation, since organisations can **motivate** people to behave in desirable ways (effective work performance) by offering them the means to fulfil their goals.

In order for learning and motivation to be effective, it is essential that **people know** exactly **what their objectives are.** This enables them to do the following.

(a) **Plan and direct their effort** towards the objectives

(b) **Monitor their performance** against objectives and adjust (or learn) if required

(c) Experience the **reward of achievement** once the objectives have been reached

(d) Feel that their tasks have **meaning and purpose,** which is an important element in job satisfaction

(e) Experience the **motivation of a challenge**: the need to expend energy and effort in a particular direction in order to achieve something

(f) Avoid the **de-motivation** of impossible or inadequately rewarded tasks. As we have in the chapter on motivation, there is a calculation involved in motivated performance. If objectives are vague, unrealistic or unattainable, there may be little incentive to pursue them: hence the importance of SMART objectives.

Some principles for devising performance measures are as follows.

Principle	Comment
Job-related	They should be related to the actual job, and the key tasks outlined in the job description
Controllable	People should not be assessed according to factors which they cannot control
Objective and observable	This is contentious. Certain aspects of performance can be measured, such as volume sales, but matters such as courtesy or friendliness which are important to some businesses are harder to measure
Data must be available	There is no use identifying performance measures if the data cannot actually be collected

Activity 2   (10 mins)

A senior sales executive has a job that involves: 'building the firm's sales' and maintaining 'a high degree of satisfaction with the company's products and services'. The firm buys sports equipment, running machines and so on, which it sells to gyms and individuals. The firm also charges fees to service the equipment. Service contracts are the sales executive's responsibility, and he has to manage that side of the business.

Here are some possible performance indicators to assess the sales executive's performance in the role. What do you think of them?

(a) Number of new customers gained per period

(b) Value of revenue from existing customers per period

(c) Renewal of service contracts

(d) Record of customer complaints about poor quality products

(e) Regular customer satisfaction survey

2   BENCHMARKING

2.1   Types of benchmarking

Definition

Benchmarking is a continuous, systematic, process for evaluating the products, services, and work processes of organisations that are recognised as representing best practices for the purpose of organisational improvement.

Through benchmarking, organisations learn about their own business practices and the best practices of others. Benchmarking enables them to identify where they fall short of current best practice and determine action programmes to help them match and surpass it.

Any activity that can be measured can be benchmarked. However, it is impracticable to benchmark every process and organisations should concentrate on areas that:

- Tie up most cash
- Significantly improve the relationship with customers, and
- Impact on the final results of the business

The choice of the activity to be benchmarked will determine the approach that needs to be taken. There are three primary types of benchmarking that are in use today.

(a) **Internal benchmarking** - in most large companies there are similar functions in different business units. One of the simplest benchmarking exercises is to compare these internal operations. It assumes there are differences in the work processes of an organisation as a result of geographical differences, local organisational history, customs, differences among business units, and relationships among managers and employees. The advantages include the information sharing that accompanies internal benchmarking and the immediate gains that can be obtained by identifying the best internal practices and transferring those to other parts of the organisation. The disadvantage of internal benchmarking is that it fosters an introverted view. It is all too easy to ignore that other organisations have the edge on you if you are concentrating on outperforming internal rivals.

(b) **Competitive benchmarking** concerns the identification of specific information about a competitor's products, processes, and business results to make comparisons with those of its own organisation. Direct competitors are the most obvious to benchmark against. The objective is to compare companies in the same markets that have competing products or services or work processes, eg Coca Cola and Pepsi.

The advantage of competitive benchmarking is that you can see what your relative performance is. The main disadvantage is that information is very hard to obtain, beyond that in the public domain. Where information may be commercially sensitive an appropriate third party can be used.

(c) **Process or activity benchmarks** - makes comparisons with organisations in different, non-competing product/service sectors but with similar core operations. They involve the identification of state-of-the-art products, services, or processes of an organisation that may or may not be a company's direct competitor. The objective of this type of benchmarking is to identify best practices in any type of organisation that has established a reputation for excellence in specific business activities such as manufacturing, marketing, engineering, warehousing, fleet management, or human resources eg, the recruitment process. The big advantage of this benchmarking is that it is easier to identify willing partners, since the information is not going to a direct competitor. The disadvantages are cost and the fact that the most renowned companies are beginning to feel overwhelmed with benchmarking visits and some are even charging a fee for access.

2.2 Benchmarking objective setting

Firms like Rank Xerox have developed employee involvement in setting their own objectives by encouraging them to benchmark their own activities against the best practice for doing their job. This is a very different approach from that used in some companies, where benchmarking is used as a 'stick' to set objectives. In the Xerox case, employees are encouraged to investigate the best practice for their activity and not only to find out what is achieved in terms of a numerical benchmark but also to discover *how* it can be achieved. The involvement is necessary to get the commitment to change required to achieve top performance.

This technique has been used to make substantial changes to systems and processes used not only in the main operational areas like sales, manufacturing and distribution but also in central areas like administration, finance and information systems.

3 FEEDBACK

3.1 Effective feedback

Definition

> **Feedback** is communication, which offers information to an individual or group about how their performance, results or behaviours are perceived or assessed by others.

Feedback relates closely to goal setting. Goals serve as targets for performance. When employees understand how they are attaining those goals, they can adjust their behaviour to perform more. Effective and timely feedback should motivate, encourage, and guide, while creating a positive environment.

Recognition, praise and encouragement create feelings of confidence, competence, development and progress that enhance the motivation to learn.

3.2 Types of feedback

There are two main types of feedback, both of which are valuable in enhancing performance and development.

(a) **Motivational feedback:** used to reward and reinforce positive behaviours and performance by praising and encouraging the individual, and allowing him or her to celebrate positive results, progress or improvements. Its purpose is to increase **confidence** and **motivation.**

(b) **Developmental feedback:** given when a particular area of performance needs to be improved, helping the individual to identify what needs to be changed and how this might be done. Its purpose is to increase **competence** and aid **learning.**

Feedback is a crucial tool in managing people – as in any control system.

(a) Positive feedback acts as a **reinforcer** or reward, which aids motivation and commitment.

(b) Negative feedback - delivered constructively provides **information for learning** processes: it supports goal setting and improvement planning.

(c) Feedback on performance **enriches work** by giving it meaning. It helps to integrate individual goals with team and organisational goals, adding to employees' satisfaction and commitment by giving them a sense of how their work is contributing to the whole.

(d) Feedback on progress helps employees to manage and adjust their **performance;** they know 'where they are' in relation to standards and targets.

(e) Ongoing feedback contributes to an effective **management style.** Rewards, sanctions and corrections are perceived to be more fair (and are less stressful for employees) if they are based on known performance standards and attainments. Feedback empowers employees to diagnose and solve their own performance problems.

Constructive feedback is designed to widen options and support development. This does not mean giving only encouraging or positive feedback when a person has done something well: feedback about undesirable behaviours or performance shortfalls, given skilfully, is in many ways more useful to the individual.

3.3 Giving feedback

Giving constructive feedback is an important leadership skill. It requires:

(a) **Assertiveness.** You must be prepared to give difficult messages and confront difficult issues where required.

(b) **Respect for others.** While being honest about other people's development/improvement needs, you must consider their right to be treated with respect.

(c) **Skill.** Giving effective feedback is a complex interpersonal skill.

The following are some general guidelines for giving constructive feedback.

(a) **Choose the right time.** Feedback should be given close to the event, so that the details are fresh in both parties' minds – but with sensitivity to the appropriate time and setting. Feedback is best given calmly and confidentially.

(b) **Start with positives.** People will more readily accept criticism as constructive if it is balanced with acknowledgement of positive aspects.

(c) **Focus on the behaviour.** Feedback needs to refer clearly to behaviours, actions and results – not the person or their personality. ('Tough on the problem, soft on the person' is a good general rule.)

(d) **Be accurate.** Feedback needs to be specific, avoiding vague and global statements (for example, not 'you're always late!' but 'on two occasions this week you have been more than fifteen minutes late for work') and avoiding inferences and assumptions.

(e) **Don't tackle everything at once.** Give the person one or two priority areas to deal with at a time.

(f) **Close with encouragement.** Balance negative feedback with positive encouragement that change is possible and will be supported by you and the organisation.

Activity 3 **(10 mins)**

Consider how easy or difficult you find it to receive feedback. See if you can come up with some guidelines for yourself on how to receive (possibly negative) feedback assertively, and how to make use of it constructively for your learning and development.

---

4 APPRAISAL PROCESSES

4.1 The purpose of appraisal

The process of appraisal is part of the system of performance management.

Definition

Performance appraisal is the process whereby an individual's performance is reviewed against previously agreed goals, and where new goals are agreed which will develop the individual and improve performance over the forthcoming review period.

The general purpose of any appraisal system is to improve the efficiency of the organisation by ensuring that the individuals within it are performing to the best of their ability and developing their potential for improvement.

(a) **Reward review.** Measuring the extent to which an employee is deserving of a bonus or pay increase as compared with his or her peers.

(b) **Performance review,** for planning and following up training and development programmes, ie identifying training needs, validating training methods and so on.

(c) **Potential review,** as an aid to planning career development and succession, by attempting to predict the level and type of work the individual will be capable of in the future.

4.2 Uses of appraisal

Jeannie Brownlow has decided to leave Gold and Silver where she has worked for five years as a supervisor. When the personnel manager asked for her reasons she said, 'I'm fed up. You don't know where you are here. No one tells you if you're doing the job well, but they jump on you like a ton of bricks if anything goes wrong. Talk about "no news is good news" – that's the way it is here'.

Monitoring and evaluating the performance of individuals and groups is an essential part of people-management. It has several uses.

(a) Identifying the current level of performance to provide a basis for informing, training and developing team members to a higher level.

(b) Identifying areas where improvement is needed in order to meet acceptable standards of performance.

(c) Identifying people whose performance suggests that they might be suitable for promotion in future.

(d) Measuring the individual's or team's level of performance against specific standards, to provide a basis for reward above the basic pay rate (in other words, individual or group bonuses).

(e) Measuring the performance of new team members against the organisation's (and team's) expectations, as a means of assessing whether selection procedures have been successful.

(f) Improving communication about work tasks between managers and team members, as a result of discussing the assessment.

(g) In the process of defining what performance should be, establishing what key results and standards must be reached for the unit to reach its objectives.

It may be argued that a particular, deliberate stock-taking exercise is unnecessary, since managers are constantly monitoring and making judgements about their subordinates and (theoretically) giving their subordinates feedback information from day to day.

4.3 Why have a system?

It must be recognised that, if no system of formal appraisal is in place:

(a) Managers may obtain random impressions of subordinates' performance (perhaps from their more noticeable successes and failures), but not a coherent, complete and objective picture

(b) Managers may have a fair idea of their subordinates' shortcomings – but may not have devoted time and attention to the matter of improvement and development

(c) Judgements are easy to make, but less easy to justify in detail, in writing, or to the subject's face

(d) Different managers may be applying a different set of criteria, and varying standards of objectivity and judgement, which undermines the value of appraisal for comparison, as well as its credibility in the eyes of employees

(e) Managers rarely give their subordinates adequate feedback on their performance. Most people dislike giving criticism as much as receiving it

Activity 4	**(15 mins)**

List four disadvantages to the individual of not having an appraisal system.

4.4 The process of appraisal

A typical system would therefore involve:

(a) Identification of **criteria** for assessment

(b) The preparation of an **appraisal report**

(c) An **appraisal interview**, for an exchange of views about the results of the assessment, targets for improvement, solutions to problems and so on

(d) The preparation and implementation of **action plans** to achieve improvements and changes agreed, and

(e) **Follow-up**: monitoring the progress of the action plan

Definition

A **criterion** (plural: **criteria**) is a factor or standard by which something can be judged or decided. For example, 'meeting output targets' is one criterion for judging work performance.

We will now look at each stage in turn. First of all, what is the basis of appraisal going to be?

4.5 What should be monitored and assessed?

Managers must broadly monitor and assess the same things, so that comparisons can be made between individuals. On the other hand, they need to take account of the fact that jobs are different, and make different demands on the jobholder. If every individual were rated on 'communication skills' and 'teamworking', for example, you might have a good basis for deciding who needed promoting or training – but what about a data inputter or research scientist who does not have to work in a team or communicate widely in your organisation?

Activity 5	**(20 mins)**
Think of some other criteria which you would want to use in assessment of some jobs – but which would not be applicable in others.	

There is also the important question of whether you assess **personality** or **performance**: in other words, do you assess what the individual is, or what (s)he does? Personal qualities like reliability or outgoingness have often been used as criteria for judging people. However, they are not necessarily relevant to job performance: you can be naturally outgoing, but still not good at communicating with customers, if your product knowledge or attitude is poor. Also, personality judgements are notoriously vague and unreliable: words like 'loyalty' and 'ambition' are full of ambiguity and moral connotations.

In practical terms, this has encouraged the use of competence or results-based appraisals, where performance is measured against specific, job-related performance criteria.

Choosing assessment criteria

So how does a manager choose what criteria to base the assessment on? Most large organisations have a system in place, with pre-printed assessment forms setting out all the relevant criteria and the range of possible judgements. (We reproduce such a form later in this chapter). Even so, a team manager should critically evaluate such schemes to ensure that the criteria for assessment are relevant to his or her team and task – and that they remain so over time, as the team and task change.

Relevant criteria for assessment might be based on the following.

(a) **Job analysis:** the process of examining a job, to identify its component tasks and skill requirements, and the circumstances in which it is performed.

Analysis may be carried out by observation, if the job is routine and repetitive it will be easy to see what it involves. Irregular jobs, with lots of 'invisible' work (planning, thinking, relationship-building and so on) will require interviews and discussions with superiors and with the job holders themselves, to find out what the job involves.

The product of job analysis is usually a **job specification** which sets out the activities (mental and physical) involved in the job, and other factors in its social and physical environment. Many of the aspects covered – aptitudes and abilities required, duties and responsibilities, ability to work under particular conditions (pressure, noise, hazards), tolerance of teamwork or isolation and so on – will suggest criteria for assessment.

(b) **Job descriptions:** more general descriptions of a job or position at a given time, including its purpose and scope, duties and responsibilities, relationship with other jobs, and perhaps specific objectives and expected results. A job description offers a guide to what competences, responsibilities and results might be monitored and assessed.

(c) **Departmental or team plans, performance standards and targets**. These are the most clear-cut of all. If the plan specifies completion of a certain number of tasks, or production of a certain number of units, to a particular quality

standard, assessment can be focused on whether (or how far) those targets have been achieved. (Personality and environmental factors may be relevant when investigating why performance has fallen short – but do not cloud the assessment of performance itself.)

Let us now look at some of the performance monitoring and reporting methods used in organisations.

5 APPRAISAL PROCEDURES

5.1 Monitoring and reporting

Overall assessment

This is much like a school report. The manager simply writes narrative judgements about the appraisee. The method is simple – but not always effective, since there is no guaranteed consistency of the criteria and areas of assessment from manager to manager (or appraisal to appraisal). In addition, managers may not be able to convey clear, precise or effective judgements in writing.

Guided assessment

Assessors are required to comment on a number of specified characteristics and performance elements, with guidelines as to how terms such as 'application', 'integrity' and 'adaptability' are to be interpreted in the work context. This is a more precise, but still rather vague method.

Grading

Grading adds a comparative frame of reference to the general guidelines. Managers are asked to select one of a number of levels or degrees (Grades 1–5 say) which describe the extent to which an individual displays a given characteristic. These are also known as rating scales, and have been much used in standard appraisal forms (for example, see the diagram of an appraisal form on the following page). Their effectiveness depends to a large extent on two things.

(a) **The relevance of the factors chosen for assessment.** These may be nebulous personality traits, for example, or clearly-defined work-related factors such as job knowledge, performance against targets, or decision-making.

(b) **The definition of the agreed standards or grades.** Grades A-D might simply be labelled 'Outstanding – Satisfactory – Fair – Poor', in which case assessments will be rather subjective and inconsistent. They may, on the other hand, be more closely related to work priorities and standards, using definitions such as 'Performance is good overall, and superior to that expected in some important areas', or 'Performance is broadly acceptable, but the employee needs training in several major areas and motivation is lacking'.

Numerical values may be added to gradings to give rating scores. Alternatively a less precise graphic scale may be used to indicate general position on a plus/minus scale.

Performance Classification

Outstanding performance is characterised by high ability which leaves little or nothing to be desired.

Personnel rated as such are those who regularly make significant contributions to the organisation which are above the requirements of their position. Unusual and challenging assignments are consistently well handled.

Excellent performance is marked by above-average ability, with little supervision required.

These employees may display some of the attributes present in 'outstanding' performance, but not on a sufficiently consistent basis to warrant that rating. Unusual and challenging assignments are normally well handled.

Satisfactory Plus performance indicates fully adequate ability, without the need for excessive supervision.

Personnel with this rating are able to give proper consideration to normal assignments, which are generally well handled. They will meet the requirements of the position. 'Satisfactory plus' performers may include those who lack the experience at their current level to demonstrate above-average ability.

Marginal performance is in instances where the ability demonstrated does not fully meet the requirements of the position, with excessive supervision and direction normally required.

Employees rated as such will show specific deficiencies in their performance which prevent them from performing at an acceptable level.

Unsatisfactory performance indicates an ability which falls clearly below the minimum requirements of the position.

'Unsatisfactory' performers will demonstrate marked deficiencies in most of the major aspects of their responsibilities, and considerable improvement is required to permit retention of the employee in his current position.

Personal Characteristics Ratings

1 – Needs considerable improvement – substantial improvement required to meet acceptable standards.

2 – Needs improvement – some improvement required to meet acceptable standards.

3 – Normal – meets acceptable standards.

4 – Above normal – exceeds normally acceptable standards in most instances.

5 – Exceptional – displays rare and unusual personal characteristics.

Personnel Appraisal: Employees in Salary Grades 5–8

Date of Review	Time on Position		S.G.	Age		Name	
	Yrs	Mths		Yrs			
Period of Review	Position Title					Area	

Important: Read guide notes carefully before proceeding with the following sections

Section One

Performance Factors	NA	U	M	SP	E	O	Section Two	Personal Characteristics				
								1	2	3	4	5
Administrative Skills							Initiative					
Communications – Written							Persistence					
Communications – Oral							Ability to work with others					
Problem Analysis							Adaptability					
Decision Making							Persuasiveness					
Delegation							Self-Confidence					
Quantity of Work							Judgement					
Development of Personnel							Leadership					
Development of Quality Improvements							Creativity					

Section Three Highlight Performance Factors and particular strengths/weaknesses of employee which significantly affect Job Performance

Overall Performance Rating (taking into account ratings given)

Prepared by: Signature .... Date .... Position Title ....

Section Four Comments by Reviewing Authority

	I R Review Initial

Signature .... Date .... Position Title .... Date

Section Five Supervisor's Notes on Counselling Interview

Signature .... Date .... Position Title ....

Section Six Employees Reactions and Comment

Signature .... Date ....

Figure 6.2 Example of an appraisal form

Results-orientated schemes

All the above techniques may be used with more or less results-orientated criteria. A wholly results-orientated approach sets out to review performance against specific targets and standards of performance, which are agreed – or even set – in advance by a manager and subordinate together. This is known as **performance management**.

5.2 Correcting under-performance

Employees do not always perform according to expectations. When there is evidence that an individual is not performing at an acceptable level, the manager should investigate the circumstances without delay and try to ascertain the reasons for the unsatisfactory performance. If, following this examination, the manager considers that the individual's performance is deficient in some material respect, an informal discussion with the member of staff will be arranged. At this meeting the manager will:

(a) Make clear the areas in which the individual's performance is below expectations (explaining the grounds/evidence for this view) with the aim of identifying any problems or reasons for the under-performance, which could be resolved. Solutions to the problem could include additional training, providing a mentor, coaching or some other kind of ongoing support to the individual.

(b) Give the individual the opportunity to explain their under-performance and to raise any concerns they may have about the job, or the support and guidance they have been given to do it. There are many reasons why people fail to deliver what is required of them. A previously good employee may be experiencing problems at home or the job may have become too tedious. The reasons for poor performance could significantly affect how this matter is resolved.

(c) Ensure that the member of staff is aware of the level of performance/ productivity required in relation to each element of the duties about which there is a concern.

(d) Set a reasonable timeframe within which improvement is expected and arrange a further meeting at the end of this time to review the situation. When establishing 'reasonable timescales' for improvement, managers must consider the complexity of the tasks involved in relation to the qualifications and experience of the individual.

The content and outcome of this meeting will be confirmed by the manager/supervisor in writing to the individual, including the type of improvement required, any additional support or training that will be provided, any other agreed actions and the timescale for improvement and review.

When discussing under-performance managers must be specific about their concerns and must demonstrate evidence and/or give examples to support their assertions. The consequences of continued under-performance need to be explained to the individual. For example, it could result in a freeze in salary, demotion or no opportunity to take part in new projects. It may be serious enough to warrant dismissal.

In introducing 'performance management', we have raised the possibility that an employee might be involved in monitoring and evaluating his or her own performance. If targets are clear, and the employee is able to be honest and objective, self-assessment may be both effective and satisfying.

5.3 Who does the appraising?

Organisations have begun to recognise that the employee's immediate boss is not the only (or necessarily the best) person to assess his or her performance. Other 'stakeholders' in the individual's performance might be better, including the people (s)he deals with on a day to day basis:

(a) The current (and perhaps previous) boss (including temporary supervisors)

(b) Peers and co-workers (peer appraisal)

(c) Subordinates; (upward appraisal)

(d) External customers or

(e) The employee him or herself (self appraisal)

5.4 360 degree feedback

360-degree feedback is an approach which collects comments and feedback on an individual's performance from all these sources (usually anonymously using questionnaires) and adds the individual's own self-assessment.

The advantages of 360-degree feedback are said to be as follows.

(a) It highlights every aspect of the individual's performance, and allows comparison of the individual's self-assessment with the views of others. (Rather revealing, in most cases.)

(b) Feedback tends to be balanced, covering strengths in some areas with weaknesses in others, so it is less discouraging.

(c) The assessment is based on real work – not artificial (eg interview) situations. The feedback is thus felt to be fairer and more relevant, making it easier for employees to accept the assessment and the need for change and development.

Activity 6   **(20 mins)**

Peter Ward, who introduced 360-degree feedback at Tesco in 1987, gives an example of the kinds of questionnaire that might be used as the instrument of 360-degree feedback. 'A skill area like "communicating", for example, might be defined as "the ability to express oneself clearly and to listen effectively to others". Typical comments would include "Presents ideas or information in a well-organised manner" (followed by rating scale); or: "Allows you to finish what you have to say".'

Rate yourself on the two comments mentioned here, on a scale of 1–10. Get a group of friends, fellow-students, even a tutor or parent, to write down, anonymously, on a piece of paper their rating for you on the same two comments. Keep them in an envelope, unseen, until you have a few.

Compare them with your self-rating. If you dare... What drawbacks did you (and your respondents) find to such an approach?

5.5 Upward appraisal

A notable modern trend, adopted in the UK by companies such as BP, British Airways and some television companies, is upward appraisal, whereby employees are rated not by their superiors but by their subordinates. The followers appraise the leader.

The advantages of this method might be as follows.

(a) Subordinates tend to know their (one) superior better than superiors know their (many) subordinates.

(b) Instead of the possible bias of an individual manager's ratings, the various ratings of several employees may reflect a rounded view.

(c) Subordinates' ratings have more impact, because it is less usual to receive feedback from below: a manager's view of good management may be rather different from a team's view of being managed!

(d) Upward appraisal encourages subordinates to give feedback and raise problems they may have with their boss, which otherwise would be too difficult or risky for them.

Activity 7 (15 mins)

Imagine you had to do an upward appraisal on your boss, parent or teacher. Suggest the two major problems that might be experienced with upward appraisal.

Having reported on an individual's performance – whether in a written narrative comment, or on a prepared appraisal form – a manager must discuss the content of the report with the individual concerned.

5.6 The appraisal interview

There are basically three ways of approaching appraisal interviews.

(a) The **tell and sell** method. The manager tells the subordinate how (s)he has been assessed, and then tries to 'sell' (gain acceptance of) the evaluation and any improvement plans.

(b) The **tell and listen** method. The manager tells the subordinate how (s)he has been assessed, and then invites comments. The manager therefore no longer dominates the interview throughout, and there is greater opportunity for

 PROFESSIONAL EDUCATION

counselling as opposed to pure direction. The employee is encouraged to participate in the assessment and the working out of improvement targets and methods; change in the employee may not be the sole key to improvement, and the manager may receive helpful feedback about job design, methods, environment or supervision.

(c) The **problem-solving** approach. The manager abandons the role of critic altogether, and becomes a counsellor and helper. The discussion is centred not on assessment of past performance, but on future solutions of the employee's work problems. The employee is encouraged to recognise the problems, think solutions through, and commit himself to improvement. This approach is more involving and satisfying to the employee and may also stimulate creative problem-solving.

EXAMPLE

A survey of appraisal interviews given to 252 officers in a UK government department found that:

(a) Interviewers have difficulty with negative performance feedback (criticism), and tend to avoid it if possible

(b) Negative performance feedback (criticism) is, however, more likely to bring forth positive post-appraisal action, and is favourably received by appraisees, who feel it is the most useful function of the whole process, if handled frankly and constructively

(c) The most common fault of interviewers is talking too much

The survey recorded the preference of appraisees for a 'problem-solving' style of participative interview, over a one-sided 'tell and sell' style.

Many organisations waste the opportunity represented by appraisal for **upward communication**. If an organisation is working towards empowerment, it should harness the aspirations and abilities of its employees by asking positive and thought-provoking questions.

(a) Do you fully understand your job? Are there any aspects you wish to be made clearer?

(b) What parts of your job do you do best?

(c) Could any changes be made in your job which might result in improved performance?

(d) Have you any skills, knowledge, or aptitudes which could be made better use of in the organisation?

(e) What are your career plans? How do you propose achieving your ambitions in terms of further training and broader experience?

5.7 Follow-up

After the appraisal interview, the manager may complete his or her report with an overall assessment and/or the jointly-reached conclusion of the interview, with recommendations for follow-up action. This may take the following forms.

(a) Informing appraisees of the results of the appraisal, if this has not been central to the review interview. (Some people argue that there is no point making appraisals if they are not openly discussed, but unless managers are competent and committed to reveal results in a constructive, frank and objective manner, the negative reactions on all sides may outweigh the advantages.)

(b) Carrying out agreed actions on training, promotion and so on.

(c) Monitoring the appraisee's progress and checking that (s)he has carried out agreed actions or improvements.

(d) Taking necessary steps to help the appraisee to attain improvement objectives, by guidance, providing feedback, upgrading equipment, altering work methods or whatever.

If follow-up action is not taken, employees will feel that appraisal is all talk and just a waste of time, and that improvement action on their side will not be appreciated or worthwhile.

5.8 Assessing potential

Definition

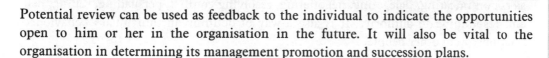
Potential review is the use of appraisal to forecast where and how fast an individual is progressing.

Potential review can be used as feedback to the individual to indicate the opportunities open to him or her in the organisation in the future. It will also be vital to the organisation in determining its management promotion and succession plans.

Information for potential assessment will include:

(a) Strengths and weaknesses in the employee's existing skills and qualities

(b) Possibilities and strategies for improvement, correction and development

(c) The employee's goals, aspirations and attitudes, with regard to career advancement, staying with the organisation and handling responsibility

(d) The opportunities available in the organisation, including likely management vacancies, job rotation/enrichment plans and promotion policies for the future

No single review exercise will mark an employee down for life as 'promotable' or otherwise. The process tends to be on-going, with performance at each stage or level in the employee's career indicating whether (s)he might be able to progress to the next step. However, an approach based on performance in the current job is highly fallible. L J Peter pointed out that managers tend to be promoted from positions in which they have proved themselves competent, until one day they reach a level at which they are no longer competent – promoted 'to the level of their own incompetence'!

Moreover, the management succession plan of an organisation needs to be formulated in the long term. It takes a long time to equip a manager with the skills and experience needed at senior levels, and the organisation must develop people continuously if it is to fill the shoes of departing managers without crisis.

Some idea of **potential** must therefore be built into appraisal. It is impossible to predict with any certainty how successful an individual will be in what will, after all, be different circumstances from anything (s)he has experienced so far. However, some attempt can be made to:

(a) Determine key **indicators of potential:** in other words, elements believed to be essential to management success; these include past track record, and also administrative, interpersonal and analytical skills; leadership; orientation towards work, and a taste for making money; or a suitable mix of any of these

(b) Simulate the conditions of the position to which the individual would be promoted, to assess his or her performance. This may be achieved using case studies, role plays, presentations or team discussions and so on. An alternative approach might be to offer some **real** experience (under controlled conditions) by appointing the individual to assistant or deputy positions or to committees or project teams, and assessing his or her performance. This is still no real predictor of his or her ability to handle the **whole** job, on a continuous basis and over time, however, and it may be risky, if the appraisee fails to cope with the situation

6 INTERPERSONAL SKILLS AND FEEDBACK

6.1 Interpersonal behaviour

Interpersonal behaviour describes interaction between people – a two way process such as communicating, delegating, negotiating, resolving conflict, persuading, selling, using and responding to authority. It is also a way of defining an individual's behaviour in relationship to other people.

The way you behave in response to other people includes:

(a) How you perceive other people
(b) Listening to and understanding other people
(c) Behaving in a way that builds on this understanding
(d) Giving and receiving feedback

We use feedback information on the results of past behaviour to make rational decisions about whether to maintain successful behaviours or modify unsuccessful behaviours in the future, according to our goals and our plans for reaching them.

Development options that improve employees' effectiveness in their current jobs are called 'position related' while those that develop opportunities for career advancement are called 'career related'.

We are going to explain three activities that could be considered appropriate for employee development – coaching, mentoring and counselling.

6.2 Coaching

Managers help employees achieve objectives on a daily basis. Coaching is a behavioural control technique used by the manager to give on-going guidance and instruction, to follow day-to-day progress, and to give feedback.

Coaching is the ability to improve the job performance of employees. It is active, instead of passive, and is involved with guiding performance. Managers, who emphasise formal training and day-to-day coaching, reap the benefits of competence, high performance, commitment and co-operative behaviour.

The coaching process includes the following steps.

(a) **Establish learning targets** – the areas to be learned about should be identified and specific, realistic goals, eg completion dates or performance standards stated by agreement with the trainee

(b) **Plan a systematic learning and development programme** – this will ensure regular progress and appropriate stages for consolidation and practice

(c) **Identify opportunities for broadening the trainee's knowledge and experience** – eg by involvement in new products, placement on inter-departmental committees, suggesting new contacts or simply extending the job by adding more tasks, greater responsibility etc

(d) **Take into account the strengths and limitations of the trainee** in learning, and take advantage of learning opportunities that suit the trainee's ability, preferred style and goals.

(e) **Exchange feedback** – the coach will want to know how the trainee sees his or her progress and future and will also need performance information to monitor the trainee's progress, adjust the learning programme if necessary, identify further needs which may emerge and plan future development for the trainee

6.3 Mentoring

Mentoring is a process where one person offers help, guidance, advice and support to facilitate the learning or development of another.

Mentors can assist in:

(a) Drawing up personal development plans
(b) Advice with administrative problems people face in their new jobs
(c) Help in tackling projects, by pointing people in the right direction

Mentoring should not be seen as an additional or supplementary management task. It is an approach to management that puts the learning and development of the person at the heart of the process, offering advice and guidance to facilitate development. It is a good way of breaking down internal barriers between departments or groups and promoting equal opportunities. Mentoring offers a constructive alternative to the more traditional development methods by:

(a) Giving structure and continuity to development in the workplace

(b) Providing learners with a sounding board and facility for trust and confidentiality

(c)   Focusing learning on the learner, not the tutor

    (d)   Transferring knowledge and skills

    (e)   Enabling quicker and more effective induction on new employees

    (f)   Providing structure for improved succession planning

    (g)   Enabling learners to focus on their own experience

    (h)   Allowing failure to be tolerated and used as a learning tool

    (i)   Helping the learner to solve real problems and make real decisions

    (j)   Providing continuous personal support and motivation

6.4 Counselling

Unlike mentoring, which focuses on learning and supporting the learner through the learning process, and coaching which focuses on the task and ensuring that the learner gains competence, counselling focuses on the person and enabling an individual to explore situations and responses.

Counselling can be defined as 'a purposeful relationship in which one persons helps another to help himself. It is a way of relating and responding to another person so that that person is helped to explore his thoughts, feelings and behaviour with the aim of reaching a clearer understanding. The clearer understanding may be of himself or of a problem, or of one in relation to the other' (Rees).

The need for workplace counselling can arise in many situations, eg:

    (a) during appraisal
    (b) in grievance or disciplinary situations
    (c) following change, such as promotion or relocation
    (d) on redundancy or dismissal
    (e) as a result of personal or domestic difficulties
    (f) in cases of sexual harassment or violence at work

Effective counselling is not merely a matter of pastoral care for individuals but is very much in the organisation's interests. The benefits include the following.

    (a)   Prevents underperformance, reduces labour turnover and absenteeism and increases commitment from employees

    (b)   Demonstrates an organisation's commitment to and concern for its employees

    (c)   Gives employees the confidence and encouragement necessary to take responsibility for self and career development

    (d)   Recognises that the organisation may be contributing to the employee's problems and therefore provides an opportunity to reassess organisational policy and practice

7 DISCIPLINARY SITUATIONS

7.1 Discipline

Definition

> **Discipline** can be considered as: 'a condition in an enterprise in which there is orderliness in which the members of the enterprise behave sensibly and conduct themselves according to the standards of acceptable behaviour as related to the goals of the organisation'.

Another definition of 'positive' and 'negative' discipline makes the distinction between methods of maintaining sensible conduct and orderliness which are technically co-operative, and those based on warnings, threats and punishments.

(a) **Positive (or constructive) discipline** relates to procedures, systems and equipment in the work place which have been designed specifically so that the employee has **no option** but to act in the desired manner to complete a task safely and successfully. A machine may, for example, shut off automatically if its safety guard is not in place.

(b) **Negative discipline** is then the promise of **sanctions** designed to make people choose to behave in a desirable way. Disciplinary action may be punitive (punishing an offence), deterrent (warning people not to behave in that way) or reformative (calling attention to the nature of the offence, so that it will not happen again).

The best discipline is **self discipline**. Even before they start to work, most mature people accept the idea that following instructions and fair rules of conduct are normal responsibilities that are part of any job. Most team members can therefore be counted on to exercise self discipline.

7.2 Types of disciplinary situations

There are many types of disciplinary situations which require attention by the manager. Internally, the most frequently occurring are these.

- Excessive absenteeism

- Poor timekeeping

- Defective and/or inadequate work performance

- Poor attitudes which influence the work of others or reflect on the image of the firm

- Breaking rules regarding rest periods and other time schedules

- Improper personal appearance

- Breaking safety rules

- Other violations of rules, regulations and procedures

- Open insubordination such as the refusal to carry out a work assignment.

Managers might be confronted with disciplinary problems stemming from employee behaviour *off* the job. These may be an excessive drinking problem, the use of drugs or some form of narcotics, or involvement in some form of law breaking activity. In such circumstances, whenever an employee's off-the-job conduct has an impact upon performance on the job, the manager must be prepared to deal with such a problem within the scope of the disciplinary process.

7.3 Disciplinary action

The purpose of discipline is not punishment or retribution. Disciplinary action must have as its goal the improvement of the future behaviour of the employee and other members of the organisation. The purpose obviously is the avoidance of similar occurrences in the future.

The suggested steps of progressive disciplinary action follow ACAS guidelines.

Step 1. **The informal talk**

If the infraction is of a relatively minor nature and if the employee's record has no previous marks of disciplinary action, an informal, friendly talk will clear up the situation in many cases. Here the manager discusses with the employee his or her behaviour in relation to standards which prevail within the enterprise.

Step 2. **Oral warning or reprimand**

In this type of interview between employee and manager, the latter emphasises the undesirability of the subordinate's repeated violation, and that ultimately it could lead to serious disciplinary action.

Step 3. **Written or official warning**

These are part of the ACAS code of practice (shown later in this chapter). A written warning is of a formal nature insofar as it becomes a permanent part of the employee's record. Written warnings, not surprisingly, are particularly necessary in unionised situations, so that the document can serve as evidence in case of grievance procedures.

Step 4. **Disciplinary layoffs, or suspension**

This course of action would be next in order if the employee has committed repeated offences and previous steps were of no avail. Disciplinary lay-offs usually extend over several days or weeks. Some employees may not be very impressed with oral or written warnings, but they will find a disciplinary layoff without pay a rude awakening.

Step 5. **Demotion**

This course of action is likely to bring about dissatisfaction and discouragement, since losing pay and status over an extended period of time is a form of constant punishment. This dissatisfaction of the demoted employee may easily spread to co-workers, so most enterprises avoid downgrading as a disciplinary measure.

Step 6. **Discharge**

Discharge is a drastic form of disciplinary action, and should be reserved for the most serious offences. For the organisation, it involves waste of a labour resource, the expense of training a new employee, and disruption caused by changing the make-up of the work team. There also may be damage to the morale of the group.

> **Activity 8** **(15 mins)**
>
> How (a) accessible and (b) clear are the rules and policies of your organisation/office: do people really know what they are and are not supposed to do? Have a look at the rule book or procedures manual in your office. How easy is it to see – or did you get referred elsewhere? is the rule book well-indexed and cross-referenced, and in language that all employees will understand?
>
> How (a) accessible and (b) clear are the disciplinary procedures in your office? Are the employees' rights of investigation and appeal clearly set out, with ACAS guidelines? Who is responsible for discipline?

7.4 Relationship management in disciplinary situations

Even if the manager uses sensitivity and judgement, imposing disciplinary action tends to generate resentment because it is an unpleasant experience. The challenge is to apply the necessary disciplinary action so that it will be least resented.

(a) **Immediacy**

Immediacy means that after noticing the offence, the manager proceeds to take disciplinary action as *speedily* as possible, subject to investigations while at the same time avoiding haste and on-the-spot emotions which might lead to unwarranted actions.

(b) **Advance warning**

Employees should know in advance (eg in a Staff Handbook) what is expected of them and what the rules and regulations are.

(c) **Consistency**

Consistency of discipline means that each time an infraction occurs appropriate disciplinary action is taken. Inconsistency in application of discipline lowers the morale of employees and diminishes their respect for the manager.

(d) **Impersonality**

Penalties should be connected with the act and not based upon the personality involved, and once disciplinary action has been taken, no grudges should be borne.

(e) **Privacy**

As a general rule (unless the manager's authority is challenged directly and in public) disciplinary action should be taken in private, to avoid the spread of conflict and the humiliation or martyrdom of the employee concerned.

7.5 Disciplinary interviews

Preparation for the disciplinary interview

(a) **Gathering the facts** about the alleged infringement

(b) **Determination of the organisation's position:** how valuable is the employee, potentially? How serious are his offences/lack of progress? How far is the organisation prepared to go to help him improve or discipline him further?

(c) **Identification of the aims of the interview:** punishment? deterrent to others? improvement? Specific standards of future behaviour/performance required need to be determined.

(d) **Ensure that the organisation's disciplinary procedures have been followed**

    (i) Informal oral warnings (at least) have been given.

    (ii) The employee has been given adequate notice of the interview for his own preparation.

    (iii) The employee has been informed of the complaint against his right to be accompanied by a colleague or representative and so on.

7.6 The content of the disciplinary interview

Step 1. The manager will explain the purpose of the interview.

Step 2. The charges against the employee will be delivered, clearly, unambiguously and without personal emotion.

Step 3. The manager will explain the organisation's position with regard to the issues involved: disappointment, concern, need for improvement, impact on others. This can be done frankly – but tactfully, with as positive an emphasis as possible on the employee's capacity and responsibility to improve.

Step 4. The organisation's expectations with regard to future behaviour/performance should be made clear.

Step 5. The employee should be given the opportunity to comment, explain, justify or deny. If he is to approach the following stage of the interview in a positive way, he must not be made to feel 'hounded' or hard done by.

Step 6. The organisation's expectations should be reiterated, or new standards of behaviour set for the employee.

    (i) They should be specific and quantifiable, performance related and realistic.

    (ii) They should be related to a practical but reasonably short time period. A date should be set to review his progress.

    (iii) The manager agrees on measures to help the employee should that be necessary. It would demonstrate a positive approach if, for example, a mentor were appointed from his work group to help him check his work. If his poor performance is genuinely the result of some difficulty or distress outside work, other help (temporary leave, counselling or financial aid) may be appropriate.

Step 7. The manager should explain the reasons behind any penalties imposed on the employee, including the entry in his personnel record of the formal warning. He should also explain how the warning can be removed from the record, and what standards must be achieved within a specified timescale. There should be a clear warning of the consequences of failure to meet improvement targets.

Step 8. The manager should explain the organisation's appeals procedures: if the employee feels he has been unfairly treated, there should be a right of appeal to a higher manager.

Step 9. Once it has been established that the employee understands all the above, the manager should summarise the proceedings briefly.

Records of the interview will be kept for the employee's personnel file, and for the formal follow-up review and any further action necessary.

Activity 9   **(20 mins)**

Outline the steps involved in a formal disciplinary procedure (for an organisation with unionised employees) and show how the procedure would operate in a case of:

(a) Persistent absenteeism

(b) Theft of envelopes from the organisation's offices

7.7 The ACAS Code of Practice

This highlights the features of a good disciplinary system.

ACAS Code of Practice

Disciplinary and grievance procedures should:

- be in written form*
- specify to whom they apply (all, or only some of the employees?)
- be capable of dealing speedily with disciplinary matters
- indicate the forms of disciplinary action which may be taken (such as dismissal, suspension or warning)
- specify the appropriate levels of authority for the exercise of disciplinary actions
- provide for individuals to be informed of the nature of their alleged misconduct
- allow individuals to state their case, and to be accompanied by a fellow employee (or union representative)
- ensure that every case is properly investigated before any disciplinary action is taken
- ensure that employees are informed of the reasons for any penalty they receive
- state that no employee will be dismissed for a first offence, except in cases of gross misconduct
- provide for a right of appeal against any disciplinary action, and specify the appeals procedure

* The ACAS code of practice does not extend to informal 'first warnings', but these are an important part of the organisation's policy: don't forget them!

NOTES

8 GRIEVANCE

Definition

> A **grievance** occurs when an individual thinks that he is being wrongly treated by his colleagues or supervisor; perhaps he or she is being picked on, unfairly appraised in his annual report, unfairly blocked for promotion or discriminated against on grounds of race or sex.

When an individual has a grievance he should be able to pursue it and ask to have the problem resolved. Some grievances should be capable of solution informally by the individual's manager. However, if an informal solution is not possible, there should be a formal grievance procedure.

8.1 Grievance procedures

Formal grievance procedures, like disciplinary procedures, should be set out in **writing** and made available to all staff. These procedures should do the following things.

(a) State what **grades of employee** are entitled to pursue a particular type of grievance.

(b) State the **rights of the employee** for each type of grievance. For example, an employee who is not invited to attend a promotion/selection panel might claim that he has been unfairly passed over. The grievance procedure must state what the individual would be entitled to claim. In our example, the employee who is overlooked for promotion might be entitled to a review of his annual appraisal report, or to attend a special appeals promotion/selection board if he has been in his current grade for at least a certain number of years.

(c) State what the **procedures for pursuing a grievance** should be.

Step 1. The individual should discuss the grievance with a staff/union representative (or a colleague). If his case seems a good one, he should take the grievance to his immediate boss.

Step 2. The first interview will be between the immediate boss (unless he is the subject of the complaint, in which case it will be the next level up) and the employee, who has the right to be accompanied by a colleague or representative.

Step 3. If the immediate boss cannot resolve the matter, or the employee is otherwise dissatisfied with the first interview, the case should be referred to his own superior (and if necessary in some cases, to an even higher authority).

Step 4. Cases referred to a higher manager should also be reported to the personnel department. Line management might decide at some stage to ask for the assistance/advice of a personnel manager in resolving the problem.

(d) **Distinguish between individual grievances and collective grievances.** Collective grievances might occur when a work group as a whole considers that it is being badly treated.

(e) Allow for the **involvement of an individual's or group's trade union** or staff association representative. Indeed, many individuals and groups might prefer to initiate some grievance procedures through their union or association rather than through official grievance procedures. Involvement of a union representative from the beginning should mean that management and union will have a common view of what procedures should be taken to resolve the matter.

(f) **State time limits** for initiating certain grievance procedures and subsequent stages of them. For example, a person who is passed over for promotion should be required to make his appeal within a certain time period of his review, and his appeal to higher authority (if any) within a given period after the first grievance interview. There should also be timescales for management to determine and communicate the outcome of the complaint to the employee.

(g) **Require written records** of all meetings concerned with the case to be made and distributed to all the participants.

8.2 Grievance interviews

The dynamics of a grievance interview are broadly similar to a disciplinary interview, except that it is the subordinate who primarily wants a positive result from it. Prior to the interview, the manager should have some idea of the complaint and its possible source. The meeting itself can then proceed through three phases.

Step 1. **Exploration**. What is the problem: the background, the facts, the causes (manifest and hidden)? At this stage, the manager should simply try to gather as much information as possible, without attempting to suggest solutions or interpretations: the situation must be seen to be open.

Step 2. **Consideration**. The manager should:

(i) Check the facts

(ii) Analyse the causes – the problem of which the complaint may be only a symptom

(iii) Evaluate options for responding to the complaint, and the implication of any response made

It may be that information can be given to clear up a misunderstanding, or the employee will – having 'got it off his chest' – withdraw his complaint. However, the meeting may have to be adjourned (say, for 48 hours) while the manager gets extra information and considers extra options.

Step 3. **Reply**. The manager, having reached and reviewed his conclusions, reconvenes the meeting to convey (and justify, if required) his decision, hear counter-arguments and appeals. The outcome (agreed or disagreed) should be recorded in writing.

Grievance procedures should be seen as an employee's right. To this end, managers should be given formal training in the grievance procedures of their organisation, and the reasons for having them. Management should be persuaded that the grievance procedures are beneficial for the organisation and are not a threat to themselves (since many grievances arise out of disputes between subordinates and their boss).

Activity 10   **(20 mins)**

Find your organisation's grievance procedures in the office manual, or ask your union or staff association representative. Study the procedures carefully. Think of a complaint or grievance you have (or have had) at work. Have you taken it to grievance procedures? If so, what happened: were you satisfied with the process and outcome? If not, why not?

---

9   RELEVANT LEGISLATION

As with other areas of employment, there are statutes that cover the disciplinary and grievance procedures in an organisation. These include dismissal and the termination of employment.

9.1   Termination of employment

The Employment Rights Act 1996 lays down minimum periods of notice for both employer and employee. A contract of employment may not permit either side to give less than the minimum period of notice. However, either party may waive his right to notice or take a payment in lieu, and the Act does not affect the right to terminate a contract without notice in the event of gross misconduct.

The contract of employment may be terminated by either party for any reason or for no reason upon giving notice of a reasonable length, unless the contract is one for a fixed term or unless it specifically restricts the reason for which it may be terminated.

At common law either party may lawfully terminate the contract summarily, eg sacking without giving any notice, if the other party has committed a serious breach of the contract. The general principle justifying summary dismissal is that the employee's conduct prevents further satisfactory continuance of the employer-employee relationship, eg misconduct including disobedience, insolence and rudeness, committing a criminal act such as stealing, or causing injury through practical jokes.

9.2   Dismissal

Dismissal is the ultimate sanction in any disciplinary procedure. However, dismissals occur most frequently in the form of redundancy. Statistics published by the Department of Employment list the major reasons for dismissal as redundancy, sickness, unsuitability and misconduct in that order. Legislation in Britain during the 1970s, notably the Industrial Relations Act 1971, the Trades Unions and Labour Relations Act 1974 and the Employment Protection Act 1975, the Employment Protection (Consolidation) Act 1978 and the Employment Rights Act 1996, makes it a difficult and costly business to dismiss employees because of the provisions for employees to challenge the employer's decision. However, in recent statistics published by the Department of Employment it was revealed that only a proportion of cases of unfair dismissal actually reach employment tribunals; the majority are dealt with by some form of conciliation and arbitration.

Dismissal may be fair or unfair:

Fair dismissal – there is a statutory obligation for an employer to show that a dismissal is fair. In this case a dismissal is fair if it is related to:

(a) **A lack of capability or qualifications** – where the employee lacks the qualifications, skill, aptitude or health to do the job properly. However, in all cases the employee must be given the opportunity to improve the position or in the case of health be considered for alternative employment.

(b) **Misconduct** includes the refusal to obey lawful and reasonable instructions, absenteeism, insubordination over a period of time and some criminal actions. In the last case, the criminal action should relate directly to the job; it can only be grounds for dismissal if the result of the criminal action will affect the work in some way.

(c) **A statutory bar** occurs when employees cannot pursue their normal duties without breaking the law, eg drivers who have been banned.

Unfair dismissal – in all cases there are two stages of proof. Firstly, the circumstances that represent fair grounds for dismissal must be established, and secondly, the tribunal must decide whether dismissal is fair in the circumstances of the case in question.

For dismissal to be automatically unfair, it must be for one of the following reasons.

(a) Trade union membership or non-membership
(b) Pregnancy
(c) Sex or race discrimination
(d) Revelation of a non-relevant spent conviction

9.3 Provisions for unfair dismissal

Where employees feel that they have been unfairly dismissed they have the right to take their case to the industrial tribunal. The tribunal will normally refer the case to ACAS (Advisory Conciliation and Arbitration Service) in the hope of gaining an amicable settlement. The possible solutions or remedies for unfair dismissal include:

(a) **Withdrawal of notice** by the employer. This is the preferred remedy as stated in the Employment Rights Act.

(b) **Reinstatement (order of industrial tribunal)** – this treats the employee as though he or she had never been dismissed. The employee is taken back to his old job with no loss of earnings and privileges.

(c) **Re-engagement (order of industrial tribunal)** – the employee is offered a different job in the organisation and loses continuity of service. Both reinstatement and re-engagement were provisions introduced by the Employment Protection Act 1975.

(d) **Compensation (order of industrial tribunal)** – if an employer refuses to re-employ then the employee receives compensation made up of a penalty award of 13-26 weeks' pay (more in the case of discrimination), a payment equivalent to the redundancy entitlement and an award to compensate for loss of earnings, pension rights and so on. Some form of compensation may also be appropriate in cases of reinstatement and re-engagement.

9.4 Prevent discrimination and value diversity

The practical implications of the legislation for employers are set out in **Codes of Practice**, issued by the Commission for Racial Equality and the Equal Opportunities Commission. These do not have the force of law, but may be taken into account by employment tribunals, where discrimination cases are brought before them. Many organisations now establish their own policy statements or codes of practice on equal opportunities: apart from anything else, a statement of the organisation's position may provide some protection in the event of complaints.

Every business wants the best person for the job. Unequal treatment, prejudice or harassment discredits the business – and can be very costly. An employee may hold the owner or manager responsible for any discriminatory action.

It is unlawful to discriminate on the grounds of someone's sex (including gender reassignment), sexual orientation, marital status, race, colour, nationality, ethnic origin, religion, beliefs or because of a disability, pregnancy or childbirth or because they are a member or non-member of a trade union. From 1 October 2004 the Government will extend the currently available protection to disabled people.

If a person feels they are discriminated against unlawfully, they may take a case to an employment tribunal. This could lead to heavy penalties for the employer and in the absence of an appropriate explanation, employment tribunals are required to infer that discrimination has occurred. It is also important to bear in mind that anti-discrimination legislation applies equally to part-time workers. It's against the law to discriminate against them because of their part-time status.

To prevent discrimination in day-to-day working practices means finding it.

- **Direct discrimination** is generally easily recognisable, where someone is denied employment because of race, gender, sexual orientation etc.

- **Indirect discrimination,** however, can be harder to detect and may often be unintentional.

Anti discriminatory practices consists of four elements.

(a) **Knowledge** – knowing and recognising how prejudice and discrimination work and understanding the processes at work. How our culture has influenced our thinking.

(b) **Values** – understanding our personal values and how this affects our attitudes and behaviour. Recognising personal prejudices and seeking to overcome them. Recognising where personal and organisational values differ. Performance can suffer and stress levels can rise.

(c) **Skills** – applying knowledge and values to practice. Using communication skills appropriately. Being self aware and dealing with people appropriately despite prejudices. Reflecting on performance.

(d) **Experience** – continuous development through experience and increased knowledge. Reflecting on experiences, both positive and negative, and learning from them. Learning from experiences of others.

Employer's responses

Most employers produce policies that set out the rules and procedures their staff need to know. A policy statement may help employees to understand what the employer expects of them, and their legal rights and obligations.

Some organisations make minimal efforts to avoid discrimination, paying lip service to the idea only to the extent of claiming 'We are an Equal Opportunities Employer' on advertising literature. To turn such a claim into reality, the following are needed.

(a) **Support** from the top of the organisation for the formulation of a practical policy

(b) A **working party** drawn from – for example – management, unions, minority groups, the HR function and staff representatives. This group's brief will be to produce a draft Policy and Code of Practice, which will be approved at senior level

(c) **Action plans and resources** (including staff) to implement and monitor the policy, publicise it to staff, arrange training and so on

(d) **Monitoring**. The numbers of women and ethnic minority staff can easily be monitored

- On entering (and applying to enter) the organisation
- On leaving the organisation
- On applying for transfers, promotions or training schemes

(It is less easy to determine the ethnic origins of the workforce through such methods as questionnaires: there is bound to be suspicion about the question's motives, and it may be offensive to some workers.)

Another response by employers is to take positive action.

Definition

Positive action: the process of taking active steps to encourage people from disadvantaged groups to apply for jobs and training, and to compete for vacancies. (Note that this is not positive discrimination.)

Examples of positive discrimination might be: using ethnic languages in job advertisements, or implementing training for women in management skills. The **Race Relations (Amendment) Act 2000** requires larger public organisations (more than 150 employees) to draw up detailed plans for achieving racial equality in all employment practices, for example.

NOTES

Chapter roundup

- Performance management suggests that people must agree performance standards, that the responsibility for performance management is principally that of line management and that it is a conscious commitment to developing and managing people in organisations. It is a continuous process.

- Benchmarking is a continuous systematic process for evaluating the products, services and work processes of organisations that are recognised as representing best practices for the purpose of organisational improvement.

- Feedback is communication, which offers information to an individual or group about how their performance, results or behaviours are perceived or assessed by others.

- There are two main types of feedback – motivational feedback and developmental feedback.

- Giving feedback requires assertiveness, respect for others and skill.

- Appraisal is part of the system of performance management, including goal setting, performance monitoring, feedback and improvement planning.

- Appraisal can be used to reward but also to identify potential, and to plan training, development and improvement programmes.

- A variety of appraisal techniques can be used to measure different criteria in different ways.

- New techniques of appraisal aim to monitor the appraisee's effectiveness from a number of perspectives, including self-appraisal, upward appraisal and 360-degree feedback.

- Coaching is a behavioural control technique used by the manager to give on-going guidance and instruction, to follow day-to-day progress and to give feedback.

- Mentoring is a process where one person offers help, guidance, advice and support to facilitate the learning or development of another.

- Discipline has the same end as motivation – ie to secure a range of desired behaviour from members of the organisation.

- Progressive discipline includes the following stages – informal talk, oral warning, written/official warning, lay-off or suspension and dismissal.

- Grievance procedures embody the employee's right to appeal against unfair or otherwise prejudicial conduct or conditions that affect him and his work.

- Grievance interviews follow: exploration, consideration, reply.

- Legislation that applies to discipline and grievance relates to dismissal and termination of employment as set out in the Employment Rights Act 1996.

Quick quiz

1 Define performance management.

2 List the steps in performance management.

3 What are the purposes of appraisal?

4 What bases or criteria of assessment might an appraisal system use?

5 Outline a results-oriented approach to appraisal, and its advantages.

6 What is the difference between performance appraisal and performance management?

7 What is a 360-degree feedback, and who might be involved?

8 When a subordinate rates his or her manager's leadership skills, this is an example of:

    (a) Job evaluation
    (b) Job analysis
    (c) Performance management
    (d) Upward appraisal

9 The most empowering style of appraisal interview is the 'tell and listen' approach. True or false?

10 What follow-up should there be after an appraisal?

11 How can appraisals be made more positive and empowering to employees?

Answers to quick quiz

1 **Performance management** is: a means of getting better results by managing performance within an agreed framework of goals, standards and competence requirements. It is a process to establish a shared understanding about what is to be achieved, and an approach to managing and developing people. (See para 1.2)

2 The steps in performance management

    (a) From the business plan, identify the requirements and competences required to carry it out.

    (b) Draw up a performance agreement

    (c) Draw up a performance and development plan with the individual

    (d) Manage performance continually throughout the year

    (e) Performance review (1.3)

3 Identifying performance levels, improvements needed and promotion prospects; deciding on rewards; assessing team work and encouraging communication between manager and employee. (4.2)

4 Job analysis, job description, plans, targets and standards. (4.5)

5 Performance against specific mutually agreed targets and standards. (5.1)

6 Appraisal on its own is a backward-looking performance review. But it is a vital input into performance management, which is forward-looking. (5.1)

7 Refer to paragraph 5.4 for a full answer.

8 (d). ((a) is a technique for grading jobs for salary-setting purposes. (b) is the process of analysing jobs for job evaluation and job description. Make sure you know what (c) is!) (5.5)

9 False. The most empowering style is 'problem solving'. (5.6)

10 Appraisees should be informed of the results, agreed activity should be taken, progress should be monitored and whatever resources or changes are needed should be provided or implemented. (5.7)

11 Ensure the scheme is relevant, fair, taken seriously, and co-operative.

Answers to activities

1 The key to performance management is that it is forward looking and constructive. Objective-setting gives employees the security in knowing exactly what is expected of them, and this is agreed at the outset with the manager, thus identifying unrealistic expectations. The employee at the outset can indicate the resources needed.

2 These measures do not all address some of the key issues of the job.

- Number of new customers. This is helpful as far as it goes but omits two crucial issues: how much the customers actually spend and what the potential is. Demand for this service might be expanding rapidly, and the firm might be increasing sales revenue but losing market share.

- Revenue from existing customers is useful – repeat business is generally cheaper than gaining new customers, and it implies customer satisfaction.

- Renewal of service contracts is very relevant to the executive's role.

- Customer complaints about poor quality products. As the company does not make its own products, this is not really under the control of the sales manager. Instead the purchasing manager should be more concerned. Complaints about the service contract are the sales executive's concern.

- Customer satisfaction survey. This is a tool for the sales manager to use as well as a performance measure, but not everything is under the sales executive's control.

3 The following are just some suggestions.

- Stay open: listen actively and demonstrate your willingness to be receptive.

- Clarify and test your understanding of what is being said. Feedback may be non-specific, ambiguous or unfair. You need to find out exactly what the problem (learning opportunity) is, by asking questions:

  ○ 'What do you mean by...?',
  ○ 'Could you give me some specific examples?'

- Don't be too quick to reject or deny. It will be your choice whether you act on the feedback or not: you can afford to hear and reflect on it first.

- Don't be too quick to defend or justify: remember it is to your benefit to learn how your behaviour or performance is perceived by others, whether or not you think it fair.

- Monitor your feelings. We usually react to negative (and sometimes positive) feedback as a threat to our self image and competence: be aware that you may feel refusal, anger and defensiveness before you move on to acceptance and problem-solving.

- Thank the person for the feedback. Giving feedback is a tough job!

4   Disadvantages to the individual of not having an appraisal system include the following. The individual is not aware of progress or shortcomings, is unable to judge whether s/he would be considered for promotion, is unable to identify or correct weaknesses by training and there is a lack of communication with the manager.

5   You will have come up with your own examples of criteria to assess some jobs but not others. You might have identified such things as:

- Numerical ability (applicable to accounts staff, say, more than to customer contact staff or other non-numerical functions)

- Ability to drive safely (essential for transport workers – not for deskbound ones)

- Report-writing (not applicable to manual labour, say)

- Creativity and initiative (desirable in areas involving design and problem-solving not routine or repetitive jobs in mass production or bureaucratic organisations).

6   Drawbacks to 360-degree appraisal include:

- Respondents' reluctance to give negative feedback to a boss – or friend

- The suspicion that management is passing the buck for negative feedback, getting people to 'rat' on their friends

- The feeling that the appraisee is being picked on, if positive feedback is not carefully balanced with the negative

7   Problems with upward appraisal include fear of reprisals or vindictiveness (or extra form-processing). Some bosses in strong positions might feel able to refuse to act on results, even if a consensus of staff suggested that they should change their ways.

8   Your own research.

9   Apart from the outline of the steps involved – which can be drawn from the chapter, this question raises an interesting point about the nature of different offences, and the flexibility required in the handling of complex disciplinary matters.

- There is clearly a difference in kind and scale between

   ○   unsatisfactory conduct (eg absenteeism)

   ○   misconduct (eg insulting behaviour, persistent absenteeism, insubordination) and

   ○   'gross misconduct' (eg theft or assault).

- The attitude of the organisation towards the purpose of disciplinary action will to a large extent dictate the severity of the punishment.

   ○   If it is punitive it will 'fit the crime'.

- If it is reformative, it may be a warning only, and less severe than the offence warrants.

- If it is deterrent, it may be more severe than is warranted (ie to 'make an example').

The absenteeism question assumes that counselling etc. has failed, and that some sanction has to be applied, to preserve credibility. The theft technically deserves summary dismissal (as gross misconduct), but it depends on the scale and value of the theft, the attitude of the organisation to use of stationery for personal purposes (ie is it theft?) etc. Communicating the situations given might best be done as follows.

(a) Telephone, confirmed in writing (order form, letter)

(b) Notice board or general meeting

(c) Fact-to-face conversation. it would be a good idea to confirm the outcome of the meeting in writing so that records can be maintained.

(d) Either telephone or face-to-face.

10 Your own research.

MANAGING ACTIVITIES TO ACHIEVE RESULTS

Chapter 7 :
BUSINESS PROCESSES AND FUNCTIONS

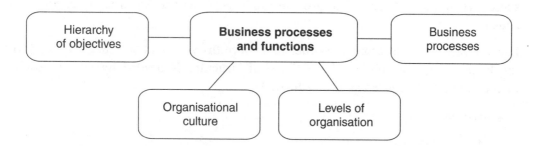

Introduction

Today you want to drive to college. You know that you can call at a BP petrol station and fill the tank, pay with your Visa credit card and go on your way along the district council's well surfaced road. If you break down you can call out the very, very nice man from the AA.

Each of the organisations involved with your drive has **objectives**. The objectives of the organisation and what it does determine the type of structure that it has. An efficient structure for a government department would be effective for an advertising agency. Changes in technology, such as the development of personal computers over the last decade or so, can radically change both the organisation's ways for working and their structures.

Your objectives

After completing this chapter you should be able to:

(a) Describe the structure and culture of an organisation and evaluate the inter-relationships between the different processes and functions of an organisation

(b) Identify the mission, aims and objectives of an organisation and analyse the effect of these on the structure and culture of the organisation

(c) Define methodology to be used to map processes to the organisation's objectives and functions and evaluate the output of the process and analyse quality gateways

First we look at the influences that shape organisations.

NOTES

1 HIERARCHY OF OBJECTIVES

Suppose that none of the organisations involved with your journey to college outlined in the **Introduction** had a formal structure. What would happen? For a start, you could not take it for granted that you could buy petrol at a petrol station. Without having people to take the decisions to drill for oil, extract it, refine it and ship the petrol to the pumps, there is no guarantee at all that it would all happen.

All organisations have some function to perform, some contribution to make. The function of the business organisation may be seen as the creation and/or supply of goods and services. This involves bringing together the factors of production and their successful mix and direction, to provide products or services in order to create value added.

It is the interaction of people, in order to achieve the aims and objectives, which form the basis of an organisation. Some form of structure is needed by which people's interactions are channelled and co-ordinated.

Organisations need:

- objectives
- people
- structure

Most writers agree with the idea that there is a hierarchy of objectives. Mintzberg uses the following:

(a) Mission – 'overriding premise' of the business
(b) Goal – 'general statement of aim or purpose'
(c) Objective – quantification or more precise statement of a goal
(d) Strategies – broad kind of action to achieve objective

Some writers ignore purpose and mission or use aims, goals, objectives and targets interchangeably. However, it is important to be able to clarify the ways in which you are using them.

1.1 Mission

Definition

> **Mission** 'describes the organisation's basic function in society, in terms of the products and services it produces for its clients' (Mintzberg).

One view of the mission is that it is a broad statement of the purpose of an organisation. It is the primary raison d'être, set in advance of strategy. It can define why the company exists or why its managers and employees feel it exists. It outlines who the organisation exists for (eg shareholders, and possibly other stakeholders such as employees and customers). Possible purposes include those below.

- To create wealth for shareholders, who take priority over all other stakeholders.

- To satisfy the needs of all stakeholders (eg including employees and society at large).

- To reach some higher goals ('the advancement of society' and so forth).

1.2 Mission statements

Definition

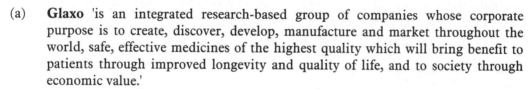

Mission statements are formal declarations of underlying purpose. They say what an organisation exists to do.

Mission statements might be reproduced in a number of places (eg at the front of an organisation's annual report, on publicity material, in the chairman's office, in communal work areas etc). There is no standard format, but they should have certain qualities

- **Brevity** will make them easier to understand and remember.
- **Flexibility** will enable them to accommodate change.
- They should be **distinctive**, to make the firm stand out.

Scott Adams, creator of Dilbert, defines a mission statement as 'a long awkward sentence that demonstrates management's inability to think clearly'. This illustrates the main problem with mission statements, which is getting people to take them seriously.

FOR DISCUSSION

The following statements were taken from annual reports of the organisations concerned. Are they 'mission statements'? If so, are they any good?

(a) **Glaxo** 'is an integrated research-based group of companies whose corporate purpose is to create, discover, develop, manufacture and market throughout the world, safe, effective medicines of the highest quality which will bring benefit to patients through improved longevity and quality of life, and to society through economic value.'

(b) **IBM (UK)**: 'We shall increase the pace of change. Market-driven quality is our aim. It means listening and responding more sensitively to our customers. It means eliminating defects and errors, speeding up all our processes, measuring everything we do against a common standard, and it means involving employees totally in our aims'.

(c) **Matsushita**: 'the duty of the manufacturer is to serve the foundation of man's happiness by making man's life affluent with an inexpensive and inexhaustible supply of life's necessities.'

(d) **Guinness Group**: 'Guinness plc is one of the world's leading drinks companies, producing and marketing an unrivalled portfolio of international best-selling brands, such as Johnnie Walker, Bell's and Dewar's Scotch whiskies, Gordon's and Tanqueray gins, and Guinness stout itself – the world's most distinctive beer. The strategy is to focus resources on the development of the Group's alcoholic drinks businesses. The objectives are to provide superior long-term financial returns for shareholders, to create a working environment in which people can perform to their fullest potential and to be recognised as one of the world's leading consumer brand development companies'.

(e)   **British Film Institute**. 'The BFI is the UK national agency with responsibility for encouraging and conserving the arts of film and television. Our aim is to ensure that the many audiences in the UK are offered access to the widest possible choice of cinema and television, so that their enjoyment is enhanced through a deeper understanding of the history and potential of these vital and popular art forms.'

1.3 Aims or goals

Aims or goals are the secondary objectives derived from the mission and also set in advance of strategy.

Organisations have definite aims (or goals); by this we mean they try to make particular things happen. An aim or goal is a future expectation – a desired future state. It is something the organisation is striving to accomplish.

Definition

> **Goals** or **aims** give a sense of direction for the activities of an organisation and are sufficient for the satisfaction of the organisation's mission.

They can be used in a very broad sense to refer to the overall purpose of the organisation, eg to produce washing machines. They may also be used to refer to more specific desired outcomes, eg to produce and sell a given number of washing machines within a given period of time.

The aims of an organisation will determine the nature of the organisation's inputs and outputs, the series of activities through which the outputs are achieved and interactions with its environment. The extent to which an organisation is successful in achieving its aims is a basis for the evaluation of organisational performance and effectiveness.

Aims serve a number of important functions.

- Aims provide a **standard of performance**. They focus attention on the activities of the organisation and the direction of the efforts of its members.

- Aims provide the **basis for planning** and management control of the activities of the organisation.

- Aims provide guidelines for decision-making and justification for actions taken.

- Aims influence the **structure** of the organisation and determine the nature of the technology employed.

- Aims or goals are the **basis for objectives and policies** of the organisation.

1.4 Objectives

In accordance with its ideology, the aims of the organisation are translated into objectives, which are expressed in a form that can be measured. All the organisation's objectives should be directed towards achieving the organisation's mission. In business organisations, a paramount consideration is profitability. The mission of a business, whether it is stated or not, must be to carry on its activities at a profit.

They should relate to the critical success factors of the organisation, which are typically:

(a) Profitability
(b) Market share
(c) Growth
(d) Cash flow
(e) Customer satisfaction
(f) Quality of the organisation's products
(g) Industrial relations
(h) Added value

Objectives are normally quantified statements of what the organisation actually intends to achieve and should fulfil the SMART criteria outlined below.

Specific

Measurable

Achievable

Results-orientated

Time-bounded

Whereas mission statements describe a value system for the organisation and some indication of the business it is in, objectives are well defined. For example:

(a) mission: deliver a quality service

(b) aim or goal: enhance manufacturing quality

(c) objectives: over the next twelve months, reduce the number of defects to one part per million

Other examples of objectives include:

(a) increasing the number of customers by x% (sales department objective)
(b) reducing the number of rejects by 50% (production department objective)
(c) responding to calls within ten minutes (hospital ambulance service)

Some objectives are more important than others. When there are several key objectives, some might be achieved only at the expense of others. For example, a company's objective of achieving good profits and profit growth might have adverse consequences for the cash flow or good product quality, or to improve market share, might call for some sacrifice of profits. There will be a trade-off between objectives when strategies are formulated, and a choice will have to be made.

1.5 Strategies

A strategy provides the commercial logic for the company and so defines the nature of the firm's business, the markets it competes in and the competencies and competitive advantages by which it hopes to prosper.

Definition

A **strategy** is a course of action, including the specification of resources required to achieve a specific objective.

Strategy is the organised development of resources (financial manufacturing, marketing, technological, manpower etc) to achieve specific objectives against competition from rival organisations. These perform a series of activities and they are all part of the inter-related sub-system of the organisation.

```
                        Task
                       /    \
                      /      \
        Technology        Management        Structure
                      \      /
                       \    /
                        People
```

Resource planning will require answers to the following questions.

- What are the key tasks that have to be completed?
- What control systems exist?
- What changes should be made to resources?

As a result of this planning, organisations may decide to change their structure to meet the strategic requirements more closely.

1.6 Policies and standards of behaviour

Policies provide the basis for decision-making and the course of action to follow to achieve objectives. For example, where the objective is to increase the number of customers by x%, the policy might be to sell to every retail outlet that is credit worthy. Some policy decisions are directly influenced by external factors, eg government legislation on equal opportunities.

Objectives and policy together provide corporate guidelines for the operation and management of the organisation. For example, specific decisions relating to personnel policy could include:

- giving priority to promotion from within the organisation

- enforcing retirement at government pensionable age

- permitting line managers, in consultation with the personnel manager, to appoint staff up to a given salary/wage level

Policies and strategies need to be converted into everyday performance. They are translated into rules, plans and procedures and relate to all activities of the organisation. For example, a service industry that wishes to be the best in its market must aim for standards of service, in all its operations, which are at least as good as those found in its competitors. In service businesses, this includes simple matters such as politeness to customers, speed at which phone calls are answered, and so forth.

Activity 1   **(10 mins)**

Set out one of your new year's resolutions in terms of:

- mission
- goal (aim)
- objectives
- strategy

1.7   Organisation structure

Clearly defined and agreed aims and objectives are the first stage in the design of organisation structure and they help facilitate systems of communication between different parts of the organisation. As we have already noted, the aims are related to the input-conversion-output cycle. To achieve its objectives and satisfy its mission and aims the organisation takes inputs from the environment, through a series of activities transforms or converts them into outputs and returns them to the environment as inputs to other systems.

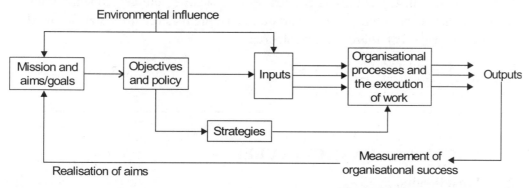

Figure 7.1 Input-output conversion

All organisations need lines of direction through the establishment of objectives and the determination of policy.

Other factors also influence the design of the structure. In total, the structure of a business organisation is determined by:

- its mission
- what it does
- its size
- where it operates
- who it deals with
- its culture
- technology
- the complexity of its operations
- its history and future expectations

For example, a hairdresser who provides haircuts to men and women within a two mile radius is clearly going to have a very different market structure to a company providing air travel globally to a global market.

1.8 The public and not-for-profit sectors

Organisations in the public and not-for-profit sectors also have structures determined by the factors listed above. The public services and local government have some additional factors which influence them:

(a) the extent and type of duties and obligations imposed by Parliament, which they must perform;

(b) the changing expectations of society;

(c) changes in government policies and priorities.

Because they are closely associated with government and depend on it for funding, quangos, much of the voluntary sector, many arts and environmental bodies and local clubs and societies that use the facilities of the local authority are all affected by these factors.

FOR DISCUSSION

Consider your college's or university's structure of faculties and departments. Which of the factors listed above have been important in shaping its structure? How do you think that they compare with those that are important for:

(a)   a news agent and sub-post office;

(b)   the Royal Air Force?

2   ORGANISATIONAL CULTURE

2.1   What is culture?

There are many factors that influence the expectations that people are likely to have of an organisation, as shown in the diagram below:

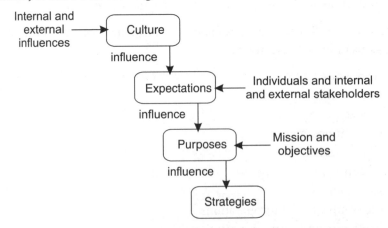

Figure 7.2 Influences on organisational culture

The aims of the organisation will have an ideology based on beliefs, values and attitudes. This ideology is a means of control through shared beliefs and determines the culture of the organisation, providing a set of principles that govern the overall conduct of the organisation's operations, code of behaviour, the management of people and its dealings with other organisations. For example, a firm's moral principles might mean refusing an assignment if it believes the client will not benefit, even though this refusal means lost revenue. A sense of mission, or emotional bond, is where employees' personal values coincide with organisational values.

Culture may be identified as ways of behaving and ways of understanding that are shared by a group of people. Handy referred to it as 'the way we do things round here'.

Definition

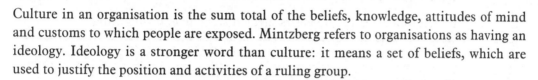

Culture is the commonly held and relatively stable beliefs, attitudes and values that exist within the organisation.

Culture in an organisation is the sum total of the beliefs, knowledge, attitudes of mind and customs to which people are exposed. Mintzberg refers to organisations as having an ideology. Ideology is a stronger word than culture: it means a set of beliefs, which are used to justify the position and activities of a ruling group.

Culture is both internal to an organisation and external to it. There are certain patterns of behaviour, assumptions and beliefs which members of the organisation have in common, because of their:

(a) citizenship of the same society or country;
(b) status or class position within that society;
(c) profession (eg as accountants, marketers);
(d) membership of the organisation.

All organisations will generate their own cultures, whether spontaneously or under the guidance of positive managerial strategy. Here are some aspects of culture.

(a) **Customs and rituals**: there may be ceremonies, whether formal or informal, such as a Christmas party and awards to high achievers.

(b) **Relationship between superiors and subordinates**: are bosses approachable?

(c) **Symbols**: status may be reflected in things like size of office, or a democratic approach may be symbolised by an open plan office.

(d) **Physical artefacts**: office layout and décor can encourage or inhibit communication.

(e) **Common language**: the slang of the Royal Navy has grown up over centuries.

(f) **Values** may be clearly stated or left unspoken and rather vague.

Trompenaars suggested that in fact there are different levels at which culture can be understood.

(a) The **observable**, expressed or 'explicit' elements of culture include:

(i) **Behaviour** – norms of personal and interpersonal behaviour; customs and rules about behaviours that are 'acceptable' or unacceptable.

(ii) **Artefacts:** concrete expressions such as art and literature, architecture and interior design (eg of office premises), dress codes, symbols and 'heroes' or role models.

(iii) **Rituals:** patterns of collective behaviour which have traditional or symbolic value, such as greeting styles, business formalities, social courtesies and ceremonies.

(b) Beneath values and beliefs lie **assumptions:** foundational ideas that are no longer consciously recognised or questioned by the culture, but which 'programme' its ways of thinking and behaving. Examples include the importance of the individual in many Western cultures: this is taken for granted in designing HR (human resources) policies, for example.

(c) Beneath values and beliefs lie **assumptions:** ideas that are no longer consciously recognised or questioned by the culture, but which 'programme' its ways of thinking and behaving. Examples include the importance of the individual in many Western cultures: this is taken for granted in designing human resources policies, for example.

Layers of culture, following Trompenaars' elements, include the following.

Item	Example
Beliefs and values, which are often unquestioned	The customer is always right'
Behaviour	In the City of London, standard business dress is still generally taken for granted and even 'dress down Fridays' have their rules.
Artefacts	Microsoft encourages communication between employees by setting aside spaces for the purpose.
Rituals	In some firms, sales people compete with each other, and there is a reward, given at a ceremony, for the salesperson who does best in any period.
Symbols	Corporate logos are an example of symbols, but they are directed outwards. Within the organisation, symbols can represent power: dress, make and model of car, office size and equipment and access to facilities can all be important symbols.

Activity 2   (10 mins)

What do you think would differentiate the culture of:

(a) A regiment in the army
(b) An advertising agency?

2.2 Categorising cultures

Deal and Kennedy (*Corporate Cultures: The Rites and Rituals of Corporate Life*) went beyond outlining the cultural elements within an organisation. They believe that the culture of a company affects its policies, decisions, activities and hence its success. Successful companies have strong and cohesive cultures where employees identify with the company goals and band together to achieve them. Alternatively, less well-performing companies have weak and disconnected cultures with minimal employee loyalty. Money is the prime motivator at work.

They suggest that an organisation is capable of being managed from a weak one to a strong one by the process of creating and implementing supporting rites, rituals and ceremonials. These act to communicate and reinforce the beliefs and values that senior management wants all employees to share.

Deal and Kennedy argue that two crucial factors shape an organisation's culture. The first is the degree of risk associated with the organisation's activities and the second is the speed of feedback provided to employees concerning the success of their decision strategy. They placed these factors on different axis to produce four distinctive types of organisational culture as shown below:

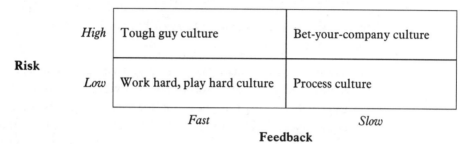

		Fast	*Slow*
Risk	*High*	Tough guy culture	Bet-your-company culture
	Low	Work hard, play hard culture	Process culture

Feedback

Figure 7.3 Deal & Kennedy's cultural grid

- **Tough guy culture** – is made up of individualists who thrive on high risks and fast feedback on their performance. Unfortunately, the short term need for feedback may divert attention from longer-term efforts. This type of culture is often found in construction, advertising and entertainment organisations.

- **Bet-your-company culture** – is characterised by high stake decisions with a delayed feedback. It is prevalent in oil and aircraft companies where the decisions that risk the company's future are made by technically competent people and necessitate attention to detail.

- **Work hard, play hard culture** – is characterised by low risk taking combined with quick feedback. High activity is the key to survival. This type of culture suits organisations with high volume sales of mass produced goods.

- **Process culture** – has little risk and little feedback. Typical process cultures include government agencies, banks and heavily regulated industries.

2.3 Analysing and comparing cultures

Developing the ideas of Roger Harrison (*Understanding your Organisation's character*) Charles Handy created a typology, which provides a useful basis for discussing and investigating variations in organisational culture.

According to Harrison, the four basic classifications of the types of culture one might expect to find in an organisation are: power; role; task; and people cultures.

Handy gave each of these types a Greek God's name:

- **Zeus** is the god representing the power culture or club culture. Zeus is a dynamic entrepreneur who rules with snap decisions. Power and influence stem from a central source, perhaps the owner-directors or the founder of the business. The degree of formalisation is limited and there are few rules and procedures. Such a firm is likely to be organised on a functional basis.

(a)   The organisation is capable of adapting quickly to meet change.

(b)   Personal influence decreases as the size of an organisation gets bigger. The power culture is therefore best suited to smaller entrepreneurial organisations, where the leaders have direct communication with all employees.

(c)   Personnel have to get on well with each other for this culture to work. These organisations are clubs of 'like-minded people introduced by the like-minded people, working on empathetic initiative with personal contact rather than formal liaison.'

- **Apollo** is the god of the **role culture** or bureaucracy. There is a presumption of logic and rationality.

(a)   These organisations have a formal structure, and operate by well-established rules and procedures. Individuals are required to perform their job to the full, but not to overstep the boundaries of their authority. Individuals who work for such organisations tend to learn an expertise without experiencing risk; many do their job adequately, but are not over-ambitious.

(b)   The bureaucratic style can be very efficient in a stable environment, when the organisation is large and when the work is predictable.

- **Athena** is the goddess of the **task culture**. Management is seen as completing a succession of projects or solving problems.

(a)   The task culture is reflected in project teams and task forces. In such organisations, there is no dominant or clear leader. The principal concern in a task culture is to get the job done. Therefore the individuals who are important are the experts with the ability to accomplish a particular aspect of the task.

(b)   Performance is judged by **results.**

(c)   Task cultures are expensive, as experts demand a market price

(d)   Task cultures also depend on variety, and to tap creativity requires a tolerance of perhaps costly mistakes.

- **Dionysus** is the god of the **existential** or **person culture**. In the three other cultures, the individual is subordinate to the organisation or task. An existential culture is found in an organisation whose purpose is to serve the interests of the individuals within it. These organisations are rare, although an example might be a partnership of a few individuals who do all the work of the organisation themselves (with perhaps a little secretarial or clerical assistance).

(a)   Barristers (in the UK) work through chambers. The clerk co-ordinates their work and hands out briefs, but does not control them.

(b)   Management in these organisations are often lower in status than the professionals and are labelled secretaries, administrators, bursars, registrars and chief clerk.

(c)   The organisation depends on the talent of the individuals; management is derived from the consent of the managed, rather than the delegated authority of the owners

---

Activity 3   **(10 mins)**

Review the following statements. Ascribe each of them to one of Handy's four corporate cultures.

People are controlled and influenced by:

(a)   the owner's personally administered rewards, punishments and plans;

(b)   the impersonal exercise of economic and political power to enforce procedures and standards of performance;

(c)   communication and discussion of task requirements leading to appropriate action, motivated by personal commitment, to achieve the goal;

(d)   intrinsic interest and enjoyment in the activities to be done, and/or concern and caring for the needs of the other people involved.

2.4   Miles and Snow

Miles and Snow analyse three strategic cultures, and a fourth 'non-strategic' culture.

(a)   **Defenders**. Firms with this culture like low risks, secure markets, and tried and trusted solutions. These companies have cultures whose stories and rituals reflect historical continuity and consensus. Decision-taking is relatively formalised. There is a stress on 'doing things right' ie efficiency. Personnel are drawn from within the industry.

(b)   **Prospectors** are organisations where the dominant beliefs are more to do with results doing the right things ie effectiveness.

(c)   **Analysers** try to balance risk and profits. They use a core of stable products and markets as a source of earnings to move into innovative prospector areas. Analysers follow change, but do not initiate it.

(d)   **Reactors**, unlike the three above, do not have viable strategies. Arguably, they do not have a strategy, either deliberate or emergent, at all, unless it is simply to carry on living from hand to mouth, muddling through.

3   LEVELS OF ORGANISATION

Organisation structure is the grouping of people into departments or sections and the allocation of responsibility and authority.

Organisation structure implies a framework intended to:

(a)   Link individuals in an established network of relationships so that authority, responsibility and communication can be controlled

(b)   Allocate the tasks required to fulfil the objectives of the organisation to suitable individuals or groups

(c)   Give each individual or group the authority required to perform the allocated tasks, while controlling their behaviour and use of resources in the interests of the organisation as a whole

(d)   Co-ordinate the objectives and activities of separate units, so that overall aims are achieved without gaps or overlaps in the flow of work

(e)   Facilitate the flow of work, information and other resources through the organisation

3.1   Hierarchy and specialisation

An organisation is a collection of groups joined in a common mission. Each group has its own specific objectives and functions. A group is unlikely to operate successfully without a leader who can take responsibility in seeing that the group performs its tasks. Current changes in management practice are leading to collective responsibility for work being given to groups themselves; however, there must still be an individual who interacts with other groups and with managers of wider groupings.

Many decisions need to be made within an organisation and someone must have the authority to make them at each of the different levels within it. This authority should be given to people who have the appropriate knowledge and experience. Along with the authority goes responsibility, and the need to ensure that decisions are carried out.

Organisations develop layers of authority to ensure that correct decisions are made and implemented. This results in the **organisation pyramid** as shown below. The more important a decision is to an organisation, the fewer are the people entrusted with the authority to make it.

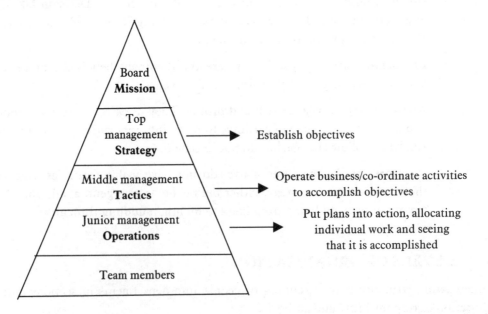

Figure 7.4 Organisational pyramid

As organisations grow, specialist individuals or groups appear. These have to be co-ordinated, so further layers of management are required. Each department develops its own pyramid of authority. There can be specialism within a department, requiring more co-ordination. Thus increasing specialisation often leads to more layers of management.

EXAMPLE: BUILDING SOCIETIES

When building societies took deposits and lent funds as mortgages they required only a few specialist departments; deposits, lending, administration, and legal. When they started to offer cheques, make personal loans and offer many types of savings, they had to develop many more specialist departments.

Activity 4 (20 mins)

Think about your local department store (or visit it if you do not know it well).

1   List the departments on all the sales floors.

2   Also list the support departments such as accounts.

3   Now suggest what advantages there are in having this degree of specialisation.

3.2   Centralisation and decentralisation

A centralised organisation is one in which authority is concentrated in one place. For example, if you meet a sales person who always says 'sorry, I'll have to refer that to head office', this implies that the organisation is centralised. We can look at centralisation in two ways.

(a)   *Geography*. It used to be the case in Russia that trivial decisions in the province had to be referred thousands of miles away to a Ministry in Moscow. In some firms decisions might have to be constantly referred to head office.

(b)   *Authority*. Centralisation also refers to the extent to which people have to refer decisions upwards to their superiors.

The table below summarises some of the key issues.

Arguments in favour of centralisation and decentralisation	
Pro centralisation	*Pro decentralisation/delegation*
Decisions are made at one point and so easier to co-ordinate.	Avoids overburdening top managers, in terms of workload and stress.
Senior managers in an organisation can take a wider view of problems and consequences.	Improves motivation of more junior managers who are given responsibility-since job challenge and entrepreneurial skills are highly valued in today's work environment.

Arguments in favour of centralisation and decentralisation	
Pro centralisation	*Pro decentralisation/delegation*
Senior management can keep a proper balance between different departments or functions – eg by deciding on the resources to allocate to each.	Greater awareness of local problems by decision makers. Geographically dispersed organisations should often be decentralised on a regional/area basis.
Quality of decisions is (theoretically) higher due to senior managers' skills and experience.	Greater speed of decision-making, and response to changing events, since no need to refer decisions upwards. This is particularly important in rapidly changing markets.
Possibly cheaper, by reducing number of managers needed and so lower costs of overheads.	Helps junior managers to develop and helps the process of transition from functional to general management.
Crisis decisions are taken more quickly at the centre, without need to refer back or, get authority	Separate spheres of responsibility can be identified: controls, performance measurement and accountability are better.
Policies, procedures and documentation can be standardised organisation-wide.	Communication technology allows decisions to be made locally, with information and input from head office if required.

There is a good argument in favour of *centralising certain specialist functions* at head office to co-ordinate the strategy of the group as a whole. Central functions might include the public relations department, and a strategic planning department. Perhaps the most important example, however, is a research and development function, which might be centralised into a single unit, or broken up into separate R & D units for each product group/major subsidiary. A drawback, though, is that R&D can become too distant from the marketing function.

3.3 Departmentation and divisionalisation

Division of labour is one of the key principles of organisation. once an organisation grows beyond a certain size, this typically involves the grouping together and allocation of specific aspects of the work to different departments. This can be done on the basis of various criteria, such as functional specialisation, geographical area or product/brand.

Basic approaches to departmentation and divisionalisation are outlined below.

Functional organisation. This is departmentation by type of work done (eg finance department, marketing department, production function).

(a) Expertise is concentrated, enabling effective division of labour.

(b) Problems include poor communication between functional specialists, who might know little about other areas of the business.

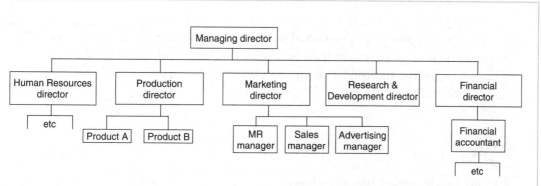

Figure 7.5 Functional organisation

Geographic/territorial organisation. Reporting relationships are organised by geography. In each area functional specialists report to an area boss, who ensures coordination.

(a) This enables greater flexibility at local level, and allows experimentation.

(b) Some managerial work is duplicated. There may be problems in ensuring consistent standards.

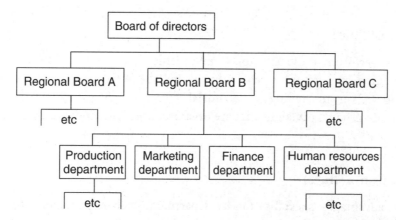

Figure 7.6 Geographic organisation

Product/brand organisation. A divisional manager for each product is responsible for marketing and production. Some divisions are effectively run as independent businesses, in which case the division's finance specialists will report to the division's head.

(a) Individual product profitability can be easily identified.

(b) There is increased managerial complexity, and problems of resource allocation.

Multinationals can also divide up their activities by product, with each product division taking responsibility for worldwide production and sales, often with a territorial structure that has, in turn, a functional structure.

International charities tend to have territorial structures. For example, the Save the Children Fund has divisions for the UK, Africa, Asia and the Americas and the Pacific.

Customer/market segment organisation: reporting relationships are structured by type of customer.

Hybrid designs. In practice, organisations may draw on a number of these approaches. Product/brand departmentation for marketing and production, say, might be combined with a centralised R&D function. This is because some activities are better organised on a functional basis (for reasons of economies of scale) whereas others are more suited, say, to product/brand departmentation (eg marketing).

A *strategic business unit* (SBU) is normally defined as a division of the organisation 'where the managers have control over their own resources, and discretion over the deployment of resources within specified boundaries' (Ward). SBUs have an external market for goods/services, distinct from those of other SBUs.

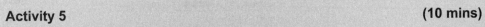

Activity 5   **(10 mins)**

What type of departmentation has:

(a) central government?

(b) independent television?

(c) your college?

FOR DISCUSSION

As you can see from these examples, an organisation can use different methods of departmentation at different levels. Why is this so? What advantages are there for a multinational firm in having a territorial structure with regional divisions each structured into product divisions that are organised into functional departments?

3.4 The matrix structure

Despite its advantages, specialisation by department leads to problems of co-ordination and control. The matrix structure was developed to ensure co-ordination between different functional departments. This structure essentially 'crosses' functional and product/project organisation, so that staff in different functional or regional departments are responsible:

- To their department managers, in regard to the activities of the department;
- To a product or project manager, in regard to the given product or project.

An example of the matrix structure is shown in the diagram below:

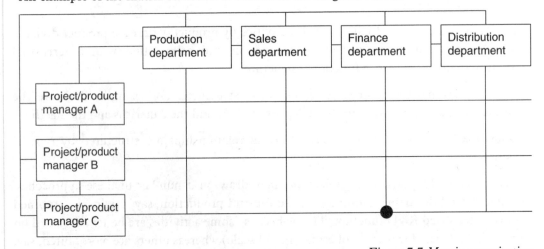

Figure 7.7 Matrix organisation

The employee represented by the dot in the above diagram, for example:

- is responsible to the Finance manager for his/her work in accounting and finance

- is responsible to the Project manager for his/her work on the project team. This may be budgeting, management reporting, and payroll relevant to the project.

The purpose is to retain functional expertise whilst ensuring co-ordination. This is similar to *project organisation* where people from different functions are drawn together in a project team: however, matrix organisation is permanent.

- Advantages include better co-ordination and communication, and focus on the task.

- Disadvantages include the potential for conflict between, say, functional and area managers, and an increase in managerial overheads.

Activity 6   **(15 mins)**

Jason, Mark, Gary and Robbie set up business together as repairers of musical instruments – specialising in guitars and drums. They are a bit uncertain as to how they should run the business, but when they discuss it in the pub, they decide that attention needs to be paid to three major areas: taking orders from customers, doing the repairs (of course) and checking the quality of the repairs before notifying the customers.

Suggest three ways in which they could structure their business.

---

4 BUSINESS PROCESSES

4.1 Business process orientation

Definition

We define a **business process** as 'a set of related activities that collectively realise a business goal'.

Business processes are valuable business assets and need to be managed and maintained in the same way as any other, more tangible, asset e.g. plant and machinery. Historically businesses have organised themselves around 'functions' such as production, sales or finance, but such functional divisions fail to recognise that many of the business processes they operate cross the artificial boundaries thus created.

The concept of business process orientation is a recent development in organising. It can be described in terms of an organisation that is oriented towards processes, customers and outcomes as opposed to hierarchies.

The components of a business process oriented organisation include:

NOTES

- a process view of the business – the cross-functional, horizontal picture of a business involving elements of structure, focus, measurement, ownership and customers;

- structures that match these processes – cross-functional process team structure, 'flat' hierarchy, process owners with leadership not control-oriented management;

- jobs that operate these processes – empowered, multi-dimensional, process team oriented – jobs that focus on processes not functions and are cross-functional in responsibility, e.g., 'product development process owner' rather than 'research manager'.

- management and measurement systems that direct and assess these processes – measures that include aspects of the process like output quality, cycle time, process cost and variability compared to the traditional accounting measures;

- customer focused, continuous improvement oriented values and beliefs (culture) that are embodied in all components.

4.2 What is a process?

A process is a transformation; it converts its inputs into its outputs.

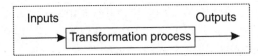

The environment

Inputs   Outputs

Transformation process

Inputs may include capital, raw materials, people, information, managerial and technical skills and knowledge.

The transformation process – Charles Handy considers these processes as sub-systems:

- Production – in a manufacturing organisation, the transformation of inputs into outputs would be the production department, in an insurance company it would be the underwriting department. The production sub-system is the heart of the organisation and all sub-systems are usually oriented towards it.

- Maintenance – keeps the organisation functioning. It may repair and service the building. Alternatively, the human resource department can be seen as a maintenance sub-system, recruiting, retiring and counselling employees.

- Boundary spanning – organisations must acquire inputs, raw materials data etc, and distribute output – the finished product or service. This sub-system can cover a variety of activities, such as purchasing and marketing.

- Adaptation – an organisation needs to adapt in order to survive. This sub-system can cover such activities as research, engineering, planning and development.

- Management – is the sub-system which co-ordinates all of the other sub-systems, by means of policies, plans, resolving conflict etc. It is the task of managers to transform the inputs, in an efficient and effective way, into outputs using the managerial functions of planning, organising, staffing, leading and controlling.

Outputs – the type of outputs will vary with the organisation. They generally include products, services, profits and rewards (the satisfaction of the goals of various claimants).

A process is not just about 'what people do', equal consideration should be given to 'what people produce'. Historically, there has been a lot of emphasis attached to the study of the way people perform their jobs, ie the activities they carry out. In process terms, the emphasis rests more heavily on the outputs a person produces – where a person does their job, the exact way they do it, what time of day they do it, or what they wear when they do it are largely irrelevant. A beach in Rio is a perfectly good office if the required output is produced on time and at the right level of quality.

Examples of processes are:

- Sales order processing
- Demand forecasting
- Sales operations planning
- Bought-ledger invoice processing
- New product development

Processes are identified from knowing an objective. If one of your objectives is to manage customer relationships effectively, you have a 'customer relationship management' process. If another objective is to bring innovative products to market ahead of the competition, you have an 'innovation' process or if the objective is to deliver product to customer on time, you have a 'delivery' process

Objectives are determined from the purpose of the organisation by establishing the factors upon which fulfilment of the purpose depends. These are the critical success factors (CSF). The CSFs indicate the capabilities needed and consequently identify the objectives to deliver these capabilities.

4.3   The components of a process

A process is performed by using a procedure to combine basic assets with explicit and tacit knowledge.

- Basic assets consist of tangible and intangible assets. Examples of tangible assets are plant, machinery and cash. Intangible assets include reputation and brand strength

- Explicit knowledge is knowledge that is in the public domain. It is formal and standardised and can be easily shared and communicated. Examples would be the legal obligations of companies and the knowledge of how to undertake stock control.

- Tacit knowledge is personal and rooted in a specific context. Skill, the ability to do something well, especially because it has been learned and practised, is one form of tacit knowledge For example, once you learn how to drive a car and have been doing it for some time, you develop certain techniques (and bad habits) and driving becomes second nature. In contrast, much of the skill in an organisation such as Tesco is organisational skill eg, how to establish profitable relationships with suppliers.

- Procedures provide the ability to co-ordinate the basic assets, explicit and tacit knowledge to perform a process.

Processes link together to form a set that delivers a product or service to the customer. Two organisations competing for the same customers are differentiated on how well they manage to perform their processes. How well, for example, they transform market research into product design and development, or prospective customer interest into sales follow-up, and raw materials into building a product. An organisation with effective processes will meet or exceed customer expectation, whereas organisations with ineffective processes will fail to meet customer expectation and will therefore fail to retain those customers.

Activity 7 (15 mins)

Give examples of the basic assets and the explicit knowledge likely to be found in a small local garage.

4.4 Process mapping

A process map is a visual aid for picturing work processes. The success of a process map rests in its ability to communicate a functional unit's core processes and key activities, how such processes and activities interrelate and the directional flow of the process. Maps are similar to flow charts, showing each step of the process in a way that is understood at every level of an organisation. An effective process map should provide a broad overview of a unit's activities – not an overly detailed description of individual tasks, responsibilities and the like. It should determine the unit's core purpose. It is vital that:

- all core processes are identified,
- all key activities are identified,
- process limits are defined.

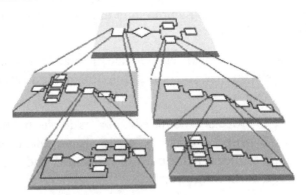

Figure 7.8 Process map

The map will identify key stakeholders that will benefit from the outputs of the unit's processes and key activities. Stakeholders may be internal and/or external to the unit.

It will also identify the inputs to the process and the outputs e.g., a service, process, a necessary outcome, process measures and/or process improvement.

The inclusion of performance measures that are related to client needs e.g. accuracy, timeliness, satisfaction, etc. should also be included.

Process maps should provide sufficient detail to allow an informed observer to understand the flow of work in the process/unit. Each step would try to show:

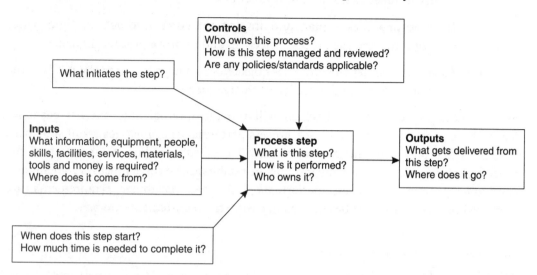

Figure 7.9 Content of a process map

4.5   Managing the processes

Business processes exist to realise business goals. By performing a business process, a necessary task is completed that contributes to the aims of the business. Thus, if a process does not make a contribution to a business goal, it should not exist.

The successful management of business processes requires the management of four different aspects of a process – process goals, performance, resources and interfaces. Process goals are derived from three sources – from business goals, from customer requirements and from benchmarking information.

There is a series of activities for managing processes effectively.

- Determine scope – identify processes, process ownership, boundaries and interfaces.

- Establish process objectives and express them in measurable terms.

- Document processes – develop process maps for all core and support processes.

- Define the key stages that convert the inputs into outputs.

- Define the resources, information and competences required to deliver the required outputs.

- Identify the risks and put in place measures that eliminate, reduce or control these risks.

- Establish measures of success – the factors that will indicate whether the objective has been achieved. Performance measures must relate to employee behaviour to tie in the strategic direction with employee action.

- Measure performance – identify customer requirements. Determine control points and specific process measures and targets. Collect data and develop statistical charts.

- Analyse performance – analyse results, determine process stability and the ability to meet customer requirements.

- Improve processes – plan and implement corrective action. Find better ways of achieving the process objectives and improve process efficiency.

- Establish whether the processes objectives remain relevant to the needs of the interested parties and if necessary change them.

Systems need to be established which will provide internal and external customer feedback on process outputs and track process performance against goals and sub-goals. Functions that play a role in the process must have feedback about their aspects of the process' performance and mechanisms must be established to solve process problems and continuously improve process performance. As new customer requirements are identified process goals must be adjusted to ensure the requirements are met.

4.6 Business process measures

The building blocks of business measures are goals (what is measured) and critical success factors (CSFs) – what has to be achieved for success. The key to effective management of processes is the correct selection of the process outcome measures to provide data that can readily determine process health-for example:

- customer satisfaction

- cost of process outcome per unit measure

- quantity of output

- reliability of quality of output

- manner of delivery of output

- reliability of delivery of process outcome to defined programme

- delivery of process outcome within the defined timescale

- success or failure of process (eg tender process, win or lose)

- quantity of rejects, cost of rework

- quantity of waste

- extent of containment of risk (eg rise/fall in number of safety/environmental incidents or unexpected results)

The actual measuring of process performance can be done in a variety of ways and for different purposes. If the measurement is part of process performance management there will need to be a comparison made between how the process is operating now and 'something else'. This could be done by measuring the process over a period of time and making the comparison between 'then' and 'now' or by benchmarking – comparing it against a similar process performed elsewhere, often external to the business.

Process measurement performed as part of process performance management must be built in to the operational processes. Where possible the information required to measure the process should be captured by an automated recording system so that it can easily extracted and reported on.

Sometimes there is a requirement to measure all or specific parts of processes to determine the amount of actual time spent performing them, or to make a comparison between operating the process manually or using automated tools. In these cases a 'time and motion' study may be required which involves observation of the process being performed by other people using a stopwatch to record actual elapsed time.

Chapter roundup

- The first stage in the design of an organisation's structure is the definition of its mission, aims and objectives.

- The structure of an organisation is determined by influences such as its mission, operations, culture, technology and external factors like changes in government policy.

- Organisations develop the typical pyramid structure because of the need to establish lines of authority and responsibility.

- Culture is the commonly held and relatively stable beliefs, attitudes and values that exist within the organisation.

- Elements of culture include observable behaviour, artefacts, rituals and symbols: underlying values and beliefs; hidden assumptions

- Types of culture and related structures were identified by Harrison and Handy as follows:

    - Power culture (Zeus)
    - Role culture (Apollo)
    - Task culture (Athena)
    - Existential or person culture (Dionysus)

- Organisation structures can be classified into the following categories:

    (a) Specialisation – the typical line and staff organisation

    (b) Departmentation – functional, product or territorial

    (c) Matrix – authority is shared between the project manager and the line managers in departments

- Business process orientation can be described in terms of an organisation that is oriented towards processes, customers and outcomes as opposed to hierarchies.

- A process is performed by using a procedure to combine basic assets with explicit and tacit knowledge.

- Processes link together to form a set that delivers a product or service to the customer.

NOTES

Quick quiz

1   Objectives should fulfil the SMART criteria. What do the letters stand for?

2   What are the elements of culture, according to Trompenaars?

3   Bureaucracy might be another name for a:

   A   Power culture
   B   Role culture
   C   Task culture
   D   Existential culture

4   A project team is most likely to be a role culture. True or false?

5   What are the three types of departmentation?

6   What are the responsibilities of project managers and department heads in a matrix structure?

7   Who is an employee's boss in a matrix structure?

8   What is a business process?

9   Explain the difference between tacit and explicit knowledge

Answers to quick quiz

1   Objectives should be: **S**pecific, **M**easurable, **A**chievable, **R**esults-orientated and **T**ime-bounded. (See Para 1.4)

2   Observable phenomena (behaviour, artefacts, rituals), values and beliefs, assumptions. (2.1)

3   B (Role culture) (2.3)

4   False – it is most likely to be a task culture. (2.3)

5   Functional, product and territorial. (3.2)

6   Project managers are responsible for all aspects of the project, including the schedule and the budget; department managers are responsible for their departments, as line managers. (3.4)

7   Both the project co-ordinator and the department head. Some matrix organisations combine territorial and functional organisation. (3.4)

8   A business process is a transformation converting inputs such as raw materials, people, information, managerial and technical skills and knowledge into outputs such as products, services, and profits. (4)

9   Explicit knowledge is formal, systemised and easily shared. Tacit knowledge is personal, formalised and rooted in specific concept. (4.3)

Answers to activities

1   Mission: have a healthier lifestyle

Aims: get fit and lose weight

Objective: lose a stone by March

Strategies: join local gym and exercise for one hour daily; eat more vegetables, fewer biscuits

2   Here are some hints. The army is very disciplined. Officers make decisions; behaviour between ranks is sometimes very formal. The organisation values loyalty, courage and discipline and teamwork. Symbols and artefacts include uniforms, medals, regimental badges and so on. Rituals include parades and ceremonies.

An advertising agency, with a different mission, is more fluid. Individual flair and creativity, within the commercial needs of the organisation, are expected. Artefacts may include the style of creative offices, awards or prizes and the agency logo. Rituals may include various award ceremonies, team meetings and social gatherings.

3   Zeus
Apollo
Athena
Dionysus

4   You will probably have found sales-floor departments such as: ladies' outer wear, gent's outfitting, sports goods, children's clothes, stationery, ladies' shoes, linens, furniture and carpets. Service departments might include: accounts, credit, personnel, transport and warehousing and marketing. The advantages of such specialisation are greater expertise and efficiency.

5   The correct answers are (a) functional; (b) territorial; (c) product.

6   The group has identified three major functions of their business (sales, repairs and quality control) and to main product areas (guitars and drums). They might decide to structure the business in the following ways.

(a)   Have one 'general manager' (whose responsibilities may include quality control) and three 'operatives' who share the sales and repair tasks.

(b)   Divide tasks by function: have one person in change of sales, one quality controller and two repairers (perhaps one for drums and one for guitars).

(c)   Divide tasks by product: have a two-man drums team (who share sales/repair/control tasks between them) and a similar guitar team.

Since there are only four individuals, each (we assume) capable of performing any of the functions for either of the products, they may decide to have a looser social arrangement. They may prefer to discuss who is going to do what, as and when jobs come in. A larger organisation would not have this luxury.

7   An example of a garage procedure is dealing with a client bringing their car in for repair, with logging the car in and estimating the cost of the repair. Where procedures are written down – and thus codified – competitors may copy them. The basic assets of a small garage would include the equipment used in the repair of cars, e.g. ramps, test equipment, its buildings and its reputation. Explicit knowledge would include car-servicing schedules and instructions describing the workings of car engines.

Chapter 8 :

PLANS FOR AREAS OF RESPONSIBILITY

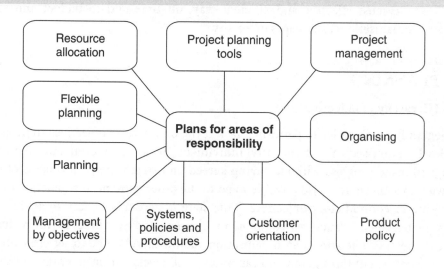

Introduction

The functions of management include **planning** – where managers establish goals, objectives, strategies, and policies and plan to achieve the stated aims of the organisation, and **organising** where managers structure the tasks that need to be performed, and decide which department and which individuals will complete which task and when. Planning helps the organisation to define its purposes and activities. It enables performance standards to be set so that results can be compared with the standard to help managers to see how the organisation is progressing towards its goals.

Because organisations have goals they want to satisfy, they need to direct their activities by:

- Deciding what they want to achieve

- Deciding how and when to do it and who is to do it

- Checking that they do achieve what they want, by monitoring what has been achieved and comparing it with the plan

- Taking action to correct any deviation

Your objectives

After completing this chapter and Chapter 9, (which is a continuation) you should be able to:

(a) Develop plans which promote goals and objectives for own area of responsibility and ensure plans are consistent with legal, regulatory and ethical requirements

(b) Use objectives which are specific, measurable, achievable, realistic and time-based to align people and other resources in an effective and efficient way

(c) Prepare and agree implementation plans which translate strategic targets into practical efficient and effective actions

(d) Manage work activities to prevent ineffective and inefficient deviations from the operational plan through effective monitoring and control

(e) Implement appropriate systems to achieve objectives and goals of the plan in the most effective and efficient way, on time and to budget and to meet organisational standards of quality

1 PLANNING

1.1 Hierarchy of objectives

It is generally much easier to perform a task if the objective or objectives to be achieved are clearly expressed. Yet frequently individuals, teams and even entire businesses attempt to make progress without having agreed and stated the performance objectives they wish to achieve. It is also possible to go to the other extreme and generate too many conflicting or contradictory objectives. This state is particularly easy to achieve in the matrix management structures common in business today, where an individual may have two 'bosses'. The aim in an organisation should therefore be to set clear objectives which are consistent throughout and can apply at all levels – from an entire enterprise to the individual.

Most writers agree with the idea that there is a hierarchy of objectives, just as there is a hierarchy of managers. At each higher level in the hierarchy the objectives are more relevant to a greater proportion of the organisation's activities so that the objectives at the top of the hierarchy are relevant to every aspect of the organisation. Plans are made at various levels in an organisation and may be stated in the form of a hierarchy. The following diagram illustrates the hierarchical relationship of mission, goals, objectives, strategy, tactics and operational plans.

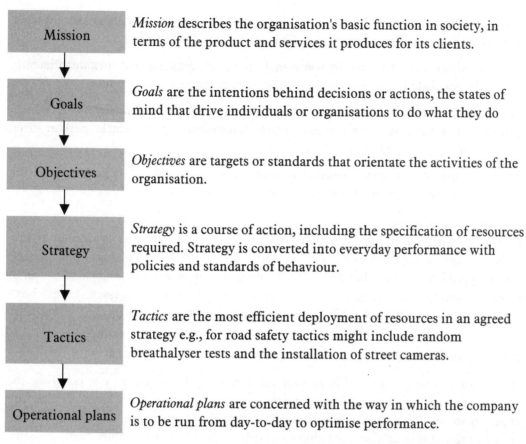

Mission	*Mission* describes the organisation's basic function in society, in terms of the product and services it produces for its clients.
Goals	*Goals* are the intentions behind decisions or actions, the states of mind that drive individuals or organisations to do what they do
Objectives	*Objectives* are targets or standards that orientate the activities of the organisation.
Strategy	*Strategy* is a course of action, including the specification of resources required. Strategy is converted into everyday performance with policies and standards of behaviour.
Tactics	*Tactics* are the most efficient deployment of resources in an agreed strategy e.g., for road safety tactics might include random breathalyser tests and the installation of street cameras.
Operational plans	*Operational plans* are concerned with the way in which the company is to be run from day-to-day to optimise performance.

Figure 8.1 Planning hierarchy

Objectives are normally quantified statements of what the organisation actually intends to achieve. Whereas mission statements describe a value system for the organisation and some indication of the business it is in, objectives are well defined, as the following example demonstrates.

(a) Mission: deliver a quality service

(b) Goal: enhance manufacturing quality

(c) Objectives: over the next twelve months, reduce the number of defects to 1 part per million

Goals and objectives are devised to fulfil the mission. The terms are often used interchangeably: if there is a difference, objectives are more likely to be quantified, and so progress towards them is more measurable. Goals and objectives can also be said to interpret the organisation's mission to a number of different client groups or *stakeholders*, all of whom have an interest in what the organisation does.

EXAMPLE

'The Co-op'

The Co-operative movement is a good example of the role of mission. The Co-operative Wholesale Society and Co-operative Retail Society are business organisations, but their mission is not simply profit.

Rather, being owned by their suppliers/customers rather than external shareholders, they have always, since the foundation, had a wider social concern.

The Co-op has been criticised by some analysts on the grounds that it is insufficiently profitable, certainly in comparison with supermarket chains such as Tescos.

The Co-op has explicit social objectives. In some cases it will retain stores which, although too small to be as profitable as a large supermarket, provide an important social function in the communities which host them.

Of course, the Co-op's performance as a retailer can be improved, but judging it on the conventional basis of profitability ignores its social objectives.

As with business planning (of which it forms an integral part) the process of setting objectives can be approached from either a 'top down' or 'bottom up' direction. The 'top down' approach ensures that the overall 'hierarchy of objectives' reflects the overall business objectives, whereas the 'bottom up' direction is necessary to establish practicality and feasibility in objectives applied at a local operational level.

1.2 The business plan

If individuals and groups within an organisation are to be effective in working for the achievement of the organisation's objectives, they need to know what it is they are expected to do. Planning allows managers to identify the objectives for which they are responsible and how far they are being successful in achieving those objectives.

Planning involves decisions about:

- What to do in future
- How to do it
- When to do it
- Who should do it

Such questions are relevant at all levels of organisational activity:

(a) At a strategic level – deciding what business the organisation should be in, and what its overall objectives should be

(b) At a tactical level – deciding how it should go about achieving its overall objectives: what products it should produce, how it will organise work and so on

(c) At the operational level – deciding what needs to be done from day to day and task to task

Strategic, or long-range, planning looks at where the business wants to be in maybe two to three years time, and works out how to get it there. This will involve consideration of environmental factors, current and potential competitors, declining and emerging markets, projected technological change, possible diversification (producing new, different products or services) and forecast movements in consumer spending. In other words, long-range planning has to deal with a lot of variables and a high level of uncertainty. The strategic plan will constantly be amended in the light of new developments.

Tactical, or short-range planning takes a shorter time period, for instance a year, and decides what needs to be done within that time period to further the strategic plan. At this level, planning will look at expansion targets, market penetration, asset purchases, financing requirements, resource requirements, and any improvements that need to be made to efficiency in order to maintain and widen the gap between costs and revenues. Improvements to efficiency will then be translated into operational planning.

Operational planning represents the lowest level of planning and involves line manager, supervisory management and foreman levels in setting specific tasks. The focus is on individual tasks, for example, scheduling individual works orders through a production planning process. Whatever it is that a supervisor intends to plan for, generally he or she will need to determine the following:

- What has to be achieved – the goal or objective?

- What jobs have to be done in order to reach that goal or objective?

- What resources are needed to do the jobs that have to be done?

- What sequence of task performance is required to progress efficiently toward the goal or objective?

- What kind of co-ordination is required?

- What has to be communicated and to whom must it be communicated?

- What has to be controlled and how must control be achieved to ensure that the plan is realised?

Planning horizon

Planning covers the long-term as well as the short-term. A planning period or time horizon is the length of time between making and implementing a planning decision. A decision to build new premises may have a time horizon of many years; a programme to develop a new product might take several years; an operating budget might span a one-year period; a production schedule might be produced weekly.

This has two main consequences.

(a) Long-term objectives might conflict with shorter-term plans, and planners should try to reconcile the two. If a company has a short-term problem with limited funds, for example, it might be tempting to cut costs to maintain profitability – but if spending on research or marketing are ignored, the company's long-term profitability might suffer.

(a) Plans, once formulated, should not be rigid, because the future is uncertain: plans might need to be changed if unforeseen circumstances arise. A compromise should be found between the need for flexibility (which suggests keeping plans short-term) and the need for commitment to decisions that have been made (which suggests planning over the whole of a long-term period).

1.3 Planning and control cycle

Planning is an activity that involves decisions about ends (organisational objectives), means (plans), behaviour (policies) and results. It is an activity which must take place against the background of the organisation's environment and which must take account of the organisation's internal strengths and weaknesses.

The stages in the planning and control cycle can be shown diagrammatically, as follows:

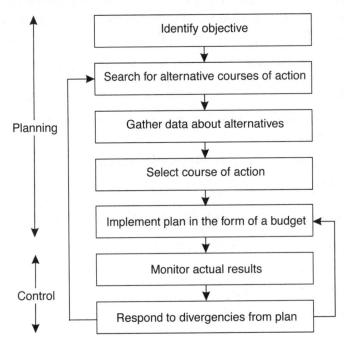

Figure 8.2 Planning process

Planning is the process of deciding what should be done. Control is the process of checking whether it has been done, and if not, doing something about it. Once the plan has been formulated and steps have been taken to carry it out, it is necessary to monitor and measure the actual results achieved. These results can then be compared to the planned results. This will show that either results are proceeding according to plan, or corrective action is necessary in order to ensure the plan is achieved.

Control is necessary because unexpected factors may arise and affect the system, so making actual results deviate from the expected results. Examples of such unpredictable factors in a business system might be:

- The entry of a powerful new competitor into the market
- An unexpected rise in labour costs
- A decline in quality standards
- A supplier going out of business
- Loss of a major customer
- New legislation affecting products
- The appearance of new technology

A good control system will provide management with rapid feedback enabling it to react appropriately to changes in the business environment.

It is as well to recognise that there always will be unpredictable factors. Given the current pace of change in finance, technology and world markets, it would be more surprising to see a long-term, or even a short-term, plan which proceeded as envisaged without any changes being made to keep it on track. It has even been argued that long-term planning is a waste of time, as the plan is bound to be overtaken by events.

An important part of planning in this regard is the consideration of contingencies. **Contingencies** are unexpected events, which may or may not happen. Contingency planning looks at how the overall plan will be affected if something unexpected happens, or if some part of the business does not proceed according to plan. As part of the contingency planning process, managers will come up with alternative solutions in response to possible problems. Contingency planning is covered in detail later in this chapter.

1.4 Purposes of planning and organising

If individuals and groups within an organisation are to be effective in working for the achievement of the organisation's objectives they need to know what it is they are expected to do. Planning allows managers to identify:

(a) the objectives for which they are responsible;

(b) what actions will serve towards achieving those objectives; and

(c) how far they are being successful in achieving those objectives.

Planning and organising are important functions in an organisation for the following reasons.

(a) **Uncertainty**. Organisations cannot deal with things ad hoc, as they occur, without chaos. The future cannot be foreseen with certainty in any case, and even the best-laid plans will go wrong to a greater or lesser degree (which is where 'control' comes in). Nevertheless, plans and structures give some direction and predictability to the work of the organisation: in other words, they are a form of risk management.

(b) **The need for co-ordination**. Organisations are collections of individuals and groups (or sub-systems): each will perceive its own part of the organisation's activity, and work towards its own objectives accordingly. Planning and organising ensures that:

(i) sub units of the organisation know what it is they need to achieve, and when;

(ii) work 'flows' from one process (or department) to another without holdups or clashes, and without idle time or overwork for staff and machinery;

(iii) the resources required for a task are available where and when they are required;

(iv) required work is being done by somebody – but not being duplicated by others, with a waste of effort;

(v) all of the above are achieved in such a way that products/services of the required quality are available to customers at the right place, at the right price and at the right time.

FOR DISCUSSION

Suggest examples of the planning/organising needed in each of the areas given in (i) to (v) above, and what would happen if planning was not carried out.

(c)   The need for objectives. Human beings are 'purposive': they like to feel that their actions have a point. If the organisation doesn't set objectives, people will set their own, according to their own interpretation of the situation: chaos ensues. Objectives are also important in learning and motivation, so people can target and adjust their behaviour according to what they want to achieve.

1.5   Measures of success

The degree to which the goals and objectives are attained is a measure of the organisation's *effectiveness*. This term should not be confused with the *efficiency* of the organisation, which is concerned with the means employed. If inappropriate means are employed the organisation could be very efficient but totally ineffective – conversely an organisation can be very effective but have sufficient organisational slack to be able to operate inefficiently.

Efficiency

Efficiency is a term often used loosely to express the idea of 'doing things well'.

Definition

Efficiency is the relationship between inputs used and outputs achieved. The fewer the inputs used to obtain a given output, the greater the efficiency. Efficiency can be expressed as: $\dfrac{\text{output}}{\text{input}}$

If a car does 400 miles on 10 gallons of petrol it does $400 \div 10 = 40$ miles per gallon. This is a measure of its efficiency at using fuel.

Efficiency is about avoiding **waste** – of effort, time and material resources – in producing desired outputs, or achieving the organisation's goals. Efficient operation might involve:

(a)   producing no less, but no more, than the demand for the product;

(b)   avoiding spoiled or unacceptable products, according to the organisation's quality standards;

(c)   avoiding overmanning (employing more people than the task requires), or improving productivity: output (or profit, say) per employee;

(d)   avoiding unnecessary movements, operations and routines (such as paperwork, task duplications, double-checks and so on) which take time, without adding value in the process;

(e)   avoiding expense of finance and resources which add no value and earn no return.

Effectiveness

It has been argued that efficiency focuses too much on controlling the 'inputs' to the organisation's activities, and not enough on the 'outputs'. (You can improve efficiency by cutting costs instead of improving sales ...)

Definition

> **Effectiveness** is the measure of how far an organisation (and its managers) achieve their output requirements, as defined by performance objectives and targets.

In other words, **effectiveness** is about 'doing the right things', not just 'doing things right'. Effectiveness-orientated managers are concerned with fulfilling objectives with regard to:

(a)   output quantity;

(b)   output quality and customer satisfaction;

(c)   added value (the value added to inputs, reflected in the sale price of the output);

(d)   innovation, or new products/services/improvements implemented.

Activity 1		**(5 mins)**
Read through and tick in the relevant columns whether the statements relate to efficiency or effectiveness.		
	Efficiency	Effectiveness
(a) A customer is satisfied	☐	☐
(b) The factory produces more cars	☐	☐
(c) Waste has been reduced	☐	☐
(d) Better quality products are produced	☐	☐
(e) Ten employees were given early retirement packages	☐	☐
(f) The company increased its dividend payment to shareholders	☐	☐

Efficiency and effectiveness require:

(a)   an idea of what outputs the organisation wants from the production system;

(b)   an idea of what inputs will be required; and

(c)   a way of monitoring and measuring performance, to ensure that it conforms to the organisation's expectations.

In essence, this is the process of planning and control.

NOTES

2 MANAGEMENT BY OBJECTIVES (MBO)

2.1 Achievement of organisational goals

Management by objectives (MBO) is a scheme of planning and control that provides co-ordination:

- of short-term plans with longer-term plans and goals;
- of the plans (and commitment) of junior with senior management;
- of the efforts of different departments.

Successful achievement of organisational goals requires the following.

(a) Each job is directed towards the same organisational goals. Each managerial job must be focused on the success of the business as a whole, not just one part of it.

(b) Each manager's targets must be derived from targets of achievement for the organisation as a whole.

(c) A manager's results must be measured in terms of their contribution to the business as a whole.

(d) Each manager must know what his or her targets of performance are.

(e) A manager's superior must know what to demand from the manager, and how to judge his or her performance.

Consequently, to ensure co-ordination, the various functional objectives must be interlocked:

(a) *vertically* from top to bottom of the business;

(b) *horizontally*, for example, the objectives of the production function must be linked with those of sales, warehousing, purchasing and R & D;

(c) *overtime*. Short-term objectives can be regarded as intermediate milestones on the road towards long-term objectives.

2.2 SMART Objectives

MBO also introduced the SMART method for checking the validity of objectives. SMART is an acronym for:

- Specific
- Measurable
- Achievable
- Realistic, and
- Time-related.

Specific	• Is the objective precise and well defined? For example, 'Answer the phone quickly' can be said to be a precise description of behaviour, you can clearly see whether someone answers the phone or not, but there is no rate, number, percentage or frequency linked to it. So, if we add 'Answer the phone within three rings' a rate has been added and the behaviour is now much more specific.
	• Is it clear?
	• Can everyone understand it?
Measurable	• How will the individual know when the task has been completed?
	• What evidence is needed to confirm it?
	• Have you stated how you will judge whether it has been completed or not? Setting an objective that requires phone calls to be answered in three rings is fine, provided a system exists which measures whether this is actually being achieved.
Achievable	• Is it within their capabilities? They need to be stretching and agreed by the parties involved. Setting targets that are plainly ridiculous does not motivate people; it merely confirms their opinion of you as an idiot.
	• Are there sufficient resources available to enable this to happen?
	• Can it be done at all?
Realistic /relevant	• Is it possible for the individual to perform the objective?
	• How sensible is the objective in the current business context?
	• Does it fit into the overall pattern of this individual's work?
	• Example: Telling the cleaners that they 'have to increase market share over the next financial quarter' is not actually something they can do anything about – it is not relevant to them. However, asking them to reduce expenditure on cleaning materials by £50 over the next three months is entirely relevant to them. It is what they spend their budget on every day.
Time-related	• Is there a deadline – in the objective somewhere there has to be a date (Day/Month/Year) for when the task has to be started (if it's ongoing) and/or completed (if it's short term or project related)?
	• Is it feasible to meet this deadline?
	• Is it appropriate to do this work now?
	• Are there review dates?

2.3 Co-ordination

Co-ordination is one of the major functions of management. Each department will have its own procedures and its own priorities. It is the job of the manager to get all of these to mesh together harmoniously and move in the direction of the common purpose.

This is nowhere more apparent than in the planning process. Each department will have its own long-term and short-term goals and purposes and targets that it wants to achieve. There may also be bonus schemes tied into this. Each department will have its own set of priorities. Effective co-ordination will cause some of these to change, in the interests of pursuing an overall set of priorities.

NOTES

As the business plan will cover all departments of the organisation, so all of the departmental plans and budgets must be co-ordinated, so that they are all working together to achieve the business plan. For instance, sales should be planning to sell the number of units that the production departments agreed to produce, otherwise there will be either unsold stock or unfilled orders.

At the production level, co-ordination will ensure that:

- Departments know what it is they need to achieve, and when

- Work 'flows' from one department to another without hold-ups or clashes, and without idle time or overwork for staff and machinery

- The resources required for a task are available where and when they are required

- There is no duplication of effort

2.4 Individual effectiveness and time management

The aim of MBO for the individual is to provide clear direction. This is the first step in delivering managerial effectiveness. There must also be a *meeting* of objectives. The individual will have personal objectives, which need to be placed in the context of the business objectives to ensure 'goal congruence' – so that the individual can work towards personal and organisational objectives simultaneously.

From then on, the effectiveness of individuals depends on how well they organise themselves. This involves competence areas like:

- Setting priorities – the organisation's operations require proper scheduling of resources to run efficiently and avoid periods of over and under utilisation. Some activities must occur at precisely the right time, eg specific day and time slot for advertising a new product. The scheduling of tasks can also affect customer service in terms of delivery.

- Skill at marshalling and utilising the resources at one's disposal – this applies to both human and material resources. For human resources the manager has to get the best out of the available resource by leading, communicating, delegating and motivating.

- Ability to communicate – this is the major key to being efficient and effective

- Efficiency in time management – the process also starts with a hierarchy of plans and objectives based on the following questions:

    - What are my long-term goals and what strategy will I employ to achieve them?

    - What are my plans for the mid term?

    - What are my daily work plans?

3   SYSTEMS, POLICIES AND PROCEDURES

3.1   Planning and co-ordination tools

The tools by which planning and co-ordination are carried out can be categorised as follows.

Systems – a system is an agreed-upon plan or process for carrying out an activity. An operating system interfaces between the hardware, programs and data in a computer. It organises and schedules the tasks. A production plant will have a system, which determines how production is organised, who does what, when the machines are serviced, how long the shifts run etc.

In a business, the accounting system will ensure that all bookkeeping and related tasks are carried out accurately and in a timely fashion. At the next level, the management information system will provide management with the financial information needed for planning and control.

Policies – are general statements or 'understandings' that provide guidelines for management decision-making. It might be company policy, for example, to offer five-year guarantees on all products, or to promote managers from within the organisation. Policy guidelines allow managers to exercise their own discretion and freedom of choice, but within certain acceptable limits.

Procedures – are chronological sequences of actions required to perform a task. They exist at all levels but are more extensive lower down the company hierarchy, where the work is more routine. They have three main advantages:

(a) **Efficiency** – procedures prescribe the most efficient way of doing a job.

(b) **Routine** – procedures remove the need for the exercise of discretion or ad hoc decision-making.

(c) **Standardisation** – this makes output more predictable and more consistent throughout the organisation.

Rules – a rule (or regulation) prescribes a specific, definite action that must be taken in a given situation. It allows no discretion – unlike a policy. For example:

(a) 'employees in department X are allowed 10 minutes exactly at the end of their shift for clearing up and cleaning their work bench'

(b) 'employees with access to a telephone must not use the telephone for personal calls'.

Programmes – are co-ordinated groups or series of plans, which together achieve a particular objective; for instance, a company might undertake a programme of expansion, computerisation or customer care, involving different aspects and stages of planning.

Budgets – a budget is a formal statement of expected results set out in numerical terms, usually summarised in money values. It is a plan for carrying out certain activities with specified resources within a given period of time, in order to achieve certain targets.

Activity 2   **(20 mins)**

Dial-a-Video Limited offers home video rental service to subscribers. Subscribers choose a video from a catalogue, phone Dial-a-Video Limited and the video is delivered by a despatch rider. The Chairman, Rajiv Bharat, says to you: 'I hope to expand the business. I've discovered a market for art movie videos. I've had to knock the directors' heads together to develop plans for building a distribution system: they've agreed a number of stages: for a new catalogue, market research and that sort of thing. We'll charge £4 per video per day including delivery. It is a premium price, but people who like that sort of movie will pay for it. We'll tell the despatch riders not to accept tips though.'

What sort of plans has Rajiv Bharat described to you?

3.2 Office procedures and systems

Office systems and procedures are designed to allow the different administrative functions to operate effectively. This diagram shows in a simplified form the flow of funds, documentation and information in an office.

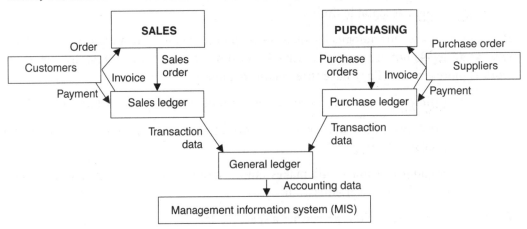

Figure 8.3 Office systems

Effective systems and procedures should ensure that:

- Relationships with customers are effectively managed
- Relationships with suppliers are effectively managed
- Office functions interrelate properly and are not duplicated

Within the overall system, which we can consider to be how each department relates to the other departments and to outside bodies, there will be sub-systems. For instance, the purchase ledger function will have its own system, which will be designed to ensure that only authorised payments are made, that no invoice ever gets paid twice and that expenses are coded to the correct accounts.

Weaknesses in office procedures may be signalled by:

- Arguments over job functions
- Missing paperwork
- Disputes with customers/suppliers
- Goods not delivered

3.3 Financial control procedures

Financial control procedures exist specifically to ensure that:

- Financial transactions are properly carried out
- The assets of the business are safeguarded
- Accurate and timely management information is produced

These are some examples of financial control procedures:

- Cheques over a certain amount to need two signatories
- Authorisation limits for purchase orders
- Authorisation for petty cash and expenses claims
- Effective credit control procedures
- Computer security procedures and access levels

Weaknesses in financial control procedures may be signalled by:

- Cash or cheques going missing
- Excessive bad or doubtful debts
- Debtors not paying within credit terms
- Suppliers not being paid on time
- Unauthorised purchases being made
- Failure to produce accounts or other reports at the specified time

3.4 Managing risk

Plans do not give managers control over the future.

(a) The future cannot be forecast with any certainty. You can only anticipate what is **likely** to happen in future, based on what has happened in the past, and any trends or tendencies that you can see in the pattern of past events.

(b) Unexpected, uncontrollable events happen. Computers break down, terrorists blow up buildings, suppliers go bust, transport strikes shut down operations for a day and so on.

Risk is the exposure to the possibility of such things as economic or financial loss, physical damage, injury or delay as a consequence of pursuing or not pursuing a particular course of action. It is the probability of an event and magnitude of its consequence.

Risk management is the process whereby an organisation anticipates the potential for adverse events that may lead to injury or loss and acts to avoid those events before they occur and/or to ameliorate them after they occur. As with all risk management, the key objective is to introduce measures that cost less than the potential damage, which might arise if the risks identified occurred. Specifically, risk management involves three steps: risk assessment, risk management and risk transference.

Risk assessment – all potential problems that can be thought of should be listed and broken down under headings eg, physical, human and systems or employees, computers, operating conditions and criminal activities.

Physical	Human	Systems
Fire, flood or terrorist action	Staff on strike	A computer virus which destroys all the files on the hard disk
Currency devaluation in your main trading country	Payroll theft	Accounting error due to posting a wrong amount
Power cut	Employee has heart attack	Snow breaks telephone lines

These risks should then be assessed as to the impact and damage they would cause to the business if they occurred. The risk should be quantified as far as possible, eg the failure of a particular computer on the network might result in the loss of half a day's sales and the time involved in re-keying information. The qualitative nature of the risk needs to be noted as well.

Risk management – once the potential damage has been assessed, steps are taken to minimise the damage. It is a vital element of risk management that the cost of the steps must be commensurate with the damage avoided. Management can attempt to reduce the risk through good work practices, quality specifications and standards, backup systems and contingency plans. The remaining risk may be an insurable risk.

Risk transference – ultimately, there are some areas where the risk is small in terms of its probability but high in the damage that would be incurred. An example might be earthquake damage in most of the UK, or losses arising due to fire, etc. Whilst steps can be taken to ensure the integrity of data, the most sensible way of dealing with the rest of the risk to the systems is to transfer, or share the cost via insurance or some other form of contingency plan covering the area of 'disaster recovery'.

Contingencies are unexpected and uncontrollable events that do not feature in the main plan of the organisation. However, some such events can be anticipated: managers do not expect them to happen, but acknowledge that they might happen, and consider what should be done if they do. Contingency plans are those which are prepared in advance to deal with a situation that may (or may not) arise.

All plans should be contingency plans to an extent, since planners must make room for:

(a) margins of error; time and resource estimates are only estimates;
(b) changes in the circumstances;
(c) slippage in the schedule which needs to be caught up elsewhere.

Remember that planning is part of the control system: plans may constantly have to be adjusted in order to correct or improve performance.

Activity 3 **(20 mins)**

What kind of contingency plans might you want to make if you were in charge of:

(a) transferring all your transactions onto a new computer system?

(b) accomplishing a project which required all the 'people hours' you have at your disposal?

(c) organising (yet another) sales conference at an external venue

---

4 CUSTOMER ORIENTATION

4.1 Managing the relationship with clients/customers

Management is not just about 'managing' the organisation and the people within it, it is also about 'managing' the relationship with clients, or customers. All organisations have customers, clients, patients, etc, and with the exception of some types of monopolies, the success and future of the organisation depends upon the continued goodwill of its clients. These clients may be individuals, businesses, governments or even other large organisations.

The customer is the basic reason for the existence of any business since without customers to sell to, a business cannot operate. Meeting the needs of those customers more effectively than competitors is the key to continued profitable existence for any business. Each customer who deals with an organisation should leave with a feeling of satisfaction. This outcome is important since it can lead to increased sales and/or a willingness to pay higher prices and thus lead to higher profits. If customers are satisfied they may:

- Buy again from the same supplier
- Buy more of the same item, or more expensive items
- Advise their friends to buy from the supplier

When anyone buys they take a risk. Everyone likes to feel that they get value for money. There is increased risk of dissatisfaction when buying a new product or buying from a new supplier. It is important that the supplier helps to reduce this risk for new customers so that they are more likely to become regular customers.

Customer loyalty is promoted, achieved and enhanced in several differing ways.

(a) The launch of specific initiatives aimed at engaging the customer in schemes which help to guarantee loyalty, eg airmiles, the Tesco ClubCard and various SMART card offers run by retailers and others.

(b) Creating a customer proposition offering something which customers may feel they cannot refuse, eg Esso's price-offer advertising campaign.

(c) Engaging the customer in a dialogue, thus ensuring that the customer feels an affinity with the product or service on offer.

Customer focus represents a major shift in marketing emphasis for many organisations, which at one time did not seem to realise that they had customers at all. Indeed, British Telecommunications plc (BT) used to call its customers 'subscribers', and kept them diligently at arm's length; many public-sector service operations were not in any sense 'customer-focused' simply because they were monopolies, supplying services like education, housing and refuse collection to 'ratepayers' whether they wanted them or not.

In most large organisations there is a customer service department, however, departments such as these were set up primarily to deal with problems or complaints. Whilst serving a useful purpose, it should, however, be considered that with a closer management-customer relationship such departments would be much less busy.

Activity 4	**(10 mins)**
Why is customer loyalty important?	

4.2 Customer orientation: internal and external customers

According to Drucker, customer orientation is ' the business seen from the point of view of its final result ie, from the customer's point of view.' To meet the customers' requirements means to listen to them and to respond to what they want and to what is agreed upon. But customers are not only external to the company – people outside the company who are the end users of a firm's products and services – they are also the internal customers.

Definition

An **internal customer** is the person within the company who receives the work of another and then adds his or her contribution to the product or service before passing it on to someone else.

In manufacturing, the internal customer is the next person down the assembly line. In a restaurant, the chef has assistant chefs, waiters, and waitresses as internal customers and the chef must meet their requirements if the diners are to be pleased.

There are two approaches to customer orientation:

(a) the market driven (reactive) approach which adapts products and services to customer expectations and preferences; and

(b) the driving markets approach which adapts customer expectations and preferences to the products and services

Figure 8.4 Approaches to customer orientation

To remain competitive today, a company must focus on quality. Product quality must encompass all aspects of a business, from superior service to turnaround time. Businesses strive to achieve quality for one main reason – customer satisfaction.

An organisation can be viewed as a series of transactions between customers and suppliers. Transfers and exchanges are observable within a team or department, and between teams, departments, divisions, or other organisational units. Therefore, every department and every person should see themselves as a customer of colleagues and a supplier to other internal customers. Viewing employees as internal customers allows the activities of the organisation to be viewed from a process management perspective. Each process within an interrelated system (and the personnel that carried out that process) is considered a customer for the preceding process as well as a supplier for the ensuing process.

Each person in the process is an important link in the chain of events. Quality failure at any stage could be catastrophic. The customer/supplier chain illustrated below shows the stages from an external customer's requirements given to a sales person, through order processing, planning and purchasing and production to dispatch and handover to the satisfied external customer.

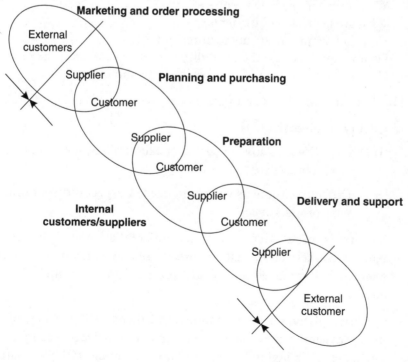

Figure 8.5 Customer/supplier chain

4.3 Quality chain

What constitutes a 'quality product or service' must, it seems, be related to what the customer wants. Indeed, quality would have no commercial value unless it delivered customer benefit, since the key reason for aiming to produce quality products is to derive extra sales, to establish competitive advantage through tangible and generally perceived superiority in particular product or service features.

John Oakland (1989) argues that meeting customer requirements is the main focus in a search for quality and the supplier/customer relationships are part of a series of quality chains throughout and beyond all enterprises.

The quality implementation process requires that all the supplier/customer relationships within the quality chain should be treated as marketing exercises, and that each customer should be carefully consulted as to their precise requirements from the product or service with which they are to be provided. Each link in the chain should prompt the following questions, according to Oakland.

Of customers:

- Who are my immediate customers?
- What are their true requirements?
- How do or can I find out what the requirements are?
- How can I measure my ability to meet the requirements?
- Do I have the necessary capability to meet the requirements? (If not, then what must change to improve the capability?)
- Do I continually meet the requirements? (If not, then what prevents this from happening, when the capability exists?)
- How do I monitor changes in the requirements?

Of suppliers

- Who are my immediate suppliers?
- What are my true requirements?
- How do I communicate my requirements?
- Do my suppliers have the capability to measure and meet the requirements?
- How do I inform them of changes in the requirements?

It should be noted that this focus on the customer does pose a number of problems.

(a) **Quality is subjective**

   (i) If quality is relative to customer expectations, it cannot be measured in an absolute sense.

   (ii) Different customers will want, need or expect different things from the same product-type

(b) **Quality is distinctive** – product differentiation and highly segmented modern markets mean that the precise requirements of a particular market segment will produce an equally precise and differentiated definition of quality.

(c) **Quality is dynamic** – expectations, and therefore definitions of quality, are highly dynamic: they change over time as a consequence of experience. A ratchet effect is highly likely, so that expectations will rise relatively easily, but will rarely and very reluctantly fall.

5 PRODUCT POLICY

5.1 Product development

By 'product' we mean everything that is used by a firm to provide consumer satisfaction. A product can be a physical commodity, or a service, a group of either of these, or a product-service combination.

It is important to bear in mind exactly what a product is to the consumer. It is really a package of satisfaction. The consumer's image of the product is frequently more significant than the physical description of the product itself. It is what it means to the consumer, not what it means to the seller, that is the key to product policy.

When the outputs of factories are virtually identical, and within a given price range, the conversion of an indifferent (even apathetic) potential customer into a buyer needs effort. Irrespective of whether the product is a toy, a pair of shoes, a lipstick or management consultancy, the existence of competition often means that the successful seller offers more than the actual product itself. The product must be surrounded by value satisfactions, which differentiate his product from others.

Developing your product line has to be based on a thorough understanding of the consumer, the market and all the various forces that make an impact upon them. The steps taken to achieve this are, broadly:

- appraising the products and their trends, in relation to those of competitors, as viewed by the consumer;

- analysing consumer needs and habits and evaluating them with respect to both present and possible future markets;

- preparing product specifications of performance, physical characteristics, quality level, dependability, serviceability, safety features, product identification, packaging and appearance that offers the benefits that our target market is seeking;

- formulating prices with the targets of volume and profit in mind;

- controlling product-lines by developing and administering policies, programmes and plans;

- processing product ideas to make plans for innovation;

- providing product information for manuals, advertising, etc;

- recommending design and redesigning;

- co-ordinating the plans and product programmes of the various chief management functions: sales, finance, production and personnel.

5.2 Marketing research

Marketing research is the systematic and objective search for, and analysis of, information relevant to the identification and solution of any problem in the field of marketing. It is not just obtaining information, but *involves*

- framing questions whose answers will provide data to help solve problems;

- asking questions to those best qualified to answer them;

- recording answers correctly;

- interpreting answers; and

- translating interpretations and making recommendations for marketing action.

It consists of

(a) *market research* (analysis of the market size, trends, market shares, etc);

(b) *distribution research* (analysis of present channels of distribution, warehouse and other storage locations, discount policy, transport needs, etc);

(c) *economic research* (analysis of trends including social and forecasting);

(d) *evaluation of product(s)* (customer requirements analysis, product life cycles, quality measurements, reliability); and

(e) *communication analysis* (of the media usage, suggested media combinations eg TV and newspaper advertising, etc).

Information required

Organisations need knowledge about

(a) *Consumers*

(i) Who is the customer and who is the consumer? (Not necessarily the same person.)

(ii) What do they desire in the way of satisfactions?

(iii) Where does the customer choose to purchase?

(iv) Why does he or she purchase?

(v) How does he or she go about seeking satisfaction in the market?

(b) Their own performance

(c) Activities of *competitors*

(d) Attitude of other *stakeholders*

FOR DISCUSSION

How are you at planning? How did you approach exam-revision, for example, or essay-writing? People must have told you how important it is to 'make a proper plan'. If you didn't do so – why not? Do you think managers suffer from the same difficulties?

---

6 ORGANISING

6.1 Structures and systems

Organising – or organisation – implies the establishment of structures, social arrangements, or systems, for the purposes of:

(a) distributing **authority and responsibility** in such a way as to ensure that each task of the organisation is facilitated and controlled: that someone is both authorised to perform it and accountable for performing it;

(b) **communication** of the information needed for the task and for control feedback;

(c) **co-ordination** of resources – including people's time and effort – towards unified objectives, via a hierarchy of objectives and targets for each sub-unit of the organisation; and

(d) the **grouping and allocation** of tasks in logical ways.

The grouping of organisational activities (into teams, departments or larger divisions) can be done in different ways. The most common are as follows.

(a) **By function,** or specialism. Primary functions in a manufacturing company, for example, might be production, sales, finance, and general administration.

(b) **By territory** or geographical area. This method of organisation occurs when similar activities are carried out in different locations. Water and electricity services, for example, operate region by region. Many sales departments are organised territorially, with regional sales areas.

The main advantage of territorial departmentation is better local decision-making at the point of contact between the organisation (eg a salesman) and its customers.

(c) **By product.** Some organisations group activities on the basis of products or product lines. Functional division of responsibility remains, but under the control of a manager with responsibility for a product, product line or brand, with authority over the personnel of different functions involved in its production, marketing and so on.

The main advantages of product departmentation are the development of specialised product knowledge, and the co-ordination of functional activities.

(d) **Matrix organisation.** As we discussed in Chapter 1, the new emphasis on flexibility has created a trend towards task-centred structures, such as multi-disciplinary project teams, which draw people together from different functions. Authority is divided between the members' departmental managers, and the team's product/project manager or co-ordinator.

Having recapped the broader implications of organising for organisation and job design, we will now look briefly at the day-to-day aspects: to whom should a manager allocate or delegate a given task.

6.2 Allocating tasks

Some decisions about division of labour will be pre-programmed by:

(a) **organisational positions and job descriptions,** which dictate who does what (although these are becoming less rigid, in favour of flexibility and empowerment); and

(b) **specialisms**. There may be an obvious expert to whom specialised tasks should be given: a payroll, legal or information technology expert, say.

However, other decisions will require management discretion.

(a) Peak periods in some tasks may necessitate redistribution of staff to cope with the workload: there should be flexibility in who does, and is able to do, non-specialist tasks.

(b) Status and staff attitudes must be considered. Flexibility in reassigning people from one job to another or varying the work they do may be hampered by an employee's perception of his own status: helping out or covering for others may be out of the question: 'I'm a secretary, not a copy typist!' etc. Task allocation must take into account people's experience and seniority – and also the fact that junior employees may want greater challenge and responsibility.

(c) Individual abilities and temperaments differ, and work should be allocated to the best person for the job. Some staff like routine work but crack under pressure, and vice versa; some are good with computers, some with people. Planning should allow for flexibility in the event of an employee proving unfit for a task – or more able than his present tasks indicate.

6.3 Align resources with objectives

Resource planning involves identifying potential resources and allocating them in order that the defined and agreed corporate objectives may be achieved. At operational level the stages in resource planning are as follows.

(a) Carrying out a *resource audit* to establish currently available or obtainable resources by category and details of any that are not available or readily obtainable.

(b) Estimating what resources would be needed to pursue a particular strategy and deciding whether there would be enough resources to pursue it successfully.

(c) Assigning responsibilities to managers for the acquisition, use and control of resources.

(d) Identifying all internal and environmental factors exerting an influence on the availability and use of resources.

Some strategies can be met from existing resources, new resources, or a mixture of existing and new resources in tandem, but the objectives and strategies that cannot be met will have to be deferred until a later time, or abandoned altogether.

The situation might be explained more simply by means of a Venn diagram.

Johnson and Scholes suggest that there are three central questions in operational resource planning that must be resolved.

(a) *Resource identification*. What resources will be needed to implement the strategy?

(b) *Fit with existing resources*. An assessment must be made of the following.

    (i) The extent to which the required resources are *already* in place.

    (ii) The extent to which any new resources that are needed can be built on existing resources.

    (iii) Whether there will have to be some *changes* to existing resources in order to implement the strategy.

(c) *Fit between required resources*. An assessment must also be made, when new resources are required to implement a strategy, of how these resources can be properly integrated with each other. For example, increasing output might require more people *and* more machines, and extra resources might be needed for training.

Planning issues

Resource plans can be prepared in detail, providing organisations know what they need to achieve.

(a) Critical success factors (CSFs) 'are those factors on which the strategy is fundamentally dependent on its success'.

(b) Key tasks are what must be done to ensure each critical success factor is achieved.

(c) Priorities indicate the order in which tasks are achieved.

For example, the critical success factor to run a successful mail order business may be speedy delivery. Some CSFs are generic to the whole industry, others to a particular firm: a generic CSF of a parcel delivery service is that it *should* be quicker than the normal post. Underpinning critical success factors are key tasks. If *customer care* is a CSF, then a key task, and hence a measure of performance, would include responding to enquires within a given time period. There may be a number of key tasks – but some might be more important than others, or come first in a sequence.

CSFs can be used to translate strategic objectives into performance targets and tactical plans. Here is an example.

(a) Dogger Bank plc has increased profit as a business objective.

(b) The strategy for increased profits is to increase revenue per customer.

(c) Increasing revenue per customer might not be possible unless customers buy other services, such as insurance from the bank.

    (i) The *critical success factor* will be the number of extra services sold to each customer.

    (ii) A *key task* might involve developing a customer database so that the firm can target customers within information about other services more effectively.

The relevance of CSFs to resource planning is that they indicate some idea of the resources that are needed. For example, if the key task for Dogger Bank plc is the development of a customer database, then the resources needed might include new hardware and the services of a systems analyst.

A resource plan will address critical success factors, key tasks and priorities – through one or more of the following planning tools:

- Budgets

- Financial plans

- HR plans

- Network analysis (project plan)- indicating how resources will be deployed in a particular sequence. This is especially relevant for one-off projects.

A resource plan will then be built up, containing detailed estimates of what is needed for the various activities of the business. The plan will contain mechanisms for testing its key assumptions, like demand, if they are liable to change.

Resource allocation includes estimates of the task requirements with regard to:

(a) how many people working for how many hours;

(b) machine hours;

(c) raw materials and components (allowing for a certain amount of wastage); and

(d) finance – that is, the cost of all the above.

It also includes estimates of the availability of all these resources.

(a) How many people with the required skills or experience are available (inside or outside the organisation)? What is their standard level of productivity, and could it be increased?

(b) What machinery is available, given the demands made on it by the task and by other tasks from other units? What is its standard level of productivity, and could it be increased?

(c) Is there sufficient stock of raw materials or components? If not, can they be bought in or made, and at what cost? Are they of the required specifications and quality? What is the expected usage rate of stock: when will stocks run out and need to be replenished? What is the standard wastage rate in the course of operations, and can this be reduced?

(d) How much money needs to be budgeted or allowed for, to complete the task? Is such an amount available and worth spending, for the expected results?

Activity 5 (20 mins)

What kind of resources might a sales conference organiser have to plan for?

6.4 Time management

A manager's use of time is affected by a number of factors.

The nature of the job

A manager's job involves regular contact with other people in the organisation: it is important to control the inevitable interruptions which this causes. Other typical causes of wasted time include prolonged or unnecessary meetings, and the preparation of unnecessary paperwork (which could be replaced with a brief oral communication).

The personality of the manager

A confident and assertive manager may be better able to resist interruptions and unnecessarily lengthy contacts than one who is diffident, and finds it difficult to 'say no'. A manager may fail to delegate, and end up with a lot of routine work on his own plate. On the other hand, he may simply be disorganised or lacking in self discipline and so be comparatively idle one minute and extremely busy the next.

The influence and demands of colleagues

There will be extra demands on the manager's time if:

(a) subordinates keep referring to the manager for decisions;

(b) subordinates require either close supervision or a consultative style of management;

(c) the culture of the organisation or department requires lots of communication, informal relationship-building, Management by Walking Around, an 'Open Door' availability policy and so on: this takes time.

Activity 6   **(10 mins)**

Suggest two ways in which the management style of a superior may make extra demands on a manager's time.

Time management will involve the following.

(a) **Identifying objectives** and the key tasks which are most relevant to achieving them – sorting out what the manager **must** do, from what he **could** do, and from what he would **like** to do.

(b) **Prioritising:** assessing tasks for relative importance, amount of time required, and any deadlines or time-spans.

(c) **Scheduling** – assigning start and end times/dates to tasks (in other words, timetabling).

(d) **Control:** avoiding, where possible, disruption by the unexpected.

NOTES

Activity 7   **(10 mins)**

Think about how effectively you manage time by answering these questions.

1   Do you often miss deadlines for activities you are responsible for?

2   Are you often late for meetings or appointments?

3   Do you have to work late regularly to get things done?

4   Do you feel you are constantly trying to beat the clock?

5   Are you too busy to find time to plan?

6   Do you seem to have more work to do than others?

7   Have you got a good balance between time spent on study or work, with family, on yourself?

---

7   PROJECT MANAGEMENT

7.1   What is project management?

Definition

A **project** is an undertaking, often cutting across organisational and functional boundaries, and carried out to meet established goals within cost, schedule and quality objectives.

Project management is directed at a particular end: achieving specific objectives within a specific time span. It is not, like general management, directed at maintaining or improving continuous work activities.

Activity 8   **(20 mins)**

See if you can think of an example of a project in each of the following areas.

(a) Building and construction.

(b) Manufacturing.

(c) Management.

(d) Research and development.

Project management therefore requires even closer attention to planning, organising and control, with regard to:

(a) **quality** – the end result should conform to specification; in other words, the project should achieve what it was meant to do;

(b) **cost** – the project should be completed without exceeding authorised expenditure (as specified in a budget) of money and other human and material resources;

(c) **time** – each stage of the project's progress must conform to schedule, so that the end result is achieved when requested or required.

7.2 Project planning

A project plan aims to ensure that the project objective is achieved within the requirements of quality, cost and time. This will involve:

(a) breaking the project down into manageable units of activity, and determining the sequence of, or relationships between, those units or tasks;

(b) estimating the resources (materials, money, time and so on) required for each unit;

(c) sequencing and scheduling each unit in the most appropriate way for co-ordinated performance.

We will now look at techniques and tools used for planning and organising interrelated and interdependent activities.

8 PROJECT PLANNING TOOLS

8.1 Work breakdown structure (WBS)

Breaking a project down into its component phases or stages is often the best way of:

(a) discovering exactly what work must be accomplished;
(b) determining the resources required; and
(c) sequencing and co-ordinating the work done.

Activity 9   **(30 mins)**

Suppose you set yourself the project of cooking a dinner party for yourself and five friends.

(a) Define the objectives of the project: devise a three course meal menu.

(b) Estimate (roughly):
    (i)   the cost and
    (ii)   the time it will take you to prepare.

(c) Establish a work breakdown structure, in the form of a detailed list of things to do, for preparing your menu.

(d) What does your WBS tell you about your cost and time estimates?

This is called establishing a work breakdown structure (WBS) for the project.

Figure 8.6 is a simple example of a **diagrammatic** work breakdown structure for a house-building project. We have only broken down two of the component stages to the second level (the foundations and the wiring), but you should get the idea. The breakdown process continues until the smallest sub-unit or task is reached, for which man and machine hours can most easily be calculated and scheduled.

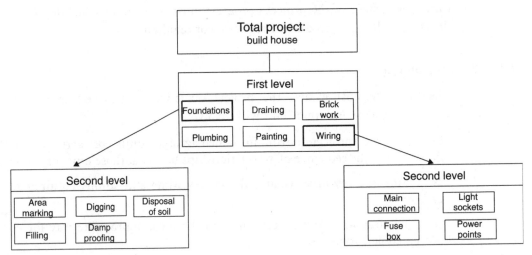

Figure 8.6 Diagrammatic work breakdown structure

Once the component activities of the project have been determined, they can be sequenced and scheduled. Here, we will show how some of the simple charts can be applied to more complex project planning.

8.2 Using charts

Bar line charts

A simple project plan can be shown on a bar line or Gantt chart. Figure 8.7 is an example of a chart for a project to build a garage.

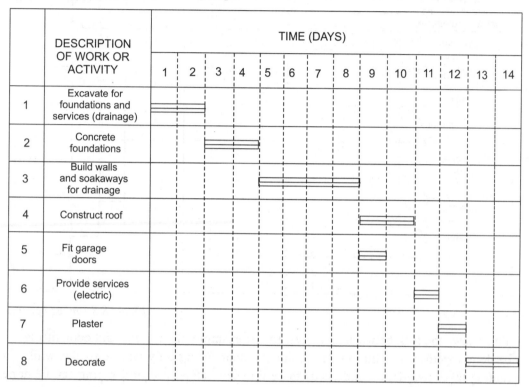

	DESCRIPTION OF WORK OR ACTIVITY	TIME (DAYS)													
		1	2	3	4	5	6	7	8	9	10	11	12	13	14
1	Excavate for foundations and services (drainage)	▭													
2	Concrete foundations			▭											
3	Build walls and soakaways for drainage					▭									
4	Construct roof									▭					
5	Fit garage doors									▭					
6	Provide services (electric)											▭			
7	Plaster												▭		
8	Decorate													▭	

Figure 8.7 Gantt chart for building a garage

This chart shows the sequence of activities to be followed, as well as the duration of each activity. You need to excavate before you can put in foundations, before you can build walls: once you've got to that stage, you can do the roof and doors together, if you have the manpower – sheltered from the elements – you can then follow the next sequence.

Activity 10 (15 mins)

How could you, very simply, turn this chart into a work schedule?

This type of chart has the advantage of being very easy to understand. It can also be used as a progress control chart, with the lower section of each bar being completed (eg shaded in) as the activity is completed.

Linked bar charts

In order to show more clearly where the activities are dependent on each other, you might prefer to use a linked bar chart, as in Figure 8.8.

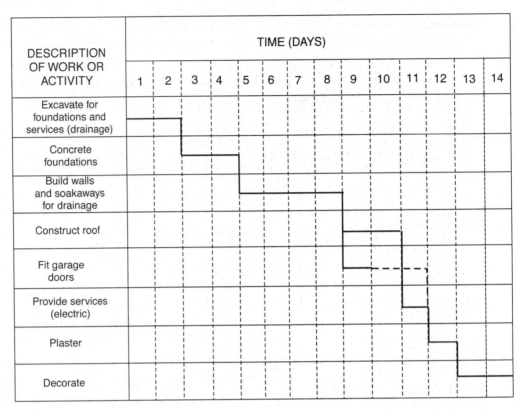

DESCRIPTION OF WORK OR ACTIVITY	TIME (DAYS)													
	1	2	3	4	5	6	7	8	9	10	11	12	13	14
Excavate for foundations and services (drainage)														
Concrete foundations														
Build walls and soakaways for drainage														
Construct roof														
Fit garage doors														
Provide services (electric)														
Plaster														
Decorate														

Figure 8.8 Linked bar chart

This shows the link between activities. In our example, the roofing and door-fitting can be done together, starting on day 9, but the door-fitting only takes one day, while the roofing takes two days – and needs to be finished before electrical wiring can be done, hopefully on day 11. The door-fitting therefore has a certain amount of leeway: it can be started late if necessary, since it does not hold up any other activity until the roofing and electrical installation are finished. This leeway is called float time, and is shown by the dotted line on the chart: the activity can be moved into the dotted area if necessary. Activities that have no float time are called critical activities: they must be completed on time in order to avoid a knock-on effect which will make the project as a whole run over time.

Activity 11 **(20 mins)**

You are the site manager of the garage construction project. You have drawn up the linked bar chart above as a guide to all your on-site staff as to the order of activities and the speed of progress required to meet the customer's two-week deadline. You decide to use the chart to monitor progress. Using a different-coloured pen, you draw a line beneath the one on your plan chart to show what your team has actually accomplished.

(a) Everything takes the time it was planned to, except that on the Wednesday (day 3) the weather is too bad to work, so that concreting of the foundations actually takes three days.

(b) The door fitting takes one day, and the door-fitter is also qualified to do roofing work. His help will knock a day off the roofing schedule.

Draw the control line onto Figure 8.8. Has your project run over time?

The big advantage of such charts is that they are easily understood by all levels of staff, and without undue calculation. However they can only display a restricted amount of information, and the links between activities are fairly crude. To overcome these limitations, when planning and organising more complex projects, we use a more sophisticated technique called network analysis.

8.3 Network analysis

Network analysis is a term for project planning techniques which aim to 'map' the activities in a particular project, and the relationship between them, including:

(a) what tasks must be done before others can be started;

(b) what tasks could be done at the same time;

(c) what tasks must be completed on schedule if the completion date for the whole project is not to slip: the critical tasks.

These relationships and sequences are represented in a network diagram, which flows from left to right. The most commonly used form of network is called an **activity-on-arrow** diagram, because activities are represented by an arrowed line, which runs between one event (start or completion of the activity) and another. Events are depicted by a node, or circle.

Hence in the following example we map activity A, which starts at a certain point (event 1) and ends at a certain point (event 2).

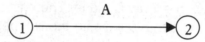

Let us tackle a more complex example. Suppose your work breakdown structure comprises six activities: we will call them activities A–G.

(a) Activities A and B can start together.

(b) You have to have done activity B before you can do activity C.

(c) Once activity A is completed, activities D and E can start, at the same time.

(d) Activity F follows on from activity D.

(e) Activity G will be completed at the same time as activity F, to end the project. However, activities C and E must be completed before G can commence.

Activity 12   **(10 mins)**

Read (a)–(e) above again. Working from left to right, draw the network diagram showing activities A–G and events 1–6.

One further complication. It is a convention in network analysis that two separate activities should not start and end at the same events. If the real activities **could** start and end at the same event, this is shown on the network by inserting a **dummy activity**, represented by an extra event node with a dotted line joining it to the next event, figure 8.9.

Incorrect

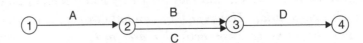

Correct

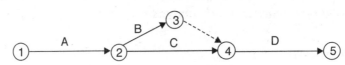

Figure 8.9 Network diagram with dummy activity

The correct version shows that activities B and C **both** have to be completed before D can begin, and the dotted line indicates that no extra activity is actually done and no extra time is taken between event 3 (completion of B) and event 4 (completion of C). The two activities therefore do start and end at the same points in the sequence, but not at the same nodes on the diagram.

Apart from pure convention, dummy activities may be needed to preserve the basic logic of the network.

Activity 13   (10 mins)

In the network produced in the previous activity, suppose that activity G depended on the completion of activity D, as well as activities C and E. Activity F still depends on activity D alone. There is no extra time or activity involved; all you need to do is to indicate the link between activities D and G. Draw the 'dummy activity' dotted line on our network diagram, to represent this scenario.

Another use of the dummy activity is to ensure that all activities end up at a single completion event, joining in any loose events.

More information can be added to a network diagram, to describe not just what happens next, but when it should happen, and how long the whole project will take if each activity takes as long as it is supposed to. This technique is called CPA, or critical path analysis.

8.4   Critical path analysis (CPA)

If Activity A takes three days, it is shown like this.

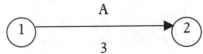

Let us say, building on our original A-G network, that:

Activity   A takes 3 days
              B takes 5 days
              C takes 2 days
              D takes 1 day
              E takes 6 days
              F takes 3 days

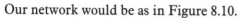

G takes 3 days.

Our network would be as in Figure 8.10.

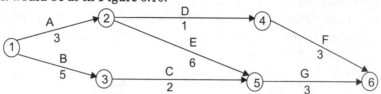

Figure 8.10 Network diagram with timings

Let us assume that you have all the resources you need to carry out the above project as drawn: in other words, you have enough workers to do activities A and B at the same time, and so on. The shortest possible time in which you can complete the project is 12 days. See if you can work out why, before reading on.

Each of the 'routes' of arrows from the first event to the last event is called a **pathway**, or **path**.

Activity 14   **(20 mins)**

List all the pathways in Figure 8.10, and add up how many days each path will take to reach event 6.

The shortest possible duration for the project is 12 days. This is the duration of the longest path (AEG), not the shortest! The activities on the longest path determine the deadline for the whole project, because if one of them runs over time, the whole project will run over time. They are therefore critical activities, and the path on which they sit is called the critical path. We show the critical path on a network by drawing double or thicker lines between the events on that path.

Activity 15   **(30 mins)**

Draw a network for the following project, and identify the critical path.

Activity	Depends on activity	Duration (weeks)
A	–	5
B	–	4
C	A	2
D	B	1
E	B	5
F	B	5
G	C, D	4
H	F	3
J	F	2

Hint: all your activities should 'tie up' at event 7.

8.5 Scheduling using the critical path

Once you have estimated activity durations and worked out the total project time, you can start scheduling. First of all, you work forwards from event 1, working out the **earliest start date** of each activity. We show the earliest start date of an activity as follows.

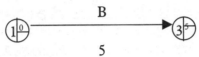

Obviously, event 1 starts at 0 (on day one): the earliest possible time for C to start, given that B takes 5 days, is at the end of day 5. If we do the same exercise with all the activities in our A-G example, we get Figure 8.11.

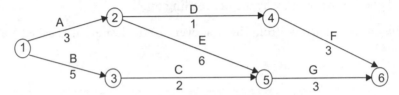

Figure 8.11 Network diagram showing start times

Note that the earliest start date for G (which has to follow A and E) is 9 days. But B and C only take 7 days: they can take two extra days, if necessary, without affecting the start of G.

We make this clear by next working backwards from event 6 to event 1, identifying the **latest start dates** when activities can start and still keep up with the timing set by the critical path. The earliest deadline of event 6 is 12 days: this is also its **latest** deadline, because it is the end of the critical path, which must not run late. Activity G takes 3 days, so its latest start date is $12 - 3 = 9$ days: again, this is the same as its earliest start date, because G is on the critical path. Activity C takes 2 days, so its latest start date (if G is to start on time) is $9 - 2 = 7$ days. However, its earliest start date (if B was on time) was 5 days: it has two days' leeway, or **float**. (Remember: activities on the critical path have no float.)

We insert the **latest** start date in the bottom quarter of the circle, as follows.

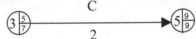

You can see just from this that Activity C can be started any time between days five and seven, giving the project manager a degree of flexibility, but that event 5 is on the critical path and must not run late!

> **Activity 16** (20 mins)
>
> Starting from event 6 and working backwards, fill in the latest start dates in Figure 7. Which activities can afford to start late, and by how much?

Attach actual dates to your days currently numbered 1-12, and you have a detailed and effective schedule.

9 RESOURCE ALLOCATION

9.1 Gantt charts

As well as plotting time to be taken (and actually taken), Gantt charts can be used to estimate the amounts of resources required for a project.

Let us take the example we have been using so far in this section. We will be starting with our final network showing earliest and latest start times for A–G, so you may like to make a clean copy of the solution to Activity 16 and keep it by you for reference.

Suppose that, in addition to the information contained on our network, we know the number of workers required to do each job, as follows.

Activity A requires 6 workers
B " 3 "
C " 4 "
D " 4 "
E " 5 "
F " 6 "
G " 3 "

Suppose that we have a team of **nine** workers, each of whom is paid a fixed wage, regardless of hours worked in a week (so we want to avoid idle time if possible). Each worker is capable of working on any of the seven activities involved in the project (so we can swap them round freely if required).

Figure 8.12 shows a Gantt chart, simply plotting the various paths against the 12-day timescale. We have assumed that activities will be started at the **earliest** start times, adding **floats** (where available) as a dotted line.

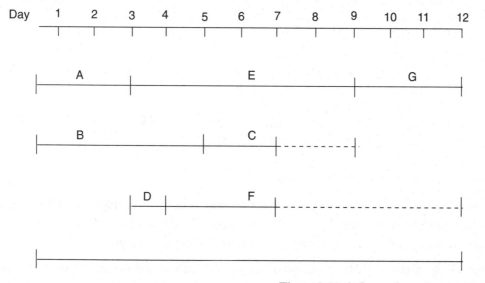

Figure 8.12 A Gantt chart showing floats

NOTES

EXAMPLE

1   On Figure 8.12 add the **number** of workers **required**, below the line under the relevant activity letter: $\frac{A}{6}$ and so on.

2   Now, label the line at the bottom of the chart '**Workers required**'.

3   Draw a line vertically through the **start and end of each activity**, from the 'Time' line (days) to the 'Workers required' line. With each activity beginning or ending, the number of workers required will change.

4   In your first section of the 'Workers required' line, which extends from day 0-3, A and B are going on simultaneously. Mark 'AB' above this section of the line.

5   Activities A and B require 6 and 3 workers respectively: that is, 9 workers. Mark '9' below the 'AB' on the 'Workers required' line.

6   Keep going until you have completed all segments of the 'Workers required' line.

ANSWER

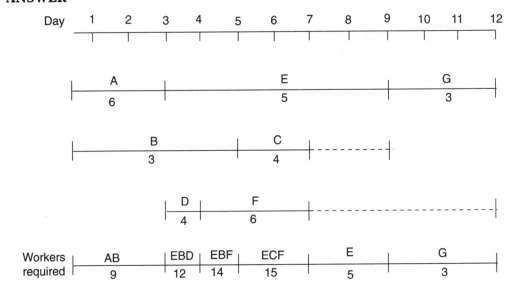

From the answer to the above activity, you may note that on days 6 and 7 you need as many as 15 workers though you only have nine. On days 8–12, you would have most of your team sitting about twiddling their thumbs. What are you going to do?

Let's look at the really busy period of days 4–7. Can you see any activities that **need** not be done during that period? We know that the path DF is **not** on the critical path. It takes four days, and need not finish until day 12: we have a full 5-day float. If we leave DF until its last possible start time (day 9), we are taking pressure off the busy period. Our Gantt chart would be redrawn as in Figure 8.13.

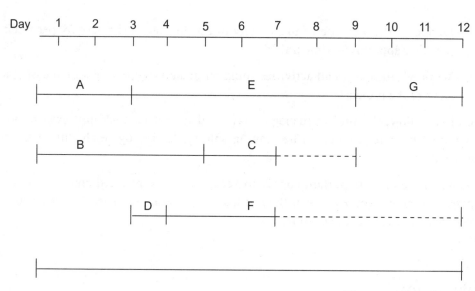

Figure 8.13 The final Gantt chart

The project can be completed without hiring any additional labour, and without running late. Good job! You can keep shuffling non-critical activities and re-calculating worker requirements like this until you are satisfied you have found the best solution. If there is too little float time at convenient stages to allow you do this, you may have to:

(a) reschedule the project to find the **minimum excess demand for labour**, and hire in extra labour for those times; **or**

(b) move critical activities as well as non-critical ones (thereby lengthening the project) to avoid excess demand for labour. The same method should be used to find the **minimum extension of the project's duration** required.

9.2 Cost scheduling

Cost estimating

It is usually not possible to say with certainty what the costs of a project will be, but some idea will be required in advance so that costs can be monitored and controlled. Estimates of costs can be based on rough guesswork (a 'ballpark' estimate), comparison with similar projects in the past, or the initial plans for the project (a 'feasibility' estimate).

The work breakdown structure will clearly be useful in devising estimates because it enables the project manager to compile a complete list of items that will attract expenditure. **Estimation forms** can be designed, based on the WBS, with columns for labour, materials, components and so on for each of the work units or tasks. This ensures that no items are forgotten, and speeds up the process of estimating, where jobs are routine or similar in type.

Cost scheduling

Costs can be scheduled, in exactly the same way as labour requirements.

(a) Draw a bar chart for the project.

(b) Estimate the cost of each activity.

(c)   Divide by the duration of the activity to get the cost of the activity per week (or other appropriate time unit).

(d)   Work out the cost of all activities going on in a given week: ie a total cost per week of the project.

For ease of cash flow, the project manager may need to restrict cash outflows in any week. As with labour requirements, he may be able to do this by rescheduling tasks which have a float.

It may, however, be more important simply to keep within the planned amount for the total expense on the project. And even then, it may be preferable to spend extra finance on a project to stop it running over time.

FOR DISCUSSION

In what kinds of project would you consider the time deadlines more important than the expenditure budget? And vice versa? (What projects do you know of which have gone way over budget, or late? Look out for examples in the press.)

Activity 17   **(20 mins)**

Find your answer to Activity 9 – your WBS for a dinner party menu.

(a)   Make up a cost estimate, based on your WBS. Draw a column marked B for budget, down the right hand side of your list, and enter your estimated amounts for each task.

(b)   Go out and find out what it would actually cost, and write down each amount in a column marked A for actual, next to your Budget column.

How was your estimating? If you gave your dinner party, you might have written down what you really paid for your ingredients in the Actual column. You could monitor how you were doing, compared to your budget. This is called budgetary control: another useful management technique!

It should be clear from our discussion of 'estimates' that project planning is inexact and uncertain: the project manager does not have a crystal ball to tell him how long an activity will take, how much it will cost or how successful it will be. Finally, in this chapter, we look briefly at this problem of uncertainty, and how it can be planned for.

10   FLEXIBLE PLANNING

10.1   Allowing for delays

As we have already discussed, activities which are not on the critical path are non-critical, and can, within limits, **start later** and/or **take longer**, without holding up the completion time of the project as a whole. This slack time is called the activity's **float**. It

allows unexpected delays to be absorbed and resources to be diverted, to avoid the late start of critical activities.

What happens if your critical activities are threatened with delays, though, and the final deadline simply cannot be extended?

10.2 Crash times

The crash time is the **minimum** time an activity can take to be completed. Crashing often involves the use of extra resources.

Job X takes one worker 1½ days – say, 12 working hours. The worker gets paid £10 per hour, so the cost of the job is £120. If the project manager needs Job X completed at the end of a single day, (s)he might ask the worker to do four hours' overtime to complete the 12 hours work in a single working day. However, the overtime rate of pay is £15 per hour. So the crash cost is (8 hours @ £10) + (4 hours @ £15) = £140.

There would be no point crashing non-critical jobs, because you would not shorten the overall project duration or affect the critical path by doing so. However, crashing can be used to shorten the critical path itself, if necessary, to:

(a)   catch up with delays; or
(b)   shorten the project duration for any reason.

You may have noted that, in most cases, we are still only talking about estimated job times or durations. What happens if you get those wrong in the first place? One answer is to take account of uncertainty and contingencies at the estimating stage. A well-known technique for doing this is PERT.

10.3 PERT

Programme Evaluation and Review Technique (PERT) recognises that the activity durations in the network are in fact uncertain. Instead of one estimate of each activity time, three estimates are used.

- The **most likely** duration of the activity, given what is known about it (which we will call m)

- The **most optimistic** (shortest) estimate, assuming that all goes well (o)

- The **most pessimistic** (longest) estimate, assuming that things that are likely to go wrong will go wrong (p)

These can be converted into a 'mean' (or middle) estimate, which takes into account the small chance that things will go entirely well or entirely badly. The mean time is calculated using the formula:

$$\frac{o + 4m + p}{6}$$

As an example, here are some more data!

NOTES

Activity	Must be preceded by activity	Optimistic (o) days	Most likely (m) days	Pessimistic (p) days
A	-	5	10	15
B	A	16	18	26
C	-	15	20	31
D	-	8	18	28

The mean times for each activity are as follows.

Activity	$(o + 4m + p)$	$\div 6 =$	Mean time
A	$5 + 40 + 15 = 60$		10 days
B	$16 + 72 + 26 = 114$		19 days
C	$15 + 80 + 31 = 126$		21 days
D	$8 + 72 + 28 = 108$		18 days

Activity 18   (20 mins)

Draw the network for A-D, using the mean times. Include earliest start and latest start times, and show where the critical path is.

Other calculations can be made using PERT, including the probability that a job will overrun by a given time. Because of their complexity, PERT systems are often run on computers, which generate the planning and control data required.

PERT is frequently used where there are a number of possible contingencies which would affect the project duration. Construction projects, for example, need to allow for delays due to unfavourable weather.

NOTES

Chapter roundup

- Plans are made a various level in an organisation and my be stated in the form of a hierarchy showing the relationship of mission, goals, objectives, strategy, tactics and operational plans.

- Planning takes place at strategic, tactical and operational levels.

- Planning is the process of deciding what should be done, by whom, when and how. It is essential for co-ordination and control and for the management of risk and uncertainty.

- Customer focus concentrates an organisation's efforts on the customer to provide satisfaction and delight.

- Customer care and service help provide a competitive advantage.

- Customer retention is important because it can be expensive to attract and retain new customers.

- The total cost of customer care has various elements.

- The heart of quality programmes is the need to define, research and respond to customer need.

- Project management is directed at a particular end, achieving specific objectives within a limited time span.

- Project planning and organisation involves

  - breaking the project into units (work breakdown structure)

  - determining the sequence and/or relationships between those units

  - estimating the resources required for each unit

  - scheduling time and allocating resources for each unit.

- Popular techniques for project planning include:

  - network analysis (including critical path analysis) and

  - Gantt charts.

- Network analysis aims to 'map' the relationships and dependencies of tasks in a project. The critical path is the longest path on the network, representing the shortest possible completion time of the project: if any activity on the critical path runs late, the project will run late. Non-critical activities may have some 'slack' time within which they can be extended without having a knock-on effect on the project duration: this is called a float.

- Estimating costs and job times is not an accurate science. One technique for taking uncertainty into account is Programme Evaluation and Review Technique (PERT) which calculates a mean time for each activity using most likely, optimistic and pessimistic estimates.

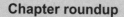

NOTES

Quick quiz

1   What is a strategic plan?

2   Why is control a necessary part of planning?

3   What is contingency planning?

4   What does co-ordination achieve?

5   If a customer suddenly went bankrupt owing the business a large sum of money from six months ago, which system would not have been operating effectively?

6   What are satisfied customers likely to do?

7   Give some examples of costs associated with attracting new customers.

8   What does customer care aim to achieve?

9   What is a work breakdown structure, and what can it be used for?

10   What are (a) a critical activity and (b) a float?

11   What is depicted by (a) nodes, (b) arrowed lines and (c) thick arrowed lines, in a network diagram?

12   In what circumstances might you add a 'dummy activity' to a network diagram?

13   Is the critical path the shortest or longest line from start to end of the project network?

14   If you know how many workers are required for each job, and all team members can do all jobs, how might you go about scheduling your manpower in an efficient manner?

15   What is a 'crash time' and why might you not want to 'crash' a non-critical activity?

16   What is the mathematical formula for calculating a mean time for a job whose duration is uncertain?

Answers to quick quiz

1   A long-term plan, taking account of known environmental factors, which formulates long-range goals for the business and works out how to achieve them. (See para 1.2)

2   Because only through feedback from an effective control system can managers know whether or not the plan is being carried out. (1.3)

3   Planning for unforeseen developments. (1.3 and 1.4)

4   Co-ordination gets all departments working in the same direction, by substituting overall for individual priorities. (2.3)

5   This would be a serious failure of the credit control system. (3.3)

6   Buy again, buy more, recommend to friends. (4.1)

7   Advertising; salesforce time; credit checks; agent commission; initial discounts. (4)

8   To close the gap between customers' expectations and their experience. (4)

9   It breaks a project down into its component phases or stages. It can be used to discover what work is needed and what resources are required and for sequencing and co-ordinating. (8.1)

10   (a)   Events
      (b)   Activities
      (c)   Critical activities (8.3)

11   When two activities could start and end at the same event. (8.3)

12   (a)   One that must be completed on time.

      (b)   The amount of leeway there is for completion of the activity. (8.4)

13   Longest. (8.4)

14   Using a Gantt chart. (9.1)

15   It is the minimum time to complete an activity. Crashing a non-critical activity would not affect the critical path or shorten the overall project time. (10.2)

16    $\dfrac{o+4m+p}{6}$ (10.3)

Answers to activities

1   The statements fit the following categories.

      Efficiency = b, c, e.

      Effectiveness = a, d, f.

      Statement (e) is an example of increased efficiency because fewer employees (inputs) are needed. Other interpretations are possible however.

2   The plans Dial-a-Video Limited propose are a strategy to exploit the 'art movie' market segment. A programme for the build-up of the distribution. The £4 charge is a tactic or policy. The 'no-tips' plan is a rule or regulation.

3   Contingency plans for the situations given would include the following.

      (a)   New systems may have 'bugs', or be unfamiliar to operators. A good contingency plan would be running the old system in parallel with the new one for a trial period.

      (b)   People get sick, or need holidays, or have problems getting to work during transport strikes, or go on strike themselves. You may have contingency plans to do with pre-notifying holidays, or laid-on transport in the event of transport strikes. A general contingency plan would be a temporary staff agency on standby to provide replacement/overflow staff.

      (c)   Again, transport may cause unexpected problems, or there could be an upset such as the venue being double-booked, the key speaker falling ill, or overhead projectors not working. Alternative transport/speaker/venue might be pre-planned, and back-up visual aids equipment (such as a flip-chart) on hand. You can't anticipate everything ...

4   Here are some suggestions.

      (a)   It means that regular customers will support the supplier. It will be difficult for competitors to attract customers away from their favoured supplier.

      (b)   Regular customers provide reliable income and turnover

(c) It is possible to build a rapport with customers over time. This helps the supplier understand their needs more easily, thus making the marketing process more straightforward.

(d) Customer loyalty is also a source of goodwill. It will enhance the supplier organisation's image and can be a source of very potent advertising in that customers may recommend the supplier to their friends or colleagues.

5 Resources for the sales conference will include the conference centre; equipment (overhead projectors etc); staffing of the conference centre; time of speakers; materials such as paper and slides; telephone and fax facilities; refreshments – and so on.

6 A superior may interfere too much in the manager's job and want constant reports: very disruptive. (Tact in warding off such attention can be a valuable attribute.) On the other hand, if the superior delegates too much, the manager's workload may be excessive.

7 If you answered yes to any of 1-6 and no to question 7, then you need to improve your time management. If you answered more than five of them this way, then time management must be a priority, particularly whilst you are trying to find time to study.

8 You will have come up with your own ideas for different projects: here are some suggestions.

(a) Construction of a motorway extension, say, or the Channel Tunnel.

(b) Limited-edition production of a car, for example, or one-off tailor-made products.

(c) Implementation of a computer system, say, or mounting a trade exhibition or conference.

(d) Ironing out bugs in a system or product, completing a market research survey and so on.

Check that your own examples have a beginning, an end, and goals.

9 The answer will depend on your menu, but your WBS may include stages such as: the purchasing of the various ingredients; washing, peeling and chopping vegetables (if any); mixing ingredients; cooking and/or preparing each dish; laying the table and preparing plates and utensils and so on. Your WBS should give you a fairly clear idea of what ingredients, in what quantities, you will need to buy: a more accurate cost estimate than trying to judge the cost of the meal as a whole. The same is true of the timetable, with the added advantage that it provides the basis for an action checklist and schedule for preparation.

10 To turn figure 8.7 into a work schedule, you could put the days of the week across the top instead of the number of days given. So the excavations should take up Monday and Tuesday, the foundations start on Wednesday and so on.

11 The control line added to figure 8.8 yields the result shown here.

DESCRIPTION OF WORK OR ACTIVITY	TIME (DAYS)													
	1	2	3	4	5	6	7	8	9	10	11	12	13	14
Excavate for foundations and services (drainage)														
Concrete foundations														
Build walls and soakaways for drainage														
Construct roof														
Fit garage doors														
Provide services (electric)														
Plaster														
Decorate														

You've made up your lost day of concreting because you had the float time on the door-fitting and were able to divert the door person to the roofing.

12

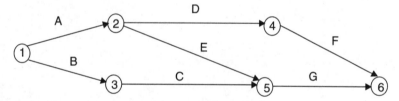

13   You should draw a dotted line from event 4 to 5.

14   There are three paths, as follows.

ADF = 3 + 1 + 3 days   = 7 days
AEG = 3 + 6 + 3 days   = 12 days
BCG = 5 + 2 + 3 days   = 10 days

15

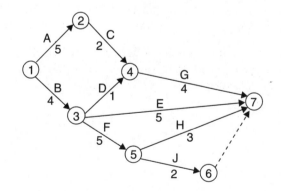

The paths are   ACG   = 5 + 2 + 4   = 11 weeks
                             BDG   = 4 + 1 + 4   = 9 weeks
                             BE   = 4 + 5   = 9 weeks
                             BFH   = 4 + 5 + 3   = 12 weeks
                             BFJ Dummy   = 4 + 5 + 2 + 0   = 11 weeks

BFH is the longest (and therefore the critical) path: the shortest time in which the project can be completed.

16

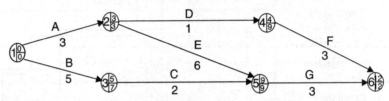

Activity C: anytime between days 5 and 7 (a 2-day float)
Activity F: anytime between days 4 and 9 (a 5-day float)

17   Did you totally underestimate your budget, and have to spend your food allowance for the next three weeks?

18

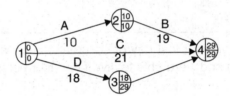

Chapter 9 :
OPERATIONAL PLANS

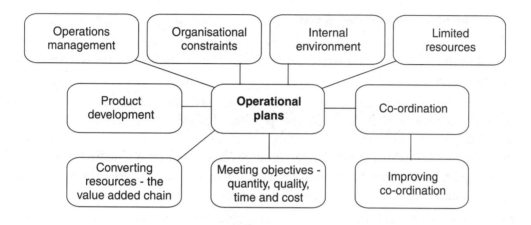

Introduction

It is generally much easier to perform a task if the objectives to be achieved are clearly expressed. This is especially important where the operational plans of an enterprise are involved, so as to ensure that the organisation's strategic purpose is supported by operational work. Production and operations management is used not only to describe factory environments, but applies to all organisations including, for example, schools and banks. It is the application of techniques to the design and operation of any system that transforms inputs into finished goods and services. Many of the techniques are applicable to service industries as well as manufacturing. Value chain analysis assesses how the business adds value to the resources it obtains, and how it delivers these resources to service customers. Just-in-Time (JIT) scheduling is a method used to reduce inventory costs and Statistical Process Control (SPC) is the continuous monitoring and charting of a process while it is operating, to warn when the process is moving away from predetermined limits.

Co-ordination ensures that within any organisation (when seen as an entity) departments, sections and individuals must all be organised in such a fashion as to ensure that the overall objectives of the organisation are attained and each department, section and individual makes a valid contribution. This must all be done within the organisational constraints and limitations that apply.

Your objectives

After completing this chapter you should be able to:

(a) Prepare and agree implementation plans which translate strategic targets into practical efficient and effective actions

(b) Manage work activities to prevent ineffective and inefficient deviations from the operational plan through effective monitoring and control

(c) Implement appropriate systems to achieve objectives and goals of the plan in the most effective and efficient way, on time and to budget and to meet organisational standards of quality

1 OPERATIONS MANAGEMENT

1.1 The importance of operations

One of the major areas in any organisation is production and operations management. The objectives, premises and strategies determine the search for and the selection of the product or service.

The term 'operations management' refers to the activities required to produce and deliver a service as well as a physical product. Production management used to be associated solely with the manufacture of goods but its expansion to operations management means that it now includes purchasing, warehousing and transportation – dealing with all the operations from the procurement of raw materials through various activities until the product is available to the buyer.

Operations are the link between the strategy and the customer and also between the different functions. The organisation's mission is only really meaningful if, at operational level, the mission is embodied in policies and behaviour standards.

The design of an operations system requires decisions on the location of facilities, the process to be used, the quantity to be produced and the quality of the product.

1.2 Operations management as a system

The production function plans, organises, directs and controls the necessary activities to provide products and services.

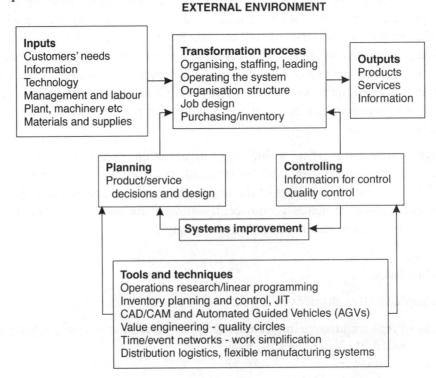

Figure 9.1 Operations management as a system

In the model shown above the inputs include the needs of the customers, information, technology, labour and management and the fixed and variable assets that are relevant to the transformation process. Managers and workers use the information and physical factors to produce the outputs. The transformation process incorporates planning, operating and controlling the system. There are many tools and techniques available to facilitate this process. The model also shows that external factors such as safety regulations and legal and ethical issues influence operations.

1.3 Relationships with other functions

Longer-term decisions, particularly relating to design and the innovation of improved products, cannot be taken by the production department alone; its activities must be integrated with other functions in the firm.

- **Product design** is co-ordinated with **R&D.** Production should advise R&D as to the consequences of particular designs for the manufacturing process.

- **Job design** will involve consultation with **human resources** specialists.

- The **marketing department** will detail expected selling quantities, timings, advertising expenditure and sales force activities.

- The **human resources department** will be involved in managing the work force.

- The **finance department** might indicate the resources available for new equipment.

1.4 Standards and procedures

Standards and procedures assist the manager with the planning and control of work.

Policies are general guidelines for management decision-making. Company policies might be, for example:

- to offer five year guarantees on all products sold and to give money back to customers with valid complaints;

- to promote managers from within the organisation, wherever possible, instead of recruiting managers to senior positions from outside;

- to encourage all recruits to certain jobs within the organisation to work towards obtaining an appropriate professional qualification;

- to be price-competitive in the market;

- that employees in the purchasing department should decline gifts from suppliers (subject, perhaps, to certain exceptions or purchase limits).

Procedures are a logical sequence of required actions for performing a certain task. Procedures exist at all levels of management; even a board of directors will have procedures for the conduct of board meetings. However, they become more numerous, onerous and extensive lower down in an organisation's hierarchy. The advantages of procedures for routine work are as follows.

- Procedures should prescribe the most *efficient* way of getting a job done.

- The absence of any need for the exercise of *discretion* in routine tasks.

- Staff will find jobs easier to do when they are familiar with established procedures.

- *Standardisation* of work. Prescribed procedures ensure that a task of a certain type will be done in the same way throughout the organisation.

- *Continuity*. The work will be done the same way even when a different person starts in a job or takes over from the previous holder.

- A written record of required procedures can be kept in a *procedures manual*. People unfamiliar with how a job should be done can learn quickly and easily by referring to the manual.

- They reduce the likelihood of *inter-departmental friction*. For example, work done by the warehousing department of a factory will affect the work of the sales force, delivery and distribution department and production department. The warehousing department will require documentation about sales orders from the sales force. It will issue delivery instructions to the delivery crews. By having established procedures, disputes between departments about who should do what, and when, and how, should be avoided.

A **rule** is a specific, definite course of action that must be taken in a given situation. Unlike a procedure, it does not set out the sequence or chronology of events. For example, the following are rules, but not procedures:

- employees in department X are allowed 10 minutes exactly at the end of their shift for clearing up and cleaning their work-bench;

- employees with access to a telephone must not use the telephone for personal calls.

Rules allow no deviations or exceptions, unlike policies which are general guidelines allowing the exercise of some management discretion.

2 PRODUCT DEVELOPMENT

2.1 Design and development

Product development is the process of creating a new product to be sold by an enterprise to its customers.

- *Design* refers to those activities involved in creating the styling, look and feel of the product, deciding on the product's mechanical architecture, selecting materials and processes, and engineering the various components necessary to make the product work.

- *Development* refers collectively to the entire process of identifying a market opportunity, creating a product to appeal to the identified market, and finally, testing, modifying and refining the product until it is ready for production. A product can be any item from a book, musical composition, or information service, to an engineered product such as a computer, hair dryer, or washing machine.

The impetus for a new product normally comes from a perceived market opportunity or from the development of a new technology.

- With a market-pull product, the company first determines that sales could be increased if a new product were designed to appeal to a particular segment of its customers. Engineering is then asked to determine the technical feasibility of the new product idea.

- With a technology-push product, a technical breakthrough opens the way for a new product and marketing then attempts to determine the idea's prospects in the marketplace.

With either scenario, manufacturing is responsible for estimating the cost of building the prospective new product, and their estimations are used to project a selling price and estimate the potential profit for the company.

2.2 Establishing specifications

During the development stage, the needs of the target market are identified, competitive products are reviewed, product specifications are defined, an economic analysis is done, and the development project is outlined.

- *Identify customer needs* – through interviews with potential purchasers, focus groups, and by observing similar products in use, researchers identify customer needs. Customer needs and product specifications are organised into a hierarchical list with a comparative rating value given to each need and specification.

- *Analyse competitive products* – an analysis of competitive products is part of the process of establishing target specifications. Rather than beginning from scratch and re-inventing the wheel with each new project, traditionally, the evolution of design builds on the successes and failures of prior work.

- *Establish target and final specifications* – based on customers' needs and reviews of competitive products, the team establishes the target specifications of the prospective new product. Target specifications are essentially a wish list tempered by known technical constraints. Final specifications are the result of tradeoffs made between technical feasibility, expected service life, projected selling price, and the financial limitations of the development project. With a new luggage product, for example, consumers may want a product that is lightweight, inexpensive, attractive, and with the ability to expand to carry varying amounts of luggage. Unfortunately, the mechanism needed for the expandable feature will increase the selling price, add weight to the product, and introduce a mechanism that has the potential for failure. Consequently, the team must choose between a heavier, more costly product and one that does not have the expandable feature. When product attributes are in conflict, or when the technical challenge or higher selling price of a particular feature outweighs its benefits, the specification may be dropped or modified in favour of other benefits.

Once the development plan is approved, marketing may begin to develop ideas for additional product options and add-ons, or perhaps an extended product family. Designers and engineers develop the product architecture in detail, and manufacturing determines which components should be made and which should be purchased, and identifies the necessary suppliers. Detail design, or design-for-manufacture, is the stage wherein the necessary engineering is done for every component of the product. During this phase, each part is identified and engineered. Tolerances, materials, and finishes are defined, and the design is documented with drawings or computer files.

3 CONVERTING RESOURCES – THE VALUE-ADDED CHAIN

3.1 Production

Production can be defined as the activity of transforming raw materials or components into finished products. Before production commences, production policies must be known and then the processes of manufacture, machine requirements, factory layout, storage and handling systems, skills required in the workforce and the method of training can be determined. These policies are largely determined by the nature of the work. The types of production are:

- Job production (or unit production) – output of single product to specific requirements (eg suit or ship). Demand is difficult to forecast, and generally production schedules can be prepared only when the customer's order arrives

- Batch production – output of a batch or quantity of a product (eg furniture). There is repetition, but not continuous production. Production is often for stock.

- Mass production – output of products of a uniform and standardised nature – production is continuous and carried out by specialised units (eg cars).

- Process (flow) production – continuous production of products of a more or less identical nature eg oil refinery

The production function plans, organises, directs and controls the necessary activities to provide products and services

Definition

> Activities are the means by which a firm creates value in its products. (They are sometimes referred to as **value activities**.)

They procure inputs and process them, adding value to them in some way, to generate outputs for customers. Activities incur costs, and, in combination with other activities, provide a product or service that earns revenue.

Activity	Example
Obtain inputs to the production 'system', such as plant facilities, materials and labour	Inputs: timber, screws, nails, adhesives, varnish, stain, templates, cutting tools, carpenters
Adding of value The activities below occupy most of the production manager's attention: Scheduling jobs on machines Assigning labour to jobs	Operations: sawing, sanding, assembly and finishing

Activity	Example
Controlling the quality of production and/or service delivery	
Improving methods of work	
Managing materials and equipment, to avoid waste	
Create outputs, ie finished products and services	Outputs: tables, chairs, cabinets etc.

Intermediate activities in all three processes include processing, inspection and storage. The linkages in the process are usually provided by information. For example the stock control system will detail movements in and out of the warehouse. To control operations, a variety of records are required.

3.2 Value-added chains

The *value chain* model of corporate activities, developed by Michael Porter, provides a bird's-eye view of an organisation's operations. *Competitive advantage*, says Porter, arises out of the way in which firms *organise and perform activities*; that is how an organisation uses its inputs and transforms them into outputs for which customers are prepared to pay.

Activities

Before we go any further, keep in mind that in Porter's analysis, business *activities* are *not* the same as business *functions*.

(a) *Functions* are the familiar departments of a business such as the production function, or the finance function, and reflect the formal organisation structure.

(b) *Activities* are what actually goes on: the work that is done. A single activity can involve work by a number of functions in sequence or concurrently.

An example should make this clear. An organisation needs many inputs of resources from the environment to function. The activity of obtaining these resources can be called procurement. However, the procurement activity may involve more than one function or department. Consider raw materials. The purchasing function may negotiate the best price and delivery terms but the production or design functions will provide the specification and the quality manager may oversee acceptance. The finance function will deal with payment, in consultation with purchasing, and if there is any dispute the legal department may be involved.

'Firms create value for their buyers by performing these activities.' Let us explain this point by using the example of a *restaurant*. A restaurant's activities can be divided into buying food, cooking it, and serving it (to customers). There is no reason, in theory, why the customers should not do all these things themselves, at home. The customer however, is prepared to pay for someone else to do all this. The customer also pays more than the cost of the food, wages and so on. The ultimate value a firm creates is measured by the amount customers are willing to pay for its products or services above the cost of carrying out value activities. A firm is profitable if the realised value to customers exceeds the collective cost of performing the activities.

There are two points to note here.

(a) Customers *purchase 'value'*, which they measure by comparing a firm's products and services with similar offerings by competitors.

(b) The business *creates 'value'* by carrying out its activities either more efficiently than other businesses, or combined in such a way as to provide a unique product or service.

Activity 1	**(10 mins)**
Outline different ways in which the restaurant can create value	

Activities that add value do not stop at the organisation's boundaries. For example, when a restaurant serves a meal, the quality of the ingredients – although the cook chooses them – is determined by the producer (grower). The producer has also added value, and success in producing ingredients of good quality is as important to the customer's ultimate satisfaction as the skills of the chef.

Porter (in *Competitive Advantage*) analysed the various activities of an organisation into a *value chain*.

Definition

Value chain. 'The sequence of business activities by which, in the perspective of the end user, value is added to the products or services produced by an organisation'

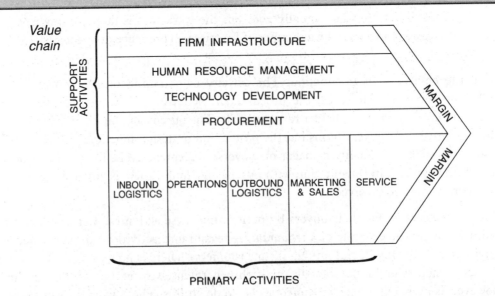

Figure 9.2 *Value chain*

The margin is the excess the customer is prepared to pay over the cost to the firm of obtaining resource inputs and providing value activities. It represents the value created by the value activities and by the management of the linkages between them.

Primary activities are those directly related with production, sales, marketing, delivery and services. The diagram shows five primary activities.

	Comment
Inbound logistics	Receiving, handling and storing inputs to the production system, including warehousing, transport and stock control.
Operations	Convert resource inputs into a final product. Resource inputs are not only materials. People are a resource especially in service industries.
Outbound logistics	Storing the product and its distribution to customers, including packaging, testing, warehousing and delivering.
Marketing and sales	Informing customers about the product, persuading them to buy it, and enabling them to do so. This includes advertising, promotion and selling.
After sales service	Installing products, repairing them, upgrading them, providing spare parts and servicing them.

Support activities provide purchased inputs, human resources, technology and infrastructural functions to support the primary activities. You will recognise them all as aspects of administration.

	Comment
Procurement	• Acquire the resource inputs to the primary activities, particularly the purchase of materials, subcomponents and equipment.
Technology development	• Product design, improving processes and/or resource utilisation. 'Technology' is used in the sense of apparatus, techniques and work organisation.
HR management	• Recruiting, training, developing and rewarding people.
Management planning	• Planning, finance and quality control: Porter believes they are crucially important to an organisation's strategic capability in all primary activities.

Analysing the value chain helps managers to decide how individual activities might be changed to reduce costs of operation or to improve the value of the organisation's offerings. Such changes will increase 'margin' – the residual value created by what customers pay minus the organising costs. For example, a clothes manufacturer may spend large amounts on:

- buying good quality raw materials (inbound logistics)

- hand-finishing garments (operations)

- building a successful brand image (marketing)

- running its own fleet of delivery trucks in order to deliver finished clothes quickly to customers (outbound logistics).

All of these should add value to the product, allowing the company to charge a premium for its clothes. Another clothes manufacturer may:

- reduce the cost of its raw materials by buying in cheaper supplies from abroad (inbound logistics)

- making all its clothes by machinery running 24 hours a day (operations)

- delaying distribution until delivery trucks can be filled with garments for a particular request (outbound logistics).

All of these should allow the company to be able to gain economies of scale and be able to sell clothes at a cheaper price than its rivals.

> **Activity 2** (10 mins)
>
> A lawn mower manufacturer has introduced some technologically advanced methods to its production but still needs to make improvements.
>
> Use Porter's value chain analysis to decide how individual activities might be changed to reduce costs of operation or to improve the value of the organisation's offerings.

Linkages connect the interdependent elements of the value chain together. They occur when one element of the value chain affects the costs or effectiveness of another. Here are some examples.

(a) More costly product design or better quality production might reduce the need for after-sales service.

(b) To deliver on time requires smooth functioning of operations, outbound logistics and service activities such as installation.

3.3 Value system

A company's value chain is not bounded by a company's borders. It is connected to what Porter describes as a *value system*.

Value system

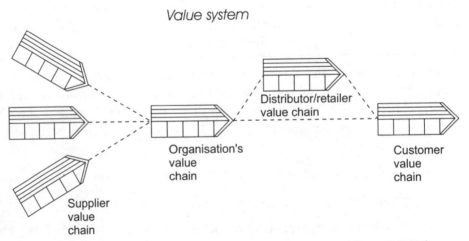

Figure 9.3 Value system

As well as managing its own value chain, a firm can secure competitive advantage by good administration of the linkages with its suppliers and customers. A company can create competitive advantage by making best use of these links and this means considering the value chains of these suppliers and customers.

Activity 3   **(10 mins)**

Sana Sounds is a small record company. Representatives from Sana Sounds scour music clubs for new bands to promote. Once a band has signed a contract (with Sana Sounds) it makes a recording. The recording process is subcontracted to one of a number of recording studio firms which Sana Sounds uses regularly. (At the moment Sana Sounds is not large enough to invest in its own equipment and studios.) Sana Sounds also subcontracts the production of records and CDs to a number of manufacturing companies. Sana Sounds then distributes the disks to selected stores, and engages in any promotional activities required.

What would you say were the activities in Sana Sounds' *value chain?*

A firm's value chain is not always easy to identify nor are the linkages between the different elements. However, it is an important analytical tool because it helps people:

    (a)   to see the business as a whole;

    (b)   to identify potential sources of competitive advantage.

3.4   Purchasing and inbound logistics

Purchasing – is generally taken to mean the procurement of the supplies for the enterprise. The buyer will study commodities, sources of supply, systems and procedures, inventory problems and market trends, methods of delivery, whether maximum discounts are being earned and the amount and use of waste materials.

The process carries many risks: materials may be purchased at too high a price, or of the wrong quality or too great a quantity, which may lead to obsolescence and loss of interest on capital. Too little purchased may mean production delays, which would also have an effect on the organisation's profits.

The purchasing mix includes quantity, quality, price and delivery. The right materials should be in the right place at the right time and at the right price.

- **Quantity** – the size and timing of the purchases will depend on delays in production as a result of stock shortages and the costs of holding the stock in terms of capital tied up, deterioration, pilferage, insurance and obsolescence.

- **Quality** – if this is very important for the manufacturing process detailed specifications of goods required and tolerances accepted must be prepared. When the goods are received there must be a system to ensure conformity with the specifications. As we have already noted in a previous chapter, some suppliers guarantee the quality of goods supplied and allow the customer access while the goods are being manufactured. This is usually done through supplier quality assurance (SQA) officers, who control the specification of the goods supplied.

- **Price** – should represent the best value considering the quality, delivery and urgency of order.

- **Delivery** – involves the supplier's lead-time and reliability.

Purchasing policy may be concerned with:

- whether to buy when required – limiting the purchases to minimum requirements

- whether to buy on contract on a medium or long-term basis – assuring continuity of supply in very important flow production

- speculative or bargain buying – where material is bought with the hope of future price rises.

Security of supplies is so important to some concerns that they have integrated backwards eg, tea producers buying tea plantations.

Inbound logistics – are the activities concerned with receiving, storing and handling raw material inputs and assets. Once the raw materials are purchased, they must be managed like any other resource. This includes stock control and security.

3.5 Stock levels

Most businesses, whatever their size, will be concerned with the problem of which items to have in stock, and how much of each item should be kept.

The principal reasons why a business needs to hold stock are:

- it acts as a buffer in times when there is an unusually high rate of consumption

- it enables the business to take advantage of quantity discounts by buying in bulk

- the business can take advantage of seasonal and other price fluctuations (eg buying oil in the summer when it is cheaper)

- any delay in production caused by lack of parts is kept to a minimum, so production processes will flow smoothly and efficiently

- it may be necessary to hold stock for a technical reason, for example whisky must be matured.

Irrespective of the nature of the business, a certain amount of stock will always need to be held. However, holding stock costs money, and the principal 'trade-off' in a stockholding situation is between the costs of acquiring and storing stocks on the one hand and the level of service that the company wishes to provide on the other hand.

The total cost of holding stock consists of the following.

- The purchase price (as affected by discounts)
- Holding costs
- Reorder costs
- Shortage costs
- Systems costs

The aim of a stock control system is to maintain the quantities of stocks held by a company at a level that optimises some predetermined management criterion (eg minimising costs incurred by the business).

There are obviously disadvantages in holding either too much or too little stock, and the problem is to balance these disadvantages against the benefits obtained.

There are two main types of stock control systems:

In a reorder level system, a replenishment order of fixed size is placed when the stock level falls to the fixed reorder level. Thus a fixed quantity is ordered at variable intervals of time.

In a periodic review system the stock levels are reviewed at fixed points in time, when the quantity to be ordered is decided. By this method variable quantities are ordered at fixed time intervals.

The economic order quantity (EOQ) approach to determining inventory levels works reasonably well when demand is predictable and fairly constant throughout the year ie, no seasonal patterns. However, where demand is likely to be intermittent, resulting in excesses at some times and inventory shortages at other times, EOQ does not work very well. The system that performs better under these circumstances is the Just-in-time system.

3.6 Just-in-time

This technique, where the supplier delivers the components and parts to the production line 'just in time' to be assembled, has revolutionised the acquisition of resources, with a resultant reduction in costs (of stock) or improvement in lead times.

Just In Time (JIT) techniques are an example of long-linked technologies which have the effect of increasing technological interdependence by removing slack from the system.

Definitions

> 'A system whose objective is to produce or to procure products or components as they are required by a customer or for use, rather than for stock. A just-in-time system is a "pull" system, which responds to demand, in contrast to a "push" system, in which stocks act as buffers between the different elements of the system, such as purchasing, production and sales.
>
> (a) **Just-in-time production.** A production system which is driven by demand for finished products whereby each component on a production line is produced only when needed for the next stage.
>
> (b) **Just-in-time purchasing.** A purchasing system in which material purchases are contracted so that the receipt and usage of material, to the maximum extent possible, coincide.

JIT emerged from criticisms of traditional responses to the problems of improving manufacturing capacity and reducing unit costs of production. These traditional responses include the techniques given below.

- Longer production runs
- Economic batch quantities
- Fewer products in the product range
- More overtime
- Reduced time spent on preventive maintenance, to keep production flowing

In general terms, longer production runs and large batch sizes should mean less disruption, better capacity utilisation and lower unit costs.

However, JIT techniques and stockless production challenge traditional views of manufacture.

- Its principles include greater flexibility in production, and matching production to meet demand.

- This in turn means shorter batch production runs and a greater product variety.

- There will be much smaller stocks of finished goods, because output is being matched more closely to demand.

- Production systems must therefore be reliable and prompt, without unforeseen delays and breakdowns. Machinery must be kept fully maintained, and so **preventive maintenance** is an important aspect of production.

The most obvious physical manifestation of JIT is a small warehouse. In other words, there are few raw materials stocks, as these are only purchased when needed. There are few finished goods stocks, as effort is not expended on production that is not required.

JIT aims to eliminate all **non-value-added costs**. Value is only added while a product is actually being processed. Whilst it is being inspected for quality, moving from one part of the factory to another, waiting for further processing and held in store, value is not being added. Non value-added activities (or **diversionary** activities) should therefore be eliminated.

Activity 4 (2 mins)

Which of the following is a value-added activity?

A Setting up a machine so that it drills holes of a certain size

B Repairing faulty production work

C Painting a car, if the organisation manufactures cars

D Storing materials

EXAMPLE

The following extract from an article in the *Financial Times* illustrates how 'just-in-time' some manufacturing processes can be. The emphasis is BPP's.

'Just-in-time manufacturing is down to a fine art at *Nissan Motor Manufacturing (UK)*. **Stockholding of some components is just ten minutes** – and the holding of all parts bought in Europe is less than a day.

Nissan has moved beyond just-in-time to **synchronous supply** for some components, which means manufacturers deliver these components directly to the production line minutes before they are needed.

These manufacturers do not even receive an order to make a component until the car for which it is intended has started along the final assembly line. Seat manufacturer *Ikeda Hoover*, for example, has about 45 minutes to build seats to specification and deliver them to the assembly line a mile away. It delivers 12 sets of seats every 20 minutes and they are mounted in the right order on an overhead conveyor ready for fitting to the right car.

Nissan has close relationships with a dozen or so suppliers and deals exclusively with them in their component areas. It involves them and even their own suppliers in discussions about future needs and other issues. These companies have generally established their own manufacturing units close to the Nissan plant.

Other parts from further afield are collected from manufacturers by *Nissan* several times at fixed times. This is more efficient than having each supplier making individual haulage arrangements.'

Problems associated with JIT

JIT should not be seen as a panacea for all the endemic problems associated with Western manufacturing. It might not even be appropriate in all circumstances.

(a) It is not always easy to predict patterns of demand.

(b) JIT makes the organisation far more vulnerable to disruptions in the supply chain.

CASE EXAMPLES

- JIT, originated by Toyota, was designed at a time when all of Toyota's manufacturing was done within a 50 km radius of its headquarters. Wide geographical spread, however, makes this difficult. Case examples

- JIT makes the organisation far more vulnerable to disruptions in the supply chain. An example of this is given in the case of Renault, the French state-owned car maker. The workforce at Renault's gear-box production plant at Cléon went on strike. The *day afterwards* a British plant had to cease production. Within two weeks Renault was losing 60% of its usual daily output a day. The weaknesses were due to:

- o   sourcing components from one plant only;

- o   heavy dependence on in-house components;

- o   low inventory;

- o   the fact '... that Japanese-style management techniques depend on stability in labour relations, something in short supply in the French public sector'.

- A similar effect was seen during the petrol supply crisis in the UK and other European countries in 2000. Prevention of tankers from making deliveries meant that petrol stations ran out of supplies within hours.

- JIT, originated by Toyota, was 'designed at a time when all of Toyota's manufacturing was done within a 50 km radius of its headquarters'. Wide geographical spread, however, makes this difficult.

3.7   Impact of JIT

JIT has a significant impact on departmental interdependence, and indeed on the interdependence between different companies in the **supply chain**. This is because there is no slack and no buffer stock. JIT massively increases the need for standardisation of quality, as there is no space for waste, and coordination of deliveries. As a result, firms are establishing long-term relationships with their suppliers.

Activity 5	(5 mins)

Batch sizes within a JIT manufacturing environment may well be smaller than those associated with traditional manufacturing systems.

What costs might be associated with this feature of JIT?

1   Increased set-up costs

2   Opportunity cost of lost production capacity as machinery and the workforce reorganise for a different product

3   Additional materials handling costs

4   Increased administrative costs

A   None of the above

B   1, 2, 3 and 4

C   1 only

D   2 and 3 only

4   MEETING OBJECTIVES – QUALITY, QUANTITY, TIME AND COST

4.1   Operating and controlling the system

Operating the system requires setting up an organisation structure, staffing the positions and training the people. Managers are needed who can provide the leadership to carry out the activities necessary to produce the desired products or services. The aim is to obtain the best productivity ratio within a time period and conforming to quality specifications.

Controlling operations requires setting performance criteria, measuring performance against them and taking action to correct unwanted deviations. Control covers production, product quality, reliability, inventory levels and workforce performance.

Output control relies upon the ability to identify specific tasks having a measurable output or criterion of overall achievement – for example, an end product, a part manufactured to agreed standards, batch production or a sub-assembly. Once outputs or criteria for achievement have been identified, management can specify output standards and targets. Rewards and sanctions can be related to performance levels expressed in output terms.

Time and money, budgets and schedules are the most basic resources within which every operation must operate. Measurement can be based on the actual start or finish times of critical activities and (especially for a project) the completion of milestones, or the timing of acceptance tests. Operation control charts use budget and schedule plans to report cumulative time and cost so that variances can be calculated. *Performance* is also monitored, by:

- inspection
- progress reviews (at regular stages)
- quality testing
- financial audit

A control limit signifies the deviation of a critical success factor that has gone beyond acceptable limits. Control limits are set to assess the severity of deviations and deviations that are larger than a predetermined value are used to trigger corrective action.

Corrective action can be taken, if deficiencies are not self-correcting. Falling behind schedule, perhaps because of some circumstance unforeseen at the planning stage, might require the rescheduling of the operation or a change in resource configuration.

4.2 Balancing the objectives

There are likely to be many objectives for the operation, which include completing the required output within a timescale and within budget; maintaining a high level of technical quality; conforming to all applicable legislation and codes; reflecting the customer's scope, standards and other requirements; incorporating applicable professional standards and practice; being responsive; maintaining an excellent working relationship with members of the value chain and others involved in the production; and continuously striving for technical excellence.

These objectives must be expressed in quantitative and qualitative measures by which the proper completion of an operation can be judged.

The four elements – cost, time, quantity and quality – should be considered together, because the optimum performance typically involves a trade-off of several dimensions, specifically what is done (scope and quality) versus the resources used to do the work (time and cost). Scope involves both stated needs (requirements or 'deliverables') and unstated needs ('expectations'). Quality involves both 'built-in' quality (internal and/or less readily noticeable aspects) and 'inspected' quality (visible and/or noticeable aspects).

Consider the performance of a department where there is a plan to improve cost-effectiveness by simply reducing costs; it may be possible to do this to some extent without affecting either the time taken, the output or the quality performance. At some stage, however, further cost reduction will either affect the ability of the department to fulfil its purpose or alternatively reduce the quality or quantity of output to a point where it is not acceptable.

4.3 Quantity objectives

Output performance objectives set for some individuals, teams and departments are relatively easy to measure. They may be sales revenue, manufacturing output, or the number of deliveries made, for example. For other support activities it is perhaps easiest to judge output by the volume of service supplied to 'internal customers' – a concept widely used in quality programmes. A personnel and training department's output may be measured in terms of recruitment activity, the number of training days delivered or some similar measurement of activity.

4.4 Cost objectives

Similarly, the cost-effectiveness or efficiency objective associated with the output objective is often easy to express, although again the measurement may be done in many different ways. It may, for instance, be expressed as total cost, or cost per unit of activity, or percentage usage (the sort of measure that reflects the efficiency with which assets are used – eg use of a machine or vehicle).

Expenditure (cost) measures – start with the establishment of budgets that refer to actual versus planned costs as outlined in the objectives. As the operation/production progresses, decisions regarding procurement, design, development, deployment etc, will be assessed with respect to their impact on expenditures. Actual expenditures will be compared to a baseline, and any variances will be reported to management for corrective action.

4.5 Time objectives

Schedule (time) performance measures – refer to the timely completion of the output of an operation as compared to a baseline schedule defined in the manufacturing/production plan. The schedules will identify all of the operation's stages, phases, and activities assigned to various employees or teams mapping them to a timeline that measures key milestones (dates) that are used to keep track of work progress. Avoiding schedule slippage is a key objective.

4.6 Quality objectives

The most difficult measure to express in numerical terms is usually quality.

(a) **Functional quality** – refers to the quality or correctness of the products and/or services features/functions delivered as a result of the operation. It can be measured by comparing the quality or correctness of the baseline product and services features/functions to the proposed deliverables. It can also be measured using the number of product and service change requests made, approved, and effectively implemented or the number of critical, serious, and non-critical defects outstanding and resolved on a weekly basis.

The customer will at some point perceive a product or service as being unacceptable if the quality declines. But the point at which that occurs depends on both the individual customer and the particular circumstances that he or she has experienced, In an organisation the ability of an individual or a department to delivery a satisfactory service is often dependent on the quality of supply of an *internal* service eg, credit controllers' ability to manage debt will be badly affected if they are served by poor quality debtor systems where the latest cash receipts have not been entered. They will lose confidence if the data is not accurate and will be less effective. More importantly, both they and the firm will lose credibility with customers if they chase payments, which have already been made.

(b) **Technical quality performance** – refers to the technical infrastructure that provides the foundation for product and service delivery. In the case of an IT operation, such indicators as system availability, downtime, problem resolution, and response time and network utilisation would measure technical quality performance.

(c) **Issue management performance** – refers to the identification and resolution of issues or exceptions that are impacting the successful delivery of the operation. Issues can be related to communications, human resources, contracts, product/service features and functions etc. The purpose of issue management is to ensure that all matters requiring resolution, decisions or direction are addressed as soon as possible to avoid negative consequences on operational objectives and deliverables.

4.7 Quality control

Quality control is the process of ensuring that goods and services are produced in accordance with specifications. The major objective of quality control is to see that the organisation lives up to the standards it has set for itself.

For many operations it is accepted that it is not possible to achieve perfection in products because of the variations in raw material quality, operating skills, different types of machines used, wear and tear, etc. but quality control attempts to ascertain the amount of variation from perfect that can be expected in any operation. If the expected variation is acceptable according to engineering requirements, then production must be established within controlled limits and if the actual variation is too great then corrective action must be taken to bring it within acceptable limits.

Quality control is concerned with trying to make sure that a product is manufactured, or a service is provided, to meet certain design specifications. It is aimed at preventing the manufacture of defective items or the provision of defective services. This means:

- establishing standards of quality

- establishing procedures or production methods to ensure that these required standards are met in an agreed proportion of cases

- monitoring actual quality

- taking control action when actual quality falls below standard.

4.8   Statistical process control

Statistical process control (SPC) is the continuous monitoring and charting of a process while it is operating, to warn when the process is moving away from predetermined limits. The goal of an SPC programme should be to minimise and eliminate if possible these variations and to operate a process such that it has the capability to produce product within a customers' specification or better.

Data obtained, manually or automatically, at the time of processing can be plotted graphically in order to provide a visual record of the performance of a process. Critical dimensions or other characteristics are measured. A typical control chart is shown in the diagram below. The horizontal axis is either time or a cumulative output volume. The vertical axis is a measure of a critical characteristic of the component such as its length or diameter. Typically the upper and lower control limits will be three standard deviations away from the mean.

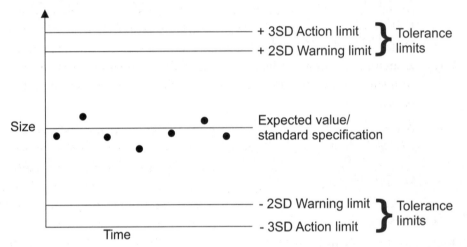

Figure 9.4 Quality control chart

The objective value of the characteristic being measured is plotted as a horizontal line. An analysis of past output will indicate the amount of random variation expected for the type of process being used. From this the standard deviation of the process from the mean (expected value) can be measured. Further horizontal lines can then be drawn on the graph at positions representing 2 and 3 standard deviations above and below the objective line. These values are derived from an analysis of the process and are control limits. It is expected that 67% of values will lie between ± 2 standard deviations hence within that part of the chart that lies between the warning limits. 99.75% will lie between ± 3 standard deviations and lie within the action limits. A control chart shows the limits within which output is expected. All points outside the control limits should be investigated and corrected.

As actual output is produced the value of the chosen dimension is plotted. This will show both random and gradual variations and also any deviations. Some output can be expected to be beyond the 2 standard deviation control limits. These are known are 'warning limits'. Some output of this type is not a problem since it is expected but successive values in this region indicate a problem that needs to be corrected. Virtually no output should occur beyond the 3 standard deviations limits. These are known as 'action limits'. If such values occur this indicates that the process is out of control and action is required to correct it.

SPC covers a wider range of topics:

- It can be used to process data to optimise plant performance. In its simplest form it is looking at the standard deviation of controlled variables and how close they are to the plant tolerance limits, and seeing if they can be pushed closer, making the plant more productive.

- It is an aspect of Total Quality Management (TQM), which is a way of managing a business to ensure complete customer satisfaction internally and externally. If the expected variation is acceptable according to engineering requirements, then production must be established within controlled limits and if the actual variation is too great then corrective action must be taken to bring it within acceptable limits.

- It can be used to control buffer stocks or inventories. These are an accumulation of stock, usually raw materials, for use in case of supply problems, or cash-flow difficulties that prevent purchase of new stock. A buffer stock, or safety stock, is an insurance against unexpected problems, but excessive hoarding ties up assets and limits supplies of the resource to other companies. The use of just-in-time techniques has reduced the requirement for buffer stock.

- It can involve the use of charts to record and monitor the accuracy of the physical dimensions of products. Representational samples of an output manufacturing process may be taken daily or even hourly, and faults in the process which are revealed may be fairly simple to correct by adjusting the appropriate machinery. If output exceeds the control limits consistently then more urgent management action would be required because this could indicate some inadequacy in production methods or quality of raw materials and components. It could even be due to inefficiency in production or excessively tight tolerances in the first place.

- Control charts can also be applied to the inspection of raw materials received from suppliers in order to confirm that the supplier is supplying materials, which conform to the size and standard specified in the purchase contract.

5   CO-ORDINATION

5.1   Organisation

Up to now in this study guide the term 'organisation' has been broadly used. Another interpretation of this term may be made if organisation is regarded as being the co-ordination of all the procedures, systems and functions within that organisation.

Co-ordination is one of the major functions of management. Each department will have its own procedures and its own priorities. It is the job of the manager to get all of these to mesh together harmoniously and move in the direction of the common purpose.

This is nowhere more apparent than in the planning process. Each department will have its own long-term and short-term goals and purposes, and targets that it wants to achieve. There may also be bonus schemes tied into this. Each department will have its own set of priorities. Effective co-ordination will cause some of these to change, in the interests of pursuing an overall set of priorities.

As the business plan will cover all departments of the organisation, so all of the departmental plans and budgets must be co-ordinated, so that they are all working together to achieve the business plan. For instance, sales should be planning to sell the number of units that the production departments agreed to produce, otherwise there will be either unsold stock or unfilled orders.

At the production level, co-ordination will ensure that:

- Departments know what it is they need to achieve, and when

- Work 'flows' from one department to another without holdups or clashes, and without idle time or overwork for staff and machinery

- The resources required for a task are available where and when they are required

- There is no duplication of effort

Definition

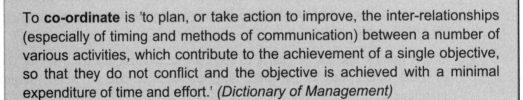

To **co-ordinate** is 'to plan, or take action to improve, the inter-relationships (especially of timing and methods of communication) between a number of various activities, which contribute to the achievement of a single objective, so that they do not conflict and the objective is achieved with a minimal expenditure of time and effort.' *(Dictionary of Management)*

5.2 Formal and informal types of co-ordination

Many organisations endeavour to set up formal systems of co-ordination to ensure that individuals, groups and functions work effectively with each other and that the parts, although existing individually, operate in harmony. This is usually attained by the setting of an overall organisational goal, which is broken down into supporting objectives for individuals, groups and functional areas. This is important – it is of little value to have a stock control system that appears to work for both raw materials and finished goods and an apparently efficient production department system if the two functional areas are not co-ordinated. If the right type of raw materials cannot be issued to the production department at the right time then however efficient the production department may be internally it will not be able to contribute effectively to the organisation as a whole. In turn such failure will mean that the production department will be unable to furnish the stores section with the required quantity of finished units to meet customers' orders. Formal systems of co-ordination are required to ensure that the goals of the organisation are achieved and not hampered.

It is to the credit of many individuals within organisations that they recognise instinctively the relationship between different procedures, systems and functional areas and implement them. This is usually achieved without formal modes, within small groups and sections where, having identified the goals of the particular group/section, the group/section leader and individuals devise suitable and logical ways of attaining the required goals. This is normally achieved informally whilst the co-ordination of a number of groups or sections requires attention of a more formal nature.

5.3 The importance of co-ordination

Remember that we defined the purpose of organisations as 'the controlled performance to achieve collective goals'. This is, in essence, what co-ordination involves. Co-ordination is important because:

(a) the organisation is a collection of individuals and groups, each with their own interests and goals; these must be given a unified, common direction if the organisation as a whole is to achieve its objectives;

(b) the organisation's activities involve a variety of:
  (i) people;
  (ii) tasks;
  (iii) resources; and
  (iv) technologies

  all of these will have to be at the right place, at the right time, working in the right way, if smooth operations are to be maintained;

(c) some activities of the organisation will be dependent on the successful and timely completion of other activities (as we saw in network analysis): someone needs to ensure that such interrelationships are taken into account in the overall activity of the organisation;

(d) some activities of the organisation will be higher priority than others: someone needs to ensure that there is an overall balance between urgent/high-priority activities and routine activities, on which the organisation nevertheless depends;

(e) resources (human, material and financial) are limited, and possibly scarce. Different units in the organisation are, in effect, in competition for their 'slice' of the resources available. Someone has to balance their demands and the organisation's priorities to ensure that overall, resources are used efficiently and effectively in pursuit of the organisation's goals.

FOR DISCUSSION

Think about a team sport you know well – say, football. What would happen if you had:

(a) no positions for each of the players to adopt?

(b) no team strategy?

(c) no team purpose – if, say, prizes were awarded to individual goal scorers, and there were no such thing as a team win?

(d) nobody in charge of providing kit, the ball, the playing field or the referee on a regular basis?

5.4 What needs co-ordinating?

From the above, we can see that, broadly, managers co-ordinate:

(a) the **timing** of activities, so that their inter-relationships are controlled without wasted time or bottlenecks;

(b) the **direction** or **purpose** of activities, so that sub-units of the organisation pull together towards common objectives, and the relative priority of activities are balanced;

(c) the **resources** (human, financial and material) required for activities, so that each sub-unit of the organisation is able to do what it should, when it should.

Activity 6   **(20 mins)**

(a) Can you immediately think of some techniques we have already discussed which might help a business in each of these areas?

(b) Give an example of a problem arising from failure to co-ordinate in each of these areas.

5.5 Symptoms of poor co-ordination

A manager might be alerted to problems of co-ordination by the following tell-tale signs.

(a) Complaints from clients, customers and other external parties, indicating that products are not being supplied on time, or that they have been given different information by different departments of the organisation.

(b) Production problems, with alternating overloads and idle time, and associated problems with labour resourcing and production costs. (The equivalent for service organisations might be missed deadlines or commitments to customers, internal paperwork failing to reach the right people at the right time and so on.)

(c) Persistent conflict within and between departments, especially the placing of blame for problems, and empire-building and power games in place of co-operation.

(d) Lack of communication between units of the organisation.

(e) Appeals to rules and red tape in an attempt to give the appearance of integrated activity.

5.6 Causes of poor co-ordination

Some of the major causes of poor co-ordination are as follows.

(a) **Poor communication** – both vertically and horizontally – so that units do not know what they are supposed to be doing, or what other units are doing, or how the two are meant to be related.

(b) **Inadequate planning and control**, so that the objectives of each unit are not clearly understood, or integrated with those of other units, within overall objectives.

(c) **Weak organisation structure,** which does not make the inter-relationships between units clear, or link them via the chain of command. This problem will be particularly acute where the organisation's task requires interdependent input across the boundaries of departments and functions.

(d) **Interpersonal and/or interdepartmental conflict**. Power and resources are limited in organisations, and there is frequently competition, rivalry, jealousies, the guarding of 'territory' and information and so on, to protect the interests of individuals and groups. This kind of activity is known as organisational politics.

(e) **Differences** between the cultures and tasks of different units. These may be differences in:

(i) the time pressures a unit works under;

(ii) the leadership style of the units' managers;

(iii) the technology used by the units;

(iv) the methods of working adopted by the units;

(v) the culture or values of the units;

and so on.

Activity 7   **(20 mins)**

Give an example of each of the types of difference between cultures and tasks of different units suggested above, which might cause problems of co-ordination.

---

6 IMPROVING CO-ORDINATION

6.1 Management strategies

Maintaining and improving communication

Communication is essential for co-ordination, ensuring that:

(a) the inter-relationship of activities and plans is understood;

(b) variations from plan in one activity are notified to, and taken into account by, other units;

(c) conflict and organisational politics are not allowed to develop, to obstruct the common goals of the organisation.

Managers should give attention to horizontal, as well as vertical, communication.

Activity 8   **(10 mins)**

Suggest three ways in which a manager might encourage horizontal communication.

Planning

Systematic planning and control is essential for co-ordination. Tasks need to be sequenced and scheduled in a way that:

(a) balances their relative urgency and priority;

(b) takes into account their inter-relationships and the dependency of one task on another;

(c) allows resources to be rationally allocated on the basis of priorities and overall objectives; and

(d) allows the plans and schedules of each unit to be integrated with those of other units, towards the organisation's overall objectives.

Controlling conflict

Managers should try to create conditions in which individuals and departments are able to co-operate instead of conflict.

Direct supervision

The manager occupies a co-ordinating role within his or her own section, as the central person responsible for all the work of the group: issuing instructions, monitoring performance and so on.

6.2 Structures and mechanisms

As well as using the co-ordinating function of managers, an organisation can aid co-ordination through its structures and various formal mechanisms.

Organisation structure

The organisation structure may be designed to provide:

(a) a **co-ordinating level of management**. Just as the individual manager acts as the 'lynchpin' of co-ordination for his own unit, so he has a superior who is responsible for co-ordinating his work with that of other units, see the diagram below;

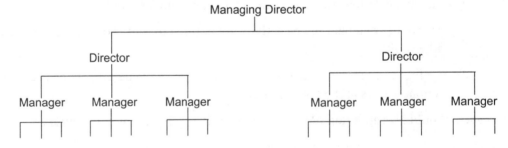

Figure 9.5 Organisation structure

(b) **liaison or integration officers** – for example, project co-ordinators, client liaison managers and so on. These posts essentially encourage communication;

(c) **multi-disciplinary teams,** committees, project groups and so on. These are matrix structures, including representation from all departments involved in a given task or activity, with a co-ordinating authority (a project manager, say) crossing functional boundaries.

Standardisation

Standardisation is an important mechanism for co-ordinating work at the operational level: it involves getting people to do things the same way, or with the same results. This adds reliability, or predictability, to work processes, allowing them to be more closely co-ordinated and controlled.

(a) **Standardisation of work processes** is possible for routine tasks, where the actual content of the task is specified or programmed. For example, think about the assembly instructions for a model or piece of furniture, or the operation of a video recorder: the task is designed to be done in the same way, regardless of who is doing it. Standardisation of forms and documents is another important aid to consistency and co-ordination.

(b) **Standardisation of output** is possible for more complex tasks, where discretion is needed in performing the work. The organisation may set standards for design, quality, cost and so on, so that its product or service is consistent, regardless of who does the work and how.

(c) **Standardisation by skill and knowledge** is possible for complex and varied work, which nevertheless requires a certain standard of performance. So, for example, a hospital sets standard requirements for the qualifications of its doctors, as an accountancy firm does for its accountants and so on.

EXAMPLE

McDonald's fast food restaurants are highly standardised in terms of work processes and outputs. This helps them to control consistency of food quality and specification in their outlets spread worldwide. You don't get lettuce in a McDonald's hamburger in the UK, because it is not possible for every hamburger made worldwide to contain lettuce, due to local variations in supply.

FOR DISCUSSION

How well co-ordinated is the course you are on? (Consider how 'smooth' your timetable is: clashes? bottlenecks? idle time? How consistent is the teaching and course material? Is there a course leader or co-ordinator, and what is his or her function?)

7 ORGANISATIONAL CONSTRAINTS

7.1 Constraints on management

In putting forward theories and techniques for managing activities, it is all too easy to give the impression that managers are in a position to make any and all decisions they think necessary to achieve their objectives, bounded only by the scope of their authority within the organisation. Of course, this isn't really so. We have already touched on the uncertainty of forecasting and planning the future; the impossibility of gathering all relevant information; the fact that power and resources are limited; the need for compromise in interpersonal relations and in business decisions alike; the importance –

and unpredictability – of human behaviour at work. All these factors act as constraints on the individual manager's right and ability to manage people and activities as (s)he sees fit, or even in the most effective way possible (in an ideal world ...). This section aims to draw together all those threads.

7.2 External stakeholders

Stakeholders are people or groups who have a 'stake' or interest in the activities and performance of an organisation and who impose certain obligations on its management. The external stakeholders of the organisation include:

(a) **its owners or shareholders** – the organisation, and its management, have a primary responsibility to look after the owners' interests and to secure them a return on their financial investment in the organisation; the shareholders of a public company have the right to vote on organisational issues in an Annual General Meeting and any Extraordinary General Meetings that may be called: ultimately, the shareholders have the say in what the organisation does and how it should be managed;

(b) **its customers** – the organisation's customers depend on it for the goods and services they need, and for the safety, value and honest marketing of those goods and services; in a free market economy, however, customers have the choice to accept or reject an organisation's offerings, and this gives them power: organisations need to tailor their products and their image to the values and wants of the market, if they are to survive competition;

Activity 9 **(20 mins)**

What sort of issues have consumer organisations focused on in the attempt to influence businesses to protect buyers' interests and values? Suggest four examples that you are aware of.

(c) **the community, or society as a whole** – society depends on businesses for employment, investment, social responsibility (eg towards the environment) and so on. It also provides the organisation with labour, with potential customers and with a reputation which may affect the organisation's position in the market, so managers need to consider whether their decisions will be socially acceptable.

In relation to external stakeholders, an organisation has:

(a) obligations or responsibilities, which it may undertake voluntarily, but which do not form a part of its internal guidance or control mechanisms; for example, value for money, charitable donations, generous wages and so on; and

(b) boundaries or constraints on its managers' freedom to act as they see fit. For example, government legislation (on pollution, health and safety at work, redundancy and so on), regulation (on financial reporting and so on) and agreements with a trade union.

Society as a whole protects its own interests formally, via laws and regulations, designed to ensure that organisations behave morally (or ethically) and responsibly.

7.3 Regulatory control

Regulatory control involves the guidance, monitoring and control of organisational practices through formal mechanisms such as laws, regulations, 'watchdog' bodies and agreed Codes of Practice. These act as constraints on managerial discretion.

Laws

Laws can affect businesses in the following different ways.

(a) *Dealings with customers* can be affected by laws on the sale of goods and services, on advertising and trade descriptions, on product safety and on shop opening hours.

(b) *How a business treats its employees* is affected by employment legislation and trade union law, largely designed to protect employees' rights. Thus there are strict rules on the dismissal of employees and on equal opportunities.

(c) *Dealings with shareholders* are affected by the Companies Acts, which lay down how information must be given in published accounts and what dividends may be paid.

(d) The *criminal law* can affect companies. Some offences can be committed by companies as separate legal persons distinct from their directors and employees.

Some laws apply to all businesses. Others apply only to particular types of business. An example is the Financial Services and Markets Act 2000, which affects firms in the financial sector dealing with investments.

Businesses are also affected by laws made outside the UK. For example, anyone doing business in the USA must take account of US law. Even a business which has no international dealings must take account of European Union law. The EU has done many things to make the sale of goods in different countries easier, and to allow the free movement of capital and labour. Here are some examples.

(a) Setting common standards on food labelling and hygiene

(b) Setting common standards for information technology

(c) Making rules to ensure that when a government needs to buy something, all EU companies have an equal chance to supply and the home country's companies are not favoured

(d) Liberalising of capital movements, so that (for example) a UK investor can freely move money to another country and invest it in a business there

(e) Removing of rules which limited access to financial services – it should soon be possible for insurance companies to sell their products anywhere in the EU

(f) Ensuring mutual recognition of professional qualifications, so that (for example) a French lawyer can practise in the UK without having to re-qualify as a UK solicitor or barrister

(g)   Giving all EU citizens the right to work anywhere in the EU

Changes in the law can affect organisations in many ways. A tightening of health and safety legislation may increase costs. Premises failing to meet the higher standards could be closed down. Particularly damaging might be the imposition of a complete ban on the organisation's product, clearly made worse should they have failed to develop a product portfolio sufficiently broad to absorb such a loss. Tobacco companies are at present faced with the prospect of a ban on advertising, if not on their products.

FOR DISCUSSION

Do you think it is necessary for governments to introduce legislation in areas such as:

(a)   health and safety at work (obliging employers to provide a healthy and safe environment and procedures)?

(b)   product safety (fire-retardant materials, no asbestos, safety belts in cars, health warnings and so on)?

If so, why? If managers were free to do what they liked or thought best for the organisation, what might standards be like? Do you think that laws encourage people to do only what is required, and not more – perhaps even lowering standards to what can be got away with?

Regulation

In some areas of decision-making, regulation has increased in recent years, where it has been felt to be in the public interest.

(a)   Regulatory bodies oversee the activities of privatised utilities like BT, British Gas and the electricity and water companies. They can influence the company's pricing policy, competitive strategy (if they feel it is unfair) and so on.

(b)   The financial services industry in the City is more heavily controlled than hitherto, though much of this is self-regulation carried out by the industry itself, with its own regulatory bodies and codes of practice, covering investment advice, 'insider dealing' and so on.

(c)   Codes of Practice may be agreed by industry representative bodies, or published by other bodies, like ACAS. They allow monitoring bodies, like the Commission for Racial Equality or the Advertising Standards Authority, to measure the behaviour of organisations against defined standards.

(d)   There is a body of regulations and standards covering the reporting of the financial performance of organisations and the verification of reports by auditors. For example, Financial Reporting Standards (FRSs) and other pronouncements by the Accounting Standards Board (ASB) and the Auditing Practices Board (APB).

Ethical obligations

Each of us has our own set of values and beliefs that we have evolved over the course of our lives through our education, experiences and upbringing. As a manager you bring with you your own concept of what is right and what is wrong. Every decision that you make, for better or for worse, is the application of these values to the question at hand. This is made more difficult by the pressures of organisational life. There are the pressures of productivity, competition and your superiors. Sometimes managers make decisions which conflict with their own or society's values because of what they see as the pressures of the business world.

Business ethics are concerned with the expectations of society, fair competition, advertising, social responsibilities and corporate behaviour (at home, as well as abroad), with how individuals interact with each other and with how organisations ought to relate to their external stakeholders and the community as a whole.

Most managers expect their organisation to develop an ethics programme or code. As with the development of other organisational programmes, it involves the input, interaction, co-operation, decision-making and ongoing commitment of many people.

There are five factors that affect ethical obligations.

(a) **The law** – this defines the minimum ethical standards in a given area of practice. For example, deceptive advertising is illegal and violators of this law are liable to large fines, court action and/or loss of goodwill. Some unethical behaviour is often not considered very illegal, such as head hunting employees from other companies, padding expense accounts etc.

(b) **Government regulations** – these are also fairly clear-cut outlining what is acceptable and what is not. These regulations set standards on issues such as unfair competition, unsafe products, etc. Failure to comply with these regulations could lead to criminal charges, or fines etc. Unfortunately, there are times when these regulations do not force ethical behaviour. In the U.S. cyclamates (artificial sweeteners) were banned because there was evidence that they were carcinogenic. Following the ban a major food manufacturer sold 300,000 cases of cyclamate sweetened food overseas. Similarly many banned food additives and pesticides etc are being sold overseas, mainly to third world countries.

(c) **Industry and company ethical codes** – are codes that clearly state the ethical standard a manager should follow within his or her organisation. These standard practices are usually followed if they are written down and the rules enforced, however many companies have 'unwritten' codes of practice or if written down, have no method of enforcing these rules. Generally, written codes clarify the ethical issues but leave the resolution to the individual's conscience

(d) **Social pressures** – exerted by society as a whole on a company to act in a humane, environmental and socially-conscious way.

(e) **Tension between personal standards and the goals of the organisation** – we can refer back to the example involving the sale of banned substances overseas. It is not illegal, but it may be against your personal values to sell these products to unsuspecting overseas clients. What would you do if this action were a direct order from a superior? Does this take away your responsibility? As with many ethical problems there are no easy answers.

Activity 10 (20 mins)

What constraints do you think were imposed on employers when the Equal Opportunities legislation was introduced?

Try to think of three main areas which were affected and why.

7.4 PEST factors

A useful acronym, widely used in the UK to describe the external environment of organisations, is PEST: Political-legal, Economic, Socio-cultural and Technological factors.

7.5 The political-legal environment

Political-legal factors which managers must take into account include the following.

(a) Law and regulation, as discussed above.

(b) The power of the government, as the nation's largest supplier, employer, customer and investor. (Consider the effect of a change of government policy on defence for the defence industry, say).

(c) Political events at home and abroad. There may be trading sanctions imposed on states (as was the case with South Africa, Iraq and Serbia) by the international community. A war or change of regime can harm industries (as happened to airlines during the Gulf War) or build them (as in the opening up of commerce in Eastern Europe after the collapse of communism).

(d) Government economic policy – for example, on public spending, borrowing and taxation (**fiscal** policy) and on interest and exchange rates and control of the money supply (**monetary** policy). Businesses are affected by taxation, and by monetary policy: high interest rates, for example, increase the cost of investment and depress consumer spending.

(e) Government industrial policy – for example, encouraging exports (by subsidies or promotion), sponsorship of businesses in depressed regions, protection of domestic industry (duty on imported goods) and so on.

(f) Government social and foreign policy – on education and training of the workforce, trade promotion overseas, obligations towards the EU and so on.

7.6 The economic environment

An organisation is affected by overall economic conditions, as these influence:

(a) the demand for its products; and

(b) the cost of its supplies.

In times of boom and increased demand and consumption, the overall planning problem will be to identify the demand. Conversely, in times of recession, the emphasis will be on cost-effectiveness, continuing profitability, survival and competition.

A company's immediate regional geographical environment is also important. It might be located in a growth area full of modern thriving industry, such as Milton Keynes; or it may be located in an area of urban decay. The economic future of the area will affect wage rates, availability of labour, the disposable income of local consumers, the provision of roads and other services and so on.

7.7 The socio-cultural environment

Social and cultural influences on management decisions include the following.

(a) **Demography**, or demographics: that is, population trends.

Definition

> **Demography** is the analysis of statistics on birth and death rates, sex and age distributions, ethnic groups and geographical movements within a population.

Conditions and changes in the local and/or national population can affect:

(i) the availability of labour of the age and skills required by the organisation in its operating area; and

(ii) the demand for its products and services in particular areas (eg if population is declining or growing) or by particular groups (eg an increasing proportion of the population of a certain ethnic group, or over retirement age).

(b) **Culture:** the beliefs and values, attitudes, customs, language and tastes of a given society or social group.

(i) Organisations need to adapt their products, marketing approach and corporate image to the values of a given group. Language and other cultural barriers may have to be overcome, especially if the organisation is operating internationally. (The custom of giving gifts to business contacts is embedded in some cultures, for example – but would be called bribery in other places!)

EXAMPLE

1 When car-manufacturer Vauxhall launched its Nova in South America, it wondered why the response was poor. Finally, someone realised that 'No va' means 'doesn't go' in Spanish ...

2 In the 1980s, Coca-Cola decided to change its flavour to compete with Pepsi. Market research, taste tests and so forth elicited positive responses to the change, and so the new formulation was introduced. A small group of consumers

vociferously opposed the change; and this opposition spread suddenly and rapidly like an epidemic, forcing Coca-Cola to re-introduce the old formula. It seemed that some consumers perceived Coke to symbolise 'American values', so changing the formula appeared to be an assault on them.

(ii) Organisations need to adapt their management styles and practices to the values prevailing in the culture from which they draw their workforce. (Having women in positions of authority is considered inappropriate in some cultures, for example.)

Activity 11 (15 mins)

Give three examples of:

(a) products tailored to a particular cultural market; and

(b) employment and management practice influenced by culture.

7.8 The technological environment

Technology is not just **apparatus** (ie tools and machines), but also **technique** (skills and procedures for the use of tools and machines) and **organisation** (the social and work structure of tasks).

Technological **change** is extremely rapid, and organisations must constantly adapt to it. Technology can affect the management of organisations by:

(a) **presenting opportunities and threats in the market for the organisation's goods and services** – compact discs, satellite dishes and home computers are 'in': records, typewriters and heavy wooden-framed tennis rackets are 'out';

(b) **changing the possibilities for how products are made** – (for example, using computer-aided design and robots) – **and services are provided** (for example, cashpoint machines instead of bank tellers);

(c) **changing the way in which labour is utilised** – technology has facilitated the delayering and downsizing of organisation structures, and created a much more knowledge-based workforce.

In general, managers will be constrained to adopt new technology – especially if the organisation's competitors have done so – in order to cut costs, enhance quality, innovate and so on.

Apart from the PEST factors, which affect all organisations, a business organisation faces competition.

7.9 The competitive environment

Business organisations compete for customers and for labour – and the price of competitive failure may be the collapse of the business. The need to compete may constrain managers to:

(a) maintain or improve the quality of products/services;

(b) control the price charged for products/services;

(c) pay more to secure a reliable supply of high-quality materials from suppliers (particularly in specialised areas);

(d) pay more for selling, advertising, promotion, sponsorship and so on;

(e) pay higher wages, salaries and benefits;

(f) implement attractive human resource practices to attract skilled labour: welfare, training, workplace crèche or whatever.

These constraints will be particularly acute if there is a new or strengthening competitor in the market.

8 INTERNAL ENVIRONMENT

8.1 Internal stakeholders

The internal stakeholders of an organisation are its members or employees.

FOR DISCUSSION

Why do employees have a 'stake' in the organisation? What kind of things do they need or want from it?

The needs, wants and expectations of the employees will act as a constraint on management decision-making because the organisation may be concerned:

(a) to harness the energy and committed co-operation of its employees;

(b) not to lose skilled and experienced employees to competitors;

(c) to maintain a reputation as a responsible or generous employer, to secure a future pool of labour.

Activity 12 **(20 mins)**

Give five examples of managerial decisions which might require careful thought because of their potential effects on the morale and attitudes of employees.

8.2 Organisation

The freedom of individual managers to make decisions as they see fit will be constrained by organisational factors such as the following.

(a) **The scope and amount of authority delegated to them:** their 'territory' and power within the organisation. A manager can only manage activities for which (s)he is responsible and has authority.

(b) **Plans, programmes, procedures, rules and so on,** which may already be in place. A manager is rarely able to plan activities and work methods from scratch: systems will have been developed for most routine sequences of activity. Managers often have to stick to plans and expenditure budgets which have been determined (with varying degrees of consultation) by more senior officials.

(c) **The existing organisation structure.** An individual manager is rarely able to organise work and workers from scratch. There may be no experience of multi-disciplinary teamworking to build on, for example, or departmental boundaries and job demarcation lines may be too firmly fixed to change.

(d) **The demand for co-ordination.** As we saw in Chapter 14, some tasks depend on others and have to be scheduled accordingly, and some processes and outputs need standardising in order to maintain co-ordination and consistency. An individual manager cannot make decisions for his or her own unit without reference to the requirements of the organisation system as a whole.

(e) **Organisation culture.** An individual manager is unlikely to be able to choose his or her own style of communication, motivation and management in general, without reference to the culture of the unit or organisation as a whole. A manager who does not 'fit' the organisational 'style' rarely lasts long ...

9 LIMITED RESOURCES

9.1 Money

Money, and the infinite variety of things it represents, is always limited and tightly controlled in organisations. Money allocated to different units represents cost to the organisation, whose financial objectives are likely to be profitability, return on investment and so on: in other words, to **maximise earnings** and **minimise costs**.

Individual unit budgets for expenditure are components of the overall organisational budget – like slices of a cake. A great deal of the politics and conflict within organisations is concerned with competing for bigger slices of the cake!

Limited financial resources therefore constrain managerial decision-making because:

(a) a limited budget can only be stretched so far, and the manager may not be able to obtain or retain all the other resources – quality materials, extra labour, new equipment and so on – that (s)he would want;

(b) a manager may be tempted to spend up to the allocated budget, even though it is not required, so as not to have the allocation reduced next time round.

9.2 Time

You may not have thought about it, but time is a limited resource.

(a) There are only so many working hours available. If these are not sufficient to accomplish everything a manager wishes, (s)he will be constrained to:

(i)   find extra labour or machine capacity, to cover the excess workload in the time available; or

      (ii)   eliminate, or simplify, tasks or 'cut corners' in order to get high-priority work done with the existing workforce; or

      (iii) allow work to run late, and adjust the work plan for the knock-on effects.

(b)   Deadlines may be imposed by customer requirements or internal co-ordination. Deadlines get closer: they make time both a limited and an increasingly scarce resource. Compromises of cost or quality may have to be made to meet deadlines.

(c)   Time for information-gathering and decision-making is also limited. This may constrain managers to make decisions which seem riskier or less informed than they might be, or which have not been subject to as much consultation with team members as the manager's style might otherwise dictate.

9.3 Information

Information is a limited resource for several reasons.

(a)   Time and money for gathering it may be limited.

(b)   There is a limit to how much a person can take in and use effectively.

(c)   Some information is simply not obtainable with any certainty – for example, how people are going to react, or what is going to happen tomorrow!

(d)   'Information is power', and individuals and units in organisations tend to hoard it if they think it will give them extra influence or a competitive edge over others.

Limited information constrains the management of activities because:

(a)   decisions have to be taken on the basis of what is known: the full range of possible options can never be known, and a certain degree of uncertainty and inaccuracy remains;

(b)   it is not possible to predict the outcome of all decisions and actions, nor the contingencies that might affect them. Changes in the PEST, competitive or physical environment of an organisation cannot always be foreseen and planned for.

If **management** information is not made available to a manager – for example, the objectives and results of the organisation, or the attitudes of employees – then the ability of the manager to make effective decisions will clearly be impaired.

NOTES

Chapter roundup

- Operations management can be described as a system. The inputs include the needs of the customers, information, technology, labour and management and the fixed and variable assets that are relevant to the transformation process. Managers and workers use the information and physical factors to produce the outputs. The transformation process incorporates planning, operating and controlling the system.

- Policies are general guidelines for management decision-making. Procedures are a logical sequence of required actions for performing a certain task and rules are specific, definite courses of action that must be taken in a given situation.

- Production can be defined as the activity of transforming raw materials or components into finished products.

- The value chain is a sequence of business activities by which, in the perspective of the end user, value is added to the products or services produced by an organisation

- Primary activities are those directly related with production, sales, marketing, delivery and services.

- Support activities provide purchased inputs, human resources, technology and infrastructural functions to support the primary activities.

- Linkages connect the interdependent elements of the value chain together. They occur when one element of the value chain affects the costs or effectiveness of another.

- JIT or zero inventory was conceived to ensure the inventory has only what is needed, when it is needed.

- The four objectives – cost, time, quantity and quality – should be considered together, because the optimum performance typically involves a trade-off of several dimensions, specifically what is done (scope and quality) versus the resources used to do the work (time and cost).

- Quality control is the process of ensuring that goods and services are produced in accordance with specifications. The major objective of quality control is to see that the organisation lives up to the standards it has set for itself.

- Statistical process control (SPC) is the continuous monitoring and charting of a process while it is operating, to warn when the process is moving away from predetermined limits.

- Co-ordination is one of the major functions of management. Each department will have its own procedures and its own priorities. It is the job of the manager to get all of these to mesh together harmoniously and move in the direction of the common purpose.

- Regulatory control involves the guidance, monitoring and control of organisational practices through formal mechanisms such as laws, regulations, 'watchdog' bodies and agreed Codes of Practice.

Quick quiz

1   Give an example of a procedure for the board of directors.

2   What does product development include?

3   How does job production differ from process production?

4   List the five primary activities in the value chain model.

5   How can performance be monitored?

6   Give three reasons why co-ordination is necessary.

7   Give three examples of the symptoms of poor co-ordination.

8   List the main causes of poor co-ordination.

9   Why is (a) communication and (b) planning helpful to co-ordination?

10 What can be 'standardised' in order to co-ordinate activities at an operational level?

11 List the main external stakeholders of an organisation.

12 What are business ethics concerned with?

13 Give three examples of (a) political and (b) cultural factors.

14 How does (a) organisation structure, (b) co-ordination and (c) organisation culture constrain management discretion?

15 What resources do managers compete for in organisations?

Answers to quick quiz

1   The conduct of board meetings will be set out as a procedure for the board of directors. (See para 1.4)

2   Development refers collectively to the entire process of identifying a market opportunity, creating a product to appeal to the identified market, and finally, testing, modifying and refining the product until it is ready for production. (2.1)

3   Job production (or unit production) is the output of a single product to specific requirements (eg suit or ship) whereas process (flow) production is continuous production of products of a more or less identical nature, eg oil refinery. (3.1)

4   Inbound logistics
    Operations
    Outbound logistics
    Marketing and sales
    After-sales service (3.2)

5   Measurement can be based on the actual start or finish times of critical activities and (especially for a project) the completion of milestones, or the timing of acceptance tests. Operation control charts use budget and schedule plans to report cumulative time and cost so that variances can be calculated. Performance can also be monitored by inspection, progress reviews (at regular stages), quality testing and financial audit. (4.1)

6   There must be a common direction for the organisation to achieve its goals; co-ordination also helps to maintain smooth operations and to balance high priority work with routine tasks. (5.1)

7   Complaints, production problems, persistent conflict. (5.5)

8   Poor communication
    Inadequate planning and control
    Weak organisation structure
    Interpersonal and/or interdepartmental conflict
    Differences between the cultures and tasks of different units (5.6)

9   (a) Communication ensures that the inter-relationship of activities and plans is understood, that variations are notified and that conflict is not allowed to develop.

    (b) Planning prioritises, understands the dependency of one task on another, allows resources to be rationally allocated and integrates, plans and schedules. (6.1)

10 Work processes, output, design, quality cost, skill and knowledge. (6.1)

11 External stakeholders include owners and shareholders, customers, the community or society as a whole. (7.2)

12 Business ethics are concerned with the expectations of society, fair competition, advertising, social responsibilities and corporate behaviour (at home, as well as abroad), with how individuals interact with each other and with how organisations ought to relate to their external stakeholders and the community as a whole. (7.3)

13 (a)   Trading sanctions, war, change of regime.
    (b)   Beliefs and values, attitudes and customs. (7.5, 7.7)

14 (a) Managers can only manage activities for which they are responsible and have authority.

    (b) Decisions are not possible without considering the requirements of the organisation system as a whole.

    (c) Decisions must 'fit in' to the organisational 'style'. (8.2)

15 Money, time and information. (9)

Answers to activities

1   The restaurant has a number of choices as to how to create value.

    (a) It can become more efficient, by automating the production of food, as in a fast food chain.

    (b) The chef can develop commercial relationships with growers, so he or she can obtain the best quality fresh produce.

    (c) The chef can specialise in a particular type of cuisine (eg Nepalese, Korean).

    (d) The restaurant can be sumptuously decorated for those customers who value 'atmosphere' and a sense of occasion, in addition to a restaurant's purely gastronomic pleasures.

    (e) The restaurant can serve a particular type of customer (eg celebrities).

    Each of these options is a way of organising the activities of buying, cooking and serving food in a way that customers will value.

2   The first step is to outline the primary activities that may be a source of advantage. Then link these to the support activities, showing how each of them cuts across all of the primary activities.

HR management	Training	Stable workforce Quality of work		Retention of best salespeople	Training service staff
Procurement		Highest quality components	Best located warehouse		Quality parts replacement
Technology development	Material handling and sorting	Unique product features	Special purpose vehicles	Engineering support	Advanced servicing techniques
Firm infrastructure	Reduced damage	Low defect rates	Quick order processing	Extensive credit to buyers	Rapid installation Service quality
	Inbound logistics	Operations	Outbound logistics	Marketing and sales	Service

Primary activities

The technology development activity at the lawn mower manufacturer, shown in the diagram, indicates material handling and sorting adding value at the inbound logistics stage. Other sources of potential advantage are sought with the unique product features at the operations stage, special purpose delivery vehicles at the outbound logistics stage and engineering support and servicing techniques in the marketing, sales and service stages.

3   Sana Sounds is involved in the record industry from start to finish. Although recording and CD manufacture are contracted out to external suppliers, this makes no difference to the fact that these activities are part of Sana Sounds' own value chain. Sana Sounds earns its money by managing the whole set of activities. If the company grows then perhaps it will acquire its own recording studios. The purpose of this exercise has been to drive the point home that a *value chain of activities* is not the same as an *organisation's business functions*.

4   The correct answer is C. The other activities are non-value-adding activities.

5   The correct answer is B.

6   Co-ordination techniques, and problems that might arise if an organisation does not co-ordinate, include the following

    (a)   Timing: scheduling, network analysis, Gantt charts.

        Direction: planning and goal-setting, priority-setting, work breakdown, network analysis.

        Resources: network analysis, resource allocation charts, budgets.

    (b)   Timing: the costing department is 'behind' in its analysis of production employees' time sheets, leaving the payroll department without the information required to prepare and pay the wages.

        Direction: the marketing department is trying to sell an 'upmarket' image of the product, while the production department is trying to increase profits by cutting down on 'frills' and packaging.

Resources: the organisation does not have enough trained staff to cope with a peak work period; there are insufficient components in store to complete a given production order on time.

7   Differences between culture and tasks might cause co-ordination problems for the reasons below.

(i)   The implementation of a computer system (devised over a period of months or years) by a project group, in an operational department with tight time schedules for ongoing work.

(ii)   The manager of one unit may inform his team of decisions, while the manager of the other consults her team, resulting in different approaches. The clash of style may also prevent effective communication between the two managers.

(iii) Incompatible computer systems in two departments, preventing them from sharing information easily.

(iv)   Two departments using different forms for the same purpose, making it difficult to share data, and encouraging different approaches (eg different criteria in staff assessment forms), which may become sources of conflict.

(v)   One unit dedicated to serving the customer at all costs, another dedicated to saving costs, and never mind the customer!

8   Horizontal communication might be beneficial if a manager encouraged in the following ways.

(a)   Not discouraging informal communication at work – even encouraging it, by providing an environment where people can talk during breaks and so on.

(b)   Teambuilding and empowerment, so that people do not see themselves as individuals in competition with other individuals, but as teams who must communicate freely in order to do their jobs.

(c)   Appointing team members to interdisciplinary or joint team meetings, so that they can exchange information with people at the same level but in different areas of the organisation.

9   Aspects of business activity on which consumer organisations have focused include:

(a)   Dangerous products and by-products (such as cigarettes and car exhaust emission)

(b)   Dishonest marketing or promotion; in the UK there is legislation designed to deal with this kind of abuse

(c)   The abuse of political and economic power by organisations (for example, ignoring international sanctions or trading with regimes with poor human rights records)

(d)   The availability of information. Consumers are anxious, for example, to be informed of any artificial additives in foodstuffs

10   Constraints on employers as a result of the Equal Opportunities legislation would involve recruitment and promotion.

In recruitment organisations can no longer specify that they only want, say male applicants (unless exempted for some reason).

In promotion and training the same opportunities have to be offered in both these areas to all employees, regardless of sex, status, race or creed.

11　(a)　Cultural products include: kosher food (to the Jewish community); magazines specifically for men, women or gays; low premium car insurance for mature drivers; cosmetics tested without cruelty to animals, for the 'green' market – eg Body Shop.

　　(b)　Employment practices affected by culture include: work hours to allow for religious holidays and observances; separate facilities and offices to differentiate managers and workers (not a cultural norm in Japan, for example); the extension of benefits previously given to 'spouses' of employees to 'partners' (including gay partners) – for example, by British Airways.

12　Managerial decisions requiring special care about morale and employee attitudes include, for example: office relocation; redundancies; change in work practices (eg introducing shiftworking); cut in benefits; cancellation of holidays in busy periods.

Chapter 10 :
QUALITY

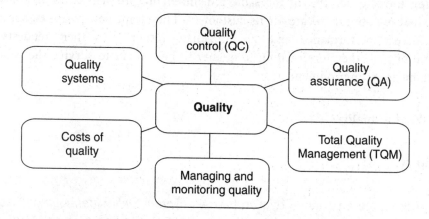

Introduction

In recent years quality has become the key in determining many organisations' positions in respect of their competitive advantage. Unfortunately, quality is difficult to define because it has a wide range of meanings, covering a wide range of businesses and processes.

Quality control is concerned with maintaining quality standards. The process goes through a cycle of establishing standards and procedures, monitoring actual quality and taking control action when actual quality falls below standard. Quality assurance, however, is the term used where a supplier guarantees the quality of goods supplied and allows the customer access while the goods are being manufactured. Total quality management is the term given to programmes that seek to ensure that goods are produced and services are supplied of the highest quality.

Your objectives

After completing this chapter you should be able to:

(a) Define resources, tools and systems required to support business process

(b) Define and implement quality audit systems/practice to manage and monitor quality to standards specified by the organisation and process operated

(c) Embed a quality culture to ensure continuous monitoring and development of the process

NOTES

1 QUALITY SYSTEMS

1.1 The importance of quality in a business environment

The modern business environment is remarkably different from the business environment of a decade or so ago. One change has been the **switch in emphasis away from quantity towards quality.** Consumers and **customers** have become **more sophisticated and discerning** in their requirements. They are no longer satisfied with accepting the late delivery of the same old unreliable products from an organisation which does not appear to care for its customers. They want new products, superior on-time delivery performance and an immediate response to their requests. Many organisations are therefore turning to quality to help them to survive the competitive modern business environment.

1.2 What is quality?

Definition

> **Quality** has been defined by Ken Holmes (*Total Quality Management*) as 'the totality of features and characteristics of a product or service which bears on its ability to meet stated or implied needs.'

In ordinary language, quality implies some degree of excellence or superiority. In an industrial context, it is defined in a much more functional way. Here, quality is more concerned with 'fitness for purpose', and quality management (or control) is about ensuring that products or services conform to specifications.

Juran defines quality as 'fitness for use', which in fact includes two elements.

    (a) *Quality of design*, which can include the customer satisfactions built into the product.

    (b) *Quality of conformance*, in other words a lack of defects in the finished goods

Quality must be considered from the viewpoint of both the consumer and the producer (or service provider).

The **consumer** – according to Deming the consumer is the most important part of the production line. Quality should be aimed at the needs of the consumer, present and future. This is driven by what the consumer wants and will pay for.

The **producer** – the product should be designed to meet or exceed the customer's expectations. Once a product has been properly designed the role of operations' managers is to ensure that the product actually produced meet the design specifications. This is done through product design, process design, process control and **conformance to specifications.**

Product design

- Assess customer needs
- Design a product to meet those needs at the least cost
- Involve customers, suppliers and manufacturing personnel
- SET – product specifications

PROFESSIONAL EDUCATION

Process Design

- Process must be designed to meet final product design specification

- Design process while product is being designed to avoid inefficiencies in production or the need to redesign the product

- SET – process limits

Process Control

- Ensure that the process actually produces a product that meets specifications.

- This will happen if the process was designed correctly and if it is kept in control

- Keep the process within limits

Activity 1   **(10 mins)**

The boss of Acme Umbrellas Ltd believes that customers want robust umbrellas, so he makes one *entirely* out of titanium apart from some gold decoration. 'It is a bit heavy I suppose', he says, showing an example, 'but it's *perfectly* made, look at the gold pins and look at the perfect, flawless finish. Why don't people want it?'

1.3 Quality systems

Quality systems include all activities that contribute to quality, directly or indirectly. Product quality depends on many variables, such as the calibre of the components or materials used; type of equipment used in design, production, handling, installation, testing and shipping; the equipment calibration and maintenance procedures employed; the training and experience of production and supervisory personnel; the level of 'workmanship'; and sometimes the environmental conditions (temperature, humidity, level of dust particles) in the area where the product is produced.

A Quality Management System (QMS) is the organised structure of responsibilities, activities, resources and events that together provide procedures and methods of implementation to ensure the capability of an organisation to meet quality requirements. To achieve this a QMS needs to be capable of:

- demonstrating continuous improvement
- preventing non-conformity
- assisting self-evaluation.

This QMS will consist of the documented rules, procedures and instructions prepared in accordance with agreed standards. These are stated in the quality manual as well as the associated core processes, procedures and work instructions. The document hierarchy is shown below.

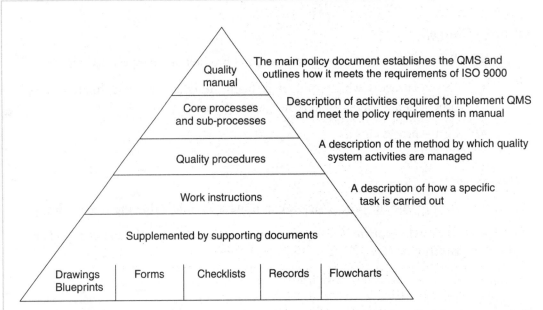

Figure 10.1 Document pyramid

1.4 Quality standards

ISO 9000 is intended to establish, document and maintain a system for ensuring the output quality of a process. It is the generic term for a series of five international standards (ISO 9000, 9001, 9002, 9003, and 9004) sponsored by the International Organisation for Standardisation (ISO), and created to standardise quality management systems for manufacturing and service industries worldwide. Each standard addresses a different aspect of quality assurance, depending on the needs of the user. ISO 9000 does not dictate the quality of *individual* goods and services, but aims to ensure that quality management *systems* of a suitable standard are in place. The standard does not cover every quality issue; it deals with quality systems. While it provides feedback about performance, it cannot guarantee that control action is taken; it is 'an indicator of potential, not of achievement'.

The ISO 9000 Standard Series is almost directly parallel to the British standard BS-5750 and is also identical, in most respects, to the European standard, EN-29000 and the American standard, Q9000. ISO 9000 certification is a tangible expression of a firm's commitment to quality that is internationally understood and accepted.

To gain certification an organisation:

- Prepares a quality manual which sets out the company's policy and procedures on quality assurance

- An assessor will visit the client company and review the facility's quality manual to ensure that it meets the standard and audit the firm's processes to ensure that the system documented in the quality manual is in place and that it is effective.

- The certificate is issued if approval is given. ISO 9000 will increasingly influence the choice of suppliers. Customers wish to avoid the cost of inspecting goods inwards.

- Once certification is obtained, the certifying body conducts audits of the facility once a year and oversees changes and evolutions of the facility's quality system to ensure that it continues to meet the requirements of the standard. ISO 9000 certification is a continuous process, and approval can be withdrawn.

1.5 The quality hierarchy

Methods of achieving quality have evolved over the years.

- Originally craftsmen individually crafted quality into the products they produced. People purchased products based on the craftsman's reputation, or 'hallmark'. The producer knew the customer directly

- Craftsmanship declined after the Industrial Revolution and volume became the goal of choice. The focus was on designing and building products for mass consumption and limiting customer choices. Quality control is maintained by inspecting and detecting bad products

- Things began to change around 1950. Japan was rebuilding and looking for markets for their products. To compete they combined low prices with improved quality. They developed new manufacturing and management techniques – a major innovation was statistical process control.

- During this time a new system was evolving based on the prevention of non-conforming products. Mistakes were not considered inevitable and could be prevented. They would be analysed and eliminated. This prevention of non-conformances is the basic concept of Quality Assurance that is promoted by ISO 9000.

- TQM was introduced to allow potential customers to determine what to design and build. Higher quality could be obtained by focusing on preventing problems and continuously reducing variability in all organisational processes.

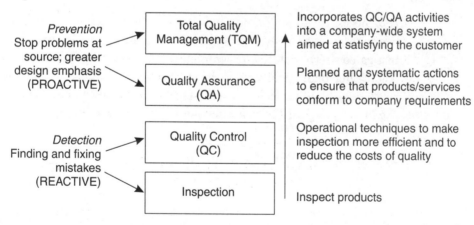

Figure 10.2 The quality hierarchy

2 QUALITY CONTROL

2.1 Inspection

In the past quality control meant *inspection* of finished output or goods inward. Quality was assured at the *end* of the process, often by specialised quality control staff. Inspection is concerned with looking at products that have been made, supplies that have been delivered and services that have been provided, to establish whether they have been up to specification. It is a technique of *identifying* when defective items are being produced at an unacceptable level. Inspection is usually carried out at three main points:

(a) receiving inspection for raw materials and bought out components;

(b) floor or process inspection; and

(c) final inspection or testing.

The problems with this inspection approach are as follows.

(a) The inspection process itself does not 'add value': if it could be guaranteed that no defective items were produced, there would be no need for a separate inspection function.

(b) The production of substandard products wastes raw materials, machine time, and human effort.

(c) The inspection department takes up space, and has to be paid.

(d) The production of defects is not compatible with newer production techniques such as just-in-time: there is no time for inspection.

(e) Working capital is tied up in stocks that cannot be sold.

2.2 Quality control and quality standards

Quality control is concerned with maintaining quality standards. There are usually procedures to check quality of bought-in materials, work-in-progress and finished goods.

In the past, failure to screen quality successfully has resulted in rejections, re-work and scrap, all of which add to manufacturing costs. Modern trends in industry of competition, mass production and increasing standards of quality requirements have resulted in a thorough reappraisal of the problem and two important points have emerged:

1. It is necessary to single out and remove the causes for poor quality goods before production instead of waiting for the end result. Many companies have instigated 'zero defects' programmes following the Japanese practice of eradicating poor quality as early in the chain as possible and insisting on strict quality adherence at every stage – as Crosby points out in his book *Quality is Free*, this is cost effective since customer complaints etc. reduce dramatically.

2. The co-ordination of all activities from the preparation of the specification, through to the purchasing and inspection functions and right up to the function of delivery of the finished product, is essential.

It is accepted that it is not possible to achieve perfection in products because of the variations in raw material quality, operating skills, different types of machines used, wear and tear, etc. but quality control attempts to ascertain the amount of variation from perfect that can be expected in any operation. If this variation is acceptable according to engineering requirements, then production must be established within controlled limits and if the variation is too great then corrective action must be taken to bring it within acceptable limits.

2.3 Quality control and inspection

A distinction should be made between quality control and inspection.

(a) Quality control involves setting controls for the process of manufacture or service delivery. It is aimed at preventing the manufacture of defective items or the provision of defective services. The procedure is:

- establishing standards of quality for a product or service;

- establishing procedures or production methods which ought to ensure that these required standards of quality are met in a suitably high proportion of cases;

- monitoring actual quality; and

- taking control action when actual quality falls below standard.

(b) Inspection is a technique of identifying when defective items are being produced at an unacceptable level. Inspection is usually carried out at three main points.

- Receiving inspection – for raw materials and purchased components
- Floor or process inspection for WIP
- Final inspection or testing for finished goods

EXAMPLE

The postal service might establish a standard that 90% of first class letters will be delivered on the day after they are posted, and 99% will be delivered within two days of posting.

- Procedures would have to be established for ensuring that these standards could be met (eg frequency of collections, automated letter sorting, frequency of deliveries and number of staff employed etc).

- Actual performance could be monitored, perhaps by taking samples from time to time of letters that are posted and delivered.

- If the quality standard is not being achieved, the management of the postal service could take control action (eg employ more postmen or advertise again the use of postcodes) or reduce the standard of quality of the service being provided.

2.4 Advantages of quality control

The advantages lie in the fact that quality control identifies why faulty work is being produced and the quantity of faulty work produced. Action taken as a result can reduce scrap and the amount of necessary re-work. It shows where a design modification could raise efficiency in manufacture. It minimises the chances of poor materials being processed.

The important factor is that quality control must be applied during processing and not after. The most effective areas where control can be usefully applied in most enterprises are:

NOTES

- goods inwards;

- inspection at the supplier's business to see the type of plant and the methods used;

- inspection of all new tools and plant;

- inspection of the first part completed at each stage;

- the first part produced at each stage should be inspected;

- inspection should take place between processes;

- a final check should be made at the end of the production line and any minor adjustments made.

It is as much a fault to produce goods of too high a quality as goods of poor quality. The requirements of the customers must be borne in mind and the sales department and market research can advise on this. They will be aware of competitor's prices and qualities and a decision must be taken whether or not to increase quality. To increase quality means increasing costs and at what point will the quality be more than the customer can afford?

3 QUALITY ASSURANCE (QA)

3.1 Acceptable standard

Quality assurance is about designing a process of which the end result is guaranteed to be of an acceptable standard, because of the checks that have been made along the way. It goes beyond inspection and quality control to embrace the whole organisation in trying to ensure that the quality of the product/service is of the required standard. In order to fulfil this objective, a company should have clear policies on quality together with precise and measurable objectives. In this way all employees will know exactly what is required in terms of product quality. Policies on quality will depend upon what standards the market requires. This means that effective quality assurance depends upon reliable market research to ascertain what the quality requirements of the customer are. Obviously, the position and sector within the market will dictate the level of quality required. Having established the quality standards, the initiative is upon the operational department management to ensure that the standards are complied with.

3.2 Supplier Quality Assurance (SQA)

Supplier Quality Assurance (SQA) is the term used where a supplier guarantees the quality of goods supplied and allows the customer access while the goods are being manufactured. This is usually done through SQA officers, who control the specification of the goods supplied. Usually, the customer and supplier agree inspection procedures and quality control standards and checks are made to ensure that they are being adhered to.

- The customer can almost eliminate goods inwards inspection and items can be directed straight to production. This can give large savings in cost and time in flow production, and can facilitate JIT production.

- The supplier produces to the customer's requirement, thereby reducing rejects and the cost of producing substitutes.

Suppliers' quality assurance schemes are being used increasingly, particularly where extensive sub-contracting work is carried out, for example in the motor industries. One such scheme is BS EN ISO 9000 (formerly BS 5750) certification. This is a nationally promoted standard, only awarded after audit and inspection of a company's operations. A company that gains registration has a certificate testifying that it is operating to a structure of written policies and procedures which are designed to ensure that it can consistently deliver a product or service to meet customer requirements. The British Standards Institution is the largest of the certification bodies.

Some companies follow Japanese practice and use supervisors, work people or quality circles to control suppliers' quality. These representatives or the SQA officer may enter the supplier's plant, to verify that production is to the correct specification, working tolerances, material and labour standards. For example, the Ministry of Defence would reserve the right to ensure that defence contractors produce to specification, since defective work could mean the failure of a multi-million pound aircraft, loss of trained pilots and possibly ground crew as well as damage to civilian life and property. Likewise, a weapons system failure could have disastrous consequences.

One great advantage of SQA is that it may render possible reduction of the in-house quality control headcount, since there will be no need to check incoming materials or sub-assemblies or components. Statistical quality control through sampling techniques is commonly used to reduce costs and production interruptions.

Activity 2 (10 mins)

Does your organisation have BS EN ISO 9000 certification? Do its competitors? Would it be worthwhile for your organisation to gain certification? If not, why not?

3.3 Quality assurance of goods inwards

The quality of output depends on the quality of input materials, and so quality control should include procedures for acceptance and inspection of goods inwards and measurement of rejects. Each supplier can be given a 'rating' for the quality of the goods they tend to supply, and preference with purchase orders can be given to well-rated suppliers. This method is referred to as 'vendor rating'.

Where a quality assurance scheme is in place the supplier guarantees the quality of goods supplied and allows the customers' inspectors access while the items are being manufactured. The onus is on the supplier to carry out the necessary quality checks, or face cancellation of the contract.

3.4 Inspection of output

This will take place at various key stages in the production process and will provide a continual check that the production process is under control. The aim of inspection is *not* really to sort out the bad products from the good ones after the work has been done. The aim is to satisfy management that quality control in production is being maintained.

The inspection of samples rather than 100% testing of all items will keep inspection costs down, and smaller samples will be less costly to inspect than larger samples. The greater the confidence in the reliability of production methods and process control, the smaller the samples will be.

3.5 Statistical Process Control (SPC)

Statistical process control (SPC) is a method of monitoring processes and process variation. The purpose is to identify causes for process variations and resolve them. Process variables may include rework, scrap, inconsistent raw materials, and downtime on equipment. It is used to monitor the consistency of processes used to manufacture a product as designed. No matter how good or bad the design, SPC can ensure that the product is being manufactured as designed and intended. Thus, SPC will not improve a poorly designed product's reliability, but can be used to maintain the consistency of how the product is made and, therefore, of the manufactured product itself and its as-designed reliability.

Statistical quality control refers to using statistical techniques for measuring and improving the *quality* of processes and includes SPC in addition to other techniques, such as sampling plans, experimental design, variation reduction, process capability analysis, and process improvement plans. A primary tool used for SPC is the control chart, a graphical representation of certain descriptive statistics for specific quantitative measurements of the manufacturing process.

A typical control chart is shown below. The horizontal axis on the graph is time, the vertical axis is the physical dimension of the product in appropriate units. Above and below the level of the expected dimension of the product are the control limits. The graph shows inner warning limits and outer action limits although in many cases only one limit is used. The limits are set such a distance from the expected dimension that a value outside the limits is very unlikely to have occurred by chance and consequently the size of the deviation from the expected dimension indicates that something may have gone wrong with the manufacturing process. Normally, the values plotted on the chart would be the mean of a small sample taken at regular points in time.

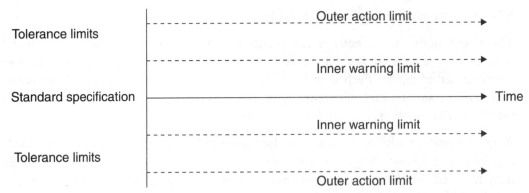

Figure 10.3 Quality control chart

Representational samples of an output manufacturing process may be taken daily or even every hour, and faults in the manufacturing process which are revealed may be fairly simple to correct by adjusting the appropriate machinery. If output exceeds the control limits consistently, more urgent management action would be called for, because this would indicate a systematic fault such as those below.

- Inefficiency in production, by labour or the machines
- Inadequacy in production methods

- Inadequate quality of raw materials and components
- Excessively tight tolerances in the first place

The ultimate goal of SPC is the reduction of variation.

4 TOTAL QUALITY MANAGEMENT (TQM)

Definition

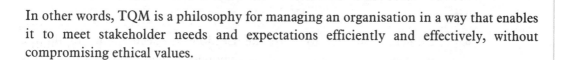
ISO 8402:1994 defines **total quality management** (TQM) as a management approach of an organisation centred on quality, based on the participation of all its members and aiming at long-term success. This is achieved through customer satisfaction and benefits to all members of the organisation and to society.

In other words, TQM is a philosophy for managing an organisation in a way that enables it to meet stakeholder needs and expectations efficiently and effectively, without compromising ethical values.

4.1 TQM philosophy

The basic principles for the Total Quality Management (TQM) philosophy of doing business are to satisfy the customer, satisfy the supplier, and continuously improve the business processes.

TQM is a management philosophy that seeks to integrate all organisational functions (marketing, finance, design, engineering, production, customer service etc) to focus on meeting customer needs and organisational objectives. It views organisations as a collection of processes.

It maintains that organisations must strive to continuously improve these processes by incorporating the knowledge and experiences of workers. The simple objective of TQM is to 'Do the right things, right the first time, every time.' Every mistake, delay and misunderstanding, directly costs the organisation money through wasted time and effort, including time taken in pacifying customers. The lost potential for future sales because of poor customer service must also be taken into account.

(a) The first and major TQM principle is to **satisfy the customer** – the person who pays for the product or service. Customers want to get their money's worth from a product or service they purchase. A company that seeks to satisfy the customer by providing them with value for what they buy and with the quality they expect will get more repeat business, referral business, and reduced complaints and service expenses. Some top companies not only provide quality products, but they also give extra service to make their customers feel important and valued.

Often in a company, there is a chain of customers, -each improving a product and passing it along until it is finally sold to the external customer. Each worker must not only seek to satisfy the immediate internal customer, but he or she must look up the chain to try to satisfy the ultimate customer.

(b) A second TQM principle is to **satisfy the supplier**, which is the person or organisation from whom you are purchasing goods or services. A company must look to satisfy their external suppliers by providing them with clear instructions and requirements and then paying them fairly and on time. It is only in the company's best interest that its suppliers provide it with quality goods or services, if the company hopes to provide quality goods or services to its external customers.

A manager must try to keep his or her workers happy and productive by providing good task instructions, the tools they need to do their job and good working conditions. The manager must also reward the workers with praise and good pay. The reason to do this is to get more productivity out of the workers, as well as to retain the good workers.

One area of satisfying the internal suppler is by empowering the workers. This means to allow them to make decisions on things that they can control. This not only takes the burden off the manager, but it also motivates these internal suppliers to do better work. Empowerment therefore has two key aspects.

- Allowing workers to have the freedom to decide how to do the necessary work, using the skills they possess and acquiring new skills as necessary to be an effective team member.

- Making workers responsible for achieving production targets and for quality control.

(c) The third principle of TQM is **continuous improvement**. Management can never be satisfied with the method used, because there can always be improvements. The aim should be to 'get it more right next time'. Certainly, the competition is improving, so it is very necessary to strive to keep ahead of the game. Some companies have tried to improve by making employees work harder. This may be counter-productive, especially if the process itself is flawed. For example, trying to increase worker output on a defective machine may result in more defective parts. Examining the source of problems and delays and then improving them is what is needed. Often the process has bottlenecks that are the real cause of the problem. These must be removed.

Workers are often a source of continuous improvements. They can provide suggestions on how to improve a process and eliminate waste or unnecessary work.

4.2 Tools and techniques

There are a number of approaches to take towards adopting the TQM philosophy. The teachings of Deming, Juran, Taguchi, Ishikawa, Imai, Oakland etc can all help an organisation realign itself and embrace the TQM philosophy. However, there is no single methodology, only a collection of tools and techniques. Examples of tools include:

- flowcharting
- statistical process control (SPC)
- Pareto analysis
- cause and effect diagrams
- employee and customer surveys

Examples of techniques include:

- benchmarking
- cost of quality
- quality function deployment
- failure mode effects analysis
- design of experiments

Measurements – after using the tools and techniques an organisation needs to establish the degree of improvement. Any number of techniques can be used for this including self-assessment, audits and SPC.

TQM initiatives have been prone to failure because of common mistakes. These include:

- allowing external forces and events to drive a TQM initiative

- an overwhelming desire for quality awards and certificates

- organising and perceiving TQM activities as separate from day-to-day work responsibilities

- treating TQM as an add-on with little attention given to the required changes in organisation and culture

- senior management underestimating the necessary commitment to TQM

4.3 Design for quality

A TQM environment aims to get it right first time, and this means that **quality, not faults, must be designed into the organisation's products, services and operations from the outset**.

Quality control happens at various stages in the process of designing a product or service.

(a) At the **product design stage**, quality control means trying to design a product or service so that its specifications provide a suitable balance between price and quality (of sales and delivery, as well as manufacture), which will make the product or service competitive.

(b) **Production engineering** is the **process of designing the methods for making a product** (or service) **to the design specification**. It sets out to make production methods as efficient as possible, and to avoid the manufacture of sub-standard items.

(c) **Information systems** should be designed to get the required information to the right person at the right time; **distribution systems** should be designed to get the right item to the right person at the right time; and so on.

As well as physical products, quality also applies to service businesses such as banks and restaurants. Quality issues arise in a number of areas.

- Customer expectations
- The process by which the service is delivered
- The attitudes and demeanour of the people giving the service
- The environment of the service encounter

4.4 Quality circles

A quality circle is a group of employees who meet regularly to discuss problems of quality and quality control in their area of work, and perhaps to suggest ways of improving quality. The main aim is to be able to offer management:

(a) ideas connected with improvement and recommendation;
(b) possible solutions and suggestions;
(c) organising the implementation of the ideas and solutions

Quality Circles have emerged as a mechanism to develop and utilise the tremendous potential of people for improvement in product quality and productivity. The development of quality circles allows the process of decision making to start at shop floor level, with the ordinary worker encouraged to comment and make suggestions, as well as being allowed to put them into practice. Circle members experience the responsibility for ensuring quality, and have the power to exercise verbal complaint. General productivity is considered as well as reduced frustration and grievances and reduced labour turnover. Quality circles may be applied at any level of organisational activity, being used to cover all aspects and could conceivably involve all employees.

The benefits arising from the use of quality circles are substantial:

- improved quality leading to greater customer satisfaction;

- greater motivation of employees;

- improved productivity;

- shop floor understand and share management/customers problems;

- a spirit of seeking improvements is generated;

- employees become more aware of opportunities for improvement because of training, in areas outside quality circles.

4.5 Continuous improvement

Quality management is not a one-off process, but is the continual examination and improvement of existing processes. The idea of continuous improvement might appear to go against the law of diminishing returns, in that it might be arguable that there is a limit beyond which there is no point in pursuing any further improvements.

Advocates of continuous improvement, however, believe that this 'law' does not always apply. Remember, that continuous improvement does not only apply to the finished product, but also to the processes which give rise to it.

- It is not easy to determine where diminishing returns set in.

- A philosophy of continuous improvement ensures that management are not *complacent*, which can be a cultural disaster.

- Customer needs change, so a philosophy of continuous improvement enables these changes to be taken into account in the normal course of events.

- New technologies or materials might be developed, enabling cost savings or design improvements.

- Rarely do businesses know every possible fact about the production process. Continuous improvement encourages experimentation and a scientific approach to production.

- It is a way of tapping employees' knowledge.

- Reducing *variability* is a key issue for quality

- Improvement on a continual, step-by-step basis is more prudent in some cases than changing everything at once.

Holmes proposes an eight-stage model for improving quality.

Step 1. **Find out the problems** (eg from customer and employees).

Step 2. **Select action targets** from the number of improvement projects identified in Step 1, on the basis of cost, safety, importance and feasibility with current resources.

Step 3. **Collect data** about the problem.

Step 4. **Analyse data** by a variety of techniques to assess common factors behind the data, to tease out any hidden messages the data might contain.

Step 5. **Identify possible causes** (eg using brainstorming sessions). No ideas are ruled out of order.

Step 6. **Plan improvement action**. Significant help might be required.

Step 7. **Monitor the effects of the improvement**.

Step 8. **Communicate the result**.

Reducing variability often requires improving the process itself, rather than changing the machines or adjusting them.

Activity 3 **(15 mins)**

You have just overheard the following conversation. The Board of a company are in a meeting and they are having a 'full and frank exchange of views' (ie a blazing row).

Chairman : Ladies and gentlemen, *please....*

Marketing director: No, he's said quite enough. Customers are our department, and all this TQM nonsense is just another, yes *another* example of those jargon-spouting boffins and bodgers in production trying to encroach on my turf! I *do* need resources. I don't need white-coated robots criticising the angles at which I fix the paper clips on to my reports!

Chairman: Ladies and gentlemen, *please....*

Production director: No, she's said quite enough. Marketing people couldn't give one hoot, let alone two, about quality and we all know it's quality that sells the goods. Remember, when we had to abandon our solar powered torch? State of the art, state of *the art* that was, and did they try and sell it? Did they?

Chairman: Ladies and gentlemen, *please....*

Finance director: No, they've both said quite enough. If all we get out of TQM is pointless rows like this, I might as well go back and count some more beans. At least it's *meaningful and* relaxing.

Chairman: Ladies and gentlemen! No, you've all said *quite* enough. Not one of you has grasped the point. I'd better get another management consultant in with a better flipchart.

What insights do each of the above characters have into TQM?

4.6 The potential benefits of quality processes

Glyn Thomas in *Accounting Technician* provides a useful summary of the benefits of TQM.

> 'It makes quality the central concern of the business. Too often, quality is either confused with addressing customer complaints which inevitably leads to it being viewed negatively, or is viewed as a direct measure of the product or service itself. Instead, all activities that are involved should be considered. Quality should be inherent in every facet of the business and not just a 'bolt-on extra'.

A key factor of [TQM] is that it can apply to all or parts of your business, so there may be scope for partially introducing it and then expanding it at a later date. Applied to the whole business however, it will allow a holistic approach to quality throughout the whole company and have an effect from shop floor through to ordering, sales and management.

It reduces wastage and mistakes, and therefore leads to contracts being completed on time without unnecessary remedial work. In addition, due to built-in fault-logging procedures, it is unlikely that problems will be duplicated in the future.

Activity 4   **(10 mins)**

(a) What are the potential benefits of training for quality?

(b) What are the potential benefits of quality control?

5   MANAGING AND MONITORING QUALITY

5.1   Organisational implications

Introducing TQM involves a significant shake up.

- TQM is associated with giving employees a say in the process (eg in the *quality survey*) and in getting them to suggest improvements.

- TQM implies a greater discipline to the process of production and the establishment of better linkages between the business functions.

- TQM involves new relationships with suppliers, which requires them to improve their output quality so that less effort is spent rectifying poor input. Long-term relationships with a small number of suppliers might be preferable to choosing material and sub-components on price.

- It requires both work standardisation and employee commitment.

5.2 Quality management

Quality management suggests a concern that the organisation's products or services meet their planned level of quality and perform to specifications. Management has a duty to ensure that all tasks are completed consistently to a standard that meets the needs of the business. To achieve this they need to:

(a) set clear standards

(b) plan how to meet those standards

(c) monitor the quality achieved

(d) take action to improve quality where necessary.

Setting standards – to manage quality everyone in the organisation needs to have a clear and shared understanding of the standards required. These standards will be set after taking account of:

(a) the quality expected by the customers

(b) the costs and benefits of delivering different degrees of quality

(c) the impact of different degrees of quality on:

    (i) the customers and their needs

    (ii) contribution to departmental objectives

    (iii) employee attitude and motivation

Having decided on the standards these must be communicated to everyone concerned to ensure that the right standards are achieved. Documentation of the standards must be clear, specific, measurable and comprehensive.

Meeting the standards – having decided on appropriate quality standards management should then:

(a) agree and document procedures and methods to meet the standards

(b) agree and document controls to ensure that the standards will be met

(c) agree and document responsibilities via job descriptions and terms of reference

(d) prepare and implement training plans for employees to ensure they are familiar with the standards, procedures, controls and their responsibilities

Monitoring the quality – after the process to achieve quality has been established, an information system to monitor the quality should be set up, which can be used constructively to improve quality and work on problem areas.

Monitoring customer reaction – some sub-standard items will inevitably be produced. Checks during production will identify some bad output, but other items will reach the customer who is the ultimate judge of quality. Complaints ought to be monitored in the form of letters of complaint, returned goods, penalty discounts, claims under guarantee, or requests for visits by service engineers. Some companies actually survey customers on a regular basis.

Employees within the organisation have a huge influence on the quality of their work and to gain their commitment and support the management should:

BPP
PROFESSIONAL EDUCATION

(a) publish the quality being achieved

(b) meet regularly with the staff involved to discuss the quality being achieved as well as the vulnerabilities and priorities as they see them and also agree specific issues and action points for them to work on to improve quality

(c) encourage ideas from the staff about improvements and consider introducing short-term suggestion schemes

Take action – it takes commitment to quality and excellence. Tom Peters' advice to managers is: 'Starting this afternoon, don't walk past a shoddy product or service without comment and action – ever again!'

In his seminars on quality he poses a situation where a brochure is going out to customers. The deadline is missed; five thousand have been printed, inserted into envelopes, addressed and sealed. They are packed and ready to take to the post office. The unit you are in charge of has a not-too-healthy cash flow. You then discover a single typo on page two, in the small print. Should you walk past it or act?

He argues that you should act and throw it out. If you knowingly ignore a tiny act of poor service or quality, you have destroyed your credibility and any possibility of moral leadership on this issue.

Activity 5   **(10 mins)**

Read the following extract from an article in the *Financial Times* in April 1993, and then explain how the bank could monitor the impact of the initiative.

'If you telephone a branch of Lloyds Bank and it rings five times before there is a reply; if the person who answers does not introduce him or herself by name during the conversation; if you are standing in a queue with more people in it than the number of tills, then something is wrong.'

'If any of these things happen then the branch is breaching standards of customer service set by the bank since last July ... the "service challenge" was launched in the bank's 1,888 branches last summer after being tested in 55 branches in 1990 ...'

'Lloyds already has evidence of the impact. Customers were more satisfied with pilot branches in 1991 than with others.'

5.3 Difficulties

Managers find some aspects of TQM particularly hard to accept.

- Social and status barriers are removed with the removal of office partitions.

- Administrative functions must now be seen as supporting the shop floor.

- The shop floor is the most important area.

- Managers are judged by their contribution to team spirit, not 'the virility of their decisions'.

- Meetings are used to gather information, not to take decisions.

- New personal skills are needed (eg the ability to listen and communicate).

- A manager's role is in supporting and training, not disciplining and restricting.

Holmes believes that managers most suited for a TQM culture will 'understand how people motivate themselves and direct this motivation towards good team results. They are concerned with achieving the goals of the team, supporting the individual members of the team, and keeping the team together'. They will 'ensure time is spent setting objectives, planning, briefing, controlling, evaluating. These activities will be conducted in a participatory or controllable way'.

5.4 Creating a culture of improvement

TQM is more than just a philosophy. It is the culture of an organisation committed to total customer satisfaction through continuous improvement and in which resources, material, equipment and quality management systems are cost effectively implemented and fully utilised.

TQM is impossible to achieve when the pervasive organisational culture is hostile to it. When the basic mechanisms of an organisational culture such as language, artefacts and symbols, behavioural patterns, basic underlying assumptions and subcultures do not operate in total accord then the whole social organisation may be in trouble. In the final analysis, a receptive organisational culture is a prerequisite of total quality management.

Guiding the change process requires an understanding of the present organisational cultures, attitudes, structures and systems.

Employees often have a poor attitude towards quality, as a system imposed 'from outside' by non-operational staff and as an implication of lack of trust in workers to maintain quality standards or to apply a control system with objectivity themselves.

Attitudes to quality control and the management of it have, however, been undergoing changes.

- As the pace of change in the environment has increased so attention to quality and a commitment to quality standards has become a vital factor for organisational adaptation and survival.

- It is being recognised that workers can be motivated by a positive approach to quality: producing quality work is a tangible and worthwhile objective. Where responsibility for quality checking has been given to the worker himself (encouraging self-supervision), job satisfaction may be increased: it is a kind of job enrichment, and also a sign of trust and respect, because imposed controls have been removed.

- Non-aversive ways of implementing quality control have been devised. Cultural orientation (the deep 'belief' in quality, filtered down to all operatives) can be enlisted. Inter-group competition to meet and beat quality standards, for example, might be encouraged.

Problems can therefore be overcome by changing people's attitudes rather than teaching them new tricks. The key issue is to instil understanding of, and commitment to, working practices that lead to quality.

5.5 Participation

Participation is important in TQM, especially in the process of continuous improvement, where workforce views are valued. The management task is to encourage everybody to contribute. When TQM is successful employees at every level participate in decisions affecting their work. Employee involvement practices include:

- Suggestion system – programme that elicits individual employee suggestions on improving work or the work environment.

- Survey feedback – attitude survey data are used to encourage, structure, and measure the effectiveness of employee participation.

- Quality circle – employees that meet voluntarily to identify and suggest work-related improvements.

- Quality of Work-Life Committee – usually focuses on issues to improve organisational performance and employee work-life

- Job redesign – to increase employee performance for example, job enlargement to increase use of employee skills, broaden the variety of work performed and provide the individual with greater autonomy.

- Self-Managing Team – group of employees given responsibility for a product or service and empowered to make decisions about assignment tasks and work methods.

However, the barriers to participation are numerous.

- An autocratic chief executive, who believes he or she is the sole key to the process.

- Individualism, in which people 'possess' ideas in order to take credit for them rather than share them for mutual benefit.

- Ideas of managers as leaders and directors rather than facilitators and supporters.

- Middle managers who feel their authority is threatened.

5.6 W. Edwards Deming

Based on his work with Japanese managers and others, Deming outlined 14 steps that managers in any type of organisation can take to implement a total quality management programme. The key points include:

- **Create constancy of purpose** – this requires innovation, investment in research and education, continuous improvement of product and service, maintenance of equipment, furniture and fixtures, and new aids to production.

- **Cease mass production** – inspect products and services only enough to be able to identify ways to improve the process.

- **Drive out fear** and build employee trust. Managers need to create an environment where workers can express concerns with confidence.

- **Break down departmental barriers** (create win-win situations). Fostering interrelationships among departments encourages higher quality decision-making.

- **Seek long-term supplier relationships** – the lowest priced goods are not always the highest quality; choose a supplier based on its record of improvement and then make a long-term commitment to it.

- **Eliminate numerical goals**; abolish annual rating or merit systems.

- **Eliminate slogans** – they provide no value in terms of improving quality.

Deming gave a new perspective to the benefits of improving quality. This he gave in the form of a chain reaction, which is illustrated below:

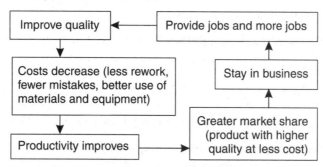

Figure 10.4 The Deming chain reaction

5.7 Barriers to quality and excellence

It has been shown that it is much easier to achieve quality and excellence in a new business, where the principles are built in from the start. It is much harder to develop and improve quality and excellence in an existing company because it may be necessary to overcome a series of barriers. These barriers may be human, technical or financial.

(a) Human barriers exist because people are naturally resistant to change. Some kind of revolutionary process is usually necessary to provide the momentum and incentive for change. This transformation of attitudes needs total commitment from the top and requires one or more champions as well as involvement at all levels.

(b) Technical barriers concern the knowledge and skills that are required to plan, implement and control the best performance practices.

(c) The finance required to sustain excellence and improve quality may be yet another barrier for the company to surmount.

5.8 Quality audits, assessments and reviews

Quality assessment is a process of identifying business practices, attitudes and activities that are either inhibiting or enhancing the achievement of quality improvement. The purpose of assessment is to:

- supply proof that quality improvement measures are necessary;
- provide a base for future measurement;
- build support for quality measures; and
- convince senior management that the issue is important.

The quality control function looks at the process as a continuous operation, a series of trends and rejection rates. Reports from the quality control department to management include:

(a) analysis of defects by cause;
(b) comparisons between processes and departments;
(c) comparison of defect levels with previous levels and standard levels;
(d) longer term trends in quality;
(e) reports on customers' complaints;
(f) developments in quality control practice; and
(g) special reports.

Apart from receiving reports, management may also commission a quality control audit to find answers to the following questions:

(a) What is the actual level of rejects?

(b) Are the standards fairly set?

(c) Are the standards achieved at the expense of excessive costs?

(d) What is the number of customer complaints?

(e) Has the quality control system been modified in accordance with changes in processing policies, materials and products?

(f) What are the costs of quality control?

(g) What is done to improve performance by eliminating causes of poor performance?

(h) Should a personnel audit on efficiency and knowledge be carried out?

Assessments and reviews of the systems and procedures are an ongoing activity in excellent companies. The responsibility for quality control cannot be isolated as we have seen and can only be effective when it is the result of joint effort. The advantages lie in the fact that quality control points out why faulty work is being produced and the extent of it. Action taken as a result can reduce scrap and the amount of necessary re-work. It shows where a design modification could raise efficiency in manufacture. It minimises the chances of poor materials being processed.

The requirements of the customers must be continually reviewed and the sales department and market research can advise on this. They will be aware of competitors' prices and qualities and a decision must be taken whether or not to increase quality. To increase quality may mean increasing costs and establishing the point at which the customer will decide that the quality is more than he or she can afford.

6 COSTS OF QUALITY

When we talk about quality-related costs you should remember that a concern for **good quality saves money**; it is **poor quality that costs money**.

Definitions

Prevention costs are the costs of any action taken to investigate, prevent or reduce defects and failures.

Appraisal costs are the costs of assessing the quality achieved.

Internal failure costs are the costs arising within the organisation of failing to achieve the required level of quality.

External failure costs are the costs arising outside the organisation of failing to achieve the required level of quality (after transfer of ownership to the customer).

EXAMPLE

Quality-related cost	Example
Prevention costs	Quality engineering
	Design/development of quality control/inspection equipment
	Maintenance of quality control/inspection equipment
	Administration of quality control
	Training in quality control
Appraisal costs	Acceptance testing
	Inspection of goods inwards
	Inspection costs of in-house processing
	Performance testing
Internal failure costs	Failure analysis
	Re-inspection costs
	Losses from failure of purchased items
	Losses due to lower selling prices for sub-quality goods
	Costs of reviewing product specifications after failures
External failure costs	Administration of customer complaints section
	Costs of customer service section
	Product liability costs
	Cost of repairing products returned from customers
	Cost of replacing items due to sub-standard products/marketing errors

EXAMPLE: COST OF POOR QUALITY

A manufacturer's inspection procedures indicate that one faulty item out of every 1,000 good items produced is sent to a customer. The management regards this as acceptable, as a replacement will be supplied free of charge. Unit sales are 10,000,000 per year, and each unit costs £20 to manufacture and makes a profit of £5. It is probable that every customer who buys a faulty product will return it, and will thenceforth buy a similar product from another company. The average customer buys two units a year. Marketing costs per new customer are £10 per year.

(a) What is your best estimate of the net cost of this policy for a year?

(b) What name(s) would you give to quality-related costs of this type?

(c) Could the situation be improved by incurring other types of quality-related cost?

ANSWER

(a) Presumed number of bad units delivered a year = 10,000,000/1,000 = 10,000

	£
Cost of defects 10,000 × £20	200,000
Cost of free replacement 10,000 × £20	200,000
Manufacturing cost	400,000
Marketing costs for replacement customers £10 × 10,000	100,000
Gross cost of poor quality	500,000
Less income from original sale	250,000
Net cost of poor quality	250,000

Although the cost of the original defective item is recovered, the company **does not get it right first time**. The company has still suffered the cost of the replacement and the cost of replacing the customer by marketing to new customers.

(b) The cost of replacements is an external failure cost; the cost of defects and the new marketing costs are internal failure costs.

(c) It appears that the manufacturer already incurs *appraisal* costs, since there are inspection procedures for goods about to be despatched. The reason(s) for the fault should be established (a further *internal failure* cost) and the extent of the problem should be more precisely ascertained (further *appraisal* costs), since it is not certain that all dissatisfied customers return their goods, though it is highly likely that their business is lost. Once this has been done it will be possible to decide whether, by spending more on *prevention*, the overall cost of poor quality can be reduced.

6.1 Traditional accounting systems and the cost of quality

Traditionally, the **costs of scrapped units, wasted materials and reworking** have been **subsumed within the costs of production** by assigning the costs of an expected level of loss (a normal loss) to the costs of good production, while **accounting for other costs of poor quality within production or marketing overheads**. So such costs are not only **considered as inevitable** but are not highlighted for management attention.

Traditional accounting reports **tend also to ignore the hidden but real costs of excessive stock levels** (held to enable faulty material to be replaced without hindering production) **and the facilities necessary for storing that stock**. The introduction of a system of **just-in-time** purchasing and manufacturing should eradicate such costs, however. A just-in-time production system is driven by demand from customers for finished products so that components on a production line are only produced when needed for the next stage of production, thereby eradicating stocks of work in progress and finished goods. In a just-in-time purchasing system, materials are not delivered until they are needed in production, thereby eradicating stock of raw materials.

To **implement a TQM programme, costs of quality** must be **highlighted separately** within accounting reports so that *all* employees are aware of the cost of poor quality.

6.2 Explicit and implicit costs of quality

Explicit costs of quality are those that are recorded in accounting records, to be separately highlighted with the implementation of a TQM programme.

Implicit costs of quality are not recorded in accounting records. They tend to be of two forms.

- **Opportunity costs** such as the loss of future sales to a customer dissatisfied with faulty goods

- **Costs which tend to be subsumed** within other account headings such as costs which result from the disruptions caused by stockouts due to faulty purchases

Chapter roundup

- Quality control happens at various stages in the process of designing a product or service.

- Quality control is aimed at preventing the manufacture of defective items or the provision of defective services. Inspection is a technique for identifying when defective items are being produced at an unacceptable level.

- The costs associated with a concern for quality are prevention costs, appraisal costs, internal failure costs and external failure costs.

- Explicit costs of quality are those that are recorded in accounting records, to be separately highlighted. Implicit costs of quality are not recorded in accounting records.

- Quality assurance procedures should not be confined to the production process but must also cover the work of sales, distribution and administration departments, the efforts of external suppliers and the reaction of external customers.

- Total quality management (TQM) is the process of applying a zero defect philosophy to the management of all resources and relationships within an organisation as a means of developing and sustaining a culture of continuous improvement which focuses on meeting customer expectations.

Quick quiz

1   What are the two elements in Juran's definition of quality as 'fitness for use'?

2   How does the quality hierarchy progress?

3   What are the three main points at which inspection is usually carried out?

4   What is statistical process control?

5   What is the simple objective of TQM?

6   What are the four aspects of the process of managing quality?

7   What are internal failure costs?

8   Provide two examples of external failure costs.

Answers to quick quiz

1   The two elements are:

  - quality of design
  - quality of conformance (See para 1.2)

2   The quality hierarchy progresses from inspection, through quality control, quality assurance to total quality management (1.5)

3   - Receiving inspection for raw materials and purchased components
  - Floor or process inspection for WIP
  - Final inspection or testing for finished goods (See para 2.1)

4   Statistical process control (SPC) is a method of monitoring processes and process variation. The purpose is to identify causes for process variations and resolve them. (3.5)

5   The simple objective of TQM is to 'Do the right things, right the first time, every time.' (4.1)

6   The costs arising within the organisation of failure to achieve the quality specified. (6)

7   Administration of customer complaints section

    Costs of customer service section

    Product liability costs

    Cost of repairing products returned from customers

8   Cost of providing replacement items due to sub-standard product or marketing errors. (6)

Answers to activities

1   The *design quality* is poor, in that it does not meet customer requirements in an *appropriate* way. The umbrella is, however, perfectly made, so its *conformance quality* is high.

2   This quality standard is aimed at manufacturing companies. It is useful to some companies because it demonstrates they are in control of their business, and have proved it to a certification body. ISO 9000 registration is a good way of measuring progress and monitoring maintenance of the standard. It reduces

the need for customer supplier demonstration of quality assurance procedures by its introduction and ensures that the organisation's product is compatible with EC and USA quality procedures.

There are many different reasons for implementing the standard.

(i)   Pressure from large customers
(ii) To maintain contracts with existing customers
(iii) To use the constraints of the standard to prevent scrap
(iv) To reduce auditing of the quality system by customers
(v) To make reference to the standard on company letterhead paper
(vi) To get the kitemark symbol on the company's product
(vii) To enforce discipline on employees

3   The chairman has got the gist. All of them miss the point as to the nature of TQM. The marketing director has a point in that TQM *does* imply a blurring of functional boundaries, but the marketing director *ought* to be pleased that, if TQM is implemented, the marketing concept will be brought into product design. The production director still has not grasped the concept. His idea of quality is 'technical excellence' not fitness for use. The finance director ought to care, as TQM has meaningful cost implications. The row is not pointless: at least the issue is being discussed, which is a beginning.

4   (a)   The potential benefits of training for quality include improved quality of output, improved productivity and greater job satisfaction and commitment on the part of employees.

        (b)   The benefits of quality control come from savings in quality-related costs, from improvements in customer relations and hopefully (because of the quality of the final product) increased sales revenue due to increased sales demand.

5   A wide variety of answers is possible. The article goes on to explain how the bank has monitored the initiative.

        (a)   It has devised a 100 point scale showing average satisfaction with branch service.

        (b)   It conducts a 'first impressions' survey of all new customers.

        (c)   There is also a general survey carried out every six months which seeks the views of a weighted sample of 350 customers per branch.

        (d)   A survey company telephones each branch anonymously twice a month to test how staff respond to enquiries about products.

        (e)   A quarter of each branch's staff answer a monthly questionnaire about the bank's products to test their knowledge.

        (f)   Groups of employees working in teams in branches are allowed to set their own additional standards. This is to encourage participation.

        (g)   Branches that underperform are more closely watched by 24 managers who monitor the initiative.

Chapter 11 :

HEALTH AND SAFETY IN THE WORKPLACE

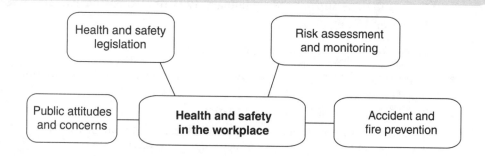

Introduction

Health and safety at work are important for several reasons.

(a) Employees should be protected from pain and suffering. (Obvious – we hope!)

(b) An employer has legal obligations for the health and safety of employees.

(c) Accidents and illness cost the employer money.

(d) The company's image in the market-place (to which it sells goods and services, and from which it recruits labour and buys in other resources) will suffer if its health and safety record is bad.

This chapter looks at the law and best practice relating to health and safety at work.

Your objectives

After completing this chapter you should be able to:

(a) Carry out risk assessments as required by legislation, regulation and organisational requirements and ensure appropriate action is taken resulting from these

(b) Identify health and safety regulations and legislation applicable in specific work situations and ensure these are correctly and effectively applied

(c) Systematically review organisational health and safety policies and procedures in order to ensure they are effective and that they comply with the appropriate legislation and regulations

(d) Ensure practical application of health and safety policies and procedures in the workplace

1 HEALTH AND SAFETY LEGISLATION

In 1972, a Royal Commission on Safety and Health at Work reported that unnecessarily large numbers of days were being lost each year through industrial accidents, injuries and diseases, because of the 'attitudes, capabilities and performance of people and the efficiency of the organisational systems within which they work'. Since then, major legislation has been brought into effect in the UK, most notably:

(a) Health and Safety at Work Act 1974 ;

(b) the regulations introduced in January 1993 implementing EU directives on Health and Safety.

Some of the most important regulations are as follows.

- Reporting of Injuries, Diseases and Dangerous Occurrences Regulations 1995
- The Health and Safety (First Aid) Regulations 1981
- The Noise at Work Regulations 1989
- The Control of Substances Hazardous to Health Regulations 1994
- The Manual Handling Operations Regulations 1992
- The Workplace (Health, Safety and Welfare) Regulations 1992
- The Provision and Use of Work Equipment Regulations 1992
- The Health and Safety (Display Screen Equipment) Regulations 1992
- The Management of Health and Safety at Work Regulations 1992
- The Personal Protective Equipment at Work Regulations 1992

We will not be able to cover their provisions in detail here. Just be aware that the framework for personnel policy in the area of health and safety is extensive and detailed!

We will begin by looking at the major legal landmarks in the area of health and safety at work. This legislation is refreshingly practical, with lots of measures to be taken and procedures to be put in place. Like other legal provisions we have discussed, the 'law is a floor': remember that these are minimum standards, not a description of best practice.

1.1 The Health and Safety at Work Act 1974

In the UK, the Health and Safety at Work Act 1974 provides for the introduction of a system of approved codes of practice, prepared in consultation with industry. Thus an employee, whatever his/her employment, should find that his/her work is covered by an appropriate code of practice.

Employers also have **specific** duties under the 1974 Act.

(a) All systems (work practices) must be safe.

(b) The work environment must be safe and healthy (well-lit, warm, ventilated and hygienic).

(c) All plant and equipment must be kept up to the necessary standard (with guards on machines and so on).

In addition, information, instruction, training and supervision should be directed towards safe working practices. Employers must consult with **safety representatives** appointed by a recognised trade union, and appoint a **safety committee** to monitor safety policy, if asked to do so. Safety policy and measures should be clearly **communicated in writing** to all staff.

The **employee** also has a duty:

(a) to take reasonable care of himself/herself and others;

(b) to allow the employer to carry out his or her duties (including enforcing safety rules); and

(c) not to interfere intentionally or recklessly with any machinery or equipment.

FOR DISCUSSION

'A baby was put on a social services 'at risk' register", reported The Times in February 1992, 'after his father, a roofer, took him to work up ladders in a sling fixed to his back.' The story continues:

After a two-hour hearing it was decided to place the boy in his godparents' care while his father goes to work. Putting [the child] on a register will allow social workers to ensure the child remains grounded. [The roofer] said that his wife... a bank clerk... was happy with the outcome.

'But I intend to fight this decision in the European Court', he said 'I should be allowed to raise my son as I want to.'

Who do you think is responsible for a person's safety? Should people be allowed to take risks if they 'want to'? Or should measures be taken to protect them 'for their own good'?

1.2   The Management of Health and Safety at Work Regulations 1999

Under the Management of Health and Safety at Work Regulations 1999 employers now have the following additional general duties.

(a) They must carry out risk assessment, generally in writing, of all work hazards. Assessment should be continuous.

(b) They must introduce controls to reduce risks.

(c) They must assess the risks to anyone else affected by their work activities.

(d) They must share hazard and risk information with other employers, including those on adjoining premises, other site occupiers and all subcontractors coming onto the premises.

(e) They should revise safety policies in the light of the above, or initiate safety policies if none were in place previously.

(f) They must identify employees who are especially at risk.

(g) They must provide fresh and appropriate training in safety matters.

(h) They must provide information to employees (including temps) about health and safety.

(i) They must employ competent safety and health advisers.

BPP
PROFESSIONAL EDUCATION

Employees are also given an additional duty under the 1999 regulations to inform their employer of any situation which may be a danger. This does not reduce the employer's responsibilities in any way, however, because his/her risk assessment programme should have spotted the hazard in any case.

Under the **Health and Safety (Consultation with Employees) Regulations 1996**, employers must consult all of their employees on health and safety matters (such as the planning of health and safety training, any change in equipment or procedures which may substantially affect their health and safety at work or the health and safety consequences of introducing new technology). This involves giving information to employees *and* listening to and taking account of what they say before any health and safety decisions are taken.

1.3 The Workplace (Health, Safety and Welfare) Regulations 1992

In replacing many older pieces of law including parts of the Factories Act 1961 and the Offices, Shops and Railway Premises Act, 1963, the Workplace (Health, Safety and Welfare) Regulations 1992 cover many aspects of health, safety and welfare in the workplace. The Regulations set general requirements in:

(a) The working environment including: temperature; ventilation; lighting including emergency lighting; room dimensions; suitability of workstations and seating; and outdoor workstations (eg weather protection).

(b) Safety including: safe passage of pedestrians and vehicles, windows and skylights (safe opening, closing and cleaning); glazed doors and partitions (use of safe material and marking); doors, gates and escalators (safety devices); floors (their construction, obstruction slipping and tripping hazards); falls from heights and into dangerous substances; and falling objects.

(c) Facilities including: toilets, washing, eating and changing facilities; clothing storage, seating, rest areas (and arrangements in them for non-smokers); and rest facilities; cleanliness; and removal of waste materials.

(d) Housekeeping including maintenance of the workplace, its equipment and facilities; cleanliness and removal of waste materials.

Guidance on the implementation of the Regulations is given in an Approved Code of Practice 17.

To augment the above the Home office is preparing regulations with regard to fire precautions in the workplace. Assessments will have to be made of risks to persons in case of fire leading to the drawing up of emergency plans and establishing reasonable means of escape. Fire fighting and detection equipment will have to be provided and maintained and persons in the workplace instructed and trained.

1.4 Health and safety (Display Screen Equipment) Regulations 1992

The *Financial Times* reported in October 1991 that RSI accounted for more than half of all work-related injuries in the USA and that in Australia it had reached almost epidemic proportions. Disorders seem to arise from poor equipment, environment and posture, which lead to muscles being starved of oxygen, the build up of waste products in the body and the compression of nerves.

Definition

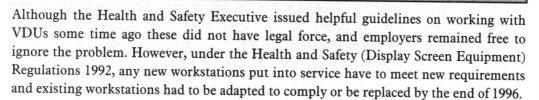

Repetitive strain injury (RSI) is the term for various complaints associated with sustained computer use, frequently including back ache, eye strain and stiffness or muscular problems of the neck, shoulders, arms or hands.

Although the Health and Safety Executive issued helpful guidelines on working with VDUs some time ago these did not have legal force, and employers remained free to ignore the problem. However, under the Health and Safety (Display Screen Equipment) Regulations 1992, any new workstations put into service have to meet new requirements and existing workstations had to be adapted to comply or be replaced by the end of 1996.

The main provisions of the directive are as follows. (You might like to check them off, if you are a regular VDU user yourself …)

(a) **VDUs:** these must not flicker, must be free from glare, and must swivel and tilt.

(b) **Keyboards:** must also tilt and be free from glare; the workspace in front of them must be 'sufficient' for the operators to rest their forearms.

(c) **Desks:** these must be free from glare; there must be enough space to allow 'flexible' arrangement of all equipment and documents. Measurements are not specified.

(d) **Chairs:** the seat must be adjustable in height, and the back in height and angle; footrests must be made available if required.

(e) **Lighting:** there must be 'appropriate contrast' between the screen and its background; windows must have some form of blinds.

(f) **Heat and humidity** levels must be 'adequate' on the one hand and not uncomfortable on the other.

(g) **Radiation,** for example from computer screens, must be reduced to negligible levels.

(h) **Breaks:** screen work must be 'periodically interrupted by breaks or changes in activity'.

(i) **Eyesight:** the employer must offer free eyesight testing at regular intervals and provide any special glasses that may be needed for screen work.

(j) **Consultation:** employees must be consulted about health and safety measures.

(k) **Training:** training in the proper use of equipment must be provided.

1.5 Working Time Regulations 1998

You should be aware that working hours are also a health and safety issue, under the Health and Safety (Young Persons) Regulations 1997. The **Working Time Regulations** have brought into effect the EU working time directive.

Young workers (between 15 and 18) must by and large have:

(a) a 12-hour rest break in every 24 hour period;

(b) a rest period of two days in every seven (consecutive if possible); and

(c) a minimum rest break of 30 minutes, where the working day exceeds $4^1/_2$ hours.

For adult workers:

(a) The Working Time Regulations 1998 limit working hours to 48 hours a week averaged over a 17-week period (or 26-week period, where continuity of work is necessary, as in health or essential services, 24-hour production or seasonal work). This *can* be extended to a year by collective workplace agreement – to preserve flexible 'annual hours' schemes, for example.

(b) If employees agree individually to work more than 48 hours a week, this should be done in writing, and a record of hours should be retained in case the Health and Safety Executive requires it.

(c) All employees are entitled to a daily rest of 11 consecutive hours in every 24, and a 24-hour rest in every seven days (averaged over 2 weeks) – with adjustments, by collective agreement where necessary.

(d) If the working day exceeds six hours, the employee is entitled to a minimum of 20 minutes' break.

(e) Staff are entitled to a health check before commencing night work, and regularly thereafter. Night work should be limited to an average of 8 in every 24 hours (over 17 weeks). If the work is hazardous, 8 hours is an absolute maximum. Protection is often reduced at night: under the regulations, health and safety protection and prevention services for night workers must be 'equivalent to those available to other workers'.

Activity 1   **(1 hour)**

Look at your own college (or workplace) from a health and safety perspective. Compare the provisions outlined in the regulations above with what you see within your college/workplace. Make a note of areas where health and safety provisions may fall short of requirements.

1.6 Further health and Safety Regulations

Other regulations that apply to the workplace include:

- **The Health and Safety (First Aid) Regulations 1981** require employers to provide adequate and appropriate equipment, facilities and personnel to enable first aid to be given to employees if they are injured or become ill at work. The minimum contents that should be found in a first aid box, for example, consist of dressings (plasters) and bandages of various sizes.

- **The Health and Safety (Young Persons) Regulations 1997** require employers to take into account the lack of experience, absence of awareness of existing or potential risks and/or the relative immaturity of young employees (aged under 18) when assessing the risks to their health and safety.

- **The Health and Safety (Safety Signs and Signals) Regulations 1996** describe the safety signs and signals that should be provided in the workplace, how they should be used and also require employers to instruct employees on their use and meaning.

2 RISK ASSESSMENT AND MONITORING

2.1 What is risk assessment?

Risk assessment is a legal requirement under Regulation 3 of the Management of Health and Safety at Work Regulations 1999. This regulation seeks to ensure that the hazards are identified and assessed by a 'competent person' and action taken to minimise the likelihood of them being realised. This person must have a sound knowledge of the working environment/activity involved, be able to recognise hazards and understand how to minimise the level of risk. Appropriate staff should be trained in how to carry out risk assessments.

Definitions

> **Hazard** – is something with the potential to cause harm. It could be a substance, a piece of machinery, an activity, the building itself or the method of work;
>
> **Risk** – is the chance, high or low, that somebody will be harmed by the hazard.

2.2 Assessing the risk

The Health and Safety Executive (HSE) has devised a logical sequence called '5 steps to Risk assessment'.

Step 1. Look for the hazards

Step 2. Decide who might be harmed and how

Step 3. Evaluate the risks and decide whether the existing precautions are adequate or more needs to be done

Step 4. Record your findings, inform affected employees

Step 5. Review your assessment on a regular basis or whenever something changes and revise if necessary

Step 1 – Look for the hazards

- Take a look at the workplace, for example awkward corners, a jutting drawer of the filing cabinet and how machinery is used. Consider the accident book; are there any accidents that could have been prevented? Be realistic and look for the obvious. In an office, is the filing stored on a high shelf? How do people place and retrieve the files? How heavy are they? How secure is the shelf?

- In a warehouse, do you know the maximum weights you can safely stack? Do employees observe them? How do they stack?

- Look at potentially dangerous substances. Do you have the safety data sheets, or manufacturer's instructions in the event of an accident?

- Look for hazards that could cause injury or affect several people. It is important to ask and involve all employees, as they know what happens on a day-to-day basis.

Step 2 – Decide who might be harmed and how

Consider how many people might be harmed and how severe the worst-case scenario would be. The more people in danger and the more serious the accident, the more important the controls become. Include specific groups of people such as young workers, trainees, or pregnant women; they may need extra consideration.

Step 3 – Evaluate the risks

Each hazard has the potential to cause harm. Once the hazards are identified a decision must be made on the likelihood of them being realised. This means:

- considering who may be harmed

- considering how likely it is that harm will arise

- considering how severe the injury may be

- considering whether or not existing procedures to avoid harm are sufficient and if not, recommending further action (control measures) to minimise the level of risk

There are many ways to evaluate the level of a risk. Risk level or rating is considered to be determined by two factors – first, the likelihood or frequency that a mishap will occur and, secondly, the severity of the consequence or outcome of the event. To aid the judgement of the level of the risk, the following simple procedure is appropriate.

The likelihood and severity of a hazard occurring are judged separately in terms of three categories.

Severity

This is the measure of the harm or damage as a result of a hazard affecting one or more persons. The three levels of severity can be shown as:

A	Death
	Major injury or disabling illness
	Major damage or major loss to property/equipment
B	Significant but non-disabling injury
	Damage to property/equipment
C	Minor injury
	Moderate damage to property/equipment

Likelihood/Frequency

This is an estimation based on all available facts of the chance that a hazard will actually occur and result in injury or damage.

1	Extremely likely to occur – probable within a month
2	Frequent – possible within a year
	Often likely to occur
3	Unlikely or remotely possible. Slight chance of occurring

Risk rating

Risk	A	B	C
1	Unacceptable – must receive immediate attention to remove/reduce risk	Urgent – must receive attention as soon as possible to reduce hazard or risk	Must receive attention to check if hazard or risk can be reduced and that systems are satisfactory
2	Urgent – must receive attention as soon as possible to reduce hazard or risk	Should receive attention to check if hazard or risk can be reduced and that procedures are satisfactory	Low priority
3	Must receive attention to check if hazard or risk can be reduced and that systems are satisfactory	Low priority	Low priority

Many activities in the workplace are covered by regulations, such as dangerous machinery, hazardous substances, manual handling, etc. A check must be made on whether the organisation is doing what the law requires. Have industry guides, good trade practice and standards been put in place?

The aim is to eliminate (if possible) and certainly reduce the risk of the hazard occurring. The law states that management must do what is reasonably practicable to make the work safe.

- Draw up a **priority action list**, with hazards that have the potential to cause the greatest harm and for the highest number of people at the top of the list.

- Look at ways to **eliminate the hazard** altogether. If that is not possible look to control the hazards so that the chance of them being realised is minimised.

- Ensure that the **controls** have suitably reduced the risk and have not created another hazard.

- **Appoint somebody** as responsible for ensuring that the action is carried out and provide a target date for completion. All of these details must be recorded. The Section Manager should ensure that the recommendations have been put into place.

When controlling risks follow the principles below:

- try a less risky option, eg change from using a hazardous substance to an alternative that is less hazardous;

- prevent access to the hazard (for example, by guarding or restricting access to qualified staff);

- organise work to reduce exposure to the hazard;

- issue personal protective equipment, but make sure it does not pose a second hazard;

- provide welfare facilities for example, washing facilities for removing contamination.

It need not be expensive; installing a mirror around a blind corner or putting non-slip mats on a slippery floor are inexpensive precautions, or arranging for fire drills, to test the organisation's fire precautions. Failure to take simple precautions can cost a lot of money if an accident does happen.

Step 4 – Record your findings

If you employ five or more people, you must record your significant findings and keep the written record in an easily retrievable format as proof for visiting inspectors or any civil liability action. It helps to demonstrate you have done what the law asks you to. Staff may also find it useful to refer to the document.

What will be recorded:

- the hazards connected with your work
- the harm if the hazard were to be realised
- who and how many people might be affected
- action taken to minimise the hazard by controlling the risk

The information arising from the risk assessment must be shared with the appropriate persons. For example if violence is identified as a hazard for staff, then the procedures and if appropriate the training for dealing with violent persons must be delivered. In other words the persons likely to be affected by the hazards must be instructed in the findings and recommendations of the risk assessment

Step 5 – Review and revision

Anything that introduces a hazard must trigger a review of the risk assessment. For example, if new machinery is purchased or if there is a change in a process or procedure, then the risk assessment must be reviewed. New hazards must be considered in their own right and, again, everything must be done to minimise or eliminate the risk.

It is good practice to review the assessment on a regular basis to check for new hazards and see if the control measures are still effective. All staff should be involved as they often work with the hazards on a regular basis.

An overview of the process is shown in the diagram below.

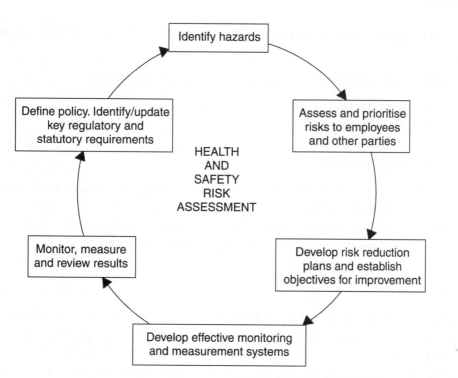

Figure 11.1 Health and safety assessment risk

2.3 Benefits of risk assessment

Apart from identifying the measures needed to comply with health and safety legislation, the main benefit of risk assessment is improved standards of health and safety for staff, service users and members of the public. Other reasons to use risk assessment include:

- Reduce accidents/injuries/fatalities

- Increase standards and efficiency

- Helps to recognise, manage and control risk

- Improved employee/employer relations

- Improved use of resources

- Fewer compensation claims

- Reduced insurance claims

- Reduction in the costs of:
    - absenteeism
    - cover for absent employees
    - loss of productivity

2.4 Monitoring health and safety

A monitoring programme for health and safety will identify existing and potential hazards and provide recommendations for appropriate corrective action. Monitoring is a pro-active action to ensure workplace health and safety is obtained. A number of monitoring methods are used – inspections and audits, benchmarking, and accident/incident reports. If performed correctly, and with sufficient frequency, health and safety inspections will help to reduce the risk of accidents and injuries, and save lives.

Health and safety monitoring/inspections are essential in order to:

- Identify hazards
- Set standards and related procedures
- Establish controls
- Monitor effectiveness

All employees should be encouraged to report unsafe working conditions to their supervisor or health and safety representative, to have the situation promptly investigated and appropriate action taken. A number of monitoring methods are used – inspections and audits, benchmarking, and accident/incident reports.

Inspections

Safety inspections should be carried out to locate and define faults in the system that allow incidents to occur. They may be carried out as a comprehensive audit, working through a checklist; or by using random spot checks, regular checks of particular risk points, or statutory inspections of particular areas, such as lifts, hoists, boilers or pipelines. It is essential that checklists used in the inspection process should identify corrective action to be taken, and allocate responsibility for that action. There should be reporting systems and control procedures to ensure that inspections are taking place and that findings are being acted on. Safety Managers will compile their own lists of relevant safety deficiencies whilst on safety inspection tours. The checklist will include:

- **Fire/emergency evacuation procedures**. The manager will check that records of employee training are kept, signage is clear and up to date, fire extinguishers are present and correct, provisions for assisting disabled persons in emergencies are in place, fire alarms are tested weekly and can be heard and are understood by all employees and a fire practice is carried out at least annually.

- **Housekeeping** – checks will cover the cleanliness and accessibility of work areas, the availability of drinking water, the safety of the equipment and storage facilities, the adequacy of the welfare facilities, the suitability of the lighting, heating and ventilation and the control of any environmental hazards that have been identified. Where ladders or towers are used they must be used correctly and maintenance checks carried out and recorded at annual intervals.

- **Electrical hazards** – all portable appliances should be tested annually for safety. Checks should identify damage to cables/extension leads, etc. and make sure they are safely routed and do not create a trip hazard.

- **Machinery** – all dangerous parts should be guarded, machinery instructions should be clear and on display, and a systematic maintenance programme should exist with records kept in a log book, which is readily available for scrutiny.

Activity 2 (10 mins)

A scene from everyday office life is shown below. Note down anything that strikes you as being dangerous about this working environment.

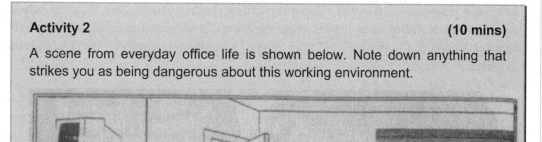

Audits

A Safety Audit is an independent, systematic examination of safety systems within each area of the organisation. All aspects of safety are checked against predetermined criteria and each category given a marked assessment. From this, an overall assessment of effectiveness is calculated, which provides managers with a benchmark of their safety performance. However, because such an audit is by necessity of limited scope, it is not highly detailed, nor is it meant to be unnecessarily critical. The purpose of the report is therefore to highlight and encourage good practice, whilst at the same time pointing out obvious shortcomings that require attention. In this way the overall 'safety culture' of an area can be assessed within the wider context.

Safety Audits give a measure of the 'health' of every area within the organisation at a specific point in time. Part of the assessment will be looking to ascertain what level of follow-up action has taken place as a result of the routine inspections.

Benchmarking

Health and safety benchmarking is a planned process by which an organisation compares its health and safety processes and performance with others to learn how to:

- reduce accidents and ill-health;
- improve compliance with health and safety law; and/or
- cut compliance costs.

Benchmarking is not just about comparing data or copying competitors. It is more about continuously learning from others, learning more about your organisation's strengths and weaknesses in the process, and then acting on the lessons learned. This is what leads to real improvement.

Accident/incident reports

Written records not only provide evidence that proper monitoring of safety is an integral part of normal procedures, but also record what actions have taken place. This is invaluable should an incident occur which involves investigation by an external agency, eg HSE, insurance company etc.

In addition to legislation, you need to be aware of helpful guidance on health and safety from other sources. The instruction manual to a piece of equipment or machinery, for example, makes all the difference between a help and a hazard. The Health and Safety Commission issues helpful booklets on matters such as working with VDUs, smoking and alcohol. But there is no substitute for common sense: care in handling chemicals, lifting heavy objects, operating machinery, moving around the workplace (and playing practical jokes) is part of every employee's own 'Safety Policy'. We will now look at some practical measures and requirements for accident and fire prevention in the workplace.

3 ACCIDENT AND FIRE PREVENTION

3.1 Accidents

Apart from obviously dangerous equipment in factories, there are many hazards to be found in the modern working environment. Many accidents could be avoided by the simple application of common sense and consideration by employer and employee, and by safety consciousness encouraged or enforced by a widely acceptable and well publicised **safety policy**.

Activity 3	**(10 mins)**

What would you expect to be the most common causes of injury in the workplace? List at least five hazards or risky behaviours.

The **cost** of accidents to the employer consists of:

    (a)   time lost by the injured employee;

    (b)   time lost by other employees whose work is interrupted by the accident;

    (c)   time lost by supervision, management and technical staff as a result of the accident;

    (d)   a proportion of the cost of first aid materials, or even medical staff;

    (e)   the cost of disruption to operations at work;

    (f)   the cost of any damage and repairs and modification to the equipment;

    (g)   the cost of any compensation payments or fines resulting from legal action;

(h)   the costs associated with increased insurance premiums;

(i)   reduced output from the injured employee on return to work;

(j)   the cost of possible reduced morale, increased absenteeism, increased labour turnover among employees;

(k)   the cost of recruiting and training a replacement for the injured worker.

An employer may also be liable to an employee in tort if the employee is injured as a result of either:

(a)   the employer's failure to take reasonable care in providing safe premises and plant, a safe system of work and competent fellow employees; or

(b)   the employer's breach of a statutory duty – say, to fence dangerous machinery.

Although the injured employee's damages may be reduced if the injury was partly a consequence of his/her own contributory negligence, due allowance is made for ordinary human failings, such as inattentiveness, tiredness and so on.

3.2   Accident prevention

The prevention of illness or accidents requires efforts on the part of employers, including workplace design, communication of health and safety policies and procedures, training and so on. Some of the steps which might be taken to reduce the frequency and severity of accidents are as follows.

(a)   Developing a safety consciousness among staff and workers and encouraging departmental pride in a good safety record.

(b)   Developing effective consultative participation between management, workers and unions so that safety and health rules can be accepted and followed.

(c)   Giving adequate instruction in safety rules and measures as part of the training of new and transferred workers, or where working methods or speeds of operation are changed.

(d)   Materials handling, a major cause of accidents, should be minimised and designed as far as possible for safe working and operation.

(e)   Ensuring a satisfactory standard from the safety angle for both basic plant and auxiliary fittings such as guards and other devices.

(f)   Good maintenance – apart from making sound job repairs, temporary expedients to keep production going should not prejudice safety.

(g)   In general, the appropriate code of practice for the industry/work environment should be implemented in full.

3.3   Accident reporting

An accident report is a management tool, designed to:

(a)   identify problems; and
(b)   indicate corrective action.

Recurring accidents may suggest the need for special investigation, but only more serious incidents will have to be followed-up in depth. Follow-up should be clearly aimed at preventing recurrence – not placing blame.

The drawing below shows the format of a **typical accident book,** which should by law be kept by any organisation which employs more than 10 people. (The one used by your organisation may be laid out differently, or it might consist of loose-leaf sheets.)

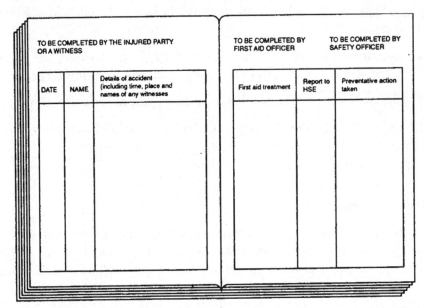

The **Reporting of Injuries, Diseases and Dangerous Occurrences Regulations 1995** (RIDDOR 95) require employers to do the following.

(a) Notify the environmental health authority or the Health and Safety Executive **immediately** if one of the following occurs.

    (i) There is an accident connected with work and either an employee or self-employed person working on the premises is killed or suffers a major injury (including as a result of physical violence) or a member of the public is killed or taken to hospital.

    (ii) There is a dangerous occurrence.

(b) Send a completed **Accident report form** to do the following.

    (i) Confirm within ten days a telephone report of an accident or dangerous occurrence (as described in (a) above).

    (ii) Notify, within ten days of the accident, any injury which stops someone doing their normal job for more than three days.

    (iii) Report certain work-related diseases.

Health and Safety at Work etc Act 1974
The Reporting of Injuries, Diseases and Dangerous Occurrences Regulations 1995

HSE
Health & Safety
Executive

Report of an injury or dangerous occurrence

Filling in this form
This form must be filled in by an employer or other responsible person.

Part A

About you
1 What is your full name?

2 What is your job title?

3 What is your telephone number?

About your organisation
4 What is the name of your organisation?

5 What is its address and postcode?

6 What type of work does your organisation do?

Part B

About the incident
1 On what date did the incident happen?

/ /

2 At what time did the incident happen?
(Please use the 24-hour clock eg 0600)

3 Did the incident happen at the above address?

Yes ☐ Go to question 4

No ☐ Where did the incident happen?

☐ elsewhere in your organisation - give the name, address and postcode

☐ at someone else's premises - give the name, address and postcode

☐ in a public place - give the details of where it happened

If you do not know the postcode, what is the name of the local authority?

4 In which department, or where on the premises, did the incident happen?

Part C

About the injured person
If you are reporting a dangerous occurrence, go to Part F.
If more than one person was injured in the same incident, please attach the details asked for in Part C and Part D for each injured person.

1 What is their full name?

2 What is their home address and postcode?

3 What is their home phone number?

4 How old are they?

5 Are they
☐ male?
☐ female?

6 What is their job title?

7 Was the injured person (tick only one box)
☐ one of your employees?
☐ on a training scheme? Give details:

☐ on work experience?
☐ employed by someone else? Give details of the employer:

☐ self-employed and at work?
☐ a member of the public?

Part D

About the injury
1 What was the injury? (eg fracture, laceration)

2 What part of the body was injured?

NOTES

3 Was the injury (tick the one box that applies)

☐ a fatality?

☐ a major injury or condition? (see accompanying notes)

☐ an injury to an employee or self-employed person which prevented them doing their normal work for more than 3 days?

☐ an injury to a member of the public which meant they had to be taken from the scene of the accident to a hospital for treatment?

4 Did the injured person (tick all the boxes that apply)

☐ became unconscious?

☐ need resuscitation?

☐ remain in hospital for more than 24 hours?

☐ none of the above?

Part E

About the kind of accident
Please tick the one box that best describes what happened, then go to part G.

☐ Contact with moving machinery or material being machined

☐ Hit by a moving, flying or falling object

☐ Hit by a moving vehicle

☐ Hit by something fixed or stationary

☐ Injured while handling, lifting or carrying

☐ Slipped, tripped or fell on the same level

☐ Fell from a height
How high was the fall?

☐ _____ metres

☐ Trapped by something collapsing

☐ Drowned or asphyxiated

☐ Exposed to, or in contact with, a harmful substance

☐ Exposed to fire

☐ Exposed to an explosion

☐ Contact with electricity or an electrical discharge

☐ Injured by an animal

☐ Physically assaulted by a person

☐ Another kind of accident (describe it in part G)

Part F

Dangerous occurrences
Enter the number of the dangerous occurrence you are reporting. (The numbers are given in the Regulations and in the notes which accompany this form.)

☐

Part G

Describing what happened
Give as much detail as you can. For instance
- the name of any substance involved
- the name and type of any machinery involved
- the events that led to the incident
- the part played by any people.

If it was a personal injury, give details of what the person was doing. Describe any action that has since been taken to prevent a similar incident. Use a separate piece of paper if you need to.

☐☐☐☐

Part H

Your signature

☐

Date

☐ / /

Where to send the form
Please send it to the Enforcing Authority for the place where it happened. If you do not know the Enforcing Authority, send it to the nearest HSE office.

For official use

Client number | Location number | Event number

☐ INV REP ☐ Y ☐ N

Definitions

Major injuries include things like fractures other than to fingers, thumbs or toes, amputation, temporary or permanent loss of sight and any other injury which results in the person being admitted to hospital for more than 24 hours.

Dangerous occurrences are 'near misses' that might well have caused major injuries. They include the collapse of a load bearing part of a lift, electrical short circuit or overload causing fire or explosion, the malfunction of breathing apparatus while in use of during testing immediately before use, and many others.

Notifiable diseases include certain poisonings, occupational asthma, asbestosis, hepatitis and many others.

The standard for the notification of injuries and dangerous occurrences is reproduced on previous pages.

Activity 4 (30 mins)

Look back at the scene from everyday office life in Activity 2.

Adopt the role of each of the three workers shown and, assuming that you have by now had one of the many accidents possible in this working environment, fill out a report in the Accident Book shown below.

Accident book

	Full name, address and occupation of injured person (1)	Signature of injured person or other person making this entry* (2)	Date when entry made (3)	Date and time of accident (4)	Room/place in which accident happened (5)	Cause and nature of injury † (6)
1						
2						
3						
4						
5						
6						
7						
8						
9						
10						

* If the entry is made by some person acting on behalf of the employee, the address and occupation of that person must also be given
† State clearly the work or process being performed at the time of the accident

3.4 Fire safety and prevention

The main provisions of the **Fire Precautions Act 1971** are that:

(a) there must be adequate means of escape kept free from obstructions;

(b) all doors out of the building must be capable of opening from the inside;

(c) all employees should know the fire alarm system;

(d) there must be an effective and regularly tested fire alarm system;

(e) there must be fire-fighting equipment easily available and in working order.

Specialised buildings are covered by other legislation such as the Fire Safety and Safety of Places of Sport Act 1987. European legislation was implemented in the **Fire Precautions (Workplace) Regulations 1997** which came into force in December 1997. These regulations require employers to:

(a) provide the appropriate number of fire extinguishers and other means for fighting fire;

(b) install fire detectors and fire alarm systems where necessary.

(c) take whatever measures are necessary for fighting fire (eg the drawing up of a suitable emergency plan of action) and nominate a sufficient number of workers to implement these measure and ensure that they are adequately trained and equipped to carry out their responsibilities;

(d) provide adequate emergency routes and exits for everyone to escape quickly and safely;

(e) ensure that equipment and facilities provided to protect workers from the dangers of fire are regularly maintained and any faults found are rectified as quickly as possible.

Apart from **fire precautions** – which are designed to protect employees in the event of a fire – there must be measures for **fire prevention:** that is, to stop it happening! The main causes of fire in industry and commerce tend to be associated with electrical appliances and installations, and smoking is a major source of fires in business premises. The Fire Protection Association (of the UK) suggests the following guidelines for fire prevention and control:

(a) management should accept that fire prevention policies and practices must be established and reviewed regularly;

(b) management should be aware of the possible effects and consequences of fires, in terms of loss of buildings, plant and output, damage to records, effects on customers and workers etc;

(c) fire risks should be identified, particularly as regards sources of ignition, presence of combustible materials, and the means by which fires can spread;

(d) the responsibility for fire prevention should be established;

(e) a fire officer should be appointed;

(f) a fire prevention drill should be established and practised.

The Fire Protection Association provides detailed guidelines for fire prevention, and checklists for use in assessing the adequacy of existing procedures and in designing new procedures.

NOTES

Activity 5 (1 hour)

Do you know what to do if fire breaks out in your college/workplace? Would you recognise the sound of a smoke alarm or fire alarm for what it was? Where is the nearest fire extinguisher? Is it safe to use a water extinguisher for any sort of fire? How do you set off the alarm? Where is the nearest fire exit? Should you leave doors open or shut? Does anybody know you are in the building? If you are not in the building does anybody think that you are?

Find out the answers to these questions!

3.5 Health and safety policy

In order to enhance safety awareness, promote good practice and comply with legal obligations, many employers have a health and safety policy for their staff. Such a policy might have the following features.

(a) Statement of principles.

(b) Detail of safety procedures.

(c) Compliance with the law (eg in siting of fire extinguishers, fire exits) should be enforced.

(d) Detailed instructions should be made available as to how to use equipment.

(e) Training requirements should be identified (eg no person who has not been on a particular training course can use the equipment), as part of the context of human resource planning.

(f) Committees of safety experts, line managers and employees can discuss issues of health and safety. There is no reason for example why safety issues should not be brought up for discussion in a firm's quality circles.

Safety policy must be implemented in detailed practice (such as fire drills and equipment checking) but it is less likely to be consistently observed if senior managers fail to set a good example, to discipline breaches of policy, or to reward health and safety suggestions. The aim is to create a culture in which health and safety are key values.

3.6 A culture of health and safety

Charles Hampden-Turner (in his book *Corporate Culture*) notes that attitudes to safety can be part of a corporate **culture**. He quotes the example of a firm called (for reasons of confidentiality) **Western Oil.**

EXAMPLE: WESTERN OIL

Western Oil had a bad safety record. 'Initially, safety was totally at odds with the main cultural values of productivity (management's interests) and maintenance of a macho image (the worker's culture)... . Western Oil had a culture which put safety in conflict with other corporate values.' In particular, the problem was with its long-distance truck

PROFESSIONAL EDUCATION

drivers (who in the USA have a culture of solitary independence and self reliance). They sometimes drove recklessly with loads large enough to inundate a small town. The company instituted Operation Integrity to improve safety in a lasting way, changing the policies and drawing on the existing features of the culture but using them in a different way.

The culture had five dilemmas.

(a) **Safety-first versus macho-individualism.** Truckers see themselves as 'fearless pioneers of the unconventional lifestyle... . "Be careful boys!" is hardly a plea likely to go down well with this particular group'. Instead of trying to control the drivers, the firm recommended that they become road safety consultants (or design consultants). Their advice was sought on improving the system. This had the advantage that 'by making drivers critics of the system their roles as outsiders were preserved and promoted'. It tried to tap their heroism as promoters of public safety.

(b) **Safety everywhere versus safety specialists.** Western Oil could have hired more specialist staff. However, instead, the company promoted cross-functional safety teams from existing parts of the business, for example to help in designing depots and thinking of ways to reduce hazards.

(c) **Safety as cost versus productivity as benefit.** 'If the drivers raced from station to station to win their bonus, accidents were bound to occur... . The safety engineers rarely spoke to the line manager in charge of the delivery schedules. The unreconciled dilemma between safety and productivity had been evaded at management level and passed down the hierarchy until drivers were subjected to two incompatible injunctions, work fast and work safely.' To deal with this problem, safety would be built into the reward system.

(d) **Long-term safety versus short-term steering.** The device of recording 'unsafe' acts in operations enabled them to be monitored by cross-functional teams, so that the causes of accidents could be identified and reduced.

(e) **Personal responsibility versus collective protection.** It was felt that if 'safety' was seen as a form of management policing it would never be accepted. The habit of management 'blaming the victim' had to stop. Instead, if one employee reported another to the safety teams, the person who was reported would be free of official sanction. Peer pressure was seen to be a better enforcer of safety than the management hierarchy.

In many companies, considerations of health and safety are not tied up so intimately and obviously with reward systems and other policies. Nor do health and safety issues relate directly to work. However, from this example, we can learn:

    (a) the importance of management practice in ensuring safety;
    (b) safety (like total quality) is everyone's responsibility;
    (c) culture and structures can either enhance or undermine safety policies.

Copies of legislation are readily available from the government and the Health and Safety Executive. Various companies produce newsletters on the issue to keep managers regularly informed. There is no real excuse for management ignorance in this matter.

FOR DISCUSSION

What are the cultural values in your nation, local community and organisation that:

(a)   promote health and safety? and

(b)   promote risk-taking and ill-health?

The diagram below shows a systematic approach to health and safety.

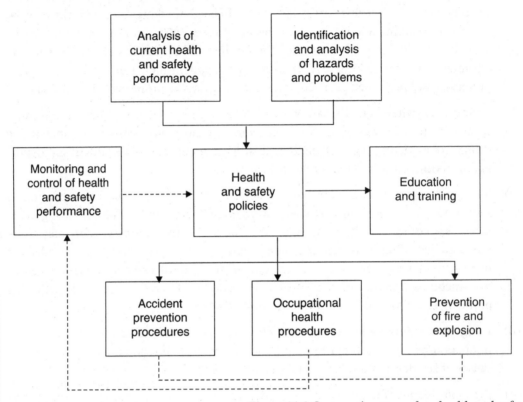

Figure 11.2 Systematic approach to health and safety

Finally, let us look at some health hazards that have recently started to cause concern.

4   PUBLIC ATTITUDES AND CONCERNS

4.1   General concerns

Many hazards in the workplace are obvious: noise, heat, vibration, odours, poor housekeeping, chemicals, dangerous goods, manual handling and hazards associated with tools or machinery.

There are also hazards in the workplace that are less obvious; these could be called *hidden hazards*. They include:

- passive smoking
- workplace stress
- workplace bullying
- alcohol and drug misuse.

These hidden hazards may *directly* affect a person 's physical or mental health, causing illness or disease. They may *indirectly* put other people at risk of a workplace incident or accident, caused by inattention, fatigue, depression, physical illness or bad judgment.

A hidden hazard may exist by itself or it may develop with other hidden hazards. For instance, a person who is under constant and significant pressure may become stressed. They might release their stress by bullying someone else, or may turn to alcohol or other drugs to cope. A victim of bullying in turn becomes stressed – and so the effect can spread throughout the workplace.

Just as employers are required to manage physical hazards in the workplace, they also need to reduce or remove the risk these hidden hazards pose to workplace health and safety.

4.2 Passive smoking

Recent public attitudes and concerns have focused on the health and comfort aspects of exposure to tobacco smoke at work. According to research done by James Repace, a health physicist based in the United States who runs a second-hand smoke consultancy, passive smoking at work kills three people every day. The study found that around 900 office workers, 165 bar workers and 145 manufacturing workers die each year as a direct result of breathing in other people's tobacco smoke at work. It also found that there are three times as many deaths a year from passive smoking at work as there are from workplace injuries.

A survey on behalf of pressure group Action on Smoking and Health (ASH) found that 85% of those questioned said that people should not be forced to breathe other people's secondhand smoke. The poll, of more than 2,000 people, also suggested that almost two-thirds of workers agreed with legislation to restrict workplace smoking.

It is the common law duty of employers to warn their staff of health hazards and to take action to protect their employees. Employers should be aware of the effects of passive smoking and take action to protect non-smokers. The Health and Safety at Work Act 1974 requires the employer to take reasonably practicable steps to ensure the health, safety and welfare at work of employees. In 1988 the Health and Safety Executive (HSE) published guidance for employers, *Passive Smoking at Work*, explaining what they should do to comply with health, safety and welfare work as it applies to environmental tobacco smoke. The guidance was last revised in 1992.

A European Union Directive required workplaces to have smoke-free 'rest facilities' for non-smokers by 1 January 1996. The HSE are currently consulting on an Approved Code of Practice (ACoP) on passive smoking at work. If adopted this will provide authoritative guidance on minimum standards employers are expected to reach.

The issue should not be about whether people smoke but about where they smoke. Some smokers might wish to cut down or give up smoking, though others will not welcome a smoking policy. A clear written policy should minimise conflict and misunderstanding between employees so that those who wish to smoke are aware of where and when they are free to do so.

4.3 Workplace stress

Stress is a term that is often loosely used to describe feelings of tension or exhaustion - usually associated with too much, or overly demanding, work. In fact, stress is the product of demands made on an individual's physical and mental energies: monotony, feelings of failure or insecurity are sources of stress, as much as the conventionally considered factors of pressure, overwork etc. It is worth remembering, too, that demands on an individual's energies may be stimulating as well as harmful: many people work well under pressure, and even require some form of stress to bring out their best performance. Excessive stress, however, can be damaging, and may be called 'strain'. This is why we talk about stress management, not 'elimination': it is a question of keeping stress to 'helpful' proportions and avenues.

Symptoms of stress (strain)

Harmful stress, or 'strain', can be identified by its effects on the individual and his performance.

(a) *Nervous tension.* This may manifest itself in various ways: irritability and increased sensitivity, preoccupation with details, a polarised perspective on the issues at hand, sleeplessness, etc. Various physical symptoms – e.g. skin and digestive disorders – are also believed to be 'stress-related'.

(b) *Withdrawal.* This is essentially a defence mechanism, which may manifest itself as unusual quietness and reluctance to communicate, or as physical withdrawal i.e. absenteeism, poor time keeping, or even leaving the organisation.

(c) *Low morale:* low confidence, dissatisfaction, expression of frustration or hopelessness etc.

(d) Signs that the individual is *repressing the problem, or* trying to deny it. Forced cheerfulness, boisterous playfulness, excessive drinking etc may indicate this. Irritability outside work (if noticed by the manager) may point to transference of the problem to the non-work environment.

The problem is exacerbated because some people tend to hide their problems. Warning signs that somebody is suffering from excessive stress can include the following – but of course this will depend on each case.

- A decline in work quality
- Absenteeism
- Regular personal emergencies
- Psychosomatic illnesses such as headaches and stomach cramps
- Use of alcohol while at work
- Persistent failure to do simple things like paperwork
- Making destructive comments or acting in a withdrawn manner in meetings
- Consistently denigrating colleagues
- Active sabotage

It is worth noting that some of these symptoms – drinking, absenteeism etc – may or may not be correctly identified with stress: there are many other possible causes of such problems, both at work (eg lack of motivation) and outside (personal problems). The same is true of physical symptoms such as headaches and stomach pains: these are not invariably correlated with personal stress. Arguably some symptoms (eg alcoholism) might be causes of stress.

The workplace factors that can cause stress include the following.

(a) **Role conflict** – this means the conflict experienced from the various roles played at work – for example the conflicting roles of boss and friend, new supervisor and ex-workmate.

(b) **Role ambiguity** – this means uncertainty about your role in your own mind and the minds of those with whom you come into contact. There is often particular uncertainty about how your work will be evaluated, how much responsibility you have and what others expect of you.

(c) **Role overload/underload** – this means having to do too much work or work which is too hard, or too little work or work which is too easy, boring and repetitive.

(d) **Responsibility for others** – higher stress is suffered by those who are accountable for success and the performance and welfare of other people.

(e) **Lack of social support** – isolation and lack of social support increases stress.

(f) **Uncertainty** – lack of control over decisions, which affect you is also a problem.

(g) **High levels of public contact** – especially if there are risks of verbal/physical confrontation, or exposure to physical or emotional suffering.

(h) **Poor interpersonal relationships** and personality clashes.

4.4 Workplace bullying

Workplace bullying is also known as 'workplace harassment' or 'mobbing'. It can be defined as a 'persistent, unwelcome, intrusive behaviour of one or more individuals whose actions prevent others from fulfilling their duties.'

Workplace bullying includes:

- persistent and repeatedly aggressive behaviour that makes someone feel victimised, intimidated or humiliated.

- any physical abuse.

- repeated verbal abuse, including yelling, screaming, personal comments, offensive language, sarcasm.

- inappropriately and unreasonably vindictive, offensive, cruel or malicious behaviour.

- gender or racial discrimination, sexual harassment.

- having your personal belongings, tools or equipment hidden or tampered with.

- initiation practices.

The bully can be an employer, peer, subordinate, or even client or supplier. The typical bully uses aggression and violence to compensate for overwhelming feelings of inadequacy. Some bullies suffer from mental health disorders but most lack self-discipline, the ability to pursue long-term goals, or to work in a team.

Bullying is a traumatic, stressful experience that often results in the mental breakdown and otherwise ill health of the victim. Physical and mental health problems, fatigue, low

NOTES

functioning, and even suicide are common. The victims can no longer be productive at work and are sometimes forced to resign.

Bullying can be unlawful. Although there is no clear single piece of legislation dealing with bullying at work, the key acts underpinning the issue of workplace bullying are:

- Health and Safety at Work Act 1974
- Criminal Justice and Public Order Act 1994
- Protection from Harassment Act 1997
- Sex Discrimination Act 1975
- Race Relations Act 1976
- Disability Discrimination Act 1995
- Employment Rights Act 1996
- Employment Relations Bill 1999

Individual responsibilities

Every employee has a personal responsibility to:

- ensure they understand the nature of harassment and bullying;

- be aware of how their behaviour may affect others, and to uphold the standards of behaviour set within the organisation;

- work within the policy guidelines;

- be aware of bullying and challenge unacceptable behaviour where appropriate.

Management responsibilities – Managers have a particular responsibility to ensure that bullying does not occur within their areas and, if it does, to deal with it swiftly and sensitively. Complaints of bullying should be taken seriously and investigated thoroughly. Confidentiality (as far as possible) should be adhered to and victimisation as a result of making a complaint, or witnessing an incident, must not be tolerated. An individual wishing to make formal complaints of bullying should do so through the grievance procedure.

4.5 Alcohol and drug misuse

All employers and managers should be aware of the problem of drugs and alcohol in the workplace – the effect on individual employees and the potential costs for employers, associated with absenteeism, poor performance, incidents of dishonesty and theft and company image. Substances that can be misused include:

- alcohol (the most commonly misused drug)
- prescription and non-prescription medication
- illegal drugs
- solvents used as inhalants
- tobacco.

A research document published by the Health Education Authority showed that 90% of the 123 Personnel Directors of large UK organisations surveyed considered that alcohol consumption was a problem for their organisation. Employers need to be aware of the

PROFESSIONAL EDUCATION

employment law implications of employees taking drugs and their responsibilities when trying to determine if there is a drugs related problem.

Keith Hellawell, former Chief Constable of West Yorkshire police has said that employers should have anti-drugs policies in the workplace and should recognise that drug taking and alcohol abuse is a problem. He also believes that 'Safety sensitive' professions, such as police forces, should introduce mandatory drugs testing.

Employers have a general duty under Section 2 of Health and Safety at Work etc Act 1974 to ensure the health, safety and welfare at work of their employees. They also have a duty under the Management of Health and Safety at Work Regulations 1999 to assess the risks to the health and safety of employees. If the employer knowingly allows an employee under the influence of drugs to continue working and his/her behaviour places himself/herself or other employees at risk then the employer could be prosecuted.

Employers also have a duty to third parties under Section 3(1) of Health and Safety at Work etc Act 1974. This states that employers must conduct their employees in a way which ensures, so far as is reasonably practicable, that people who are affected by the operation of those employees are not exposed to health and safety risks. There is a potential criminal liability for all employers who knowingly allow or at the very least tolerate, the use of controlled drugs on company premises under the Misuse of Drugs Act 1971.

Some employees are subject to specific laws covering drug testing, such as offshore oil workers and those working in transport systems – guards, drivers, conductors and signalmen.

Activity 6   **(15 mins)**

Since we have broadened our awareness of what constitutes a potential threat to health and safety, take some time to think about what other issues personnel policies might cover? Suggest five areas for consideration. (If you are currently employed, check your organisation's manual on health and safety.)

Chapter roundup

- The major piece of legislation covering health and safety at work is the Health and Safety at Work Act 1974, which places duties on both employers and employees.

- Regulations under the Act and under EU directives place additional responsibilities regarding health and safety on employers.

- Machine safety, fire prevention, chemicals' handling and so on are obvious areas for attention. However, the average workplace contains many potential hazards, and working conditions (including stress, VDU use and long working hours) can jeopardise health. Detailed safety policies must be formulated and communicated to all staff. It is also important to create a culture in which health and safety are a priority.

NOTES

Quick quiz

1   Give reasons for the importance of health and safety at work.

2   What are the duties placed on an employee by the HASAW Act 1974?

3   Outline the powers of safety committees.

4   What additional duties have been placed on employers by recent regulations?

5   Explain the term Repetitive Strain Injury.

6   What does the cost of accidents to an employer consist of?

7   What preventive action could be taken to reduce the possibility of illness or accidents at the workplace?

8   What are the main causes of fire in the workplace?

9   What are the main objectives of a smoking policy?

10 What are the major work-related causes of stress?

Answers to quick quiz

1   To protect employees from pain and suffering; legal obligations; the cost of workplace accidents; to improve the company's image. (See Introduction)

2   To take reasonable care of self and others; to allow employers to carry out their duties; not to interfere with machinery/equipment. (1.1)

3   Safety committees can insist that the employer produces a written statement of safety measures and consults with safety representatives. (1.1)

4   Risk assessment; risk control; information on risks and hazards; revise and initiate safety policies; identify 'at risk' employees; training; competence of advisers. (1.2)

5   A syndrome involving back ache, eye strain, stiffness in the neck, shoulders, arms and hands. (1.4)

6   Time lost by employees and management; cost of first aid and staff; cost of disrupted work. (3.1)

7   Safety consciousness; consultation and participation; adequate instruction; minimal materials handling; safety devices on machines; good maintenance; codes of practice. (3.2)

8   Electrical appliances and installations; smoking. (3.4)

9   To provide smoke-free air in most areas where smokers and non-smokers meet; to identify areas where people can smoke; to minimise conflict between smokers and non-smokers. (4.2)

10 Job demands; role conflict; role ambiguity; role overload and underload; responsibility for others; lack of social support; non-participation in decision making. (4.3)

Answers to activities

1   Obviously we do not know the shortcomings of safety measures at your college or work place. Your answer will depend on your following the checklist and identifying what you see in your informal inspection. If you do spot anything which you think might represent a health and safety risk, you should report it to your course tutor or your boss in the first instance.

2   You should have spotted the following hazards

(a)   Heavy object on high shelf.
(b)   Standing on swivel chair.
(c)   Lifting heavy object incorrectly.
(d)   Open drawers blocking passageway.
(e)   Trailing wires.
(f)   Electric bar fire.
(g)   Smouldering cigarette unattended.
(h)   Overfull waste bin.
(i)   Overloaded socket.
(j)   Carrying too many cups of hot liquid.
(k)   Dangerous invoice 'spike'.

If you can see others, you are probably right.

3   (a)   Slippery or poorly maintained floors.
(b)   Frayed carpets.
(c)   Trailing electric leads.
(d)   Obstacles in gangways.
(e)   Standing on chairs (particularly swivel chairs!) to reach high shelving.
(f)   Staircases used as storage facilities.
(g)   Lifting heavy items without bending properly.
(h)   Removing the safety guard on a machine to free a blockage.

NOTES

4

Accident book

Full name, address and occupation of injured person (1)	Signature of injured person or other person making this entry* (2)	Date when entry made (3)	Date and time of accident (4)	Room/place in which accident happened (5)	Cause and nature of injury † (6)
1 TIM SMILEY 22 SPRING ROAD, LONDON OFFICE MANAGER	*Tim Smiley*	14/9/2000	10/9/2000 17.00	OFFICE FLIT POWDER CO	CAUGHT RIGHT HAND ON INVOICE SPIKE. NEEDED STITCHES
2 FRANCES FINLEY 14 SILVER ST, LONDON DATA ENTRY CLERK	*Fran Finley*	15 Nov 2000	8 Nov 2000	OFFICE FLIT POWDER CO	TRIPPED ON TRAILING WIRE AND SPRAINED ANKLE
3 FINBAR MCINTOSH 151 QUEEN STREET, LONDON PROGRAMMER	*Finbar McIntosh*	29 Nov 2000	24 Nov 2000	OFFICE FLIT'S	FELL OFF CHAIR WHILE GETTING EQUIP OFF SHELF - BROKE ARM
4					
5					
6					
7					
8					
9					
10					

* If the entry is made by some person acting on behalf of the employee, the address and occupation of that person must also be given

† State clearly the work or process being performed at the time of the accident

5   This answer is specific to your college/workplace. As an interesting additional piece of learning, though, note how difficult or easy it was to **find out** about fire prevention and safety measures in the organisation.

6   Some areas you might have thought of include:

(a) alcohol on the premises;

(b) drug taking (including prescription drugs) on the premises;

(c) horse play and practical jokes;

(d) noise (or 'acoustic shock'), particularly from headset use. (In a recent case, 20 BT telephone operators claimed that faulty equipment damaged their hearing: PM 15 May 98);

(e) workplace behaviour: running, throwing things, etc;

(f) tiredness (dangerous objects, dust, slippery objects etc).

Chapter 12 :
IMPROVE ORGANISATIONAL PERFORMANCE

Introduction

Organisational control is the process whereby an organisation ensures that it is pursuing strategies and actions that will enable it to achieve its goals. The measurement and evaluation of performance are central to control and involve posing four basic questions

- (a) What has happened?
- (b) Why has it happened?
- (c) Is it going to continue?
- (d) What are we going to do about it?

The first question can be answered by performance measurement. Management will then have to hand far more useful information than it would otherwise have in order to answer the other three questions. By finding out what has actually been happening, senior management can determine with considerable certainty which direction the company is going in and, if all is going well, continue with the good work. Or, if the performance measurements indicate that there are difficulties on the horizon, management can then make adjustments or even alter course altogether with plenty of time to spare.

Change in organisations is always the result of some external influence. Even seemingly small internal changes can be traced back to an external source. In this chapter we shall consider the environment of the organisation, specifically those influences stemming from political, economic, social and technological forces.

Your objectives

After completing this chapter you should be able to:

(a) Monitor systems and work activities and identify problems and opportunities for improvement

(b) Recommend improvements which align with the organisation's objectives and goals and which result in a reduction in the variation between what customers and other stakeholders want and what products, processes and services deliver

(c) Identify the wider implications of proposed changes within the organisation

(d) Plan, implement and evaluate changes within an organisation

1 MONITORING SYSTEMS

1.1 Monitoring and control

Monitoring in simple terms means watching over something that is happening. Generally the word also carries a sense of warning: detecting things that are going wrong. Active monitoring systems ensure that the organisation is quickly aware of changes in the market place (competitors' actions, changes in customer tastes etc). This is probably best achieved by both formal and informal information collection methods. The organisation will keep abreast (as far as it can) of what its competitors are doing and someone will have an eye on general economic trends, the opinions of political commentators and the progress of scientific research at the *pure* as well as the *applied* stage, in addition to any more specific research work the company may itself be engaged in.

An organisation is a system, and any system must be controlled to keep it steady or enable it to change safely: each system must have a control system. Control is required because unpredictable disturbances arise and enter the system, so that actual results, the outputs of the system, deviate from the expected results or goals. Examples of disturbances in a business system would be the entry of a powerful new competitor into the market, an unexpected rise in labour costs, a decline in quality standards, the failure of a supplier to deliver promised raw materials, or the tendency of employees to stop working in order to chatter or gossip. A control system must ensure that the business is capable of surviving these disturbances by dealing with them in an appropriate manner.

To have a control system, there has to be a plan, standard, budget or any other sort of target or guideline towards which the system as a whole should be aiming. Control is dependent on the receipt and processing of *information*, both to plan in the first place and to compare actual results against the plan, so as to judge what control measures, if any, are needed.

1.2 Process of control

The managerial process of controlling is the measurement and correction of performance to make sure that the enterprise objectives and the plans devised to attain them are accomplished. Control techniques and systems are essentially the same for cash, office procedures, morale or product quality. The basic control process involves three steps:

- establishing standards, ie criteria of performance
- measuring performance against these standards and
- correcting variations from standards and plans

1.3 Feedback

Feedback is information about actual achievements. In a business organisation, it is information about actual results, produced from within the organisation (for example, management accounting control reports) with the purpose of helping with control decisions.

A feature of feedback is that it is information that is gathered by measuring the outputs of the system itself, as distinct from environmental information, which comes from outside the system. For some control systems, notably for control by senior management at a strategic planning level, control information will be gathered from both environmental sources and internal sources. For example, a company might be unable to judge the success or failure of its activities without putting them into the context of the national economy (Is it booming? Is it in recession? How high is the rate of inflation?) and its markets (How well are competitors doing? Is the number of potential customers rising or falling?).

Some form of internally generated feedback is essential if there is to be any effective monitoring within an organisation and the most common types of monitoring systems in businesses, such as budgetary control, stock control and production control systems, are all based on feedback cycles.

A **feedback system** measures the outputs of a process and then provides information regarding corrective action to the process or the inputs, after the outputs have been produced. In most management problems, because of time lags in implementing the corrective process, this is not good enough. For example, if the manager is informed in August that the administration department has overspent against budget due to a purchase in June, there is nothing that can be done.

Feed forward control will inform management of deviations in time for them to take corrective action. It is used to overcome the time lag problems often encountered by feedback systems. This type of system monitors the inputs into the process to ascertain whether the inputs are as planned; if they are not, the inputs, or perhaps the process, are changed in order to ensure the desired results. In the above example, the administration department would have to submit an estimate for the item they wish to purchase. The organisation would then have to decide whether to refuse the request or change the budget in order to allow the purchase to be made. The diagram below shows feedback/feedforward control.

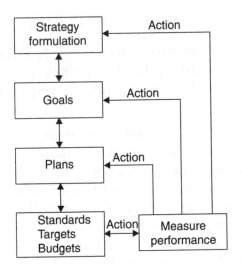

Figure 12.1 Feedback/feedforward control

1.4 Critical control points and standards

Actual or expected performance is measured against standards or yardsticks. If the operation is simple, a manager might control through observation of the work being done. However, in most situations this is not possible because of the complexity of the operations and the fact that a manager has better things to do. He or she must choose critical points for special attention and monitor them to be sure that the operation is proceeding as planned. The principle of critical point control states that effective control requires attention to those factors critical to evaluating performance against plans. Managers need to select these points after asking themselves:

- what will best reflect the goals of my department?
- what will best show me when these goals are not being met?
- what will best measure critical deviations?
- what will tell me who is responsible for any failure?
- what standards will cost the least?
- for what standards is information economically available?

1.5 Taking corrective action

Where these are critical deviations from the plan, the action to be taken will vary from organisation to organisation according to the managerial style employed and the structure adopted.

A problem analysis exercise will be carried out, which will cover the following issues.

- Why are current methods and working practices used?
- What problems are restricting the effectiveness of the current system and the reasons for their existence?
- Are alternative methods available to achieve the same or better results?
- What changes can be introduced?
- What performance criteria are required from the system and how they can be measured?

It must be appreciated that some failures to attain standards are symptomatic of more fundamental causes and that tinkering with the system may not lead to any real improvement. Changes in standards and overall objectives should not be ruled out.

2 PERFORMANCE MEASUREMENT

2.1 What is evaluated?

Performance measurement aims to establish how well something or somebody is doing in relation to the planned activity and desired results. It is a vital part of control and generates the results, which are fed back for comparison with objectives. The 'something' may be a machine, a factory, a subsidiary company or an organisation as a whole. The 'somebody' may be an individual employee, a manager, or a group of people.

Performance measurement is a highly topical issue at present. The factors that have given rise to this interest include the following.

(a) The move away from the traditional emphasis on increasing volume and reducing costs towards a focus on quality and customer satisfaction.

(b) Increasingly competitive world markets, requiring a 'world class' response.

(c) Recognition that the way to achieve (a) and (b) is through the empowerment of those who have most direct control over the product or service, so that responsibility is devolved as far down the line as possible.

(d) The impact of advanced manufacturing technology and information technology on methods of working.

(e) The opportunities presented by activity based approaches to management.

(f) A government intent on achieving excellence and value for money in the public sector through target setting and performance evaluation.

A typical business requires performance measurement in the following areas.

(a) In terms of its relations with external parties, that is its customers or market, suppliers and competitors

(b) Across the organisation as a whole (divisional performance measurement)

(c) *Within* each of the main sub-divisions of the business

(d) At the level of individual activities

Three possible points of reference for measurement are profitability, activity and productivity.

(a) *Profitability*. Profit has two components: cost and income. All parts of an organisation and all activities within it incur costs, and so their success needs to be judged in relation to cost. Only some parts of an organisation receive income, and their success should be judged in terms of both cost and income.

(b) *Activity*. All parts of an organisation are also engaged in activities that cause costs. Activity measures could include the following.

- Number of orders received from customers, a measure of the effectiveness of marketing

NOTES

- Number of deliveries made, a measure of the effectiveness of distribution

- Number of production runs achieved by a particular factory

- Number of machine breakdowns attended to by the repairs and maintenance department.

Each of these items could be measured in terms of physical numbers, monetary value, or time spent.

(c) *Productivity.* This is the quantity of the product or service produced in relation to the resources put in, for example so many units produced per hour, or per employee, or per tonne of material. It defines how *efficiently* resources are being used. The dividing line between productivity and activity is thin, because every activity could be said to have some 'product'. The concept of value is important for assessing activities: that is, to what extent do they add value to the overall output of the organisation?

Activity 1 (10 mins)

An invoicing assistant works in a department with three colleagues. She is paid £18,000 per annum. The department typically handles 10,000 invoices per week.

One morning she spends half an hour on the phone to her grandfather, who lives in Australia, at the company's expense. The cost of the call proves to be £32.

Required

From this scenario identify as many different performance measures as possible, explaining what each is intended to measure. Make any further assumptions you wish.

2.2 Quality measures – importance of prevention rather than correction

The **cost of quality** attempts to provide a single measure of all the costs of ensuring a product meets specifications as well as the costs incurred because of the failure of the product to meet specifications. These costs can be classified into four categories, *prevention, appraisal, internal failure* and *external failure*:

Prevention costs – are incurred in order to prevent the production of non-conforming products. They include:

- Costs of designing and administering a quality assurance programme.
- Costs of development of improved production processes.
- Costs of equipment to produce higher quality products.
- Costs of ensuring supply of quality raw materials and component parts.
- Costs of tooling, calibration and preventative maintenance programmes.

Appraisal costs – are incurred to identify those products that do not meet specification before the product leaves the factory. They include:

- Cost of inspecting and testing programmes for purchases, work in process and finished goods.

- Cost of quality audits and statistical quality control programmes.

- Cost of field-testing.

Internal failure costs – are the costs incurred to rework defective products before the product is delivered to customers. These costs include:

- Cost of scrap, repair and rework.
- Cost of downtime associated with trouble-shooting a process.
- Cost of discounts on sale of seconds.

External failure costs – are the costs incurred when defective products reach the customer. They include:

- Cost of handling customer complaints and claims.
- Warranty and replacement costs.
- Product liability costs.
- Loss of customer goodwill.

The *quality of a service* could be measured by the level of complaints or by favourable reaction. The quality of a training course, for example, could be monitored by asking trainees to complete an assessment form when the course has finished. The training manager's performance could be assessed on the basis of the responses. It would be far more difficult to measure actual achievement in terms of improved performance, as there are so many other variables involved.

Management may be surprised to learn how much is spent on quality-related costs. Because of the importance of prevention rather than correction, there may be high payoffs from shifting quality costs from the last three categories to the prevention category.

2.3 Profit and other objectives

A traditional view has been that a desire to achieve greater profitability often entails a sacrifice in some other aspect of performance. One obvious example is quality: if cheaper materials are used to make a product or less highly trained workers deliver a service, money will be saved (increasing profits), but quality will fall. It is now widely recognised that economising on quality has an adverse effect in the longer term.

In other cases there may not be a clear link between an objective and the profitability objective. A company may aim to improve working conditions for its staff, and measure its success in terms of the cost of improved facilities, falls in staff turnover, or absenteeism and so on. Some of the successes are directly contrary to profitability, while others can only with difficulty be linked to extra productivity.

A third example is where a company aims to fulfil its social and moral responsibilities, for example by incurring costs to make a manufacturing process more environmentally friendly or by keeping a loss-making facility open so as not to cause undesirable unemployment in a depressed area.

2.4 Critical success factors

Some CSFs that cover both financial and non-financial criteria are outlined below.

Sphere of activity	Critical factors
Marketing	Sales volume
	Market share
	Gross margins
Production	Capacity utilisation
	Quality standards
Logistics	Capacity utilisation
	Level of service

2.5 System resource approach

An effective organisation is one which does the right things and is thus able to satisfy the needs of its client group. However, effectiveness is often difficult to measure.

The system resource model bears some relationship to the systems approach, which views an organisation as a system, which obtains inputs and processes them into outputs. System resource effectiveness covers the ability to do the following.

(a) *Obtain scarce and valued resources from the environment*. Oil companies need to secure oil reserves. So, for an oil company indicators of future success are the volume of reserves.

(b) *Sustain day-to-day activities*. An example is the UK's voluntary blood donor scheme.

(c) *Respond to environmental changes and sustain the environment*. Business organisations which fail to ensure they have the ability to remain in business *in future* are not effective.

At first sight, this might seem a rather bizarre way of measuring effectiveness. However, effectiveness in obtaining resources *now* might be essential in meeting clients' needs *in future*. Consider the following example.

Parents often judge prospective schools in part on their academic record (eg proportion of 'A' GCSE and 'A level' passes obtained, number of ex-pupils going to university etc). A school, which attracts the right pupils, will find it easier to meet these exacting targets: attracting the right mix of pupils is a measure of success. It is a vicious circle. Similarly, the ability to attract a high quality teaching staff indicates effectiveness.

Obviously, there are many better ways of measuring organisation effectiveness – but in cases where *outputs* are hard to measure quantitatively, this approach is all there is.

2.6 Internal process approach

The internal process approach really refers to efficiency and the internal workings of the organisation, rather than effectiveness as we have defined it. However, it assumes that *because* the organisation is healthy and efficient in its internal processes, *therefore* it is effective. Internal efficiency and health is an outward sign of organisational effectiveness in meeting client needs.

There are problems with this approach:

(a) *Ignores customers.* You could run a factory making asbestos ceiling tiles with incredible efficiency and a deeply satisfied workforce: but customers' needs are not satisfied.

(b) *Ignores strategy.* Concentration on internal processes is never enough; you might want to be close to your customer – but is this the *right* customer, and, furthermore, does the customer value the relationship as much as you do?

(c) *Assumes status quo.* Managers may not be *objective* judges of internal health. The soft systems approach suggests that managers are 'actors' in a problem situation with their own objectives and perspectives.

(d) *Ignores environment.* The organisation's relationship with the environment is not addressed by this approach.

Possible performance indicators include:

(a) Ratio of inputs to outputs, in other words, economic *efficiency* in the use of scarce resources (eg revenue per employee, units of output per labour hour).

(b) Strong corporate culture.

(c) Team spirit, loyalty etc.

(d) Good communications, horizontally and vertically, and between workers and management.

(e) Swift, flexible decision-making.

(f) Reward systems that encourage optimum performance.

(g) Successful resolution of conflicts in favour of the overall well-being of the organisation.

(h) Quality.

2.7 The goal approach

The 'goal approach' measures 'effectiveness' by comparing the actual performance of the business with its *stated* objectives and goals. It is quite easy to use and it is possible, for example, to use output measures as measures of effectiveness.

(a) Profitability
(b) Growth
(c) Market share
(d) Innovation
(e) Staff turnover (as a measure of employee satisfaction)
(f) Quality, as measured.

If the goals and objectives are congruent with the organisation's purpose, then reaching them can indicate that an organisation is effective. But there are problems.

(a) *Comparisons.* Organisations do not exist in isolation. Their output effectiveness can only be realistically measured in comparison with *other* organisations.

(b) Effectiveness can only be measured across a *wide* variety of indicators. There may have to be *trade-offs* between them.

(c) *Subverting the goal setting process.* Managers may set goals which they can *easily* achieve.

(d) *Measurability does not equal significance.* There may be a bias towards goals that can be *measured*. Not all the aspects of effectiveness can be easily measured. In a service organisation, it is hard to measure staff courtesy, although this is vitally important for organisation effectiveness.

(e) '*What gets measured gets managed*'. Managers may only *care* about what is measured, to the detriment of other aspects of performance.

Finally, we must assume that the objectives chosen are the right ones, and that they do stand in successfully for effectiveness. And here is the nub of the problem. *Who* decides what is *effective*?

(a) For a *business*, the issue is reasonably clear cuts shareholders have the ultimate say, as the business is run on their behalf.

(b) For other organisations, this is not so easy to determine.

2.8 The stakeholder view approach

The stakeholder view is a way of looking at an organisation that holds that many different groups of people have an interest in what the organisation does. From their various perspectives they have different objectives, which they would like to see the organisation fulfil. There are three broad types of stakeholder in an organisation, as follows.

(a) Internal stakeholders (employees, management).
(b) Connected stakeholders (shareholders, customers, suppliers, financiers).
(c) External stakeholders (the community, government, pressure groups).

The *ecology model of effectiveness* brings the issues of stakeholders into the foreground by identifying the extent to which the organisation *depends* (or is reliant) on a stakeholder group at *any particular time*. For example, a firm with persistent *cash flow problems* might depend on its *bankers* to provide it with money to stay in business at all.

In the long term, any firm depends on its customers. Their strategic importance will vary depending on:

(a) *customer bargaining power* in the industry as a whole;

(b) the *relationship of customers* to the firm. For example, much of the defence industry depends on the procurement decisions of a small number of government officials.

The *degree of dependence or reliance* can be analysed according to these criteria.

(a) *Disruption.* Can the stakeholder disrupt the organisation's plans or operations (eg a bank withdrawing overdraft facilities)?

(b) *Replacement.* Can the firm replace the relationship (eg find another bank)?

(c) *Uncertainty.* Does the stakeholder cause uncertainty in the firm's plans? A firm with healthy positive cash flows and large cash balances need not worry about its bank's attitude to a fixed asset investment. A firm which has to borrow money might be concerned about the bank's attitude.

In this model, measuring organisational effectiveness depends on identifying:

(a) the key stakeholders

(b) the degree of dependence

(c) the goals of each stakeholder group

(d) potential conflicts between them

(e) the organisation's ability to satisfy key stakeholder groups

2.9 The competing values approach

The *competing values* approach suggests that organisational goals and performance indicators are defined by top and middle managers. However, different groups of managers have different sets of priorities. These can be modelled on two dimensions.

(a) *Organisational focus*

- *External.* This group of managers are focused on the environment and the organisation's well-being within it.

- *Internal.* Managers with an internal focus are concerned with internal issues such as efficiency or employee well-being.

(b) *Organisation structure*

- *Stability.* Managers who favour stability prefer an ordered environment, with top-down control, as in a bureaucracy, or any organisation run according to classical or scientific management principles.

- *Flexibility.*

The key issue is that different groups of managers are concerned about different things. For example, the marketing manager will have the external, customer focus, whereas a production manager will have an internal focus. In some organisations, marketing managers have more power than production managers. In others, the reverse is true.

In practice, an organisation contains features of *all* approaches in different degrees. Employees cannot be ignored, even if managers are more concerned with customers. Much depends on the *values* of the senior executives and key decision-makers in the organisation. Currently, many managers are emphasising flexibility and responsiveness.

3 PERFORMANCE MEASURES

3.1 Quantitative and qualitative performance measures

It is possible to distinguish between *quantitative* information, which is capable of being expressed in numbers, and *qualitative* information, which can only be expressed in numerical terms with difficulty.

An example of a quantitative performance measure is 'You have been late for work *twice* this week and it's only Tuesday!' An example of a qualitative performance measure is 'My bed is *very* comfortable'.

The first measure is likely to find its way into a staff appraisal report. The second would feature in a bed manufacturer's customer satisfaction survey. Both are indicators of whether their subjects are doing as good a job as they are required to do.

Qualitative measures are by nature subjective and judgmental but this does not mean that they are not valuable. They are especially valuable when they are derived from several different sources because then they can be expressed in a mixture of quantitative and qualitative terms which is more meaningful overall: 'seven out of ten customers think our beds are very comfortable' is a *quantitative* measure of customer satisfaction as well as a *qualitative* measure of the perceived performance of the beds. (But it does not mean that only 70% of the total beds produced are comfortable, nor that each bed is 70% comfortable and 30% uncomfortable: 'very' is the measure of comfort.)

3.2 Financial performance measures

Financial measures (or *monetary* measures) are very familiar to you if you read the business pages of a quality newspaper. Here are some examples, accompanied by comments from a single page of the *Financial Times*.

(a) *Profit* is the commonest measure of all. Profit maximisation is usually cited as the main objective of most business organisations: 'ICI increased pre-tax profits to £233m'; 'General Motors ... yesterday reported better-than-expected first-quarter net income of $513 (£333m) ... Earnings improved $680m from the first quarter of last year when GM lost $167m.'

(b) *Revenue*: 'the US businesses contributed £113.9m of total group turnover of £409m'.

(c) *Costs*: 'Sterling's fall benefited pre-tax profits by about £50m while savings from the cost-cutting programme instituted...[last year]...were running at around £100m a quarter'; 'The group interest charge rose from £48m to £61m'.

(d) *Share price*: 'The group's shares rose 31p to 1278p despite the market's fall'.

(e) *Cash flow:* 'Cash flow was also continuing to improve, with cash and marketable securities totalling $8.4bn on March 31, up from $8bn at December 31'.

The important point to note here is that the monetary amounts stated are only given meaning in relation to something else. Profits are higher than last year's; revenue for one part of the business is so much compared with the total for the group; costs are at a lower level, in keeping with a planned reduction and in the light of changing economic conditions; share price is relative to the market; cashflow has improved compared with last quarter's.

We can generalise the above and give a list of yardsticks against which financial results are usually placed so as to become measures.

- Budgeted sales, costs and profits

- Standards in a standard costing system

- The trend over time (last year/this year, say)

- The results of other parts of the business

- The results of other businesses

- The economy in general

- Future potential (for example, the performance of a new business may be judged in terms of nearness to breaking even).

3.3 Non-monetary measures

The term non-monetary (or more commonly 'non-financial') needs care. It means *either* 'quantitative (but not in money quantities)' *or* 'qualitative', and we suggest that you use these more precise terms.

Quantitative non-monetary measures are either expressed in units other than money, such as units of product, hours or weight, or in a relative form such as percentages, ratios and indices.

Ratios – are a useful way of measuring performance for a number of reasons.

(a) It is easier to look at changes over time by comparing ratios in one time period with the corresponding ratios for periods in the past.

(b) Ratios are often easier to understand than absolute measures of physical quantities or money values. For example, it is easier to understand that 'productivity in March was 94%' than 'there was an adverse labour efficiency variance in March of £3,600'.

(c) Ratios relate one item to another, and so help to put performance into context. For example the profit/sales ratio sets profit in the context of how much has been earned per £1 of sales, and so shows how wide or narrow profit margins are.

(d) Ratios can be used as targets. In particular, targets can be set for ROI, profit/sales, asset turnover, capacity fill and productivity. Managers will then take decisions that will enable them to achieve their targets.

(e) Ratios provide a way of summarising an organisation's results, and comparing them with similar organisations. For example:

   (i) the results of one investment centre or profit centre can be compared directly with the results of another by means of ratio analysis;

   (ii) the results of one company can be compared with the results of similar companies.

Percentages – a percentage expresses one number as a proportion of another and gives meaning to absolute numbers. Examples are as follows.

(a) *Market share.* A company may aim to achieve a 25% share of the total market for its product, and measure both its marketing department and the quality of the product against this.

(b) *Capacity levels* are usually measured in this way. 'Factory A is working at 20% below full capacity' is an example which indicates relative inefficiency.

(c) *Wastage* is sometimes expressed in percentage terms. 'Normal loss' may be 10%, a measure of *in*efficiency.

(d) *Staff turnover* is often measured in this way. In the catering industry for example, staff turnover is typically greater than 100%, and so a hotel with a lower percentage could take this as an indicator both of the experience of its staff and of how well it is treating them.

4 OPERATIONAL PERFORMANCE INDICATORS

4.1 Financial and non-financial indicators

In this section we are going to look mainly at performance measurement under conventional headings: sales, material, labour and overheads. These are financial terms and we shall be considering what you may think of as financial measures such as standard costs and variances.

You will by now appreciate that financial measures do not convey the full picture of a company's performance, especially in a modern manufacturing environment.

'In today's worldwide competitive environment companies are competing in terms of product quality, delivery, reliability, after-sales service and customer satisfaction. None of these variables is directly measured by the traditional responsibility accounting system, despite the fact that they represent the major goals of world-class manufacturing companies.'

Many companies are discovering the usefulness of quantitative and qualitative non-financial indicators (NFIs) such as the following.

(a) Quality
(b) Number of customer complaints and warranty claims
(c) Lead times
(d) Rework
(e) Delivery to time
(f) Non-productive hours
(g) System (machine) down time, and so on

Unlike traditional variance reports, measures such as these can be provided quickly for managers, per shift or on a daily or even hourly basis as required. They are likely to be easy to calculate, and easier for non-financial managers to understand and therefore to use effectively.

4.2 Performance measures for sales – a customer-focused culture

Traditionally sales performance is measured in terms of price and volume variances, and also perhaps a sales mix variance. Other possible measures include revenue targets and target market share. These are all highly valid measures and there is no reason to suppose that they will not remain the principal measures for sales. They may, of course, be analysed in some detail: by country, by region, by individual products, by salesperson and so on.

However, in organisations with a customer-focused culture the basic information 'Turnover is up by 14%' can be supplemented by a host of other indicators.

(a) *Customer rejects/returns: total sales.* This ratio helps to monitor customer satisfaction, providing a check on the efficiency of quality control procedures.

(b) *Deliveries late: deliveries on schedule.* This ratio can be applied both to sales made to customers and to receipts from suppliers. When applied to customers it provides an indication of the efficiency of production and production scheduling. The term 'cycle time' is used in this context: total cycle time is the length of time between receipt of an order and delivery of the product.

(c) *Flexibility* measures indicate how well able a company is to respond to customers' requirements, not only in terms of delivering the goods on time, but also in terms of speed of launching new products and changing old procedures to meet market needs.

(d) *Number of people served and speed of service,* in a shop or a bank for example. If it takes too long to reach the point of sale, future sales are liable to be lost.

(e) *Customer satisfaction.* You have probably filled in questionnaires in fast-food restaurants or on aeroplanes without realising that you were completing a customer attitude survey for input to the organisation's management information system. Horngren cites the 'Customer Satisfaction Target' used by Holiday Inns where information is measured by evaluating scores (A – F) on guest inspection cards and imposing a limit of 0.457 guest complaint letters per 1,000 room-nights sold.

(f) *Marketing* measures might include number of sales per enquiry, amount of new business brought in, share by sales territory of the organisation's total market share and so on.

(g) Customer profitability analysis

In certain circumstances a useful approach to performance evaluation may be the analysis of profitability by customer or customer group. Profitability can vary widely between different customers because various overhead costs are, to some extent, variable and 'customer-driven'. These overheads include:

- discounts;

- sales force (eg telesales are cheaper and more time-efficient than a field sales force);

- quality control (some customers demand higher quality);

- merchandising;

- distribution (full-pallet transactions are cheaper than breaking bulk);

- promotions;

- financing costs;

- enquiries.

The task of customer profitability analysis is to relate these variabilities in cost to individual customers or customer groups. Managers can use this information to check whether individual customers are actually profitable to sell to, and to assess whether profitability can be improved for any customer by switching effort from one type of overhead activity to another, or by reducing spending on some overhead activities.

Customer profitability analysis can provide valuable management accounting information.

(a) It helps a firm to identify unprofitable customers as well as unprofitable products.

(b) It draws attention to the *three* ways of improving profitability, both for individual customers and so for products in total. These are:

- productivity improvements to reduce product costs;

- higher sales volumes to customers, to increase total contribution;

- more efficient use of 'overhead' resources to improve customer profitability.

4.3 Performance measures for materials

Traditional measures are standard costs for materials, and price and particularly usage variances. Many traditional systems also analyse wastage, although as we have seen elsewhere, wastage is to some extent *encouraged* by systems that regard a certain level of loss as 'normal' and acceptable.

Other relevant measures include the following.

(a) *Stock turnover.* This is a traditional measure, but a particularly relevant one in a Just-in-Time production environment, where the aim is to minimise all stocks.

(b) *Physical qualities* of materials may be crucially important to the final product, and if so the performance of materials should be measured. They may have to demonstrate a certain degree of smoothness, hardness, pliability, or stickiness; they may have to be a consistent shade of a certain colour or a consistent smell. Do they retain their shape, or do some get misshapen in transit or during production?

4.4 Performance measures for people

Labour costs are traditionally reported by rate and efficiency variances against standards. Many other staff-related measures have already been mentioned such as sales per salesperson; almost any aspect of an organisation's performance can be measured in terms of the different individuals or groups who actually do the job.

Qualitative measures of labour performance concentrate on matters such as ability to communicate, interpersonal relationships with colleagues, customers' impressions ('so and so was extremely helpful/rude'), and levels of skills attained. Some matters are extremely difficult to measure, notably staff morale, but attempts can be made.

4.5 Performance measures for overheads

Apart from standards for variable overheads and efficiency variances, a variety of time-based measures are available. Here are just two examples.

(a) *Machine down time: total machine hours.* This ratio could be used to monitor machine availability and can provide a measure of machine usage and efficiency.

(b) *Value added time: production cycle time.* Value added time is the direct production time during which the product is being made and value is therefore being added. The production cycle time includes non-value-added times such as set-up time, downtime, idle time etc. The optimum ratio is 100%, but in practice this optimum will not be achieved. A high ratio will help a company to satisfy customer orders more quickly.

Overhead expenses may also be measurable in qualitative terms: is the light adequate? Is the office or factory warm enough? Does the general state of cleanliness detract from workers' performance?

4.6 The balanced scorecard

A technique which has been developed to integrate the various features of corporate success is the **balanced scorecard**, developed by Kaplan and Norton.

It can be defined as 'a set of measures that gives top managers a fast but comprehensive view of the business'. The balanced scorecard includes financial measures that tell the results of actions already taken and it complements these with operational measures on customer satisfaction, internal processes, and the organisation's innovation and improvement activities – operational measure that are the drivers of future financial performance.'

The reason for using such a system is that 'traditional financial accounting measures like return on investment and earnings per share can give misleading signals for continuous improvement and innovation – activities today's competitive environment demands'.

The balanced scorecard allows managers to look at the business from four important perspectives:

Financial perspective: reflecting how the business looks to shareholders and typically would include familiar measures such as asset turnover and earnings per share.

Customer perspective: how the business looks to customers, indicated by market share and customer satisfaction for example.

Internal business processes: pointing to what the organisation must excel at, response times and product quality for instance.

Innovation and learning: focusing on the ability to change and improve and will be reflected in employee attitudes and morale, organisational culture and so forth.

(a) **Financial perspective** – from the financial perspective, the question to be asked is: 'How do we appear to shareholders?' Financial performance indicators indicate 'whether the company's strategies, implementation, and execution are contributing to bottom line management.'

(b) **Customer perspective** – 'How do customers see us?' Given that many company mission statements identify customer satisfaction as a key corporate goal, the balanced scorecard translates this into specific measures. Customer concerns fall into four categories.

- *Time.* Lead time is the time it takes a firm to meet customer needs from receiving an order to delivering the product.

- *Quality.* Quality measures not only include defect levels – although these should be minimised by TQM – but accuracy in forecasting.

- *Performance* of the product. (How often does the photocopier break down?)

- *Service.* How long will it take a problem to be rectified? (If the photocopier breaks down, how long will it take the maintenance engineer to arrive?)

NOTES

(c) **Internal business perspective**

Findings from the customer's perspective need to be translated into the actions the firm must take to meet these expectations.

- The internal business perspective identifies the business processes that have the greatest impact on customer satisfaction, such as quality and employee skills.

- Companies should also attempt to identify and measure their distinctive competences and the critical technologies they need to ensure continued leadership. Which processes should they excel at?

- To achieve these goals, performance measures must relate to employee behaviour, to tie in the strategic direction with employee action.

- An information system is necessary to enable executives to measure performance. An *executive information system* enables managers to drill down into lower level information.

(d) **Innovation and learning perspective**. The question is 'Can we continue to improve and create value?' Whilst the customer and internal process perspectives identify the *current* parameters for competitive success, the company needs to learn and to innovate to satisfy *future* needs. This might be one of the hardest items to measure. Examples of measures might be these.

- How long does it take to develop new products?

- How quickly does the firm climb the experience curve to manufacture new products?

- What percentage of revenue comes from new products?

- How many suggestions are made by staff and are acted upon?

- What are staff attitudes? Some firms believe that employee motivation and successful communication are necessary for organisational learning.

- Depending on circumstances, the company can identify measures for training and long-term investment.

Continuous improvement measures might also be relevant here.

An example of how a balanced scorecard might appear is offered below.

Financial – How do we look to our shareholders?	**Process** – What must we excel at?
• Return on capital employed	• Hours with customer on new work
• Cash flow	• Tender success rate
• Project profitability	• Rework
• Profit forecast reliability	• Safety incident index
• Sales backlog	• Project performance index

Customer – How do our customers see us?	Innovation and Learning – Can we continue to improve and create value?
• Pricing index • Customer ranking survey • Customer satisfaction index • Market share	• Percent revenue from new projects • Rate of improvement index • Staff attitude survey • Number of employee suggestions • Revenue per employee

In each perspective, sets of measures are chosen that both provide the appropriate balance as well as capturing the cause and effect relations inherent in a coordinated strategy. For example if Return on capital employed (ROCE) was the prime financial measure, then to increase that indicator would require retention and loyalty of customers so customer loyalty would be measured as the cause of high ROCE. Perhaps for the customers, the key determinant of their loyalty might be on time delivery that would be the driver of customer loyalty. To achieve on time delivery, quality and cycle time would have to be improved, which in turn would require an increase in employee skills.

Activity 2	**(20 mins)**

Draw up a balanced scorecard for the organisation for which you work.

5 TYPES OF CHANGE

Organisational change can be initiated deliberately by managers, it can evolve slowly within a department, it can be imposed by specific changes in policy or procedures or it can arise through external pressures. The forces for change may come from:

- the environment external to the organisation
- changes in technology
- changes in structure
- changes in culture

5.1 Environmental change

Environmental change can affect the strategy, structure or culture of an organisation. It may affect a combination of them all. Environmental changes are sometimes dramatic, such as a sudden change in public opinion, but it is more frequently the case that changes are insidious and gradual. Organisations which communicate effectively with their environment are well placed to become aware of changes as they occur. Organisations that have become insular may take longer to pick up on such changes.

Pressure for change can come from a variety of sources – political, economic, social and technological.

Social pressures for change. There are many examples of changes brought about by social pressures for change.

EXAMPLES: CHANGE THROUGH SOCIAL PRESSURE

Green issues

Recent changes in the awareness of the public concerning the potential destruction of various parts of the flora or fauna of our planet have had an impact on many industries. In some of these both the products made and the production processes have had to be changed. For example, paper production may now be from sustainable forests, and canned tuna may be caught by methods that are dolphin friendly.

The National Health Service

The National Health Service has undergone major changes in terms of waiting times and clients' expectations of level of service. Whilst some of this change can be attributed to changes in government policy (political pressures), it is the pressure from the population that has increased the impetus for change.

Communication is important in enabling social pressure for change to grow and to have an effect. Effective communication within the organisations concerned is essential to enable these changes to occur. It is also the case that growth in worldwide communication has increased the social pressures themselves.

> ### Activity 3   (20 mins)
>
> Make a list of four products or industries which have been forced to change in the last ten years as a result of social pressures
>
> In each case, give the reason for the change and indicate in what direction the changes have been made.

Social and political pressures are often interrelated. Here we focus on the effects of political pressures emanating from outside the UK.

Political pressures for change. European directives have considerable effect on the way UK organisations are run, especially as many UK companies now have links outside this country. The integration process that is occurring between EU member states in respect of working conditions within organisations is forcing many established firms to rethink their staff management policies.

> ### Activity 4   (1 hour + research)
>
> In the 1990s the European Union issued a directive concerning works councils. Although the UK has not become party to the Maastricht Treaty from which this directive stems, the directive has had implications for UK firms. For the purpose of this activity, assume that the directive is equally valid in the UK as in other European countries.

> The directive instructs that all organisations over a specified size (based on number of employees) must set up works councils through which employees will be kept informed of anything affecting them (directly or indirectly) and at which employees can have their say over working conditions. The works councils will not deal with remuneration matters or other subjects covered by existing collective bargaining agreements.
>
> Write a short essay (500-1000 words) on how you think this directive changed the emphasis of communication within UK organisations.

For organisations to be successful in introducing these changes in a beneficial way, there must be effective communication between all those involved.

Economic pressures for change. External competition has always been a driving force behind changes in product design and innovation of new products. However, in the economic climate of the recent past, there has been even greater pressure on organisations to find ways to change and to adapt to fierce competition. One of the ways some organisations have achieved this is by the use of strategic alliances. One example is the alliance between Rover and Honda. This alliance was driven by two factors.

(a) The desire by Honda to move into the European market at a time when quotas for non-EU imports were in place.

(b) The declining ability of the UK car manufacturing industry in general, and Rover in particular, to compete in the market, and the necessity of improving competitiveness in order to survive.

The alliance of these two companies allowed them both to achieve their objectives. The continued success of the Rover/Honda alliance depended upon trust built from effective communications. Once these communications broke down, the alliance was doomed to failure.

FOR DISCUSSION

Discuss the following statement in groups.

Increasing competitive pressure will result in greater openness in communications between rivals. The eventual outcome will be such close alliance that each sector of the market will become an effective monopoly.

One of the greatest recent changes in the environment of organisations is in the area of technological advances. Technological changes have also had impacts on the strategy, structure and culture of organisations.

5.2   Technological change

Technology has had an impact on the whole strategy of organisations. The globalisation of organisations would have been impossible without present day means and methods of communications. Similarly, the concept of selling to a customer you never see would have remained a small niche market if technological innovation had not allowed television and internet shopping. The growing interest of the UK food retailing industry in the concept of home shopping is testament to the viability of such changes.

The use of IT-based data collection systems to determine where there are areas of waste has allowed organisations to realise their ambitions to cut costs. This represents a change in the values of the organisation and thus a change in its culture.

Improved communications technology has helped to improve partnership relationships with suppliers to such an extent that raw materials and components can now be delivered exactly when they are needed. This reduces the need for manufacturers to hold large stocks and thus saves money. This is one of the few areas when it is easy to quantify the benefits of highly developed and effective communications systems.

Activity 5 (15 mins)

How has improved communications technology facilitated the expansion of the global organisation? Make a list of the factors you consider to be important.

Activity 6 (45 mins)

Robert and Son is a small factory producing components for the electrical industry. Their system of production has for many years taken the form of a series of production lines, with each line producing a different sub-section of the finished component.

The development of new technology, which partly automates the production of the subsections, now means that it is possible to increase the production capacity. The old system required a large factory floor to house the production lines and a final assembly line where the components were put together and packaged. The new technology reduces the amount of space required, so that all operations can be housed in one building. The production manager has put forward two separate layout plans for the 'new look' plant as shown in Figures 2 and 3 overleaf. Figure 1 shows the existing layout.

Based on what you know about communications, draw up an advantages and disadvantages list for each of the three layouts. Make a final decision as to which layout to choose. Give reasons for your choice.

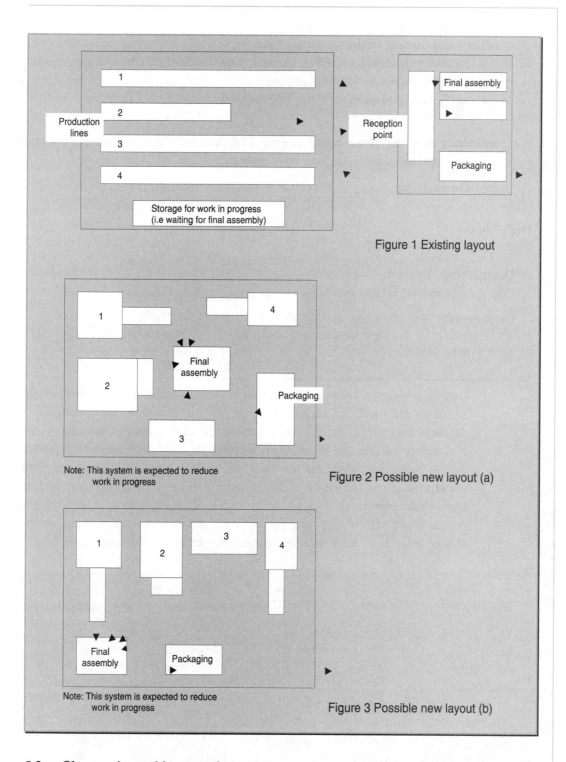

Figure 1 Existing layout

Note: This system is expected to reduce work in progress

Figure 2 Possible new layout (a)

Note: This system is expected to reduce work in progress

Figure 3 Possible new layout (b)

5.3 Changes in working practices

Changes in working practices can be a simple as introducing a new information collection form or as complex as transferring from a paper to computer-based system. However great or small the change, communication plays its part in its introduction and ultimate success.

Effective communication will:

(a) allay fear and suspicion about the motivation for the change;

(b) involve the workforce and gain their commitment;

(c) highlight potential problems;

(d)   ensure that the change is appropriate;

(e)   encourage feedback regarding unexpected side effects of the change;

(f)   monitor the results of the change;

(g)   facilitate the adaptation of the original plans.

We concentrate here on three contemporary and far reaching changes to working practices – downsizing, outsourcing and outworking.

(a)   **Downsizing**

Definitions

> **Downsizing:** the term used to describe the contraction of an organisation so that it concentrates on its core activities.
>
> **De-layering:** the removal of one or more layers of middle management, accompanied by the devolving of responsibility and authority further down the organisation structure.

It is important to note the distinction between downsizing and de-layering. Although they are quite separate concepts, both can have similar effects on the motivation of the workforce, although within differing groups of workers. If communications are poor, the workforce do not understand the strategy that is being followed and the only effect they see is redundancies. This undermines their security and their commitment to the organisation, and, in turn, their performance is likely to suffer. Effective communications can reduce these effects and actively generate a stronger commitment to the change from those workers who remain after the process is complete.

> **Activity 7**   **(25 mins)**
>
> You are the chief executive officer of a large group of companies. You have decided that, in order to consolidate your business with a view to expansion of your core activities in the future, you must sell off some of your smaller enterprises. Make a list of who you think you should communicate with in your environment to ensure that this will be a positive action for your company. Give reasons for communicating with each individual, group or organisation on your list.

(b)   **Outsourcing**

Definition

> **Outsourcing:** the term used to describe the process of employing outside contractors to perform tasks which, although not core activities of the organisation, were formerly performed in house. Examples can be cleaning, security, legal work and occupational health.

Outsourcing is often the result of downsizing and, as such, can encounter the same problems. Effective communication is especially important to ensure that the outsourced service is to the same standard, or better, and at lower cost than that previously provided in house. Partnership relationships are required with these service providers, and effective communications are the only way to achieve these. (There can be other influencing factors, but without effective communications they will not ensure success.) A great deal of outsourcing has been carried out in public sector organisations, especially as a result of compulsory competitive tendering.

Activity 8 (25 mins)

Consider the following

(a) A local hospital

(b) The council for your locality

Make a list of any activities associated with the above which are outsourced.

Make a second list of activities that you think could be outsourced.

(c) **Outworking**

Definition

Outworking: the term used to describe a formerly office-based function being carried out primarily from the home of the job holder. This form of working has become popular in the financial services and data processing industries. The effects on the organisation are (a) to reduce overheads on expensive office accommodation and (b) to access the pool of (predominantly) female labour who have child care commitments that prevent them from taking office-based work. Outworking should not be confused with outsourcing.

The advent of the home computer and advances in telecommunications have facilitated the move towards home working. Critics of this working method claim that it will be a passing phase, as the effects of lack of communication on the worker become more evident. However, advances in all technological communication methods mean that the only area that cannot be satisfied is that of face-to-face personal interaction with others. Whilst there is debate as to the importance of interpersonal communication on the performance of the worker, it is clear that it does play a part in job satisfaction and motivation. It remains to be seen whether communications can be so carefully structured and facilitated as to remove this problem.

5.4 Continual improvement culture

Continual improvement is a type of change that is focused on increasing the effectiveness and/or efficiency of an organisation to fulfil its policy and objectives. It is far more than a set of techniques and for many organisations it involves a radical change in attitudes. A continual improvement culture requires the commitment of the organisation's leaders. Clearly, there can be no continual improvement or business strategy without the direct commitment and involvement of the leadership. Organisations which practice continual improvement are truly focused on continually enhancing customer and stakeholder value. The defence of the status quo, and resistance to innovation, cannot be treated as normal management behaviour. A fear of reprisals for reporting problems has to be replaced by congratulating staff for identifying an opportunity to improve. People will be encouraged to share their knowledge and experience in the search for greater collective success.

We have already noted (in Chapter 10) its relationship with TQM and ISO 9000. Continual improvement is one aspect of a TQM philosophy. It can also be an element of an ISO 9000 quality system. ISO 9000:2000 will in fact include requirements for continual improvement. However, continual improvement is not limited to quality initiatives. It can apply to improvement in business strategy, business results, customer, and employee and supplier relationships.

It should focus on enablers such as leadership, communication, resources, organisation structure, people and processes and lead to better results such as price, cost, productivity, time to market, delivery, responsiveness, profit and customer and employee satisfaction.

There are three types of improvement.

1. Continuous improvement is gradual never-ending change

2. Continual improvement is incremental change

3. Breakthroughs are improvements but in one giant leap – a step change that tends to arise out of chance discoveries and could take years before being made

All managerial activity is either directed at control or improvement. Managers are either devoting their efforts at maintaining performance, preventing change or creating change, breakthrough or improvement. If businesses stand still they will lose their competitive edge, so improvements must be made to keep pace and stay in business.

Every system, programme or project should have provision for an improvement cycle. Therefore when an objective has been achieved, work should commence on identifying better ways of doing it.

There are ten steps to undertaking continual improvement.

1. Determine current performance

2. Establish a need to improve

3. Obtain commitment and define the improvement objective

4. Organise the diagnostic resources

5. Carry out research and analysis to discover the cause of current performance

6. Define and test solutions that will accomplish the improvement objective

7. Produce improvement plans which specify how and by whom the changes will be implemented

8. Identify and overcome any resistance to the change

9. Implement the change

10. Put in place controls to hold new levels of performance and repeat step one

6 MANAGING CHANGE

6.1 Framework for managing change

A framework for managing change will involve:

- continually looking for areas where improvements can be made
- assessing the benefits against any problems caused by the changes
- consulting with all concerned to get them to agree to the changes
- implementing your plans for change
- evaluating whether improvements have been achieved.

It can be helpful to take four steps to ensure that you manage change effectively:

1. Ensure that everyone understands why change is necessary. If people are dissatisfied with the way that things are, they will be more likely to welcome change.

2. Show those affected how things will be better in the future.

3. Ensure that they understand the plan.

4. Try to ensure that there can be no way of going back to previous ways of doing things: ensure that only new forms are available, that computer systems reflect the new way of working, and that procedures work smoother under the new system than the old.

6.2 Identifying opportunities for improvement

To keep up to date with developments in your sector you must make sure you monitor and evaluate your operations continuously – always looking for areas where improvements can be made, getting relevant, valid, reliable information from various sources on developments in materials, equipment, technology and processes and taking appropriate action. You can then use the information to identify opportunities for growth, improvements in procedures or improvements in quality, using your experience of previous improvements to help identify new ones. By identifying any obstacles to change, appropriate measures can be taken to alleviate any problems that may prevent improvements being made.

6.3 Assessing the benefits and problems of change

Make sure you have sufficient, reliable information on both current and proposed services, products and systems to allow you to make a reliable assessment using qualitative and quantitative techniques to assess the advantages and disadvantages of current and proposed services, products and systems.

The implications of introducing changes will be assessed – changes may affect cash flow, working practices and conditions, health and safety, team morale, supply and distribution networks and customer loyalty. You can look at how realistic previous assessments turned out to be and use these to modify your current assessment.

You will then be in a position to present your recommendations to the appropriate people – make your recommendations to senior managers or specialists in a way that helps them make a decision and in time to allow the decision to be put into effect. In the light of responses you get from senior managers and specialists you can make appropriate alterations to your recommendations.

6.4   Proposing the introduction of change

Presenting the plans on projected change involves communicating the changes, and the anticipated benefits for your organisation and for individuals, to team members, colleagues, senior managers and others in order to gain their support. Negotiations will be conducted in a spirit of goodwill to make sure you retain people's support and find mutually acceptable ways of settling any disputes. It may be necessary to make compromises to accommodate other priorities, but make sure these compromises are consistent with your organisation's strategy, objectives and practices.

You need to reach an agreement in line with your organisation's strategy and revise your implementation plans accordingly. It is advisable to keep complete and accurate records of negotiations and agreements so that they are available for others to refer to if necessary.

Where you could not secure the changes you anticipated, tell those affected in a positive manner; sometimes you are disappointed in not being able to obtain the changes you wanted due to other organisational priorities; explain the reasons for this in a way which maintains people's morale and motivation. Encourage all relevant people to understand and participate in the changes – explain the changes and their effects to people, and gain their support.

6.5   Planning change

When planning change it helps to get people involved – giving them the chance to comment on the proposed change and help in the planning. Clear and accurate information should be provided to let those affected know about the proposed change in time for them to prepare effectively. This will help you make the case for change and you can give a clear and convincing rationale for the change and support this with sound evidence.

You may identify potential obstacles to change so must find effective ways of avoiding or overcoming these obstacles before developing the plan for the change.

The plan will include:

- the rationale
- the aim and objectives of the change
- how it will be implemented
- who will be involved and their individual roles
- the resources required
- the time scale
- how the plan will be monitored
- how you will know that the change has been successful.

Once you have worked out the details of your plan, the next stage is to decide whether it will work and its impact. Often you may find that a plan may have unexpected effects, either positive or negative.

You may also find that when you cost the plan, and compare this against the benefits achieved, that the plan is simply not worth carrying out. This can be frustrating after the hard work of detailed planning, however it is much better to find this out now than when you have invested time, resources and personal standing in the success of the plan. Evaluating the plan now gives you the opportunity to either investigate other options that might be more successful, or to accept that no plan is needed or should be carried out.

6.6 Implementing change

You should now be in a position to present details of implementation plans to all concerned. Make sure that you brief everyone involved, or affected by, the changes on their role in the changes and the possible impact on their area. Encourage people to seek clarification, check on their understanding of their role and encourage them to ask questions.

A systematic approach should be established, for planning and implementing changes.

Step 1. **Determine** need or desire for change in a particular area.

Step 2. Prepare a tentative **plan**.

Brainstorming sessions a good idea, since alternatives for change should be considered (Lippitt 1981)

Step 3. Analyse **probable reactions** to the change.

Step 4. Make a **final decision** from the choice of alternative options.

Decision taken either by group problem-solving (participative) or by manager on his own (coercive)

Step 5. Establish a **timetable** for change.

- 'Coerced' changes can probably be implemented faster, without time for discussions.

- Speed of implementation that is achievable will depend on the likely reactions of the people affected (all in favour, half in favour, all against etc).

- Identify those in favour of the change, and perhaps set up a pilot programme involving them. Talk with the others who resist the change.

Step 6. **Communicate** the plan for change.

This is really a continuous process, beginning at Step 1 and going through to Step 7.

Step 7. **Implement** the change. **Review** the change.

Continuous evaluation and modifications

6.7 Plan evaluation

At this stage you can monitor the changes – checking to see that the changes have been implemented according to plan and that they result in the improvements anticipated. You can also modify the way you implement changes to cope with unforeseen problems.

It is important to keep clear and accurate records of your monitoring and evaluation activities and the results. They will help you to review the change process – the whole process of identifying, assessing, negotiating, agreeing, implementing and evaluating change; note ways of doing it better next time and make appropriate recommendations to senior managers, colleagues and specialists.

There are a number of ways in which you can evaluate your plan:

Cost/Benefit Analysis

This is probably one of the simplest ways of evaluating a plan. During the implementing process above you should have carried out an analysis of the costs involved with each activity within the plan. Simply add up these costs, and compare them with the expected benefits.

Cost/benefit analysis is a strategy evaluation technique often used in the public sector, where many of the costs and benefits of a project are intangible.

(a) The project and its overall objectives are defined.

(b) The costs and benefits are analysed in detail. It is not always easy to put a value on social costs. For example, a new road might result in excessive noise for local residents. They can be asked how much, in principle, they would be able and prepared to pay to move to a quieter dwelling. This gives a very rough estimate of the value of tranquillity.

(c) The net benefits for the project are estimated, if possible. A road might reduce journey times, and so save money. These are compared with costs, and the project is appraised by:

- discounted cash flow methods such as Net Present Value (NPV) and Internal Rate of Return (IRR);

- cost/benefit ratios.

PMI – 'Plus/Minus/Implications'

Once you have carried out a cost/benefit analysis, you may find it useful to mix its financial information with an assessment of the intangible or non-financial aspects of the decision. An effective way of doing this is with a PMI analysis. To use the technique, draw up a table with three columns headed Plus, Minus and Implications. Within the table write down all the positive points of following the course of action, all the negatives, and all the interesting implications and possible outcomes.

If the decision is still not obvious, you can then score the table to show the importance of individual items. The total score should show whether it is worth implementing the decision. A strongly positive score shows that an action should be taken, a strongly negative score that it should be avoided.

Force Field Analysis

Similar to PMI, force field analysis helps you to get a good overall view of all the forces for and against the change that you want to implement. This allows you to see where you can make adjustments that will make the plan more likely to succeed. By carrying out the analysis you can plan to strengthen the forces supporting a decision, and reduce the impact of opposition to it.

To carry out a force field analysis, follow these steps.

.

(a) List all forces for change in one column, and all forces against change in another column.

(b) Assign a score to each force, from 1 (weak) to 5 (strong).

(c) Draw a diagram showing the forces for and against change. Show the size of each force as a number next to it.

For example, imagine that you are a manager deciding whether to install new manufacturing equipment in your factory. You might draw up a force field analysis like the one in diagram below:

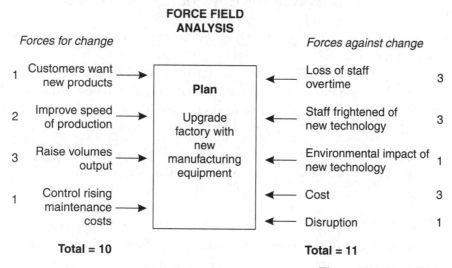

Figure 12.2 Force field analysis

Once you have carried out an analysis, you can decide whether your project is viable. In the example above, you might initially question whether it is worth going ahead with the plan.

Where you have already decided to carry out a project, Force Field analysis can help you to work out how to improve its probability of success. Here you have two choices:

- To reduce the strength of the forces opposing a project, or
- To increase the forces pushing a project

Often the most elegant solution is the first: just trying to force change through may cause its own problems. People can be unco-operative if change is forced on them.

If you had to implement the project in the example above, the analysis might suggest a number of changes to the initial plan:

- By training staff (increase cost by 1) you could eliminate fear of technology (reduce fear by 2)

- It would be useful to show staff that change is necessary for business survival (new force in favour, +2)

- Staff could be shown that new machines would introduce variety and interest to their jobs (new force, +1)

- You could raise wages to reflect new productivity (cost +1, loss of overtime, –2)

- Slightly different machines with filters to eliminate pollution could be installed (environmental impact, –1)

These changes would swing the balance from 11:10 (against the plan), to 8:13 (in favour of the plan).

Cash Flow Forecasts and Break Even Analysis

Where a decision has mainly financial implications, such as in business and marketing planning, preparation of a Cash Flow Forecast can be extremely useful. It allows you to assess the effect of time on costs and revenue, and it also helps in assessing the size of the greatest negative and positive cash flows associated with a plan, and provides the basis for accurate break-even analysis. When it is set up on a spreadsheet package, a good Cash Flow Forecast also functions as an extremely effective model of the plan, allowing the effect of variance in assumptions to be examined.

Risk Analysis & Contingency Planning

All of the above analyses broadly assume that the plan functions correctly. None of them assess the risks associated with carrying the plan out and the potential costs should those risks damage the plan. Risk management involves three stages.

(a) *Risk assessment* requires the identification and quantification of risks. They must then be categorised in terms of potential loss. The importance of some attempt to *quantify* potential loss in financial terms is that this is a measure against which the cost of safeguards can be assessed.

(b) *Risk minimisation*

- Selection of counter-measures. Insignificant risks may not justify the cost of setting up and operating controls.

- Implementation of counter-measures

- Draw up contingency plans (eg backup if counter-measures are ineffective)

Scenario analysis is a technique whereby descriptions of a number of possible loss-causing events are circulated to the relevant functional managers who assess which are the most probable. Security measures are taken against any events that are thought likely to result in loss.

(c) *Risk transfer (insurance)* It is impossible to eliminate all risk. Risks that cannot be covered by security measures should be insured against, so that at least the financial consequences are not too severe.

A contingency plan sets out what needs to be done to restore normality after something has gone wrong. The plan needs to provide for:

(a) standby procedures so that some operations can be performed while normal services are disrupted;

(b) recovery procedures once the cause of the problem has been addressed;

(c) the personnel management policies to ensure that (a) and (b) above are implemented properly.

6.8 Wider implications of change

It is important to ensure that you do not rely exclusively on the results of numeric analysis as the basis of your plan evaluation. Many factors that are important to the evaluation of your plans cannot practically be quantified. These factors include:

(a) **Ethical considerations** – this should include an assessment of likely changes in public ethics over the lifetime of the plan.

(b) **Shareholders** – how will the shareholders, owners, or trustees of the organisation view the plan?

(c) **Members/employees** – what effects will the plan have on the organisation's members or employees? Should these effects stand in the way of improving efficiency?

(d) **Customers** – will the plan change the way in which your organisation's customers view it? Will this affect their likelihood of reordering?

(e) **Suppliers** – how will your plan affect relations with suppliers?

(f) **Public relations** – will the plan have a positive or negative effect on your organisations relations with the public, press and politicians?

(g) **Environment** – will it enhance or damage the environment?

Any analysis of your plan must be tempered by common sense. It is much better to change a beautifully crafted plan that analysis shows will not work than deal with the consequences after a failed attempt at implementation.

7 BUSINESS PROCESS RE-ENGINEERING

Definition

> **Business process re-engineering:** 'the fundamental rethinking and radical redesign of business processes to achieve dramatic improvements in critical contemporary measures of performance, such as cost, quality, service and speed.' (Hammer and Champy)

Investment in technology can be wasted if the fundamental processes of the business remain unaltered. In other words, the apparatus might change and even the techniques, but not the organisation behind it. This might be a reason why, despite all the investments in information technology, the productivity of office workers has not matched the dramatic improvements in manufacturing productivity of recent years.

Business process re-engineering (BPR), is also known as process innovation and core process re-design.

7.1 Development

The concept of BPR was originally formulated in 1990 by Michael Hammer in a seminal article for the *Harvard Business Review*. He contended that: 'In a time of rapidly changing technologies and ever-shorter product life cycles, product development often proceeds at a glacial pace. In an age of the customer, order fulfilment has high error rates and customer enquiries go unanswered for weeks. In a period when asset utilisation is critical, inventory levels exceed many months of demand. The usual methods of boosting performance – process rationalisation and automation – have not yielded the dramatic improvements companies need. In particular, heavy investments in information technology have delivered disappointing results – largely because companies tend to use technology to mechanise old ways of doing business. They leave the existing processes intact and use computers simply to speed them up.'

7.2 How it works

The chief BPR tool is a clean sheet of paper. Re-engineers start from the future and work backwards. They are unconstrained by existing methods, people or departments. In effect, they ask, 'If we were a new company, how would we run the place?' Re-engineers ask two fundamental questions about everything that happens in organisations: 'Why?' and 'What if?'. Only when they receive satisfactory answers to these questions do they then begin to explore better ways of doing things. The critical questions they then ask are:

- What is done?
- How is it done?
- Where is it done?
- When is it done?
- Who does it?

- Why do it?
- Why do it that way?
- Why do it there?
- Why do it then?
- Why that person?

7.3 Processes

By process which Hammer and Champy mean 'a collection of activities that takes one or more kinds of input and creates an output that is of value to the customer.' For example, order fulfilment is a process that takes an order as its input and results in the delivery of the ordered goods. Part of this process is the manufacture of the goods, but under BPR the aim of manufacturing is not merely to **make** the goods. Manufacturing should aim to **deliver** the goods that were **ordered**, and any aspect of the manufacturing process that hinders this aim should be re-engineered. The first question to ask might be 'Do they need to be manufactured at all?'

A **re-engineered process** has certain characteristics.

- Often several jobs are combined into one.

- Workers make decisions.

- The steps in the process are performed in a natural order.

- The same process has different versions depending on the market, or the inputs etc.

- Work is performed where it makes most sense.

- Checks and controls are reduced.

- Reconciliation is minimised.

- A case manager provides a single point of contact.

- The advantages of centralised and decentralised operations are combined.

7.4 Principles of BPR

Hammer presents seven principles for BPR.

(a) Processes should be designed to achieve a **desired outcome** rather than focusing on **existing tasks**.

(b) Personnel who **use the output from a process should perform the process**. For example, a company could set up a database of approved suppliers; this would allow personnel who actually require supplies to order them themselves, perhaps using on-line technology, thereby eliminating the need for a separate purchasing function.

(c) Information processing should be included in the work which produces the information. This **eliminates the differentiation between information gathering and information processing**.

(d) **Geographically dispersed resources should be treated as if they are centralised**. This allows the benefits of centralisation to be obtained, for example, economies of scale through central negotiation of supply contracts, without losing the benefits of decentralisation, such as flexibility and responsiveness.

(e) **Parallel activities should be linked rather than integrated**. This would involve, for example, co-ordination between teams working on different aspects of a single process.

(f) **'Doers' should be allowed to be self-managing**. The traditional distinction between workers and managers can be abolished: decision aids such as expert systems can be provided where they are required.

(g) **Information should be captured once, at source**. Electronic distribution of information makes this possible.

7.5 Characteristics

Because of its strong links to overall strategic planning, BPR cannot be planned meticulously and accomplished in small and cautious steps.

- It tends to be an **all-or-nothing proposition**, often with an uncertain result. It is therefore a **high risk** undertaking and not worth attempting unless there is a pressing need to rethink what the organisation is doing overall or in a major area.

- Many organisations trying BPR do not achieve good results because they **fail to think it through**, do not engage **hearts and minds** sufficiently, act on **bad advice or cannot override established departmental/functional power groups** which have a vested interest in the *status quo*, or in incremental change rather than radical revolution.

- Business process re-engineering has received a great deal of attention in the UK over the last couple of years and there are now concerns that it has been promoted to such an extent that it has become misunderstood. According to a recent independent study of 100 European companies, the Cobra report, BPR has become allied in managers minds with narrow targets such as reductions in staff numbers and cost-cutting measures.

- Champy suggests that management itself should be re-engineered. Managers are not, according to Champy, used to thinking in systems terms, so, instead of looking at the whole picture (which might affect their own jobs), they tend to seize on individual aspects of the organisation, such as re-engineering of processes.

CASE EXAMPLES

Barr & Stroud, a Glasgow engineering firm, had to introduce radical changes in response to new business conditions and demands. The changes implemented through BPR included a focus on core competencies, a reduction in management layers from nine to four, and the establishment of multi-disciplinary teams with a brief to strip time and waste out of the organisation.

Many of the more celebrated BPR case histories come from the USA. *Ford* re-engineered its whole accounts payable process, covering the separate functions of purchasing, material control and accounts, with the result that the have introduced a system of invoiceless processing and have reduced their accounts payable staff headcount by 75%. *Union Carbide* eliminated $400 million of fixed costs in just three years; *Mutual Benefit Life* reduced its turnround of customer applications from 5-25 days to 2-5 days and jettisoned 100 field office positions. *IBM Credit* cut their time for preparing quotes from 7 days to one. *Bell Atlantic* reduced its delivery times from 15 days to just one.

NOTES

Chapter roundup

- By monitoring the system, managers can identify deviations from the plan and introduce alternatives.

- Performance measurement is highly fashionable because of market pressures and because information technology makes it possible.

- Measurement can take place at various levels ranging from external comparisons to reports on individual activities. Profitability is often a key objective but other 'success factors' are also critical.

- An imaginative approach to performance measurement is becoming a necessity in the modern business environment, and many businesses now recognise the need to supplement traditional financial measures like standard costs with other indicators.

- The balanced scorecard allows managers to look at the business from four important perspectives: financial, customer, internal business and innovation and learning.

- Continual improvement is a type of change that is focused on increasing the effectiveness and/or efficiency of an organisation to fulfil its policy and objectives.

- By identifying any obstacles to change, appropriate measures can be taken to alleviate any problems that may prevent improvements being made.

- Management sometimes must introduce change to the organisation. A variety of forces will promote or resist the change. Force field analysis is a way of identifying these factors.

- Where you have already decided to carry out a project, force field analysis can help you to work out how to improve its probability of success. Here you have two choices:

  - To reduce the strength of the forces opposing a project, or
  - To increase the forces pushing a project

- A contingency plan sets out what needs to be done to restore normality after something has gone wrong.

- BPR is the fundamental rethinking and radical redesign of business processes to achieve dramatic improvements in critical contemporary measures of performance such as cost, quality, service and speed. The aim of the process is to reorganise business around processes rather than around functions or departments. BPR reorganises workflows, eliminating waste.

Quick quiz

1   What general issues govern the approach to performance evaluation?

2   What is productivity?

3   List seven financial yardsticks.

4   What are the advantages of ratios in performance measurement?

5   List five traditional measures of sales performance.

6   List the four perspectives of the balanced scorecard.

7   What external factors can give rise to the need for change?

8   Define 'outworking'.

9   List the differences between outworking and outsourcing

10   What is a scenario analysis?

Answers to quick quiz

1   • What is evaluated?

   • Who decides what constitutes 'performance' and whether it is good or bad?

   • Does an organisation have a single unambiguous purpose which can be translated into specific goals?

   • Are the measures that will be used quantitative and qualitative? (See para 2)

2   This is the quantity of the product or service produced in relation to the resources put in, for example so many units produced per hour, or per employee, or per tonne of material. It defines how efficiently resources are being used. (2.1)

3   (a)   Budgeted sales, costs and profits
    (b)   Standards in a standard costing system
    (c)   The trend over time (last year/this year, say)
    (d)   The results of other parts of the business
    (e)   The results of other businesses
    (f)   The economy in general
    (g)   Future potential (3.2)

4   Ratios are a useful way of measuring performance.

   • it is easier to look at changes over time by comparing ratios in one time period with the corresponding ratios for periods in the past.

   • it is easier to understand than absolute measures or physical quantities or money values.

   • can be used as targets.

   • can provide a way of summarising an organisation's results, and comparing them with similar organisations. (3.3)

5   Customer rejects/returns, Deliveries late: deliveries on schedule, Flexibility, Number of people served and speed of service, Number of people served and speed of service. (4.2)

6   The balanced scorecard allows managers to look at the business from four important perspectives: customer; financial; internal business; and innovation and learning. (4.6)

7   Any change in the environment of the organisation – political, social, technological or economic. (5)

8   Outworking is when a job is done from home rather than from an office. (5.3)

9   Outworkers are (a) employed directly by the organisation, (b) may perform core activities and are usually individuals. Outsourcing is the practice of contracting out work; such work is usually peripheral or a support activity and is often contracted out to another organisation. (5.3)

10   Scenario analysis is a technique whereby descriptions of a number of possible loss-causing events are circulated to the relevant functional managers who assess which are the most probable. (6.7)

Answers to activities

1   Invoices per employee per week: 2,500 (activity)

        Invoices per employee per day: 2,500/5 =500 (activity)

        Staff cost per invoice: £0.14 (cost/profitability)

        Invoices per hour: 2,500/7 = 71.4 (productivity)

        Cost of idle time: £32 + £4.94 = £36.94 (cost/profitability)

        You may have thought of other measures and probably have slight rounding differences.

2   This will depend on your own organisation.

3   Here are four products/industries that have been forced to change in the fast ten years. You may have thought of other equally valid examples.

        (a) The major players in the retail food industry have had to change the focus of their product ranges as a result of pressure from consumers to reduce prices. They have done this by introducing 'own brand' labels.

        (b) Building societies have found that they cannot compete against the range of services provided by high street banks, and have thus changed from the traditional mutual society.

        (c) Lucozade became less fashionable as concern regarding the sugar contents of food and drink grew. The target market of the drink changed away from the wider consumer towards the young and sporting fraternity.

        (d) Fewer fur coats are now sold in the UK as a result of social pressures regarding animal cruelty.

4   Your essay should include the following points.

        (a) Works councils could raise the awareness of management regarding the importance of communication with their workforce.

        (b) The workforce could begin to feel that their views are important.

(c) Adversarial relationships between workers and management should begin to be broken down.

(d) Greater commitment towards the organisation may result.

(e) No change may occur in attitudes.

(f) Works councils may be 'window dressing' with no substance or commitment from management.

(g) Adversarial relationships could be created between works council and unions.

(h) Union power could be further decreased.

5   Technology has facilitated the expansion of the global organisation by:

(a) speeding up the communication process;
(b) increasing the ability to co-ordinate activities;
(c) facilitating data collection to raise awareness of customers' needs;
(d) allowing standardisation of response;
(e) enabling decision making to be better informed.

6   The relative merits of the two possible new layouts are as follows.

	Advantages	Disadvantages
Present layout (Figure 1)	Logical sequence to production Production lines do not interfere with each other	Cost of larger premises Communication difficult between production lines Isolation from final assembly stops workers from feeling part of the final product Communication difficult along assembly lines
Layout (a) (Figure 2)	Savings on space Less work-in-progress Central final assembly gives all workers a feeling of completing the product Communication between all workers easier 'Shorter' and 'fatter' production lines make communication and team building easier	All workers will be affected by disruption to one area, even if only mentally
Layout (b) (Figure 3)		Lines 3 and 4 are more isolated from final assembly Communication between lines 3 and 4 and final assembly more difficult

Based on these factors, your choice of layout should be layout (a) (Figure 2.) The reasons are that communications are easier, work-in-progress is reduced, team spirit is facilitated and there is a lower cost from the size of the facilities.

7 You could have included the following in your list.

   (a) Trade unions – Effective communications with unions can avoid misinterpretation of your actions and the militant reaction that often accompanies such misunderstandings.

   (b) Shareholders, including the money markets in general if a Plc is involved - you may need the agreement of shareholders in order to carry out your strategy. Failure to have your reasons for change understood may result in the strategy being seen as a symptom of financial difficulties. The effects of this on share prices would be detrimental to the proposed sale.

   (c) The media – much of the potential misinterpretation can be averted if regular accurate information is communicated to the media.

   Note. The activity asked for communication with your environment, so your answer should not include internal communication, such as with the workforce.

8 Your lists could have included the following:

   (a) Hospital: security, cleaning services, laundry, sterilisation of instruments, non-emergency transport, portering.

   (b) Council: gardening, refuse collection, street lighting, house and footpath maintenance, snow clearance and road gritting, library services, the running of any leisure facility.

MANAGING COMMUNICATIONS, KNOWLEDGE AND INFORMATION

Chapter 13 :
INFORMATION AND KNOWLEDGE NEEDS

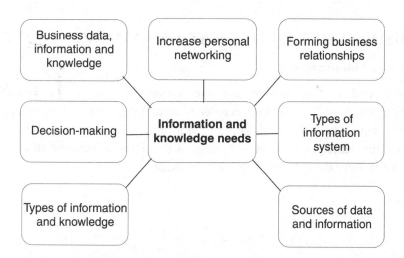

Introduction

In this chapter we introduce the concept of an information system. We start with the information requirements of the modern organisation and consider various aspects of the use of information systems to address corporate needs and make decisions.

The information system of an organisation is essential to allow the day-to-day activities to take place. Management and staff need information for decision-making. We describe the different types of decisions that are made within organisations and demonstrate how these dictate the type of information and information system required by the decision-makers.

Relationships are critical to success; so often, knowing the right person to ask is as valuable as knowing the answer yourself, if not more so. Being well connected is the ultimate source of personal effectiveness and advantage. And it is now a case of shared success – with what you can give being as important as what you get out of your networking success.

Personal networking provides a straightforward approach to building and working within networks. It delivers a practical guide to creating the kind of network that you need, and becoming a natural and effective networked communicator.

Your objectives

After completing this chapter you should be able to:

(a) Assess information and knowledge needs internally and externally to improve decision-making and taking

(b) Identify the range of decisions to be taken

(c) Review information and knowledge needed to ensure effective decision taking

(d) Assess internal and external sources of information and understanding

(e) Identify personnel from stakeholders and other areas of expertise

(f) Make contact with those identified and develop business relationships

(g) Involve those identified in decision making as appropriate

1 BUSINESS DATA, INFORMATION AND KNOWLEDGE

1.1 Data and information

Information and communication are the means by which the activities of an organisation are co-ordinated. Information is sometimes said to be processed data. In normal everyday speech, the term 'data' and 'information' are often used interchangeably, as meaning the same thing. However, there are stricter definitions of the two terms, which make an important distinction between them.

Definitions

Data is the complete range of raw facts and measurements eg, letters, numbers, symbols, sounds and/or images, relating to events in the organisation or its environment. Data is collected and then processed into information.

Information is data that has been processed ie, organised and arranged into a form that people can understand and use.

1.2 Knowledge

Knowledge is commonly distinguished from data and information. Data represents observations or facts out of context, and therefore not directly meaningful. Information results from placing data within some meaningful context, often in the form of a message.

Definitions

Knowledge is information within people's minds.

Knowledge management describes the process of collecting, storing and using the knowledge held within an organisation.

Knowledge Work Systems (KWS) are information systems that facilitate the creation and integration of new knowledge into an organisation.

Knowledge workers are people whose jobs consist primarily of creating new information and knowledge. They are often members of a profession such as doctors, engineers, authors, lawyers and scientists.

We have come to believe that knowledge is based on the meaningfully organised accumulation of information (messages) through experience, communication or inference. General knowledge is broad, often publicly available, and independent of particular events. Specific knowledge, in contrast, is context-specific. Knowledge can be viewed both as a *thing* to be stored and manipulated and as a *process* of simultaneously knowing and acting – that is, applying expertise. As a practical matter, organisations need to manage knowledge both as object *and* process.

1.3 Range of purposes

An organisation is composed of resources – people, materials, machines and money – and the activities it carries out to achieve its objectives. Information is necessary to convert these resources for use in the organisation's activities.

Often when data is processed the information is communicated immediately to the person who wishes to use it. If it is kept for later use it must be stored and then retrieved when required.

Organisations require information for a range of purposes. These can be categorised as follows.

- **Planning** – requires knowledge of the available resources, possible time scales and the likely outcome under alternative scenarios. Information is required that helps decision-making and how to implement decisions taken.

- **Monitoring and controlling** – once a plan is implemented, its actual performance must be controlled. Information is required to assess whether activities are proceeding as planned or whether there is some unexpected deviation from plan. It may consequently be necessary to take some form of corrective action.

- **Recording transactions** – information about each transaction or event is required. Reasons include:

  (a) Documentation of transactions can be used as evidence in a case of dispute

  (b) There may be a legal requirement to record transactions eg, for accounting and audit purposes

  (c) Operational information can be built up, allowing control action to be taken.

- **Performance measurement** – comparisons against budget or plan can be made. This may involve the collection of information on e.g., costs, revenues, volumes, time scales and profitability.

- **Decision-making** – just as decision-making can be analysed into three levels, so information necessary to make decisions within an organisation can be analysed in the same way.

NOTES

2 DECISION-MAKING

2.1 Decisions

A decision is a choice whereby a person forms a conclusion about a situation. Within an organisation, it is the point at which plans, policies and objectives are translated into concrete actions. Planning leads to decisions guided by company policy and objectives and implies the selection from alternative objectives, policies, procedures and programmes. The purpose of decision-making is to direct human behaviour towards a future goal. If there were no alternatives, there would be no need for a decision.

2.2 Types of decisions

Drucker distinguishes between 'tactical' and 'strategic' decisions. We will be examining these in the next section. Other classifications include a division between organisational and personal decisions:

(a) **Organisational decisions** are those made in the role of an official of the company and reflect company policy.

(b) **Personal decisions** refer to those made by a manager as an individual and cannot be delegated.

Another classification is between *basic* and *routine* decisions:

(a) **Basic decisions** are long-range in scope, e.g. the location of factory in a Development Area, or deciding what product to make. Wrong decisions on these matters can be costly.

(b) **Routine decisions** are made repetitively and need little thought.

Decisions may be classified as:

(a) **structured** – they are programmed eg, stock re-ordering

(b) **unstructured** – 'fuzzy' complex problems with no clear cut solutions eg, introducing a new product line

(c) **semi-structured** – some standard procedures are applied, but also some individual judgement eg, production scheduling

A final, similar, classification by H A Simon distinguishes between programmed and unprogrammed decisions:

(a) Automatic decision-making in a computerised control system means that the elements of some (or all) of the factors needed to make the decision have been programmed into the computer, thus allowing the computer to choose 'automatically'. Programmed decisions are routine and repetitive eg, reordering stock, and have procedures set up to deal with them. Risks involved are not high and they therefore can be more easily delegated.

(b) Any decision that requires management judgement will be a non-programmed decision, so that automatic decision-making would not be appropriate. Unprogrammed decisions are new and non-repetitive, where risks involved are high and they cannot easily be assessed in numerical terms. There are many courses of action possible and decisions made will mean a greater expenditure of resources.

2.3 Management decision-making

Within an organisation, different types of decision are taken at different levels. Senior management will be involved in decisions that affect the business as a whole; decisions that affect only one aspect of the business will be delegated to lower levels of management. As we explained in Chapter 8 planning and control decisions are taken at the strategic, tactical and operational levels of organisational activity.

Strategic planning is a process of deciding on objectives of the organisation, on changes in these objectives, on the resources used to attain these objectives and on the policies that are to govern the acquisition, use and disposition of these resources.

Strategic decision-making:

- is medium- to long-term
- involves high levels of uncertainty and risk (the future is unpredictable)
- involves situations that may not recur
- deals with complex issues

Tactical planning/control (also called management control) means ensuring that resources are obtained and used effectively and efficiently in the accomplishment of the organisation's objectives.

- Efficiency means that resources input to a process produce the optimum (maximum) amount of outputs.

- Effectiveness means that the resources are used to achieve the desired ends.

Tactical decisions are routine, usually contain few alternatives and relate to the economic use of resources.

Operational control ensures that specific tasks are carried out effectively and efficiently. It focuses on individual tasks, and is carried out within the strictly defined guidelines issued by strategic planning and tactical control decisions. Managers at this level decide what needs to be done from day to day and task to task

It may help to clarify the above to consider it in terms of how well **structured** the problem situation is. Examples of unstructured and structured decisions at the different levels of management are shown in the following table.

Decision level	Structured	Semi-structured	Unstructured
Operational	Stock control procedures	Selection of new supplier	Hiring supervisor
Tactical	Selection of products to discount	Allocation of budget	Expanding into a new design
Strategic	Major investment decisions	Entry to new market; new product line	Reorganisation of whole company

2.4 Decision making and decision-taking

Poulton (1982) distinguishes decision making from decision taking. Decision makers are all those who have an interest (active or passive) in a particular decision. Decision takers are 'those charged with reaching decisions and making specific commitments'. Decision-making, therefore, comprises the whole process (e.g., problem identification, analysis, discussion, negotiation) that involves decision-makers up to the point at which the issue is decided. Decision taking is the function or activity of the responsible authority, as in the case of a manager deciding on a course of action.

Identifying stakeholders and examining their respective interests in the issue – in other words stakeholder analysis – is an essential part of the overall decision-making process. Satisfying stakeholders is a complicated task that begins with including their involvement in the process. The steps involved in stakeholder analysis are shown in the following diagram.

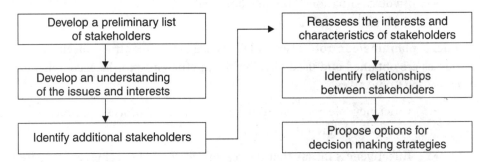

Stakeholders may have multiple and overlapping interests, so not all stakeholders will be obvious at first. To accommodate this situation we might ask the initial group of stakeholders to identify other groups who they think should be included. After we include additional stakeholders, we can reassess their interests. This will give an idea of how different groups interact and what role they will play in decision-making.

Customers and final consumers will want the product or service to live up to expectations and expect a quick response to any complaints and replacements for any defective items. For example, if an organisation wishes to follow a strategy that increases the quality of a product at the same time as increasing the price, there may be problems with both existing and potential new customers. Existing customers may not be willing to pay more for the product, while new customers are not attracted to a product that they still view as being of low quality.

Suppliers are generally concerned with being paid promptly for goods and services delivered and receiving regular repayments of any capital provided (e.g. banks). For example, if an organisation wishes to follow a strategy that improves working capital management by paying suppliers late, existing suppliers may decide to stop supplying the organisation, leading to the increased cost of finding new suppliers.

A robust communications and stakeholder involvement programme includes communicating with and engaging stakeholders before making final decisions on significant changes so that you can determine stakeholder response and incorporate stakeholder considerations into planning. Stakeholders have a wealth of relevant experience and knowledge to contribute. Feedback is also considered when making decisions and stakeholders are told how the input was used. If stakeholders feel that their suggestions are ignored or dismissed, the process can be undermined and future communications can be unproductive.

Stakeholder involvement is most effective when it encourages stakeholders to describe their underlying concerns and issues. Establishing a common ground can facilitate the resolution of difficult issues.

Below are listed some of the advantages that come with collaboration in decision making.

- All parties have a chance to be part of the solution

- Businesses gain public approval and trust for dealing with their less powerful adversaries in a reasonable manner and considering alternative options

- Problems are handled more effectively when information is available to all parties

- Long-term working relationships are formed, which aid in the resolution of future problems/issues

---

Activity 2   **(5 mins)**

Consider management decisions as they affect work in a purchase ledger department. Classify each of the following three decisions according to the three types of decision identified above.

(a) The payment cycle will be extended by five days to improve cash flow.

(b) On receipt of an invoice, the purchase order form and goods received note relating to the order must be checked to the invoice. Specified details must be checked, and the invoice stamped to show that the checks have been carried out fully and satisfactorily.

(c) Suppliers who supply over £50,000 worth of goods per annum will be asked to join the company's EDI network.

---

3 THE TYPES OF INFORMATION AND KNOWLEDGE

3.1 Types of management information required

A manager needs to know, basically, three things:

1. What are his resources? (Finance, stocks of raw materials, spare machine capacity, labour availability, the balance of expenditure remaining for a certain budget, target date for completion of a job.)

2.   At what rate are his resources being consumed? (How fast is his labour force working, how quickly are his raw materials being used up, how quickly are other expenses being incurred how quickly is available finance being consumed?)

3.   How well are the resources being used? (How well are his objectives being met?)

A manager uses resources in the light of information given to him. The board of a company decides how much of available funds should be allocated to any particular activity, and the same problem faces the manager of a factory or department, or even a foreman (ie which machines should he use, which men should he put on certain jobs etc). Having used information to decide what should be done, a manager then needs feedback (or else control information from the environment) to decide how well it is being done.

3.2   Levels of information

Information *within* an organisation (as distinct from information provided by an organisation to external users, such as shareholders, the general public, pressure groups, competitors, suppliers, customers etc) can be analysed into three levels.

(a)   **Strategic information** – is mainly used by directors and senior managers to plan the organisation's overall objectives and strategy and to measure whether these are being achieved. The characteristics of strategic information are as follows:

- derived from internal and external sources
- summarised at a high level
- relevant to the long term
- deals with whole organisation
- often prepared on an *ad hoc* basis

Such information includes overall profitability, the profitability of different segments of the business, future market prospects, the availability and cost of raising new funds, total cash needs, total manning levels and capital equipment needs etc. Much of this information must come from environmental sources, although internally generated information will always be used. Strategic information will be used for the management decision-making previously described as *strategic planning*.

(b)   **Tactical information** – is used by managers at all levels, but mainly at the middle level for tactical planning and management control activities, such as pricing, purchasing, distribution and stocking. These managers require information and instructions from the strategic level of management and information from the operational level of management. Tactical management are able to adopt a management-by-exception approach, needing only summary reports from subordinates. As a rule, information is forwarded by tactical to strategic management, in summary report format, to assist decision-making.

A large proportion of the information used at this level will be generated from within the organisation (ie as feedback) and is likely to have an accounting emphasis. Tactical information is usually prepared regularly – perhaps weekly, or monthly (whereas strategic information is communicated irregularly) and it is used for the decision-making previously referred to as 'management control'. The information would also be in a summarised form, but detailed enough to allow for tactical planning of resources and manpower.

Such information includes productivity measurements (output per man hour or per machine hour) budgetary control or variance analysis reports, and cash flow forecasts, manning levels and profit results within a particular department of the organisation, stock levels and labour turnover statistics within a department, short-term purchasing requirements etc.

(c) **Operational information** is used by 'front-line' managers such as foremen or head clerks to ensure that specific tasks are planned and carried out properly within a factory or office etc. In the payroll office, for example, operational information relating to day-rate labour will include the hours worked each week by each employee, his rate of pay per hour, details of his deductions, and for the purpose of wages analysis, details of the time each man spent on individual jobs during the week. In this example, the information is required weekly, but more urgent operational information, such as the amount of raw materials being input to a production process, may be required daily, hourly, or in the case of automated production, second by second. Other examples of operational information include:

- listings of debtors and creditors
- listings of customer complaints
- machine output statistics
- delivery schedules, etc

Operational information relates to the level of decision-making previously referred to as operational control. The characteristics are as follows:

- derived entirely from internal sources
- highly detailed
- relates to immediate/short term
- task-specific
- prepared frequently, routinely

The amount of detail provided in information is likely to vary with the purpose for which it is needed, and operational information is likely to go into much more detail than tactical information, which in turn will be more detailed than strategic information.

What is information to one level of management or one department may be raw data (needing to be processed) to another. A foreman, for example, will check the output of each of the men or machines within the area of his responsibility but his superior may only wish to know about the performance of the section as a whole.

Activity 3 (5 mins)

What type of information are the following examples?

- listings of debtors and creditors
- payroll details
- raw materials requirements and usage
- listings of customer complaints
- machine output statistics
- delivery schedules, etc

3.3 Information in different sectors

Organisations can be divided into four sectors – manufacturing, service and public sectors and not for profit/charities.

Manufacturing – commercial organisations are influenced by the need to make and monitor profit. Examples of information requirements at the strategic, tactical and operational level include:

- strategic level include future demand estimates, new product development plans and competitor analysis
- tactical level include information on variance analysis and stock turnover
- operational level include material and labour used and stock levels

Service – increased customer and results orientation for all sectors lead to similar information requirements with activities measured in similar ways. Examples of information requirements at the strategic, tactical and operational level include:

- strategic level include forecast sales growth, profitability and market share
- tactical level include resource use and customer satisfaction rating
- operational level include customer waiting time and individual customer feedback.

Public – information requirements depend on objectives chosen. Information may compare actual performance with standards, targets, indices and activities over time as trends. Examples include:

- strategic level – population demographics and expected government policy
- tactical level – average class sizes and percent of reported crime solved
- operational level – staff timesheets and student daily attendance records

Not for profit/charities – performance is usually assessed in terms of economy, efficiency and effectiveness. A key measure for charities is the amount spent on the cause rather than on administration or advertising. Examples of information requirements at the

- **strategic level** include the activities of other charities and public attitudes
- **tactical level** include percent of revenue spent on admin and average donation
- **operational level** include donations, banking documentation and households approached and collected from.

3.4 Past, present and future information

Another useful categorisation of information is between past, present and future information.

(a) *Past information.* This is *record keeping*, the storing of information about what has been done or what has happened in the past. This historical information will subsequently be used again at some time in the future. Much past information is information of a transaction processing nature.

- In the case of a company, there is a statutory requirement of the Companies Act for a company to maintain proper accounting records of past transactions.

- Records that are kept of past transactions might be used to generate further routine operations at a later date. For example, a record of a sale to a customer, and details of the invoice sent out, will be kept, and if the customer does not pay on time, a statement or reminder will be sent out, chasing payment.

(b) *Present information.* This is information about what is happening now, so that decisions can be taken about what, if anything, to do next. Present information is therefore most readily associated with *control information,* which is the feedback in a management information system.

(c) *Future information.* This is *forecasting information* about what is expected to happen in the future. It is most readily associated with planning decisions, possibly for a budget, but also for longer-term strategic information. Future information is also likely to include a significant proportion of environmental information, because the future of any organisation will not be secure unless it continues to adapt to changes in its environment.

Past information should be the most accurate of the three categories, and future information the least accurate of the three. The degree of accuracy expected from information should therefore vary according to whether it is past, present or future.

3.5 Quantitative and qualitative information

Quantitative information consists of measurable information – hard facts, numbers, weights and measures, percentages, statistics, estimates, specifications.

Methods of gathering this type of information focus on numbers and frequencies rather than on meaning and experience. Examples of quantitative methods of gathering information include surveys, laboratory experiments, questionnaires, psychometric tests and consulting and analysing records. They provide information that is easy to analyse statistically and fairly reliable.

Qualitative information is difficult (or even impossible) to measure in quantitative terms. It consists of facts about opinions, preferences and perceptions. Examples of qualitative information may be employee morale, motivation, customer loyalty, goodwill or attitudes of the general public.

Methods of gathering this type of information were originally developed in the social sciences to enable researchers to study social and cultural phenomena. Examples of qualitative methods are: case study research, participant observation, interviews and questionnaires, analysing documents and texts produced by others, and the information gatherer's own impressions and reactions.

To assist management decision-making, an attempt may be made to provide a quantitative evaluation of qualitative 'phenomena'. For example, accountants may try to evaluate:

- goodwill for the purpose of agreeing the sale price of a business;

- the cost of poor employee morale, in terms of labour turnover (and the cost of training, etc or low productivity);

- the cost of poor motivation, in terms of lost output and profits.

In certain areas progress has been made in *creating* quantitative information, ie in measuring qualitative information. For example:

- *uncertainty,* which inevitably surrounds any decision, can be measured in terms of sensitivity analysis, probability distributions or a 'margin of safety';

- *attitudes* can be measured according to their strength.' For example, a scale of 0-6 might be used to quantify the motivation of employees, with 0 representing poor morale and 6 high morale.

Quantitative information is preferred to qualitative information because it can be built into mathematical models and formulae. Mathematical computer models (such as financial planning models, operation research models and simulation models) that are used extensively by management require some method of quantifying 'variables' in the situation under review.

Qualitative information depends on the experience and judgement of a manager, whereas quantitative information simply depends on the accuracy of the measured data and the assumptions used in a mathematical formula or a computer model.

When qualitative factors will influence a decision, the manager should either:

- use his or her *judgement* in reaching the final decision, trying to balance quantitative and qualitative factors;

- use a technique, if one is available in the organisation, for converting qualitative values into quantitative values, and making the decision on the strength of estimated quantified costs and benefits. This is the principle underlying so-called 'cost-benefit analysis' or CBA, which is sometimes used by a government to make decisions (eg about road-building) by putting money values to *social* costs and benefits.

3.6 Tacit and explicit knowledge

There are two types of knowledge:

- **Explicit** – this is formal and standardised and can be easily shared and communicated. For example, knowing the basics of how to drive a car is explicit. You could explain it to someone else.

- **Tacit** – is personal and rooted in a specific context. Once you learn how to drive a car and have been doing it for some time, you develop certain techniques (and bad habits) and driving becomes second nature. However, this phase is more difficult to articulate.

When we speak of 'knowledge', most people assume that this refers to knowledge that is written in books and discussed in classrooms and conference rooms, a form referred to as 'explicit' knowledge. But knowledge is in:

- Presentations, reports, journals
- Patents and licences
- Databases, software
- Libraries, archives and catalogues
- Manuals, policy documents and memos
- Individual ability, memory, know-how and experience

- Teams, communities, groups and networks
- Meetings, training materials and management information.

Tacit knowledge is subconsciously understood and applied, developed from direct experience and action, and usually shared through highly interactive conversation, story-telling and shared experience. It is tacit knowledge that enables us to recognise the correct 'feel' eg, the right way to hold and use a hammer or a kitchen knife. It is tacit knowledge that is critical to producing a desired outcome when the task is complex. Hence, we recognise that tacit knowledge is involved in a task when we are reduced to trying to explain the 'feel' of something, particularly the way that it feels when it feels 'right'. In many cases, this feel eludes all of our attempts to describe it, and so success in tacit domains comes, ultimately, to a matter of doing it.

Explicit knowledge, in contrast, is easier to identify, can be stored as a written procedure or as a process in a computer system and is re-usable in a consistent and repeatable manner – for decision- making and/or exercising judgement. Therefore, although more abstract, it can be more easily codified, documented, transferred or shared.

Knowledge *about* something is called **declarative knowledge**. A shared, explicit understanding of concepts, categories, and descriptors lays the foundation for effective communication and knowledge sharing in organisations. Knowledge of *how* something occurs or is performed is called **procedural knowledge**. Shared explicit procedural knowledge lays a foundation for efficiently co-ordinated action in organisations. Knowledge *why* something occurs is called **causal knowledge**. Shared explicit causal knowledge, often in the form of organisational stories, enables organisations to co-ordinate strategy for achieving goals or outcomes.

Using these two types of knowledge – tacit and explicit, we can see that there could be four ways of acquiring or creating knowledge:

(a) Explicit to explicit – is the standard way that management information is created and amalgamated eg, monthly sales figures.

(b) Tacit to tacit – the data capture skills eg, keying in the invoice details from different suppliers, can be transferred to a trainee whilst sitting next to someone who has been doing it for a while.

(c) Tacit to explicit – this is where the knowledge can be articulated to another person and understanding takes place.

(d) Explicit to tacit – individuals take in the knowledge and it becomes a part of their expertise ie, internalised. Experience and learning enables individuals to make connections between events and to increase their knowledge and understanding of certain situations.

To ensure than the interchanges between individual tacit and shared explicit knowledge take place, tacit knowledge has to be tapped and articulated.

4 THE SOURCES OF DATA AND INFORMATION

4.1 Internal and external data

Internal information is necessary for all management levels, in every function in the organisation. It will relate to activities or transactions performed within the organisation, such as administrative tasks, the production of products and services, or the sale of those products. Often these activities generate costs and revenues and so a lot of the internal data collected will be quantitative.

The internal sources include:

- The **accounting ledgers**, which are used for predicting future events eg, budgeting and analysing the stock control system eg, speed of delivery, quality of supplies

- **Personnel and payroll systems** are used for costing a project and ascertaining the availability and rate of pay of levels of staff and also for keeping detailed records of time spent on various activities

- **Production departments** are a source of information on machine capacity, fuel consumption, work in progress, maintenance requirements and the movement of people

- **Marketing departments** provide information on opinions and buying habits of customers and potential customers.

Gathering data/information from inside the organisation involves:

- establishing a system for collecting or measuring data eg, measuring output, sales, costs, cash receipts and payments, asset purchases, stock turnover etc. In other words, there must be established procedures for what data is collected -how frequently, by whom and by what method – and how it is processed and filed and communicated;

- relying to some extent on the informal communication lines between managers and staff eg, word of mouth and conversations at meetings.

Knowing the source helps the user to compensate for systematic bias. If for example the managing director of an organisation receives a sales forecast from the sales director and another from the finance director, knowledge of the two individuals involved will allow adjustments to be made to the data. In doing so, the managing director would probably consider their personal biases and those placed upon them by their positions within the firm.

External information emanates from official and unofficial sources, the latter having to be assessed for reliability. It concerns such matters as official areas (tax, regulations, etc), the economy, suppliers and customers.

There are a wide range of sources including the government, consultants, newspapers and magazines, the Internet and other electronic sources such as Reuters.

4.2   Formal and informal information

Obtaining information from outside the organisation may be formal or informal. Formal sources include statements from the organisation's officials, published documents and company advertising. Informal sources include rumours, meetings with suppliers or customers and reports compiled for personal use.

Informal gathering of data/information from outside sources goes on all the time, consciously or unconsciously, because we all learn what is going on in the world from newspapers, television or radio.

The formal collection of data from outside sources may be entrusted to particular individuals within the organisation. For example:

- a tax specialist within the organisation will be expected to gather facts about changes in tax law and determine whether it will affect the organisation;

- a responsible person will need to obtain data about any new legislation relating to health and safety at work or employment regulations. For example, companies registering under the Data Protection Act should appoint a data registration officer with the responsibility for finding out the procedure for keeping personal details on computer;

- research and development work needs someone to co-ordinate data on similar work being done by other companies;

- market research is undertaken by specialists to find out about the opinions and buying attitudes of potential customers.

Activity 4	(5 mins)

What sort of data is collected by staff in a purchasing department?

4.3 Primary and secondary data

Organisations frequently need to make use of data obtained outside the organisation itself. For example:

- a survey may have been commissioned to determine customer satisfaction with service arrangements in a large store;

- when determining the number of potential customers for a product, data on the size and the characteristics of a section of the population is useful;

- if a company is to remain successful and competitive, details on the activities (sales, reinvestment, etc.) of its competitors are necessary.

This data will fall into the categories of primary and secondary data.

Primary data – any data that is used solely for the purpose for which it was collected is termed primary data. Some problems can only be solved by collecting primary data and this involves carrying out an inquiry or survey.

Businesses are particularly interested in *market research* surveys. The ideal survey will cover 100 per cent of the items to be surveyed. In practice, a *sample* of this total may be used. The Census of Population in the UK is based on 100 per cent of the population. Other surveys must decide upon a suitable size of the sample to be used and also upon the methods of collection of the information.

Secondary data – is data that is taken from some other source is called secondary data. An important distinction is made here since information collected for one purpose by a company and then, at a later date, used again for another purpose would no longer be primary data. Internal sources of secondary information include:

Accounts department	• Procedures manual • Management accounts – balance sheets • Financial data
Sales and marketing department	• Sales reports by region • Sales by customer and product • Competitor intelligence • Market prospects and reports • Customer complaints • Marketing research reports
Production and operations	• Operations data • Efficiency and capacity detail • Process flow charts • Input prices
Human resources	• Number of employees • Training programmes • Staff turnover details • Details of pay

External sources of secondary information include:

- Books

- Journals and articles

- The Internet is an excellent source of secondary data if used with care. For example, you can use a search engine that will bring up websites of interest. Your Internet service provider may also refer you to magazines and on-line newspapers.

- Government agencies are good sources of economic and other statistical information. Most countries have an agency that provides national statistics.

- Regulatory bodies and industry associations – there are many quasi-government and other public sector bodies that can provide data on particular industry sectors.

Statistics compiled from secondary data are termed secondary statistics. For example, the government publish tables of unemployment figures (these are secondary data): when this *data* is used for calculations, they are termed secondary *statistics*.

Government statistics are widely available and are produced to measure the effects of their policies and the effect external factors have on them. Trends can also be noted and this assists future planning. The Central Statistical Office co-ordinates the government's statistical services.

Activity 5   **(15 mins)**

Give an explanation of primary and secondary information with a quantitative and qualitative example for each.

4.4 Official and unofficial secondary sources

We can loosely divide secondary data sources into two categories: *official* and *unofficial*. Official secondary data comprise all information collected, processed and made available by legally constituted organisations, primarily by government departments and statutory authorities. Official statistics abound in all developed societies. Governments collect data about their operations, usually for valid reasons, such as for efficient long- and short-term planning.

Unofficial secondary data comprises all other forms of secondary information sources. Examples include:

- **Private research results** – many organisations and private consultants generate potentially useful secondary data. The major problem is access: the commercial confidentiality that is usually thought to attach to such material means that they are rarely available for public scrutiny.

- **Research reports, research papers, textbooks** – academic research and publication forms a major body of secondary data sources.

- **Opinion polls** – the process of collecting public opinion via surveys and questionnaires has been developed to a high level of sophistication in recent decades, and the results of such surveys (if made public) can be an important contextual source.

- **Market research** – like opinion polls, most market research is carried out by private organisations on behalf of specific clients. Depending on the requirements of the client, the results of such surveys may or may not be made public. The commercial orientation of most surveys tends to limit their general applicability.

- **On-line databases** – may range from bibliographic information to census data.

- **Anecdote/hearsay** – making due allowance for exaggeration and hyperbole, we will sometimes find that we need to use anecdotal information. Such sources are obviously best used as 'backup' to other, perhaps more reliable, sources; but there will be occasions when they represent the only source open to us.

4.5 Customers and other stakeholders

Very often the most valuable knowledge that an organisation has is in the heads of its people, and those of its stakeholders, especially customers. However, 'people walk', so forward looking companies continually to seek ways of locking it in to their organisation. The two complementary approaches are:

- Converting it to a more explicit form – in documents, processes, databases etc. This is often referred to as 'decanting the human capital into the structural capital of an organisation'. It is also called the 'Western tendency' since it is the main emphasis of many European and US knowledge programmes.

- Enhancing tacit knowledge flow through better human interaction, such that the knowledge is diffused around the organisation and not held in the heads of a few. In Japan various 'socialisation' activities support this kind of knowledge flow that by its very nature also sparks the generation of new ideas and knowledge. Add some basic elements of good human resource management, including a stimulating environment, personal development plans, motivation and suitable reward and recognition systems (such as knowledge sharing awards and stock options), then there is less chance of the best knowledge workers wanting to leave.

5 TYPES OF INFORMATION SYSTEM

A modern organisation requires a wide range of systems to hold, process and analyse information. So far we have talked a good deal about the need to gather and analyse *information* without stopping to consider how that information can be organised. An overall strategy or any of its component strategies could be undermined by an inadequate or non-existent information strategy. We will now examine the various Information Technology (IT) systems that deliver information to different levels in the organisation.

5.1 Transaction processing systems

Transaction processing systems (TPS), or data processing systems, are the lowest level in an organisation's use of information systems, serving the operational level and supporting highly structured decisions.

They are used for routine tasks in which data items or transactions must be processed so that operations can continue. Handling sales orders, purchase orders, payroll items and stock records are typical examples.

Transactions processing systems provide the raw material that is often used more extensively by management information systems, databases or decision support systems. In other words:

(a) Transaction processing systems might be used to produce management information, such as reports on cumulative sales figures to date, total amounts owed to suppliers or owed by debtors and so on.

(b) However, the main purpose of transaction processing systems is as an integral part of day-to-day operations.

5.2 Knowledge Work Systems (KWS)

Knowledge work means creating new knowledge or information by research, experimentation and investigation into existing trends and products. There are many different areas of knowledge work, and each one can be supported by its own collection of knowledge work systems (KWS).

Examples are shown in the following table.

Areas of knowledge work	Examples
Knowledge distribution	Office automation systems (OAS)
Knowledge sharing	Group collaboration systems eg, Groupware, Intranets and Extranets
Knowledge creation	Knowledge work systems • Computer Aided Design (CAD) • Virtual Reality
Knowledge capture and codification	Artificial intelligence systems Expert systems

Groupware

Groupware is a term used to describe software that provides functions for the use of collaborative work groups.

Typically, groups using groupware are small project-oriented teams that have important tasks and tight deadlines Perhaps the best-known groupware product at present is Lotus Notes.

Features might include the following.

(a)   A scheduler allowing users to keep track of their schedule and plan meetings with others.

(b)   An address book.

(c)   'To do' lists.

(d)   A journal, used to record interactions with important contacts, record items (such as e-mail messages) and files that are significant to the user, and record activities of all types and track them all without having to remember where each one was saved.

(e)   A jotter for jotting down notes as quick reminders of questions, ideas, and so on.

(f)   File sharing and distribution utilities.

There are clearly advantages in having information such as this available from the desktop at the touch of a button, rather than relying on scraps of paper, address books, and corporate telephone directories. However, it is when groupware is used to share information with colleagues that it comes into its own. Here are some of the features that may be found.

(a)   Messaging, comprising an e-mail in-box which is used to send and receive messages from the office, home, or the road and routing facilities, enabling users to send a message to a single person, send it sequentially to a number of people (who may add to it or comment on it before passing it on), or sending it to everyone at once.

(b)   Access to an information database, and customisable 'views' of the information held on it, which can be used to standardise the way information is viewed in a workgroup.

(c)   Group scheduling, to keep track of colleagues' itineraries. Microsoft Exchange Server, for instance, offers a 'Meeting Wizard' which can consult the diaries of everyone needed to attend a meeting and automatically work out when they will be available, which venues are free, and what resources are required.

(d)   Public folders. These collect, organise, and share files with others on the team or across the organisation.

5.3   Management information system (MIS)

A management information system (MIS) converts data from internal and external sources into information, and communicates that information in an appropriate form to

managers at all levels. This enables them to make timely and effective decisions for planning, directing and controlling the activities for which they are responsible.

An MIS provides regular formal information gleaned from normal commercial data. For example, an MIS might provide information on the following.

(a) **Product information**. On-line, categorised information at the fingertips.

(b) **Sales ledger**. Information will be immediately available relating to customer turnover and payment records. Trend analysis will identify customers whose business is growing or has fallen away.

(c) **Marketing**. As enquiries and sales arise, the MIS can summarise this data to assist in forward planning. Customer satisfaction can be measured by post-purchase surveys and questionnaires. This information will be processed by the MIS and summarised for use by the management, both in report and graphical form.

(d) **Supplier information**. Information such as amount spent with each supplier, and reliability indicators (cancellations by the supplier, satisfaction of the customers) will prove useful when negotiating and making strategic decisions.

(e) **Accounting**. Because the transactions of the company are on the system, information will be available to trial balance stage of the nominal ledger. This will be available to the accounts department with comparable budget and prior year information, through drill down enquiry and also available in report formats.

(f) **Modelling**. Key data from the above areas can be combined into reports, possibly via spreadsheets, the create strategic and 'what if' models.

While a *management information system* (MIS) may not, in principle, be able to provide all the information used by management, it should however be sufficiently flexible to enable management to incorporate unpredictable, informal or unstructured information into decision-making processes. For example, many decisions are made with the help of financial models such as spreadsheets, so that the effect of new situations can be estimated easily.

Operational level MIS

Operational decisions are essentially small-scale and programmed, and operational information is often highly formal and quantitative. Many operational decisions can be incorporated into routine computer processing, for example allowing a sale subject to a credit limit. Most MIS are used at operational level for processing transactions, updating files and so forth.

Tactical level MIS

A variety of systems can be used at tactical level, and there may be a greater reliance on:

(a) exception reporting;
(b) informal systems;
(c) investigation and analysis of data acquired at operational level;
(d) externally generated data.

The MIS at tactical level will interact with the same systems as that at operational level, and in fact tactical information may be generated in the same processing operation as operational level information. For example, tactical level information comparing actual costs incurred to budget can be produced by a system in which those costs are recorded. Functional MIS at tactical level are typically related to other functional MIS. Information from the sales MIS will affect the financial accounting system, for example.

Strategic level MIS

At strategic level the information system is likely to be informal, in the sense that it is not possible always to quantify or program strategic information, and much of the information might come from environmental sources. The MIS will provide summary level data from transactions processing. Human judgement is used more often at this level, as many strategic decisions cannot be programmed.

Highly sophisticated *enterprise resource planning* systems such as SAP are used at this level. They may in fact be essential, depending on the complexity of the undertaking and the degree of competition. *Executive information systems* (EIS) are discussed below.

EXAMPLE: THE FINANCE SUBSYSTEM

In a finance subsystem, the operational level would deal with cash receipts and payments, bank reconciliations and so forth. The tactical level would deal with cash flow forecasts and working capital management. Strategic level financial issues are likely to be integrated with the organisation's commercial strategy, but may relate to the most appropriate source of finance.

5.4 Decision support systems

Decision support systems (DSS) have the potential to integrate data, methods, models, and other tools, within a framework that explicitly addresses the process of making decisions. They are used by management to help in making decisions on issues that are unstructured, with high levels of uncertainty about the true nature of the problem, the various responses which management could undertake or the likely impact of those actions.

- Decision support systems are intended to provide a wide range of alternative information gathering and analytical tools with a major emphasis upon flexibility and user-friendliness.

- DSS include a range of systems, from fairly simple information models based on spreadsheets to expert systems.

Decision support systems *do not make decisions*. The objective is to allow the manager to consider a number of alternatives and evaluate them under a variety of potential conditions. A key element in the usefulness of these systems is their ability to function interactively.

5.5 Executive information system (EIS)

An EIS – sometimes called Executive Support Systems (ESS) – is an information system for senior managers, which gives them easy access to key internal and external data. It is designed to be easy to use. An EIS is likely to have the following features.

(a) Provision of summary-level data captured from the organisation's main systems.

(b) A facility that allows the executive to 'drill-down' from summaries of information to supporting detail.

(c) Data manipulation facilities like comparison with budget or prior year data and trend analysis.

(d) Graphics, for user-friendly presentation of data.

(e) A template system. This will mean that the same type of data, for example sales figures, is presented in the same format, irrespective of changes in the volume of information required.

An EIS summarises and tracks strategically critical information from the MIS and DSS and includes data from external sources eg, competitors, legislation and databases such as Reuters. The basic design philosophy of EIS is that they should be easy to use as they may be consulted during a meeting.

The significance of an EIS is that it is not only a tool for analysis, but also a tool for *interrogating* data.

5.6 Expert systems

Expert systems are computer programs that allow users to benefit from expert knowledge, information advice. An expert system holds a large amount of specialised data, for example on legal, engineering or medical information, or tax matters. The user keys in the known facts, perhaps responding to cues from the system if more data are required and the system then provides an expert solution or advice.

(a) A user without a legal background can obtain guidance on the law without having to consult a solicitor – for example, on property purchase matters, or for company law guidance.

(b) A user without much tax knowledge could consult an expert system for taxation for guidance on particular matters of tax.

(c) As a non-business example, doctors can use an expert medical system to arrive at a diagnosis.

(d) Banks use expert systems to assess the credit-worthiness of loan applicants.

Activity 6	**(5 mins)**

What do you consider is the importance of some of the management information systems discussed above for organisation hierarchy?

6 INCREASE PERSONAL NETWORKING

6.1 Personal networking

Personal networking begins with family and friends, co-workers and people we socialise with and then everyone they know. Through these connections, trustworthy relationships are developed that generate information, referrals, advice, support, energy, and much more. However, the true value of personal networking is found through the movement beyond one's immediate network and exploiting other people's networks, perhaps far removed from one's own.

Networking is based on good will between people. Research that has been done into networking practice in business shows that in terms of good will from other people:

- 10% of the people you know will actively help you, no matter what

- 80% are not particularly interested in your personal development, but would be willing to help if you take the initiative

- 10% of the people who know you don't like you and will actively hold you back or try to stop you.

Networking is one of the most beneficial ways for people to help each other develop their ideas and professional careers. It increases the opportunity for people to talk with each other and share ideas, information and resources and can serve to enhance both the personal and professional aspects of one's life. Building a strong network requires the effort of everyone involved.

Effective networking requires people to:

- effectively communicate
- keep pace with developments and trends in their fields
- be prepared and willing to share information
- keep in touch with others
- nurture friendships and relationships
- listen carefully and show interest in what others are saying
- exhibit curiosity – ask questions
- continue to learn – it is a life-long process
- stay visible – attend industry and community functions

Once you begin to make contacts you may find that you will become part of a group, meeting together to develop mutual interests or communicating via email and the Internet.

6.2 Stakeholders and useful contacts

Networking means staying in touch with organisations and key individuals who can affect your work or help you to achieve your goals. It can serve many purposes and help you to:

1. Build alliances that will strengthen your work
2. Stay in touch with developments in your area of work
3. Get access to information that will help your work
4. Influence other organisations to take up and support your issues
5. Influence individual decision-makers

NOTES

Networking is about connections. In the business sense, it is nothing more complicated than working out ways to get other people to send you business, based on word of mouth or direct introduction.

Definitions

> **Networking** – is consciously developing contacts in an effort to increase the number of referrals you get for your business.
>
> **Contacts** are people with whom you have developed, or are developing, an ongoing relationship of trust and mutual respect, specifically regarding business matters.
>
> **Referrals** are the recommendation of a business to a person who knows the prospective customer well enough to have developed some level of established trust.

Stakeholders can be internal (top management, line managers, functional heads, service and support workers) or external (regulators, environmental and legal entities, the general public). They are clients, project managers and teams, contractors and subcontractors, distributors and suppliers, and everyone else with a stake in an outcome.

This is how to arrange to meet with others who may be interested:

- Send e-mails to appropriate discussion lists.
- To colleagues.
- To people in other organisations.
- Ask if anyone is interested in meeting locally.
- On which dates they would like to meet.
- Will they forward the e-mail to anyone who might be interested?

Networking organisations can provide access to members in a wide range of fields and give you the ability to pursue additional areas of business.

Because of the careful selection of people accepted for membership, you will find that you never want for access to the best services and products available in your area. If a member cannot supply what you need, there is a high degree of likelihood that he or she can refer you to someone who can supply just about any thing you need.

6.3 Internal and external contacts

Networking includes interaction with outsiders and socialising/politicking inside and outside the organisation; routine communication activities include exchanging information and handling paperwork; traditional management activities consist of planning, decision making and controlling; and human resource management includes motivating/reinforcing, disciplining/ punishing, managing conflict, staffing and training/developing.

Networking in the sense that we use the word here is a deliberate, planned process. It involves the open exchange of leads and introductions. It is a completely honest process.

Where and how you network can add value professionally and personally:

PROFESSIONAL EDUCATION

- Professional contacts
- Information sources
- Friends

Potentially you can network anywhere – socially, locally, at work, nationally and within the profession. Virtual networks are also important via promotional literature, e-mail discussion lists and newsletters

Network at work – reception staff are the first point of contact in the organisation. They are very important people to network with. You can also network:

- Informally, over lunch or a coffee
- Formally, in your professional capacity
- In person
- By phone
- E-mail
- Greet and meet
- Walk and talk

Network via the canteen and the works sociable club. Every so often let the people you support know that you are there, what you do and what you can do for them.

All new staff should have an induction, ensure staff know:

- Where you work
- When you are available
- What you can do for them (even for simple queries)

Networking outside of your workplace includes:

- networking with other professional groups that are relevant to the work you do

- attending social events away from work. They are a good opportunity to network and enjoy yourself at the same time

- being interested in the professional bodies that relate to you at work and your organisation

6.4 Direct or via media

The most fundamental act of networking occurs when you give someone a referral or get a referral from someone based on the relationship of trust that has been built between the two of you. That connection is a simple network. And that is, in the end, all that is involved in even the most sophisticated networks. People exchanging connections, or leads, based on trust.

Networking can be done anywhere that two or more people get together. It is important to be aware of what is appropriate in the setting. Sometimes a direct approach is appropriate, others it is more acceptable to simply ask a person what they do and ask them for a business card 'in case I run into anyone who could use your services.'

Professional networking groups exist to create an exchange of leads between members. They are structured to ensure that this is effective for all the members.

The basic concept is simple. The group meets at regular times at a specific place, usually once a month or once a week. Each member tells the group exactly what would be their best customer/contact, and they keep an eye out for possible leads for the other members during the course of the week. At each meeting they exchange leads.

These groups are the best source for referrals. They limit membership, in most cases, to one person from any specific profession. This alone makes for a more certain result. The better groups also check carefully to make sure that prospective members are businesses operated with integrity and a good record of customer satisfaction. And they require a fee for membership. While the fees aren't usually anything huge, they do discourage the curiosity seekers.

What this all means is that you can be confident in the quality of work that will be done for someone when you refer them to a member of the group. Since each member has the same level of assurance, it is easier for them to send people to you.

Social networking is the latest hot application to hit the Internet world. Basically, it is a kind of search engine for people and relationships, and is based on the theory that 'a friend of my friend is my friend'. The concept revolves around connections – who you know, what you know, and who knows you.

There are also several business-oriented social networking websites and software packages available eg,www.network.monster.com where you join the website (some eg, LinkedIn.com – by invitation only) and add your list of contacts. On Ryze.com, you set up your own networking homepage, and you can contact other members directly. At Tribe.net, you can join a public 'tribe' or be invited to join a private 'tribe.' At Monster Networking, simply fill in a profile with your job title and personal information and start networking. Your list then expands to the contacts of your friends and so on, to an ever-widening circle of possible business contacts. The idea is to find links between people and create trustworthy paths for contacting others, all in an effort to increase efficiency in establishing business contacts and cut down on cold calling.

6.5 Formal and informal networking prospects

Although we are looking at networking as it applies to business, it is a practice that can cover a lot of ground. In its simplest form, networking simply means making connections to make exchanges easier. This can be social, personal, professional, or even technical.

In the professional setting, networking is getting to know people and businesses, and developing trust and communication to make the process of business easier and more profitable. This usually involves the exchange of 'leads', or referrals to potential customers, between businesses.

This can be by formal agreement, as happens in a networking group, or through the development of personal contacts over the course of time.

Identifying networking prospects among your friends, neighbours and acquaintances can pay off. They may have a useful contact in an industry you are interested in.

6.6 Relating and interacting trust and confidentiality

Effective business networking is the linking together of individuals who, through trust and relationship building, become walking, talking advertisements for one another.

- Keep in mind that networking is about being genuine and authentic, building trust and relationships, and seeing how you can help others.

- Ask yourself what your goals are in participating in networking meetings so that you will pick groups that will help you get what you are looking for. Some meetings are based more on learning, making contacts, and/or volunteering rather than on strictly making business connections.

- Visit as many groups as possible that spark your interest. Notice the tone and attitude of the group. Do the people sound supportive of one another? Does the leadership appear competent? Many groups will allow you to visit a couple of times before joining.

- Hold volunteer positions in organisations. This is a great way to stay visible and give back to groups that have helped you.

- Ask open-ended questions in networking conversations. This means questions that ask who, what, where, when, and how as opposed to those that can be answered with a simple yes or no. This form of questioning opens up the discussion and shows listeners that you are interested in them.

- Become known as a powerful resource for others. When you are known as a strong resource, people remember to turn to you for suggestions, ideas, names of other people, etc. This keeps you visible to them.

- Have a clear understanding of what you do and why, for whom, and what makes your doing it special or different from others doing the same thing. In order to get referrals, you must first have a clear understanding of what you do that you can easily articulate to others.

- Be able to articulate what you are looking for and how others may help you. Too often people in conversations ask, 'How may I help you?' and no immediate answer comes to mind.

- Follow through quickly and efficiently on referrals you are given. When people give you referrals, your actions are a reflection on them. Remember, there are three sides to every referral. Your side, as the person who is being trusted by both to arrange a good match. The customer's side, since they are trusting you to get them someone to handle a problem for them – the right way the first time. And of course the other businessperson's side, since they are expecting that this customer will pay on time and not create more problems than the job is worth. Respect and honour that and your referrals will grow.

- Call those you meet who may benefit from what you do and vice versa. Express that you enjoyed meeting them, and ask if you could get together and share ideas.

- Never talk about something shared in confidence. If you have a reputation for discretion, your network will grow.

- Share the credit with other individuals who helped you earn it. When others congratulate you, mention your colleague's contribution. Write letters of appreciation to his or her boss.

Remember that networking should have a purpose and should be with people who have the same interests as your organisation, or decision makers who can affect your work.

7 FORMING BUSINESS RELATIONSHIPS

7.1 Stakeholder contacts

Stakeholders have been defined as 'any group or individual who can affect or is affected by the achievement of the firm's objectives.'

- Primary stakeholders have interests that are directly linked to the fortunes of a company. They typically include shareholders and investors, employees, customers, suppliers, and residents of the communities where the company operates.

- Secondary stakeholders have an indirect influence on an organisation or are less directly affected by its activities. They include the media and pressure groups, regulators, competitors, and others that form the social ecology of an organisation.

Building relationships with clients, stakeholders and organisational members means following through on commitments, respecting confidentiality, and demonstrating an interest in their work-related issues and activities. **Collaborative relationships** with stakeholders can increase an organisation's stability in a turbulent environment and enhance its control over changing circumstances. For example, suppliers will be more likely to show optimal responsiveness to company needs (as well as flexibility in demanding payment in times when cash flow is limited) if there is a trusting relationship. Similarly, if a company has a good working relationship with the community, it is more likely to get co-operation when it comes to expanding facilities or engaging in activities that will affect the community. When a company establishes collaborative relationships with stakeholder groups it is much like the process individuals go through to find and develop lasting interpersonal relationships. We decide what we want from a relationship, consider how our existing relationships measure up or fall short, and decide whether there is some obvious gap.

Establishing powerful collaborative relationships is not easy or quick. Time is needed for people to get to know one another, build trust, deal with organisational issues, negotiate agreements, and manage the logistics of working together.

Partners must clarify their expectations ('What's in it for me?'); they must develop structures, roles, and responsibilities that work for everyone; and they must establish milestones to evaluate progress.

People must also be willing to learn from each other and have the skills to communicate effectively. Communication ground rules should be set early in the process to create a safe environment within which individuals feel free to express their views.

But where can you find network contacts? Start with Websites of customers, suppliers, professional associations, trade magazines or companies in your target industry. You will eventually find lists of people who can help you.

Networking should be an ongoing and systematic part of your work. Networking is not just diplomacy and public relations – it should be meaningful communication and co-operation between organisations with shared interests.

There are many different ways to network. Some of the methods are informal or form part of your normal work; others are part of setting up a networking system. Here are some examples:

- Send your newsletters and information pamphlets to organisations and individuals you want to network with.

- Get to know key people in organisations that share your interests and talk to them regularly about common issues and problems.

- Attend the meetings, AGMs and events of other organisations.

- Attend political and community events where key organisations and decision-makers will be present.

- Attend conferences, seminars, consultation meetings, etc. Make sure your organisation is represented by someone who can speak for and raise the profile of your organisation. Lots of informal networking happens at these events.

- Offer support and advice to other organisations when you can and ask for it when you need it.

- Use your skills, contacts and expertise to help key decision-makers and organisations – networking happens naturally when you work together.

- Always have copies of your brochures and contact details so that you can hand it out to any useful contacts you meet.

- Use email and the Internet to network with national or international organisations who are working on similar issues.

7.2 Relationships with customers

Relationship marketing is grounded in the idea of establishing a learning relationship with customers. At the lower end, building a relationship can create cross-selling opportunities that may make the overall relationship profitable. For example, some retail banks have tried selling credit cards to less profitable customers. In determining which customers are worth the cost of long-term relationships, it is useful to consider their lifetime value. This depends on:

- Current profitability computed at the customer level

- The propensity of those customers to stay loyal

- Expected revenues and costs of servicing such customers over the lifetime of the relationship

Building relationships makes most sense for customers whose lifetime value to the company is the highest. Thus, building relationships should focus on customers who are currently the most profitable, likely to be the most profitable in the future, or likely to remain with the company for the foreseeable future and have acceptable levels of profitability. The goal of relationship management is to increase customer satisfaction and to minimise any problems. By engaging in 'smarter' relationships, a company can learn customers' preferences and develop trust. Every contact point with the customer can be seen as a chance to record information and learn preferences. Complaints and errors must be recorded, not just fixed and forgotten. Contact with customers in every medium, whether over the Internet, through a call centre, or through personal contact, is recorded and centralised. Many companies are beginning to achieve this goal by using customer relationship management (CRM) software. Data, once collected, can be used to customise service. In addition, the database can be analysed to detect patterns that can

NOTES

suggest better ways to serve customers in general. A key aspect of this dialogue is to learn and record preferences. There are two ways to determine customers' preferences: transparently and collaboratively.

Discovering preferences transparently means that the marketer learns the customers' needs without actually involving them. For example, the Ritz Carlton Hotel makes a point of observing the choices that guests make and recording them. If a guest requests extra pillows, then extra pillows will be provided every time that person visits. At upmarket retailers, personal shoppers will record customers' preferences in sizes, styles, brands, colours and price ranges and notify them when new merchandise appears or help them choose accessories.

7.3 Supplier relationships

An organisation and its suppliers are interdependent and a mutually beneficial relationship enhances the ability of both to create value.

Key benefits include:

- Increased ability to create value for both parties.

- Flexibility and speed of joint responses to changing market or customer needs and expectations.

- Optimisation of costs and resources.

Applying the principles of mutually beneficial supplier relationships typically leads to:

- Establishing relationships that balance short-term gains with long-term considerations.

- Pooling of expertise and resources with partners.

- Identifying and selecting key suppliers.

- Clear and open communication.

- Sharing information and future plans.

- Establishing joint development and improvement activities.

- Inspiring, encouraging and recognising improvements and achievements by suppliers

Tight bonds between companies and their key suppliers have been created in many industries.

For example, IKEA, the Swedish furniture retailer, commits to long-term relationships with its suppliers, and helps the suppliers to improve their products by leasing them equipment, providing technical assistance, and helping to find sources of raw materials.

BPP
PROFESSIONAL EDUCATION

Chapter roundup

- Organisations require information for recording transactions, measuring performance, making decisions, planning and controlling.

- An organisation's information requirements will be influenced by the sector they operate in.

- Information may be strategic, tactical or operational.

- There are many systems available to hold, process and analyse information. Examples include ESS, DSS, KWS, OAS and TPS.

- An information system should be designed to obtain information from all relevant sources – both internal and external.

- Effective information systems are vital at all levels of an organisation to assist in decision-making.

- Decision support systems allow managers to consider a number of alternatives and evaluate them under a variety of potential conditions.

- Executive information systems have summary level data and more detailed levels and other data manipulation and analysis facilities, graphics and templates.

- Expert systems are computer programs that allow users to benefit from expert knowledge and information.

- Networking – is consciously developing contacts in an effort to increase the number of referrals you get for your business.

- Networking should be an ongoing and systematic part of your work. Networking is not just diplomacy and public relations – it should be meaningful communication and co-operation between organisations with shared interests.

- Relationship marketing is grounded in the idea of establishing a learning relationship with customers.

Quick quiz

1   Give a brief definition of knowledge.

2   Distinguish between strategic, tactical and operational information.

3   Give two examples of strategic, tactical and operational information relevant to an organisation operating in the manufacturing sector.

4   Which is easier to measure – qualitative information or quantitative information?

5   What are the two types of knowledge?

6   Decision support systems are used for routine decisions. TRUE or FALSE?

7   What are decision support systems used for?

8   What are some applications of expert systems?

9   Give three examples of primary stakeholders and three examples of secondary stakeholders.

Answers to quick quiz

1   Knowledge is information within people's minds. (See para 1.2)

2   Strategic information is used to plan the objectives of the organisation. Tactical information is used for management control activities and operational information is used to ensure that specific tasks are executed properly. (3.2)

3   Two examples of strategic information:

(i)   Communication of corporate objectives to the management of the business expressed in terms of profit targets and measures of wealth such as earnings per share.

(ii)   Communicating information on strategy for future acquisitions of companies in different fields as a hedge against risk.

Two examples of tactical information:

(i)   A twelve-month budget of sales analysed by product group.

(ii)   A manufacturing plan for the next twelve months.

Two examples of operational information:

(i)   An 'aged' analysis of debts showing all customers whose deliveries have been stopped pending settlement of overdue balance.

(ii)   A list of all purchase orders outstanding with the financial evaluation of total purchase order commitment. (3.3)

4   Qualitative information is difficult (or even impossible) to measure in quantitative terms. (3.5)

5   Tacit and explicit. (3.6)

6   False. (5.4)

7   A decision support system (DSS) is normally an interactive system that helps people make decisions, use judgement and work in ill-defined areas. It supports decision-making in semi-structured and unstructured situations and provides information, models, or tools for manipulating and/or analysing information. It enables managers to focus on the real business problems, by automating the process of gathering, summarising and analysing information relevant to a particular decision area, and enables one-off ad hoc problem situations to be resolved. Its most likely usage is in the area of producing information to aid in tactical decision-making. (5.4)

8   The ES will be used for:

- diagnosing problems
- strategic planning
- internal control planning
- maintaining strategies.

The system is able to make complex and unstructured decisions. It can offer managers advice and explanation, and is able to integrate with other systems such as MIS, DSS and EIS.

Examples of expert systems include:

- Advice on legal implications during labour-management negotiations
- Tax computations
- Selection of training methods (5.6)

9 Primary stakeholders include shareholders and investors, employees, customers, suppliers, and residents of the communities where the company operates. Secondary stakeholders include the media and pressure groups, regulators and competitors. (7.1)

Answers to activities

1 There are many possible suggestions, including those given below.

(a) The organisation's bankers take decisions affecting the amount of money they are prepared to lend.

(b) The public might have an interest in information relating to an organisation's products or services.

(c) The media (press, television etc) use information generated by organisations in news stories, and such information can adversely or favourably affect an organisation's relationship with its environment.

(d) The government (for example the Department of Trade and Industry) regularly requires organisational information.

(e) The Inland Revenue and HM Customs and Excise authorities require information for taxation and VAT assessments.

(f) An organisation's suppliers and customers take decisions whether or not to trade with the organisation.

2 The first is a tactical control decision, the second is an operational control decision and the third is a strategic planning decision.

3 They are examples of operational information.

4 The data will be related to:

- Suppliers – the standing of the organisation (you do not want to be dealing with a company that is on the verge of bankruptcy), the quality of their service, the discounts they offer, their after-sales service, the delivery charges and times etc.

- Products and services – the prices, availability, quality assurance, quantities supplied,

5

	Secondary information	Primary information
What it is	Data neither collected directly by the user nor specifically for the user, often under conditions unknown to the user- in other words, data collected not by you but by someone else for their own purposes or for general use.	Data that is collected specifically by or for the user, at source, in other words by you.
Quantitative, 'factual' or 'objective' example	A company's published financial statements summarise and interpret company transactions data for the benefit of shareholders, not necessarily for your precise needs.	A survey you conduct with a questionnaire you have designed, with regard to a sample. You aim to get a statistically significant result.
Qualitative example	An article in a student publication or in a book about theories of motivation.	A focus group you have conducted to talk about a specific topic.

6 (a) Expert systems bring the power of expertise to the desk. Say a person wants a loan from a bank. An expert system can be used for credit scoring, so the request will not have to be directed back to a superior.

 (b) Executive information systems mean that senior management can focus easily on operations so the middle management function of information processing might disappear.

This points to delayering of management hierarchies, counterbalanced by the creation of new jobs in information management.

Chapter 14 :
DEVELOP COMMUNICATION PROCESSES

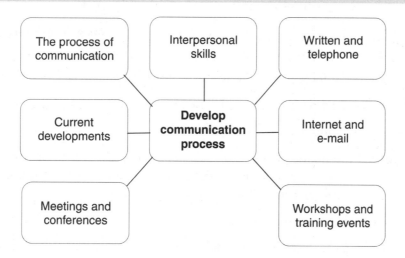

Introduction

The efficient running of organisations requires that all the members of the organisation work together towards the achievement of the organisation's objectives. This working together requires the adequate understanding of what others are doing. It requires a high level of co-ordination and control, and fundamentally it requires communications, which are efficient and effective.

This chapter focuses on communication in the organisation, its nature and operation. The design of the formal communication system is considered as well as the types of informal communications channels that probably will exist in an organisation. If management is the art of 'achieving results through other people' then interpersonal skills are a key part of the job.

This chapter deals with the use of the Internet and the World Wide Web in business. It will consider the impact of e-commerce and the growing use of intranet by organisations in order to manage their information.

Your objectives

After completing this chapter you should be able to:

(a) Review existing processes of communication

(b) Evaluate appropriateness of communication processes

(c) Implement improvements to ensure greater integration of systems of communication

(d) Identify weaknesses and develop personal and interpersonal skills of communication

1 THE PROCESS OF COMMUNICATION

1.1 Functions and objectives of communication

Communication in an organisation can serve a number of functions.

(a) It can be a vehicle for the exchange of information, so that people are told about an event or state of affairs, or what other people are doing.

(b) It can be a vehicle for instruction (eg a superior communicating by giving orders to a subordinate).

(c) It can be a vehicle of persuasion in which a person can be won over to a particular viewpoint or proposal.

(d) It can reinforce (by encouragement) existing behaviour.

(e) It may be directed towards the establishment of relationships.

(f) It can publicise needs and requirements.

The objective of communication by a manager or administrator is to exchange, impart or receive *information*. This does not mean that unedited data should be transmitted to all and sundry. Good information will have the following qualities.

(a) Relevance to a user's needs

    (i) *Identifying the user*. Information must be suited and sent to the right person (one who needs it to do a job, make a decision etc).

    (ii) *Getting the purpose right*. Information is effective only when it helps a user to act or make a decision. If you ask someone the way to the nearest train station, you do not expect or need to be told that the weather is fine, or even that there is a very interesting train station in another town some miles away.

    (iii) *Getting the volume right*. Information must be complete for its purpose, ie not omitting any necessary item: it should also be no more in volume than the user will find helpful or be able to take in.

(b) *Accuracy within the user's needs*. Information should be 'accurate' in the sense of 'correct': downright falsehood and error are fatal to effective communication of any sort. It may, however, be impossible – or at least time-consuming and expensive – to gather, process and assimilate information that is minutely detailed. An approximation or an average figure is often sufficient to our needs. If you asked: 'Is it hot in Brighton in August?' because you were planning a holiday, you would be happy to hear that it 'averaged 78 F': you would not waste time and effort poring through a sheet of daily temperature readings for the last five years.

(c) *Inspiring the user's confidence*. Information should not give the user reason to mistrust, disbelieve or ignore it, eg because it is out-of-date, badly presented or from an unreliable source. It should be *verifiable* by reference, or by application (which risks finding out the hard way, if the information is incorrect).

(d) *Timeliness*. Information must be readily available within the time period, which makes it useful: ie it must be in the right place at the right time.

(e) *Appropriately communicated.* Information will lose its value if it is not clearly communicated to the user in a suitable format and through a suitable medium.

(f) *Cost effective.* Good information should not cost more than it is worth. Gathering, storing, retrieving and communicating an item of information may require expense of time, energy and resources: if the expense is greater than the potential value of the item, re-consider whether the information is necessary to such a degree of accuracy, completeness etc – or even necessary at all.

1.2 A model of the process

Effective communication is a two-way process, perhaps best expressed as a cycle. Signals or 'messages' are sent by the communicator and received by the other party, who sends back some form of confirmation that the message has been received and understood. This is enormously complicated in practice, especially in face-to-face communication: you may send a letter and receive an acknowledgement back, which would correspond to a single cycle of communication, but face-to-face, the workings of two or more minds and bodies (nodding understanding, gesturing and so on) complicate the picture. A basic interpretation of the process of communication might be as follows.

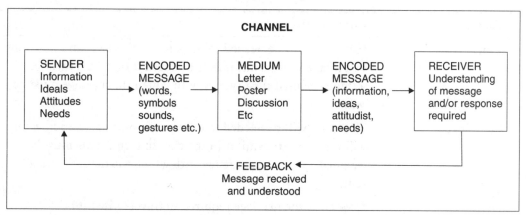

Figure 14.1 Communication process

Activity 1   **(10 mins)**

One definition of business communication is 'the transmission of information so that it is received, understood and leads to action'. Evaluate the key items included in this definition.

Feedback is the reaction of the receiver that indicates to the sender that the message has (or has not) been received and enables him to assess whether it has been understood and correctly interpreted.

Feedback can range from a **smile** or a **nod** to a **blank look** or a **shrug,** or from the desired action being taken to no action or the wrong action being taken.

Within the communication process it is also important to note the problem of 'noise' ie, anything in the environment that impedes the transmission of the message, is significant. Noise can arise from many sources eg factors as diverse as loud machinery, status differentials between sender and receiver, distractions of pressure at work or emotional upsets. The effective communicator must ensure that noise does not interfere with successful transmission of the message.

Activity 2   **(10 mins)**

Give five examples of what you would interpret as:

(a) Negative feedback (a sign that your message was not having the desired effect)

(b) Positive feedback (a sign that your message was received and understood)

1.3 Choosing the communication channel

Choosing the right method of communication is important. How information is communicated will impact on how it is interpreted. A channel that will help the receiver correctly interpret the information should be used. The choice of medium will depend on numerous factors, including the following:

Factor	Considerations
Time	How long will be needed to prepare the message, and how long will it take to transmit it in the chosen form? This must be weighed against the urgency with which the message must be sent.
Complexity	How long will be needed to prepare the message, and how long will it take to transmit it in the chosen form? This must be weighed against the urgency with which the message must be sent.
Distance	How far is the message required to travel? Must it be transmitted to an office on a different floor of the building, or across town, or to the other end of the country?
Written record	A written record may be needed as proof, confirming a transaction, or for legal purposes, or as an aid to memory. It can be duplicated and sent to many recipients. It can be stored and later retrieved for reference and analysis as required.
Feedback/interaction	Sometimes instant feedback is needed for effective communication eg when you are questioning a customer to find out his precise requirements (small, medium or large) (green, red or blue).
Confidentiality	Telephone calls may be overheard; faxed messages can be read by whoever is standing by the fax machine; internal memos may be read by colleagues or by internal mail staff; highly personal letters may be read by the recipient's secretary. On the other hand a message may need to be spread widely and quickly to all staff: the notice-board, or a public announcement or the company newsletter may be appropriate.

Factor	Considerations
Recipient	It may be necessary to be reserved and tactful, warm and friendly, or impersonal, depending upon the desired effect on the recipient. If you are trying to impress him, a high quality document may be needed.
Cost	Cost must be considered in relation to all of the above factors. The aim is to achieve the best possible result at the least possible expense.

As regards **confidentiality**, remember:

- Telephone calls can be overheard
- Faxed messages can be read by whoever is standing by the fax machine
- Internal memos may be read by colleagues or internal mail staff
- Personal letters may be read by the recipient's secretary
- E-mail may not be completely secure

An overview of the features and limitations of common communication tools are outlined in the following table.

Tool	Features /Advantages	Limitations
Conversation	Usually unstructured so can discuss a wide range of topics Requires little or no planning Gives a real impression of feelings	Temptation to lose focus May be easily forgotten
Meeting	Allows multiple opinions to be expressed Can discuss and resolve a wide range of issues	Can highlight differences and conflict if not managed efficiently – have been known to turn into time-wasting confrontations
Memorandum	Provides a permanent record of an internal message Adds formality to internal communications	If used too often or the message is too general people may ignore it Can come across as impersonal
Letter	Provides a permanent record of an external message Adds formality to external communications	If inaccurate or poorly presented provides a permanent record of incompetence May be slow to arrive depending on distance and the postal service
Report	Provides a permanent, often comprehensive written record Use a clear, simple structure	Complex messages may be misunderstood in the absence of immediate feedback

Tool	Features /Advantages	Limitations
Presentation	Complex ideas can be communicated Visual aids such as slides can help the communication process The best presentations will leave a lasting impression	Requires planning and skill Poorly researched or presented material can lead to an audience
Telephone	Good for communications that do not require (or you would prefer not to have) a permanent written record Can provide some of the 'personal touch' to people in geographically remote locations Conference calls allow multiple participants	Receiver may not be available Can be disruptive to receiver if in the middle of another task No written record gives greater opportunity for misunderstandings
Facsimile	Enables reports and messages to reach remote locations quickly	Easily seen by others Fax machine may not be checked for messages Complex images do not transmit well
Electronic mail	Provides a written record Attachments can be included Quick – regardless of location Automated 'Read receipts' or a simple request to acknowledge receipt by return message mean you know if the message has been received Can be sent to multiple recipients easily, can be forwarded on to others	Requires some computer literacy to use effectively People may not check their e-mail regularly Lack of privacy – can be forwarded on without your knowledge Is impersonal

Activity 3 **(10 mins)**

Because of the advantages and disadvantages associated with each type of communication, organisations use more than one method in conjunction. What methods would you suggest for the sales launch of a new product?

2 CURRENT DEVELOPMENTS

2.1 Changing environment

The changing economic and business climate is likely to put increased pressures upon communication systems. The challenges require an enhanced commitment to quality, profitability and the ability to manage change.

- The changing demographic profile is introducing *new working practices*, with more job sharing, full-time women workers and multi-skilling becoming standard. These new working practices inevitably mean different values, attitudes, skills and aspirations for the future. Workers of the future will require more challenging occupations, more variety and continual development together with increased flexibility to balance family and working life.

- The *flatter management structures* currently fashionable are encouraging a more dynamic and interactive working environment, which will precipitate the need for closer and more personal communication systems that contribute to maintaining the competitive position of the organisation.

- The growth of *multi-national enterprises* will ultimately require the establishment of global information systems that can effectively integrate differing cultures, languages and operating systems throughout the organisation.

- Increased numbers of *people working from home* will mean that more effort must be directed towards fostering a feeling of belonging to the organisation, since such workers may well suffer a sense of isolation. Electronic media will undoubtedly assist in the maintenance of links (both formally and informally) between worker and employer.

- Recent years have witnessed unprecedented *downsizing*, both within the manufacturing base and also the service sector, where jobs are being sacrificed in pursuit of improved efficiency and profitability. Consequently, employees are increasingly concerned with job security and less confident in the competence of senior level management. Those responsible for stabilising a climate of distrust need to engender greater levels of confidence and openness within the organisation. Indeed, criticism of downsizing has emerged: so-called 'corporate anorexia' inhibits growth.

2.2 Changing communication

In the last few years, the infrastructure and tools of communication have radically changed. The phone is swiftly being overtaken by e-mail as the most popular method of remote interpersonal communication. The Internet has changed the way people access information. Even 'old' media like the television and telephone are being transformed by new data transmission infrastructures and integration with computer systems.

Broadly, communication has changed in the following ways.

(i) **Higher speed** – the development of 'facsimile transfer' (fax) was breakthrough in its day: enabling documents, which previously had to be posted, to be transferred down a phone line. Now, messages can be transferred via a local computer network or the Internet almost instantly, to

NOTES

the point where real time conversations can be held using online messaging and chat rooms. Recent infrastructure innovations such as ISDN (Integrated Systems Digital Network), DSL (Digital Subscriber Lines), satellite transmission (for telephone and television signals), fibre optic cabling and increased 'band width' (allowing more data to pass through networks more swiftly) have supported this process.

(ii) **Wider access to information** – once you are connected to the Internet, you have instant access to an almost indescribable wealth of information. Through electronic mail and bulletin boards (newsgroups) you can use a different kind of resource: a worldwide supply of knowledgeable people, some of whom are bound to share your interests, no matter how obscure... There are also more (and better) resources, including museums, exhibitions, art galleries and shops.

(iii) **24-7 global communication** – information and communications technology (ICT) has enabled 24-hour 7-day global communication: across working or office hours, time zones and geographical distances. Telex, fax and answer machines were a start in this direction – but they required (possibly delayed) human intervention to initiate a response. The Internet allows users to access information/services and perform transactions at any time of any day. Nor is there any distinction between local and international sites, in terms of speed or cost of access. (Physical delivery of products ordered will, of course, re-erect some of the geographical barriers.)

(iv) **Interactivity and multi-media** – Interactivity is mutual responsiveness. Consumers are increasingly demanding in terms of interactivity in accessing and responding to promotional messages. Consumers are also increasingly demanding in terms of the stimulation provided by promotional messages. Multi media communication implies the use of written, visual and audio elements to enhance a message's impact and interest. The Internet and related technologies have habituated people (particularly young media and IT consumers) to multi-media presentations, high-level animated/video-based graphics and interaction with material. Although the impact of such trends may be limited by the power of the individual user's PC and the speed of the modem, printed matter may seem relatively unstimulating in comparison: some of the features of online and multi-media presentation are being added to traditional print advertising and information: simulated 'links' and buttons, multi-directional graphics and so on.

(v) **Personalisation** – database, document generation and web technologies have improved the ease and sophistication of targeting and personalisation of contact between organisations and customers. Examples include:

- Allowing users to customise web pages for their personal interests and tastes

- Making individually-targeted product offers and recommendations based on browsing/buying behaviour

- Sending personally addressed and targeted-content messages to customers

- Encouraging users/customers to form 'virtual communities' (for example, using chat rooms, discussion boards and newsgroups)

Activity 4   **(10 mins)**

Suggest the most effective medium for communication in the following situations.

(a) New printer cartridges are urgently required from the office goods supplier.

(b) The managing director wants to give a message to all staff.

(c) Fred Bloggs has been absent five times in the past month and his manager intends to take action.

(d) You need information quickly from another department.

(e) You have to explain a complicated operation to a group of people.

---

3 MEETINGS AND CONFERENCES

3.1 Meetings

Meetings play an important part in the life of any organisation. Meetings include:

(a) **Formal meetings** required by government legislation or the Articles of a company.

(b) **Regular or 'one-off' internal management meetings**. These may involve the gathering of, communication of, or review of, information. Alternately, the meeting may have a problem-solving or decision-making purpose.

(c) Some **discussions** held informally may 'qualify' as a meeting – there are no hard and fast rules as to what constitutes an informal meeting.

Face-to-face communication is necessary at all levels of an organisation. Communication does not happen by chance – it requires structure and discipline! While meetings can be time consuming, effective meetings use that time to drive to specific outcomes, utilise the input of all participants, and assign accountability for business results.

The face-to-face meeting can be formal or informal, vertical, horizontal, or diagonal, but it is always the richest communication medium. Here the full play of verbal and non-verbal cues is available to both sender and receiver. Meetings take place in offices and boardrooms, but many meetings are the more informal ones in the hallways at work (by chance or by design); breakfast, lunch or dinner meetings; and those that take place at the club or on the golf course. These more informal meetings should not be underestimated for their importance to activities at work, for it is here that many relationships are built and deals are made.

Organisational members who are excluded from such meetings by their sex or age are discriminated against because they do not have the same opportunities to communicate, as do others. This discrimination can be as simple as the men at a meeting taking a washroom break and continuing to discuss business while women present at the meeting are excluded.

3.2   Formal meetings – structured

Most managers seem to spend half of their life in meetings, so understanding how they work and how to make them more effective is very important.

Definition

> A **meeting** is a group of people coming together for the purpose of resolving problems or making decisions.

Meetings can be held for a wide range of purposes, but it is important that the purpose of the meeting is made clear to the participants in advance. If this is done, the meeting is more likely to be a success.

A well-organised, well-aimed and well-led meeting can be extremely effective in many different contexts.

- The relaying of decisions and instructions (eg briefings)
- The dissemination of information and the collection of feedback
- Participative problem solving
- Brainstorming: free exchanges with a view to generating new approaches and ideas
- Co-ordinating the efforts of a large number of people from different interest groups

A meeting may be responsible for taking a final decision on an issue of great importance.

Formal meetings – are planned and structured and include Board meetings, committees, working groups, public meetings, conferences, Annual General Meetings (AGMs) and EGMs, team meetings, appraisals, interviews and brainstorming.

Formal meetings, such as the Board meeting of a company, the Annual General Meeting (AGM) of a society, or a Local Council meeting, are governed by strict conventions. These may establish procedure on such matters as:

(a)   attendance rights (for members of the public, shareholders etc)

(b)   adequate notice of forthcoming meetings

(c)   the minimum number of members required to hold the meeting (the 'quorum')

(d)   the timing of meetings

(e)   the type of business to be discussed

(f)   the binding power of decisions made upon the participants

Formal meetings generally conform to a system where there is usually a chairperson who guides the proceedings and aims to maintain order. They generate formal documentation for the announcement, planning, conduct and recording of the proceedings. These include the following:

- **Notice** – the invitation or announcement of the meeting, which is prepared and circulated in advance. The communication can be by e-mail, a personal letter, a memo, a notice on the internal notice board or an official card like an invitation.

- **Agenda** – the items of business to be discussed at the meeting. This is often attached to the notice to give participants a guide to the business that will be discussed and the preparations they will need to make. The minutes of the previous meeting might also be included so that any queries or objections relating to them may also be prepared.

- **Minutes** – the written record of the proceedings at the meeting, approved by those present. They provide a source of reference, particularly with regard to decisions and action points agreed by participants.

3.3 Project meetings

Project team members should meet regularly to maintain and improve team relationships and to ensure project objectives, progress and current priorities are communicated and understood.

(a) **Project status meetings** – should be held regularly to keep project stakeholders informed of project status and plans. The attendees of such a meeting would usually include:

- Project manager
- Team members
- Customer/client representatives

A typical agenda of a project status meeting may include the following items:

- Objectives achieved since the previous meeting
- Current project status
- Expected future project progress
- Current expenditure/resource use compared to forecast
- Task assignment with due dates

(b) **Project problem-solving meetings** – it may be necessary over the course of a project to call additional meetings to address specific problems. If a problem that has the potential to impact on project progress is identified, a meeting of all those affected may be the best way to establish an effective course of action. The project manager should ensure all are aware of the level of authority the problem-solving team has to make decisions, and it is clear who is responsible for ensuring the action decided on is carried out.

(c) **Project evaluation meeting** – at the end of a project the project manager should meet each team member to thank him or her for their work, assess their contribution to the project and consider how this may be improved on future projects. The project manager should also call the whole project team together for a project evaluation meeting to see what lessons can be learnt from the project that may help with future projects.

A typical agenda of a project evaluation meeting may include the following items:

- Was the overall objective achieved?
- Resource use compared with the budget
- Time taken compared with the schedule

- The effectiveness of the project plan and management
- Problem identification and resolution
- Team relationships and working arrangements
- Customer liaison, communication and satisfaction

The results of the meeting should be incorporated into the post-completion audit report.

3.4 Conference – a co-ordinated approach

A conference is a specific method of communication. It can serve several purposes and involve visual, written and verbal communication techniques. Most conferences consist of one-way communication only. Conferences should be recognised as being distinctly different from normal meetings. They tend to be several months apart and require a major planning effort to ensure smooth running.

- **Public conferences** – are held for speakers to present lectures to an audience drawn from many companies and many industries. Such conferences are usually one-way communication with limited opportunity to raise questions from the floor. The main purpose of such conferences must be to inform. So Cabinet ministers can use a conference to explain government thinking, an accountant can use the platform to explain the effects of the latest tax regulations; a scientist can explain the methods used in and the results of his research programme.

- **In-house conferences** – are more common. They can be:

    (a) *Horizontal*, ie a member of a certain status level. An example would be a partners' conference where all partners of an accountancy firm may convene to discuss business trends and policy. Frequently such a conference would also include information sessions where an outside expert would be invited to present a topic or one partner may explain developments in his/her area.

    (b) *Vertical*, ie members of different status levels from one department or one division of a company. An example could be the announcement of the company results to its workers or announcement of a major policy change, eg a progress report during a management buyout.

Sales conferences – a company's sale conference is usually held annually and includes all sales representatives above a certain status level or performance level. If we take as an example a company launching a new product such as a pharmaceutical company launching a new drug that is to be sold ´over the counter` at chemists shops, as well as being available on prescription through the Health Service.

We can readily trace the different communication approaches used in such a conference.

    (a) Firstly, the visual communication techniques of video, slide projection and handling of product packages would be used to arouse attention and achieve maximum impact. Explanations from the platform would be brief, relying on the visual images as the main focal thread.

    (b) The next stage would involve mainly verbal communication when the selling attributes of the product would be explained. The selling message would be extolled and the approach to customers would be made clear. This session would be structured to encourage maximum involvement of delegates with questions periods and discussion groups established to achieve two-way flow. This is the persuasive stage when face-to-face, two-way communication will motivate the salesforce and prepare them for any customer queries.

(c) The final stage is the written communication when the salespeople will be issued with product information packs. This pack will summarise all major aspects discussed during the day including details of advertising programmes, product benefits, the selling approach, competitors' strengths/weaknesses and sales targets. This provides the permanent record that can be referred to in the future as the need arises.

3.5 Teleconferencing

Teleconferencing uses communications network technology to connect participants' voices. Teleconferences are similar to telephone calls, but they can expand discussion to more than two people. In many cases, speaker telephones are used for conference calls among the participants. A two-way radio system can also be used. In some remote areas, satellite enhancement of connections is desirable.

Teleconferencing is a method in use to connect a small to large number of people so that they can talk together. Fax machines can also be connected so that documents can be distributed to everyone in the conference at once. Documents can be e-mailed, put in a shared computer window, or posted to the web so everyone can see them at once. Teleconferencing can save organisations money by reducing travel costs. It can also be a strategic method used by organisations to reach their employees, customers, and clients. The travelling executive with a cellular-modem laptop can stay in constant communication by fax and e-mail.

The World Wide Web is used as a medium for holding conferences on specific topics. Those who are interested can visit the conference web site to read posted documents, make contributions, and read the comments of others. This method does not require participants to be physically in the same location or to be communicating at the same time.

3.6 Videoconferencing

Videoconferencing can transmit pictures as well as voices. It is the use of computer and communications technology to conduct meetings in which several participants, perhaps in different parts of the world, are linked up via computer and a video system.

Much productive time can be lost travelling to meetings. Face-to-face meetings usually provide the best channel for discussion, information exchange and relationship building. These benefits should be balanced against the lost productive time. In general a mixture of physical and virtual meetings provides the best compromise.

Arranging telephone conferences should be simple. Most major organisations already have facilities available. Alternatively, the telephone service provider should be able to make the arrangements.

There are two main styles of Videoconferencing: using specialist videoconference facilities or using desktop software from your PC. The ideal scenario is to be able to hook up with other participants through the network at any time without leaving your desk. Although this is technically feasible, relatively few organisations have the bandwidth and controls to operate it efficiently.

The alternative is for attendees to gather at their nearest videoconference suite (internally or externally – eg conference centres, press agencies). Two-way links are just dialled directly. Multiple link ups can be achieved through 'bridges' – everyone connects to the bridge which combines and controls the multiple video and audio links.

4 WORKSHOPS AND TRAINING EVENTS

4.1 Verbal communication

Verbal methods from a major channel in business communications. Some examples of verbal methods are purely voice-to-voice as in telephone conversations and public address announcements. Most methods are face-to-face:

(a) Interviews
(b) Lectures and presentations
(c) Sales visits
(d) Formal group meetings
(e) Informal contact and discussions
(f) Briefing sessions
(g) The grapevine

Verbal methods have several important advantages when used in workshops or training sessions:

- There is the personal touch of seeing the face and/or hearing the voice.

- There is instant feedback with the opportunity to respond quickly to questions of misunderstanding and disagreement.

- Because of the strong personal aspect, it is a good persuasive medium encouraging people to take a certain course of action.

- The message can be unique to you as an individual; no one else is likely to select your mix of words or emphasise the same key phrases.

The obvious disadvantages are:

- There is no permanent record, so disagreement can easily arise as to what was said.

- Vocabulary shrinkage occurs, in that we use only 66% of our full vocabulary when communicating verbally. The full vocabulary is available to us only when writing.

- We do not have the facility, as with writing, to go back, cancel out and replace an earlier sentence because we wish to amend its meaning.

4.2 User workshops

A workshop may be conference style or skill development style. In conference- style events, the trainer stands at the front of the room and speaks, using audio-visual or other props where appropriate. Participants learn what they can from the performance and from the distributed handouts. In skill development workshops, participants have the opportunity to practice and develop specific skills throughout the course of the event. This type of workshop is a meeting with the emphasis on practical exercises.

User workshops are often used in systems analysis to help establish and record user requirements.

At this type of user workshop, user input is obtained by the analyst to analyse business functions and define the data associated with the current and future systems. An outline of the proposed new system is produced, which is used to design more detailed system procedures.

Depending on the complexity of the system, the workshop may devise a plan for implementation. More complex systems may conduct a workshop early in the design stage and hold a later workshop with the aim of producing a detailed system model. Prototyping may be used at such a workshop to prepare preliminary screen layouts.

User workshops should be facilitated by a facilitator. The facilitator co-ordinates the workshop activities with the aim of ensuring the objectives of the session are achieved.

The facilitator would most likely be a systems analyst with excellent communication and leadership skills. The skills of the person in this role are critical to the success of the workshop.

Many user workshops also utilise a scribe. The scribe is an active participant who is responsible for producing the outputs of the workshop.

4.3 Training events

There are many training methods available to choose from. Some of these methods are well established – lecture talks and discussions are the obvious examples of this sort. Others are found to be useful but need to be properly designed and administered – these include all forms of simulation, eg, business games. The method chosen should match the needs of the particular training event and be based upon sound learning principles. It should generally speaking allow for the following:

    (a)   the trainee's participation;

    (b)   the provision of feedback to the trainee about his or her performance;

    (c)   the transfer of the training experience to the job;

    (d)   reinforcement for desired behaviour;

    (e)   practical application of things learned;

    (f)   improved performance through motivation.

Training may be given on, or off, the job and either within the firm or outside (for example, a training scheme at a college workshop). The place of training may well, of course, have a bearing on the method(s) of training used, the structure of the training programme and its content. On-the-job training is a systematic approach for a particular job, normally used by supervisors when training those who report to them. It consists of four steps:

    (i)   preparing the trainee;

    (ii)   giving the trainee the necessary knowledge or information and demonstrating how the job is to be done;

    (iii) allowing the trainee to do the job; and

    (iv) checking the trainees' performance.

4.4 Types of training methods

The training arrangements and methods available include the following.

(a) *The lecture method* – this is regarded as an economical way of giving a large amount of information to many people. Some people prefer listening to reading and good lecturers can help learning and assist understanding. Lectures are of little value if the aim of training is to change attitudes, or develop job or interpersonal skills.

(b) *Discussion methods* – discussion and participation are known ways of securing interest and commitment. Discussion methods in this respect are useful ways of shaping attitudes, encouraging motivation and securing understanding. Discussion methods can also underline the nature, and the difficulties of group problem solving.

(c) *Case study method* – in this approach to training, learning occurs through participation in the definition, analysis and solution of the problem or problems. It demonstrates the nature of group problem solving activity and usually underlines the view that there is no one best solution to a complex business problem.

(d) *Role-playing* – this method requires trainees to project themselves into a simulated situation that is intended to represent some relevant reality, say, a confrontation between management and a trade union. The merit of role-playing is that it influences attitudes, develops interpersonal skills and heightens sensitivity to the views and feelings of others.

(e) *Business games* – games simulate realistic situations, mergers, takeovers, etc in which groups compete with one another and where the effects of the decision taken by one group may affect others. The benefits are said to include development of an appreciation of the complex character of decision taking; understanding of risk and the nature of teamwork.

(f) *Films and closed circuit television (CCT)* – Films are useful as explanatory devices for, say, describing company situations, how the different functions of an organisation relate to one another, or for presenting an overview of production. They are of little use in the teaching of craft and technical skills. CCT is used increasingly in management training to illustrate how managers behave and to show how such behaviour can be modified to enable beneficial changes in their interpersonal and problem solving skills.

(g) *Computer based training (CBT) and computer assisted learning (CAL)* – Some training packages and skills training can be designed for use on computers. User-friendly systems enable trainees to work at their own pace, working on set programmes.

4.5 Presentations

A presentation is a combination of both verbal and visual form of communication that is used by managers at some meetings, training sessions, lectures and conferences.

Before any presentation is made it is necessary to establish the objectives of the presentation, why it is being done and what you want it to achieve. Once these things have been identified, the best way to achieve the objectives can be established.

Compiling a presentation that holds the audience's interest and drives the point home with clarity is not as easy as it looks. Some professional presenters advise that you divide your presentation into three sections.

A presentation is a combination of both verbal and visual form of communication that is used by managers at some meetings, training sessions, lectures and conferences.

Before any presentation is made it is necessary to establish the objectives of the presentation, why it is being done and what you want it to achieve. Once these things have been identified, the best way to achieve the objectives can be established. Compiling a presentation that holds the audience's interest and drives the point home with clarity is not as easy as it looks. Some professional presenters advise that you divide your presentation into three sections

(a) The *introduction* summarises your overall message and should begin with a title slide, or transparency, that succinctly states the purpose of the presentation.

(b) The *main section*, sometimes called the *rationale*, delivers your main points. In general, each point should be made in a simple, powerful text slide and then bolstered with more detail from charts and subsidiary text slides. For some reason, three items of supporting data for each main point seems to work best for most audiences and most arguments.

(c) Section three winds up with re-emphasis, starting with a summary, moving on to a *conclusion* and leaving the audience with a message that will persuade them to act – this may be to applaud your department's progress or to buy your scheme. The final line of the presentation must be a definite close.

The presentation must be summarised throughout, because you cannot rely on the audience having read any handouts prior to the presentations.

The audience should be given the opportunity to ask questions and whether this is done at regular intervals or at the end of the presentation will depend upon the topic of the presentation and the audience to which it is addressed.

Graphics, in the form of still or moving pictures, can be a particularly effective method of communication. They have *advantages* in that they are attention-catching, have a dramatic impact, they facilitate the understanding of complex material and are comprehensive to those of poor linguistic ability.

4.6 Coaching

Coaching is a specialised form of communication that is concerned with training. Its need becomes apparent to management when there is a need to extend the depth and range of an employee's knowledge very quickly for reasons which may range from the introduction of new techniques to the need to train for a particular job, perhaps on the unexpected retirement of the present job holder.

Planning of the scheme of work so that any coaching is done on a systematic basis is an important aspect of the process and the teaching undertaken should be directly related to the style preferred by the student. This is usually a one to one learning situation and care should be taken to hold the attention of the student very closely throughout the coaching process. As individuals differ in their response to alternative learning styles,

BPP
PROFESSIONAL EDUCATION

coaching may take any form from the academic, where the student is geared to research and knowledge based learning, to activity based learning – such as projects.

Coaching is a considerable drain on managerial time. Support has to be given from the planning stage and will continue during the learning process, with the value of constructive criticism being particularly relevant. There is a need for clear goals to be set and agreed by both the management and the student with regular evaluation and feedback being incorporated in the coaching plan.

Well planned coaching is an effective way of communicating information in a concentrated form.

5 INTERNET AND E-MAIL

5.1 The Internet

The **Internet** (also known as 'the Net', the 'information super-highway' or 'cyberspace') is a vast computer network offering the ability for computers across the world to communicate via telecommunications links. Information can be exchanged either through e-mail or through accessing and entering data via a website: a collection of screens providing information in text and graphic form, any of which can be viewed by clicking the appropriate link (shown as a button, word or icon) on the screen.

The '**World Wide Web**' (or 'Web') is a navigation system within the Internet. It is based on a technology called 'hypertext' which allows documents stored on host computers on the Internet to be linked to one another. When you view a document that contains hypertext links, you can view any of the connected documents or pages simply by clicking on a link. The web is the most powerful, flexible and fastest growing information and navigation service on the Internet. In order to 'surf' or navigate the web, users need a web client (called a 'browser') which interprets and displays hypertext documents and locates documents pointed to by links. Internet Explorer is the browser from Microsoft: alternatives include Netscape Navigator, Mosaic, WebSurfer and others.

Access to the Internet will become easier and easier. Most new PCs now come pre-loaded with the necessary hardware and software, and cheaper Internet devices are beginning to reach the market: Microsoft and America Online (AOL) – among others – have been exploring inexpensive 'set-top' TV/Internet connections. Developments in telecom networks are already rendering modems unnecessary. Personal digital assistants (PDAs) such as the Palm Pilot, wireless Internet-compatible cellular phones and wireless laptop connections allow users to surf the Web and send and receive e-mail from almost any location, without cords or cables.

5.2 The Internet as a promotional communication

The Internet can be used across the promotion mix.

Advertising	• Dedicated corporate websites, banner/button advertising, ranking on Internet search engines (to increase site exposure)
	• The forecast global penetration of the Internet over the next few years would give it a significantly larger audience than any of the television networks, print media outlets or other advertising vehicles
	• Studies show that brand awareness increases some 5% after using banner advertising
Direct marketing	• E-mail messages sent to targeted mailing lists (rented, or developed by the marketing organisation itself)
	• 'Permission marketing' (targeting consumers who have opted to receive commercial mailings)
Direct response advertising	• Immediate contact (information/transaction facilities) to follow up customer responses to TV/radio/print advertising
Sales promotion	• On-line prize draws and competitions
	• On-line discounts (offset by lower transaction costs)
	• Downloadable or e-mailed discount vouchers
Customer loyalty programmes	• Value-added benefits that enhance the Internet buying experience
	• User home page customisation
	• Virtual communities (chat rooms etc)
	• Free e-cards/SMS messages
Media/press relations	• Online media/press kits
	• E-mailed media releases
	• 'About us' and 'contacts' pages
	• Technical briefings and articles on key issues
Public relations	• 'About us' and 'FAQ' (frequently asked question) features
	• News bulletins (eg for crisis or issues management)
	• Publicity/information for sponsorships, exhibitions and events
	• Sponsorship of popular/ useful information sites
Relationship marketing	• Customisation of Web pages and targeting of offers/promotions
	• E-mail follow-up contacts
	• E-zines – special interest newsletters published on the Web, or distributed by e-mail direct to subscribers and mailing lists
Grass roots marketing	• Generating word of mouth promotion and recommendation among customers
	• Online chat or message board forums and 'introduce a friend' schemes/incentives

Direct distribution	• Of products (through online shopping) and services (including access to information databases)
	• Products can be ordered via the Net
	• Some can also be delivered via the Net, by downloading direct to the purchaser's PC: examples include music, computer software, Clipart, product catalogues and instruction manuals
Partnership development	• Strategic promotional collaborations with synergistic content-specific sites or 'portals' (search engines, Web directories or other high-traffic sites such as Yahoo! or MSN)
Customer service and technical support	• E-mail contact
	• FAQs (frequently asked questions)
	• Access to databased information
	• Online messaging or voice interruption for interactive support
Market/ customer research	• Gathering information on customers and visitors for the purposes of market segmentation, personalisation/customisation of future contacts
	• Site monitoring
	• Online or e-mailed feedback questionnaires and surveys
Corporate identity	• Website and e-mail messages must be designed to create a unified and coherent marketing message alongside all other marketing messages for marketing synergy

5.3 On-line shopping

The Internet is, subject to a few remaining security concerns, a potential means of direct selling and distribution to potential customers.

Definition

E-commerce is an abbreviation of 'electronic commerce': it means business transactions carried out online via the Internet.

A transaction-based website is a virtual warehouse (or supermarket, or bookstore – or whatever its creators wish). Customers can take a virtual browsing tour; download catalogues; explore products; put items in 'shopping baskets'; proceed to 'checkout' and pay by debit or credit card (in some cases with one click of the mouse, enabled by a database containing the customer details); select delivery options; print out accompanying documentation; monitor the progress of their order; receive e-mailed confirmations and notifications and so on.

Although online shopping has not lived up to initial (inflated) forecasts, surveys now suggest that it is growing at a steady rate, particularly in the business-to-business market and for products such as niche market/rare items (such as craft supplies and out of print books), books, CD/cassettes, software, transport/travel and groceries. (You will need to monitor the quality press and marketing magazines for up-to-date figures and projections.)

As an alternative to e-commerce through the organisation's own transaction-based website, the following options may be considered.

(a) **Storefronts**: getting online stores such as Amazon or Yahoo! to catalogue and sell your products or services online through their sites. (In other words, an online distribution channel, with the associated benefits – and the drawbacks of competing with other brands, losing margins and so on.)

(b) **Auction sites**: putting merchandise (surplus products, used products, limited-supply items and so on) up for auction on sites such as eBay. Most auction sites charge a transaction fee, but the marketing organisation has no processing costs: it merely has to set a 'reserve' (lowest acceptable) price, write a marketing blurb and upload pictures for the auction site, and ship out the product when sold. Products may be put up for auction for promotional purposes, using the blurb, photos and a link to the company's own website. Check out: www.ebay.com.

5.4 E-mail

The term 'electronic mail', or e-mail, is used to describe various systems for sending data or messages electronically via a telephone or data network and a central 'server' computer. E-mail has replaced letters, memos, faxes, documents and even telephone calls – combining many of the possibilities of each medium with new advantages of speed, cost and convenience.

E-mail offers many advantages for internal/external customer communication.

- Messages can be sent and received very **fast** (allowing real time messaging dialogue)

- E-mail is **economical** (estimated 20 times cheaper than fax): often allowing worldwide transmission for the cost of a local telephone call (connecting to the local service point of the Internet Service Provider).

- The recipient gets a '**hard copy**' message, and the sender has documentary evidence of message transmission and retrieval by the recipient (for legal/logistical purposes).

- Messages can be sent **worldwide** at any **time**.

- The user can prepare **complex documents** (spreadsheets, graphics, photos) for sending as 'attachments' to e-mail covering messages. These can be printed out by the recipient, as a convenient alternative to fax.

- E-mail **message management** software (such as Outlook Express) has convenient features such as: message copying (to multiple recipients); integration with an 'address book' (database of contacts); automatic alert messages sent when the target recipient is unable to access his or her e-mail immediately, with alternative contact details; stationery and template features, allowing corporate identity to be applied; facilities for mail organisation and filing.

5.5 Intranet and extranet

'Inter' means 'between': 'intra' means 'within'; 'extra' means 'outside'. This may be a useful reminder of some of the inter-related terminology in this area.

- The **Internet** is used to disseminate and exchange information among the public at large.

- An **intranet** is used to disseminate and exchange information 'in-house' within an organisation. Only employees are able to access this information. The firewall surrounding it fends off unauthorised access.

- An **extranet** is used to communicate with selected people outside the organisation.

The idea behind an Intranet is that companies set up their own mini versions of the Internet, using a combination of their own networked computers and Internet technology. Each employee has a browser and a server computer distributes corporate information as well as offering access to the global Net.

Typical intranet content

- **Performance data**: linked to sales, inventory, job progress and other database and reporting systems, enabling employees to process and analyse data to fulfil their work objectives

- **Employment information**: online policy and procedures manuals (health and safety, disciplinary and grievance), training and induction material, internal contacts for help and information

- **Employee support/information**: advice on first aid, healthy working at computer terminals, training courses, offered, resources held in the corporate library and so on.

- **Notice boards** for the posting of message to and from employees: notice of meetings, events, trade union activities

- **Departmental home pages**: information and news about each department's personnel and activities to aid identification and cross-functional understanding

- **Bulletins or newsletters**: details of product launches and marketing campaigns, staff moves, changes in company policy – or whatever might be communicated through the print equivalent, plus links to relevant databases or departmental home pages.

- **E-mail facilities** for the exchange of messages, memos and reports between employees in different locations

- **Upward communication**: suggestion schemes, feedback questionnaires

- **Individual personnel files**, to which employees can download training materials, references, certificates and appraisals

Benefits of intranet

- Cost savings from the elimination of storage, printing and distribution of documents that can instead be exchanged electronically or be made available online

- More frequent use made of online documents than printed reference resources (eg procedures manuals) and more flexible and efficient interrogation and updating of data

- Wider access to corporate information. This facilitates multi-directional communication and co-ordination (particularly for multi-site working). It is also a mechanism of corporate culture and *esprit de corps*. The term '**virtual team**' has been coined to describe how ICT can link people in structures which emulate the dynamics of teamworking (identity, solidarity, shared goals and information) despite the geographical dispersion of team members in different locations or constantly on the move (as, for example, sales representatives).

Definition

An **extranet** is an intranet that is accessible to authorised outsiders.

Whereas an intranet resides behind a firewall and is accessible only to people who are members of the same company or organisation, an extranet provides various levels of accessibility to outsiders. Only those outsiders with a valid username and password can access an extranet, with varying levels of access rights enabling control over what people can view. Since information will not be available to the public in general, it can be used as part of a relationship marketing strategy. Examples include the member-only pages of professional bodies (and their student equivalents), which make information and downloads available only to registered members.

Extranets are useful tools for **business partners**. They can share data or systems to provide smoother transaction processing and more efficient services for customers. Extranets therefore allow better use of the knowledge held by an organisation – by facilitating access to that knowledge. An extranet may be used to:

- Provide a 'pooled' service which a number of business partners can access

- Exchange news that is of use to partner companies and clients

- Share training or development resources

- Publicise loyalty schemes, sponsorships, exhibition attendance information and other promotional tools

- Exchange potentially large volumes of transaction data efficiently

- Provide online presentations to business partners and prospects (and not competitors)

5.6 Electronic Data Interchange (EDI)

Electronic Data Interchange (EDI) is the exchange of transactional data between organisations by electronic means as a replacement for documents.

EDI is the electronic transfer of business information, with the information being sent in a format that conforms to certain standards. It introduces the possibility of 'paperless' trading and promises the end of repetitive form filling, stock orders and other forms of 'paper shifting'. EDI is used predominantly between large business customers and their suppliers eg, General Motors in the automobile industry use EDI as a part of the 'just-in-time' (JIT) organisation of the supply of components and raw materials to their assembly plants.

EDI is also of growing significance in the retail trade, enabling a large superstore such as Tesco to organise supplies from a central warehouse (and from external suppliers) to its chain of retail stores. Using EDI and electronic point of sale (EPOS) technology, Tesco deals with over 1,000 suppliers across computer networks so that stocks can be replenished exactly when needed, forecast sales patterns can be passed on to suppliers and invoices forwarded.

In banking and financial industries, EDI and related applications of IT are revolutionising the entire system of moving funds, encouraging the emergence of global or fully-internationalised money and securities markets in which the electronic transmission of funds is fast replacing 'paper-shifting'. In another thirty years, in an almost 'cashless society', most transactions to do with borrowing. paying, receiving, depositing and moving money will probably be done on wallet-sized personal communicators.

6 WRITTEN AND TELEPHONE

6.1 Written methods of communication

Although verbal communication is the most common form of day-to-day communication, by its nature it is transitory and is often informal. Hence a verbal agreement is commonly supplemented by written confirmation – the written communication serves as a permanent formal record of what passed in what might have been a relatively informal manner (eg in a telephone conversation).

Written methods of communication of all sorts – letters, memos, bulletins, files, circulars – are the norm in many companies. The dominant characteristic of many managers' working day is paperwork and meetings. They do have the advantage that being in permanent or hard copy form they are less open to misinterpretation. With meetings, for instance, formal minutes may be taken, circulated and agreed to as the definitive written evidence of the meeting. Written methods of communication can be very flexibly used. When trying to reach a number of workers in one place notice boards are often used, typically to announce current events, meetings and similar matters which are not of crucial significance.

The advantages of written messages include the following.

(a) They provide a *permanent record* of a transaction or agreement, for confirmation and recollection of details. Evidence may also be necessary in legal affairs.

(b) They provide *confirmation* and *clarification* of verbal messages, again in case evidence should be needed, but also as an aid to memory.

(c) They are easily *duplicated* and sent out to numerous recipients: this ensures that information, operating instructions etc will be consistent.

(d) They enable a difficult piece of communication to be re-worded and rewritten over a period of time, so that the exact shade of meaning can be conveyed.

(e) They can be *stored* and later *retrieved* for reference and analysis as required.

(f) They are the cheapest form of contacting a range of individuals.

The main disadvantage is that there is no means of knowing whether the message has been received and understood by the person notified.

Other disadvantages include:

- *Time*. A written message can take time to produce, and to send (eg by post), if expensive technology is beyond the user's reach. Instant feedback is not available, and so errors in interpretation may not be corrected immediately. Because of the time factor, swift 'interactive' exchanges of opinion, attitudes etc are impossible.

- *Inflexibility*. Once sent, the message cannot immediately be altered or amended, even though circumstances change, errors are discovered etc. Written communication also tends to come across as formal and impersonal, so in situations requiring greater sensitivity or persuasion, the personal presence or voice of the sender may be more effective.

- *Perceived irrelevance*? Written messages do not have the immediacy of the phone call and so may not be read.

- *Poor drafting*. Written messages that are poorly drafted may not be understood.

6.2 Written formats – planned communication

As well as e-mail, written communications formats commonly used in business include the following.

Letters	• Used for interpersonal communication via the external mail system (eg from the organisation to external stakeholders)
	• Flexible for use in a wide variety of situations
	• Often used to provide 'covering' or confirming details
	• May be used within the organisation for confidential or personal matters
Memos	• Equivalent of a letter in internal communications within the organisation
	• Flexible for use in a wide variety of work situations
	• Efficient, especially where pre-printed stationery or e-mail formats are used
	• Can be overused, where a phone call or note would suffice

NOTES

Handbooks and journals	• Used for employee communications
	• Can be used to set out work-relevant information, policies and regulations, procedures
	• Can be used to brief and update employees on performance, results, staff news and meetings
Reports	• Enable a number of people to review complex facts and arguments, for decision-making
	• Should be objective in content and impersonal in style
	• May be formal (subject to strict structural conventions) or informal (in the form of a memo or e-mail)

Reports are meant to be *useful*. There should be no such thing as 'information for information's sake' in an efficient organisation: information is stored in files and retrieved for a purpose. The information contained in a business report might be used:

- as a permanent record and source of reference; or

- as a management tool – a source of information prepared in order to assist in management decision-making. Often more junior managers do the 'legwork' in obtaining information on a matter and then prepare a report for more senior managers to consider. This saves senior managers' time and ensures that the information on which they base their decision is more objective than if it had all been gathered and used by one person only.

Depending on its ultimate purpose, a report may consist of:

(a) *information*, retrieved from files or other sources as a basis for management activity;

(b) *narrative* or *description*, eg of one-off events or procedures, such as a takeover target or the installation of new equipment;

(c) *analysis*, that is a further processing of data and information to render it more useful; or

(d) *evaluation* and *recommendation*, directly assisting in the decision-making process.

Different types of information may be presented in a report.

- *Descriptive or factual information.* This consists of a description of facts and is objective: inferences can be drawn from the facts, but they must be logical and unbiased.

- *Instructive information.* This is information that tells the report user how to do something, or what to do. A recommendation in a report is a form of advice, and is therefore instructive information.

- *Dialectical information.* This consists of opinions and ideas, based on an objective assessment of the facts and with reasons for why these opinions and ideas have been reached.

The value of recognising these different types of information is that it can help to make clear what a report writer is trying to say.

PROFESSIONAL EDUCATION

- 'These are the facts' (*factual*).

- 'This is what the facts seem to suggest is happening, has happened or will happen' (*dialectical*).

- 'This is what should be done about matters to sort out the situation' (*instructive*).

6.3 Telephone – informal communication

The telephone has been an informal medium that implies that personal contact is important in the sending of the message. The message sender has had control in when to initiate this contact. The message receiver has often been willing to give the telephone message priority over a face-to-face meeting. Most people have had the experience of talking to someone who interrupts the conversation to answer the telephone. Advances in telecommunications technology have changed the relationship between the caller and the called. Call display, call block, call return, and other services mean that the person called can now screen calls, know who called, and block incoming calls from a certain number. The widespread use of mobile telephones and computerised communication networks has changed the nature of the telephone. It is losing its personal nature and is becoming a more formal tool used to accomplish routine work.

For example, a salesperson on the road can use a mobile phone in the car to contact buyers, suppliers, and a support person at head office who is tied into the computer systems that track orders and deliveries. The telephone is used as a tool to get the latest information to the salesperson, to schedule appointments, and to relay data on orders and information on clients back to head office. The sales agent is using the telephone not as an informal way to chat but as an indispensable tool to perform the work.

The services available to users are increasing all the time, making the mobile phone a tool of **promotion** and **e-commerce** as well as interpersonal communication. Communication services include:

Messaging	• Voice mail
	• Short message service (SMS) which allows text messages of up to 160 characters to be transmitted over a standard digital phone
	• Paging services
	• Access to e-mail messages, downloaded from the Internet
Call management	• Call barring
	• Conference calls
	• Call divert
Corporate services	• Integrated numbering, so that people have a single contact number for their desk and mobile phones
	• Virtual private networks that incorporate mobile phones as well as conventional desktop phones

6.4 Computer Telephony Integration (CTI)

Computer Telephony Integration (CTI) systems gather information about callers such as their telephone number and customer account number or demographic information (age, income, interests etc). This is stored on a customer database and can be called up and sent to the screen of the person dealing with the call, perhaps before the call has even been put through.

Thus sales staff dealing with hundreds of calls every day might appear to remember individual callers personally and know in advance what they are likely to order. Order forms with key details entered already can be displayed on screen automatically, saving time for both the sales staff and the caller.

Alternatively a busy manager might note that an unwelcome call is coming in on the 'screen pop' that appears on her PC and choose to direct it to her voice mailbox rather than dealing with it at once.

As another example, a bank might use CTI to prompt sales people with changes in share prices and with the details of the investors they should call to offer dealing advice.

Activity 5 (30 mins)

'Effective communication enhances the administrative function'. Comment on this statement and highlight guidelines for effective communication.

---

7 INTERPERSONAL SKILLS

7.1 Personal and Interpersonal skills

Interpersonal skills involve inspiring, motivating, leading and controlling people to achieve goals that are often poorly defined.

Definition

Interpersonal skills are the skills used in interactions and relationships between two or more people.

They include:

(a) Building rapport or a sense of 'being in tune with' another person, which draws them into a relationship

(b) Building trust and respect, so that the relationship is maintained and co-operation facilitated

(c) Managing conflict in such a way that the relationship is preserved

(d) Persuading or influencing another person to do what you want them to do or to share your beliefs

(e) Negotiating or bargaining in order to reach mutually acceptable or compromise solutions to problems

(f) Communicating assertively, so that you uphold your rights and get your needs met -without violating the rights or ignoring the needs of others

(g) Communicating informatively, so that you give (and receive) relevant and timely information

(h) Communicating supportively, so that you encourage the other person and gain their commitment

People need these skills to:

- understand and manage the roles, relationships, attitudes and perceptions operating in any situation in which two or more people are involved

- communicate clearly and effectively

- achieve their aims from an interpersonal encounter (ideally allowing the other parties to emerge satisfied too)

Issues to consider in interpersonal communication and work relationships

Issue	Comment
Goal	What does the other person want from the process? What do you want from the process? What will both parties need and be trying to do to achieve their aims? Can both parties emerge satisfied?
Perceptions	What, if any, are likely to be the factors causing 'distortion' of the way both parties see the issues and each other? (Attitudes, feelings, expectations?)
Roles	What 'roles' are the parties playing? (Superior/subordinate, customer/server, complainer/soother) What expectations does this create of the way they will behave?
Resistances	What may the other person be 'afraid of? What may he or she be trying to protect? (His or her self-image/ego, attitudes?)
Attitudes	What sources of difference, conflict or lack of understanding might there be, arising from attitudes and other factors that shape them (sex, race, specialism, hierarchy)?
Relationships	What are the relative positions of the parties and the nature of the relationship between them? (Superior/subordinate? Formal/informal? Work/non-work?)
Environment	What factors in the immediate and situational environment might affect the issues and the people? (eg competitive environment: customer care; pressures of disciplinary situation: nervousness; physical surroundings: formality/informality)

7.2 Why are interpersonal skills important?

Good working relationships and good interpersonal skills can assist in the following areas.

Area	Comment
Motivation	Work can satisfy people's social needs because it provides relationships
Communication	Poor interpersonal relationships can cause a barrier to communicating effectively -messages will be misinterpreted
Team working and team-building	Good working relationships and good interpersonal skills can develop a climate in which people can communicate openly and honestly
Customer care	Good interpersonal skills are recognised as being increasingly important when dealing with customers
Career development	Good interpersonal skills are increasingly necessary to get promotion
Managerial roles	Many of the managerial roles require interpersonal skills
Power and persuasion	Interpersonal skills can be a source of personal power in an organisation and can make a manager more effective
Team management	Interpersonal skills are required for the manager's tasks of appraisal, interviewing etc

7.3 Communication skills

In addition, a range of communication skills will be deployed. The following checklist identifies and classifies communication skills.

Oral	Written	Visual/non-verbal
Clear pronunciation	Correct spelling	Understanding of control over body language and facial expressions
Suitable vocabulary	Suitable vocabulary	Drawing ability
Correct grammar/syntax	Correct grammar/syntax	
Fluency	Good writing or typing	
Expressive delivery	Suitable style	

Skills in sending messages include the following.

- **Selecting and organising your material** – marshalling your thoughts and constructing your sentences, arguments etc

- **Judging the effect of your message** on the particular recipient in that particular situation

- **Choosing language and media** accordingly

- **Adapting your communication style** accordingly – putting people at their ease, smoothing over difficulties (tact) or being comforting/challenging/ informal/formal as the situation and relationship demand

- Using **non-verbal signals** to reinforce (or at least not to undermine) your spoken message

- Seeking and interpreting **feedback**

Skills in receiving messages include the following.

- **Reading attentively** and actively making sure you understand the content, looking up unfamiliar words and doubtful facts if necessary and evaluating the information given: is it logical? correct? objective?

- Extracting **relevant information** from the message and filtering out the non-essentials.

- **Listening attentively** and actively – concentrating on the message and **not** on what you are going to say next; questioning and evaluating what you are hearing.

- **Interpreting** the message's underlying meaning, if any, and evaluating your own reactions. Are you reading into the message more or less than what is really there?

- Asking **questions** in a way that will elicit the information you want **to obtain.**

- Interpreting **non-verbal signals** and how they confirm or contradict **the** spoken message.

- Giving helpful **feedback** if the medium is appropriate (eg poor telephone line) or the message is unclear, insufficient etc.

Activity 6   **(15 mins)**

Which written formats do you use most often in interpersonal communication (a) with colleagues or team members, (b) with your superiors and (c) with friends at work?

(a) What do you find most convenient about each of these formats?
(b) What factors or guidelines do you have to bear in mind when using them?

7.4   Effective negotiation skills

Negotiating is an activity that seeks to reach agreement between two or more starting positions.

The skills of a negotiator can be summarised under three main headings.

(a) **Interpersonal skills** – the use of good communicating techniques, the user of power and influence, and the ability to impress a personal style on the tactics of negotiation

(b) **Analytical skills** – the ability to analyse information, diagnose problems, to plan and set objectives, and the exercise of good judgement in interpreting results

(c) **Technical skills** – attention to detail and thorough case preparation

There are behaviours that are typical of successful negotiations and distinguish them from the less successful.

Successful negotiators	Less successful negotiators
• avoid criticising or attacking the other person and concentrate instead on 'attacking' the problem in a no nonsense but constructive way.	• are more likely to get locked into an attacking spiral where one side attacks the other, which provokes a counter attack and so on.
• ask many more questions than the less skilled. The skilled negotiator asks questions not only to gain more information and understanding but also as an alternative to disagreeing bluntly, and as a means of putting forward suggestions.	• tend to assume that they understand the other person's point of view and that the other person has the same basic information. This makes asking questions redundant.
• summarises and tests understanding, knowing that being explicit aids common understanding and leads to quality agreement that is more likely to stick.	
• keep the emotional temperature down by sticking to the facts.	• are inclined to exaggeration, using expressions such as 'an offer you can't refuse' and 'mutually beneficial'
• is more likely to say things that reveal what he or she is thinking, intending and feeling than the less skilled.	• feel vulnerable to losing the argument and are more likely to 'keep their cards close to their chests'.

7.5 The process of consultation

Consultation is the process where, on a regular basis, management genuinely seeks the views, ideas and feelings of employees before a decision is taken.

Definition

> **Consultation** is where one party seeks the views of another party before either party takes a decision

Consultation is not the same as negotiation. Negotiation implies acceptance by both parties that agreement between them is required before a decision is taken. Consultation implies a willingness to listen to the views of another while reserving the right to take the final decision, with or without agreement on both sides.

For the effective manager, using his or her interpersonal skills, a way of consulting subordinates is to discuss proposals with them. The 'I have decided to give you X approach is nowhere near as effective as the 'I've been thinking – do you feel that you can tackle X approach?'

The advantages that can be associated with consultation include the following.

- Improved quality of decisions because the manager is using the collected knowledge and ingenuity of those who are most affected by the decisions.

- Better co-operation between managers and employees because people will accept even those decisions that they do not like if their views have been taken into consideration, assuming they have been told why the decision has been taken.

- It serves as a valuable preliminary to negotiation. When representatives have been involved in the discussion of 'how' they will be better informed when it becomes a matter of 'how much'?

- Increased efficiency of the entire organisation by involving employees in achieving a better product or service.

- Help industrial relations by allowing managers and their subordinates the opportunity to understand each other's views and objectives.

For a process of consultation to be genuine, it must not be used when a manager has already reached a decision. His or her mind will then be closed to alternatives, the meeting will sense that it is an insulting charade of 'guess what's in my mind'. Instead of gaining commitment to the decision, the pseudo-consultation will alienate. There will be resentment, which might result in non co-operation.

Consulting implies decisions are only made after consultation. However, the final decision may not include any or all of the ideas put forward. Subordinates may feel cheated and not truly involved.

NOTES

Chapter roundup

- The objective of communication by a manager or administrator is to exchange, impart or receive *information*.

- Effective communication is a two-way process, perhaps best expressed as a cycle.

- The changing economic and business climate is likely to put increased pressures upon communication systems. The challenges require an enhanced commitment to quality, profitability and the ability to manage change

- Communication has changed in recent decades with the development of technologies offering higher speed, wider access to information, 24-hour, 7-day global communication (and commerce), greater interactivity and multi-media presentation and greater personalisation/customisation of communication

- A meeting is a group of people coming together for the purpose of resolving problems or making decisions.

- The face-to-face meeting can be formal or informal, vertical, horizontal, or diagonal, but it is always the richest communication medium.

- The Internet is used to disseminate and exchange information among the public at large. An intranet can be used to perform the same function within an organisation, and an extranet within a network of selected customers, prospects, members or business partners.

- The Internet (with related tools such as e-mail and website marketing) is a complex and powerful promotional tool for a wide range of promotional activities.

- E-mail has replaced letters, memos, faxes, documents and even telephone calls – combining many of the possibilities of each medium with new advantages of speed, cost and convenience.

- Electronic Data Interchange (EDI) is the exchange of transactional data between organisations by electronic means as a replacement for documents.

- The main disadvantage of written communication is that there is no means of knowing whether the message has been received and understood by the person notified.

- Interpersonal skills involve inspiring, motivating, leading and controlling people to achieve goals that are often poorly defined.

- Negotiation implies acceptance by both parties that agreement between them is required before a decision is taken. Consultation implies a willingness to listen to the views of another while reserving the right to take the final decision, with or without agreement on both sides.

Quick quiz

1   Draw a model of the communication process

2   What do you understand by the term '24-7 global communication'?

3   What is a quorum?

4   How will electronic media help people working from home?

5   E-mail is cheaper than fax for transmitting hard copy messages to remote locations

    True   ☐

    False ☐

6   What do the following stand for?

    (a)   E-mail

    (b)   V-mail

    (c)   SMS

    (d)   EDI

Answers to quick quiz

1   The process of communication can be modelled as follows:

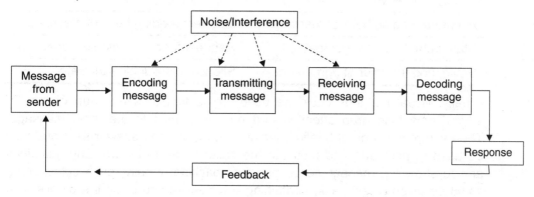

(See para 1.2)

2   Information and communications technology (ICT) has enabled 24-hour 7-day global communication: across working or office hours, time zones and geographical distances. The Internet allows users to access information/ services and perform transactions at any time of any day. Nor is there any distinction between local and international sites, in terms of speed or cost of access. (Physical delivery of products ordered will, of course, re-erect some of the geographical barriers.) (2.2)

3   A quorum is the minimum number of members required to hold the meeting. (3.2)

4   Increased numbers of *people working from home* will mean that more effort must be directed towards fostering a feeling of belonging to the organisation. Electronic media will help in the maintenance of links (both formally and informally) between worker and employer. (2.1)

5   True. (5.4)

6   (a) Electronic mail
      (b) Voice mail
      (c) Short Message Service
      (d) Electronic Data Interchange (5)

Answers to activities

1   The main items are:

- 'transmission' ie: onus on the sender to sent the information;

- 'information' not data. Data is dead, historic or irrelevant; information tells the recipient something he does not know;

- 'received and understood' ie, in the sense intended by the sender;

- 'leads to action' ie, if it does not lead to action was communication necessary?

2

Positive feedback	Negative feedback
Action taken as requested	No action taken or wrong action taken
Letter/memo/note confirming receipt of message and replying in an appropriate way	No written response where expected
Accurate reading back of message	Incorrect reading back of message
Statement: 'Yes, I've got that.'	Request for clarification or repetition
Smile, nod, murmur of agreement	Silence, blank look, frown etc

3   Initially, visual methods could be used, eg, a film or a mock-up of the TV advertisement, to grab attention and provide impact to the main message. Then verbal methods of briefing, lectures, question and answer sessions may be used to persuade and motivate the sales team, to answer any questions and to show top management's personal backing. Finally, each salesperson could be given a fact pack, containing a written record of all the details, test results, etc for later reference.

4   (a) Telephone, confirmed in writing later (order form, letter) – or e-mail order (if both parties have access)

      (b) Noticeboard (or employee Web page, if available) or general meeting: depending on the sensitivity of the topic and the need for staff to ask questions.

      (c) Face-to-face private conversation – but it would be a good idea to confirm the outcome in writing so that records can be maintained.

      (d) Telephone, email or face-to-face (if close by).

      (e) Face-to-face, supported by clear written notes. You can then use visual aids or gestures to help explain. This will also give you the opportunity to check the group's understanding – while the notes will save the group having to memorise what you say, and enable them to focus on understanding

5   Administration is closely concerned with the processing and conveying of information and effective communication can only help this. Communication itself is necessary for a variety of reasons including:

- to exercise day-to-day control;
- to facilitate planned change;
- to cope with unplanned changes and unforeseen circumstances.

The better and more effective the communication the more efficient will be the administrative function. The three reasons shown immediately above may be broken down into more specific purposes including:

- to convey information about what is happening internally and externally;

- to explain the nature and implications of current and anticipated problems;

- to establish guidelines, policies and procedures of dealing with a number of differing situations;

- to stimulate action;

- to enhance the quality of staff relationships.

Downward communication is concerned with planning and control and upward communication is usually concerned with feedback from all levels within the organisation, together with information from external sources such as customers.

If communication is poor then it is likely that the result will be poor, with inadequate control and faulty co-ordination. This could result in:

- poor understanding of working instructions and responsibilities;
- poor awareness of organisational objectives;
- lack of warning of problems;
- lack of employee participation;
- isolation of management from other staff;
- disregard of real problems.

Overall the organisation will not be working as a whole but as a group of isolated individuals and sections of individuals and obviously this cannot be good for the organisation.

6   The answer to this will depend on your own situation.

BPP
PROFESSIONAL EDUCATION

Chapter 15 :
DESIGN AND IMPROVE APPROPRIATE SYSTEMS

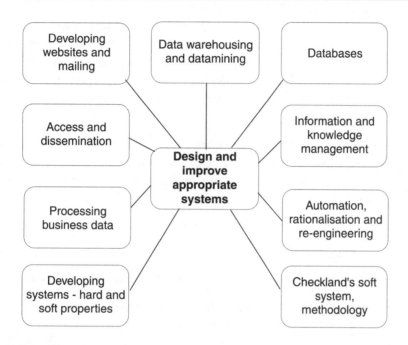

Introduction

This chapter describes how new information systems are developed, with special attention to organisational design issues and business re-engineering. It describes systems analysis and design and other core activities involved in the building of any information system. Different methodologies emphasise different aspects of the development process. For example, Soft Systems methodology concentrates on the problem formulation stage, while structured methodologies emphasise the design of solutions.

As information systems have developed, they have allowed organisations to gather and store vast amounts of data and knowledge. Making information available quickly and easily to those who could act on it is a challenging and important task. In this chapter we explain the concepts of information management and knowledge management before identifying and evaluating various systems available for the management of knowledge.

Your objectives

After completing this chapter you should be able to:

(a) Analyse existing approaches to the collection, formatting, storage and disseminating of information and knowledge

(b) Justify and implement appropriate changes to the collection, formatting, storage and disseminating of information and knowledge

(c) Consider ways of improving access to your systems of information and knowledge to others as appropriate and implement

1 PROCESSING BUSINESS DATA

1.1 Processing features

Processing business data can be said to have the following features for both manual as well as electronic data processing.

(a) *Collecting data in the first place.* There must be data to process and this may arise in the course of operations. There has to be a system or procedure for ensuring that all the data needed for processing is collected and made available for processing. Collecting data is an important step that must not be overlooked because the quality, accuracy and completeness of the data will affect the quality of information produced.

(b) *Converting the data into information,* perhaps by summarising it or classifying it and/or producing total figures etc. For example, a sales ledger system might be required to process data about goods despatched to satisfy customer orders so as to:

- produce and send out invoices;

- record the invoices sent out in the customers' personal ledgers;

- produce a report of the total value of invoices sent out in the day/week etc;

- record the total value of invoices sent out in the debtors' control account in the nominal ledger.

The output consists of invoices and figures for sales totals (ie management information). Updating the personal ledgers and the debtors' control account are file updating activities to keep the sales ledger records up to date.

(c) *Updating files to incorporate the processed data.* The example of sales ledger work has already been mentioned. Updating files means bringing them up to date to record current transactions.

(d) *The dissemination of information to users.* This includes a variety of reports (on-screen, or hard copy), for example:

- scheduled reports, routinely prepared on a regular basis (eg payroll report) and reviewed to ensure that any control information it contains is used;

- exception reports which delineate deviations from plan;

- reports produced on demand (ie only when requested, but not as a matter of course);

- planning reports (eg forecasts).

1.2 Information in the organisation

Since the source of action within any organisation is decision-making, the object of communicating information within an organisation should be to serve those persons taking the relevant decisions. It is therefore natural to consider the type and level of decisions each manager has to take. Only then can the following be considered:

(a) What information is required?

(b) How should it be collected and by whom?

(c) When and from where should it be collected?

A great deal of interpreted information is disseminated within an organisation for use by its members. The organisation as an information-processing entity is shown below.

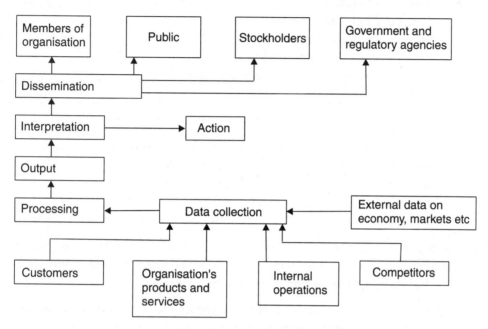

Figure 15.1 Organisation as an information-processing entity

The typical information requirements of organisations that are operating in different sectors such as manufacturing, service, the public sector and non-profit organisations such as charities will all be similar. They all have customers (sponsors, contributors, members), products or services, internal operations, competitors and the environment to obtain information from.

2 DEVELOPING SYSTEMS – HARD AND SOFT PROPERTIES

Systems thinking is central to collaboration, placing the organisation within the web of relationships that define and sustain it. A systems view of the world implies a focus on the whole – not just the constituent parts. To identify and establish productive relationships, an organisation and its employees must understand how they fit into the larger systems of which they are a part.

2.1 Hard and soft properties

Systems theory explores the nature of systems and the characteristics of systems and approaches that are suited to different situations. Organisations are social systems. All social systems are open to a wide range of influences, which means they are sensitive to a wide variety of environmental factors and are often exposed to unstructured problems.

Unstructured problems are sometimes referred to as 'soft' problems. Different people might have different views of what the problem that needs to be addressed is, and a solution might have to satisfy a variety of different objectives.

On the other hand, a 'hard' approach is based on structured, logical problems, where the objective is clear.

A **hard** approach is suitable in circumstances when:

- The problem can be clearly defined
- Objectives are clear
- The problem is self-contained
- Information needs are known
- A solution can be recognised
- Standard solution techniques are applicable

A **soft** approach is suitable in circumstances when:

- The problem is difficult to define
- Tastes, values, judgement and opinions are involved
- It is not clear what is known and what is needed
- It is not clear what the solution should achieve
- The problem is 'people' oriented
- There are no standard solution techniques available

Many problems or situations have both hard and soft properties, for example an information systems project. Properties can be classified as either hard or soft – although in practise the two will, in some circumstances, be related.

The hard properties would include the specifications of the system, for example processing speeds, the space required to accommodate the system and the budget available to develop the system. Soft properties are usually people related.

2.2 Hard systems approach

Different approaches to systems development place differing emphasis on hard or soft areas. Early systems development approaches, such as the systems lifecycle, tended to be 'harder' in their approach than more modern approaches.

In the early days of business computing, computers were used to automate processing activities. To a large extent, the systems that were developed simply matched previous manual procedures. However, the process of managing information systems development has moved on from being a matter of technical control over a few computer programmers to being a major management operation involving large parts of an organisation and elements of its environment.

2.3 Systems lifecycle

The systems lifecycle (sometimes referred to as the Systems Development Lifecycle or SDLC) is a traditional method of building information systems. This disciplined approach to systems development identifies several stages of development. (Note that the number and name of the stages varies depending on the author or organisation referred to – but the principle of a structured approach is consistent.)

NOTES

Definition

> The term **'systems lifecycle'** describes the stages a system moves through from inception until it is discarded or replaced.

Stage	Comment
Project definition	Involves an investigation and analysis of the organisation's information requirements to decide if a new or modified information system is required. If a new project is identified its objectives, scope and project plan are developed.
Feasibility study	This involves a review of the existing system and the identification of a range of possible alternative solutions. A feasible (technical, operational, economic, social) solution will be selected – or a decision not to proceed made. Findings are usually contained in a feasibility study report that describes the activities required in the remaining lifecycle phases.
Design	The logical and physical design specifications are produced in a detailed specification of the new system.
Programming or software selection	If bespoke software is to be produced, analysts work with programmers to prepare program specifications and then the programs. If off-the-shelf software is suitable, packages are evaluated (perhaps in a report) and selected.
Installation	Steps are taken to put the system into operation. Testing, file conversion and user training are carried out. A formal conversion plan is developed.
Post-implementation	The system is used and evaluated. A formal post-implementation audit determines how well the system has met its objectives and whether any modifications are required.

2.4 Drawbacks of the lifecycle approach

The systems lifecycle is considered a hard systems approach as it has a narrow focus. The approach efficiently automates existing procedures within easily defined processing requirements. The resulting systems are modelled on the manual systems they are replacing.

Sequential models (such as the lifecycle model) restrict user input throughout much of the process. (A sequential model is one where a stage is not started until the previous stage is complete.) This often results in substantial and costly modifications late in the development process. It becomes increasingly difficult and expensive to change system requirements the further a system is developed.

Time overruns are common. The sequential nature of the process means a hold-up on one stage would stop development completely – contributing to time overruns. Time pressures and lack of user involvement often result in a poor quality system.

Because of these drawbacks the lifecycle approach is not as widely used today as in the past. However, it is still used with success for building systems where requirements are highly structured and well-defined eg large transaction processing systems.

2.5 Soft systems approach

The soft systems approach to systems development aims to take into account the soft properties of the implementation – this approach looks at the wider picture. Some examples of soft properties that should be considered during systems development and implementation are:

- **Job security and status** – employees might think that a new system will put them out of a job, because the computer will perform routines that are currently done manually, and so reduce the need for human intervention. In some cases, the resistance to a new system might stem from a fear that it will result in a loss of status for the department concerned. For example, the management of the department might believe that a computer system will give 'control' over information gathering and dissemination to another group.

- **Career prospects** – managers and staff might think that a new system will damage their career prospects by reducing the requirement for middle managers and therefore reducing opportunities for promotion.

- **Social change** – new systems might disrupt the established social system in the office. Individuals who are used to working together might be separated into different groups, and individuals used to working on their own might be expected to join a group.

- **Fear of depersonalisation** – staff may be afraid that the computer will 'take over' and they will be reduced to being operators chained to the machine, losing the ability to introduce the 'human touch' to the work they do. This is not wholly unrealistic.

Another fear is that the new system will expose how inefficient previous methods of information gathering and information use had been. Individuals may feel that they are being criticised by the revelation of any such deficiencies.

To overcome the human problems with systems design and implementation, management and systems analysts must recognise them, and do what they can to resolve them.

3 CHECKLAND'S SOFT SYSTEMS METHODOLOGY (SSM)

3.1 Complex relationships

Checkland's 'soft systems methodology' is a response to difficulty in applying the approach of hard systems (engineering) thinking to business problems. Hard systems engineering tends to emphasise:

- measurable system objectives
- top down decomposition of systems into sub-systems.

Advanced systems engineering may show systems with unexpected and counter-intuitive behaviour and complex feedback loops between components but systems engineering when applied to 'human systems' leads to problems.

Organisation goals may be in dispute. It is wrong to assume that all organisational members accept the views and goals of top management.

Formal methods usually begin with a problem statement but fixing the problem too early tends to hide problems. The method itself can restrict what will be elicited – conclusions will reflect methods and starting positions.

With SSM the process is as important as the outcome. The experience itself of applying an SSM approach will change the organisation. This will arise from changed views about the problem and possible solutions.

SSM is based on a number of assumptions:

- People attempt to place a *meaning* on their observations and experiences

- This meaning is the individual's *interpretation* of the event/situation

- The interpretation leads to the intention to follow a particular course of action

- Once the course is decided, *purposeful action* is taken – altering the event or situation leading to the action and creating a cycle of activity

- SSM involves a circular process of enquiry leading to action – shown in the diagram below:

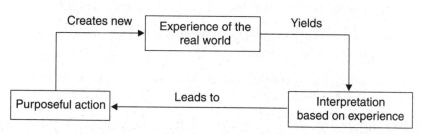

Figure 15.2 Soft systems methodology

3.2 Seven stage process

In principle, an SSM project is done by the people of the organisation, with a consultant-facilitator. It is divided into seven distinct stages. These are:

1 **Problem situation** – finding out about the problem situation. This is basic research into the problem area. Who are the key players? How does the process work now?

2 **Analysis** – expressing the problem situation in three steps – intervention, prevalent culture and power relationships. (Rich picture)

3 **Root definition** of relevant systems – selecting how to view the situation and producing root definitions. From what different perspectives can we look at this problem situation?

4 **Conceptualisation** – based on the root definition for each area defined, build a conceptual model of the required capabilities

5 **Comparison** of the conceptual models with the real world. Use gap analysis, compare scenarios, and tables of comparisons and key-players' contrasting opinions to identify what part(s) of the conceptual models are lacking or poorly supported in the existing problem situation

6   **Changes** – identify culturally feasible and systemically desirable changes. Are there ways of improving the situation?

7   **Action** – the decision to implement the defined changes thus changing the problem situation itself and restarting the cycle.

A key feature of SSM is to keep the project vague and wide ranging for as long as possible – don't jump to conclusions, and don't ignore the current situation by concentrating on some idealised future.

There may be checklists of things to look for, models and frameworks of consideration may be used but without getting stuck with one model. Typically brainstorming techniques and force-field analysis may be used.

3.3   Streams of enquiry

SSM incorporates two related streams of enquiry:

(a)   The logic-driven stream of enquiry
(b)   The cultural stream of enquiry

The cultural stream of enquiry

There are three types of analysis involved in the cultural stream of enquiry:

(a)   An analysis of the relationship between the client, the would-be problem solver and the problem owner.

(b)   The second analysis considers the evolving set of relationships between roles, norms and values.

(c)   The third analysis focuses on how different interests reach accommodation and how power is expressed.

In combination all three types of analysis complement and enrich the logic-based stream of analysis.

This examination of the background of the problem can be expressed in the form of a rich picture, which is a representation of the situation showing the relevant relationships. It can be any sort of picture, a diagram or a cartoon – it can be funny, sad or political. It shows:

- Structural elements eg, departmental boundaries, product types and activities
- Process elements indicating what actually takes place in the system
- Relationships – indicated by arrows and symbols

The rich picture:

- provides an idea of the 'climate' of the situation

- includes components such as clients, people involved, tasks performed, environment

- is an important communication tools

- has a focus on perspectives and shared understanding

We can use the following example to try to draw a rich picture:

A local choral society always has difficulty in obtaining nominations for its officers and committee and attracting people to participate in choral related works. As it is a performing society a number of non-choral tasks must be managed. How can this difficulty be addressed and examined?

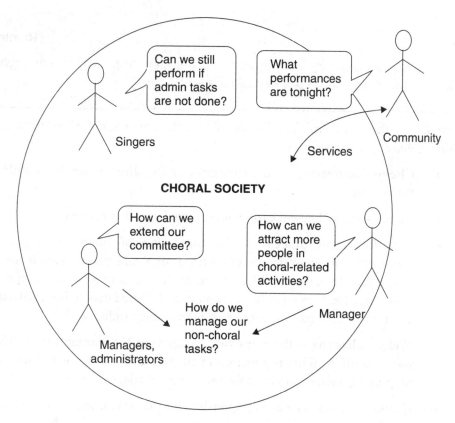

Figure 15.3 Example rich picture

Checkland describes his rich pictures as diagrams 'without rules'. Rich pictures have some distinguishing features. They show:

- the people involved

- their stated purposes

- their desires and fears (usually in think bubbles)

- more environmental detail than most diagrams (human activities, like processes, cross organisational boundaries)

- how interests agree or conflict

The logic-driven stream of enquiry

Under the logic-driven stream of enquiry the core purpose of the system is established. This is known as the root definition. A root definition is a statement defining:

- what a system is,
- who will be in it,
- persons who could be affected by it,
- persons who could affect it, and
- persons who are taking part in it.

NOTES

In the choral society example, activities such as: identify needs of local community; attract membership; generate funds; attract audiences; could be used for the problem situation.

Activity 1	**(10 mins)**

Root definitions can vary. As well as being a system to punish criminals, what other root definitions for a prison could there be?

In formulating the root definition, Checkland uses the mnemonic CATWOE to describe the human activity and its situation.

- **Clients** (customers) – those who more or less directly benefit or suffer from the system

- **Actors** – those that will carry out the transformation process

- **Transformation process** – the conversion of input to output. What transformations, movements, conversions of X take place? What is the nature of the transformations? What is the content and process of transformation from ingredients to a sandwich, from mixed, varied data to information, from an idea to a performance concept or marketable product etc?

- **Weltanschauung** – the worldview underlying the assumptions behind the root definition. What is going on in the wider world that is influencing and shaping the system and need for the system to adapt?

- **Owner** – the person who is responsible for the system and could also stop the transformation process

- **Environmental** (the political, legal, economic, social, demographic, technological, ethical, competitive and natural) constraints – fixed elements outside the system

Transformation example

Checkland offers the case of an aircraft landing system. The transformation involves getting the incoming aircraft from a height and a distance safely on the runway. The actors would be the pilots (human and auto), the clients would be the passengers and crew, the owners the owners of the airline, and the environment: the air traffic controllers, air lanes, traffic conditions and geographic features. The Weltanschauung may involve competition between international airports, the airport-housing environment, and high concern for safety and high technology operations.

3.4 Conceptual model

Once the SSM team has agreed on a root definition and the CATWOE participants, a conceptual model of the relevant system is created.

The steps involved in building a conceptual model from a root definition are:

- Use the root definition and CATWOE elements to form an impression of the system carrying out a transformation process

- Decide on key verbs to describe the fundamental activities in the system

- Structure key related activities in groups

- Connect the groups with arrows to indicate logical dependencies

- Check that the root definition and conceptual model together give a clear impression of what type of system it is and what the system does.

In our example, the choral society manages fluid relationships between those involved with choral and non-choral related tasks in order to perform outstanding choral performances.

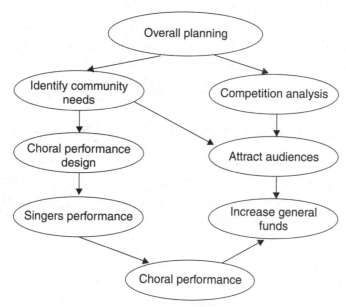

Figure 15.4 Conceptual model

The success or failure of the transformation process in the model is assessed.

Checkland's – Five Es for selection criteria are:

- efficacy (will it work at all?)
- efficiency (will it work with minimum resources?)
- effectiveness (does it contribute to the enterprise?)
- ethicality (is it moral?)
- elegance (is it beautiful?)

3.5 Comparison

Comparing the model to the real world should stimulate debate about whether the model improves the current situation. The comparison process might include:

- Formal questioning
- Informal discussion
- Event reconstruction
- Model overlay

The aim is to:

- understand the problem and the gaps better and be able to identify potential improvements

- determine mismatches between the actual situation and the model

- raise questions about which models should exist in reality

- evaluate the models in terms of the 3Es

- determine which models are workable

- compare the models with one found in practice

At this point, the changes that would improve the problem situation are defined and agreed and measures are taken to implement these changes.

4 AUTOMATION, RATIONALISATION AND RE-ENGINEERING

4.1 Forms of organisational change

Developing and introducing a new information system can lead to organisational change, enabling organisations to redesign their structure, scope, power relationships, work flows, products, and services.

Four types of change, encouraged by IT, have been identified.

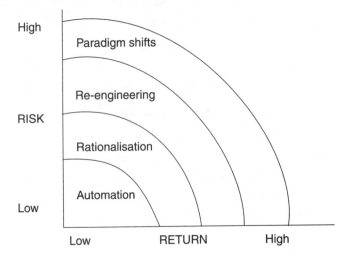

Automation

Business automation is the use of computerised working methods to speed up the performance of existing tasks. The first applications of automation using IT were introduced to help employees perform their tasks more efficiently and effectively eg, calculating pay.

Rationalisation

Rationalisation involves streamlining operating procedures and eliminating obvious bottlenecks and inefficiencies that are revealed by automation, for enhanced efficiency of operations.

As well as automating a process, rationalisation includes efficient process design. An automated banking system needs standardised account numbers and rules for calculating the daily balances.

Business process re-engineering (BPR)

BPR is the fundamental rethinking and radical redesign of business processes to achieve dramatic improvements in critical contemporary measures of performance such as cost, quality, service and speed.

The aim of the process is to reorganise business around processes rather than around functions or departments. BPR reorganises workflows, eliminating waste.

Davenport and Short's five-step approach to BPR

- (a) Develop the business vision and process objectives
- (b) Identify the processes to be redesigned
- (c) Understand and measure the existing processes
- (d) Identify IT levers
- (e) Design and build a prototype of the new process

Why focus on processes?

Many businesses recognise that value is delivered through processes, but still define themselves in terms of their functional roles. To properly harness the resources within a business a clear agreement of the management and implementation of processes is needed. Without this focus on processes:

- (a) It is unclear how value is achieved or can continue to be achieved.

- (b) The effects of change on the operation of the business are hard to predict.

- (c) There is no basis to achieve consistent business improvement.

- (d) Knowledge is lost as people move around or out of the business.

- (e) Cross-functional interaction is not encouraged.

- (f) It is difficult to align the strategy of an organisation with the people, systems and resources through which that strategy will be accomplished.

The relationship between **strategy**, **processes**, **people** and **technology** is shown below.

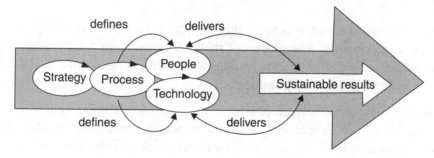

Figure 15.5 Relationship between strategy, processes, people and technology

4.2 Paradigm shifts

A paradigm shift involves rethinking the nature of the business and the nature of the organisation itself. In terms of knowledge and knowledge management, the transformation from the old world of business to the new world of e-business includes transitions that are paradigm shifts.

These changes have implications for turning the 'tried and tested' management theories and assumptions on their head. They change how managers think about:

- business strategy
- information technology
- organisational knowledge processes
- corporate assets
- organisational design
- the role of senior management

4.3 The effect of computers on information systems

Computers have revolutionised information systems for the following reasons:

Speed – Computers are ideal for dealing with repetitive processes. The limiting factors, for example, in processing a payroll by computer are not the speed of calculation by the computer, but the speed with which data can be input and the speed of the printer at the output.

Accuracy – In general, computers do not suffer from errors, or lapses of concentration but process data perfectly. Any mistakes which computers make nowadays are not caused by electronic error, but by human error, for example at the input stage, or in designing and programming software.

Volume – Not only do computers work fast, but also they do not need to rest. They can work twenty-four hour days when required. They are therefore able to handle vast volumes of data.

Complexity – Once subsystems are computerised they can generally function more reliably than human beings. This makes it easier to integrate various subsystems. Computers are therefore able to handle complex information systems efficiently. However, one of the problems with this is that when the computer does fail, there is often a major breakdown in the system, with many personnel unable to perform their work functions.

Cost – All the above advantages mean that computers have become highly cost-effective providers of information. The process of substituting computers for human beings has revolutionised information-oriented industries such as accountancy, banking and insurance and this process is continuing.

Presentation – More recently, emphasis has been placed on displaying information in as 'user-friendly' a way as possible. Modern packages containing sophisticated word processors, spreadsheets and graphics combined with the development of the laser printer now enable boring reports to be presented in new and exciting ways!

Judgement – It is necessary, however, to remember the advantages that human beings have as providers of information. Chief amongst these is judgement of reasonableness. Human beings can usually see when an item of information looks unreasonable. Although it is possible to program limited reasonableness tests into computer systems, it is still very difficult to program judgement. The computer remains a highly trained idiot, which is particularly apparent when a programming error is made or it is subject to a computer virus.

Activity 2   **(5 mins)**

Why does a computer system process information better than a manual system?

---

5 INFORMATION AND KNOWLEDGE MANAGEMENT

5.1 Information management

Information must be managed just like any other organisational resource.

Information management entails the following tasks.

(a) Identifying current and future information needs.

(b) Identifying information sources.

(c) Collecting the information.

(d) Storing the information.

(e) Facilitating existing methods of using information and identifying new ways of using it.

(f) Ensuring that information is communicated to those who need it, and is not communicated to those who are not entitled to see it.

Developments in technology provide new sources of information, new ways of collecting it, storing it and processing it, and new methods of communicating and sharing it.

5.2 Knowledge management

Knowledge management (KM) describes the process of collecting, storing and using the knowledge held within an organisation.

Definition

Knowledge Management is a strategy, framework or system designed to help organisations create, capture, analyse, apply, and reuse knowledge to achieve competitive advantage

Knowledge is now commonly viewed as a sustainable source of **competitive advantage**. Producing unique products or services or producing products or services at a lower cost than competitors is based on superior knowledge.

Knowledge is valuable as it may be used to create new ideas, insights and interpretations and for decision-making. However knowledge, like information, is of no value unless it is applied. As the importance of knowledge increases, the success of an organisation becomes increasingly dependant on its ability to gather, produce, hold and disseminate knowledge.

There are dozens of different approaches to KM, including document management, information management, business intelligence, competence management, information systems management, intellectual asset management, innovation, business process design, and so on.

Many KM projects have a significant element of information management. After all, people need information about where knowledge resides, and to share knowledge they need to transform it into more or less transient forms of information.

But beyond that, KM does have two distinctive tasks:

- To facilitate the **creation** of knowledge – designing and creating environments and activities to discover and release **tacit knowledge** (expertise held by people within the organisation that has not been formally documented).

- To manage the way people **share** and **apply** it – designing and installing techniques and processes to create, protect and use **explicit knowledge** (knowledge that the company knows that it has eg, facts, transactions and events that can be clearly stated and stored in management information systems).

The **motivation to share** hard-won experience is sometimes low; the individual is 'giving away' their value and may be very reluctant to lose a position of influence and respect by making it available to everyone.

Organisations should encourage people to share their knowledge. This can be done through a culture of openness and rewards for sharing knowledge and information.

Companies that prosper with KM will be those that realise that it is as much about managing people as about information and technology.

EXAMPLE: HOW TO FACILITATE KNOWLEDGE SHARING

The business trend for the new millennium might well be summed up as, 'Tradition is out, innovation is in.' World-class companies now realise that the best ideas do not necessarily come from the executive boardroom but from all levels of the company; from line workers all the way through to top management.

Companies that have cultures that encourage best practice sharing can unlock the rich stores of knowledge within each employee: sharing promotes overall knowledge, and facilitates further creativity. World-class companies are innovatively implementing best practice sharing to shake them of out of the rut of 'the way it's always been done.' Programs such as General Electric's Work-Out sessions or Wal-Mart's Saturday meetings help employees challenge conventions and suggest creative new ideas that drive process improvement, increased efficiency, and overall, a stronger bottom line.

The fundamental goal of knowledge management is to capture and disseminate knowledge across an increasingly global enterprise, enabling individuals to avoid repeating mistakes and to operate more intelligently – striving to create an entire learning organisation that works as efficiently as its most seasoned experts.

Best Practices recently updated report, '*Knowledge Management of Internal Best Practices*', profiles innovative methods used by world-class companies to communicate best practices internally. The study provides recommendations for how to create a best-practice-sharing culture through all levels of the organisation, how to use both external and internal sources to find best practices and how to capture that knowledge and communicate it to all employees.

Best Practices contacted over fifty leading companies at the vanguard of knowledge management to compile its report. Some of the vital issues these thought leaders addressed include measurement and management of intellectual assets, best practice identification and recognition systems, best practice prioritisation systems, communication of best practices, and knowledge sharing through technology. For example, in the area of best practice communications, the report examines how General Electric spreads best practices with regular job rotations.

Adapted from Chapel Hill, N.C. (Business Wire) Feb 2000 via News Edge Corporation

---

5.3 Where does knowledge reside?

There are various actions that can be taken to try to determine the prevalence of knowledge in an organisation.

- One is the identification and development of informal networks and communities of practice within organisations. These self-organising groups share common work interests, usually cutting across a company's functions and processes. People exchange what they know freely and develop a shared language that allows knowledge to flow more efficiently.

- It is then possible to 'map' a knowledge network and make it available to others in the organisation. Knowledge maps are guides that assist employees to ascertain who knows what. This methodology involves the discovery of tacit knowledge in order to facilitate eventual sharing.

- Expert databases are similar to mapping the knowledge. They map experts by identifying knowledge of each expert and providing a guide map to help employees find those experts. Knowledge databases, similar to standard document databases facilitates the storage and sharing of explicit knowledge.

- Another means of establishing the prevalence of knowledge is to look at knowledge-related business outcomes. One example is product development and service innovation. While the knowledge embedded within these innovations is invisible, the products themselves are tangible.

Every day companies make substantial investments in improving their employees' knowledge and enabling them to use it more effectively. Analysis of these investments is a third way of making KM activities visible. For example how much technical and non-technical training are individuals consuming? How much is invested in competitive and environmental scanning, and in other forms of strategic research?

Japanese companies have a strong focus on **tacit knowledge**. They motivate knowledge creation through visions of products and strategies coupled with organisational cultures that promote sharing, transparency and proactive use of knowledge and innovation.

Human resource policies such as rotation of employees through different jobs and functions support the expansion of knowledge.

The process by which an organisation develops its store of knowledge is sometimes called organisational learning.

A learning organisation is centred on the **people** that make up the organisation and the **knowledge** they hold. The organisation and employees feed off and into the central pool of knowledge. The organisation uses the knowledge pool as a tool to teach itself and its employees.

5.4 Systems that aid knowledge management

Information systems play an important role in knowledge management, helping with information flows and helping formally capture the knowledge held within the organisation.

Any system that encourages people to work together and share information and knowledge will aid knowledge management.

Distributing knowledge

Office automation systems (OAS) – are the systems that create, store, modify, display and communicate the correspondence of the business. Communication can be written, verbal, facsimile or in video form.

Now that most computers are networked there is the ability to share computer files and send messages to one another via the communications network. This service is provided by electronic mail systems and electronic bulletin boards. The electronic bulletin boards are a public sector service whereby public messages can be posted.

OAS also includes voice mail systems, image processing systems, collaborative writing systems, and video conferencing facilities.

Knowledge work is dependant on the efficient production and distribution of documents and other forms of communication such as voice messaging systems.

Document imaging systems convert documents and images to digital form, reducing the amount of paper required. Electronic information should be easier to retrieve as electronic searches should be quicker than hunting through a mountain of paper.

Knowledge workers themselves perform many essential tasks within an organisation including:

- Keeping the organisation up-to-date with new knowledge as it develops outside the company, in areas such as technology, science and the humanities.

- Providing advice inside the organisation on the use of new knowledge.

- Acting as change agents by actually recommending and implementing change within an organisation.

Knowledge sharing

We have already discussed Groupware and its uses in Chapter 13. Typically, groups utilising groupware are small project-oriented teams that have important tasks and tight deadlines Perhaps the best known groupware product at present is **Lotus Notes**. However, there are many related products and technologies.

Creating knowledge

Knowledge work systems (KWS)

Knowledge Work Systems (KWS) are information systems that facilitate the creation and integration of new knowledge into an organisation. They provide knowledge workers with tools such as:

- Analytical tools
- Powerful graphics facilities
- Communication tools
- Access to external databases
- A user-friendly interface

The workstations of knowledge workers are often designed for the specific tasks they perform. For example, a design engineer would require sufficient graphics power to manipulate 3-D Computer Aided Design (**CAD**) images; a financial analyst would require a powerful desktop computer to access and manipulate a large amount of financial data (an investment workstation).

The components of a KWS are shown in the following diagram.

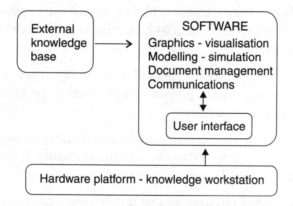

Figure 15.6 Components of a knowledge work system

Virtual reality systems are another example of KWS. These systems create computer-generated simulations that emulate real-world activities. Interactive software and hardware (eg special headgear) provide simulations so realistic that users experience sensations that would normally only occur in the real world.

EXAMPLE: VIRTUAL REALITY

Burger King has used virtual reality stores to test new store designs.

Volvo has used virtual reality test drives in vehicle development.

PROFESSIONAL EDUCATION

Capturing and codifying knowledge

Artificial intelligence (AI) is the development of computer-based systems designed to behave as humans. Artificial intelligence systems are based on human expertise, knowledge and reasoning patterns.

The field of AI includes:

- Robotics
- Natural language' programming tools
- Perceptive systems
- Expert systems (ES)

The main commercial applications of AI have involved **expert systems**.

An **expert system** is a computer program that captures human expertise in a limited domain of knowledge. An organisation can use an expert system when a number of conditions are met.

(a) The problem is **well defined**.

(b) The expert can define **rules** by which the problem can be solved.

(c) The **investment** in an expert system is cost-justified.

The system enables a person with expertise in a particular situation to transfer knowledge into the computer from where someone needing that expertise can receive advice. An ES must have:

- A way of storing the information that is fed into it (the knowledge base). The **knowledge base** contains facts (for example 'Postcode AX9 9ZZ had 104 reported burglaries in 2003') and rules ('next year the burglary rate is likely to be 5% higher than last year'). These facts and rules enable the system to make a 'judgement' such as; 'In 2004 homes in postcode AX9 9ZZ have a 6% chance of being burgled'.

- A way of transferring information from the expert into the knowledge base (a knowledge acquisition program which enables the expert system to acquire new knowledge and rules).

- A way of reaching conclusions in a particular situation (the inferencing engine is the software that executes the reasoning. It needs to discern which rules apply, and allocate priorities).

- An easy to use interface so that a non expert can interrogate the system (a user interface).

The knowledge base of an expert system must be kept up-to-date. Expert systems are not suited to high-level unstructured problems, as these require information from a wide range of sources rather than simply deciding between a few known alternatives.

Activity 3 (15 mins)

Why do you think organisations wish to automate reasoning or decision-making tasks which humans are naturally better able to perform than computers?

Neural networks

Neural networks are another application of AI, seen by some as the 'next step' in computing. Neural computing is modelled on the biological processes of the human brain.

Neural networks can learn from experience. They can analyse vast quantities of complex data and identify patterns from which predictions can be made. They have the ability to cope with incomplete or 'fuzzy' data, and can deal with previously unspecified or new situations.

Neural techniques have been applied to similar areas as expert systems eg credit risks. They are more advanced in that they don't rely on a set of hard rules, but develop a 'hidden' layer of experience and come to a decision based on this hidden layer.

5.5 Diagrams and text

Any successful company must react quickly to changing trends in the market. New products should be designed and manufactured quicker and cheaper than competitors do. A shorter design time provides a distinct competitive advantage. In many cases, communication may best be achieved if information is presented in a visual form such as a chart or a graph. CAD provides the means for capturing system requirements and for the visual modelling and design of systems on a high level of abstraction.

Graphs and charts can be complex and highly technical, so they should, like any other medium of communication, be adapted to suit the understanding and information needs of the intended recipient: they should be simplified and explained as necessary, and include only as much data as can clearly be presented and assimilated.

6 DATABASES

6.1 What is a database?

The way in which data is held on a system affects the ease by which the data can be accessed and manipulated. To maintain data in a database, data must be organised and stored in a consistent, reliable, and efficient manner. Many modern software packages are built around a database. A database provides a comprehensive set of data for a number of different users.

Definitions

A **database** is a collection of data organised to service many applications. The database provides convenient access to data for a wide variety of users and user needs.

A **database management system** (DBMS) is the software that centralises data and manages access to the database. It is a system that allows numerous applications to extract the data they need without the need for separate files.

Other key terms associated with databases include the following:

- The logical structure of a database refers to how various application programs access the data. The physical structure relates to how data is organised within the database.

- The independence of data items from the programs which access them is referred to as data independence.

- Duplication of data items is referred to as data redundancy.

- In a database environment, the ease with which applications access the central pool of data is referred to as integration.

- Integrity relates to data accuracy and consistency.

- Data independence and integration should reduce data redundancy resulting in improved data integrity.

6.2 Consistency and reliability

In the database approach the three data requirements that are much-emphasised are: integrity of data; data integration and data independence.

(a) A database must have integrity. This means that it must be consistent, accurate and reliable. *Integrity* signifies that a single user cannot be permitted to amend the data on file and thereby ruin the usage of the database for other users. Yet users must be able to make valid amendments to the stored data by updating. Furthermore there is no inconsistency occurring due to wrongly duplicated data held in different files, because a single update proffers new data to all database users.

(b) *Data integration* – means that information retrieved from various files must be accessed and subjected to co-ordination and manipulation exactly as though it originated from a single file. In logical terms the data is centralised, but it is very probably stored in devices that are located in a number of organisational areas. The concept of centralisation/integration must be actively maintained to allow links between data, normally utilising direct-access approaches.

(c) *Data independence* – is the characteristic existing when amendments are made to both the organisation and content of the stored (physical) data without any effect upon the applications utilising the data. In other words, there is no need for reprogramming.

6.3 The characteristics of a database system

A database system has the following characteristics.

- **Shared.** Different users are able to access the same data for their own processing applications. This removes the need for duplicating data on different files.

- **Controls** to preserve the **integrity** of the database. Users should not be able to alter the data on file so as to **spoil** the database records for other users. However, users must be able to make **valid** alterations to the data.

- **Flexibility.** The database system should provide for the **needs of different users**, who each have their own processing requirements and data access methods. The database should be capable of **evolving** to meet **future** needs.

The **advantages** of a database system are as follows.

(a) **Avoidance of unnecessary duplication of data** – it recognises that data can be used for many purposes but only needs to be input and stored once.

(b) **Multi-purpose data** – from (a), it follows that although data is input once, it can be used for several purposes.

(c) **Data for the organisation as a whole, not just for individual departments** – the database concept encourages management to regard data as a resource that must be properly managed just as any other resource. Database systems encourage management to analyse data, relationships between data items, and how data is used in different applications.

(d) **Consistency** – because data is only held once, it is easier to ensure that it is up-to-date and consistent across departments.

(e) **New uses for data** – data is held independently of the programs that access the data. This allows greater flexibility in the ways that data can be used. New programs can be easily introduced to make use of existing data in a different way.

(f) **New applications** – developing new application programs with a database system is easier as a central pool of data is already available to be drawn upon.

(g) **Flexibility** – relational systems are extremely flexible, allowing information from several different sources to be combined and providing answers to *ad-hoc* queries.

The **disadvantages** of a database system relate mainly to security and control.

(a) There are potential problems of **data security** and data privacy. Administrative procedures for data security should supplement software controls.

(b) Since there is only one set of data, it is essential that the data should be accurate and **free from corruption**. A back-up routine is essential.

(c) Initial development **costs** may be high.

(d) For hierarchical and network structures, the **access paths** through the data must be specified in advance.

(e) Both hierarchical and network systems require **intensive programming** and are **inflexible**.

7 DATA WAREHOUSING AND DATAMINING

Two techniques designed to utilise the ever-increasing amounts of data held by organisations are **data warehousing** and **datamining**.

7.1 Data warehousing

Definition

> A **data warehouse** consists of a database, containing data from various operational systems, and reporting and query tools.

A data warehouse contains data from a range of external (customer care systems, outside agencies or websites) and internal (eg sales order processing system, nominal ledger from newer channels such as customer care systems, outside agencies or websites) sources. It is loaded with a database product such as Oracle or Microsoft SQL server. This database is configured to hold the key information you want to look at and is interfaced with the 'transaction processing' systems.

For larger volumes of data a toolset has been developed called OLAP (on-line analytical processing) which allows summary information to be created and stored across the different business performance metrics. As a consequence of this, on-line and instant enquiries can potentially be made on the balances of any combination of customer/product/regional performance by date/period range.

The performance of the transaction-processing systems will not be affected by heavy use of the data warehouse for a complex set of enquiries, as you will not be working with the live information.

Once this warehouse has been set up, information can be combined from the different operations systems into a consistent format and can be accessed by a wide variety of reporting/analysis/web tools.

Data is copied to the data warehouse as often as required – usually daily, weekly or monthly. The process of making any required changes to the format of data and copying it to the warehouse is usually automated.

The result should be a coherent set of information available to be used across the organisation for management analysis and decision-making. The reporting and query tools available within the warehouse should facilitate management reporting and analysis.

7.2 Features of data warehouses

A data warehouse is subject-oriented, integrated, time-variant, and non-volatile.

- **Subject-oriented** – a data warehouse is focused on data groups not application boundaries. Whereas the operational world is designed around applications and functions such as sales and purchases, a data warehouse world is organised around major **subjects** such as customers, supplier, product and activity.

- **Integrated** – data within the data warehouse must be consistent in format and codes used – this is referred to as integrated in the context of data warehouses. For example, one operational application feeding the warehouse may represent gender as an 'M' and an 'F' while another represents gender as '1' and '0'. While it does not matter how gender is represented in the data warehouse (let us say that 'M' and 'F' is chosen), it must arrive in the data warehouse in a consistent integrated state. The data import routine should 'cleanse' any inconsistencies.

- **Time-variant** – data is organised by time and stored in 'time-slices'. Data warehouse data tends to deal with **trends** rather than single points in time. As a result, each data element in the data warehouse environment must carry with it the time for which it applies.

- **Non-volatile** – data cannot be changed within the warehouse. Only load and retrieval operations are made.

Organisations may build a single central data warehouse to serve the entire organisation or may create a series of smaller data marts. A data mart holds a selection of the organisation's data for a specific purpose.

A data mart can be constructed more quickly and cheaply than a data warehouse. However, if too many individual data marts are built, organisations may find it is more efficient to have a single data warehouse serving all areas.

The components of a data warehouse are shown in the following diagram.

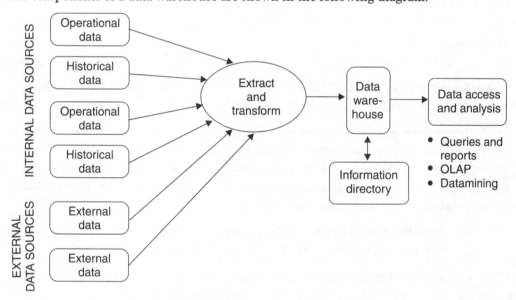

Figure 15.7 Components of a data warehouse

7.3 Advantages and limitations of data warehouses

The advantages of setting up a data warehouse system include the following.

(a) Decision makers can access data without affecting the use of operational systems.

(b) Having a wide range of data available to be queried easily encourages the taking of a wide perspective on organisational activities.

(c) Data warehouses have proved successful in some businesses for:

- Quantifying the effect of marketing initiatives.

- Improving knowledge of customers.

- Identifying and understanding an enterprise's most profitable revenues streams.

NOTES

Some organisations have found they have invested considerable resources implementing a data warehouse for little return. To benefit from the information a data warehouse can provide, organisations need to be flexible and prepared to act on what they find. If a warehouse system is implemented simply to follow current practice it will be of little value.

Other limitations exist, particularly if a data warehouse is intended to be used as an operational system rather than as an analytical tool. For example:

(a) The data held may be outdated.

(b) An efficient regular routine must be established to transfer data into the warehouse.

(c) A warehouse may be implemented and then, as it is not required on a day-to-day basis, be ignored.

7.4 Datamining – Trends, patterns and relationships

New data management techniques have been developed to provide managers with better and quicker access to data analysis.

Definition

> **Datamining** is a set of statistical techniques that are used to identify trends, patterns and relationships in data

Datamining techniques have been available for many years, but they have only recently grown popular, as more data is being created, data processing power (in the form of computers) is becoming more accessible and datamining software tools are becoming available. Most datamining models are either:

- **Predictive**: using known observations to predict future events (for example, predicting the probability that a recipient will opt out of an e-mail list)

- **Descriptive**: interrogating the database to identify patterns and relationships (for example, profiling the audience of a particular advertising campaign).

Datamining software looks for hidden patterns and relationships in large pools of data.

True datamining software discovers previously unknown relationships. The hidden patterns and relationships the software identifies can be used to guide decision-making and to predict future behaviour.

EXAMPLE: DATAMINING

(1) The American retailer Wal-Mart discovered an unexpected relationship between the sale of **nappies** and **beer!** Wal-Mart found that both tended to sell at the same time, just after working hours, and concluded that men with small children stopped off to buy nappies on their way home, and bought beer at the same time. Logically therefore, if the two items were put in the same shopping aisle, sales of both should increase. Wal-Mart tried this and it worked.

(2) Some credit card companies have used datamining to predict which customers are likely to switch to a competitor in the next few months. Based on the datamining results, the bank can take action to retain these customers.

Datamining uses statistical analysis tools as well as neural networks, fuzzy logic and other **intelligent techniques**.

The types of relationships or patterns that datamining may uncover may be classified as follows.

Relationship\Discovery	Comment
Classification or cluster	These terms refer to the identification of patterns within the database between a range of data items. For example, datamining may find that unmarried males aged between 20 and 30, who have an income above £50,000 are more likely to purchase a high performance sports car than people from other demographic groups. This group could then be targeted when marketing material is produced/distributed.
Association	One event can be linked or correlated to another event – such as in Wal-Mart example (1) above.
Forecasting	Trends are identified within the data that can be extrapolated into the future.

8 DEVELOPING WEBSITES AND MAILING

8.1 Website design

Websites are now a key form of corporate communication. Almost every major company has some type of web presence. Increasingly, advertisers are using websites as key marketing tools – and using their conventional media advertising (especially print) to point consumers to the website. (Some print/poster ads now simply feature a prominent web address.)

Website design is a relatively new skill and the technology is constantly changing. The following, however, are some of the key issues.

Design issues	Comments
House style	The website should be consistent with corporate identity guidelines and other promotional messages.
Interest	The website should offer content that is relevant, original or regularly changing/expanding, in order to encourage repeat visits. This may be product information, links, news features, and free e-cards or chat communities.

Design issues	Comments
Interactivity (and/or entertainment)	Colour, graphics, audio, video and movement add impact and entertainment value. Information can be presented as database applications, search tools, notice boards, calculators and other interactive formats.
'Stickiness'	Website 'stickiness' refers to (a) how often visitors return to a site and (b) how long they spend there. Stickiness can be improved by continually updated content, and also by promotional techniques such as chat rooms, games and reviews. Keeping visitors longer at the site gives you more time to build up awareness, and gives them more time to take in promotional messages and/or make purchases.
Credibility	Websites often contain 'about us' pages to bolster consumer confidence (and public relations) by providing information about the company.
Transaction efficiency	As well as encouraging 'browsing' with mechanisms such as virtual 'shopping trolleys' and 'wish lists', websites can offer 1 Click or other convenient order mechanisms, automatic e-mail order confirmations and order tracing. A secure site for transactions (using various forms of encryption) is also important.

8.2 Current and valid

Once a website is 'live' on the Internet, it can be used as a 24 hour source of information on your products, services and organisation news. The more up-to-date it is, the more likely your customers will come. One of the most important parts of having a website is to make sure that the information on the site is current. A website is a work in progress and a reflection of the business. As the business grows and changes, so should the website – it should always be up to date. For example, when including a press release area on the site, you should make sure that you are regularly adding press releases. Visitors who hit the site and find that the last press release is dated a year ago may think that the site has not been updated since then. It is better to have no dates than old dates. If you are selling products on your site, make sure that your prices are current. Customers may very well use your site as a point of reference before calling. Should they get one price on the phone and another on the site, they will not be very impressed with your company.

The domain registration must also be kept current and valid because the company that it is registered with may need to contact you to renew your registration. This information is also used when you try to transfer your domain from one hosting company to another.

8.3 Mailing

E-mail is one of the most popular uses of the Internet. According to Allen *et al (One-to-One Web Marketing)* 'there are more people in the world with access to e-mail than with access to the World Wide Web. This means e-mail marketing can grab attention and interest without requiring users to even start their web browsers.

E-mail lists can be obtained by buying or renting suitably targeted/segmented lists (of willing subscribers) from list brokers or permission marketing agencies. Organisations can also build their own lists, by inviting people to subscribe to an online e-mail list (to participate in two-way discussion or receive one-way announcements) or by inputting customer and contact data from other sources (such as trade exhibitions, sales promotions and so on).

Various software-based tools exist to enable marketing organisations to maintain and manage e-mail lists and to send **mass mailings** (batched to avoid over-loading individual servers). There are even tools available online, free of charge (but supported through the placing of advertisements at the bottom of the e-mail messages).

Using e-mail as an alternative to (or support for) direct mail and direct response advertising has the following advantages.

- **Cost-effectiveness**. E-mail is one of the least expensive ways to reach people in a highly targeted, personalised manner – whether one person in the office across the hall or millions of people all over the world.

- **Speed of delivery/response**. Apart from instant transmission (unlike postal direct mail packages), most e-mail campaigns are said to elicit 5% of their responses within 24 hours and 15% of their responses within 72 hours.

- **Targeting**. E-mail messages can be written for the interests of a highly targeted audience, using integrated address books and databased information to personalise content for individual recipients.

- **Acceptability**. 'People look forward to receiving e-mail from friends, relatives and co-workers. This means that their attitude is more open and accepting than in more advertising-oriented media, such as advertising-supported websites, as well as traditional print and electronic media and direct mail.' (Allen *et al*)

Almost all commentators on e-mail marketing note the fine line that exists between legitimate use of the medium and 'spam' – unsolicited, untargeted mass e-mail broadcasts. Much of the controversy comes from companies 'harvesting' e-mail addresses from web pages, discussion lists, newsgroups and other sources and using them to target users. (It is now illegal in the UK to disclose or sell these addresses to third parties without users' permission.) Spam not only annoys recipients (and the complaint departments of their Internet Service Providers), but also frequently causes network traffic problems.

9   ACCESS AND DISSEMINATION

9.1   Accessing information

We are seeing massive changes in the way that researchers/specialists in different countries communicate with one another and in how they produce and gain access to information. If they are 'connected' to various information and communication technologies (ICTs), and have access to some essential skills, they can keep in touch with their peers at the click of a few buttons, rapidly publish and disseminate their own work, and browse through whole libraries of reports and data, downloading the latest ideas needed for their work.

We have also seen changes in the information management 'business.' Fifteen years ago, information 'handling' and its management was the job of professionals and specialists (in publishing, libraries, archives, computers). Usually located in specialist units inside organisations (sometimes specialist information organisations), these people tracked down and organised scarce information.

This situation is different today. More access to more powerful and easier to use ICTs has turned us all into information specialists, allowing us to handle our own information management needs. Around the world, researchers build websites, manage databases, publish newsletters, organise workshops, and find their own information. The old information professionals are still around, sometimes re-branded as 'knowledge' specialists, and struggling to provide services and products to people who appear to have their own access to the same technical tools.

9.2 Research information

Researchers in general wish to make the results of their work widely and easily available to their colleagues because the whole edifice of progress is built on the gradual build-up of information and ideas from the whole community. Journal articles have been the traditional form of this dissemination and over time specific journal publishing has become a sophisticated operation offering (in print on paper) quality assurance through peer review and effective distribution. It has become highly competitive with some journals commanding important positions in their field by using subjective criteria for material that is particularly important and topical.

The system has also become very expensive as journals have proliferated and print numbers declined, so that even the biggest libraries have found it impossible to maintain subscriptions to all the available journals, while smaller institutions and in particular developing countries have been effectively priced out of the market.

Electronic publishing provides a whole new range of opportunities to improve the information chain, of which wide and apparently free dissemination via the Internet is one of the most obvious. It has encouraged more and more self-publication through individual websites, through institutional information providers, and through subject oriented preprint servers.

9.3 Legal and confidentiality concerns

Keeping some information confidential is an important **legal requirement**. It may also be part of your organisation's **policy**.

Some requirements are pure common sense. For example, most of us would expect details of our wages, salaries, health etc to be kept confidential. Others are less obvious. For example some information about your organisation may be valuable to competitors. This is known as **commercially sensitive information**.

The Data Protection Act 1998 lays down strict rules about the storage, purposes or uses, accuracy, processing and transfer of personal data.

Due to the explosion in the use of computers, concerns were expressed about:

- Access to personal information by unauthorised parties

- The likelihood that an individual could be harmed by the existence of computerised data about him or her which was inaccurate or misleading, and which could be transferred to unauthorised third parties at high speed and little cost

- The possibility that personal information could be used for purposes other than those for which it was requested and disclosed

The list of people that have the organisational and technical opportunity to collect information about users and their computers includes resource owners, e-mail recipients, Internet providers who control users' access to the net and maintain information about them, third persons with the widest range of motives, up to and including criminal intentions, and other parties.

When connected to the Internet there is the potential to collect the following information, whether comprehensively or in part:

- The IP address of a computer that is connected to the Internet, and information about the Internet provider and services rendered to the user.

- The user's e-mail address.

- Information about installed software and computer configuration.

- Information obtained through the use of cookies, indicating the users' access to websites, and their activities on those sites, including all sorts of information on logins and passwords required for access to resources and services.

- Personal data entered by the user while using various Internet sites and resources.

- User information that the provider maintains incident to rendering telecommunications services, including passwords and logins for access to the provider's information systems.

The **Data Protection Act 1998** applies to information held in any form. Therefore it does not matter whether the information is held on paper, in computer files or in another form – it is all covered by the Act. The strictest requirements of the Act apply to '**sensitive data**' such as racial origin, health, sexual orientation or political or religious beliefs. The processing of sensitive data is generally forbidden without the consent of the subject.

So who does the Act effect? You must firstly look at the definitions under the Act.

Definitions

'**Data**' is any information processed by automated equipment or recorded so that it forms part of a relevant filing system or accessible record.

'**Personal Data**' is information pertaining to a living individual who can be identified from that data. It also includes any expression of opinion about them.

A '**Data Subject**' is a living individual, so we are all to that extent data subjects. Organisations or businesses cannot be data subjects.

A '**Data Controller**' is any legal person who alone or jointly determines the manner or purposes of processing of any data.

A '**Data Processor**' is any employee other than an employee of the data controller who processes data.

Definitions (continued)

> A **'Recipient'** is anyone to whom information is disclosed.
>
> **'Data users'** are organisations or individuals which use personal data covered by the Act.

The most obvious use is actually processing the data. However use also includes controlling the contents of personal data files.

Processing covers 'obtaining, holding, recording, carrying out operations such as the organisation, adaptation and alteration of information, the retrieval, consultation or use of the same, disclosure, transmission or dissemination thereof, and the alignment, combination, blocking, erasure or destruction of information'. Consequently there are very few if any business practices which will not need to be notified under the Act.

Data subjects can **sue** data users for **damage** or **distress** caused by inaccurate data, loss of data or unauthorised disclosure. They also have a legal right to see their own personal data.

9.4 Internal requirements

Within an organisation, the policy manual will often lay down other confidentiality rules. For example, some organisations forbid employees to talk to the press without authorisation, or to publish their research results. You can imagine that businesses planning large redundancies or the launch of a new product will not want the information to become public prematurely.

Paper files with **restricted access** should be

- Listed
- Stored securely
- Only accessible by specific people

Computer systems often use **passwords** to restrict access to information that is held on computer. You should never divulge your password to an unauthorised person or keep it in view on your desk. Think of your password as needing as much secrecy as your bank PIN number.

Use of the **Internet** can pose particular problems in maintaining confidentiality. Many companies have a policy on the purposes for which the Internet should and should not be used. The law surrounding Internet information and its protection is still developing.

If you have access to restricted information in any form, you are responsible for protecting it to comply with company policy and the law. You should lock confidential papers or computer disks away when you are not using them. You should not leave them lying around on your desk (or in the photocopier!).

You should also **not provide confidential information** to **others** outside your department without checking with a supervisor.

Activity 4 **(5 mins)**

Your company's planning department asks for a copy of the monthly research cost reports for the last six months. Your computer password does not give you access to this information. What should you do?

A Refer the query to your supervisor

B Ask someone what the password is that will access the information

C Ask for your password to be changed so that it will access the information

D Try and find a hard copy of the information

Chapter roundup

- Organisations are social systems that are exposed to a wide range of influences and environmental factors. Organisations are often exposed to unstructured or 'soft' problems.

- The Systems Development Lifecycle (SDLC) is a disciplined, hard approach to systems development that identifies several stages of development.

- The soft systems approach to systems development aims to take into account the soft properties of the implementation – this approach looks at the wider picture.

- Checkland's Soft Systems Methodology (SSM) is a way of analysing situations in systems – such as an organisation. It provides an organised approach which can be used to tackle unstructured and poorly defined problems.

- The purpose of SSM is to enhance understanding of complex social situations which entail many divergent perspectives.

- In SSM the root definition is a concise description of a human activity system that states what the system is and what the system does. The root definition is established using the mnemonic CATWOE.

- A rich picture is a diagrammatic representation of a situation compiled through examining elements of structure, process and the situation climate.

- Knowledge management describes the process of collecting, storing and using the knowledge held within an organisation.

- Knowledge is now commonly viewed as a sustainable source of competitive advantage. Producing unique products or services or producing products or services at a lower cost than competitors is based on superior knowledge.

- Information systems play an important role in knowledge management, helping with information flows and helping formally capture the knowledge held within the organisation.

Chapter roundup (continued)

- A database is a collection of data organised to service many applications. The database provides convenient access to data for a wide variety of users and user needs.

- Advantages of a database system include the avoidance of data duplication, management is encouraged to manage data as a valuable resource, data consistency across the organisation, and the flexibility for answering *ad-hoc* queries.

- A data warehouse consists of a database, containing data from various operational systems, and reporting and query tools.

- Organisations may build a single central data warehouse to serve the entire organisation or may create a series of smaller data marts.

- Datamining software looks for hidden patterns and relationships in large pools of data. Datamining uses statistical analysis tools as well as neural networks, fuzzy logic and other intelligent techniques.

Quick quiz

1   List five characteristics of problems or situations that would make a hard approach to problem solving suitable.

2   The term 'systems lifecycle' describes the stages a system moves through from inception until it is discarded or replaced. What are the six stages of the lifecycle?

3   List five examples of soft properties that should be considered during the development and implementation of an information system.

4   Although SSM is not intended to follow a rigid sequential approach, some writers have identified 'stages of SSM'. Briefly outline these seven stages.

5   List the steps involved in building a conceptual model from a root definition.

6   Distinguish between business automation and business rationalisation.

7   Business process re-engineering involves computerising tasks previously done by people. TRUE or FALSE?

8   Under what circumstances can data subjects sue data users?

9   Why should companies have a policy on Internet use?

10   What should you do with confidential papers?

Answers to quick quiz

1   Any five of those given below. You may have thought of others.

Objectives are clear
The problem is self-contained
The problem can be clearly defined
Information needs are known
A solution can be recognised
Standard solution techniques are applicable (See para 2.1)

2   The model used in this Course Book has the stages Project definition; Feasibility study; Design; Programming or software selection; Installation and Post-implementation. (2.3)

3   Any five of those given below. You may have thought of others.

Tastes, values, judgement and opinions are involved
It is not clear what is known and what is needed
The problem is difficult to define
It is not clear what the solution should achieve
The problem is 'people' oriented
There are no standard solution techniques available (2.1)

4   SSM is divided into seven distinct stages. These are: Problem situation, Analysis, Root definition, Conceptualisation, Comparison, Changes and Action. (3.2)

5   Step 1. Use the root definition and CATWOE elements to form an impression of the system carrying out a transformation process.

Step 2. Decide on a number of key verbs that describe the fundamental activities necessary in the system.

Step 3. Structure key related activities in groups.

Step 4. Connect the groups of activities by arrows which indicate logical dependencies.

Step 5. Check that the root definition and conceptual model together give a clear impression of what the system is and what the system does. (3.4)

6   Business automation is the use of computerised working methods to speed up the performance of existing tasks. Business rationalisation is the streamlining of operating procedures to eliminate obvious inefficiencies. Rationalisation usually involves automation. (4.1)

7   FALSE. BPR uses IT to allow a business to do things that it is not doing already. (4.1)

8   Data subjects can sue data users who have caused them damage or distress by loss of data, inaccurate data or unauthorised disclosure of data. (9.3)

9   Companies need a policy on Internet use because it is a potential source of breaches of confidentiality. (9.4)

10 Confidential papers should be locked away unless in use, used discreetly and not copied to unauthorised people without checking with a supervisor. (9.4)

Answers to activities

1   •   A system to punish criminals by locking them up (the victim's perspective).

        •   A system to rehabilitate offenders by showing them the error of their ways in order to help them adjust to society (the state's perspective, perhaps).

        •   A system to train criminals and increase criminal behaviour by bringing criminals' into contact with one another so that they can share their skills (the 'criminal' perspective).

        •   A system to produce mailbags by using a captive workforce in order to utilise cheap labour (the Post Office's perspective).

        •   A system to store people by keeping them in cells (the architect's perspective perhaps).

        •   A distribution system for narcotics (the Mafia's perspective).

        •   An opportunity for profit (as in the case of privatised prisons).

2   The functions of computers in information processing include:

        •   processing information more quickly;

        •   handling bigger volumes of processing;

        •   undertaking complex operations;

        •   processing information more reliably ie, with less chance of errors and mistakes;

        •   processing information at less cost than a manual system;

        •   improving the scope and quality of management information.

3   The primary reason has to do with the relative cost of information. A human expert builds up a specialised body of knowledge over time. This knowledge has a commercial value. With human resource 'time is money'. Expert systems aim to use this expertise without requiring the human expert to spend time making the decision. The system also protects the organisation against loss of this expertise should the human expert leave the organisation.

        Capturing knowledge in a computer system means that more people can access this wisdom. Thus, the delivery of complicated services to customers, decisions whether or not to extend credit and so forth, can be made by less experienced members of staff if the expert's knowledge is available to them.

        If a manufacturing company has a complicated mixture of plant and machinery, then the repair engineer may accumulate a lot of knowledge over a period of time about the way it behaves: if a problem occurs, the engineer will be able to make a reasoned guess as to where the likely cause is to be found. If this accumulated expert information is made available to less experienced staff, it means that some of their learning curve is avoided. An expert system is advantageous because it saves time, and therefore costs less. It is particularly useful, as it possesses both knowledge and a reasoning ability.

4   Refer the query to your supervisor.

PART D: UNIT 13

PROFESSIONAL DEVELOPMENT

Note

Although Unit 13, *Professional Development*, forms part of the Management Endorsed Title Route, it is a unit which in theory could be done at any time during study for the HND/HNC qualification.

Therefore we have included this unit at the end of the book, so that the 'pure' management units are dealt with first.

Chapter 16 :

PERSONAL AND CAREER DEVELOPMENT

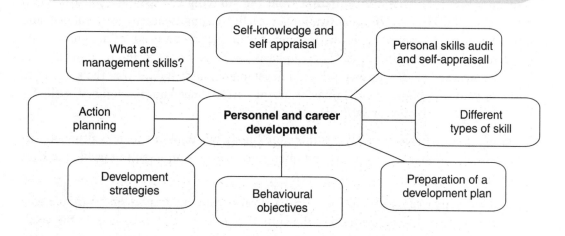

Introduction

Specialist Unit 13 is unusual, not just in the context of the HND and HNC qualification, but in the context of all exam syllabuses, because it requires you to carry out a detailed self analysis and self-evaluation.

This Unit is also unusual in that it is likely that you will develop it throughout the course and your study of other units, so that it reflects your career and personal development over a period of time.

You are required to carry out four different activities in order to achieve the Unit.

- Undertake responsibility for your own personal and career development

- Evaluate your progress and monitor the achievement of your personal development and learning targets

- Develop a range of interpersonal and transferable skills

- Demonstrate self-managed learning in a professional context

The assessment for the Unit consists of three different requirements.

1 For the **personal profile**, you must self-evaluate your current skills and experiences by means of a **skills audit**, and then construct a **personal portfolio**

2 For the **career development** you should keep a **personal journal or skills log** throughout the programme, based on your own personal and career aims and needs

3 Assessment of your **interpersonal and transferable skills** should involve **role play** at your college and the **study of examples of 'real life' situations**

The demonstration of self-managed learning can be regarded as an ongoing process, which will happen throughout the process of studying for this Unit and any others that you may have outstanding.

Pedler, Burgoyne and Boydell (2001) give a brief definition of personal development in the context of self development. They say:

'Self development is personal development, with the person taking primary responsibility for his or her own learning and choosing the means to achieve this.'

Therefore this process is very different from the studying process that you have seen hitherto in the HND/HNC qualification or earlier exams, whereby you studied and learned a specific series of topics with a view to completing an exam or assignment. As the description of the Unit says, 'The emphasis is on the needs of the individual'. The Unit is concerned with your own personal development and enables you, the student, to build on your existing skills to enhance current performance and develop new skills for your future personal and career development.

From that point of view, this Unit is therefore highly personal to you, and although this Course Book can make suggestions and offer guidance, it is up to you to tackle the Unit honestly.

As well as being very personal, this Unit will also have an impact on your role as a member of a team. The description of the Unit stresses that the emphasis is on the needs of the individual but this is 'within the context of how the development of self-management corresponds with effective team management in meeting objectives'.

1 WHAT ARE 'MANAGEMENT SKILLS'?

There is no universally accepted definition of management skills. The demands made on managers differ according to the structure, culture and environment of the organisation *and* over time, with the impact of constant change on the business environment. Whetten, Cameron and Woods (2000) surveyed a number of research studies which cite different lists of 'skills' recognised as key contributors to managerial effectiveness and career success. Personal qualities ('enthusiasm' and 'determination') are listed alongside behaviours ('hard work'), activities ('processing paperwork') and 'technical competence'. Even where researchers appear to be talking about the same thing, their terminology varies. Some lists use the phrase 'human relations', while others refer to 'managing people' or 'working well with others'.

How might it be possible to describe 'management skills' in a meaningful way?

FOR DISCUSSION

Independently brainstorm your own answers to the following questions.

- What skills do you need to be an effective manager?
- Can you group these into different categories in any way?
- Can you prioritise which are the most important skills?

If possible, invite at least one other person to contribute his or her own answers to these questions, and compare your views. Consider any differences of viewpoint and where they may come from: your gender or cultural values? personal perceptions? definition of terms? different past experiences of managers or managing?

1.1 Skills

Whetten and Cameron (2002) suggest that management skills can be differentiated from other kinds of 'managerial characteristics' (such as ambition or integrity) and 'management practices' (such as hiring and firing) because they are:

- *behavioural:* observable and identifiable sets of actions that individuals perform, with certain outcomes;

- *controllable:* able to be consciously demonstrated, practised, improved or restrained by individuals;

- *developable:* amenable to learning, practice and feedback towards higher levels of competency; and

- *inter-related and overlapping:* integrated sets of complex responses, which support one another for behavioural flexibility – rather than simplistic, repetitive behaviours.

Renewed emphasis on management education, training and development has focused attention on specific **skills** and **competences** which are amenable to analysis, modelling, development and assessment. In the UK, competence-based Management Standards, supported by government initiatives such as Investors in People and National Vocational Qualifications (NVQs) are at the forefront of what Adair and Allen (1999) identify as:

'a drive towards lifetime learning, flexible self-development, continuous improvement and competence or core skills based training, linked directly to business goals'.

1.2 People skills

Management skills may also be differentiated from purely technical/operational skills (such as using statistics, typing or welding) because they are inherently bound up with *people* and influenced by *personal factors*.

- *Intrapersonal skills* involve processes within people themselves: self awareness, time management, stress management, problem-solving and decision-making.

- *Interpersonal skills* involve interactions between two or more people: communication, leadership, influencing, assertiveness, negotiation, conflict management, team-working and so on.

EXAMPLE

Rosemary Stewart's real-world survey of research into how managers actually behave highlights the 'human dimension' of management.

'The picture that emerges from studies of what managers do is of someone who lives in a whirl of activity, in which attention must be switched every few minutes from one

subject, problem and person to another; of an uncertain world where relevant information includes gossip and speculation about how other people are thinking and what they are likely to do; and where it is necessary, particularly in senior posts, to develop a network of people who can fill one in on what is going on and what is likely to happen. It is a picture, too, not of a manager who sits quietly controlling but who is *dependent upon many people*, other than subordinates, with whom reciprocating relationships should be created; who needs to learn how to trade, bargain and compromise; and a picture of managers who, increasingly as they ascend the management ladder, live in a political world where they must learn how to *influence people* other than subordinates, how to manoeuvre, and how to enlist support for what they want to do. In short, it is a much more *human activity* than that commonly suggested in management textbooks.' [Italics ours]

(Quoted in Mullins 1999)

Reflection: What impressions of the manager's role have *you* got from 'management textbooks' so far? How do they compare to the real world of work in your own experience?

There are many ways of classifying management roles and skills, and describing how they work together for successful performance. However, it is generally agreed that **interpersonal skills underpin managerial competence** in the key process of 'getting things done through other people'.

1.3 Developing skills for your HND/HNC

Unit 13 effectively underpins the entire HND/HNC programme by focusing on **self development** in the context of **interpersonal skills and processes.**

- Pedler, Burgoyne and Boydell (2001) identify '**balanced learning habits and skills**' as one of the 'meta qualities' which allow managers to develop and deploy *all* the other skills, behaviours and resources they require for successful performance.

- Management involves **working through and with other people**, and interpersonal competence comprises the range of skills required to do this effectively.

- Effective managerial decision-making is not just about making the 'right' decisions, but about effective **management of the processes** by which decisions are made, communicated, implemented and responded to in a given organisation or work group.

This is particularly true in a business environment which increasingly relies on collaborative working in networks, teams and flexible organisation structures – and on continuous learning and adaptation to change.

Self-development, process awareness and interpersonal skills can be applied to all the other units in the HND programme. As you learn and apply strategic planning techniques, for example, you will be taking responsibility for your skill and career development. And you will also need to give attention to your effectiveness in the relevant interpersonal processes of networking, participating in meetings, communicating visions and goals, managing potential for conflict and resistance, negotiating for resources... and so on.

The HND module is designed to help you to develop a double focus, or 'dual channel' awareness, so that ultimately you can monitor and manage interpersonal processes at the same time as working towards any specific business decision or outcome.

1.4 Developing skills for life

Learning how to manage statistical data, market dynamics, business systems and resources is likely to be useful in your professional life. Learning how to manage your behaviours and relationships, and your ongoing development in both areas, is potentially useful in *all* areas of your life – and on a lifelong basis.

Don't leave your skills at the office!

While the aim of Unit 13 is to enhance your competency in a managerial role, the interpersonal and learning skills developed through the module should be applicable in other areas of your life: family, friendships, study and leisure activities. This is explicitly acknowledged in the setting of life – as well as career – goals as the framework for development. Non-work relationships and activities also provide essential scope for practising and applying your developing interpersonal skills – even (and especially) if you are not yet operating professionally in a managerial role.

Learning itself is a life skill

Peter Honey and Alan Mumford (1992) suggest that:

'Learning is perhaps the most important of all the life skills, since the way in which people learn affects everything else. We live in the post industrial 'information' age where data have a shorter shelf-life and where transformational changes are less predictable and occur more rapidly than ever before. Clearly learning is the key, not just to surviving but to thriving on all these changes....'.

Learning to learn enables you to *keep* on learning far beyond any particular study text, training event – or HND unit! It is a framework for on-going self-development.

Learning is a constant, cyclical process

Research by David Kolb (1984) and its implications for management (Honey and Mumford, 1992) suggests that effective learning is a cyclical process of experimentation and adjustment.

- We perform an action or have an experience

- We reflect on the experience, its results and any feedback we may have obtained

- We formulate a hypothesis about what we might be able to do differently next time

- We plan to test our hypothesis in action

- We perform the action – and so continue the cycle.

The following *(Figure 16.1)* is a simple diagram of the learning cycle, as put forward by Honey and Mumford (1992).

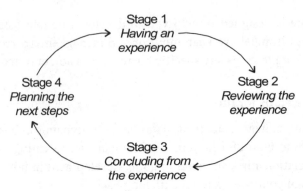

Figure 16.1 The learning cycle

We covered the learning cycle – and the learning styles associated with each stage – in Chapter 4 of this Course Book, as we discussed and applied ideas about management development.

New learning needs emerge all the time. Developing the kind of management skills that are needed to manage a business, a team – and, indeed, one's own life and relationships – is a lifelong process: a journey, not a destination. While it is helpful to set goals and yardsticks for measuring your progress along the way, it is important to stay open to further learning and not to become frustrated that you never seem to 'arrive': the journey is in many ways more valuable than the destination itself.

FOR DISCUSSION

"If asked to think about how we have learned, most of us may think first of when attempts have been made to teach us. If, on the other hand, we are asked about problems we have solved, we think about difficult situations we have faced and managed to overcome. However, in solving problems we don't just deal with the immediate difficulty, we discover a solution which we can use again in some form, and we may also become better at solving problems generally. Problem solving is, to a large extent, learning." *Pedler, Burgoyne and Boydell* (2001)

How have you learned various interpersonal skills? (Think about communication, leadership, assertiveness, influencing, negotiation and team working – not necessarily in a work setting.) Think about what you have learned through being 'taught', for example courses, workshops etc., and what skills you have learned and developed through experience.

1.5   The HND approach

A focus on behaviour

While the learning objective of content-oriented learning is *knowledge* or *understanding*, the learning objective of skill development is *application:* **intentional behaviour** and **behavioural change**.

This unit is designed to get you to think about how you (and others) behave, so that you can make changes to your behaviour if you wish to do so, in order to achieve your purposes more effectively, efficiently or consistently. While you need to understand the determinants of behaviour – what influences people to behave the way they do – you will be encouraged to focus your development planning on the behaviour itself.

Gillen (1999) defines behaviour as 'the link between what we want and what we get'. He uses the vivid example of learning to play pool or snooker.

Making notes

Observations, impressions and intuitions provide valuable data for self reflection, but in order to make them a durable, flexible and practical source of information, you need to capture and record them! Get into the habit of making notes – verbal or visual, paper or electronic – during or shortly after any meeting or discussion you are involved in.

These will probably not be the kind of notes you might usually make (content-based minutes of the discussion, decisions reached, action to be taken and so on), but **process notes** about:

- repeated patterns of behaviour which you notice in a group or individual

- changes or interruptions to the 'usual' patterns of behaviour, and their effects

- thoughts or feelings that come up for you in response to others' behaviours or changes in behaviour

- how you 'automatically' react to others' behaviour, and what happens

- how you make a controlled and intentional response to others' behaviour, and what happens

- others' responses to your 'usual' behaviours

- others' responses when you experiment with new behaviours

- what happened in the course of *critical* incidents and interactions (those which impact on you and appear to highlight a problem or issue)

These notes will provide the raw material for reflection and self-evaluation. If you rely solely on your memory, you will probably have insufficiently detailed data to go on.

Collecting and filing data

Next, get into the habit of collecting and filing data. If you take notes on loose sheets of paper, put them (as soon as possible) somewhere where you'll find them again! The same applies to:

- the outputs of completed self-report questionnaires and feedback forms

- the outputs of various exercises you undertake as you work through this textbook, your wider reading and other training activities

- copies of reports from performance appraisals or development planning sessions

- feedback-bearing messages of all kinds (for example: commendation or thank-you letters; complaints; personal or employment references)

- draft mind-maps, objectives, action plans and other records of your on-going thinking about your interpersonal skills development

- any other data relating to the impact and effectiveness of your interpersonal skills

If it represents information about your attributes, behaviours or attainments in any area of interpersonal skill – save it! There will be plenty of opportunities to prioritise and organise the data into a more systematic 'portfolio' format as it builds up, and as you get a better sense of what you need.

2 SELF KNOWLEDGE AND SELF APPRAISAL

2.1 Reasons

Every manager needs clear images of his or her personal skills and characteristics for the following reasons.

(a) **Interacting with other people and developing interpersonal skills.** People's perceptions of themselves and others, and the roles they play, are crucial in the process of communication and relationship-building. A supervisor will be better able to identify and solve problems with teamworking and leadership, if he is able to be objective about his own perceptions, role and behaviour.

(b) **Goal-planning and self-development.** An individual will be more able to take control of his future development if he has a realistic picture of his aspirations, capabilities, and potential at a certain point in time. There would be no point planning to take professional exams and become an assistant supervisor in five years, if you did not have the ambition, capacity for hard work or leadership qualities required. On the other hand, many people have a low opinion of themselves and do not attempt to plan a positive course for their careers and lives – which an objective appraisal of their strengths and weaknesses might indicate.

(c) **Motivation and performance.** If you do not know what you are capable of, you may not be motivated to fulfil your potential to perform at a higher level. If you are not performing well, it is too easy to shift the blame on to 'fate', 'the system' or other people. You could be aware of weaknesses in yourself that contribute to the problem – and overcome them.

The organisation obviously has an interest in assessing its employees' skills and characteristics as well: for selection, training, promotion planning and pay awards. Formal performance appraisal is a critical and well-established part of this, and you should be aware that the process can be used to further self-knowledge and is therefore of value to the individual as well as to the organisation.

(a) An appraisal report, for example, may require the employee's assessor to grade him on a number of personal characteristics and skills, to assess particular strengths and weaknesses which affect his job performance and to recommend areas for development. If the employee accepts the assessment (and he should have opportunity to discuss it in an interview or counselling session), he can add the information to his own picture of himself.

(b) Potential assessment techniques are designed to gauge:

(i) the employee's strengths and weaknesses in existing skills and qualities;

(ii) potential for improvement, correction and development; and

(iii) the goals, aspirations and attitudes of the appraisee, with regard to career advancement and the acceptance of responsibility.

Various techniques can be used, including written tests, simulated desk-top tasks or case studies, interviews and personality tests.

(c) **Group assessment** and training techniques are particularly useful to help supervisors and managers to gain an accurate picture of how they relate to other people, and how people react to them. Role-play exercises allow people to participate in situations requiring negotiating or influencing skills, conflict resolution or team leadership, with subsequent feedback from the trainer and other group members: participants are made aware of their own patterns of behaviour and how these affect others, how they are perceived and what responses they get.

(d) **Assessment centres**. An assessment centre is a place where a person's behaviour and performance in job-related tasks and activities can be conveniently evaluated. Candidates are brought to a central location such as an hotel for a period and are tested and observed by a panel of assessors: exercises include leaderless group discussion, role play and business games. They are used in recruiting outsiders and assessing existing employees for advancement.

There are ways, however, in which an individual can engage informally in the same process of developing self awareness, which may involve two broad activities:

(a) compiling a personal dossier in order to build up an accurate self-image;

(b) carrying out a strengths and weaknesses analysis.

These are the procedures that are an essential part of this Unit.

2.2 Building an accurate self-image

Humans are self-conscious creatures: we behave partly in accordance with the image or concept that we have of ourselves. That self-image is something we mainly learn from interacting with other people; a reflection of their behaviour and attitudes towards us. It is formed by experience over time and is constantly adjusted. For example, repeated failure or criticism at work might tend to create a low self-image spreading into other areas of the individual's life, where it may be completely unjustified. Every individual has a self-image, but very few people attempt to confirm, refute or change their self-image in any systematic or objective fashion. In other words, they are not self-aware.

2.3 Developing self-awareness

In order to become more self-aware, you might try out the ideas below.

(a) Acquire knowledge about human beings and their behaviour in general. Your own studies of motivation, people in groups, interpersonal skills etc will help you to observe and understand what is going on when you act or interact with other people.

NOTES

(b) Gather the opinions of trusted individuals who know you well. On the basis that, in dealing with other people, 'you are what they think you are', this is a practical way of finding out about yourself. For example, even if you have low self-confidence, you may appear to others to be aggressive and overbearing, perhaps because you try to cover up your lack of confidence.

(i) In this process, you are using other people as a mirror which reflects your image back to you. You see yourself as others see you. This can be quite a daunting prospect, so you would need to talk to someone whom you could trust to be honest but supportive: bolstering – or crushing – your ego is not only unhelpful, but downright dangerous, since your self-image will get further distorted. The other person also needs to trust you: they will not be honest with a criticism if they think you will never speak to them again!

(ii) A friend or partner, relative or colleague might be consulted. They would be in a position to help you with those aspects of your personality and behaviour that are displayed in contact with other people in various situations ('you tend to snap at people when you are under pressure'; 'you're not a good listener in meetings'; 'you're a good person to have around in a crisis').

(c) Compare yourself to role models in your life. All individuals consciously or unconsciously select models or ideals for themselves, for the various roles that are relevant to their lives. Parents, school teachers, colleagues or superiors at work are often influential in giving the individual a picture of what he should aspire to be like at different stages in his life. You may choose your model because of your view of his or her charisma, knowledge or expertise (the appeal of the teacher or more experienced colleague); success (as with a hero or celebrity or tycoon); or dominating personality. Festinger suggested that most people seek to evaluate their own performance through comparison with other individuals rather than by using absolute standards. So having a role model to measure yourself against helps to formulate your self-image and your aspirations to change and grow.

(d) Take tests – independently, or as part of the appraisal or training processes of the organisation. You might take an IQ test, or aptitude test (for particular skills). If you wanted to know more about your personality, there are various kinds of test for that too – although it is uncertain how scientifically accurate and objective some of them really are.

(e) Analyse incidents at work or outside work. A particular problem with the work group, for example, may give you insight into your own behaviour in that situation. A new challenge might bring out in you a quality you had not displayed before.

BPP
PROFESSIONAL EDUCATION

> **Activity 1** (30 mins)
>
> Whom do you look up to – at work or outside work, whether you know them personally or not? Do you want to be like them – and if so how? Compare yourself to this 'role model': what areas of yourself would you have to change in order to be more like them – and how could you go about it?
>
> Does your employer have a system of mentoring? If you do not have, or are not yourself, a mentor, ask your superior whether there is mentoring at more senior levels. If there is, what is the mentor expected to do? How useful is it in practice?

It is a good idea to compile the findings from such an investigation into a written self profile. You could start with information from your discussions with others, and your own observations. Take Rodger's 'Seven Point Plan' personnel specification, which includes such features as aptitude, disposition, interests and physical attributes – or consider what aspects are likely to be important to you in your own life: your impact on other people, your motivation, your confidence level, whether you are introvert or extrovert and so on. Test results and copies of assessment reports can be added to the file as they are acquired, along with any changes, for instance, if you gain some further insight from a particular incident, or you get training in some area which enhances your skills or attributes.

2.4 Self appraisal: strengths and weaknesses analysis

Strengths and **weaknesses** analysis is a technique used for corporate appraisal – the self-awareness exercise for a whole organisation. It is sometimes added to an analysis of the **opportunities** and **threats** facing the organisation: hence the abbreviation SWOT.

A personal SWOT is equally valuable for individuals.

(a) Identify your **strengths**, and your **positive assets**: physical, mental, behavioural and emotional. You may dress well, have a good memory, be good with the telephone, be honest, calm under pressure, a good listener and so on.

(b) Identify your **weaknesses**, or **liabilities**. You may have no head for numbers, have a tendency to fidget, be subject to stress, or impatient with other people.

This is a useful exercise. You may gain confidence and set higher goals for yourself as a result of appraising your strengths. You may need to find more realistic goals, or plan to practise/train to minimise your weaknesses. You may decide that you are not in the job – or are not doing enough outside work – to make the most of your strengths. You may identify in your weaknesses the root of certain problems you have had, say, with passing exams or leading a group.

NOTES

Activity 2　　　　　　　　　　　　　　　　　　　　　　　　**(20 mins)**

Draw up a two-columned chart and list some of:

(a) your strengths; and

(b) your weaknesses,

that are relevant to your present job, or studies.

Do the strengths outweigh the weaknesses? Can you identify ways in which your weaknesses can be overcome or at least minimised?

There are a number of dimensions to this analysis for individuals.

(a) Do you have the skills necessary to do the job **today?** (You should have – but if not, training is essential.)

(b) Do you have the skills to do the job **tomorrow?** (This may be because of a change in the environment or an expansion of the department – if not, pro-active training should be planned to ensure you are prepared.)

(c) Do you have the skills to do **tomorrow's job?** (Will you be promoted? If so, what new skills and knowledge will be needed? This is development and would be a pro-active approach to succession planning, or a personal strategy to increase the chances of promotion.)

(d) Do you have the skills for a different job tomorrow? (What will be the alternative employment options in the future and what skills and qualifications will be needed? This is the personal career development planning and investment for which many managers are today taking personal responsibility.)

Activity 3 (30 mins)

You have already undertaken a personal strengths and weaknesses analysis of your current management competences. You can add to that an **opportunities** *and* **threats** assessment which will encourage you to think about career prospects and future opportunities. This external analysis of your own personal job market should help you to extend and prioritise the areas of skill development you want to focus on.

You are already undertaking your HND or HNC qualification so are clearly committed to personal development. Your study time can have considerable added value if you use it to develop additional and specific management skills.

Select four skill areas you want to work on or your boss suggests might be beneficial.

(a) These may be areas of weakness like time management or presentation skills.

(b) They may be areas of strength like analysis and problem solving which you want to develop further.

Using the grid overleaf identify each area, set a **quantified** objective for the next 6 months and give some thought to how (your strategy) to achieve this improvement. The next section of this chapter has ideas on training and development which may stimulate some thoughts on strategy. Here is our example.

NOTES

Area	Objectives	Strategy
Time management	• To hit at least 90% of deadlines set over the last 6 months • To find at least 6 hours per week for HND/HNC studies	• To spend time every morning planning my time • Agreeing a study plan and sticking to it • Taking measures to reduce timewasting

	Area	Objectives	Strategy
1			
2			
3			
4			
5			
6			
7			

Review Dates   1......................2......................3......................

PROFESSIONAL EDUCATION

3 PERSONAL SKILLS AUDIT AND SELF-APPRAISAL

The personal skills audit and self-appraisal requires you to identify, review and assess your own performance of current management skills.

EXAMPLE: MANAGEMENT SKILLS

Look at the following list of skills. We will be discussing some of them later on in this Course Book, but for the moment, for each identify why you think it is important or relevant for the business manager:

Skill   *Importance*

1   Time Management

2   Prioritisation

3   Delegation

4   Communication

5   Negotiation

6   Leadership

7   Motivation

8   Team Building

ANSWER

1   **Time management**. Fewer managers means more responsibility for those in the business. Time management is essential to avoid stress and to get everything done.

2   **Prioritisation** is an integral part of time management. In marketing, managers may have to prioritise markets or customers and need to understand the process and criteria by which priorities can be established. At BPP we have to prioritise our work according to when each range of books is to be published, which depends on such external factors as the exam timetables of the various examining bodies.

3   **Delegation** is essential:

   (a)   in ensuring that tactical details of activities are attended to;

   (b)   to give younger managers and staff experience and chance to develop their skills;

   (c)   to act as a motivator.

4   **Communication**. The essence of the manager's job is communicating, both sending messages and listening to them. It must be done professionally both inside and outside the organisation.

5   **Negotiation** with clients and staff is a key aspect of bringing buyers and sellers, employees and the organisation together in a way which satisfies everyone's needs.

6   **Leadership**. The business manager is often a figurehead and must share the organisation's vision in order to communicate it effectively to others. Managers are in the business of leading the business down the path of customer orientation.

7   **Motivation**. Management roles can be very isolated and motivation has to be clear and effective to get the best out of those working at the customer interface.

8   **Team building**. Management is about co-ordination. Satisfying customers has to be a team effort. Managers have to be able to build teams even when they have no line authority, for example teams with advertising agencies and distributors as well as with operations and distribution.

3.1   Self-appraisal

Take each of the headings listed in the exercise above, and consider to what degree you have each of the skills. You should spend at least five minutes on each one, and jot down your thoughts on each one on the following few pages of this book. Consider these factors about each one:

*   Is it relevant to you in your current job? If it is not relevant now, is it likely to be in the future?

*   If it is a skill which is relevant now, how well do you think that you exercise it?

*   Think of specific examples of ways in which you have used that skill

*   Could you use the skill better than you do at the moment, or differently?

*   Would it improve your ability to do your job if you improved your use of that skill?

- What impact would it have on your management skills generally if you exercised this skill better

- In summary, do you use that skill effectively or is there room for improvement?

- Do you use or have any other management skills which are not included in our list? Think of the nature of your own job, and consider whether you carry out any tasks which are unique to your own role.

You may find it helpful to take a short break after each one so that you tackle the next one with a refreshed mind.

It is vital that you are honest in assessing your skills! You will only be deluding yourself and wasting your time if you are not honest.

TIME MANAGEMENT

PRIORITISATION

DELEGATION

NOTES

COMMUNICATION

NEGOTIATION

LEADERSHIP

MOTIVATION

TEAM BUILDING

Once you have thought through each of the skill headings, and made rough notes, make a more formal record of your deliberations. This will be useful for two reasons:

- It will form a key part of journal or skills log and provide important evidence which can be assessed as part of the Unit

- It may form the basis of the personal development plan which you will need to draw up with your line manager as part of this Unit.

You could draw up a chart like this:

Area for development	Level of skill before (1-5)	Activities completed	Level of skill now	Comments on the process	New Goals
1.					
2.					
3.					
4.					
5.					

NOTES

3.2 Personal development plans

Definition

> A **personal development plan** is a clear developmental action plan for an individual which incorporates a wide set of developmental opportunities, including formal training.

Personal development implies a wide range of activities with the objectives of:

- improving performance in an existing job
- improving skills and competences, perhaps in readiness for career development or organisational change
- planning experience and pathways for career development and/or advancement within the organisation
- acquiring transferable skills and competences for general 'employability' or change of direction
- pursuing personal growth towards the fulfilment of one's personal interests and potential

Activity 4   **(20 mins)**

What mechanisms and programmes are there in your organisation to help you:

(a) assess your job requirements, current competence and training requirements?

(b) identify and plan relevant training and development activities?

(c) access or implement training resources?

How do you mobilise these procedures?

How far are you encouraged to get actively involved in the process of development?

A systematic approach to personal development planning

A systematic approach to planning your own development will include the following steps.

Step 1.   Select an **area for development**: a limitation to overcome or a strength to build on. Your goals might be based on your need to **improve performance** in your current job and/or on your **career goals**, taking into account possible changes in your current role and opportunities within and outside the organisation. You might carry out a personal SWOT (strengths, weaknesses, opportunities, threats) analysis along similar lines to the one we saw earlier in this chapter. One helpful tool is an interest/ aptitude and performance matrix, on which you can identify skills which you require (don't do well) but for which you can build on your aptitudes and interests (like).

PROFESSIONAL EDUCATION

596

		Performance	
		High	Low
Aptitude/ interest	High	Like and do well	Like but don't do well
	Low	Dislike but do well	Dislike and don't do well

Step 2. Set a SMARTER (specific, measurable, agreed, realistic, time-bounded, evaluated and reviewed) **learning objective**: what you want to be able to do or do better, and in what time scale.

Step 3. Determine how you will move towards your objective:

- **Research** relevant learning resources and opportunities

- **Evaluate** relevant learning resources and opportunities for suitability, attainability and cost-effectiveness

- Secure any **support or authorisation** required from your manager or training department

Step 4. Formulate a comprehensive and specific action plan, including:

- The SMARTER objective

- The learning approaches you will use, described as **specific actions** to take. (Ask a colleague to provide feedback; watch a training video; enrol in a course.) Each action should have a **realistic time scale** or schedule for completion.

- A **monitoring and review plan**. Precisely how and when (or how often) will you assess your progress and performance, against your objectives? (Seek feedback? review results? pass an end-of-course test?)

Step 5. Secure **agreement** to your action plan (if required to mobilise organisational support or resources)

Step 6. **Implement** your action plan.

The following is an example of a completed Personal Development Action Plan for someone who is focusing on improving his interpersonal skills.

Objective	Methods	Timescale	Monitoring and review
To be able to utilise a range of influencing strategies and styles to achieve successful outcomes: by end December.	*Reading:* Gillen 'Agreed: Improve your powers of influence'	End March	Review progress in June and December with manager
	Coaching: Meet with manager. Discuss key decision makers in the organisation. Identify examples of successful strategies.	By end March	Monthly meetings with mentor
			Seek feedback on influencing style from colleagues
	Project: Take responsibility for agreeing timescales for delivery of budget reports with department heads	Agreement reached by October	
	Reflect on day-to-day influencing experiences: note in Personal Development Journal and discuss with mentor.	Monthly	
To remain calm when faced with aggressive behaviour (not raise voice, use sarcastic tone or make un-controlled gestures): by end August	Meet with John before next accounts meeting: ask him to observe and give feedback on my behaviour. At accounts meeting, try to implement assertiveness skills (broken record, count to 10) if Paula becomes aggressive.	Meet with John by end April	Seek regular meeting with John for on-going feedback.
	Meet with John after the meeting to get feedback. Identify from this meeting further action points.	Further action points by mid May	Reflect on accounts meetings in PDJ: evaluate results of assertiveness behaviours

NOTES

Activity 5 (20 mins)

Draw up an action plan sheet, using the columns shown in our example. Select one immediate training need for yourself (perhaps related to some aspect of the HND syllabus) and formulate an action plan.

Activity 6 (20 mins)

Aim:

To help you to identify your priority development needs in the light of your career goals.

Instructions:

- Write down your highest priority career goal.

- List the *three* interpersonal skills which you feel are most relevant to successful achievement of this goal.

- Identify and list any *five* specific strengths *and* weaknesses you perceive or have identified in your behaviours or skills in these areas. (If you highlighted 'listening' as a key interpersonal skill, for example, you might identify strengths such as 'patience' and 'open-mindedness' and weaknesses such as 'passive listening behaviours' and 'insufficient feedback giving'.)

- Now restate these strengths and weaknesses as *development needs*: behaviours that need to be adjusted or skills that need to be improved in order for you to achieve your goal. (If your strength is 'patience', for example, you might restate it as a need 'to maintain patience in conflict situations' or 'to be assertive where patience allows discussion to get off track'. If your weakness is 'passive listening behaviours', for example, you might restate it as a need 'to adopt active listening behaviours'.

- *Rank* your development needs in order of (a) urgency, (b) importance and (c) leverage, by assigning each a score from 1 (least urgent, important, cost-effective) to 10 (most urgent, important, cost-effective).

Goal: _____

BPP PROFESSIONAL EDUCATION

	How urgent? (1-10)	How important? (1-10)	How cost-effective? (1-10)	Total
Development needs: building on interpersonal strengths				
1	☐	☐	☐	....
2	☐	☐	☐	....
3	☐	☐	☐	....
4	☐	☐	☐	....
5	☐	☐	☐	....
	How urgent? (1-10)	How important? (1-10)	How cost-effective? (1-10)	Total
Development needs: overcoming interpersonal limitations				
1	☐	☐	☐	....
2	☐	☐	☐	....
3	☐	☐	☐	....
4	☐	☐	☐	....
5	☐	☐	☐	....

- Total the ranking scores for each development need. Those with the highest scores may represent your highest priorities for obtaining that goal.

4 DIFFERENT TYPES OF SKILL

The Edexcel Guidelines require you to carry out a skills audit, evaluating your:

- Self-management
- Leadership and
- Interpersonal skills

How do you think you should classify each of the skills you have been considering under those three headings?

Activity 7	(5 mins)

Set the three categories of skill out as three headings and allocate each type of skill to one of the headings.

Self-management   *Leadership*   *Interpersonal*

5 PREPARATION OF A DEVELOPMENT PLAN

The Edexcel Guidelines say you must prepare a development plan covering:

- Career and personal development
- Current performance
- Future needs
- Aims, objectives and targets
- Review dates
- Achievement dates
- Learning programme/activities
- Action plans

The scope of the plan is obviously very wide-ranging, and it is likely to take you some time to devise it. The Guidelines do not indicate with whom, if anyone, you should produce or agree your development plan, but if possible the most likely person would be your line manager at work. This is because the plan will encompass many of the objectives that are directly relevant to your work, and the plan will be vital not only for your success in this Unit of the HND/HNC qualification but also very useful as part of your overall career development.

If you are not currently in employment, don't worry! You could consider producing the plan with your college tutor or supervisor. If this is not an option, you could enlist the help of a friend or a member of your family who would be willing to discuss the plan with you.

Bear in mind that the development plan can include a wide range of targets, not just improvements in the management skills identified in the self-appraisal covered earlier in this chapter. The Edexcel guidelines refer to 'personal development targets' and devising a 'personal development plan'. The emphasis on the word 'personal' indicates that this area of the Unit will be very specifically geared towards you as an individual. You may find that the production of the development plan provides you with the ideal opportunity to think seriously about your current situation and future plans. You should regard it as an opportunity which could pay considerable personal dividends, and not a chore.

5.1 Set, prioritise and agree targets

Targets establish what you are aiming for. They can be short, medium or long term. If you can set and then meet a target, you are demonstrating that you have acquired the skill of managing yourself, the main theme of this Unit.

5.2 Targets

Decide what you would like to achieve over a specified time, for example one year. This book cannot tell you exactly what targets you should set for yourself, because they are intensely personal to you and to your own particular set of circumstances, but we can make suggestions.

Some of these may be relevant:

- Complete Unit 13 of the HND/HNC qualification by a certain date. What date? Perhaps it should be by a forthcoming holiday or by Christmas or within a fixed number of weeks.

- Complete the entire HND/HNC qualification by a certain date, for example this time next year or the end of 2006.

- Gain promotion at work, for example by your next birthday

- Improve your standard of French or another foreign language

- Acquire additional computer skills, for example learn a new package, or how to do something that you cannot do at the moment, such as draw tables

- Try to delegate more

- Go on a course on presentation skills

5.3 Prioritise

Once you have established a list of targets, allocate numbers to them to indicate how important they are, with 1 as the highest, 2 as the next highest and so on.

You may find it difficult to decide which order they should go in. The targets could be prioritised in terms of

- Importance to your job
- Importance to you as an individual
- How much you want to achieve them
- How quickly you need to achieve them
- Cost to you or your employer
- Enjoyability and potential satisfaction arising
- How realistic it is that you will achieve them

This is an aspect which you should perhaps discuss with your manager: remember that your personal development plan is to be devised with him or her.

The order in which you put your targets may change a number of times before it is finalised. You may want to prioritise improving your command of French, but if you do not use the language at work it would not be regarded as a high business priority. However, if it is something which you personally have a burning desire to do, it should not necessarily be consigned to the bottom of the heap, as it would pay dividends in terms of personal satisfaction and sense of achievement.

Similarly, you may well want to be promoted or given the chance to work in a different department before a certain date, but that may not be realistic from a business planning point of view. Alternatively, your promotion may depend on your passing exams and gaining qualifications, or on someone ahead of you being promoted themselves, so that the matter is not entirely under your control.

5.4 Short and long term learning objectives

Note that the Edexcel guidelines require you to think in terms of learning both in the short and the long term.

Your short tem learning objectives probably include completing this and other HND/HNC Units, but your long term learning objectives could encompass more or less anything, for example qualifying as an accountant or with the Chartered Institute of Marketing or Institute of Personnel Management. The only limit really is that you must be realistic in terms of timing and your own abilities.

6   BEHAVIOURAL OBJECTIVES

Behavioural objectives are specific descriptions of what you want to be able to do or do differently. They are therefore *not* to be confused with:

- A 'wish list' of desired changes which are not directly within your control or choice.

  ✗   *Wish:* 'To get my boss to be more supportive'

  ✓   *Behavioural objective:* 'To request support from my boss in an appropriately assertive manner (using 'I statements', 'broken record' and other assertive behaviours) when work problems arise.'

- A vague or global wish for improvement, divorced from any specific behaviour or context.

  ✗   *Wish:* 'To be better at communication'

  ✓   *Behavioural objective:* 'To communicate calmly and confidently (to speak clearly without hesitating or pausing and to maintain eye contact) when confronted with aggressive behaviour'

- A wish that your personality, attitudes, thoughts or feelings were different than they are.

  ✗   *Wish*: 'To feel less stressed when leading team meetings'

  ✓   *Behavioural objective:* 'To utilise confidence-building techniques (eg affirmation, preparation, rehearsal) and to adopt confidence-projecting non-verbal behaviours (eg appearance, relaxed posture, controlled gestures, steady eye contact) when giving presentations.'

- The means by which you may plan to achieve your objectives.

  ✗   *Means:* 'To attend an influencing skills course'

  ✓   *Behavioural objective:* 'To be able to utilise a range of influencing strategies and styles, as appropriate to different contexts and relationships.'

Behavioural objectives are important for effective development because they:

- Give you a *specific* measure against which you can gather feedback and evaluate your progress and success. ('Have I achieved this behaviour or behavioural change?')

- Express your aims in terms of *behaviours* – specific things that you want to *do* – which are observable, learnable, changeable, and within your control to change.

- Help you identify the type of action you can take to achieve the desired changes.

6.1 SMARTER objectives

You may have heard of the 'SMART' framework for formulating effective business objectives. Adair and Allen (1999) suggest that objectives need to be SMARTER. (You might use this as a checklist when formulating your behavioural objectives.)

- ☐ **Specific**. What exactly do you hope to achieve, and in what contexts? Can it be broken down into smaller, more specific steps?

- ☐ **Measurable**. How will you recognise success in pursuing the objective? How will you measure your progress along the way?

- ☐ **Agreed**. Whose support or authority do you need to pursue the objective? (Note for planning stage: arrange an opportunity to discuss it with them.)

- ☐ **Realistic**. Are you able to achieve the objective within the constraints of your current abilities and commitments, your available time and resources?

- ☐ **Time-bounded**. By what date do you want to achieve the objective? (Check 'realistic'...)

- ☐ **Evaluated**. Is the objective worth pursuing, given the investment in time or effort it will require?

- ☐ **Reviewed**. When and how will you review your progress? (Note for planning stage: specify monitoring methods and review dates.)

Activity 8	**(20 mins)**

Aim:

To help you to apply the SMARTER framework to your own development objective-setting.

Instructions:

Draft a behavioural objective for one of the development needs you identified in Activity 6.

Ask yourself each of the SMARTER questions in relation to your objective. Redraft your objective and add planning notes, as required, after each answer.

7 DEVELOPMENT STRATEGIES

7.1 Identifying development options

The first step in formulating a development strategy is to brainstorm a range of options.

Broadly speaking, you might plan to:

- increase your **knowledge** of skills: reading, analysing case studies, observing others, receiving instruction, going on courses and so on; *in order to*

- seek and exploit opportunities to **do things differently**: using role plays or real work interactions to attempt apply new behaviours and skills; observing and reflecting, seeking feedback, integrating your experience with theoretical concepts, generating alternative options, planning to apply them – and so on round the learning cycle.

Knowledge will *support* behavioural change – but will not, by itself, bring it about. You need to identify specific ways in which you can adapt or change the way you behave for real development to take place.

7.2 Learning methods and media

There are many formal and informal learning methods and media.

- Some learning activities are accessible via specialist education or **training providers** (such as Edexcel or BPP), and others via more **experienced or skilled individuals** in your professional context (such as instructors, coaches or mentors). Others still are generated by *you*, through **your own experiences** and the reflections, conclusions and adjustments you make as a result of them.

- You may have access to **'on-the-job'** or work-based learning activities, utilising real-life work settings, equipment, teams and tasks to observe, practise and apply skills. For example: you may accept job rotations or secondment to another department; undertake project or committee work; be temporarily promoted, or occupy an 'assistant to' position. All of these are opportunities to gain and learn from new experiences. Alternatively, there are **'off-the-job'** methods, which allow knowledge acquisition and skill practice without the distractions and risks of real work demands. For example, you may attend courses, observe demonstrations or simulations, study case studies, practise role plays and so on.

- Different **technologies** may be used, including: face-to-face presentations, demonstrations or workshops; paper-based self-study programmes (like this Course Book and further reading); television, radio and video presentations; and interactive video-, computer- and Internet-based learning.

Activity 9   **(20 mins)**

Aim:

To encourage you to think about available development opportunities and resources.

Instructions:

Select one interpersonal skill which you have identified as a development need. Brainstorm a list of options for accessing or creating learning activities designed to improve your skills in this area.

Do not evaluate or place any limitations on the options you put forward at this stage: try to think freely and creatively. Write down all your suggestions as they emerge on a large sheet of paper: allow ideas to prompt other ideas.

Once you feel that the 'flow' of suggestions has stopped, move to evaluation. Consider the possibilities of each method. How would it work? What resources would it require? What benefits and drawbacks would it present?

> Identify which learning style or styles (Activist, Pragmatist, Theorist, Reflector) each method would best suit in identifying options.

7.3 Evaluating the options

Having identified a range of options, you need to select those you will adopt in your development plan. The following are some of the issues you may wish to consider.

Available resources

- What resources (materials, equipment, venues, opportunities, people, finance) would you require to pursue each option? How readily available are they?

- What other people could help or support you in each option? (Whom could you ask for information, contacts, expertise, time, feedback, authorisation?)

- What time frame would each option require? How would this fit with your other commitments and schedules?

Learning preferences

- Which option(s) are most likely to suit your learning style preferences (as an Activist, Pragmatist, Reflector or Theorist)?

- Which option(s) are likely, on all other grounds, to be most effective? Is it worth stretching yourself and expanding your learning skills by undertaking an activity that does *not* suit your learning style preferences, in order to benefit from this learning opportunity?

Pros and cons

- What are the advantages, benefits, payoffs or likely positive consequences of pursuing each option?

- What are the disadvantages, risks, tradeoffs or likely negative consequences of pursuing each option?

You may have your own preferred techniques for planning and decision-making. Some people like to use mind-maps and other visual aids. Some like to discuss options with others for input and debate. Use whatever method works for you.

One of the simplest techniques is to compile a **two-column list**, with arguments for and against each option set side by side.

- Rule out any option which has a longer and/or more compelling list of points on the 'against' side of the equation.

- Select the options which have the longest and/or most compelling list of points on the 'for' side of the equation.

8 ACTION PLANNING

8.1 An action plan

Again, you may have your own preferences in regard to formatting and recording action plans: timetables, diaries, checklists and so on. Feel free to use whatever works for you.

We recommend a simple, systematic format such as the following.

Objective	Methods	Timescale	Monitoring & review
Statement of SMARTER behavioural objective	List of specific methods/activities selected	Target completion date for each listed method/activity	How, with whom and how often you will check your progress?

We show an example of a completed action plan, using this simple framework, in Section 8.4 below, following a brief discussion of some of the key issues.

8.2 Defining realistic time scales

It is generally unrealistic:

- to attempt massive behavioural changes in a short time frame; and
- to attempt to work on too many areas of change at a time.

It may take time to acquire the underpinning knowledge and concepts relevant to a given skill; to arrange to receive coaching, or feedback on your competence; to practise the skill repeatedly in low-risk environments (perhaps in study settings), learning by trial and error; to find an opportunity to apply the skill at work; to repeat the application in order to consolidate your learning; and to gather feedback through which you can evaluate your success. Set realistic time scales for each stage of this process.

Remember that this is likely to be only one of the plans and schedules operating in your life – and in the lives of those whose help, counsel and feedback you may require. There will be other demands on your time, attention and resources – and theirs. Some of the steps in your plan may be dictated by external events: scheduled meetings (for example, with your mentor), or opportunities arising to put skills into practice (an interview, negotiation or team meeting).

There is nothing wrong with planning for **gradual, incremental changes** or improvements over time. Indeed, it may be beneficial to make one or two small, realistic steps towards your goal, and to consolidate them before moving on to the next steps. Whetten and Cameron (2000, p. 125) call this a 'small wins' strategy. It is a valid, confidence-building and stress-reducing approach to problem-solving, particularly when tackling large and complex tasks. It is also central to the concept of continuous improvement (in Japanese, *kaizen*): a way of sustaining on-going development over time.

8.3 Identifying ways to monitor and review progress

In order to benefit from any development activity, you need to know:

- whether your progress is on schedule in relation to your plans.

  Your activity or resources may need adjusting in order to bring them into line with your schedule or performance targets.

- whether, or how far, your planned activity is effective in achieving your objectives.

  Your plan may need adjusting in order to achieve the objective more effectively. The objective itself may need adjusting if it turns out to have been unrealistic or unattainable in its original form.

The control process may involve *regular monitoring* of your activity and/or *periodic review* of your results.

- What **progress markers** are built into your objectives, which you can check for in your performance? What are your criteria for success at each stage of your plan?

- What types of **information** will you use for monitoring? Your own observations and reflections? Performance results? Feedback from other people?

- What **other people** might you involve in the monitoring and review process? A mentor? Your line manager or appraiser? Selected feedback-givers? Your learning partners or study group?

- How **often** will you review/sample your activity and its results? Periodically? By random sampling? At key stage deadlines? At completion date?

Activity 10	**(20 mins)**

Aim:

To offer a guided process for action planning.

Instructions:

Select one of your SMARTER development objectives (output from Activity 8) or formulate one now.

Complete the action planning sheet overleaf.

ACTION PLANNING SHEET

SMART objective: _____

_____

Identified strengths which will facilitate my attaining the objective
•
•
•
•
•

Identified limitations which may hinder my attaining the objective
•
•
•
•
•

Rewards/payoffs for achieving the objective (rank in terms of value):

1
2
3
4
5

SMART objective: _____

_____

Blockages/barriers/risks/downsides to achieving the objective	Strategies for overcoming blockages/barriers/ risks/downsides
•	•
•	•
•	•
•	•
•	•

Steps for achieving the objective (starting now)	Time deadline
•	•
•	•
•	•
•	•
•	•

Indicators that you have achieved the objective	How/when evaluated?
•	•
•	•
•	•
•	•
•	•

8.4 Example of a completed action plan

Figure 16.2 is an example of the kind of action plan you may formulate using the framework suggested in Section 8.1 above.

Objective	Methods	Timescale	Monitoring and review
To be able to utilise a range of influencing strategies and styles to achieve successful outcomes: by end December.	*Reading:* Gillen 'Agreed: Improve your powers of influence'	End March	Review progress in June and December with manager
	Coaching: Meet with manager. Discuss key decision makes in the organisation. Identify examples of successful strategies.	By end March	Monthly meetings with mentor
			Seek feedback on influencing style from management team colleagues
	Project: Take responsibility for agreeing franchise arrangements with prospective partners	Agreement reached by October	
	Reflect on day-to-day influencing experiences: note in PDJ and discuss with mentor.	Monthly	
To remain calm when faced with aggressive behaviour (not raise voice, use sarcastic tone or make un-controlled gestures): by end August	Meet with John before next marketing meeting: ask him to observe and give feedback on my behaviour. At marketing meeting, try to implement assertiveness skills (broken record, count to 10) if Paula becomes aggressive.	Meet with John by end April	Seek regular meeting with John for on-going feedback.
	Meet with John after the meeting to get feedback. Identify from this meeting further action points.	Further action points by mid May	Reflect on marketing meetings in PDJ: evaluate results of assertiveness behaviours.

Figure 16.2 Example of a completed action plan

610

Chapter roundup

- This area of the Unit is geared specifically to you as an individual and provides an opportunity to think seriously about your current situation and future plans.

- The process of self-managed learning can be regarded as an ongoing process throughout your studies and career.

- Pedler, Burgoyne and Boydell identify balanced learning skills as one of the meta qualities which allow managers to develop and deploy all the other skills, behaviour and resources they require for effective performance!

- Every manager needs clear images of his or her personal characteristics in order to perform effectively. This chapter gives you guidance on how to evaluate your self awareness.

- A personal skills audit requires you to identify, review and assess your own performance of management skills. The Edexcel guidelines specifically state you must evaluate your personal effectiveness in such areas as self management, leadership and interpersonal skills.

- Behavioural objectives are important for effective development because they:

  - give you specific measures against which you gather feedback and evaluate progress

  - express your aims in terms of observation and learnable behaviours

  - help to identify the type of action you can take to achieve the desired change

- A personal development plan is a clear development action plan for an individual which incorporates a wide set of developmental opportunities, including formal training, against SMART criteria.

Quick quiz

1 What resources are available for building up a good self-appraisal?

2 What is a personal development plan?

3 List some formal and informal learning methods and media.

4 What resource considerations should you make when evaluating self-development options?

5 What criteria do the Edexcel guidelines say your personal development plan can include?

6 What methods should you use to monitor and evaluate your progress?

Answers to quick quiz

1   Your list could include: Appraisal reports; potential assessments; role play, team participation, games and case studies; assessment centres; developing a personal portfolio; carrying out an individual SWOT analysis. (See para 2.1)

2   A clear development action plan for an individual which incorporates a wide set of developmental opportunities.

3   Your list could include: specialist education from dedicated centres; coaches; analysing own experience; on the job learning including rotations, secondments and deputisation; off-the-job learning including courses, simulations; knowledge acquisition (lectures, presentations etc); home study programmes in a variety of media including print, TV, audio, PC and Internet. (7.2)

4   What resources are needed and how readily are they acquired?

    Who is available to support you, and how?

    What timeframe does each option require and how does this fit in with your schedules and other commitments? (7.3)

5   Your list should include:

    Career and personal development
    Current performance
    Future needs
    Aims, objectives and targets
    Review dates
    Achievement dates
    Learning programme/activities
    Action plans

6   You should ensure that: your progress is on schedule (and amend if necessary); your planned activity is meeting your stated objectives; you have clearly identified the measures you will be using for evaluating your progress; you have clearly identified who can help you assess your performance and on what basis; you have built in review dates on a regular basis or at critical stages in your programme.

Answers to activities

1   This will be completely specific to you.

2   This will be completely specific to you.

3   This will set out your own quantified objectives.

4   This will be completely specific to you.

5   This will be completely specific to you.

6   This exercise does not take into account all your goals, nor all the interpersonal skills that may be relevant in achieving them. It may or may not reflect your own sense of priorities, or those suggested to you by a supervisor or mentor. That's fine: take only what you can use.

It may be harder to state the development 'needs' represented by your strengths than by your limitations. As our examples show, however, there may be a need to:

- recognise a 'down side' to your strengths and preferences: 'patience' may helpfully enable you to avoid interrupting people when listening, but it may prevent you from interrupting or redirecting a speaker when you need to;

- increase your flexibility, so that you can choose the most effective behaviour in a given situation, rather than relying on your strengths: being assertive rather than patient, or being patient but directive, as the need arises;

- increase the scope or level of your competence in your strength: to be patient in more difficult situations, for example.

The mix of urgency, importance and leverage in your ranking may highlight some development needs which are urgent, important *and* cost-effective to attempt. This is a great place to start! If your top priorities are all urgent and important, but relatively low on cost-effectiveness, you may not want to tackle them all at once in your initial development planning. Select a manageable mix of urgent/important *and* cost-effective changes to work on.

7   Here is a suggestion as to how you could have classified the skills.

Self-management	*Leadership*	*Interpersonal*
Time management	Delegation	Communication
Prioritisation	Motivation	Negotiation
	Leadership	
	Team building	

Did you find yourself wanting to allocate some of the skills to more than one category? Time management, for example, can relate to the management of your own time (hence a self-management skill), but also the management of other people's time, so also qualifying as a leadership skill. Communication and negotiation are also skills that can be classified as leadership skills as well as pure interpersonal skills. The purpose of this activity is to show you that in the context of management skills not everything can be classified in terms of black and white.

8   It is helpful to redraft your objective (if required) in answer to each question, in order to become aware of any weaknesses in your objective-setting skills. Highlight areas in which your objective was initially lacking, and consider their implications. Might you have a *tendency* to be unrealistic in your expectations of yourself? Or to forget to consider the need for authorisation? Or to enter into projects which you can't sustain, because the rewards were not sufficiently worthwhile?

It may also be helpful to share this process with your learning community. They may contribute some alternative perspectives on your objective, as well as allowing you to observe the issues they face in their own objective-setting exercise.

9   You might usefully repeat this exercise on your other development needs as you identify them. You might also like to try the exercise with one or more other people, if you get the opportunity. A brainstorming group is very effective in generating options, and perhaps offering access to resources and contacts as well.

10   Note that the planning sheet highlights the motivational value (rewards/payoffs) of your behavioural objective (SMART objective). You can use the *objective, methods, timescales* and *indicators* elements of your sheet in compiling an action plan such as that shown in the chapter.

Chapter 17 :

INTERPERSONAL AND TRANSFERABLE SKILLS

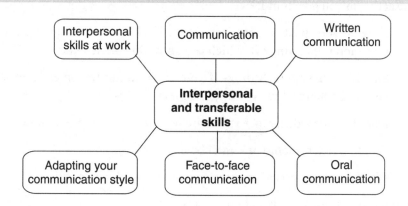

Introduction

One of the main objectives of Unit 13 is to develop your abilities to organise, manage and practise a range of approaches to improve your performance as a self-organised learner. In this chapter, we look at a variety of interpersonal and transferable skills which will be of value both in your HND studies and in your professional career beyond.

Your objectives

In this chapter you will learn about the following:

   (a)   Interpersonal skills

   (b)   Communication

   (c)   Written communication

   (d)   Oral communication

   (e)   Face-to-face communication

   (f)   Adapting your communication style

1 INTRODUCTION

There are certain skills that are key to effective participation in the workplace:

- courtesy and respect for others;

- you need to influence or negotiate with others if you want them to do something that is beyond your authority to 'demand';

- you need to give information and support to colleagues.

So *how*, exactly, do you go about it?

- How do you speak supportively/persuasively/assertively to someone – or is it more about listening? In which case, how do you do *that*?

- Should your approach differ if you are speaking to someone above or below you in the hierarchy? At work or among friends?

- Does it make a difference if you are face to face or on the phone?

- Would a letter, memo or e-mail be more appropriate?

- What makes an effective letter, memo or e-mail message?

Interpersonal communication is a complex business...

Fortunately, others have wrestled with these questions before us, and have come up with techniques, tools, guidelines and conventions for:

- **understanding and managing** what is going on in interpersonal interactions (or communication events)

- **choosing** appropriate communication **formats and media** for your purposes and audience

- **using** a range of communication formats, media and technologies **effectively and efficiently**

- **planning and adapting** the **structure and style** of your message so that it achieves the effects you want

We look at some of these techniques, tools, guidelines and conventions in this chapter. Bear the following points in mind.

- This is a *vast* topic of study, and we can only scratch the surface here. You may wish to make specific interpersonal or communication skills the focus of your self-development planning for this Unit.

- Your organisation may have its own specific requirements, guidelines and 'house style' of communication. For each model or example we give, ask yourself: 'how do *we* do that?'

2 INTERPERSONAL SKILLS AT WORK

2.1 What are interpersonal skills?

Interpersonal skills are skills used in interactions and relationships between ('inter') two or more people.

They include such skills as:

- building **rapport** or a sense of 'being in tune with' another person, which draws them into a relationship

- building **trust** and **respect**, so that the relationship is maintained and co-operation facilitated

- managing **conflict** in the relationship in such a way that it is preserved.

- **persuading** or **influencing** another person, to do what you want them to do or to share your beliefs

- **negotiating** or bargaining in order to reach mutually acceptable or compromise solutions to problems

- communicating **assertively**, so that you uphold your rights and get your needs met – without violating the rights or ignoring the needs of others

- communicating **informatively**, so that you give (and receive) relevant and timely information

- communicating **supportively**, so that you encourage the other person

These are essentially communication skills. We discuss many aspects of communication in this chapter, including some of the particular 'styles' mentioned above (in Section 8).

2.2 Why are interpersonal skills important?

You need interpersonal skills in order to:

- Understand and manage the **roles, relationships, attitudes** and **perceptions** operating in any situation in which two or more people are involved

- **Communicate** clearly with other people

- Achieve your **aims** from any interpersonal encounter (ideally, allowing the other parties to emerge satisfied as well).

In a business context, interpersonal skills are particularly important for processes such as:

- **Motivation**: persuading and inspiring employees to committed performance (often identified with 'leadership')

- **Team-building**: building trust, encouraging communication, forming co-operative relationships and managing conflict

- **Customer care** (including internal customers): winning trust, managing conflict, exchanging information and persuading

- **Negotiation**: maintaining relationships despite conflicting interests, working towards mutually acceptable solutions

- **Workload management**: being able to delegate effectively, negotiate assistance, say 'no' assertively

---

Activity 1   **(10 mins)**

Using the following grid, monitor all the various conversations or interactions you have at work in the course of one day. For each one, put a tick in the appropriate column.

	Technical/ work-related with colleagues	Technical/ work-related with customers/ clients/ enquirers	Organisational/ team/ 'membership'	Asking for help or advice	Getting support/ encouragement /challenge	Non work-related: just friendly/ courteous
During work time						
During breaks/ lunch/ after work etc						
	Total:	Total:	Total:	Total:	Total:	Total:

What does this information tell you about the contexts in which your interpersonal skills are required?

---

3   COMMUNICATION

Communication is – at its most basic – the transmission or exchange of information.

Communication underpins everything you do at work.

It is so basic to our lives that you may never have thought about what is actually going on when we communicate. There is no need to go too deeply into the theory, but it is worth examining **why** we communicate and **what has to happen** for effective communication to take place.

3.1   Why we communicate

The general purpose of most communications will be as follows.

- **To inform**: to give people data that they require

- **To persuade**: to get somebody to do something

- **To request**: to ask for something

- **To confirm**: to check that information is correct and that both parties have the same understanding of it

- **To build the relationship**: giving information in such a way as to acknowledge and maintain the relationship between the sender and receiver – mutual trust, loyalty, respect, benefit and so on

In addition, you may have a specific purpose for communicating. Think in terms of the **outcome** that you want from the communication event: what do you want to happen, and when?

Knowing the **purpose of your communication** – what you want to achieve – is the first step in planning any message (as discussed later in the chapter).

3.2 The communication process

Effective communication is a **two-way process**, often shown as a 'cycle'. Signals or messages are sent by the communicator and received by the other party who sends back some form of confirmation that the message has been received and understood.

CHANNEL

Phone line, postal services noticeboard,

FEEDBACK
Message received and understood?

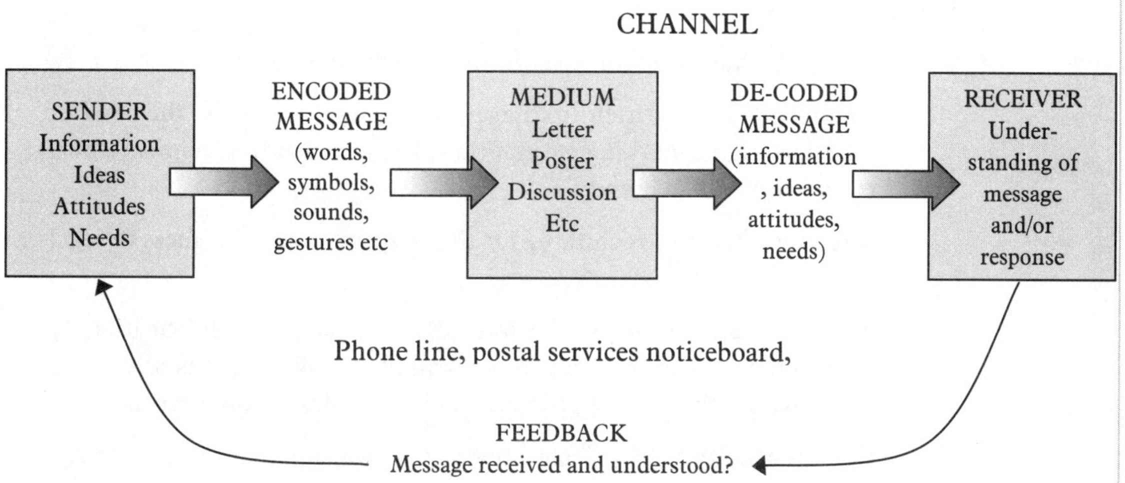

Figure 17.1 The communication cycle

Key

- **Encoding** and **decoding**

- Words are only symbols or stand-ins for your ideas or intentions in communicating. In other situations a gesture, pictures, symbols or numbers will be the most appropriate code to use. The important thing is that both parties understand the code.

- **Feedback**

  Feedback is the reaction of the receiver which indicates to the sender that the message has (or has not) been received and enables him to assess whether it has been understood and correctly interpreted.

  Feedback can range from a **smile** or a **nod** to a **blank look** or a **shrug,** or from the desired action being taken to no action or the wrong action being taken.

  It is the **responsibility of the communicator** to adjust his message, in response to feedback, until he is satisfied that it has been understood. In a sense, the meaning of a communication is only what the other person understands by it. If you want a **result** from your communication (as opposed to just 'getting it off your chest'), it is up to you to make sure that you have communicated effectively.

Activity 2 (10 mins)

Give five examples each of what you would interpret as:

(a) negative feedback (a sign that your message was not having its desired effect); and

(b) positive feedback (a sign that your message was received and understood).

- **Media**

  The choice of an appropriate medium for communication depends on a number of factors.

  - **Speed.** A phone call, for example, is quicker than a letter

  - **Complexity.** A written message, for example, allows the use of diagrams, figure working etc and time for perusal at the recipient's own pace, repeated if necessary.

  - **Need for a written record**: eg for the confirmation of business or legal transactions

  - **Need for interaction** or the immediate exchange of information or questions and answers. Face-to-face and phone discussion is often used to resolve conflicts, solve problems and close sales for this reason.

  - **Confidentiality** (eg a private interview or sealed letter) or, conversely, the **need to disseminate** or spread information widely and quickly (eg via a notice board, public meeting or website).

  - **Cost**: for the best possible result at the least possible expense.

Activity 3 (10 mins)

Suggest the most effective medium for communication in the following situations.

(a) New printer cartridges are urgently required from the office goods supplier.

(b) The managing director wants to give a message to all staff.

(c) Fred Bloggs has been absent five times in the past month and his manager intends to take action.

(d) You need information quickly from another department

(e) You have to explain a complicated operation to a group of people.

3.3 Planning a message

In some circumstances, your organisation's policies, procedures and culture – its '**house style**' will have made many of your communication decisions for you.

- There may be **standard formats and rules** for communications: memo stationery, for example, or controls over the use of e-mail.

- There will be **standard documents** for a variety of routine communication tasks: payroll forms, report forms, standard letters to clients (eg on the opening of credit accounts, for debt collection, acknowledgement of payments etc).

- Your organisation will have its own **house style** for communications – and your national culture will have its own **conventions** for style and presentation.

The following is a very simple **framework for planning any message**, linked to an easy-to-remember mnemonic: **PASS**.

Purpose — What do you wish or need to achieve as a result of the communication task or event?

Audience — What factors in the intended recipient(s) of the message, or their situation, will affect whether they receive, understand and/or respond to the message in the way you intend?

Structure — What content, emphasis, order and format will be most suitable to achieve your purpose, given the audience factors?

Style — What vocabulary, sentence structure, visual elements and 'tone of voice' will be most suitable to achieve your purpose, given the audience factors?

Purpose

It is a good idea to analyse your objectives before you communicate in order to have:

- A guide for the **content, structure** and **style** of the message: a checklist of points to be made, and what order to put them in

- A criterion against which each element of your message can be assessed for suitability and relevance to its intended **audience** and

- A way of determining whether and how far your message is actually **successful** in getting the outcome you wanted

Audience

Some of the factors to take into account include:

- Recipients' information needs and capacities

  - What are their priorities: what information will be important or urgent to them?

  - How much information or detail will they require?

  - How much do they already know?

  - How much will they be able to understand (if you use your technical knowledge and vocabulary)?

- Recipients' attitudes, interests and opinions

- What 'common ground' can you anticipate and use to build rapport?

- What 'sensitive areas' should you avoid or handle carefully in order to avoid conflict?

- What language or vocabulary will they find easy to understand – but not patronising?

- What factors of age, background or personality might interfere with effective communication?

- Recipients' professional role

  - Is your message suitable to their expertise and experience?

  - Is your message suitable to their position in the organisation?

  - Is your message suitable to your respective roles (eg supplier/client)?

Structure

Having identified your purpose and relevant audience factors, you are in a position to make decisions about **what** you are going to say in your message, and **how**.

Structure involves decisions about how information is **selected** (for relevance) and **organised** (for clarity and impact).

- What points you consider relevant and important – for you and for the recipient

- What order you cover the points in, for maximum impact (eg building up suspense, grabbing attention at the beginning, or leaving the recipient with a key message at the end)

- How you divide your message into paragraphs and subsections that will help the recipient to digest and understand

Style

Style involves elements such as:

- **Vocabulary:** the words you use. Are they interesting? emotional or factual? technical (jargon) or something that could be understood by someone not familiar with the subject matter?

- **Tone:** the total effect on the reader or listener of your way of communicating. Do you 'sound' friendly or officious? Assertive or aggressive? Formal or informal? Positive or negative? Humorous or serious?

The style you adopt should be appropriate to your purpose, the nature of the information you are communicating, the needs and expectations of the recipient and the role you occupy in relation to him or her.

Activity 4 (20 mins)

Two important values in persuasive communication are:

- **Credibility**: the message inspires trust and belief in the recipient; and

- **Congeniality**: the message is appealing to the recipient, offering satisfaction or confirmation.

How credible and congenial do you find the following A5 flyer, which was posted through the door of a private home?

DECORWISE
SERVICES
Est. 1968
999 Upper Richmond Road, Putney, London, SW39 6TH
0181 777 6621

Dear *Householder,*

My name is Jim Smith.

I decorate houses for a living.

I came from Australia in 1966 and have been in the business in this area since then.

I won't go into a big sales talk beyond this:
- A business is as good as its owner
- I'm a straight guy
- I was raised on hard work and honest dealings
- You'll get pretty solid service from me at a moderate price

Please ring for a free quotation.

Jim Smith

Jim Smith
MANAGER

PS We do all aspects of property maintenance and small construction, to supplement the decorating.

QUALITY PAINT FINISHES • PAPER AND VINYL HANGING • INTERIORS AND EXTERIORS
COMMERCIAL AND DOMESTIC. ASSOCIATED REPAIR WORK - CARPENTRY + PLASTERING.

3.4 Communication methods

We will now go on to look in detail at some of the main communication methods you might use at work:

- **Written communication**: letters, memos, e-mails, faxes and other documents
- **Visual communication**: including various charts and graphs
- **Oral communication**: including the telephone
- **Face to face communication**: including body language

4 WRITTEN COMMUNICATION

4.1 The letter

The letter is a very **flexible and versatile medium of communication**. It can be used for many different purposes.

- Request, supply and confirm information and instructions
- Offer and accept goods and services
- Convey and acknowledge satisfaction and dissatisfaction

Standard letter format

The modern business letter contains various **standard elements**, and you will need to know what these are and where they are located on the page. Here is a skeleton format and a full example. (Later we shall see some alternative layouts.) (Remember, these are only common conventions: be sure to follow the **guidelines** and **house style** of your own organisation.)

Hi-Tech Office Equipment Ltd

Micro House, High St, Newtown, Middlesex NT3 0PN
Telephone: Newtown (01789) 1234   Fax: (01789) 5678

Directors:	Registered Office:
I. Teck (Managing)	Micro House, High St, Newtown
M. Ployer	Middlesex NT3 0PN
D. Rechtor	Registered No 123 4 56 789
N. Other	Registered in England

Our Ref: IW/cw
Your Ref: JB/nn   7th June 20X0

Private & Confidential

J. M. Bloggs, Esq
Administrator
Toubai Forze Timber Yard
Wood Lane Industrial Estate
SUSSEX
SX1 4PW

Dear Mr. Bloggs

WORD PROCESSING EQUIPMENT

Thank you for your letter of 3rd June 20X0, in which you request further details of Hi-Tech's range of personal computers with word processing software packages. I am delighted to hear that our earlier discussions were of some help to you.

Please find enclosed our list of hardware and software with current prices. I have also included our leaflet entitled 'Desktop', which outlines some of the options for word processing on PCs: I trust this will answer your questions and give you an idea of the exciting possibilities.

I would also take this opportunity to remind you that two of your old printers are currently under maintenance contract with us, and that both of them become due for routine servicing within the next month. Perhaps you would contact my secretary to arrange a convenient date for our engineer to call at your offices.

I look forward to hearing from you, when you have thought about the word processing option. If you have any queries or need further information on accessories do not hesitate to let me know.

Yours sincerely

I. M. Wright
SALES MANAGER
Enc

NOTES

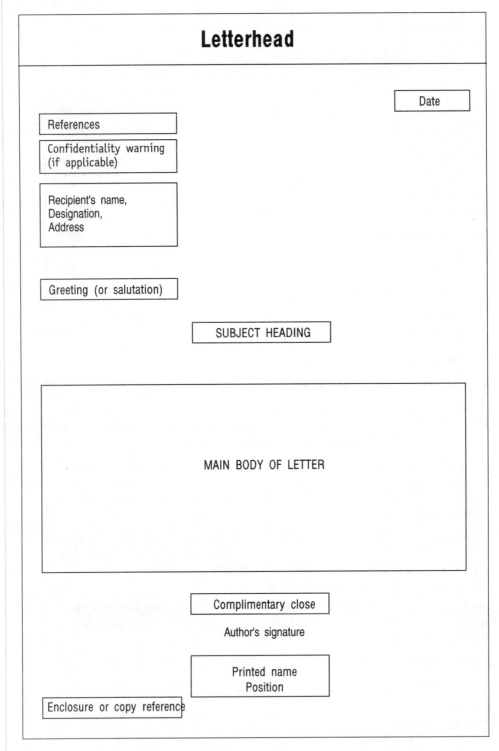

Key

- **Greeting and complimentary closes**

    By convention, the following greetings and complimentary closes should be used together.

Greeting	Close	Context
Dear Sir/Madam/Sirs (*Name not used*)	Yours faithfully	Formal situations Recipient not personally known Recipient senior in years, position
Dear Dr/Mr/Mrs/Miss Cake Dear Sir Keith/Lady Jane (formal name used)	Yours sincerely	Friendly (or would-be friendly, eg for selling or conciliatory letters) Established relationships
Dear Joe/Josephine	Yours sincerely	Close, informal relationships
My dear Joe/Josephine	Kind regards	More various, because more personal
	Best wishes	
	Affectionately	

- **Signature**

  If an assistant or secretary is signing a letter on behalf of the writer, the writer's name is preceded by 'For' (or its equivalent from legal terminology 'pp.' which stands for **per procurationem**).

  For I Cantwell
      Accounts Manager

- **Enclosure reference**

  If you are putting something other than the letter in the same envelope, such as a cheque, price list or leaflet, use an enclosure reference to make sure that the reader or the person opening the mail does not overlook (and possibly discard) it: 'Enc' (or Encs for more than one item) is the standard form.

- **Copy reference**

  If a duplicate of a letter has been sent to an interested third party, it is **courteous to acknowledge the fact to the letter's recipient** with a similar footnote:

  Copies to (3rd party names) *or* cc: (3rd party names)

- **Follow-up sheets**

  The second sheet, and all subsequent sheets, of a letter will be on plain (un-headed) paper. In case they should get detached or confused, therefore, **continuation sheets** are headed as follows.

  Name of recipient, page number in letter, date.

Alternative layouts

Simplicity and attractiveness are general guidelines to good layout, and there are two main styles currently in use.

FULLY BLOCKED *style* is the easiest to type and therefore increases the typist's productivity. Everything starts at the left-hand margin. This style is becoming increasingly common.

```
_____
Date _____
Ref: _____
Recipient _____
_____
_____
_____

Dear _____

SUBJECT

Main body_____
_____
_____
_____
_____

Yours _____


Name _____
```

```
_____
              Date _____
Ref: _____
Recipient _____
_____
_____
_____

Dear _____
        – SUBJECT –

Main body_____
_____
_____
_____
_____

          Yours _____



          Name _____
```

SEMI-BLOCKED *style* is much like fully blocked, but selected elements are moved over for balance. The date is against the right hand margin: the *complimentary close* starts from the centre: the subject header may be centralised.

Letter content

A letter (and indeed, any written message) should have a beginning, a middle and an end.

- **Opening paragraph**

    The reader will not be as familiar with the context of the message as you are. Offer:

    – A brief **explanation** of why you are writing. ('Thank you for your letter of 3rd March, in which you requested information about auditing services.')

    – An **acknowledgement** of relevant correspondence received. ('As requested [or agreed] in our telephone conversation [or meeting] of 4th September, I am sending you our brochure of services.')

    – Important **background** details. ('I have been asked by my colleague, George Brown, to contact you in regard to your enquiry about auditing services.')

- **Development of the message**

  The middle paragraph(s) should contain the substance of your response to a previous message, details of the matter in hand, or the information you wish to communicate. If you are making several points, start a new paragraph with each, so the reader can digest each part of your message in turn.

- **Closing paragraph**

  Your letter will not be effective unless it has the desired result of creating understanding or initiating action. Summarise your point briefly – or make clear **exactly what response is required.**

  - I look forward to meeting you to discuss the matter in more detail.
  - If you require any further information, please call me.
  - I will be contacting you in the next few days to arrange a meeting.

Activity 5   **(30 mins)**

The following is a detailed plan, showing how you might use the PASS framework to plan a letter replying to a client complaint.

Purpose: To show you have considered the complaint seriously

             To soothe the complainant's anger, disappointment etc

             To offer redress that will be acceptable to both parties

             To keep a positive relationship

Audience: Will want to have been taken seriously

             Will be resistant to avoidance of responsibility

             May be cynical about 'sincere' apologies

             Will have to be motivated to accept what you feel able to offer

Structure and style

Context. Acknowledgement of receipt and understanding of the complaint. Expression of regret.	Briefly reconfirm the details. Apologise gracefully but simply: overdo it and you will only sound insincere.
• Explanation. Results of an investigation into why the problem occurred. • Indication of what is being done to put things right.	Don't make **excuses**, or try to blame other people. Explain why the error occurred. Show that you were concerned to find out. Don't sound grudging. You are making amends gladly, and swiftly.
Restatement of apology. Assurance of non-recurrence. Hope that good relations not damaged (especially with client, customer, employee).	You want to be conciliatory, as you do **not** want to lose customers. Smooth things over, but again, don't go over the top and grovel.

Make a similar plan, showing PASS factors, for a **covering letter** to be sent to a colleague at another office with a parcel of brochures for an upcoming Accounting Conference.

Activity 6 (30 mins)

You work in a bank. Your manager has passed you the following letter and wants you to draft a reply for typing.

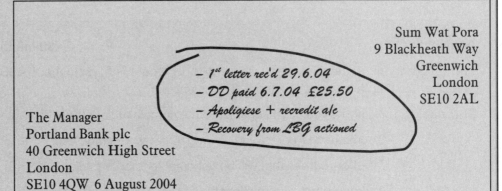

Sum Wat Pora
9 Blackheath Way
Greenwich
London
SE10 2AL

– 1ˢᵗ letter rec'd 29.6.04
– DD paid 6.7.04 £25.50
– Apoligiese + recredit a/c
– Recovery from LBG actioned

The Manager
Portland Bank plc
40 Greenwich High Street
London
SE10 4QW 6 August 2004

Dear Sir,

Account no. 0139742 – S Wat Pora Esq

I wrote to you on 27 June 2004 instructing you to cancel the monthly direct debit from the above account in favour of the London Borough of Greenwich with immediate effect.

Upon receiving may bank statement for July 2004 I find that my instructions were not carried out.

I should be grateful if you would rectify this matter at your earliest convenience.

Yours faithfully

Sum Wat Pora

Sum Wat Pora

If possible, prepare your answer using computer with word processing software (rather than writing by hand).

4.2 Memoranda (memos)

The **memorandum** or '**memo**' performs internally the same function as a letter does in external communication by an organisation. It can be used for reports, brief messages or 'notes' and any kind of internal communication that is more easily or clearly conveyed in writing (rather than face-to-face or on the telephone).

Format of memos

Memorandum format will vary slightly according to the **degree of formality** required and the organisation's policy on matters like filing and authorisation of memoranda by their writer. **Follow the conventions of house style in your own organisation**. A typical format, including all the required elements, is illustrated below – but get hold of your own organisation's memo pad (or computer template for memos) and start using that, if you do not already do so.

Organisation's name (optional)

MEMORANDUM

To: (recipient's name or designation) **Ref**: (for filing)

From: (author's name or designation) **Date**: (in full)

Subject: (main theme of message)

The message of the memorandum is set out like that of a letter: good English in spaced paragraphs. Note that no inside address, salutation or complimentary close are required.

Signed: (optional) author signs/initials

Copies to: (recipient(s) of copies)

Enc: to indicate accompanying material, if any

Forrest Fire Extinguishers Ltd

MEMORANDUM

To:　All Staff　　　　　　　　　　　　　　　　**Ref**: PANC/mp

From:　P A N Cake, Managing Director　　　　**Date**: 13 January 2003

Subject:　Overtime arrangements for January/February

I would like to remind you that thanks to Pancake Day on and around the 12th February, we can expect the usual increased demand for small extinguishers. I am afraid this will involve substantial overtime hours for everyone.

In order to make this as easy as possible, the works canteen will be open all evening for snacks and hot drinks. The works van will also be available in case of transport difficulties late at night.

I realise that this period puts pressure on production and administrative staff alike, but I would appreciate your co-operation in working as many hours of overtime as you feel able.

Copies to: All staff

Structure and style of memos

The structure and style of the message will vary according to its nature, the number of people it is addressed to, who those people are and what position they occupy. The flexibility of the medium means that some memos can be less formal than others. **The same guidelines apply as with a letter**.

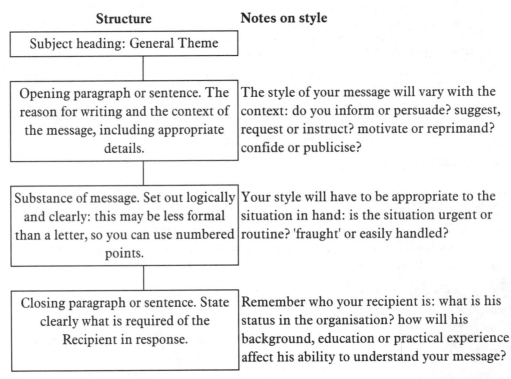

Structure	Notes on style
Subject heading: General Theme	
Opening paragraph or sentence. The reason for writing and the context of the message, including appropriate details.	The style of your message will vary with the context: do you inform or persuade? suggest, request or instruct? motivate or reprimand? confide or publicise?
Substance of message. Set out logically and clearly: this may be less formal than a letter, so you can use numbered points.	Your style will have to be appropriate to the situation in hand: is the situation urgent or routine? 'fraught' or easily handled?
Closing paragraph or sentence. State clearly what is required of the Recipient in response.	Remember who your recipient is: what is his status in the organisation? how will his background, education or practical experience affect his ability to understand your message?

The **audience** of a memo will be people **within your organisation** or business network.

- You may be writing to a fellow-specialist, and so be able to use technical language and complex ideas. Think first, however: a memo to all staff might cover a vast range of fields and abilities, from tea lady to accountant to engineer.

- If you are reporting to, or making a suggestion to, someone **higher in the hierarchy** than yourself, your tone will have to be appropriately formal, businesslike and tactful.

- If you are dashing off a handwritten note on a memo pad to a **colleague** with whom you enjoy an informal working relationship, you can be as direct, familiar and friendly as you like.

- If you are instructing or disciplining **junior personnel**, you will have to retain a certain formality for the sake of authority; a more persuasive and less formal tone might be appropriate if you are congratulating, motivating or making a request.

Activity 7 **(30 mins)**

You were made responsible for ordering stationery in The Accounts Department of Modus Operandi Ltd a month ago. The system requires anybody who notices that stationery stocks are running low or are exhausted to fill in a standard requisition form and pass it to you in room 32. This is clearly stated in a notice on the door of the stationery cupboard. You have not received any requisition forms during your month in office but you have frequently been interrupted in your work by heads popping round the door making remarks like 'Why aren't there any yellow highlighters in the cupboard?' and 'Who is it that does the stationery then?'

This is annoying and you have decided to send a memo to all staff in your department reminding them of the system.

Required:

Draft the memo, using your own name.

4.3 E-mail messages

Many organisations now conduct both internal and external communications via e-mail systems. E-mail can be used for a wide variety of communication purposes, in place of letters, circulars, internal memos, notes and other brief messages. Lengthier messages (such as briefs and reports) and graphic messages (such as diagrams and maps) can be attached as file attachments.

Most organisations have guidelines for the use of e-mail.

- E-mail messages have a legal effect. Firms can be sued for libellous, offensive or misleading remarks made in e-mail, and e-mail messages can be cited as evidence in court.

- E-mail can be used excessively, to the exclusion of other forms of communication which might be more appropriate. Excessive personal use (or

NOTES

abuse) is also an issue for many organisations (as it has been with the telephone).

- E-mail is not private, and remains on the server. There are thus dangers in using it to send confidential messages.

Using e-mail software

The most common e-mail software is Microsoft Outlook. In Outlook, depending on which version you use, a new (empty) mail message looks something like this (Figure 17.2).

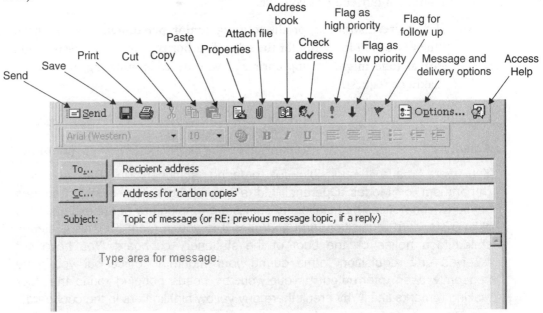

Figure 17.2 Email 'page'

You will need to become familiar with the functions and capabilities of whatever software your organisation uses.

Composing effective e-mail messages

The following are general hints on composing e-mail messages.

Do not commit to e-mail any message that is private or confidential. As mentioned above, it is not a secure medium in general: a co-worker may cover someone's e-mail while (s)he is absent, the system administrator may access messages and companies may monitor e-mail.
Do not send illegal or offensive messages. (This should not be on your agenda anyway – especially for marketing purposes – but abusive, discriminatory and harassing messages do get sent.) E-mails can be traced to their source, and systems administrators can be liable for the misdeeds of users.
Beware of informality. Writers of e-mails may dash off a friendly note, but the recipients may (quite rightly) regard it as a written (and legally valid) response which may imply contract terms.

BPP
PROFESSIONAL EDUCATION

Beware of 'tone of voice'. Sarcasm and irony do not come across well in brief, typed, computer-mediated messages. If you wish to be humorous (in an informal context), there are conventions: adding 'emoticons' such as 'smiley faces' (☺) or the typed equivalent :).
Use mixed case letters. All uppercase (ie capitals) IS INTERPRETED AS SHOUTING!
Keep the line-length reasonably short, to ensure that it displays effectively on most recipient terminals.
Ensure that you give the recipient's address correctly and that you state a subject. The first will avoid getting the message returned to you (remember that computers are very literal) and the second will avoid getting the message deleted by the recipient as possible junk or virus mail.
Remember that sending e-mail is instant and that you cannot usually re-call a message. Check your message carefully before you click on 'send'.

Activity 8 **(15 mins)**

How often do you use e-mail at work, and for what purposes?

What guidelines are there in your organisation for:

(a) How to use the e-mail software?

(b) How to format and compose e-mail messages (disclaimers, signatures, style)?

(c) Restricting the use of e-mail?

4.4 Other written formats

There are a number of other formats you may need to use in the course of your work, including a variety of:

- **notices** or posters

- **reports**: highly-structured formal reports, or short informal reports (which may be submitted as memos or e-mails, say)

- **forms**: eg accident reports forms, payroll forms, expenses sheets

In addition, there will be different **technologies** available for **producing** and **transmitting** written messages.

- **Handwriting** of messages: a personal letter or telephone message, say

- **Word-processing** for the **production** of documents (including letters, memos, notices, reports and forms) which may be:

    – Typed on a computer using a word-processing package

    – Saved to computer disk for storage and retrieval

    – Printed out if hard copy is required and

– Sent either electronically (via e-mail) or physically (via internal or external post or delivery)

- **Facsimile transfer (fax)** of documents. Any **hard-copy** message (letter, memo, report, form, diagram or chart) can be **transmitted** via fax, which allows it to be printed out as an exact copy, almost instantaneously, at the remote fax machine.

  Make sure that you prepare (or use) a **fax header sheet** approved by your organisation, setting out:

  – The target recipient (name, position, organisation, fax number)

  – The sender (name, position, organisation, contact details)

  – The date

  – The number of pages being sent (including the header) in case of loss or damage

  – Any accompanying notes (like a covering letter) to explain or direct attention to the documents being faxed

  An example of a Fax header sheet is reproduced below.

Fax

To	_____
Company	_____
From	_____
cc	_____
Fax No	_____
Tel No	_____
Date	_____ Total pages_____ (including this header)
Re	_____

BPP House
Aldine Place
142-144 Uxbridge Ro:
London
W12 8AA

Tel: +44 (0)20 8740 2
Fax: +44 (0)20 8740 2

info@bpp.com
www.bpp.com

If you haven't received all pages shown above, or find any are illegible, please contact us immediately

- **E-mail** of documents. Any message produced on (or scanned into) a computer can be attached to an e-mail message and **transmitted** via the Internet or computer network to a remote computer, even faster and more cheaply than fax.

The guidelines given in this chapter will be useful in composing *any* written message effectively.

Activity 9 **(20 mins)**

You want to fax a draft of the memo you composed in Activity 7 to John Agabon, the Purchasing Manager of Modus Operandi, prior to circulating it to the Accounts department. (John's office is at another site.)

You think that as Purchasing Manager, he might be able to give you some advice about making the requisitioning system more efficient.

His fax number is: 208 123 4567.

Prepare a fax header sheet with the relevant information (inventing any other details necessary).

4.5 Visual communication

If you are preparing a report or giving a presentation, you may need to use **visual aids** of some kind:

- to convey large amounts of data more accessibly. ('A picture paints a thousand words.')

- to add interest and appeal

Examples of visual communication

Examples of visual communication you might use include:

- The **presentation** of text in documents: using layout, colour, spacing, different typefaces, logos and so on.

- **Tables** of data: a simple way of presenting **numerical information**.

- **Bar charts**: a visually appealing way of **showing or comparing magnitudes** of an item (eg amount of money, hours, sales) according to the length of the bars on the chart.

Pollution complaints

Number of complaints

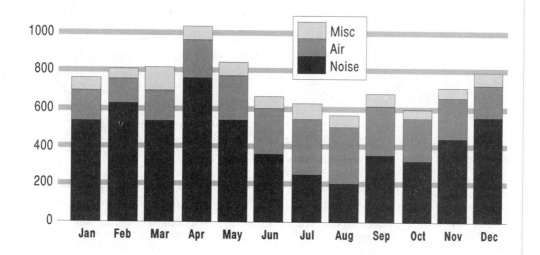

NOTES

- **Pie charts**: a visually effective way of showing the relative sizes of **component elements** of a total value or amount (represented by the 360 degrees of the circle or 'pie').

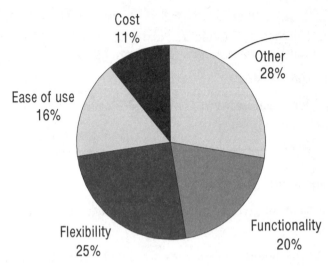

Choice of software

- **Flow charts**: a form of diagram used to show **processes**. Actions or positions are connected by lines and arrows which depict work flows, communication channels and so on.

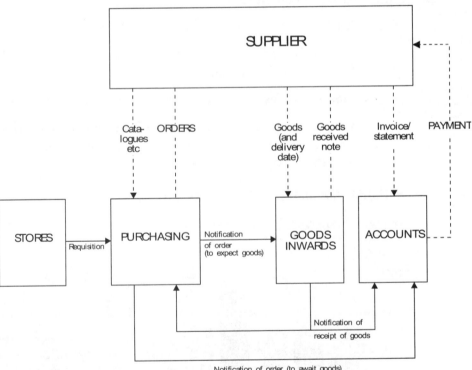

Flow chart showing information flows

- **Line graphs**: showing the **relationship between two variables** (represented by horizontal and vertical axes) by plotting points and joining them by straight or curved lines. These are particularly useful for demonstrating **trends**.

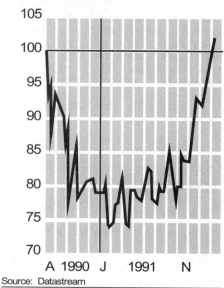

British Airways

Share price relative to the
FT~A All~Share Index

Source: Datastream

- **Illustrations**: from technical drawings to simple pictures which **highlight basic lines and features** of an object.

Basic principles of visual communication

Of course, preparing the various charts, graphs and diagrams mentioned above (and others), requires statistical competences not covered in this Text. However, the general principles of visual communication include the following.

- Give a clear and meaningful **title**.

- Cite the **source** of the data, where relevant.

- Clearly **label** all axes, columns, symbols and other elements: either on the visual itself, or in a separate 'key'.

- Keep narrative elements (labels, explanatory text) brief and simple

- Keep the presentation as **simple** as possible: cut down on unnecessary lines and elements to avoid overcrowding and confusion.

- Use the **size** and **spacing** of the visual to make it easy to read.

BPP
PROFESSIONAL EDUCATION

NOTES

Activity 10 (45 mins)

The table below shows a company's sales figures for 2000.

Prod	Jan £'000	Feb £'000	Mar £'000	Apr £'000	May £'000	Jun £'000	Jul £'000	Aug £'000	Sep £'000	Oct £'000	Nov £'000	Dec £'000	Total £'000
T470	800	725	725	400	415	405	410	605	590	700	845	900	
S332	210	210	180	170	175	160	195	200	195	210	220	230	
V017	480	510	510	510	520	515	510	385	420	475	460	465	
J979	25	50	60	95	125	140	145	145	165	180	190	190	
B525	615	600	505	430	445	430	485	560	650	700	695	610	
Z124	370	360	370	385	370	350	380	375	375	360	325	355	

Tasks

Add up the columns and rows and then (making your presentation as simple or elaborate as you wish) construct the following.

(a) A graph of the year's sales

(b) A bar chart of the year's sales

(c) A pie chart, showing whatever information you think is most appropriate to be shown in this form

(d) Which method did you find most effective in presenting this information?

---

5 ORAL COMMUNICATION

5.1 Oral communication

Oral communication is communication 'by speech'. It is sometimes also called 'verbal communication': communication in spoken words.

Oral or verbal communication is the most basic and generally-used way of sending a message to another person: think of all the people you talk to in a day, in person or on the phone.

The same process occurs in oral communication as in written: a message is conceived, encoded, transmitted, decoded, interpreted and acknowledge by feedback. However, in oral communication there is:

- **More immediate interaction**: you switch between 'sending' (speaking) and 'receiving' (listening) very quickly, as you ask and answer questions and exchange information.

- **More going on**! In addition to the meaning of the words themselves, there is an additional **non-verbal** element to the communication process. You will be sending and receiving messages through tone of voice and (if you are communicating face-to-face) through facial expressions, gesture and appearance. These 'signals' are collectively known as '**body language**'.

Oral communication can be:

- Face-to-face: as in a discussion, interview or presentation (see Section 7 below) or

- Remote, or audible only: as by telephone.

5.2 Speaking skills

The following are key skills in effective spoken communication – whether face-to-face or on the phone.

- **Clear articulation** is vital: not because it is associated with a particular region, section of society or level of education, but because you want to be understood immediately and unambiguously by *any other person*, in order to get a response that you require. Be **considerate** to the recipient of your message: don't use or pronounce words in a way that he or she will not understand, and don't speak too quickly. If you are satisfied that your speech is clear, unambiguous and not mannered just for the sake of it: fine.

- If you are articulating clearly, you will be much more audible, but you will also have to consider how to **project your voice**. Speaking softly or even at a normal **volume** will be ineffective in a large room with a high ceiling and heavy curtains.

- **Intonation** affects *how* your message reaches its recipient, as much as volume affects *whether* it does. Be aware of how the placing of **emphasis** on different words alters the meaning of a sentence: the stress *implies* something to the listener. How does your voice sound? Cheery? Gloomy? Disapproving? Encouraging? Affectionate? Enthusiastic? Indifferent? Hostile? Stay alert: if your voice is not **expressive**, you may come across as bored or indifferent.

- **Pace and pauses** are further elements in fluent but clear delivery. Don't garble your words or string together long breathless sentences. Avoid excessive use of 'um' or 'er' and phrases like 'sort of' and 'I mean'.

5.3 Assertiveness

Definition

Assertiveness may be described as clear, honest and direct communication.

Assertive, aggressive and passive (non-assertive) behaviours

Assertive behaviour is a considered response to frustration, conflict or threat which seeks to satisfy the needs and wants of all parties involved in the situation. According to Back and Back (*Assertiveness at Work*), such behaviour involves:

(i) Standing up for your own rights in such a way that you do not violate another person's rights

(ii) Expressing your needs, wants, opinions, feelings and beliefs in direct, honest and appropriate ways

An example of an assertive response to an inconvenient demand by a supervisor, for example, might be: 'I appreciate that you would like this task done immediately. However, I would prefer to complete the project I'm working on first. Will tomorrow morning work for you?'

Aggressive behaviour is a 'fight' reaction to frustration, conflict or threat. It usually takes the form of a verbal or physical attack on another person or object. According to Back and Back, aggression implies:

(i)   Standing up for your rights in such a way that you violate the rights of others

(ii) Ignoring or dismissing the needs, wants, feelings or viewpoints of others

(iii) Expressing your own needs, wants and opinions in inappropriate ways

An example of an aggressive response in the circumstances cited above might be: 'I'm not going to disrupt my work just because you've left the job late. Get someone else to do it!'

Passive (or non-assertive) behaviour is a 'flight' reaction to frustration, conflict or threat. It usually takes the form of giving in to others' demands. According to Back and Back, non-assertion implies:

(i)   Failing to stand up for your rights, or doing so in such a way that others can easily disregard them

(ii) Expressing your needs, wants, opinions, feelings and beliefs in apologetic, diffident or self-effacing ways

(iii) Failing to express honestly your needs, wants, opinions, feelings and beliefs

An example of a non-assertive response in the circumstances cited above might be: 'Well, I'm very busy at the moment ... but I suppose I could work late and fit it in, if you really need it.'

Assertion, aggression and non-assertion each have specific characteristic verbal and non-verbal behaviours which reflect these underlying orientations.

Techniques of assertion

Asking for what you want

(a) **Decide what it is you want or feel, and express it directly and specifically.** Don't assume that others will know, or work out from hints, what it is that you really want.

(b) **Stick to your statement.** If you are ignored, refused or responded to in some other negative way, don't back down, 'fly off the handle', or enter into arguments designed to deflect you from your purpose. Stick to your position, and repeat it calmly, as often as necessary: repetition projects an image of determination and reinforces your own confidence and conviction.

(c) **Deflect responses from the other person.** Show that you have heard and understood the other person's response, but are not going to be sidetracked.

Saying no without upsetting yourself or your colleagues

Saying 'no' can be very difficult for people: they feel it is selfish, or will cause offence.

(a) **Don't be pushed.** If you are at all hesitant about whether to say 'yes' or 'no' try asking for time to decide, to think or obtain more information. Why should you make an instant decision? Acknowledge your doubts: ask your questions. Feel free to change your mind.

(b) **Say 'no' clearly and calmly, if that is your answer.** Explain why, if you think it appropriate – not because you are anxious to excuse yourself, as if it were not your right to say 'no'. Don't express regret unless you feel regretful. Remember that when you say 'no', you are refusing a request, not rejecting a person.

(c) **Acknowledge your feelings**. If you feel awkward about refusing, or under pressure to accept, say so: the other person will be reassured that you are giving him or her due consideration.

(d) **Watch your body language.** If you have said 'yes' when you wanted to say 'no', don't start giving 'no' signals by sulking. If you are saying 'no', don't give contradictory signals by smiling ingratiatingly, lingering as if waiting to be talked out of it etc.

Receiving criticism and feedback

Distinguish between **valid criticism** (which you know to be legitimate), **invalid criticism** (which you now to be untrue) and a **put down** (intended to be hurtful or humiliating).

(a) **Invalid criticism and put-downs** should be handled simply and assertively with a straightforward denial: 'I don't accept that at all'.

(b) **Valid criticism** should be regarded positively as a potentially helpful experience.

    (i) **Negative assertions:** learning how to agree with a criticism if it does in fact apply to you, without growing defensive or abjectly apologetic. You simply acknowledge the truth in what the critic is saying, together with your response to the situation.

    (ii) **Negative enquiry:** learning how to take the initiative, to **prompt** specific criticism, in order to use the information if it is constructive **or** expose an attempt to put you down or be negative.

Giving criticism

Expressing negative feelings to others so that they hear what you are saying but do not feel personally attacked or rejected is not easy. Effective communication will be impossible if you make the other person defensive or aggressive, or if you let your own feelings get in the way. Guidelines are as follows.

(a) Describe the **behaviour** and express your feelings about the behaviour – to the individual personally.

(b) **Ask for a specific change of behaviour**. Being specified separates constructive criticism (which involves give and take) from attack or complaint.

(c) **End on a positive note.** This does not mean backing off your criticism ('it's not that important, really: I just thought I'd mention it'), but stating something positive that you feel. For example: 'I'm glad I've had a chance to say this', or 'In all other areas, you're doing fine, so I hope we can get this sorted out'.

NOTES

> **Activity 11** (10 mins)
>
> Think about incidences of conflict you have observed or been involved in at your work-place or college.
>
> What can you see as the (a) immediate or apparent benefits ('payoffs') and (b) the actual longer term results of:
>
> - Behaving passively or non-assertively?
>
> - Behaving aggressively?
>
> - Behaving assertively?

Assertiveness and the role of women at work

Assertiveness training is popularly seen as a prime means of remedying underachievement in women, or of helping women to avoid exploitation at work. It is likely to be a part of a 'Women Into Management' or similar training and education programme. The techniques and insights involved are likely to be of benefit to men as well, but it has been recognised that it is primarily women who are disadvantaged in western society by the failure to distinguish between assertion and aggression, submission and conflict-avoidance.

5.4 Listening skills

Many benefits are available from effective listening.

- It is a **quick, direct source of information**, which may be useful to you.

- It offers the opportunity to use the speaker's **tone of voice** to help you interpret underlying messages. (One example is knowing when someone is serious or joking.)

- It is **interactive** and **flexible**, so you can ask questions or add information of your own, to make the communication process more effective.

- It **builds relationships**, by encouraging (and demonstrating) understanding of another person's feelings and point of view.

The following are some guidelines on being a good listener.

What to do	How to do it
Be ready	Get your attitude right at the start, and decide to listen. You might even be able to do some background research so that you have established a context for the message you intend to receive.
Be interested	Don't try to soak up a message like a sponge: make it interesting for yourself by asking questions: how is this information relevant to me and how can I use it?

PROFESSIONAL EDUCATION

What to do	How to do it
Be patient	Try to hold yourself back from interrupting if you disagree with someone, and don't compete to get your view in before the speaker has properly finished. Wait until a suitable opening (ie while your point is still relevant to the immediate discussion, but not while the speaker is just drawing a breath between phrases). Don't be so preoccupied with how you're going to respond that you forget to listen to what is said in the meantime.
Keep your mind on the job	Concentrate. It is very easy to switch off as attention wanders or you get tired. Don't get side-tracked by irrelevancies in the message: co-operate with the speaker in getting to the point of what he is trying to say.
Give feedback	For example, try an interested and attentive look, a nod, a murmur of agreement or query ('Yes... Really?'). If there are opportunities, use some verbal means of checking that you have understood the message correctly: ask questions, referring to the speaker's words in a way that demonstrates your interpretation of them ('You said earlier that...' 'You implied that...'). The speaker can then correct you if you have missed or misinterpreted something.

You may be interested in the results of a Gallup poll in which American adults were asked how they felt about others' **talking habits**.

Talking habit	Extremely annoyed	Not annoyed	Don't know
	%	%	%
Interrupting while others are talking	88	11	1
Swearing	84	15	1
Mumbling or talking too softly	80	20	0
Talking too loudly	73	26	1
Monotonous, boring voice	73	26	1
Using filler words such as 'and um', 'like um' and 'you know'	69	29	2
A nasal whine	67	29	4
Talking too fast	66	34	0
Using poor grammar or mispronouncing words	63	36	1
A high-pitched voice	61	37	2
A foreign accent or a regional dialect	24	75	1

> **Activity 12** (1 hour)
>
> Practise your skills by interviewing some friends. Ask them (a) what talking habits annoy them, and (b) how they respond (extremely annoyed, not annoyed, don't know) to the habits listed in the Gallup poll.
>
> Part (a) allows you to practise listening, encouraging and clarifying while your friends talk in their own way. Part (b) allows you to practise your questioning, defining and leading skills.

5.4 Ways of listening

Like reading, listening may have a number of purposes, which should be borne in mind as you listen.

Listening for content

If you trust the source of the message to be correct and objective, or you only want to know what the source's viewpoint is (in which case it doesn't matter if it is incorrect or subjective), listening for content will be a straightforward receiving activity – but still requires skilful listening in order to:

(a) **Receive** physically as much as possible of what is said (ensuring that it is audible, and that your attention doesn't wander).

(b) **Interpret** as much as possible of what is said, in the way the speaker intends (understanding the message).

(c) Give appropriate **feedback** to achieve both of the above (asking for repetition or louder delivery, asking questions, encouraging the speaker to continue and so on).

In addition, you may want to make an effort to **remember** the content of the message. The surest way is to write down the important points, but the way you listen – noticing key words, for example, or listening just as hard to repetitions and summaries – will make recall easier.

5.5 Critical listening

If you require an objective viewpoint or accurate information, and you do not have absolute confidence that the source is able and intending to give it to you, you will need to listen critically. This is essentially like evaluating a piece of writing.

(a) Be **alert** to things you know to be factually false, and reappraise the source's credibility.

(b) Appraise the speaker's **vocabulary** and way of speaking for attempts to distract or persuade you. Tone of voice and **body-language** – if you can see the speaker – will be an additional source of guidance in this.

(c) Question the speaker's **assumptions** and logic (if only to yourself). Consider whether an illogical argument is the product of muddled thinking or an attempt at manipulation – and whether the conclusion is therefore invalid, or may still be true.

(d)   Look for **balance** – or bias – in the argument. It may or may not be conveniently signalled verbally ('On the one hand ... On the other hand ...').

(e)   Appraise the **supporting evidence** given, if any.

(f)   Consider the source's **credibility** and purpose in communicating.

(g)   Bear in mind your own biased **perceptions** as you respond critically to the message and to the speaker: don't dismiss the message because you dislike the voice!

Listening to the tone of voice of the speaker adds an extra dimension to the process of interpreting (is he being ironic, for example, or serious?) and evaluating (is he carried away by emotion, or trying to be persuasive?).

5.6   Empathetic listening

'**Empathy**' is defined as 'the power of understanding and imaginatively entering into another person's feelings'.

Empathetic listening is a highly active form of listening, which goes a step beyond critical listening in the attempt fully to understand the message and what lies behind it. In effect, the listener must engage with the speaker, interpreting in the content and style of the message both the surface and underlying meanings and the feelings and motives which prompted them: a third, unspoken 'message' in its own right. Questions to ask yourself when listening empathetically include the following.

(a)   **What** do the speaker's vocabulary, tone, manner and selection of content say over and above the surface message?

(b)   **Why** is the speaker saying this, and in this way (vocabulary/tone of voice)?

(c)   How does the speaker **feel** about this – whether or not it is actually said?

(d)   How would **I** feel in the same situation?

(e)   How might this idea/information **apply to me**, to my life?

(f)   What **feedback** can I give that would be helpful to the speaker, both to improve and encourage communication (say, asking a question) and to meet the underlying motives and needs (for encouragement, respect, friendliness, comfort or whatever)?

5.7   Attentive listening

Here are some brief hints to being a good listener, whether it be in one-to-one discussions, lectures, meetings or telephone conversations. In the context of your Research and Analysis Project, you will listen mainly to your mentor and your peer group.

(a)   **Be ready**. Get your attitude right at the start, and decide to listen. You might even be should have done some background research for the meeting or discussion so that you have established a context for the message you intend to receive.

(b)   **Be interested**. Don't try to soak up a message like a sponge, and then complain that you found it dull. Make it interesting for yourself by asking questions: how is this information relevant to me and how can I use it?

(c) **Be patient.** Try to hold yourself back from interrupting if you disagree with someone, and don't compete to get your view in before the previous speaker has properly finished. Wait until a suitable opening (while your point is still relevant to the immediate discussion, but not while the speaker is just drawing a breath between phrases). Don't be so preoccupied with how you're going to respond that you forget to listen to what is said in the meantime.

(d) **Keep your mind open.** Be aware of your negative reactions to the speaker's message, delivery or appearance. Control them, and don't jump to conclusions: you may miss something.

(e) **Keep your mind going.** Being open-minded does not mean accepting everything blindly. Use your critical faculties: test the speaker's assumptions, logic and evidence. Also test your own interpretation of words and ideas, making sure they make sense in their context.

(f) **Keep your mind on the job.** Concentrate. It is very easy to switch off as attention wanders or you get tired. Don't be distracted by details of the speaker or the room. Don't get side-tracked by irrelevancies in the message: co-operate with the speaker in getting to the point of what he is trying to say. Listen for main points, and the summary or conclusion.

(g) **Give feedback.** You can encourage the speaker and ensure your own understanding by sending feedback signals, particularly during pauses in the speech or message. For example, try an interested and attentive look, a nod, a murmur of agreement or query ('Yes... Really?'). If there are opportunities, use some verbal means of checking that you have understood the message correctly. Ask questions, referring to the speaker's words in a way that demonstrates your interpretation of them ('You said earlier that...' 'You implied that..'): the speaker can then correct you if you have missed or misinterpreted something. Remember, you're not trying to score points for cleverness or clairvoyancy: co-operate with the speaker, and if you don't understand something, or you think you've got something wrong, say so.

(h) **Use non-verbal cues (if available).** Be aware of the messages given by gestures, factual expression, tone of voice and so on.

(i) **Avoid interruptions**: if you interrupt it will disturb the speaker's flow, and can cause the conversation to go right off the rails. There are different reasons for interruptions:

    (i) boredom

    (ii) failure to understand

    (iii) a burning desire to state your own case and not hear out the other person

but they can all cause communication to break down completely.

(j) **Allow silence:** many people are embarrassed by silence and think that it is a sign of weakness or conversation drying up. In a complex, technical conversation, however, nothing could be further from the truth. Participants must have time to formulate their thoughts, mentally come to a conclusion and prepare what they are going to say, and this cannot happen instantaneously.

Try to indicate that you are happy with silence when it does occur, by looking relaxed and not pre-empting the speaker's next remarks.

5.8 The telephone

The telephone is still the most used item of office equipment. There are bound to be many situations in which you find yourself having to communicate via the phone with internal – and external – customers.

The following guidelines may seem obvious: good! Make sure that you use them – or any guidelines given by your organisation: they ensure that you promote a positive and consistent image, as well as being efficient and effective.

5.9 Prepare before you make a call

Know what result you are aiming at. What action or information will satisfy you, and where and when must you get them? (You might *say* 'I was just wondering...' to sound tactful, but make sure you have done all your wondering before you pick up the receiver.)

Know to whom you should be talking. Find out names and extension numbers if possible, and keep them handy in a personal directory.

Know what you want to say, and the order and style in which you want to say it.

- A **checklist** of points will be a helpful reminder
- Have all relevant **documents** and **reference material** to hand.

Make sure you will not be **interrupted, distracted or disturbed** once you have dialled the number.

5.10 Tactics and techniques

When you get through to the dialled number, wait for a greeting and identification from the answering party. **Seek** the identification if necessary. ('Good morning. To whom am I speaking?') It is time-wasting and embarrassing to launch into the subject of your call, only to be interrupted two minutes later by: 'I'm sorry. You need to speak to ... ' or even 'Thank you. I'll put you through.'

If the target recipient of your call is out or otherwise unavailable, carry out your 'Plan B', which may be any one of the following.

- Ask to speak to **someone else** who might be knowledgeable enough to help you.

- Leave a **message** with the secretary, or switchboard operator. Make it a brief one, but dictate clearly all essential details of who you are, where you can be contacted, and what the main subject of your call was to be. State whether you wish to be called back.

- Arrange to **call back** at a convenient time, when it is anticipated that the target will be available.

Once through to the appropriate person, the business of the call should be covered as **succinctly** as possible (consistent with rapport-building and courtesy).

Greet the other person by **name**: if you do not already know it – find out first!

Prepare the ground by briefly explaining the context of your call, what it is about, any relevant details.

Remember that the other person **cannot see you** to lip-read, judge your facial expression, or see you nod your head. Speak clearly, spell out proper names and figures; use your tone of voice to reinforce your message.

Pace your message so that the other person can refer to files or take notes.

Check your own notes as you speak and make fresh ones of any information you receive.

You may easily be **misheard** or misinterpreted over the telephone line, so you will have to seek constant feedback. If you are not receiving any signals, ask for some ('Have you got that?', 'Can you read that back?', 'Am I going too fast for you?', 'OK?')

Close the call effectively. Emphasise any action you require, and check that the other person has understood your expectations.

5.11 Receiving calls

It is very important that those who **answer** the telephones in an organisation should be **efficient, courteous and helpful**. A voice on the telephone may be the **first** or only **impression** of the organisation that an outsider receives: remember that you will have to create the impression you make with your voice and responsiveness alone.

Give a **courteous greeting** and **identify yourself** in whatever way is appropriate (name, department, organisation): there may be 'house rules' about this.

Identify and **note** the caller's name and organisation as soon as possible

Listen carefully to the message: it may require instant action or response.

Check your understanding. If the other person speaks too fast, or you do not catch something, are not sure that you have heard it right, or simply do not understand, say so: a courteous interruption to ask for a repetition or spelling is helpful to the caller.

Never leave callers hanging. If you have to transfer them to another extension or put them on hold, tell them what you intend to do.

Speak clearly and with a certain **formality**, and keep your **tone** appropriately helpful, courteous and alert. (It is easy to sound brusque when you intend to sound efficient).

Take **concise notes** of any details you may require in order to follow up the conversation. If you are giving information, pace it so that the caller can also take notes.

Co-operate with the caller. If you can resolve the matter in the course of the call, for example, by providing information, do so. If there are still matters to be resolved – further action to be taken or information to be sent to the caller by post – make sure that you are both clear as to what is required, and within what timeframe.

6 FACE-TO-FACE COMMUNICATION

You may communicate face-to-face with people in:

- informal discussions
- interviews

- meetings or
- presentations

The key difference between face-to-face communication and other forms of oral communication is the addition of **non-verbal signals**.

6.1 Non-verbal communication

Non-verbal communication is, as its name implies, communication without words, or other than by words.

We convey **more than half our meaning** by means of body language (Figure 17.3)

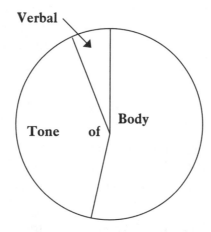

Figure 17.3 The proportion of a message conveyed by non-verbal communication

We can control and use non-verbal behaviour:

- **Instead** of words (eg storming out of a room or pointing something out)

- To **confirm or add** to the meaning of our words (eg nodding and saying 'yes', or pointing something out and saying 'look')

- To give appropriate **feedback** to another communicator (eg yawning, fidgeting or applause)

- To **create a desired impression** (smart dress, firm handshake)

Be aware, though, that body language can also **undermine** our spoken messages (eg wearing a grim expression while saying 'Everything's fine') – and studies show that people believe the body language more then the words!

If you can be aware of **other people's body language**, and **interpret** its meaning, you can:

- Receive **feedback** from listeners and modify your message accordingly

- Recognise people's **real feelings** when their words are constrained by politeness or dishonesty

- Recognise **interpersonal problems** (eg an angry silence, refusal to look someone in the eye)

- Read situations so you can **modify your communication/response strategy**. (Is the boss irritated by a delay? Reassure – and hurry. Is a colleague on the point of tears? Support and soothe.)

6.2 Body language 'cues'

What is it that we see and interpret when we say 'He looked upset', 'I could tell he was nervous', or 'She didn't say anything, but I could tell she was pleased'?

Sign	Meaning and interpretation
Facial expression	The eyebrows, eyes, nose, lips and mouth, jaw and head position all contribute to the expression on someone's face: lips can be tight or slack, eyes narrowed or widened, the eyebrows lowered or raised, the whole face moving or still, pale or flushed.
Gestures	People make gestures unconsciously: jabbing a finger in the air for emphasis, tapping the fingers when impatient. They also make conscious gestures – and not only impolite ones: a finger against the lips for silence, a jerk of the head to indicate a direction, a shrug to indicate indifference.
Movement	Watch how people move, at what pace, and to what effect. Someone who walks briskly conveys determination; someone who shuffles along, laziness or depression; someone who can never sit still, nervousness or impatience.
Positioning	You will probably find you sit closer to the people you like and trust, face them directly, or even lean towards them. You may keep a 'respectful' distance between yourself and someone with whom you have a more formal relationship.
Contact	Shaking hands is acceptable for transmitting greeting in most contexts but, for example, nudging or prodding for emphasis, or clapping on the back, implies familiarity and ease.
Posture	Consider the way you sit and stand. Lounge, hunch or sit/stand up straight and you convey relaxation, negativity or alertness. Lean forward when you listen to someone, and you transmit interest: lean well back and you convey weariness or boredom.
Sounds	A sceptical grunt, a sympathetic murmur and a delighted whoop are particularly useful non-verbal feedback signals.

Be aware that no non-verbal cue **by itself** is enough to make an accurate diagnosis of someone's meaning or mental state! A frown may be caused by irritation *or* perplexity *or* a headache! Consider the **whole body language** of the person, take the context into account – and test out your theories before acting on them!

You should also be aware that body language **means different things in different cultures.** An assertive level of steady eye contact, for a Westerner, would be regarded as aggressive and offensive to some Eastern cultures – just to give one example. Beware of making assumptions!

Activity 13 **(10 mins)**

How might you interpret (or use) the following non-verbal cues?

(a) A clenched fist

(b) Stroking the chin slowly, with furrowed brow

(c) Head in hands

(d) Sitting elbow on knee, chin resting on fist

(e) Tapping toes

(f) Turning or leaning away from another person while talking

(g) A sigh, whole facial muscles relax and mouth smiles

(h) A sigh, while body sags and face 'falls'

7   ADAPTING YOUR COMMUNICATION STYLE

There are several different 'styles' of communication which could be used for different purposes. This is a vast area of study, and we cannot do it justice here, but the following guidelines will give you a starting point.

7.1   Informing

Consider the **information needs and priorities** of others: what do they need and want to know (which may not be the same thing)?

Consider how much others **know already**: what background or explanation will (or will not) be required? As the range statement for this Unit points out, some people will be familiar with your subject matter, and some will not.

Avoid 'jargon': technical terminology which you use in your specialism, but may not mean anything to others.

Communicate as **clearly, simply** and **directly** as possible – even (or especially) if the topic is complex.

Use **visual aids** if this will help to make points more appealing, accessible or understandable.

Provide an appropriate **volume** of information. This means:

- Not **overloading** people with information they will not be able to get through or take in, in the time available.

- Not giving people more information than is **relevant** to them (or you).

- Not giving people **less** information than they need, or you want them to have

Consider the degree of **accuracy** required. All information should be accurate in the sense of **correct** – without falsehood – but need not be minutely detailed: a summary or average figure may be all that is needed.

Present factual information **objectively:** without emotional colour, exaggeration or bias.

Activity 14 (10 mins)

As a business person, who are the people you deal with regularly at work who:

(a) are familiar with the subject matter of accountancy work and communications?

(b) are not familiar with this subject matter?

If you were in a multi-disciplinary team meeting, with both groups of people, and you had to give a report on an accounting procedure, how might you adapt you communication style to accommodate the needs of both?

7.2 Influencing

Lee Bryce (*The Influential Woman*) suggests two main types of influencing strategy.

Push	Pull
1 Identify the problem/opportunity and propose your solution.	1 State your view of the problem/opportunity.
2 Invite reactions.	2 Clarify how the other person sees the situation.
3 Check that you understand each other's arguments.	
4 Deal with objections:	3 Work towards agreement on the nature of the problem/opportunity.
– by persuasion (if you want commitment)	4 Look for solutions, using as many of the other person's ideas as possible.
– by authority (if you only need compliance)	5 Come to joint agreement on outcome and action plan.
5 Agree on the outcome and action plan.	
• Directive	• Supportive/collaborative
• Effective where you are clear about problem/solution	• Effective where consensus, input desired
• Quick decisions where authority works to secure compliance, or where decision routine	• Slower decisions, but secures commitment
• **Can appear authoritarian**	• **Can appear weak**

7.3   Being assertive

Assertive behaviour is a considered response to a problem which seeks to **satisfy the wants and needs of all parties involved** in the situation – and to **preserve the relationship** between them.

Assertive communication involves:

- Standing up for **your own rights** – but in such a way that you do not violate another person's rights.

- Expressing your **needs, wants, opinions, feelings** and **beliefs** in direct and honest – but appropriate – ways.

For example:

- Asking specifically and directly for what you want: not assuming that others will know, or work it out from hints. ('I would like the day off' *not* 'I'm just so tired...')

- Acknowledging your feelings, using 'I' statements instead of blaming ('I feel let down' *not* 'You let me down')

- Using specific statements instead of exaggeration, especially when giving criticism ('I feel let down when you deliver work late, as you did on Tuesday' *not* 'You *always* let me down)

- Sticking to statements, repeating them as often as necessary until you feel heard, without raising your voice or entering into arguments. ('I have booked a day off... Yes, I realise you're under staffed, but I have booked a day off.')

- Defusing criticism by accepting what is valid, without becoming defensive ('You're right: I've been late twice this month' *not* 'I am not late all the time! I come in on time more than *you* do!')

- Saying 'no', when you need to, without being apologetic ('My schedule is full right now' *not* 'Oh, I'm sorry, I'm not sure... well, I suppose I *could...* if you were really desperate... But... Oh, well, never mind...)

An example of an assertive response to an inconvenient demand by a supervisor, for example, might be:

'I appreciate that you would like this task done immediately. *[Show respect for the other person's needs]* However, I would prefer to complete the project I'm working on first. *[Clearly stating own wants in the matter.]* Will tomorrow morning work for you? *[Inviting the other person to work with you in coming up with a solution that will satisfy you both]'*

Assertive behaviour must be carefully distinguished from aggressive behaviour, which takes the form of a verbal or physical attack:

- Standing up for your rights in such a way that you violate the rights of others
- Ignoring or dismissing the needs, wants, feelings or viewpoints of others
- Expressing your own needs, wants and opinions in inappropriate ways

An example of an aggressive response in the circumstances cited above might be: 'I'm not going to disrupt my work just because you've left the job late. Get someone else to do it!'

7.4 Negotiating

Negotiating is a process of:

- **Purposeful persuasion**: each party attempts to persuade the other to accept its case, by marshalling persuasive arguments.

- **Constructive compromise**: each party accepts the need to move closer towards each other's position , so that they can explore common ground and areas where concessions and compromises can be made while still meeting the key needs of both parties.

Negotiation is a **problem-solving** technique. Its objective is that both parties reach **agreement**, so that they both go away with a **decision they can live with** – without damaging the **relationship** between them.

This is not just a useful skill for purchasing departments! You can use it as a style of communication to reach agreement and solve problems in all kinds of areas: asking your boss for permission to decorate your work space; asking your tutor for more time to complete an assignment; sorting out the demands of different people asking you to do things at the same time – and so on.

A basic 'win-win' approach to negotiating (using the example of a purchasing negotiation, for relative simplicity) is as follows.

Step 1. Map out, in advance, what the needs and fears of both parties are. This outlines the psychological and practical territory.

Step 2. Define your desired outcome and estimate the worst, realistic and best case scenarios. ('If I can pay £500, it would be ideal, but I'd settle for £600. Above £700, it's just not worth my while.') Start with the best case and leave room to fall back to the realistic case. Keep your goal in sight.

Step 3. Look for mutual or trade-off benefits. How might you both gain (for example, by getting a higher discount in return for prompt or direct-debit payment). What might be cheap for you to give that would be valuable for the other party to receive or vice versa?

Step 4. Spell out the positive benefits to the other party and support them in saying 'yes' to your proposals by making it as easy as possible. (Offer to supply information or help with follow-up tasks, for example.) Emphasise areas of agreement and common ground.

Step 5. Overcome negativity by asking questions such as:

- 'What will make it work for you?'

- 'What would it take to make this possible?'

Step 6. Overcome side-tracks by asking questions such as: 'How is this going to get us where we need/want to go?'

Step 7. Be hard on the issue/problem but soft on the person. This is not personal competition or antagonism: work together on problem solving (eg by using flip chart or paper to make shared notes). Show that you have heard the other person (by summarising their argument) before responding with your counter argument.

Step 8. Be flexible. A 'take it or leave it' approach breaks relationships. (However, saying 'no' repeatedly to sales people is a good way of finding out just how far below the list price they are prepared to go!) Make and invite, reasonable counter offers.

Step 9. Be culturally sensitive. Some markets thrive on 'haggling'. Some cultures engage in a lot of movement up and down the bargaining scale (eg Asian and Middle Eastern), while others do their homework and fix their prices.

Step 10. Take notes, so the accuracy of everyone's recollection of what was proposed and agreed can be checked.

Step 11. Summarise and confirm the details of your agreements to both parties (by memo, letter, contract) and acknowledge a mutually positive outcome.

Activity 15   **(30 mins)**

Get together with fellow students (or friends) in pairs or teams to prepare and role-play a negotiation.

Scenario:

You want to go on holiday with the whole family to a coastal resort this summer. Your (role-play) partner wants to have some quiet time at home redecorating the bathroom, knowing that the two teenage (role-play) kids are keen to spend time with friends. These projects are important to both (or all four) of you. Negotiate! If you really can't find role-play partners, make notes on the possible strategies, win-win potential, and best-realistic-worst positions for all participants.

Chapter roundup

- Interpersonal skills for building and maintaining relationships include: rapport building, influencing, building trust and co-operation and managing conflict. These are underpinned by skills in communication.

- Communication is the transmission and exchange of information. It is a two-way process: feedback is the signal returned from the recipient of a message, indicating whether (and how accurately) the message has been received.

- Written communication formats include letters, memoranda, fax, e-mail and reports. Each has specific requirements for:

  - the format and structure of the message
  - the suitability of the medium for its intended use and recipient
  - competent use of any equipment involved in the medium

- Oral communication is the least formal, most common way of communicating. It includes face-to-face and telephone discussions. There are particular techniques involved in:

  - using the telephone efficiently
  - being an effective listener

- Face-to-face communication involves body language: facial expression, eye contact, gesture, position, posture) in confirming, emphasising or undermining verbal messages.

- It is important to adapt the content and style of your communication to your purpose and the likely response of the other person. Different styles of communication include:

  - information
  - influence
  - assertion
  - negotiation

Quick quiz

1   The appropriate 'complimentary close' to the salutation 'Dear Sir' is:

A   Yours sincerely
B   Yours faithfully
C   To whom it may concern
D   Dear Sir or Madam

2   From your knowledge of body language, what might be conveyed by the following?

(a)   clenched first
(b)   drumming fingers on the table
(c)   stroking the chin

Why might you use caution in making this diagnosis?

3   The best means of conveying bad news to someone is via e-mail. True or false?

4   Your manager comes to you late on a Friday afternoon and tells you that she needs a piece of work from you 'urgently'. You are in the middle of something else. You say (loudly): 'There's no way I can do it now: I'm busy. Get someone else to do it!'

This would be defined as:

A   an assertive response
B   a non-assertive response
C   an aggressive response
D   an informative response

5   Which of the following written formats would typically require a handwritten signature at the end?

Letter	Y	N
Memorandum	Y	N
E-mail	Y	N
Authorisation form	Y	N

6   What type of chart is used to show pictorially the relative sizes of component elements of a total value or amount, as a proportion of the 360% of a circle?

7   Label the numbers in the following diagram of the communication process.

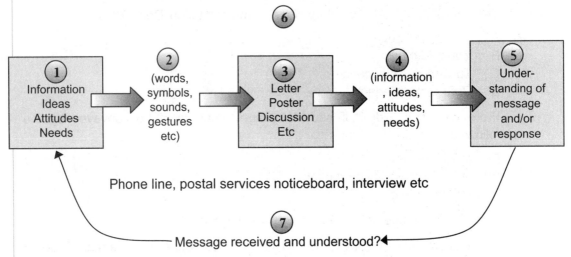

Phone line, postal services noticeboard, interview etc

Message received and understood?

8   Effective listening means *not* thinking your own thoughts until the other person has finished speaking. True or false?

Answers to quick quiz

1   B. (See para 4.1)

2   (a) Anger (b) Boredom or impatience (c) Deep in thought or perplexity. Caution is required because these signals by themselves cannot be accurately diagnosed, and may mean different things in different cultures. (6.2)

3   False, in general. Face-to-face would be preferable, allowing sensitivity and supportive communication. If the news was very urgent, a telephone call would still be preferable to e-mail, which can come across as very cold and abrupt. (4)

4   C. Many people confuse 'assertive' with 'aggressive': make sure you know the difference! (5.3)

5   Letter: yes. By convention, and to give authorisation/identification, in person-to-person letters.

Memorandum: no. Identifying details are contained in the header: initials, if required, would suffice.

E-mail: no. Identifying details are contained in headers and trailers.

Authorisation form: yes. A signature acts as formal identification for the purposes of authorisation. (4)

6   Pie chart. (4.5)

7   (1) Sender, (2) Encoded Message, (3) Medium, (4) De-coded message, (5) Receiver, (6) Channel and (7) Feedback. (3.2)

8   False. You may have had to think carefully about this. The point is not to *distract* yourself or *interrupt* the other person with your thoughts (or your impatience to say them). However, you need to *keep thinking*: consider whether what you are hearing is true/relevant, come up with questions, further information requests, feedback signals etc. (5.4)

Answers to activities

1   Your answer will reflect your interpersonal activities on the day you chose: no two answers will be alike.

What could you learn from this data? You would expect technical/work-related conversations to dominate during work time, and friendly/courteous conversations during breaks. (If not, are you wasting the organisation's time? Or becoming a workaholic?)

You would expect to ask for advice and help sometimes, but not as a large proportion of your interactions. (If not, are you avoiding seeking help when you ought to do so? Or are you constantly in crisis, or asking for help needlessly?)

You would expect to receive some supportive and encouraging words occasionally. (If not, where can you get some?)

2

	Positive feedback		Negative feedback
1	Action taken as requested	1	No action taken or wrong action taken
2	Letter/memo/note confirming receipt of message and replying in an appropriate way	2	No written response where expected
3	Accurate reading back of message	3	Incorrect reading back of message
4	Statement: 'Yes, I've got that.'	4	Request for clarification or repetition
5	Smile, nod, murmur of agreement	5	Silence, blank look, frown etc

3   (a)   Telephone, confirmed in writing later (order form, letter) – or e-mail order (if both parties have access)

(b)   Noticeboard (or employee Web page, if available) or general meeting: depending on the sensitivity of the topic and the need for staff to ask questions.

(c)   Face-to-face private conversation – but it would be a good idea to confirm the outcome in writing so that records can be maintained.

(d)   Telephone, email or face-to-face (if close by).

(e)   Face-to-face, supported by clear written notes. You can then use visual aids or gestures to help explain. This will also give you the opportunity to check the group's understanding – while the notes will save the group having to memorise what you say, and enable them to focus on understanding.

4   You may not have to draft marketing communications, but this is a useful exercise in evaluating the elements (and effects) of style and tone in written messages.

Decorwise's letter may be considered credible because of its:

(a)   imposing letterhead and long-established business

BPP
PROFESSIONAL EDUCATION

(b)   link to the Guild of Master Craftsmen

    (c)   Modest tone: not trying to raise inflated expectations

    (d)   Offer of a free quotation: implies trust that you will be satisfied (and low risk to you)

It may be considered congenial because of its:

    (a)   simple design and straightforward content
    (b)   no-nonsense, colloquial style and informality
    (c)   air of a personal communication from Jim himself
    (d)   appeal to solid working-class values (presumably Jim's target audience)

5   **Purpose**:   To introduce other enclosed items (goods, documents)

                      To highlight helpful aspects of the items (important points, instructions)

    Audience: They may or may not be expecting items (may be perplexed or resistant)

                      They may or may not need guidance or motivation to use/read items

Structure and style

Context. What you have sent (a CV, Brochure, a press release, a delivery etc) and why, with relevant details.	A letter may be sent to accompany items not expected by the recipient, so putting it clearly in context will be important.
Explanatory notes, if required, or Comments drawing the recipient's attention to particular features of the accompanying item.	If your enclosure is something you need to 'sell', a summary of its most attractive and relevant features may be appropriate. If it is being delivered late, explanation and apology may be required.
What is to be done next: you will follow-up with a phone call? Recipient to act or respond?	If no follow-up action is required, a courteous word of thanks for the reader's attention may be offered – especially if the item sent was unsolicited in the first place.

6

N E Name
Branch Manager
Portland Bank plc
40 Greenwich High Street
London
SE10 4QW

10 August 2004

Dear Mr Wat Pora,

Account no. 0139742

Thank you for your letter of 6 August 2003 regarding the above account.

I have looked into the matter that you raised and I am afraid that your letter of 27 June was indeed overlooked.

I apologise for this error. I have arranged for your account to be recredited with the sum of £25.50, the amount of the direct debit paid in July. I confirm that the direct debit instructions have now been cancelled.

Yours sincerely

Your Name

Clerk

7

MEMORANDUM

To: All staff in The Accounts Department   Ref: STAT/1

From: Your name   Date: 24 September 2004

Subject: Stationery

Please note that I am now responsible for ordering stationery for The Accounts Department.

The normal procedure appears to have lapsed and as a gentle reminder I attach a copy of the standard stationery requisition form. I should be grateful if you would complete a form and pass it to me whenever you become aware that stocks of any item are running low.

I shall ensure that there is always an ample supply of requisition forms and pens in the stationery cupboard.

8   We have provided no solution to this activity, as it depends on your own organisational practices and policies. Make sure that you are aware of any guidelines that exist in regard to: security, liability (eg disclaimer messages), presentation (eg signatures, stationery), content (eg non-offensive) and usage (eg work use only).

9

Fax

To	John Agabon, Purchasing Manager	**Modus**
Company		**Operand**
From	Your Name, Accounts Assistant	
cc		
Fax No	208 123 4567	
Tel No		
Date	[today] Total pages 2 (including this header)	
Re		

If you haven't received all pages shown above, or find any are illegible, please contact us immediately

I thought you might like to see the following memorandum, which I am planning to circulate to all Accounts Staff.

It is intended to tighten up stationery requisition procedures, for which I have taken over responsibility.

If you have anything to add, which might facilitate your stationery ordering – or help me to make our procedures more effective – I would be grateful.

You can contact me by e-mail (yname@modusoperandi.co.uk) or by phone on extension XXX.

Thank you.

YN

10

The totals you should have arrived at are as follows.

Product	T470	S332	V017	J979	B525	Z124
Total	7,520	2,355	5,760	1,510	6,725	4,375

Month	Total £'000
January	2,500
February	2,455
March	2,350
April	1,990
May	2,050
June	2,000
July	2,125
August	2,270
September	2,395
October	2,625

November	2,735
December	2,750
	28,245

Tutorial note. We have laid out the answer like this to make you aware that it is more difficult to check information presented in one way against information presented in another. It would have been kinder of us if we had simply reproduced the table with totals. Note, also, how much more effectively the table uses space.

(a)

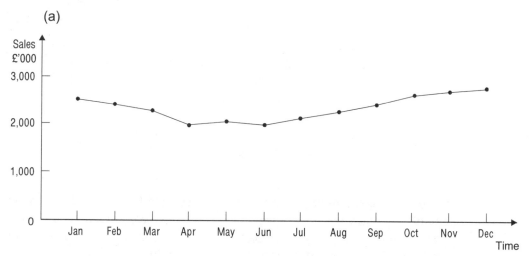

(b) We have divided our bar chart into segments for each product. Do not worry if you did not think of this, but notice how much more information you get if you present the data in this way.

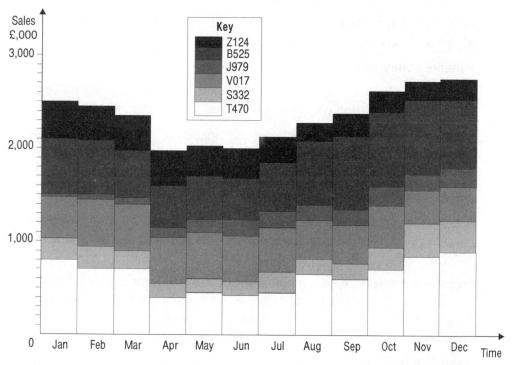

(c) We think that the share of total sales by product is the most appropriate information to show in pie-chart form. To arrive at the percentages for each segment divide the total for each product by the overall total and multiply by 100. To arrive at the number of degrees take the relevant percentage of 360°.

For example, T470: 7,520/28,245 × 100 = 27%; 27% × 360°= 96°

Total annual sales by product

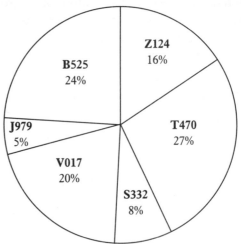

We do not think that any of the methods show the full range of information completely effectively. The graph is perhaps the worst (individual lines for each product could have been plotted but the graph would have been very crowded). The bar chart is probably the best method.

In practice, of course, there is no reason why all four methods (including the table) should not be used.

11   This activity should have made you think.

You may have come up with some of the following points. Note that assertiveness is an effective strategy for interpersonal relations!

Passive behaviour

Apparent/immediate payoffs: you avoid conflict and unpleasantness; you get to feel good for sacrificing your needs to others; people may like you.

Longer-term results: you do not get our needs met; you may feel angry and resentful later; others may lose respect for you; dominant people may feel they can exploit you whenever they wish

Aggressive behaviour

Apparent/immediate payoffs: you get your way; you may enjoy dominating people; you can let off some steam or anger; you may be respected for your 'forthrightness'.

Longer-term results: others may resent or fear you; others may withdraw from relationship with you; if others are equally dominant, conflict may escalate; you may feel guilty later; you may suffer anger-related problems such as high blood pressure.

Assertive behaviour

Apparent/immediate payoffs: you get your needs met; you have the satisfaction of expressing your feelings; you don't need to feel guilty or resentful later; interpersonal relationships are maintained or improved; new solutions to problems can be reached.

Longer-term results: as apparent/immediate payoffs, precisely because assertive behaviour takes this into consideration in deliberately managing communication for long term benefits.

12   This was a 'live interaction' activity. Your answer is: whatever results you heard and observed. (Do think about how successfully you listened and questioned: what might you do differently next time?)

13   (a) Anger or tenseness
      (b) Perplexity or thoughtfulness
      (c) Despair or exhaustion
      (d) A rather negative (tired? bored?) attempt to show attention
      (e) Impatience
      (f) Unease or coldness, even hostility
      (g) Relief, relaxation
      (h) Sadness, wistfulness

14   People familiar with your subject matter would include: your colleagues in the accounts department; people in related disciplines (eg if the payroll or finance functions were separate); other functional managers who are share certain aspects of your work (eg budgeting, costing, management and financial reporting); other people who might have some accounting training (for marketing or general business qualifications, say).

      People unfamiliar with your subject matter would include most of colleagues in marketing, legal services, production, HR and so on – especially for the more advanced aspects of your role – and many clients or customers.

      If you were in a mixed meeting, you would need to think about:

      •   making your information accessible to those unfamiliar with your subject, while

      •   not boring or patronising those who *are* familiar with it.

      Some ways you may have come up with for doing this are:

      •   using technical terms where necessary – but explaining them, briefly, for those who do not know them

      •   using visual aids that are simple and accessible – while explaining complex concepts verbally

      •   handing out explanatory notes for those who would like to look them over (at their own pace) later

      •   carefully monitoring feedback from those who might get 'lost': pacing yourself more slowly, or adding explanations if necessary

      •   giving frequent opportunities for questions: perhaps after the main meeting (so as not to waste the time of the experts)

15   Just do it – it's fun!

Chapter 18 :
SELF MANAGED LEARNING

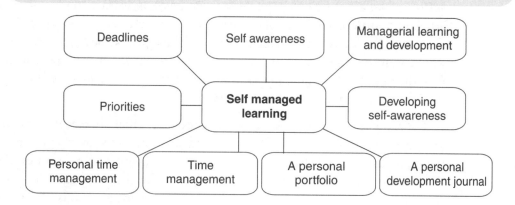

Introduction

This is a key – and intensely practical – chapter, which aims to equip you with the methodology and approaches to embark on the first stage of self development: developing self awareness and formulating a coherent and objective evaluation of your own interpersonal behaviours. You will learn and practise the key development skills of observation, description and reflection.

Learning outcomes

On completing this chapter you should be able to:

(a) Identify the relevance of the learning cycle and learning style preferences as a framework for self development

(b) Explain the importance of observing, describing and reflecting on behaviour for developing management skills

(c) Explain the role of questionnaires and feedback in increasing your self awareness

(d) Start to develop a Personal Portfolio and produce Personal Development Journals (PDJs)

(e) Understand the key principles of time management, using time effectively and prioritising

1   SELF AWARENESS

1.1   Self awareness and professional development

Self awareness is one of the key dimensions of emotional intelligence (Goleman, 1998). It can be invaluable tool for self development in several ways.

- **Self awareness motivates change**. 'All workplace competencies are *learned habits* – if we are deficient in one or another, we can learn to do better. The arrogant and impatient person *can* learn to listen and take other views into account... But those improvements will never happen without the first step, which is to become aware of how these habits damage us and poison our relationships. With no glimmer of what these behaviours do to us, we have no motive to change them.' (Goleman, 1998)

- **Self awareness implies openness to feedback**, which is essential to the process of continuous learning and improvement. Studies show that there are telling discrepancies between how managers rate themselves on abilities like listening and adaptability and how their peers rate them: in general, when there are such discrepancies, it is the *external* feedback that is the more accurate predictor of actual job performance. (Goleman, 1998)

- **Self awareness includes knowing one's strengths and weaknesses and approaching work accordingly**: a key characteristic of 'star' performers (Goleman, 1998). Managers can function more effectively and less stressfully by making allowances for their underlying personality traits and type preferences. They can also plan skill development activities to address particular strengths and limitations.

- **Self awareness enables self control** (Goleman, 1998). Recognising how events or circumstances 'trigger' unhelpful behaviours enables us to be more intentional about generating alternative, and more helpful, responses.

- **Self awareness helps us to identify, manage and appreciate difference**. If we recognise how our preferred behaviours suit us for particular team roles and communication styles, we can utilise the complementary strengths of others and manage the potential for incompatibility. If we are aware of our values, attitudes and perceptions, we will be more ready to acknowledge that – in an increasingly diverse work place – others may be operating from a different view of the world.

- **Self awareness helps us to clarify our values and goals** so that we are more motivated, intentional and congruent in our behaviours.

Among the personal competencies included in self awareness is **accurate self-assessment,** defined (Goleman, 1998) as:

- a candid sense of our personal strengths and limits,
- a clear vision of where we need to improve, and
- the ability to learn from experience.

This is the aim of self reflection and self evaluation in this Unit.

EXAMPLE

Goleman (1998) reports the following anecdote, which indicates the effects of a lack of self-awareness, and the impact of feedback.

'He was promoted to the top tier of a large manufacturing company, bringing with him a reputation as a kick-ass turnaround artist because of the ruthless reengineering and job cutting he had conducted in the past. "He never smiled – there was a scowl on his face all the time," Kathryn Williams, an executive coach with KRW International, told me. "He was always impatient and quick to anger. When people brought bad news, he would attack the messenger, so people stopped telling him things. He had no idea he frightened people. His gruff, intimidating demeanour may have worked while he was the turnaround artist, but now it was undermining him."

'Williams was called in to consult with the executive. She videotaped him in action and then replayed the tape for him, *pointing out the effect his habitual forbidding facial expression had on people*. It was a revelation...'

1.2 Selective self perception

The 'self' is, for practical purposes, only a 'self image': the mental picture we have of ourselves. Self image is influenced by:

- how we see ourselves, based on what we think of our appearance, behaviour, attributes and so on;

- the reactions we get from other people, and the conclusions we draw from those reactions about the sort of person we are;

- how we would like to be (or see ourselves) – our 'ideal self image' – and how we would like others to see us;

- the culture of our family, organisation and/or society, which determines the values we attach to particular attributes – and indeed how we regard the 'self'.

Self-image is highly subjective.

- Many of its components will be based on **selective self-perception**. There will be areas of our personality and behaviour that we are not aware of, and may not wish to become aware of. These 'blind spots' may be created by seeing only what we expect to see (aspects of ourselves that conform to our self image) and ignoring inconsistent information; or by seeing only what we want to see (aspects of ourselves that conform to our ideal self image) and ignoring dissonant information. Thus blind spots may relate to our strengths (if we have a low self-image) or to our weaknesses (if we have a high ideal image).

- Many of its components will be loaded with **value judgements**: whether you see yourself as an attractive or 'good' person, how you rate your abilities and so on. Guirdham (1995) notes that: 'These half-conscious self-assessments of strengths and weaknesses will influence what you try to do, whether you hope for success or fear failure in your dealings with others, and your expectations about how other people will or should behave towards you and respond to you.' (People with low self esteem, for example, often seek out interactions with discouragers and critics, in order to maintain the consistency of their self-image. Because they tend to be unambitious, non-assertive and self-critical, they actively encourage others to respond to them in the negative ways they expect or feel they deserve.)

Because self-image is so subjective and selective, and because its influence on behaviour is largely subconscious, the checking of our self-perceptions is vitally important.

We discuss how to check and challenge self perceptions using observed data, feedback and self-report questionnaires later in the chapter.

1.3   Through the Johari Window

A useful framework for looking at self-awareness, blind spots, and perception-checking is the 'Johari window' (Luft 1961). It classifies behaviours on a simple matrix: the horizontal axis representing what is known-unknown to self and the vertical axis representing what is known-unknown to others (Figure 18.1).

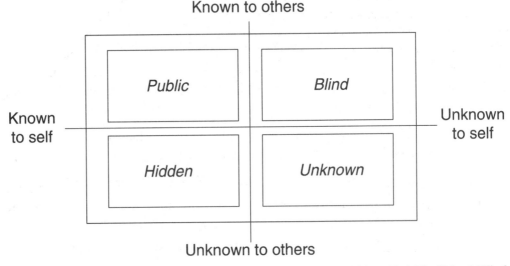

Figure 18.1 The Johari Window

- Some behaviours are obvious to you and to others: these are your **public** behaviours. They can be used effectively in interpersonal interactions because both parties are able to perceive and take them into account.

- Other behaviours are things you are aware of in yourself, but do not communicate to other people: these are **hidden** behaviours. They include private feelings and thoughts which you decide not to share, or which you fail to convey effectively. For example, you don't show your anger, or don't express it in a way people understand, so others don't 'know' that you are angry. Hidden behaviours can limit interpersonal interactions, because they create potential for misunderstanding and neglect opportunities for feedback.

- Some behaviours are obvious to other people, but you yourself are not aware of them: these are **blind** behaviours. They are often non-verbal behaviours and action tendencies: patterns of behaviour and habitual mannerisms. For example, you do not realise that you adopt a sarcastic tone of voice in conflict situations. **Blind** behaviours can limit interpersonal interactions, because they may undermine your conscious intentions and messages.

- Some behaviours are not consciously noticed by you or by others: these are **unknown** behaviours. These factors are a potential wasted resource in interpersonal interactions: not currently available for use. For example, you may have leadership abilities that neither you nor others are aware of.

The process of developing self awareness involves:

- Reducing *unknown* behaviours, by bringing them into your awareness through **self-observation**, **reflection** and **assessment** (for example, using self-report questionnaires).

- Reducing *blind* behaviours of others' perceptions of you through **feedback-seeking**.

- Managing *hidden* behaviours, through more – or less – **self-disclosure** to others, as relevant to the requirements of the interaction and appropriate to the level of trust and intimacy in the relationship.

Note that while the general aim is to increase *public* behaviours, we are *not* advocating indiscriminate self-disclosure! It is possible to disclose too little, and so limit both the collaborative and learning potential of an interaction. It is, however, possible to disclose too much – and this may be irrelevant to the information needs of others, inappropriate to the cultural/relational/communication context, and at worst psychologically unsafe for the discloser.

FOR DISCUSSION

How far do you think you should seek to increase your 'public' behaviours? Are there situations in your work context in which it would be advisable to keep certain behaviours hidden?

---

2 MANAGERIAL LEARNING AND DEVELOPMENT

2.1 The nature of managerial learning and development

Organisations are favouring approaches to management education, training and development which place greater emphasis on:

- managers' own responsibility for identifying and satisfying their learning needs

- competence-based training, allowing individuals to identify and take advantage of learning opportunities in the work-place

- experiential learning (learning by 'doing') rather than knowledge-based curricula and

- continuous-self development, aimed at personal competence and employability rather than job-specific performance improvement.

A self development approach based on increasing self-awareness takes these elements into account by giving you flexible competencies and approaches which allow you to:

- set your own life- and career-relevant learning and problem-solving goals;

- plan to exploit development opportunities in your work place (as well as in other settings);

- apply the experiential learning cycle to utilise *any* experience or action as a learning opportunity

- incorporate theoretical knowledge, reflection, practise and application for effective competence development and

- practise balanced learning habits and skills which will enable on-going development throughout your lifetime

2.2 The experiential learning cycle

Earlier in this book, we introduced the simple model of the learning cycle (Kolb, 1984; Honey and Mumford, 1992) which we will explore in more detail here. Kolb suggested that as well as learning from abstract concepts and theories, people can *learn from experience*, or learn by 'doing'. Learning should not be 'a special activity cut off from the real world and unrelated to one's life': instead, it should be an integrated part of life.

Building on Kolb's work, Honey and Mumford proposed the learning cycle.

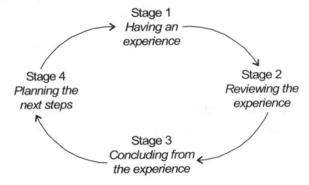

Figure 18.2 Honey and Mumford's learning cycle

Learning from experience is a process of:

- *Having an experience:* being fully involved in an action or interaction, utilising your current knowledge and skills.

- *Reviewing the experience:* looking back at what happened, describing it, reflecting on the causes and effects of your behaviour.

- *Concluding from the experience:* forming generalisations, concepts and theories that will enable you to integrate your observations and reflections into your behaviour on future occasions or in other contexts.

- *Planning the next steps:* planning ways in which you can apply and test your conclusions in further action.

Say you interview a client (having an experience): you are fully engaged in the activity. Afterwards, however, you are able to think more objectively about the behaviour you observed in the interaction: reflecting on the client's resistance to persuasion, you realise that your responses failed to take into account the concerns suggested by her non-verbal behaviours (reviewing the experience). You hypothesise that more empathetic responses may be more persuasive (concluding from the experience). You plan to try out some new empathy behaviours in your next interview (planning the next steps). This provides you with an experience with which to start the cycle over again.

Activity 1 **(20 mins)**

Aim: To highlight the role of learning the cycle in your interpersonal skills development.

Instructions:

For each stage of the learning cycle discussed above, what are the implications for your self development in the area of interpersonal skills? What will you need to do in order to progress through the stages?

[We will answer these questions in this chapter, but it is worth your thinking through the requirements yourself first, so that you clearly grasp the nature of the learning cycle.]

2.3 Learning styles

Kolb (1984) recognised that people tend to have a preference for a particular phase of the cycle, which he identified as a preferred **learning style**.

Honey and Mumford (1992) also noted that 'people vary not just in their learning skills but also in their learning styles. Why otherwise might two people, matched for age, intelligence and need, exposed to the *same* learning opportunity, react so differently?' Honey and Mumford formulated a popular classification of learning styles in terms of the attitudes and behaviours which determine an individual's preferred way of learning.

Style	Characteristics	Learning preferences
ACTIVIST *'I'll try anything once'*	Activists involve themselves fully in new experiences. They are open-minded and enthusiastic about new things – but easily bored by long-term implementation and consolidation: act first and think about consequences later. They prefer to tackle problems by brainstorming. They easily get involved with others – but tend to centre activities on themselves.	Learn best from activities which: • present new experiences/problems • involve short 'here and now' activities • offer excitement, drama and variety • have high visibility/limelight • allow them to generate ideas without constraints of structure or feasibility • challenge/throw them in at the deep end • involve them with other people • allow them to 'have a go'

Style	Characteristics	Learning preferences
		Learn least from activities which: • involve passive roles and processes • don't allow involvement • require the handling of 'messy' data • require solitary work • involve precise instructions, repetition (practice) and 'theoretical' concepts • require follow-up or attention to detail
REFLECTOR *'Look before you leap'*	Reflectors like to stand back to observe and ponder new experiences, preferring to consider all angles and implications, and to analyse all available data, before reaching any conclusions or making any moves. When they do act, it is from awareness of the big picture. They tend to adopt a low profile, taking a back seat in meetings and discussions – though listening and observing others carefully – and tend to have a slightly distant, tolerant, unruffled air.	Learn best from activities which: • encourage observation and reflection • allow them to stand back from events • allow them to think before acting • involve painstaking research • offer an opportunity for review • help them to exchange views with others without risk, with structure • allow them to arrive in their own time Learn least from activities which: • force them into the limelight • require action without warning/planning • give insufficient data • give unanalysed practical instructions • impose time pressures, especially if these necessitate shortcuts

Style	Characteristics	Learning preferences
THEORIST *'If it's logical it's good'*	Theorists are keen on basic assumptions, principles, theories, models and systems thinking. They are detached and analytical and like to analyse and synthesise facts and observations into coherent theories. They think problems through systematically and logically. They are interested in maximising certainty, and so tend to be rigidly perfectionist and uncomfortable with subjectivity, ambiguity, lateral thinking and flippancy.	Learn best from activities which: • relate to a system, model or theory • allow time to grasp underlying logic • display rationality or logic • have clear purpose and structure • allow analysis/generalisation of reasons for success/failure • stretch them intellectually Learn least from activities which: • have no context or apparent purpose • emphasise emotions or feelings • involve ambiguity and uncertainty • require them to act or decide without a basis in policy, principle or concept • skim the surface of the subject • lack theoretical or evidential support • appear shallow or gimmicky • involve them with people with less intellectual styles (eg activists)
PRAGMATIST *'If it works, it's good (but there is always a better way)'*	Reflectors are eager to try out ideas, theories and techniques to see if they work in practice. They like to get on with things, acting quickly and confidently on ideas that attract them – and tending to be impatient with ruminating and open-ended discussion. They are down to earth: enjoying practical decisions and responding to problems and opportunities 'as a challenge'.	Learn best from activities which: • relate to work problems/opportunities • offer techniques with obvious practical applications/advantages • allow practise with coaching/feedback from a credible expert • expose them to role models to imitate • allows them to concentrate on practical issues (plans, tips etc)

Style	Characteristics	Learning preferences
		• are followed up with immediate opportunities to implement learning
		Learn least from activities which:
		• are not related to immediate needs
		• are too theoretical or distant from reality
		• offer no practical guidelines
		• waste time 'going round in circles'
		• offer no apparent benefits or rewards
		• cannot be implemented due to personal or organisational obstacles

Source: compiled from Honey and Mumford (1992)

Each style 'connects' with a stage on the continuous learning cycle (*Figure 18.3*).

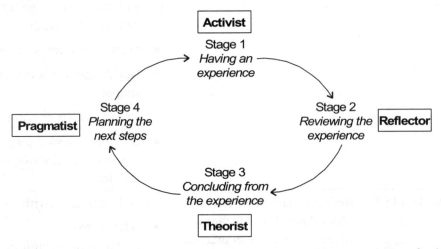

Source: Honey and Mumford (1992)

Figure 18.3 The learning cycle with learning styles

'People with Activist preferences, with their 'I will try anything once' approach, are well equipped for Experiencing. People with Reflector preferences, with their predilection for mulling over data, are well equipped for Reviewing. People with Theorist preferences, with their need to tidy up and have 'answers' are well equipped for Concluding. Finally, people with Pragmatist preferences, with their liking for things practical are well equipped for Planning.' (Honey and Mumford, 1992)

Activity 2 **(20 mins)**

Aim: to consider the implications of your preferred learning style(s) for managing your own development.

Instructions:

Consider your preferred learning style(s). On the basis of your preferences:

- Identify which stages of the learning cycle you are *best* and *worst* suited to.

- Identify what you could do to ensure you learn effectively from experiences.

2.4 Using learning styles in your development planning

A knowledge of your learning style enables you to select learning activities and opportunities that are congruent with your preferences and that work to their associated strengths and limitations. Honey and Mumford (1992, p. 49) suggest two possible strategies.

- **Seek activities which suit your preferred style**: those which *work* for you. 'This avoids the likelihood of people being exposed to learning experiences in a form which they find unhelpful. It reduces frustration.' It does not, however, maximise the opportunity for learning. The fact that a learner has a strong preference for a style does not mean that (s)he necessarily actually uses the style to full effect, but it does often mean that potential areas of learning – which might be accessed by a less-preferred style – are being missed.

- **Seek activities which are *not* suited to your preferred style**: those which *stretch* you. This builds a wider range of learning effectiveness, by developing competence in the learner's less preferred styles. No one style is 'better' or 'worse' than any other, but different styles may be better able to maximise particular learning opportunities. Developing flexibility may therefore be helpful – not just to become 'a better learner' but to be able to get out of any given learning activity or opportunity (whether or not suited to your preferred learning style) something that will contribute to your effectiveness.

It may be helpful for you to articulate your learning style preferences to others – tutors, mentors, coaches, superiors involved in your development planning – in order to help them to help you to maximise your learning.

Activity 3 **(30 mins)**

Aims:

To begin to build your awareness of potential learning opportunities available for inclusion in your development planning

To allow you to practise your use of learning style preferences in planning developmental activities for yourself and others

Instructions:

(a) Brainstorm a list of all the learning activities you can (currently) think of for improving your interpersonal skills.

(b) For each activity you have listed, consider which learning style it would suit *best*. Mark each style with an R (for reflector), P (for pragmatist), A (for activist) or T (for theorist).

(c) Highlight the activities that match *your* learning style.

(d) Highlight the activities that you consider would be particularly *useful* for your development (for example, analysing actual interactions at work) but which do not suit your learning style.

3 DEVELOPING SELF AWARENESS

3.1 An outline approach

In the rest of this chapter, we outline a systematic approach, based on the learning cycle, for:

- *gathering data* on the impact and effectiveness of your behaviours in interpersonal interactions: observing and describing interpersonal events; gathering feedback; and using self-report questionnaires.

- *reflecting* on the data and its implications for your effectiveness, using key self-development tools: a personal development journal and a personal portfolio.

- formulating *conclusions* in the form of a coherent *evaluation* of your strengths and limitations in key areas, as a framework for your development planning.

- You may choose to start a continual process of event/interaction sampling, observing and describing and feedback-gathering. From the gathered data, you can then select specific areas of interest for reflection and self evaluation (and subsequent development planning). We might call this a *self-awareness* approach (Figure 18.4), since the focus is on gathering data about your behaviour and performance.

- You may, however, choose to start with specific areas or hypotheses as the focus of your event/ interaction sampling, observing and describing, feedback-gathering, reflection and self evaluation. We might call this a *problem-solving* approach (Figure 18.5), since the focus is on investigating apparent or potential weaknesses/threats – or strengths/opportunities.

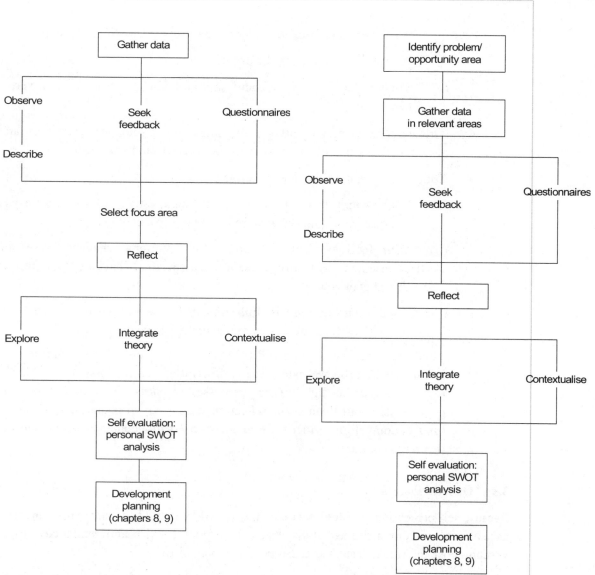

Figure 18.4 A self-awareness approach   *Figure 18.5 A problem-solving approach*

Either approach may be appropriate, depending on your needs, and they are not mutually exclusive. We set out the self-awareness approach below. If you prefer a problem-solving approach, simply tackle the stages in the appropriate sequence.

3.2   Observation and description

In order to learn from your experience, you will need firstly to **observe** and **describe** interpersonal interactions (specific behaviours and their outcomes in specific contexts). This may be done in any structured and accessible way, including the use of Personal Development Journals (PDJs): see Section 4 below.

Your observation and description should focus on:

- *External*, observable behavioural events in the course of an interpersonal interaction. 'Observable' means, primarily, what you see and hear, but may also include other sensory data such as touch (for example, a firm handshake).

(a)   What happened immediately before the event (its 'antecedents')?

(b)   What happened during the event?

(c)   What did each party do and say, and how (verbal and non-verbal behaviours)?

- This description may be used as raw material for your own learning – and also as feedback for the other party in the interaction, if appropriate.

- Your own *internal*, subjective processes.

(a)   Your **thoughts**: what was going through your mind, how were you interpreting things, what were you 'telling yourself'?

(b)   Your **feelings**: what emotions (and emotional changes) were you experiencing and in response to what specific behaviours by others or thoughts of your own?

(c)   Your **intentions and inclinations**: how you wanted to behave – not necessarily the same as how you actually behaved.

This is personal data, which will help you to reflect on the event and identify its underlying processes later. At the description stage, it may not be helpful to speculate about the internal processes of *others*. (You may choose to hypothesise about them at the reflection stage – but with caution, and on the basis of compelling evidence from their observable behaviours and relevant theoretical models…)

3.3 Questionnaires

Because self-perceptions are highly subjective, it will be helpful to **seek more objective assessment** of your attitudes, skills, traits, behavioural styles and tendencies, using psychometric instruments such as self-report questionnaires.

We have already presented you with a number of formal and informal models designed to classify or describe your style or the ways you typically behave. Questionnaires can be useful as a 'reality check' on your self-perceptions, as a well-designed and validated questionnaire offers a reasonably reliable picture of your action tendencies or preferences. However, when using questionnaire data for reflection and self evaluation, it is important to be clear what they can and cannot tell you.

In interpreting questionnaire data, it is important to remember the following points.

- Questionnaires are not 'tests': there are no right and wrong answers. No style or type (or whatever) is 'better' than any other. A certain style or type may merely be more effective in certain situations: remember that behavioural flexibility and competence development is possible, whatever your action tendencies.

- Questionnaires are designed to help you to develop self insight. You do not have to agree with the conclusions of the questionnaire.

- Do, however, be open to the challenge the results may pose to your self-perception. This is a useful reality check. If you disagree with the results of a questionnaire, try and identify why. Were you honest in completing the questionnaire? Did you think too long over the questions, rather than giving your first response? Did you try to give the 'right' answer in terms of how you would like to be, or how you think you should be, rather that stating how you actually behave? Did the questionnaire genuinely not offer responses that accurately reflected your behaviour? Is your self-image (or behaviour) genuinely ambiguous at the moment – perhaps because of some major changes occurring in your life.

- Questionnaire data alone can never give a full picture of an complex individual. They are intended to provide a common language for talking about differences and similarities between individuals: not to stereotype people or suggest that you will or must always behave in a certain way. Don't allow a questionnaire to 'label' you: take only what you can use.

- Questionnaire data should always be considered alongside other information: feedback from others, personal reflections on experience and so on.

- Always check to make sure you understand fully what questionnaire terminology means: technical labels are often used which differ from the meaning you may assume. (For example, in the Myers-Briggs model, 'judging' is not about 'being judgemental' but about a preference for a particular set of cognitive functions.)

- Remember that types and styles are merely statements about what behaviours you tend to *prefer*: they do not evaluate your *ability* or *skill development* in those behaviours. A theorist learning style does not imply that you necessarily use that style well to maximise learning – nor that you learn poorly by pragmatic means.

FOR DISCUSSION

Think about a questionnaire you have recently completed regarding your behaviour or preferences. You could consider the Learning Styles Questionnaire.

- Did you feel that the questions accurately reflected your behaviours and attitudes – or did you have to choose the 'least inaccurate' option?

- Did you (honestly) give answers that reflected your actual behaviours and attitudes – or were you tempted to give the 'right' answer?

- Do you fit the profile of the style or type in which the questionnaire placed you – or is it not 'really you'?

- How have you been able to *use* the results of the questionnaire, so far, to improve your effectiveness?

3.4 Feedback

Seek feedback information from other people who observe or experience your behaviours.

Feedback is simply communication which offers information to an individual or group about how their behaviour is *perceived* by the feedback-giver and how it *affects* him or her.

The purpose of feedback is to help people learn by increasing their awareness of what they do, how they do it and its impact on other people.

Whetten *et al.* (2000, p. 48) point out that: 'It is almost impossible to increase skill in self-awareness without interacting with and disclosing ourselves to others. Unless one is willing to open up to others, to discuss aspects of the self that seem ambiguous or unknown, little growth can ever occur.'

There are two main types of feedback, both of which are valuable in enhancing performance and development.

- **Motivational feedback** is used to reward and reinforce positive behaviours and performance by praising and encouraging the individual. Its purpose is to increase *confidence*.

- **Developmental feedback** is given when a particular area of performance needs to be improved, helping the individual to identify what needs to be changed and how this might be done. Its purpose is to increase *competence*.

Motivational feedback may contribute to a person's development. (S)he may not realise that (s)he has certain skills, and receiving positive feedback on performance may help to highlight areas of under-utilised potential.

Constructive feedback is designed to widen options and encourage development. This does *not* mean giving only positive or 'encouraging' feedback about what a person did well: feedback about undesirable behaviours and their effects, given skilfully, is in many ways more useful.

Activity 4 (15 mins)

Aim: to help you to identify areas of difficulty in giving feedback.

Instructions: Consider a situation in the past when you have had to give feedback to someone about their performance or behaviour.

(a) How did you feel about it?

(b) What do you think makes giving:

- positive feedback on good performance and

- negative feedback on poor performance

difficult for you (and others)?

3.5 Reflection

Reflection is simply 'thinking over' the data you have gathered. This deceptively simple skill is a key element in the experiential learning cycle. While observation, description, questionnaires and feedback bring our behaviours into conscious awareness, reflection gives them **meaning** and helps to **evaluate** our behaviour and impact on others.

Select areas for reflection and evaluation

How do you decide which areas to reflect on? The areas you choose may be based on:

- **Gathered data**. From your regular observations and descriptions of interpersonal processes, (plus questionnaires, feedback and so on) you identify a pattern of behaviour which does or does not appear to be effective in helping you to achieve your aims.

- **Critical incidents** in which you participated: specific incidents which highlight a given behaviour – for example, by illustrating it particularly clearly, or by eliciting particularly positive or negative outcomes.

- **Examination of goals**. You consider a particular desired outcome or objective which you are or are not (yet) achieving effectively, and identify the behavioural strategies you have been using to pursue it: these may represent potential areas for problem-solving and development.

- **Impressions**: you feel generally satisfied or dissatisfied with your performance in a given area.

Note that the highlighting factors may be positive (indicating a possible strength/opportunity) as well as negative (indicating a possible limitation/threat)

Explore

Reflect on the issues raised by your gathered data in your chosen areas. There is an infinite number of questions you might usefully ask yourself, but as a thought-prompter, you may like to consider:

- your *action tendencies* or patterns of behaviour (how you 'usually' behave or react), and whether you did anything *different* this time;

- what might have *triggered* and *influenced* your behaviour, thoughts or feelings. (Assumptions, perceptions, past experience, expectations? Trait/type preferences?);

- the *outcomes* you wanted from your behaviour – and those you actually got;

- whether the behaviour and its results are the same in all *contexts*, or only in some;

- the *value* and *relevance* of the feedback and assessments you obtained, and how you felt about them;

- any *discrepancies* which emerged between feedback/assessments and your self-perception, and what might account for them.

Incorporate relevant theoretical concepts

Relevant theoretical models and research findings may help you to formulate some ideas as to:

- factors which may be influencing your (and others') behaviour in the situation

- why particular behaviours might be resulting in the observed outcomes

- what you might need or be able to do differently for better outcomes

Theoretical concepts may support or challenge your self perceptions and hypotheses about your behaviours: a useful reality check.

Integrating your practice/observation with theoretical concepts also allows you to move to the next stage of the learning cycle: to draw **conclusions** about your experience. This in turn allows you to **transfer your learning** to different situations. This is the key to genuine learning and on-going development.

Contextualise

This is an opportunity to reflect on the **need** for behavioural change, and its **feasibility**, in the light of:

- your *desired outcomes* and how important they are to you (congruence with your terminal values)

- *opportunities* in the situation, which might be better exploited if you change your behaviour

- *threats* in the situation, which might cause problems if you maintain your present behaviour

- *constraining factors* in the situation which might limit your ability to change your behaviour

- *potential side-effects* of changing your behaviour (impacts on others, change in relationships)

- *restraining factors* within yourself: sources of resistance and reluctance (congruence with instrumental values)

You may like to think of this as an '**ecology check**': anticipating some of the impacts of behavioural change on your environment.

3.6 Self evaluation

It may facilitate the development planning process if you summarise your **conclusions**. Identify specific behaviours which you perceive to be strengths and limitations:

- in a given context and
- in light of your desired outcomes.

We will now look at two key managerial tools for developing self awareness: a personal development journal and personal portfolio.

4 A PERSONAL DEVELOPMENT JOURNAL (PDJ)

4.1 What is a 'PDJ'?

A 'journal' is a book (or note pad, or whatever) in which you regularly record your experiences and actions, events and interactions in which you have participated *and* your reflections on them.

A PDJ is a structured approach to recording your experience, providing you with data which will enable you:

- to bring your experience into your conscious awareness, opening up the possibility of different and more intentional behaviours;

- to reflect on and analyse your behaviours and their outcomes, enabling you to learn consciously and intentionally from your experience, maximising your learning opportunities;

- to monitor and track your development.

Recording your external and internal observations of events and interactions on a regular basis captures your experience while it is fresh in your mind. If you do not do this, you will be relying on longer-range memories, which are likely to be less detailed, coherent and accurate – and will accordingly make a lesser contribution to your development.

4.2 Structuring your PDJ

A PDJ make take the form of a notebook, loose leaf folder, computerised file or whatever you prefer. However, it is intended to be more than a diary of occasional, miscellaneous jottings: it requires a coherent *structure*.

Pedler *et al* (2001, p. 80) propose a model which focuses on the following aspects of experience (*Figure 18.6*).

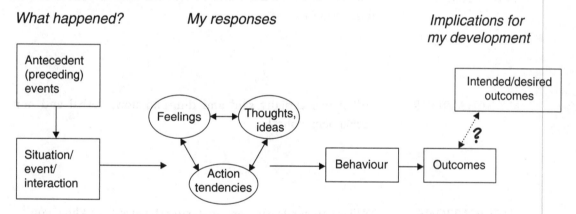

Figure 18.6 Focus of PDJ entries

A suggested format for exploring your experiences in a structured PDJ are shown in the blank specimen which follows. This structure is based around the model in Pedler *et al.* (2001).

BPP
PROFESSIONAL EDUCATION

PERSONAL DEVELOPMENT JOURNAL

Date:

WHAT HAPPENED   [A brief description of events, with the emphasis on objective facts, and including what led up to the situation]

MY EMOTIONS   [Be specific about the emotions you experienced during the event eg: anger, irritation, fear, anxiety, happiness, satisfaction, sadness – and how they changed during the event]

MY THOUGHTS/ IDEAS   [What was going through your head during the events.]

MY ACTION TENDENCIES   [What you usually do in similar circumstances. What you 'wanted' to do. What other factors influenced your action or non-action.]

MY BEHAVIOUR   [What you actually said and did, and how: verbal and non-verbal behaviours]

IMPLICATIONS FOR MY DEVELOPMENT   [What you can learn from analysing the event, and how you might change your behaviour for the future.]

Activity 5   **(20 mins)**

Aim:

To help you get started on completing a PDJ.

Instructions:

Using the format given above, select a specific interaction or interpersonal activity you participated in recently, and complete one complete journal entry following the guidelines given. What did you find difficult about completing the PDJ? What did you learn about your interpersonal behaviour by completing the PDJ?

5   A PERSONAL PORTFOLIO

5.1   What is a Personal Portfolio?

A portfolio is simply a folder for keeping documents, which is organised in its presentation. Designers, architects and artists, among others, have long kept portfolios of their work for systematic storage, easy access, and presentation to interested parties. A portfolio for management education and development works the same way: it represents a filing system *and* a potential résumé.

The intended benefits of compiling a portfolio are as follows.

- It encourages you to become more reflective about your work performance and your impact on other people, heightening your awareness of your personal/interpersonal behaviour and effectiveness. As a conscious gathering of information about your experience, it will increase your self awareness and insight.

- It enables you to evaluate your competence over a period of time, and to plan and evaluate action for your development.

- It provides you with ideas and evidence about your strengths, limitations and development goals which you can use when applying for jobs, attending selection interviews or assessment centres, participating in appraisal and development planning sessions and so on.

5.2   What should go in a portfolio?

The portfolio provides a record of interactions and events which you have observed and participated in, and of your development in relevant skills and competences. It is a dynamic document which will develop as you progress through your HND/HNC – and this module in particular.

Your portfolio might include:

- PDJ entries

- The outputs of questionnaires and activities you have completed *and* your reflections on them

- Observations that you have made of others' reactions to you

- Feedback from your peers and others

- Other materials that you think relevant to your personal development

5.3 Organising your portfolio

You may start by saving data more or less indiscriminately. However, you will need to review your collected material periodically, in order to select and utilise information for self evaluation and development planning.

It does not matter how you organise your material – but it does need to be organised, so that you can:

- *Find and access items of information when you want them.* Classify them in any suitable way and label them accordingly, as you put them into the folder, so you can sort them later.

- *Understand the information readily.* 'Raw' notes made during or shortly after interactions and events may need to be re-drafted (while your memory is reasonably fresh) – especially if you have a tendency to use shorthand note forms!

Activity 6	(30 mins)

Aim:

To get you started on compiling and organising a Personal Portfolio

Instructions:

You were encouraged in Chapter 16 to start collecting evidences and observations immediately. If you undertook this activity, you should have a file of material available.

Review and organise your filed material and turn it into the beginnings of a portfolio.

6 TIME MANAGEMENT

On any given working day, you might have a large number of tasks to perform: your 'work load'.

- **Routine tasks,** which you perform on a regularly daily, weekly or monthly cycle, according to well-defined procedures.

  Depending on your work role, examples may include: dealing with correspondence; filing, daily banking procedures; completing sales and purchase ledgers; preparing sales invoices; and so on.

- **Unexpected or non-routine tasks,** which are delegated to you by others or imposed on you by events.

  Depending on your work role, examples may include: being asked to prepare a one-off report or presentation; being asked to help or replace a colleague in completing a task; having to deal with a technical problem or customer complaint; taking action on a health and safety problem; and so on.

Some tasks can be planned in advance into a schedule or routine – and some will require one-off or urgent attention. Some tasks will be easily placed in an 'in-tray', presenting themselves for your attention – and some may emerge from situations as more complex problems without a clear-cut 'to do' list. Some tasks can be completed and filed – and some may require complex problem solving over a long period.

How do you know what **order** to tackle these tasks in? Which are more **important**? Do you interrupt your routine tasks to handle **unexpected** tasks? How do you keep track of complex **on-going** tasks without their getting lost in the flow of smaller, clearer tasks? How do you **keep up**? How do you know if you are **falling behind** – and what do you do about it?

If you are to manage your work load efficiently and effectively, there needs to be some kind of **framework of planning, decision-making and problem-solving** which will enable you to:

- Assign relative importance and urgency to different tasks, so you know what order you need to tackle them in, and which tasks take precedence when non-routine matters crop up: this process is called **prioritisation**

- Set or take into account target dates by which given tasks must be completed: these dates are called **deadlines**.

- Schedule work time and co-ordinate relevant resources so that tasks can be completed by the deadline, allowing for unforeseen events where necessary: this process is called **work planning**.

- Make the most efficient use of your available time, by prioritising, planning and methodical working: this is called **time management**.

In Section 8 of this chapter, we add the topic of **information handling**, since this is a major component of work methods and practices in an administrative role.

7 PERSONAL TIME MANAGEMENT

7.1 What is time management?

Time is a resource, like money, information, materials and so on. You have a fixed and limited amount of it, and various demands in your work (and non-work) life compete for a share of it. If you work in an organisation, your 'time is money': you will be paid for it, or for what you accomplish with it.

Time, like any other resource, needs to be managed, if it is to be used efficiently (without waste) and effectively (productively).

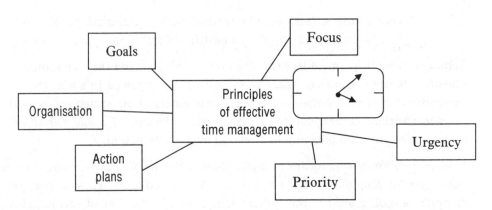

Figure 18.7 Principles of effective time management

To be a truly effective time manager you must apply these principles to your personal life with the same enthusiasm that you apply them to your job – in fact, this is one aspect of the priorities principle, as we shall see.

7.2 Goals

If you have no idea what it is you are supposed to accomplish, or only a vague idea, all the time in the world will not be long enough to get it done. Nor is there any way of telling whether you have done it or not. To be useful, goals need to be SMART:

S pecific

M easurable

A ttainable

R ealistic and

T ime-bounded

In work terms you could probably set **specific goals** by reference to your job description: 'prepare and despatch invoices for all goods sold'; 'issue monthly statements'; 'monitor slow paying customers' and so on.

However, **measurable** and **time-bounded goals** are very important for **effective time management**. If you say 'My goal is to see that invoices are issued and despatched for all goods sold *on the day of sale*' you have a very clear and specific idea of what it is that you have to achieve and whether you are achieving it or not.

The same applies to personal goals. 'I'd like a promotion' is just a wish. 'I aim to be promoted to General Manager by the end of my first year' is a goal, but not a realistic or attainable one. 'I aim to be promoted to supervisor of my section by the end of next year' gives you something to aim at. (We will discuss career goals further in chapter 9.)

Set SMART goals for all aspects of your work, large and small. It may seem silly at first to set yourself a goal of, say, always answering the phone before the third ring, but by the end of the first day you will have impressed everybody you speak to with your prompt service, besides having the personal satisfaction of having achieved something that you set out to do.

7.3 Action plans

Now you must make **written action plans that set out how you intend to achieve your goals**: the timescale, the deadlines, the tasks involved, the people to see or write to, the resources required, how one plan fits in with (or conflicts with) another and so on. These need not be lengthy or formal plans: start with **notes, lists** or **flowcharts** that will help you to capture and clarify your ideas and intentions.

7.4 Priorities

Now you can set priorities from your plan. You do this by deciding which tasks are the most important – what is the most valuable use of your time at that very moment.

Which task would you do if you only had time to do one task? That is your first priority. Then imagine that it will turn out that you have enough time to do one more thing before you have to leave. What would you do next? That is your second priority. Continue in this vein until you have identified three or four top priorities. Then get on with them, in order. Anything else is a waste of time that could be used in a more valuable way.

We discuss prioritising in more detail in Section 8 below.

7.5 Focus: one thing at a time

Work on **one thing at a time** until it is finished, where possible.

- If a task cannot be completely finished in one 'session', complete everything that it is in your power to complete at that time and use a **follow-up system** to make sure that it is not forgotten in the future. Correspondence, in particular, will involve varying periods of delay between question and answer, action and response.

- **Make sure that everything that you need is available before you start work.** If it isn't, you may not be able to do the task yet, but one of the things on your to do list will be to order supplies of the necessary forms or stationery, or to obtain the required information or do whatever it is that is holding you up.

- **Before you start a task clear away everything from your desk that you do *not* need for that particular task.** Put irrelevant things where you will be able to retrieve them instantly when you come to deal with the tasks that you need them for. If they are not needed by anyone throw them away.

  It is quite hard to discipline yourself to do this because it might take some time, initially, and you might feel that that time could be spent doing other things. However, once tidy working becomes a habit, it will take no time at all, because your desk will always be either clear or have on it only the things you are using at that precise moment. Moreover, one of the best ways of helping yourself to concentrate and handle things one at a time is to remove less important distractions.

7.6 Urgency: do it now!

Do not put off large, difficult or unpleasant tasks simply because they are large, difficult or unpleasant. If you put it off, today's routine will be tomorrow's emergency: worse, today's emergency will be even *more* of an emergency tomorrow. Do it now!

Think for a moment about how you behave when you know something is very urgent. If you oversleep, you leap out of bed the moment you wake up. If you suddenly find out that a report has to go out last post today rather than tomorrow afternoon, then you get on with it at once. We are saying that you should **develop the ability to treat everything that you have to do in this way**. Procrastination is a natural tendency – fewer than 2% of people are reckoned to have a true sense of urgency – but procrastination really is the thief of time.

7.7 Organisation

Apart from working to plans, checklists and schedules (discussed in Chapter 6), your work organisation might be improved by the following.

- **An ABCD method of in-tray management.** When a task or piece of paper comes into your in-tray or 'to do' list, you should never merely look at it and put it back for later. This would mean you would handle it more than once – usually over and over again, if it is a trivial or unpleasant item! Resolve to take one of the following approaches

  (**A**)ct on the item immediately

  (**B**)in it, if you are sure it is worthless, irrelevant and unnecessary

  (**C**)reate a definite plan for coming back to the item: get it on your schedule, timetable or 'to do list'

  (**D**)elegate it to someone else to handle

- **Organise your work in batches** of jobs requiring the same activities, files, equipment and so on. Group your filing tasks or word processing tasks, for example, and do them in a session, rather than having to travel to and fro or compete for equipment time for each separate task.

- **Take advantage of your natural work patterns.** Self-discipline is aided by developing regular hours or days for certain tasks, like dealing with correspondence first thing, or filing at the end of the day. If you are able to plan your own schedules, you might also take into account your personal patterns of energy, concentration, alertness etc. Large or complex tasks might be undertaken in the mornings before you get tired. Friday afternoon is usually not a good time to start a demanding task in the office...

Activity 7	**(20 mins)**

Which of the statements overleaf apply in your case and which do not? Add explanatory notes where applicable.

	True	False	Explanatory notes
I work with a tidy desk.	☐	☐	
All my drawers, shelves and cabinets are tidy.	☐	☐	
Items that I use frequently are always ready to hand.	☐	☐	
Whenever I have finished with a file or a book I put it back where it belongs immediately.	☐	☐	
I write everything down and never forget anything.	☐	☐	
I work on one task at a time until it is finished.	☐	☐	
I do daily tasks daily except in very exceptional circumstances, in which case I catch up the next day.	☐	☐	
Every routine task that I do is done at a regular time each day.	☐	☐	
I never pick up a piece of paper without taking action on it (writing a reply, filing it, binning it, whatever).	☐	☐	
I organise my work into batches and do all of one type of work at the same time.	☐	☐	
I never run out of stationery that takes a while to obtain: I keep an eye on this and order in advance.	☐	☐	
My routine work could easily be taken over by someone else if I were unavoidably absent because I keep proper notes of what I am doing.	☐	☐	
I try to anticipate likely work and I ask my boss what is expected of me over the next week or so, so that I can plan out my work.	☐	☐	
I am able to estimate how long any task will take fairly accurately.	☐	☐	
I never miss deadlines.	☐	☐	
I do not panic under pressure.	☐	☐	

BPP
PROFESSIONAL EDUCATION

8 PRIORITIES

8.1 What is 'prioritising'?

Prioritising basically involves arranging all the tasks which may face an individual at the same time (this week, or today) in order of '**preference**'. Because of the individual's responsibility to the organisation, this will not just be what he would 'like' to get done (or do first), but what will be most valuable to the attainment of his immediate or long-term goals.

8.2 What makes a piece of work 'high priority'

A piece of work will be **high priority** in the following circumstances.

- **If it has to be completed by a deadline.** The closer the deadline, the more urgent the work will be. A report which is to be typed for a board meeting the following day will take precedence in planning the day's work over the preparation of an agenda to be circulated in a week's time: **routine work comes lowest on the list,** as it can usually be 'caught up with' later if necessary.

- **If other tasks depend on it**: if the preparation of a sales invoice, or notes for a meeting, depends on a particular file, the first task may be to send a request for it to the file registry. Work can't start unless the file is there. Begin at the beginning!

- **If other people depend on it**. An item being given low priority by one individual or department – for example, retrieval or reproduction of a particular document – may hold up the activities of others.

- **If it is important**. There may be a clash of priorities between two urgent tasks, in which case relative **consequences** should be considered: if an important decision or action rests on a task (for example, a report for senior management, or correction of an error in a large customer order) then that task should take precedence over, say, the preparation of notes for a meeting, or processing a smaller order.

Activity 8   **(20 mins)**

Devise a mnemonic, using the letters 'P-R-I-O-R-I-T-Y', that will help you remember when a piece of work is high priority.

8.3 Routine and unexpected priorities

Routine priorities, or regular peak times include:

- Preparation of the weekly payroll
- Monthly issue of account statements
- Year end accounts preparation

They can be planned ahead of time, and other tasks postponed or redistributed around them.

Non-routine priorities occur when **unexpected demands** are made: events crop up, perhaps at short notice, or errors are discovered and require corrective action. If these are also **important** (as well as sudden) they should be regarded as high priority.

8.4 Priority and urgency

Just because a task is **urgent** (that is, its deadline is close), it does not necessarily mean it is **high priority**. A task may be urgent but **unimportant**, compared to a task which has a more distant deadline.

On the other hand, as we noted earlier, you should **treat all important tasks as if they were urgent**.

In other words, you need to be aware of changing priorities. You need to:

- **Monitor** incoming work for unexpected or non-routine demands.

- Immediately **prioritise** each new task in relation to your existing list of tasks: it may not belong at the bottom of your 'to do' list but at the top!

- **Adapt your schedule** accordingly.

  This may simply involve changing the order of your 'to do' list in order to tackle new priorities before lesser ones.

  If your schedule is 'tight', however, there may be less room to manoeuvre. You may find that if you tackle the new high-priority task first, you will have difficulties completing a lesser-priority (but potentially still important) task by your target or deadline. In this case you may need to:

  - Ask your supervisor to confirm that your priorities are correct.

  - Notify your supervisor, and any other people affected, of potential difficulties in meeting previously-arranged commitments. (We discuss this in more detail in Section 5 below.)

  - Request assistance with meeting the new or previous demands. (We discuss this in more detail in Section 7 below.)

- Adapt any relevant resource allocations accordingly.

  Again, this may simply involve re-allocating your own time (or that of others under your authority), machine hours or services (eg secretarial support) to the new priority. Again, however, this may have to be authorised and/or negotiated with your supervisor and others affected by the change.

Activity 9 (20 mins)

You are the accounts assistant at Modus Operandi Ltd.

It is three o'clock on a Friday afternoon, and you are performing your routine end-of-week tasks, including issuing pay slips to staff, printing them out on the department's one printer and planning to distribute them to workers' departmental pigeon holes prior to the end of work at 5.00. (The office is closed over the weekend.)

> The department manager, Mrs Tancredi, comes to you and requests a print out of a confidential report that she will need by lunch time on Monday for a meeting. You calculate that the report will take three hours to print.
>
> What will you do?

9 DEADLINES

9.1 What is a deadline?

A deadline is the **latest date or time** by which a task **must be completed** in order for its objectives to be fulfilled.

The important points about deadlines are:

- They have been set for a reason
- They get closer!

The need to 'meet specific demands and deadlines' (Element 23.1) effectively underlies **all** the elements of competence and performance criteria. If you are the type of person who is so 'in the moment' that you are not aware of time passing or deadlines approaching, do whatever it takes – alarm clocks, diary follow-up systems, daily work checklists, visualisations of time lines or charts – to get you deadline-minded!

9.2 Reasons to avoid missing a deadline

Delay on your part delays other people from getting on with their work, and creates a bad impression of you and the organisation you work for.

If you are late in producing a piece of work then you will tend to hurry it as the deadline draws near or passes, and its **quality will suffer**.

You will have **less time to do your next piece of work.** That too will be late or below standard.

You may get a **reputation** as someone who misses deadlines, and may not be trusted with responsibility in future.

On the other hand, there may be a problem if you find that you get a reputation as being someone who always **beats his or her deadlines**: you may find that you end up with a much larger workload than slower colleagues. This will have to be discussed with your superior: perhaps you are ready for more responsibility!

9.3 How to meet your deadlines: basic principles

Different people approach their work in different ways. You may like to get the easy tasks out of the way first. On the other hand you may prefer to get the difficult bits out of the way first.

As soon as possible after you are allocated a task and a deadline **think it through** (with a colleague if necessary) **from beginning to end.**

Then you can **plan out how you are going to achieve it in the time specified.** If you set aside one day for gathering information, say, two days for inputting and processing, and one day for analysing and preparing the results for presentation, you would comfortably meet a Friday deadline for a task allocated on Monday morning. **This planning stage is the time to renegotiate the deadline if it appears that the work cannot be done in the time that has been allocated.**

Your plan should **indicate what input, if any, you will need from others**. Before you do anything else, make sure that others are aware of the deadline you are working to and how their work fits in with your overall plan.

Batch together any tasks that are similar and routine and do them all in one go. For example, you may have to write to those buyers of a certain product who share a certain characteristic. It is likely to be more efficient to identify all of the customers with the characteristic first, and then to write to them all, rather than writing to each customer as you come across his case.

Monitor your progress constantly. Something may take far longer than you anticipated: how will this affect your ability to complete the task on time?

9.4 Difficulties meeting deadlines

As soon as you know or can anticipate that a deadline is likely to be missed **tell the person who is relying on you** and explain why.

- If you are being delayed because you are **awaiting input from others**, the person you report to may have the authority to hurry them along.

- If **unforeseen difficulties** have arisen, your manager may be able to arrange for your workload to be shared, to make sure that the job comes in on time.

- If you are late because you have **not worked hard enough** you will naturally be reluctant to explain this to your superior. Own up earlier rather than later, while there is still a chance of salvaging the situation.

The **appropriate person** to whom you need to report anticipated difficulties may be:

- The line manager to whom you are responsible for the task's completion – and the one who retains ultimate responsibility for seeing it done. The line manager has the authority to:

  - adjust the plan (eg by extending the deadline)

  - mobilise extra resources (eg allocating more machine time or extra staff to help you)

  - influence other people (especially in other teams or departments) whose performance is causing your difficulties

  - communicate with other people (especially in other teams or departments) whose performance will be affected by your difficulties

- The project manager, if you are a member of a project team and the task is part of a project rather than routine departmental work. The project manager will have similar authority to the line manager, within the scope of the project: in addition, (s)he may be able to negotiate with your line manager to free you from departmental duties while the difficulties are met.

- Any colleagues who may be relying on your completion of the work, and whose schedules and deadlines may be co-ordinated with yours. These colleagues may not have authority to help you with your difficulties, but they may be in a position to adjust their plans – or to inform their own line and project managers of a possible delay. Be realistic about revising your target deadline – or about the likelihood of overcoming the difficulties in time to make the original deadline: *repeated* changes of plan swiftly erode working relationships!

Activity 10 (20 mins)

You are a member of the Accounts Department of Modus Operandi Ltd, headed by the Chief Accountant, Mrs Tancredi.

For a three week period, as part of the Development Plan agreed at your last performance appraisal, you have been seconded to a Task Force auditing the organisation's data security practices and compliance with Data Protection requirements. The head of this task force is the IT manager, Mr Sproule. You have been given a work area in the IT department and your routine accounting duties have been re-allocated for the three weeks.

It is coming up to the end of week two of your secondment, and you are aware that you are going to have problems completing your report on the employee database, as agreed, by the end of week three. You are having trouble obtaining the information you require on Personnel Records from the HR assistant, Jenny Gomez: she has been busy preparing an induction course. Jenny is unable to say when she will have time to prepare your data – but without it, you can go no further in preparing your report.

Meanwhile, your colleague Parvinder in the Accounts Department, who has been undertaking your routine accounting duties while you have been on secondment, is due to go on his annual holiday the day after you return to the department, giving him a day to brief you on what has been going on and what tasks are as yet unfinished.

Required:

(a) Outline your problem, and what its effects might be.

(b) Whom do you need to inform – and of what?

(c) Write a brief memo to the person (or each of the persons) you decide to inform.

NOTES

Chapter roundup

- Self awareness is a key tool for self development, as it motivates and supports behavioural change.

- Self image is highly subjective, due to selective self-perception and value judgements. In addition, some behaviours are unknown to the individual.

- A useful tool for considering self-awareness is the *Johari window,* which suggests that behaviours may be known or unknown to oneself *and* known or unknown to others. Developing self awareness involves bringing more behaviours into the public (known to self and others) or hidden (known to self, unknown to others) areas, as appropriate.

- An approach to self development based on increasing self-awareness allows managers to take responsibility for relevant, flexible and continuous experiential learning. It can be expressed as a *learning cycle,* incorporating four stages: having an experience; reviewing the experience; concluding from the experience; planning the next steps.

- People tend to have a preference for a particular phase or phases on the learning cycle, or a *preferred learning style(s).* Honey and Mumford (1992) identify four learning styles: Activist, Reflector, Theorist, Pragmatist.

- A systematic approach based on the learning cycle may include:

  – observation and written description of interpersonal events and behaviours

  – the use of questionnaires to support or challenge self-perceptions

  – the seeking of feedback from others

  – reflection on selected experiences and their development implications

  – integrating relevant theoretical concepts

  – summarising conclusions in a coherent evaluation of strengths and limitations

- Two key tools for managing self development are a Personal Development Journal and a Personal Portfolio.

- Time management is a critical skill in any form of self-managed learning.

Answers to activities

1   Some of the issues you may have raised include:

- the need to seek out *experiences* of interpersonal interactions. Your development plan will need to identify opportunities to *do* things (or do them differently) – not just to gather more knowledge.

- the need to *review* the experience. This may have raised questions about how to *observe* behaviours and processes; how to capture the data for later review (eg by taking notes or making a written *description* of the event); what kind of *reflection* you will need to do, what areas you will focus on, whether you'll write out your thoughts.

- the need for *theoretical concepts* that will enable you to draw conclusions or make hypotheses about the experience.

- the need for *planning* to *apply* your learning in further experience: practical action plans.

2   Low activist style: be more willing to experiment and take advantage of new experiences.

Low reflector style: spend more time thinking through what you do and how you do it. Asking for feedback can help this process.

Low theorist: make use of concepts, models and theories in evaluating your behaviour and understanding what you could do differently.

Low pragmatist: spend time working out in very specific ways how you could adopt more effective behaviours. Identify specific actions and timescales.

3   Don't forget to consider methods which:

- increase your knowledge/ awareness: formal courses (T), reading, observing expert practitioners (R)

- allow you to experiment/practice: on-the-job courses (P), 'live' interpersonal interactions (P, A), coaching (P), assistant-to-positions (A), teaching/coaching others

- use different media and technologies: books and distance learning programmes (T, R); Internet-, computer- or video-based training programmes (A if sufficiently 'new', P if sufficiently relevant)

- use solo learning (reading, reflection, writing: R, T) and group learning (discussion groups, role plays, teaching others, A) and so on.

4   You may have come up with some of the following difficulties or barriers.

Positive feedback: disliking giving compliments (embarrassment?); the fear of sounding insincere or as if you want something from the other person; the feeling that the person is 'only doing their job', so why should they get praise (perhaps some hostility?); the fear of being thought to have 'gone soft' (clinging to a 'hard' image?)

Negative feedback: fear of being disliked, and even disrupting the relationship; dislike of 'causing a scene'; not wanting to hurt the person's feelings; convincing yourself that the problem is not important or will go away by itself.

Note that many of these difficulties are based on a misconception about what giving feedback is for, and that it can be done in a skilled and appropriate manner.

5   There is no 'answer' to this activity – other than to attempt it. You may find that the requirement to write a PDJ entry makes you more observant of antecedent events, behaviours, thoughts and feelings. Don't neglect the 'Implications' section: although you may not be in a position to complete it immediately. Many people find the experience of journalling so helpful that they continue indefinitely, applying the observe-describe-reflect model to other areas of their work and life.

6   There is no answer to this activity – other than to attempt it.

Consider alternative uses for your portfolio as you organise it. How might you use selections or summaries in performance appraisal or selection interviews?

7   Again your answer will be specific to you, so there can be no suggested solution.

Each of the statements is an *ideal* of work organisation. Wherever you have ticked the 'False' box you should have some kind of comment explaining why the ideal is not possible in the circumstances under which you work.

Where you have ticked a *false* box, is there anything you can do about it? For example, if you have said 'I sometimes miss deadlines because others do not deliver their input to me in time', is this really a problem of your relationship with others? If you said 'I am not always able to work on one task at a time until it is finished: sometimes there is a delay because I have to get information from elsewhere', is this the full story? Perhaps you do not plan out your work properly when you start.

This is an opportunity to reappraise the way you work. Take action on any suggestion that strikes you as being a more efficient way of working for you. You will soon begin to appreciate the time and effort saved by good personal organisation.

8   **Note:** Just our suggestion: The devising of the mnemonic was the point of the exercise.

Priority?

Relative consequences

Importance

Other people depend on it

Required for other tasks

Immediacy (urgency)

Time limits (deadlines)

Yes!

9   **The problem**

Your task of preparing and issuing the pay slips is routine (weekly schedule) – but also high priority because it has to be done by a certain time (distributed by 5 pm) and it is an important matter (since it affects the rights and morale of employees).

The new task is high-priority, in that it has been set by your manager – and the deadline is urgent: given that the office is closed over the weekend, Monday lunchtime is not many working hours away.

Resources are limited for accommodating both priorities: there is only one printer in the department. You are in the middle of printing the pay slips – and the report will require three hours of printing.

Options

Interrupting pay slips and staying late to print the report today? – Not an option (pay slips first priority).

Leaving report printing overnight, for collection Monday? – Not a good option from point of view of security (confidential report left open on the printer)

Raising the matter of limited print resources with Mrs Tancredi: possibility of her negotiating use of secretariat or other department printer for use today? – Not an ideal option, as it would mean you (or other staff) would have to stay very late.

Review tasks for Monday morning: reschedule routine tasks in order to get report job under way; negotiate with colleagues to book 3 hours printer time first thing Monday morning; if not possible, book time on printer(s) in secretariat. Notify Mrs Tancredi of this plan: confirm that 12 o'clock delivery of the report will be sufficient time for her meeting.

10 (a) **Problem**

Due to Jenny Gomez's workload (and possible lack of co-operation?) you are unable to complete your task to deadline – or to estimate when it might be completed. You lack the direct authority to enforce co-operation from a member of another department. Moreover, you have a further deadline imposed by Parvinder's departure: you need to return to your accounting duties on the day planned, and so cannot lengthen your secondment to 'stretch' the deadline – even if this were possible.

(b) Informing appropriate people

(i) You will need to inform Mr Sproule of the problem with getting the HR information, as it is his project deadline you are in danger of overrunning – and he may have the authority (as a cross-functional project manager) to influence the HR department.

(ii) You will need to inform Mrs Tancredi that there may be a scheduling conflict that will require you to extend your secondment in order to complete your report. It is up to Mrs Tancredi and Mr Sproule to negotiate how your time will be co-ordinated between them.

(iii) You should inform Parvinder that there may be a question mark over the date of your return to the department, so that he can make alternative arrangements to brief you, if necessary. (Note that you have not got the authority – or the right – to ask him to postpone his holiday!)

(c) Memoranda

MODUS OPERANDI LTD
MEMORANDUM

From: Your Name

To: Mr Sproule, IT Manager; Mrs Tancredi, Chief Accountant

Date: [Today's date]

Subject: Report on Employee Database

I thought it advisable to inform you that I am currently experiencing some delays in accessing the information on Personnel Records which I require to complete my report on the Employee Database.

With six working days remaining until the report deadline, and the end of my agreed secondment, I have been unable to obtain the information from Jenny Gomez, the HR assistant, who is engaged in preparing an induction course. Jenny has been unable to say when she will have time to prepare the Personnel Records information, despite my best efforts to impress upon her the urgency of my task.

I have scheduled five days' work to analyse the information and compile the report. If the information is not immediately forthcoming, my concern is that:

(a) I will be unable to meet the agreed deadline for submitting the report

(b) the period of my secondment will over-run (subject to agreement between you as my project and line managers), conflicting with my commitments to the Accounts Department

(c) any prolonged absence from the Accounts Department will affect my colleague Parvinder, who has been covering my duties.

May I leave it with you both to determine what you think best in regard to the possible prolonging of my secondment? I will personally contact Parvinder to make a contingency plan for the handover of duties.

Meanwhile, Mr Sproule, I would appreciate your advice about how the Personnel Records information might more swiftly be obtained. I would be happy to discuss the matter with you at your convenience.

YN

MODUS OPERANDI LTD

MEMORANDUM

From: Your Name

To: Parvinder

Date: [Today's date]

Subject: Handover of accounting responsibilities

As you know, I am scheduled to return to the accounts department on Monday week. I'm sure you have been doing a great job in my absence: thank you for looking after things for me.

I just thought you ought to know that I am currently facing some delays (beyond my immediate control) in completing my report for the DP Task Force. I have brought the matter to Mr Sproule's and Mrs Tancredi's attention, and they are going to decide whether it might be necessary to extend my secondment.

I know you are going on holiday on the Tuesday, and wanted to spend the Monday briefing me on what has been going on and what tasks are unfinished. I'm not sure now whether that is going to be possible.

I'd like to talk to you about some kind of contingency plan, in case I can't get back to the department before you go. Perhaps you could prepare a briefing or checklist for me – or hand over to someone else (whom Mrs Tancredi will nominate) as an interim measure. I don't want to put you to unnecessary work. Give me a call on extension 573 some time next week, if it's convenient, and we can discuss the matter.

Everything may, after all, go as originally planned, but it's just as well to be prepared.

Thanks.

YN

ASSIGNMENTS

UNIT 14

Assignment 1 (1 hour)

Broadside Retail Services

Broadside Retail Services of Leeds has a vacancy for an assistant accountant. The post is located in the financial accounting section of the company's large finance department which, among other things, is responsible for the preparation of interim and published accounts and the maintenance of the computerised nominal ledger records from which these accounts are compiled. The person appointed to the post is responsible for updating these records and this entails the supervision of a number of clerks. For these reasons the Chief Accountant is seeking to recruit a certified accounting technician.

(a) Prepare a draft of an appropriate advertisement for the post and indicate what you consider would be the most appropriate media of communication to prospective applicants.

(b) Define 'job description'.

(c) Specify the types of information that you consider should be incorporated into the job description for the post.

Assignment 2 (1¹/₂ hours)

Biotherm PLC

You are the Personnel Director for Biotherm PLC, a detergent and washing powder manufacturer based in Bootle, Merseyside. You have a staff of nine reporting to you, from junior clerks to senior managers, and you are just preparing for the annual round of appraisal interviews. One of your senior personnel officers, Alan Heath, has become a real problem child of late. You have never particularly warmed to this individual; he never really seems part of the team, his attendance record is poor and he never works beyond contracted hours. You know that Alan is not especially fit and healthy, but you rather feel he is playing on his physical condition.

You would describe yourself as a 'person-oriented' leader, although you acknowledge that with difficult staff you tend to become *laissez faire*. This has been the case with Alan: you have never tackled him on his absence record (29 days sickness in the past year) nor on his desire to work to contract. Apart from yourself, he is the only person with extensive and detailed knowledge of employment law, which is valuable in your organisational environment. You secretly admit that this is the main reason for your reticence in handling him: in spite of his difficult demeanour you would be lost without him.

However, you must now grasp the nettle and deal with the situation at his appraisal interview. Prepare a plan for the interview which not only reviews his past performance but also proposes a set of acceptable objectives for the forthcoming year. Remember that your meeting should not, if possible, degenerate into a disciplinary case! Your plan should be organised according to the following headings:

- assessment of performance
- how to improve current performance
- how to motivate Alan Heath
- how to assess him for promotability
- how to tackle unsatisfactory performance areas

Throughout this plan, you should anticipate questions, issues and objectives which he will raise, and resolve how to deal with them.

UNIT 15

Assignment 3   (2 hours)

Take an organisation that you know, or on which you can get the basic information required.

1   Draw an organisation chart for the organisation.

2   Explain the structure shown in the chart with reference to:

    (a)   the organisation's mission;
    (b)   its products;
    (c)   its markets;
    (d)   its method of production;
    (e)   any particular external influence.

Write up a list of your findings in the form of a list of bullet points for a presentation to be made to new recruits to the organisation.

Assignment 4 (1¹/₂ hours)

Duntoiling Nursing Homes

You are the personnel officer for Duntoiling Nursing and Retirement Homes PLC, a chain of residential complexes for senior citizens in the West Midlands region. Recently, Gareth Cheeseman, the bullish, entrepreneurial director, sent a brief memorandum to all staff informing them that all premises now constitute 'No Smoking' areas for patients, visitors and staff alike. Notices to this effect have gone up all round the homes. Duntoiling is also declaring its 'No Smoking' policy in recruitment advertisements.

The abruptness with which Cheeseman introduced this policy is now causing problems. It seems that some staff are continuing to smoke 'behind closed doors', and visitors and patients are flouting the ban in the corridors and toilets. Staff rebuking them have been subject to verbal abuse. Some staff also complain of suffering from stress because they cannot give up the craving.

The crunch came last week, when one supervisor issued a formal oral warning to a member of his staff caught 'red-handed' smoking in her office, and stated that if she repeated the offence she would be dismissed. The employee in question resigned in a fit of pique and is now claiming constructive dismissal, with union support.

Cheeseman has asked you to brief him on what action needs to be taken:

(a)   to deal with the disciplinary case; and
(b)   to ensure that the policy is complied with in the future.

What advice will you give? Present your answer in the form of a memorandum to Gareth Cheeseman.

UNIT 16

Assignment 5 **(1 hour)**

Managers need to assess the **quality** and **value** of information provided to them.

What attributes might they consider when they are doing this?

Assignment 6 Part 1 (30 minutes)

Read the following case study. As you read, make notes of any important information about the company (for example, size, type of organisation). Take particular note of any information regarding the forms of communications within this organisation. Try to structure your notes into issues that arise and actions which you think should be taken. (You will need these notes for this chapter's assignment).

John Gibb, the owner of Gibbs Motors, a small second-hand car garage, needed to invest in more stock. John usually obtained his cars from Wally's Car Auctions, a local auctioneers, but although John never had any problems with the cars he bought, rumour had it that some of the cars Wally's sold were of dubious ownership. He decided to look around for a more reputable car auctioneer.

After visiting many car auctions, John came across Quality, a car auctioneer selling second-hand cars of extremely high quality. John told Peter Gold, the owner, that he was interested in obtaining cars and said he would phone them the next day to confirm his order and specify which cars he wanted.

John spent a couple of days deciding which cars he wanted to buy. Before he could contact Quality, Peter Gold rang to ask John whether he still wanted to place an order. John specified the models he wanted and told Peter his price limit was two thousand pounds for each car, There was a lot of interference on the phone lines that day and the parties found it difficult to understand each other. John told Peter that he would fax through a confirmed order in writing. Before leaving the office that day, John left a note for his secretary to confirm the order.

Within the week five cars were delivered to John's garage. John was delighted with the quality of these cars and thought them good value for money. He advertised them in the local paper the next evening. Before the paper came out, the invoice for the cars arrived. To John's amazement the invoice was for £15,000. Thinking that there must be some mistake, John rang Peter Gold and asked why the bill was for £15,000 when it should have been for a maximum of £10,000. Peter said that once the vehicles were delivered to their new owner, whether it was a member of the public or another garage, they could not be returned and must be paid for. John sought legal advice, and found that, as he had confirmed the order in writing, Quality would either have to charge him the agreed price or accept the cars back. When John spoke to his secretary she denied all knowledge of his note and said she had not confirmed the order at all. John realised that short of being able to prove a verbal contact over the agreed price, he was stuck with five cars he could barely afford to pay for.

Part 2 (1½ hours)

From your notes above, write a report for John identifying the communication problems within his company. Make recommendations as to how communications could be improved to prevent a similar situation in the future.

ANSWERS TO ASSIGNMENTS

Answer to Assignment 1

Broadside Retail Services

Helping hand

For (a) include all the essential items you would expect to see in an advertisement.

For (b), a simple definition is all you need. Listing the key features of what a job description sets out would be a suitable approach.

For (c), use your answer to (b) as a list of the contents of a job description and then think about how to apply them to the situation in the question.

(a)

Guidance

You are asked to draft an advertisement for a job vacancy, and in examination conditions, you cannot be expected to devise a 'perfect' advertisement. However, you will be expected to include all the essential data items, and it is worth listing what these are before you start to write your advertisement.

1   Who is offering the job?

2   What, as a 'headline' for the ad, is the job?

3   What is the salary? Are there any other 'perks' with the job?

4   What are the qualifications needed for the job?

5   What does the job consist of?

6   Are there good career prospects?

7   How to apply for the job.

BROADSIDE RETAIL SERVICES

(Company logo)

ASSISTANT ACCOUNTANT

Salary £xxxx

Broadside Retail Services, a fast-growing company based in Leeds, needs an Assistant Accountant to join its large accounts department and to be responsible for maintaining the company's computerised nominal ledger records and for the preparation of interim and published accounts.

The successful applicant will be a certified accounting technician with some previous experience of working with computerised financial accounting systems. Experience in the supervision of staff would be an advantage.

Career prospects for hard-working and well-motivated accountants are outstanding, and conditions of employment are all that you would expect from a successful company.

For further information about the job, or for an application form, please telephone or write to

        John Smith

        Personnel Manager

        Broadside Retail Services

        (address)

        (telephone number)

The media used to advertise the job vacancy should reach the 'target audience' of certified accounting technicians, probably in the Leeds area only.

Two media

(i)   An advertisement in a professional accountancy magazine, such as Accountancy Age might be considered useful,

(ii) A 'space' advertisement in one or more local newspapers in the Leeds area, which will be read by local residents, including accounting technicians.

(b)   A job description is a document or record which sets out in a standardised format:

(i)   the job title and the purpose of the job;

(ii) details about the scope and contents of the job and the tasks performed;

(iii) the responsibilities involved;

(iv) the skills, training and/or qualifications required;

(v)   the organisational relationships between the duties of the job and other jobs.

(c)

Guidance

Do not forget that the question is not asking about what, in general terms, are the contents of a job description. You are being asked to specify the type of information that should go into the job description for the assistant accountant at Broadside Retail Services. Try to specify the main duties of the job in some detail - about five duties would probably be sufficient. The format of a job description can vary, but should contain somewhere at least most of the information given in the suggested answer.

Job title: Assistant accountant

Department: Accounts department

Job Code Number: 1234

Responsible to: Senior accountant

Job summary:

The job holder is responsible for the preparation of the company's interim and published accounts and for the maintenance of the computerised nominal ledger records from which these accounts are compiled.

The computer system consists of a multi-user system of [type of computer] using [type of software].

Main duties:

(1)   Maintain up-to-date nominal ledger records.

(2)   Provide for the security of the nominal ledger accounts by maintaining suitable back-up files.

(3)   Supervise the work of the three input clerks.

(4)   Provide the management accountant with data for budgetary control.

(5) Assist the senior accountant in the preparation of the interim and published accounts.

Responsible for:

(1) The budget for the nominal ledger section of the accounts department.

(2) Three input clerks in the nominal ledger system.

(3) Liasing with IT suppliers.

Co-operative relationships: with the management accountant for budgetary control.

Reporting to: senior accountant

Experience required for the job:

(1) Working experience with financial accounting microcomputer systems.

(2) Professional qualification as an accounting technician.

Job description:

Prepared by   J Smith, senior accountant

Agreed by   W Brown, chief accountant

Date of preparation   ....

Answer to Assignment 2

Biotherm PLC

The overall purpose of the appraisal interview should be to encourage Alan Heath to become more a part of the personnel team (after all he has specialist knowledge which cannot be replaced). You cannot ignore his sickness record because it impacts on performance. However, you should attempt to understand the reasons behind his poor attendance rather than tackling it at this stage (this is best left for a separate occasion). You should ensure at all costs that the appraisal interview does not become a disciplinary one.

Your plan should include the following:

(a) discussion on achievement of past objectives;

(b) reasons behind failure to achieve objectives;

(c) problems and successes in current performance (you should have consulted in advance with the main people Alan interacts with, eg line managers, colleagues, external clients);

(d) attempts to understand Alan's personal needs (he may be motivated by his 'expertise' for example, rather than any additional pay award);

(e) a discussion of Alan's job aspirations; this will follow on from the previous point but you should have done your homework in advance on the requirements of the job immediately senior to his;

(f) a commitment not to duck difficult issues but to explore; you may find out some very good reasons behind his refusal to work beyond contracted hours, for example;

(g) an attempt to agree a set of SMART objectives.

Your approach to this interview should be 'problem-solving', rather than 'tell and sell' or 'tell and listen'.

Answer to assignment 3

An example is Jones Brothers Department Store

It is organised in sales departments and support departments such as accounts and warehouse.

1   The mission is to be the best department store in town providing high quality goods and services to our customers.

2   Products are household goods and furniture, clothes, gardening goods, electrical and kitchen goods, hairdressing and haberdashery.

3   The market is the area around the town.

4   Purchase from original manufacturers and contract making of clothing.

5   The retail park ten miles away.

Answer to Assignment 4

Duntoiling Nursing Homes

To deal with this difficult situation effectively you need to do the following:

(a)   introduce a disciplinary procedure if none currently exists;

(b)   consider the Health and Safety at Work legislation, particularly the employer's obligations of duty and care towards staff;

(c)   define constructive dismissal (this means where an organisation has changed terms and conditions of employment to such an extent that the employees feel they have no other option but to resign);

(d)   consider the wisdom of unilateral changes in terms and conditions without notice (ie Cheeseman imposing these changes without any consultation);

(e)   consider reinstating the employee with possible concessions (eg counselling to give up smoking);

(f)   prepare your ideal and 'fall-back' positions when negotiating;

(g)   question why the policy was introduced in the first place;

(h)   ask why there was no involvement from the personnel function in implementing the smoking policy;

(i)   develop a 'best practice' model showing how to introduce a smoking policy and do it again (remember the employer's duty to protect employees from the effects of passive smoking). The model should include:

    (i)   a consultation period (say 3 months);
    (ii)   establishing a consultative committee;
    (iii)   conducting a staff attitude survey;
    (iv)   making provision for special cases;
    (v)   make formal changes to terms and conditions;
    (vi)   retrain line managers in disciplinary matters;
    (vii)   review and monitor the policy.

Again remember that the question asks for your answer to be in the form of a brief to Mr Cheeseman.

Answer to Assignment 5

Quality

A manager should weigh up the quality of information he or she receives against certain theoretical qualities of 'good information'. These include [*five of*] the following.

(a) **Relevance**

Information must be relevant to the purpose for which a manager wants to use it. Far too many reports fail to 'keep to the point' and contain purposeless, irritating paragraphs which only serve to vex the managers reading them.

(b) **Completeness**

An information user should have all the information he needs to do his job properly. If he does not have a complete picture of the situation, he might well make bad decisions.

(c) **Accuracy**

Information should obviously be accurate because using incorrect information could have serious and damaging consequences. However, information should only be accurate enough for its purpose and there is no need to go into unnecessary detail for pointless accuracy.

(d) **Clarity**

Information must be clear to the user. If the user does not understand it properly he cannot use it properly. Lack of clarity is one of the causes of a breakdown in communication, which is referred to in information system theory as 'noise'.

(e) **Consistency**

An important quality of information (especially in accounting) is that it is prepared consistently, for instance so that it is valid to compare reports from two different periods.

(f) **Reliability**

Information must be trusted by the managers who are expected to use it. Information sources will not be used if they have proved unreliable in the past. Information relating to the future or to the external environment is uncertain.

(g) **Communication**

Information that is needed might be communicated to a person who does not have the authority to act on it, or who is not responsible for the matter and so does not see any need to act on it. Sometimes one method of communication is better than another, for instance a telephone call as compared with a letter.

(h) **Conciseness**

There are physical and mental limitations to what a person can read, absorb and understand properly before taking action. An enormous mountain of information, even if it is all relevant, cannot be handled. Reports to management must therefore be clear and concise and in many systems, control action works basically on the 'exception' principle. This is especially true of tactical information for management control.

NOTES

(i) **Timeliness**

Information, to be of any use, must be produced when it is needed. Information which is not available until after a decision is made will be useful only for comparisons and longer-term control, and may serve no purpose even then.

(j) **Costs and benefits are dealt with below.**

Value

The **value** of information can also be assessed by reference to certain theoretical ideas.

Basically, information is only worth collecting if the **benefits** obtainable from it exceed the **costs** of collection. There are many ways in which information might give value. For example, it might lead to a **decision to take action** which results in reducing costs, eliminating losses or increasing sales - or it might lead to a **better utilisation** of **resources**, or **prevent fraud**.

As the value of information lies in the action taken as a result of receiving it, an assessment of value may be reached by asking the following questions:

(a) **what** information is provided?

(b) what is it **used** for?

(c) **who** uses it?

(d) **how often** is it used?

(e) does the frequency with which it is used coincide with the frequency with which it is provided?

(f) what is **achieved** by using it?

(g) what **other** relevant information is available which could be **used instead**?

An assessment of the value of information can be derived in this way, and the cost of obtaining it should then be compared against this value. On the basis of this comparison, it can be decided whether certain items of information are worth having.

Answer to Assignment 6

Part 1

Your notes could include the following points.

- Gibbs Motors seem to be a small company; there is an owner and a secretary, but no one else is mentioned.

- Gibbs has used a local supplier and never had any problems.

- John Gibb listens to rumours.

- John Gibb has time to visit many auctioneers.

- John Gibb is not in a hurry for new stock.

- John Gibb placed the order when prompted.

- John Gibb did not confirm his own order.

- John Gibb communicated by a note to his secretary.

- The cars were of good quality.

- John Gibb is in a hurry to sell them.

- Is his secretary telling the truth?

- Gibbs Motors has low cash flow.

- Communications – John Gibb does not seem to like written communications.

Part 2

Check your report against the following guidance:

The Terms of reference are given in the questions:

(a) identify communication problems;
(b) make recommendations for the future.

Your Introduction should not retell the story, but should outline the salient points: the size and nature of the organisation, the individuals, and the circumstances.

In the Main body of your report, you should highlight any problems, such as:

(a) the owner of Gibbs Motors listens to rumours and ignores his own experience

(b) there is an over reliance on verbal communication

(c) there is a reluctance on the part of the owner to enter into written communication with his supplier

(d) the owner of Gibbs Motors does not encourage feedback from suppliers or staff. (You may also identify other problems.)

You may have decided that some of these problems are symptoms of a deeper problem. You should draw all this together into your Conclusion.

In your Recommendations you should have included the need to:

(a) identify appropriate media for the message;
(b) use written communications where records are needed;
(c) encourage and listen to feedback;
(d) ensure that the message actually reaches its intended recipient.

Your recommendations should be detailed and focused on the case. They must be backed up by reasoned argument.

BIBLIOGRAPHY

Adair, J. and Allen, M. (1999) *Time Management and Personal Development*. London: Hawksmere.

Goleman, D. (1998) *Working with Emotional Intelligence*. London: Bloomsbury.

Guirdham, M. (1995) *Interpersonal Skills at Work* (2nd ed.) Harlow, Essex: Prentice Hall.

Honey, P. and Mumford, A. (1992) *The Manual of Learning Styles*. Maidenhead: Peter Honey.

Kolb (1984) *Experiential Learning*. New York: Prentice Hall.

Luft, J. (1961) The Johari window, *Human Relations Training News*, No. 5.

Pedler, M., Burgoyne, J. and Boydell, T. (2001), *A Manager's Guide to Self Development* (4th ed.) Maidenhead: McGraw Hill.

Rogers, C. (1961) *On Becoming a Person*. Boston: Houghton Mifflin.

Whetten, D. and Cameron, K. (2002) *Developing Management Skills* (5th ed.) New Jersey: Prentice Hall.

INDEX

NOTES

See overleaf for information on other
BPP products and how to order

HND/HNC Order

To BPP Professional Education, Aldine Place, London W12 8AW
Tel: 020 8740 2211. Fax: 020 8740 1184
E-mail: Publishing@bpp.com Web: www.bpp.com

Mr/Mrs/Ms (Full name) _____

Daytime delivery address _____

Postcode _____

Daytime Tel _____ E-mail _____

5/04

Course Books

MANDATORY (£9.95 each)

Unit 1 Marketing ☐

Unit 2 Managing Financial Resources and Decisions ☐

Unit 3 Organisations and Behaviour ☐

Unit 4 Business Environment ☐

Unit 5 Common Law I ☐

Unit 6 Business Decision Making ☐

Unit 7 Business Strategy ☐

Unit 8 Research Project ☐

Special offer: Buy all 8 Mandatory Texts for £70 ☐

ENDORSED TITLE ROUTES (£14.95 each)

Units 9-12 Finance ☐

Units 13-16 Management ☐

Units 17-20 Marketing ☐

Units 21-24 Human Resource Management ☐

Units 25-28 Law ☐

Special offer: Buy any 2 Endorsed Title Routes for £25 ☐

SUBTOTAL £ _____

TOTAL FOR PRODUCTS £ _____

POSTAGE & PACKING

Texts	First	Each extra	Online
UK	£5.00	£2.00	£2.00
Europe*	£6.00	£4.00	£4.00
Rest of world	£20.00	£10.00	£10.00

TOTAL FOR POSTAGE & PACKING £ _____

Grand Total (Cheques to *BPP Professional Education*)

I enclose a cheque for (incl. Postage) £ _____

Or charge to Access/Visa/Switch

Card Number ☐☐☐☐ ☐☐☐☐ ☐☐☐☐ ☐☐☐☐

CV2 No ☐☐☐ last 3 digits on signature strip

Expiry date _____ Start Date _____

Issue Number (Switch Only) _____

Signature _____

We aim to deliver to all UK addresses inside 5 working days; a signature will be required. Orders to all EU addresses should be delivered within 6 working days. All other orders to overseas addresses should be delivered within 8 working days. * Europe includes the Republic of Ireland and the Channel Islands.

Review Form & Free Prize Draw – HND Specialist Units 13 - 16 – Management (9/04)

All original review forms from the entire BPP range, completed with genuine comments, will be entered into one of two draws on 31 January 2005 and 31 July 2005. The names on the first four forms picked out on each occasion will be sent a cheque for £50.

Name: _____   Address: _____

_____

_____

How have you used this Course Book?
(Tick one box only)

☐ Home study (book only)

☐ On a course: college _____

☐ Other _____

Why did you decide to purchase this Course book? *(Tick one box only)*

☐ Have used BPP Texts in the past

☐ Recommendation by friend/colleague

☐ Recommendation by a lecturer at college

☐ Saw advertising

☐ Other _____

During the past six months do you recall seeing/receiving any of the following?
(Tick as many boxes as are relevant)

☐ Our advertisement

☐ Our brochure with a letter through the post

Your ratings, comments and suggestions would be appreciated on the following areas

	Very useful	Useful	Not useful
Introductory pages	☐	☐	☐
Topic coverage	☐	☐	☐
Summary diagrams	☐	☐	☐
Chapter roundups	☐	☐	☐
Quick quizzes	☐	☐	☐
Activities	☐	☐	☐
Discussion points	☐	☐	☐

	Excellent	Good	Adequate	Poor
Overall opinion of this Course book	☐	☐	☐	☐

Do you intend to continue using BPP HND/HNC Course books?   ☐ Yes   ☐ No

Please note any further comments and suggestions/errors on the reverse of this page.

The BPP author of this edition can be e-mailed at: pippariley@bpp.com

Please return this form to: Pippa Riley, BPP Professional Education, FREEPOST, London, W12 8BR

Review Form & Free Prize Draw (continued)

Please note any further comments and suggestions/errors below

Free Prize Draw Rules

1   Closing date for 31 January 2005 draw is 31 December 2004. Closing date for 31 July 2005 draw is 30 June 2005.

2   Restricted to entries with UK and Eire addresses only. BPP employees, their families and business associates are excluded.

3   No purchase necessary. Entry forms are available upon request from BPP Professional Education. No more than one entry per title, per person. Draw restricted to persons aged 16 and over.

4   Winners will be notified by post and receive their cheques not later than 6 weeks after the relevant draw date.

5   The decision of the promoter in all matters is final and binding. No correspondence will be entered into.